JOHN L. THOMAS, the editor of this volume in the Eyewitness Accounts of American History Series, is the author of *The Liberator*, a biography of William Lloyd Garrison which won both the Allan Nevins Prize and the Bancroft Prize in American history. He did his undergraduate work at Bowdoin college and received his Ph.D. from Brown University. Dr. Thomas is Associate Professor of American History at Brown.

SLAVERY ATTACKED:

THE ABOLITIONIST CRUSADE.

SLAVERY ATTACKED:

THE ABOLITIONIST CRUSADE.

EDITED BY:

JOHN L. THOMAS,

Associate Professor of American History

at

BROWN UNIVERSITY.

A SPECTRUM BOOK

published by

PRENTICE-HALL, Incorporated

ENGLEWOOD CLIFFS, NEW JERSEY

LIBRARY OF CONGRESS CATALOG CARD NO.: 65-12170

Current printing (last digit):
11 10 9 8 7 6 5 4

Printed in the United States of America—C
81276-P

For

JOHN and JANE.

CONTENTS

PART IV. CONVERTING THE NORTH.

PART V. SCHISM.

PART VI. THE ANTI-SLAVERY ENTERPRISE.

PART VII. THE GATHERING CRISIS.

PART VIII. ARMAGEDDON AND AFTER.

INTRODUCTORY ESSAY.

THE ABOLITIONIST CRUSADE.

BY JOHN L. THOMAS

THE ABOLITIONIST CRUSADE began during the first administration of Andrew Jackson with a declaration of holy war against slavery, and it ended nearly thirty-five years later when Abraham Lincoln signed the Emancipation Proclamation. Three turbulent decades witnessed a continuing moral assault on Southern institutions and hard-fought encounters with Northern resistance, sharp skirmishes with mob rule, major engagements against both political parties, and, finally, an insurrection within the abolitionist camp itself. From beginning to end abolitionism was a militant movement.

The first strategic objective in the abolitionists' attack was the destruction of the American Colonization Society. Organized in 1817, the Colonization Society aimed at the complete removal of the Negro from the United States. Some Southern planters supported the Society in the hope that exporting free Negroes would strengthen the institution of slavery, while Northern philanthropists endorsed colonization in the equally futile expectation that it would purify American democracy by ridding the country of slaves. Thus colonization embraced two irreconcilable points of view. On one crucial issue, however, both Northern and Southern colonizationists were agreed—the Negro was inherently inferior to the white man and had no place in a democratic society.

It was precisely this sweeping assumption of inferiority and unfitness which the pioneer abolitionists rejected. Their argument proved devastatingly simple: slavery was a sin and a crime, a sin because it denied to the Negro the status of a human being, a crime because it violated the natural rights to life, liberty, and the pursuit of happiness guaranteed in the Declaration of Independence. These two beliefs—in the spiritual equality of all believers and the political equality of all Americans—served as the chief moral weapons in the attack on slavery.

To destroy the power of slavery the abolitionists relied on the equally simple strategy of conversion. In the beginning they tried to change the minds of slaveholders and gain sympathizers by appealing directly to the individual conscience. They broadcast their indictment in their own press, organized societies and wrote pamphlets, compiled statistics and circulated petitions, all with the purpose of bringing their moral argument directly to bear on the presumed guilt of the American people. The American Anti-Slavery Society, organized in 1833, functioned chiefly as a clearinghouse for a huge propaganda campaign mounted by agents and agitators who looked to moral suasion for their power. Its program, however variously interpreted in later years, originally called for moral agitation directed at individual citizens in both sections of the country to make them see and feel the sinfulness of slavery. Change people's hearts, they believed, and the people would soon change their habits.

The years immediately following the organization of the American Anti-Slavery Society saw a furious burst of abolitionist energy. Thousands of petitions with hundreds of thousands of signatures deluged Congress. Hundreds of anti-slavery agents swept over New England, New York, and the Ohio Valley lecturing and distributing tracts. A dozen state auxiliaries and twice as many abolitionist newspapers sprang up in the North. By 1836 the crusade against slavery had succeeded in turning the course of American politics.

Such an outburst of moral indignation against a deeply rooted institution was bound to provoke a sharp reaction. Northerners and Southerners alike countered the abolitionist attack by resorting to political suppression. Congress found a way of shutting off the deluge of anti-slavery petitions. The Postmaster General helped Southern states close the mails to abolitionist literature. State legislatures in both sections of the country considered "gag" laws restricting the activities of the opponents of slavery. Worst of all, mobs whipped up by local demagogues, disrupted anti-slavery meetings, destroyed abolitionist property, and threatened the lives of the leaders. In Boston in 1835 a mob dragged William Lloyd Garrison through the streets until he was rescued by his friends. In New York gangs of waterfront toughs roamed the city's Negro district looting and burning. In Louisville, Amos Dresser, an abolitionist agent, was publicly whipped and driven out of town. And in Alton, Illinois, Elijah Lovejoy was killed while defending his press from a mob.

The abolitionists responded to these repressive tactics with a firm and effective defense of civil liberties. If some of them seemed to enjoy their notoriety and a few openly to court martyrdom, all of them insisted on their right to hold and preach unpopular opinions. The alliance between abolition and civil rights, struck early in the fight against slavery, survived until the Civil War.

The stiff public resistance to any discussion of the slavery question precipitated a crisis within the abolitionist movement. When the American Anti-Slavery Society was first organized, the founders had assumed that some kind of political action would be required eventually, but they saw their task as one of educating the people to the need for action rather than defining its scope. In 1833 the time for political programs and platforms seemed far off. The public outcry and the organized repression which threatened their crusade, however, convinced many abolitionists that a change in strategy was required. In the first place, both the petition and the pamphlet campaigns proved costly failures. Moreover, a vague and diffused opposition to slavery was spreading through the North faster than the national society's network of control. By 1837 the American Anti-Slavery Society consisted of a loose web of semi-autonomous state and local auxiliaries, each more concerned with converting its own section than with supporting the national organization.

This recognition that moral suasion had reached an impasse produced a division in the abolitionist ranks. One phalanx, led by James G. Birney, Joshua Leavitt, and Myron Holley, turned to politics. Their road led toward the Liberty Party and the Free Soil movement, and eventually to the confused anti-slavery politics of the Republican Party. The political abolitionists hoped to use compromise and concession to build an anti-slavery platform broad enough to support candidates and win elections. They were willing to accept the role of a political minority and exploit party politics in behalf of the slave.

A smaller but more militant group of abolitionists, led by William Lloyd Garrison and Wendell Phillips, took another and—so they believed—a higher route to emancipation. Insisting that proscription and repression branded the American church and state as hopelessly corrupt, they demanded that abolitionists have "no union with slaveholders." They refused to seek office, vote for anti-slavery candidates, or in any way support the political abolitionists whom they denounced as traitors to the cause of moral suasion. With their intransigent "come-outer" beliefs the Garrisonians carried moral suasion to its limits in Christian nonresistance and woman's rights. The logic of their position, if not of all their activities, pointed toward secession.

By 1840, then, the abolitionists were engaged in a civil war of their own, with both political abolitionists and Garrisonians struggling for control of the nearly moribund national society. When Garrison imported a boatload of women delegates from Massachusetts for the annual meeting in New York that year and won control, his opponents seceded, some of them to form the rival American and Foreign Anti-Slavery Society.

others to enter the political arena with the Liberty Party.

Thus the year 1840 marked a turning point in the abolitionist crusade. Its institutional phase was over. Although Garrison's "Old Organization" (as his followers called themselves) and the secessionist "New Organization" (as they contemptuously referred to their opponents) continued to agitate for immediate emancipation, an effective national organization ceased to exist after 1840.

If abolitionist organization had been eclipsed by the time of the Mexican War, the anti-slavery enterprise flourished. Agitators stepped up their attack on the slave system, and reformers intensified their efforts to improve the lot of the free Negro in the North. Meanwhile, Manifest Destiny and an expansionist war translated the slavery question into an acute political one which split Whigs and Democrats in the election of 1848 and brought new converts to anti-slavery principles if not to abolitionist methods—Charles Francis Adams, Charles Sumner, Henry Wilson, Salmon P. Chase, and other Northern moderates now fearful of a "slave power" plot to nationalize the peculiar institution. The principal beneficiaries of this new Northern fear were the Free Soilers, although by now even the Garrisonians enjoyed an unexpected tolerance. When the Compromise of 1850 tied the territorial question and the fugitive slave issue together, the stage was set for a ten-year sectional struggle that ended with the firing on Fort Sumter. Though few Americans were prepared to accept all of the abolitionists' premises, Northern convictions that slavery must be checked grew rapidly. The abolitionists had done part of their work well.

The Compromise of 1850 set in motion a train of events which, given the impetus toward sectional conflict provided by the Mexican War, proved irreversible. The Fugitive Slave Law was met throughout the North with state personal-liberty laws. A series of daring slave rescues dramatized the futility of attempting to enforce a law which the moral sense of one half the nation would not support. The Nebraska Act and the doctrine of "squatter sovereignty" touched off a race for control of the new territories culminating in violence and fraud. The Dred Scott decision seemed the fulfillment of abolitionist predictions of the triumph of slavery until in one desperate act John Brown tried to reverse the balance of power.

The reactions of the abolitionists to the gathering crisis of the 1850's were as varied as their personalities. Some of them, like Theodore Parker in Boston and Samuel May in Syracuse, organized vigilance committees to thwart slave-catchers. Others, like Eli Thayer and Henry Ward

Beecher, concentrated on the problem of making Kansas free soil. In Sumner, Wilson, Chase, and Seward abolitionists found political voices to denounce slavery. The Garrisonians stuck to their disunionist standard and as late as 1857 held a convention calling for the peaceful dissolution of the Union. Disunionism, however, remained largely discredited in the North; and peaceful secession, as it turned out, was neither realistic nor beneficial to the slave. When the Civil War came, the Garrisonians who had been most anxious for Northern secession joined in a war to preserve the union and abolish slavery.

Throughout the decade, political abolitionists ran the constant risk of diluting the moral content of their program. Free Soil leaders were forced to appeal to Northern opinion, which was anti-Negro as well as anti-slavery; and the territorial problem as argued by Republican politicians generated more sectional heat than moral light.

All of the abolitionists contributed to the crisis: attacking Douglas and "squatter sovereignty"; arraigning the Pierce and Buchanan administrations; interpreting every development in light of their theory of the great slave-power conspiracy. When the Confederate batteries stopped firing on Fort Sumter, few abolitionists doubted that the coming war would somehow—they did not know quite how—destroy slavery. None of them had expected their crusade to end in bloodshed. They had accepted responsibility for a moral struggle, but for the eventuality of total war they, like the nation, were unprepared. Yet they accepted the Civil War, a few gladly, most of them reluctantly, as a war for the slave even though they were not sure what emancipation would bring. When Lincoln signed the Emanicipation Proclamation on January 1, 1863, they concluded that the divine will which seemingly had directed their crusade had finally triumphed.

PART I.

THE ABOLITIONIST INDICTMENT.

WILLIAM LLOYD GARRISON ABANDONS COLONIZATION (1830).

ALTHOUGH THE ATTITUDE OF the abolitionists toward slavery and their program for eliminating it were diametrically opposed to the views of the American Colonization Society, many of the early leaders like William Lloyd Garrison, Theodore Weld and James G. Birney began their anti-slavery careers as colonizationists. In the fall of 1829 Benjamin Lundy brought Garrison, then only twenty-three years old, to Baltimore to help edit his anti-slavery paper, the *Genius of Universal Emancipation*. While Lundy advertised his scheme for Haitian colonization, Garrison undertook an editorial investigation of the Colonization Society which ended six months later in his decision to abandon Lundy and attack slavery with his own weapons. The immediate occasion for this decision was a speech defending colonization by Henry Clay, the most eminent supporter of the Society. In a series of three editorials entitled "Henry Clay's Colonization Address," which appeared in the *Genius of Universal Emancipation* on February 12 and 19, and March 5, 1830, Garrison analyzed the colonization argument only to reject it and announce his determination to use "strong, indignant, vehement language" in indicting the slaveholders and their crime.

FEBRUARY 12, 1830

THERE ARE FEW INDIVIDUALS, I am persuaded, who cherish a higher regard for Henry Clay, or who look forward to his ultimate elevation to the Presidency with more satisfaction than I do. . . .

In reviewing his recent address before the Colonization Society of Kentucky, it is more than probable that I shall have occasion to differ widely from his views of slavery—perhaps to be somewhat personal, even pointedly so—and therefore I have deemed it necessary to avow my partiality, in order to escape the charges of political hostility. . . .

. . . I find, therein, many liberal concessions relative to the evils of slavery—many hearty desires to see our country free from this foul blemish,—something about expediency, and safety, and gradual manumission—but no where do I see the claims of justice enforced with becoming fearlessness or candor—no personal application—no direct allusion to the awful guilt of debasing the physical, and defiling the moral workmanship of the great God—creatures made a little lower than the angels, and capable of the highest intellectual attainments:—not a word—Therefore my dissatisfaction.

The episode, at the commencement of the address, relative to the persecuted Indians, is replete with tenderness, truth, humanity, justice—spoken at an eventful crisis, and calculated to unite many discordant views. One cannot help remarking how much more freely Mr. Clay breathes in defending these poor red men, than in speaking of the Africans. Yet his notion about the *natural* physical and intellectual superiority of the whites over the Indians, is unphilosophical and absurd. I deny the postulate, that God has made, by an irreversible decree, or any inherent qualities, one portion of the human race superior to another. No matter how many breeds are amalgamated—no matter how many shades of color intervene between tribes or nations—give them the same chances to improve, and a fair start at the same time, and the result will be equally brilliant, equally productive, equally grand. . . .

But let these wandering tribes be universally reclaimed, and civilization pour in upon them its renovating light, and the "glorious gospel of the blessed God" dispel the mist of superstition, and who shall put limits to their progress in knowledge, in virtue, in the arts and sciences, or in any moral or intellectual improvement? . . .

February 19, 1830

It is morally impossible, I am convinced, for a slaveholder to reason correctly on the subject of slavery. His mind is warped by a thousand prejudices, and a thick cloud rests upon his mental vision. He was really taught to believe, that a certain class of beings were born for servitude, whom it is lawful to enthral, and over whom he is authorized—not merely by the law of his native state, but by Jehovah himself—to hold unlimited dominion. His manhood, perhaps, may detect the absurdity of the doctrine, but interest weakens the force of conviction, and he is never at a loss to find palliatives for his conduct. He discourses eloquently, it may be, upon the evils of the system—deprecates its continuance as a curse upon the country—shudders when he contemplates individual instances of barbarity—and rejoices in gradual emancipation. Interrogate him relative to his own practices, and you touch the apple of his eye. If not disposed to resent your freedom, he takes shelter in the ignorance and helplessness of his slaves; and, dextrously relinquishing the authority of an oppressor, assumes the amiableness of a philanthropist! "The poor creatures are pennyless—benighted—without a home! Freedom would be a curse, rather than a blessing to them—they are happy now—why should I throw them upon an unpitying world?" Will a christian reason in this manner? Yes—if a christian can be a slaveholder—but the two characters differ so widely, that I know not how they can unite in one man. Yet this wicked cant obtains as readily at the north as the south, and with many it is as impregnable as the rock of Gibralter. Does not every tyrant make the welfare of his subjects a plea for his conduct?

What evidence—besides mere words—does that slaveholder give me, or the world, that his benevolence is sincere? Have not his slaves toiled early and late, through summer's heat and winter's cold, faithfully, steadily, year after year, for his own aggrandizement? Yes. What recompense have they received? A bare maintenance. To whom does the property, in equity, belong? To those who accumulated it—the slaves. If the account were fairly adjusted, who would be pennyless? The master. *Let him, then, at least divide his substance.* But the blacks are ignorant, and cannot safely be liberated! Then is moral degradation a crime! Then is slavery eternal! Did that *benevolent* and *christian* master ever strive to elevate their minds—to illumine their understandings—or lead their souls to God? Never! Is he now, in the copiousness of his sympathy, teaching them the way to heaven, or preparing them to enjoy the blessing of liberty? No—they are scarcely more intelligent than his cattle. But they are happy! Horrible perversion of the term! mockery of mockeries! and by an American—a Christian, too! . . .

MARCH 5, 1830

. . . Although Mr. Clay deeply laments the existence of slavery as an evil of gigantic size, and sympathises with the unfortunate beings who groan in bondage, yet he says:

> If the question were submitted, whether there should be either immediate or gradual emancipation of all the slaves in the United States, without their removal or colonization, painful as it is to express the opinion, I have no doubt that it would be unwise to emancipate them.

I can hardly credit my senses that this is the language of Henry Clay. The alternative here presented is shocking. It would lead to the most disastrous consequences. It would make slavery eternal. For, be it remembered, Mr. Clay believes Africa to be the only feasible, safe and proper spot on which to colonize our colored population. Now, talk as we may of the abilities of government—of colonization societies, and charitable donations, and facilities of transportation, and our multitude of ships—the scheme is as delusive and hopeless as any that was ever projected by a civilized people. Mr. Clay, it is true, thinks otherwise: but, if it fail, he would prohibit *gradual* emancipation. In his sight, a free black is a nuisance,—and a community of slaves more tolerable than a community of colored freemen. He consults nothing but policy, and forgets that justice should be first interrogated.

And here a word or two in relation to the American Colonization Society.

I do not place myself in a hostile attitude to this Society, neither do I choose to rank among its warmest advocates. Its policy or impolicy—its good or evil, in the aggregate, is a question which has constantly agitated but never satisfied my mind, and which time alone can solve. On a few points, however, my judgment is clear.

Granting—what, perhaps, is no longer problematical—that the colony is built on a stable foundation; granting, moreover, that its infancy is rich in promise, and that its kindly influences may penetrate to a considerable extent into the interior of Africa—is the Colonization Society calculated to promote or retard the abolition of slavery in our own country? That is the question.

The friends of the Society reply in the affirmative—its enemies take the negative—the neutrals constitute a majority.

What has the Society accomplished? Much, unquestionably, for a single association, engaged in a hazardous enterprise, and supported by the uncertain charities of the public. But has it, in any degree, sustained its high pretensions? or made good one of its numberless and extravagant proclamations? or taken away a fraction from the "sum total"? or made any visible impression upon the growth of slavery? Assuredly not.

It has been in existence about thirteen years—a term amply sufficient to test its capacity and usefulness. Its annual transportation to Liberia, I believe, has averaged *one hundred* souls. During the same period, the *increase* of the colored population has amounted to upwards of *five hundred thousand*. And yet such is the colonization mania—such the implicit confidence reposed in the operations of the Society—that no demonstration of its inefficiency, however palpable, can shake the faith of its advocates.

Let me be understood. I would not utterly discard the Colonization Society, as an auxiliary in the cause of African emancipation. My complaint is, that its ability is overrated to a disastrous extent—that this delusion is perpetuated by the conduct and assurances of those who ought to act better—the members of the Society. I complain, moreover, that the lips of these members are sealed up on the subject of slavery, who, from their high standing and extensive influence, ought to expose its flagrant enormities, and actively assist in its overthrow. But they dare not lead to the onset—and if *they* shrink from the battle, "by whom shall the victory be won?"

In the same issue Garrison announced his intention to quit the *Genius* and strike out on his own, a decision which led to the founding of the *Liberator* a year later.

. . . My views on the subject of slavery have been very imperfectly developed in the Genius,—the cares and perplexities of the establishment having occupied a large share of my time and attention. Every pledge, however, that I have made to the public, shall be fulfilled. My pen cannot remain idle, nor my voice be suppressed, nor my heart cease to bleed, while two millions of my fellow beings wear the shackles of slavery in my guilty country.

In all my writings, I have used strong, indignant, vehement language, and direct, pointed, scorching reproof. I have nothing to recall. Many have censured me for my severity—but, thank God! none have stigmatized me with luke-warmness. "Passion is reason—transport, temper here."

ELIZUR WRIGHT, JR.

DEFINES IMMEDIATE EMANCIPATION (1833).

MORAL OUTRAGE WAS SHARED by all of the pioneer abolitionists who denounced slavery as a sin and called for "immediate emancipation." The phrase was variously interpreted during the 1830's to mean "immediate emancipation gradually accomplished" and "gradual emancipation immediately begun." For all of the abolitionists, however, the doctrine signified a moral imperative to begin at once their redemptive work. Elizur Wright, Jr. was a young professor of mathematics and moral philosophy at Western Reserve when he first read Garrison's *Thoughts on African Colonization* (1832), a savage indictment of colonization. Converted to immediate emancipation, Wright left the college to join a group of New York abolitionists led by the philanthropists Arthur and Lewis Tappan who were planning a national anti-slavery society. Wright's first anti-slavery pamphlet, *The Sin of Slavery and its Remedy* (1833), employed nearly all of the arguments and techniques which came to comprise the standard abolitionist indictment: an appeal to guilt and reliance on repentance and reformation; an arraignment of Southern society and culture; warnings of imminent slave uprisings; challenge to the American churches; a distrust of politics and a preference for Old Testament methods. Elizur Wright, Jr., *The Sin of Slavery and its Remedy; Containing Some Reflections on the Moral Influence of African Colonization* (New York, 1833), ch. V.

IMMEDIATE ABOLITION.

. . . UNDER THE GOVERNMENT of God, as exhibited in this world, there is but one remedy for sin, and that is available only by a *repentance*, evidenced by reformation. There is no such thing as holding on to sin with safety. It is not only to be renounced, but the very occasions of it are to be avoided at whatever sacrifice. If thy right hand cause thee to offend, cut it off—if thy right eye, pluck it out. The dearest human relationships are to be broken through when they interfere with the relation which a man bears to God, and through him to his rational creatures. This being the case, we might certainly expect that the entire agency which God has provided to reclaim the world should be adapted to produce *immediate repentance.* It certainly is so, if we take the testimony of the Bible. . . . Those men who are so excessively cautious not to disturb prejudice, who would remove sin while the wicked are asleep, stealing around the bed and effecting a *reformation* beforehand, so that the sinner may repent at his leisure without hindrance when he wakes, derive their authority elsewhere than from the word of God, as indeed they must derive their hope of success elsewhere than from the natural history of man. The doctrine of the immediate abolition of slavery asks no better authority than is offered by scripture. It is in perfect harmony with the letter and spirit of God's word.

The doctrine may be thus briefly stated. It is the duty of the holders of slaves immediately to restore to them their liberty, and to extend to them the full protection of law, as well as its control. It is their duty equitably to restore to them those profits of their labor, which have been wickedly wrested away, especially by giving them that moral and mental instruction—that education, which alone can render any considerable accumulation of property a blessing. It is their duty to employ them as voluntary laborers, on equitable wages. Also, it is the duty of all men to proclaim this doctrine—to urge upon slaveholders *immediate emancipation,* so long as there is a slave—to agitate the consciences of tyrants, so long as there is a tyrant on the globe.

Though this doctrine does not depend, in regard to the slave-holder, upon the safety of immediate emancipation, nor, in regard to the non-slave-holder, on the prospect of accomplishing any abolition at all, but upon the commands of God, yet I shall attempt to establish it upon those lower grounds. I am willing to rest the cause on the truth of the following propositions.

1. The instant abolition of the whole slave system is safe, and the substitution of a free labor system is safe, practicable and profitable.

2. The firm expression of an enlightened public opinion, on the part of non-slave-holders, in favor of instant abolition, is an effectual, and the only effectual means of securing abolition in any time whatsoever.

1. *Immediate abolition is safe.*

. . . The immediate abolition of slavery is safe, because, without giving to the slaves any motives to injure their masters, it would take away from them the very strong ones which they now have. Why does the white mother quake at the rustling of a leaf? Why, but that she is conscious that there are those around her, who have been deeply enough provoked to imbrue their hands in her blood, and in that of the tender infant at her breast? And this, while all is cringing servility around her—while every want is anticipated, and the most menial services are performed with apparent delight. But well she knows that it is a counterfeited delight. Well enough she knows, that were *she* subjected to the same degradation to which she subjects others, vengeance would fire her heart, and seek the first occasion to do its fellest deed. All the instincts of animal nature cry out, that oppression is dangerous. The natural history of man cries out, that there is a point, beyond which endurance would be miraculous. . . .

There is another very striking point of view in which these movements may be regarded. So long as the slaves are left entirely to the control of individual masters, some are kind and lenient, freeing now and then a slave, and promising freedom to others, and exercising a sort of patriarchal authority, while others are, each in his own way, more harsh and severe, the unity of the slaves, as a body, is broken. They have no common cause. Every conspiracy will be detected early, by means of those who, being kindly treated, have a blind attachment to their masters. But these legislative enactments are a common oppression. They form the slaves into a single body, give them a common interest, and break the claim of individual kindness, as well as attach, in the view of the slaves, an immeasurable importance to a knowledge of letters. Go on, then, tyrants—connect into one mine the explosive materials beneath you—dry the powder—increase the pressure—lay trains of the best fulminating mixtures, and wait for the spark, or the blow that is to annihilate you. Already have your abused, outraged vassals such motives to rid themselves of your yoke, that your knees smite together in spite of the boasted stoutness of your hearts. Go on, then, refuse to emancipate, add insult to injury—add stings to desperation—make death easier than bondage—for, in so doing, you assuredly hasten the day, when the American bill of rights shall mean what it says.

But if you recoil at the prospect—if sanity has not yet bid adieu to your heads, and the milk of human kindness is not quite dried up from your breasts—look at the other side. Immediate emancipation would reverse the picture. It would place a motive to love you in the room of every one which now urges the slaves to hate you. They would then become, for you well know how grateful they are for even the slightest favors, your defenders instead of your murderers. The law which now represses their crimes, would then more effectually secure their good behavior, not being counteracted by the exasperating influence of individual irresponsible oppression. Your fields which now lie sterile, or produce but half a crop, because the whip of the driver, although it may secure its motion, cannot give force to the negro's hoe, would then smile beneath the plough of the freeman—the genial influence of just and equitable wages. Mark, that I say nothing of the amount of human happiness which might be reared by Christian instruction on this ground of justice, mercy and equal rights applied to 2,000,000 of men. Your own estates would be worth double the cash. The capital which you have expended in slaves—scarcely less than the value of your land—is sunk; for your slave labor after all costs more than free. And, besides, the waste arising from involuntary labor is prodigious. Make all labor free, and the purchaser can afford to pay for your land what he must now pay for the land and slaves together. Even in a pecuniary point of view the change from the slave to the free labor system would be profitable, and that upon your own comparison. . . .

Holders of stolen men! do you still point us to the degraded free blacks of the South, and say they are more miserable than the slaves? We deny the assertion. We appeal to yourselves whether there be any suffering even unto death which you would not endure rather than be slaves—rather than be fed and fattened slaves—rather than to wear a single link of a slave's chain—rather than to submit to slavery even in the abstract principle, apart from all matters of reality. But granting the assertion to express a fact. You are not the men to plead it. You have made this fact with your own blood-stained hands—made it for the very purpose of discouraging the slave's freedom in the view of the slave, and the view of the world! This shall be proved from your own lips. . . .

But what if it were true, that the free black at the South is more miserable than the slave? It would be no argument against that sort of emancipation for which we plead. We plead for no *turning loose, no exile, no kicking out of house and home, but for complete and hearty* JUSTICE. Justice requires that the masters who have shut out the light of knowledge from their slaves, should now freely communicate it; that they should follow up their acts of emancipation by giving *employment* and affording the means of *education.* A wise and vigorous system of free labor and of primary instruction, should be immediately erected on the dark pile of oppression, which we urge them instantly to demolish. Nothing like this has been done heretofore, either at the South or the North, on any extensive and liberal scale. Is it a wonder, then, that these poor enslaved men, when thus *turned adrift,* have in so many instances missed the path of moral and mental improvement? Is it not rather marvelous that they have not sunk, as a class, deeper in vice than we find them? We hold the masters bound, individually and in the aggregate, first to LIBERATE and then to ENLIGHTEN the IMMORTAL MINDS that have been abused and debased by their avarice and lust! JUSTICE hitherto has been clogged, defaced, mutilated; but the day of her power rolls on.—Her sun is above the horizon!

Shame on you, *proprietors of men!* Do not add to your inhuman cruelty the useless hypocrisy of professing to wish the free blacks away for their own good! Say, in plain English, for we cannot be much longer deceived, that your sole object is to rid yourselves of colored freedom, lest your slaves should be provoked to think themselves men, and discover that they too have *rights*. Shame on you too, benevolent colonizers! Do not add to your unchristian prejudice the gratuitous sycophancy of doing their foulest deeds for menstealers! Say in plain English, for it will be believed whether you say it or not, that you succumb to arrogance, and are recreants to the Master in whose name you have been baptized! . . .

2. *The firm expression of an enlightened public opinion on the part of non-slave-holders, in favor of instant abolition, is an effectual, and the only effectual, means of securing abolition in any time whatsoever.*

Many men, very wise men in their own estimation, dismiss abolition as a "wild" project, a "theory," a mere closet theory. Colonization is a *practical* business—therefore they are for colonization. But is speaking *truth* a theory? Is calling things by their right names a closet theory? How passing strange that one of our state legislatures should offer $5,000 for the abduction of a mere theorist! For my own part, I had supposed that such large pecuniary transactions involved practical business. I had supposed that this reward might be viewed in the light of a steam-gage, which indicates the efficiency of the moving force. I had supposed it might be a necessary and *practical* part of the business of reclaiming wicked men, to say something which they would not choose to have us.

If northern men, as a body, would become abolitionists, and if they will not, what security have we that they will not become slave-holders? If they would speak out as abolitionists, would the people of the South regard it as a mere unpractical *theory?* May it not be that they now hold their slaves by virtue of our *theory* against *immediate emancipation,* expressed a thousand times through the Colonization Society and in other ways? If we, that is to say, all our *wise* and *prudent* men, have justified slavery, why should they condemn it? But if the cry, *cum tacent, clamant,* of 2,000,000 of oppressed men should enter our ears; if all our philanthropic men and women should be moved from the bottom of their hearts, and pour out the deep current of their united sympathy for the slave; and if the cautious and the timid, and the immovably *prudent,* should be, as they always are, borne along with the tide, might it not have a very practical bearing on the common sense and conscience of the southern people? How do we know that there are not hundreds and thousands among them, who need only to be backed by northern sentiment to become martyrs in the cause of humanity? Are we to be told that the most benevolent men at the South deprecate any interference on our part? Let us have the proof that they are benevolent men. We cannot take their word for it, nor any man's word for it, till it is shown that those men are not slave-holders, and that they have no sympathy with slave-holders as such; otherwise, we are merely told of benevolent robbers,—a thing incredible, especially on the testimony of the robbers themselves. But, waiving this point, it is said that they are on the ground, and know better than we what ought to be done, and how it ought to be done. "Why should men who have never set foot south of the Potomac or Ohio, pretend to know more about slavery and its remedy, than those who have been born and bred in the midst of it? Insufferable presumption!" This reminds me of a certain person—a *minister of the gospel,* reader—in this vicinity, who, on being asked to subscribe for an abolition newspaper, said he had not yet *read enough* on the subject to know whether a man could have a right of property in man or not! accordingly, he very sagely concluded *not* to take the newspaper till he had investigated the matter more thoroughly,—probably, to see whether or not it was worthy of investigation! Should such a man visit the South, and see with his own eyes, he would doubtless be well satisfied that man *can* have property in man. What is a man's *honesty* good for, if he needs to make a pilgrimage to Georgia to learn whether stolen property ought to be given up?

Others exclaim, "But how can your scheme of *immediate instant abolition* be practicable? Can a handful of northern men, or even the combined North, expect to overturn southern society from its foundation in a *moment?*—in the *twinkling of an eye?* What fools! Forsooth you will do nothing against slavery, unless you can do every thing, all at once! Heaven deliver *us* from such Quixotism! We are for the gradual abolition, for not attempting more than we can effect." What a pity that the great body of evangelical preachers of the gospel cannot learn wisdom of such counsellors. *They* preach *immediate, entire* repentance; of course they *expect,* "what fools!" to convert the whole world at a blow! Why do *they* not confine themselves to the doctrine of *gradual* repentance, and not attempt more than they are able to effect?

Now if I may be allowed to make a distinction too elementary to be overlooked by an infant, a *doctrine* is one thing, and a *plan* is another. When we say that slave-holders ought all to emancipate their slaves *immediately,* we state a *doctrine* which is *true.* We do not propose a *plan.* Our *plan,* and it has been explained often enough not to be misunderstood, is simply this: To promulgate the true *doctrine* of human rights in high places and low places, and all places where there are human beings. To whisper it in chimney corners and to proclaim it from the house-tops—yea from the mountain-tops. To pour it out like water from the pulpit and the press. To mix it up with all the food of the inner man, from infancy to gray hairs,—to give "line upon line and precept upon precept," till it forms one of the foundation principles and parts indestructible of the public soul. Let those who contemn this plan, renounce, if they have not done it already, the gospel plan for converting the world; let them renounce every plan of moral reformation, and every plan whatsoever, which does not terminate in the gratification of their own *animal* natures.

By prosecuting the plan described, we *expect* to see the benevolent, one by one at first, and afterwards in dense masses, awaking, gathering up their armor and rushing to the standard with the resolution to make up for lost time; we expect to see, at length, the full tide of public sympathy setting in favor of the slave. We expect to see him, when escaped from his cruel servitude, greeted by the friends of liberty, at the North, equally with the more courtly refugee of European tyranny. We expect to see the free colored American so educated and elevated in our own land, that it shall be notorious that the slave is BROTHER TO A MAN! In the meantime we expect to see the great body of slave-holders exasperated, foaming with rage and gnashing their teeth, threatening loudly to secede from the Union! madly prating about the invasion of sacred rights, the disturbance of their domestic quiet, and the violation of solemn compacts; and with blind infatuation, riveting tighter the fetters of their helpless victims. Nevertheless, we expect to *see* some tyrants, conscience-stricken, loosen their grasp; we expect, with God's good help, to hear the trumpet of the world's jubilee announcing that the *last fetter* has been knocked off from the heel of the *last slave*. . . .

WILLIAM JAY

DISMISSES THE PRO-SLAVERY ARGUMENT (1836).

THE ABOLITIONISTS REFUSED to give serious consideration to Southern theories of the origins of slavery or to the elaborate moral arguments justifying the "peculiar institution." Instead, they persisted in condemning it as a specifically American deviation from the enlightened and humanitarian standards of the nineteenth century. The effect of their criticism, notwithstanding the development of modern sociological and anthropological analysis by pro-slavery theorists, was to isolate the Southern argument as a medieval and barbaric set of assumptions. The most powerful anti-slavery weapon in countering the "positive good" theory was a none too subtle irony that exploited the contrast between the ideal of a great civilization resting on an essentially beneficent institution and the reality of an inhuman labor system as it existed in the South.

One of the most mordant of abolitionist polemicists was William Jay, the son of John Jay and a New York jurist who also served as corresponding foreign secretary of the American Anti-Slavery Society from 1835 to 1837. When Professor Thomas R. Dew of William and Mary published the first comprehensive American defense of slavery, *Review of the Debate in the Virginia Legislature of 1831 and 1832* (1832), Jay reviewed it for Elizur Wright's *Anti-Slavery Quarterly.* Dew's moderate arguments were directed to those members of the Virginia legislature—the last of the Jeffersonian critics of slavery—who voted for conpensated emancipation and colonization in a last futile effort to end slavery in the Old Dominion. Jay's caricature of Dew as the Don Quixote of slave society was a measure if the respect which he accorded the "true faith" in slavery. William Jay, Esq., "Remarks on Professor Dew's Vindication of Perpetual Slavery," *Quarterly Anti-Slavery Magazine,* vol. I, no. 3 (April 1836), 211-227.

THE MASSACRE AT SOUTHAMPTON in 1831 naturally directed public attention in Virginia, to the danger and consequences of servile insurrections. In the succeeding legislature, a portion of the members were led by the recent tragedy, to suggest the expediency of extinguishing slavery in the State at some distant period, and to propose plans for effecting this object. . . .

. . . The debates were published, and they disclosed the alarming fact, that there were native Virginians, men of character and influence, who believed slavery to be a moral and political evil which ought to be removed at some future day. It was important to the permanency of the institution, that this dangerous heresy should be at once assailed and vanquished, and Mr. Thomas R. Dew, Professor of History, Metaphysics, and Political Law, in William and Mary College, immediately buckled on his armor, and sallied forth a champion for the true faith. And never did a knight-errant exhibit a more gallant bearing; nor did even the hero of La Mancha, rush upon the windmills with more reckless intrepidity, than does our chivalric Professor battle with history and experience, and reason, and the moral sense of mankind. . . .

Our author now enters upon the defence of slavery, and satisfactorily proves that it is not a modern institution. Indeed he traces it to very high antiquity, and shews that it has prevailed over a large portion of the globe. In these respects, however, it must yield the palm to murder, since the latter crime dates its commencement in the family of Adam, and has been more or less perpetrated among every people from the time of Cain to the present hour.

The *origin* of slavery is next discussed, and *four* distinct sources are pointed out. We will examine them in their order:—

First. The Laws of War. Under this head we are treated with a fervid description of the horrors of savage warfare, and in contemplating the awful picture his own pencil had drawn, Mr. Dew exclaims, "what is there, let us ask, which is calculated to arrest this horrid practice, (killing and eating prisoners of war,) and to communicate an impulse towards civilization? Strange as it may sound in modern ears, it is the institution of property, and the existence of slavery." p. 12. . . .

Savage warfare, then is one source of slavery—let us see *how* the source sanctifies the stream. "Judging from the universality of the fact we may assert that domestic slavery seems the ONLY means of fixing the wanderer to the soil, moderating his savage temper, mitigating the horrors of war, and abolishing the practice of murdering the captives." p. 13.

We commend this new plan for effecting civilization, to our missionary boards, and suggest to them the expediency of instructing their missionaries in savage countries, to direct all their efforts in the first instance, to the establishment of domestic slavery, as preparatory to the introduction of the Gospel. . . .

We are next taught, that the great men of antiquity had none of the modern fastidiousness, on the subject of slavery, and the instances given to prove this point, furnish us, accidentally as it would seem, with the following beautiful illustration of the civilizing, humanizing influence of the practice of enslaving prisoners of war. "Julius Caesar had been reckoned one of the mildest and most clement military chieftains of antiquity, and yet there is very little doubt that the principal object in the invasion of Britain was to procure slaves for the Roman markets. When he left Britain, it became necessary to collect together *a large fleet* for the purpose of transporting his captives across the channel. He sometimes ordered the captive chiefs to be executed, and he butchered the whole of Cato's Senate, when he became master of Utica. Paulus Emilius acting under the special orders of the Roman Senate, laid all Epirus waste, and brought 150,000 captives in chains to Italy, all of whom were sold in the Roman slave-markets." p. 16.

Thus it would seem that the invasion of Britain, and the devastation of Epirus were caused by the influence of slavery, and that although Caesar was so distinguished a patron of this humanizing institution, he could nevertheless slaughter not only captive chiefs, but even the whole Utica Senate.

But to proceed—"If we turn from profane history to Holy Writ, that sacred fountain whence are derived those pure precepts and holy laws and regulations by which the christian world has ever been governed, we shall find that the children of Israel under the guidance of Jehovah, massacred or enslaved their prisoners of war." p. 16. When the Creator and Almighty Governor of the Universe shall devote the British nation to destruction for their sins, and shall by a series of stupendous miracles, require and enable the southern planters to execute his wrath, they will no doubt be excusable in killing or enslaving as many Englishmen as possible; but it is not clear to us, that in an ordinary war, the rights of victors over their prisoners, are thus extensive. The Professor indeed, does not explicitly contend for this right as belonging to *civilized* belligerents, but seems chiefly to rely on the *rights* of *savage* warriors, to make out his first source of slavery. Now it will be recollected, that it is part of the very essence of slavery, that it is perpetuated by descent. Let us suppose that one of the ancestors of our Virginia Professor had been captured by the royal but savage father of Pocahontas, and had, after the peace effected by that generous damsel, been sold as a slave to one of the Colonists. The whole transaction, according to the teacher of "Political Law" in William and Mary College, would have been strictly legal, sanctioned not only by innumerable instances in savage warfare, but by the example of Julius Caesar, Paulus Emilius, and other great men of antiquity, and above all, by the conduct of "the children of Israel under the guidance of Jehovah." The posterity of the hapless captive, would of course through successive generations have been lawfully held in bondage, and the Professor, instead of publishing theories about slavery, would at the present day, by his own shewing, be fairly, justly and honestly experiencing in his own person the blessings of hopeless interminable servitude, with the assurance that his own fate would be the inheritance of his children after him. . . .

But in the catalogue of blessings conferred by slavery, the most extraordinary, and we venture to say, the one least anticipated by our readers, is its influence "ON THE CONDITION OF THE FEMALE SEX"! That we may not do injustice to the Professor, we will permit him to speak for himself. "Slavery changes the hunting into the shepherd and agricultural states—gives rise to augmented productions, and consequently furnishes more abundant supplies for man: the labor of the slave thus becomes a substitute for that of the woman: man no longer wanders through the forest in quest of gain; and woman, consequently, is relieved from following on his track, under the enervating and harrassing burthen of her children: she is now surrounded by her domestics, and the abundance of their labor, lightens the toil and hardships of the whole family; she ceases to be a mere beast of burthen." p. 36.

It seems to have escaped Mr. Dew's recollection while penning this argument, that there were such beings in the world as *female* slaves. Where slavery prevails, we are told that woman ceases to be "a mere beast of burthen," and yet it so happens that in the slave states, there are more than ONE MILLION OF WOMEN, who in consequence of slavery, are mere beasts of burthen, exposed and sold like cattle in the public market, deprived of the rights and endearments belonging to the relations of daughter, wife and mother, unprotected from violence, and kept in ignorance and degradation.

Such is the influence of slavery on the "female sex." But our author refers to its influence on the LADY, and not on the *"domestics,"* by whom she is "surrounded." She, we are assured, "becomes the charming and animating centre of the family circle—time is afforded for reflection, and the cultivation of all those mild and fascinating virtues which throw a charm and delight around our homes and firesides, and calm and tranquilize the harsher tempers and more restless propensities of the male." p. 36. Far be it from us to question the charms and virtues of the southern ladies, to whatever cause Mr. Dew may ascribe them; but surely no one acquainted with northern society, will dare to assert, that it is necessary to brutalize one portion of the sex, in order to elevate the other to the highest degree of purity and loveliness, of which the female character is susceptible. . . .

Having explained the principle which is to determine the continuance or abolition of slavery, he proceeds to apply it, by asserting that the free blacks taken as a whole, "must be considered the most worthless and indolent of the citizens of the United States—the very drones and pests of society"; and we are assured, that this character does *not* arise "from the disabilities and disfranchisements by which the law attempts to guard against them." p. 88. After dwelling much on their idleness and profligacy, he proposes the important question, "Why are our colored freemen so generally indolent and worthless, among the industrious and enterprising citizens of even our northern and New England states?" p. 92. Now to this question *we* would reply, because they are deprived by unjust laws, and cruel prejudices, of almost every incentive to vigorous and honorable exertion, and are *kept* in ignorance, depravity and idleness. We conscientiously believe that had Mr. Dew been reared and treated from infancy, just as most of the southern free blacks are usually reared and treated, great as his natural endowments unquestionably are, he would himself have been a drone and a pest. But let us attend to the answer he gives to the question. "It is because there is an *inherent* and *intrinsic* cause at work which will produce its effect under *all circumstances.* In the free blacks, the *principle of idleness and dissipation* triumphs over that of accumulation, and the desire to better our condition: the animal part of man gains the victory over the moral." p. 92. Such is the solution of this moral phenomenon, given by our Professor of Metaphysics; and what does it amount to? Why, that God has implanted in the constitution of the black man, "a principle of idleness and dissipation," which is "inherent and intrinsic," and which of course does not belong to the white man. Unfortunately for this inherent and intrinsic principle, the Professor cites the example of the liberated serfs of Poland, Livonia, and Hungary, to prove that emancipated slaves will not work. These serfs who were in fact *white* slaves, he describes as being in the lowest state of degration [*sic*] and wretchedness. . . .

Mr. Dew proceeds at great length to vindicate the *moral influence* of slavery on the character and condition of both master and slave. We will not contest the matter with him. His own book, were other testimony wanting, would settle the question with us. Such heartlessness, such balancings of dollars and cents against the social and intellectual enjoyments and everlasting happiness of millions of his countrymen; such complacency in the contemplation of perpetual bondage, ignorance and degradation; such strange estimates of duty, cannot, we are persuaded, be the natural outpourings of his heart, but are the baneful fruits of the institution in which he has been nurtured. . . .

PART II.

ORGANIZING THE CRUSADE AGAINST SLAVERY.

THE AMERICAN ANTI-SLAVERY SOCIETY SENDS INSTRUCTIONS TO THEODORE WELD (1834).

THE AMERICAN ANTI-SLAVERY SOCIETY was organized in December, 1833, with Arthur Tappan as president and Elizur Wright and William Lloyd Garrison secretaries, on the principle that "the right to enjoy liberty is inalienable." "Every man," the Society's Declaration of Principles asserted, "has a right to his own body—to the products of his own labor—to the protection of law—and to the common advantages of society. . . ." Capitalizing on the organizational genius of agents like Theodore Weld and new mass propaganda techniques, the Society grew rapidly, until by 1838 it claimed 1,350 auxiliaries and some 250,000 members. Still, the organization was national in name only; until the schism of 1840 it remained a loosely constructed league of local and state societies—a clearinghouse for anti-slavery activities rather than a policy-making directory. Both the Society's strengths and its weaknesses can be seen in its printed commission to Theodore Weld and the accompanying hand-written "Particular Instructions." "American Anti-Slavery Society Commission to Theodore D. Weld," Gilbert H. Barnes and Dwight L. Dumond eds., *Letters of Theodore Dwight Weld, Angelina Grimké Weld and Sarah Grimké, 1822-1844* (New York: Appleton-Century-Crofts, Inc., 1934), 2 vols., I, 124-128. Reprinted with the permission of Dwight L. Dumond and the American Historical Association.

DEAR SIR:

You are hereby appointed and commissioned, by the Executive Committee of the American Anti-Slavery Society, instituted at Philadelphia in 1833, as their Agent, for the space of one year commencing with the first day of January, 1834, in the State of Ohio and elsewhere as the Committee may direct.

The Society was formed for the purpose of awakening the attention of our whole community to the character of American Slavery, and presenting the claims and urging the rights of the colored people of the United States; so as to promote, in the most efficient manner, the immediate abolition of Slavery, and the restoration of our colored brethren to their equal rights as citizens.

For a more definite statement of the objects of your agency, and the methods of its prosecution, the Committee refer you to their printed "Particular Instructions," communicated to you herewith; a full acquaintance and compliance with which, according to your ability, you will, on accepting this commission, consider as indispensable.

The Committee welcomes you as a fellow-laborer in this blessed and responsible work; the success of which will depend, in no small degree, under God, on the results of your efforts. Their ardent desires for your success will continually attend you; you will have their sympathy in trials; and nothing, they trust, will be wanting, on their part, for your encouragement and aid.

They commend you to the kindness and co-operation of all who love Zion; praying that the presence of God may be with you, cheering your heart, sustaining you in your arduous labors, and making them a means of a speedy liberation of all the oppressed.

Given at the Society's Office, No. 130 Nassau-street, New-York, the twentieth day of February in the year of our Lord eighteen hundred and thirty-four.

Arthur Tappan
Chairman of the Executive Committee

Attest,
E. Wright Jr.
Secretary of Domestic Correspondence

PARTICULAR INSTRUCTIONS.

To Mr. T. D. Weld

Dear Sir: You have been appointed an Agent of the American Anti-Slavery Society: and will receive the following instructions from the Executive Committee, as a brief expression of the principles they wish you to inculcate, and the course of conduct they wish you to pursue in this agency.

. . . Our object is, the overthrow of American slavery, the most atrocious and oppressive system of bondage that has ever existed in any country. We expect to accomplish this, mainly by showing to the public its true character and legitimate fruits, its contrariety to the first principles of religion, morals, and humanity, and its special inconsistency with our pretensions, as a free, humane, and enlightened people. In this way, by the force of truth, we expect to correct common errors that prevail respecting slavery, and to produce a just public sentiment, which shall appeal both to the conscience and love of character, of our slave-holding fellow-citizens, and convince them that both their duty and their welfare require the immediate abolition of slavery.

You will inculcate every where, the great fundamental principle of IMMEDIATE ABOLITION, as the duty of all masters, on the ground that slavery is both unjust and unprofitable. Insist principally on the SIN OF SLAVERY, because our main hope is in the consciences of men, and it requires little logic to prove that it is always safe to do right. To question this, is to impeach the superintending Providence of God.

We reprobate the idea of compensation to slave holders, because it implies the right of slavery. It is also unnecessary, because the abolition of slavery will be an advantage, as free labor is found to be more profitable than the labor of slaves. We also reprobate all plans of expatriation, by whatever specious pretences covered, as a remedy for slavery, for they all proceed from prejudices against color; and we hold that the duty of the whites in regard to this cruel prejudice is not to indulge it, but to repent and overcome it.

The people of color ought at once to be emancipated and recognized as citizens, and their rights secured as such, equal in all respects to others, according to the cardinal principle laid down in the American Declaration of Independence. Of course we have nothing to do with any *equal* laws which the states may make, to prevent or punish vagrancy, idleness, and crime, either in whites or blacks.

Do not allow yourself to be drawn away from the main object, to exhibit a detailed PLAN of abolition; for men's consciences will be greatly relieved from the feeling of present duty, by any objections or difficulties which they can find or fancy in your plan. Let the *principle* be decided on, of immediate abolition, and the plans will easily present themselves. What ought to be done can be done. If the *great* question were decided, and if half the ingenuity now employed to defend slavery were employed to abolish it, it would not impeach the wisdom of American statesmen to say they could not, with the Divine blessing, steer the ship through.

You will make yourself familiar with FACTS, for they chiefly influence reflecting minds. Be careful to use only facts that are well authenticated, and always state them with the precision of a witness under oath. You cannot do our cause a greater injury than by overstating facts. Clarkson's "Thoughts," and Stuart's "West India Question," are Magazines of facts respecting the safety and benefit of immediate emancipation. Mrs. Child's Book, Stroud's Slave Laws, Paxton's and Rankin's Letters, D. L. Child's Address, are good authorities respecting the character of American slavery. The African Repository and Garrison's Thoughts will show the whole subject of expatriation.

The field marked out by the Committee for your agency is the State of Ohio.

The Committee expect you to confine your labors to that field, unless some special circumstances call you elsewhere. And in such case you will confer with the Committee before changing your field, if time will allow. And if not, we wish immediate notice of the fact.

In traversing your field, you will generally find it wise to visit first several prominent places in it, particularly those where it is known our cause has friends. In going to a place, you will naturally call upon those who are friendly to our objects, and take advice from them. Also call on ministers of the gospel and other leading characters, and labor specially to enlighten them and secure their favor and influence. Ministers are the hinges of community, and ought to be moved, if possible. If they can be gained, much is gained. But if not, you will not be discouraged; and if not plainly inexpedient, attempt to obtain a house of worship; or if none can be had, some other convenient place—and hold a public meeting, where you can present our cause, its facts, arguments and appeals, to as many people as you can collect, by notices in pulpits and newspapers, and other proper means.

Form Auxiliary Societies, both male and female, in every place where it is practicable. Even if such societies are very small at the outset, they may do much good as centres of light, and means of future access to the people. Encourage them to raise funds and apply them in purchasing and circulating anti-slavery publications gratuitously; particularly the Anti-Slavery Reporter, of which you will keep specimens with you, and which can always be had of the Society at $2.00 per 100. You are at liberty, with due discretion, to recommend other publications, *so far* as they advocate our views of immediate abolition. We hold ourselves responsible only for our own.

You are not to take up collections in your public meetings, as the practice often prevents persons from attending, whom it might be desirable to reach. Let this be stated in the public notice of the meeting. If you find individuals friendly to our views, who are able to give us money, you will make special personal application, and urge upon them the duty of liberally supporting this cause. You can also give notice of some place where those disposed can give you their donations. Generally, it is best to invite them to do this *the next morning*.

We shall expect you to write frequently to the Secretary for Domestic Correspondence, and give minute accounts of your proceedings and success. If you receive money for the Society, you will transmit it, *by mail,* WITHOUT DELAY, to the Treasurer.

Always keep us advised, if possible, of the place where letters may reach you.

Believing as we do, that the hearts of all men are in the hand of Almighty God, we wish particularly to engage the prayers of all good men in behalf of our enterprise. Let them pray that *we* and our agents may have Divine guidance and zeal; and slave-holders, penitence; and slaves, patience; and statesmen, wisdom; so that this grand experiment of moral influence may be crowned with glorious and speedy success. Especially stir up ministers and others to the duty of making continual mention of the oppressed slaves in all social and public prayers. And as far as you can, procure the stated observance of the LAST MONDAY EVENING in every month, as a season of special prayer in behalf of the people of color.

We will only remind you, that the Society is but the almoner of the public—that the silver and the gold are the Lord's—that the amount as yet set apart by his people for promoting this particular object is small—our work is great and our resources limited—and we therefore trust that you will not fail to use a faithful economy in regard to the expenses of traveling, and reduce them as low as you can without impairing your usefulness.

JAMES THOME AND JOHN ALVORD

WITHSTAND A BARRAGE OF EGGS (1836).

WHEN THEODORE WELD RECEIVED his commission and instructions from the American Anti-Slavery Society in 1834, he had abandoned colonization and was already deeply involved in the abolitionist enterprise. A convert of the great revivalist Charles G. Finney and an agent in Christian reform movements, Weld brought to abolition an infectious zeal and a talent for gaining supporters unmatched in anti-slavery circles. Within a year after his appointment he had engineered a student revolt at Lane Seminary in Cincinnati against President Lyman Beecher's ban on free discussion of slavery, led the exodus from Lane to Oberlin, and organized a group of anti-slavery agents, known as "Weld's Band," to abolitionize the whole upper Mississippi Valley. Two of Weld's band of seventy were James Thome and John Alvord, both of whom had deserted to Oberlin after the famous Lane Debates. Enrolled at Oberlin, they spent their summer vacations and the year following their graduation traveling the anti-slavery circuit in Ohio. Like all of Weld's evangelicals, they thought of themselves as latter-day Luthers completing the Reformation by carrying the doctrine of the equality of true believers to its ultimate conclusion. Their report on their activities in 1836 reveals both the religious ardor and the keen sense of the antic aspects of moral agitation which marked the true believer in the anti-slavery cause. Barnes and Dumond, *Weld-Grimké Letters,* I, 256-262. Reprinted with the permission of Dwight L. Dumond and the American Historical Association.

Middlebury, Portage Co. [Ohio] Feb. 9, 1836

VERY DEAR BRO. WELD:

I am about to bore you with another long sheet. Here's a hand. How are you? In good spirits, I trust, and flushed with triumph. You have bearded the Lion in his den, there at Utica, and I trust you have smitten him. Well I suppose you want to hear how your *weak brother* has succeeded since he last wrote. I will tell you. I went to Akron pursuant to invitation. The citizens were rampant for discussion. They were certain (so they intimated to the Abolitionists of the place) that if they only had a chance to reply to my arguments they could prove, to a demonstration, the absurdity and danger of Abolition. I was a little disappointed at finding this state of feeling; for, until the Lyceum had met, I supposed that it was expected that I would deliver an *address.* Accordingly I had prepared a Lecture on the *Reasons for discussion.* However at the opening of the Lyceum, it was moved that I should be restricted to the ordinary time of a debater—20 mins. and that the opposition should have the privilege of answering me. So I was called upon, unexpectedly, to open the debate, on the Question "Ought the present abolition Societies to be sustained?" I remarked that before the Lyceum could intelligently decide upon this Question, they must know what the *principles and designs* of Abolition Societies were.

I therefore gave an exposition of Abolition principles and measures. First I was particularly careful to *disclaim* certain things which are confounded with abolitionism; such as social intercourse, amalgamation, etc. I further stated that we did not claim for the slave the right of voting, immediately, or eligibility to office. Also that we did not wish them *turned loose,* having the possession of unlicensed liberty; nor even to be governed by the same *code* of Laws which are *adapted* to intelligent citizens. That on the contrary we believed that it would be necessary to form a *special code* of Laws restricting them in their freedom, upon the same general principles that apply to foreigners, minors, etc. By the time I had got through with the *negative* part of the subject, my 20 [minutes] were up. I was replied to by a lawyer. He expressed his astonishment at the *disclaimers* which I had made. Said he didn't know but that he was ready to go *all lengths* with *me;* but he protested that I was a NEW abolitionist and had disowned every distinguishing feature of modern abolitionism. He proceeded then to give *his* view of abolition, and after he had dressed it up in a bear-skin, he fell upon it like a whole kennel of hell-hounds, and he tore it to pieces most adroitly. I complimented him for his skill and *voraciousness,* and hoped that he would have a *happy digestion* of his *bear-skin and straw.* I then proceeded to state what abolition *was;* and I blazed and threw sky-rocketts, talked of human rights, touched upon the Amer. Revolution and brought heaven and earth together. I did all the speaking on our side—spoke four times—followed each time by some lawyer or other important personage. Each successive opponent emulated the first dog, in barking at the man of straw, and tearing bear-skins. The Lyceum room was full and tho' the discussion was continued till 10 ocl. there was unabated interest to the last. The discussion was adjourned to Monday evening. . . . On Monday eve. the Lyceum Room was full again. The neg[ative] had the floor. The gentleman—a merchant—tried to demolish my Bible Argument. He untied a handkerchief full of Commentaries, and read from Scott, Henry, Clarke, and thus he demonstrated, like an Episcopalian minister in Cleveland, that the *modern commentator* was in error. Things went pretty much as on the first evening. Quite as much interest, quite as much confidence on the part of the opposition that they could explode Abo. and quite as great a failure. The discussion was adjourned to Tuesday Eve. I dwelt on the safety of Emancipation. The Facts went like chain shot, *heated red hot.*

On Wednesday Eve, after a sharp encounter the enemy filed off and retreated—the *call for Question* being, of course, synonymous with a *cry for Quarter*. The vote was taken in the Lyceum. It stood 12 for Abolition and 9 against. The vote of the house was then called for. It was taken and stood for Abolition 40 to 22. Lectured the following evening in the Pres. Church. The evening was intensely cold, and the house had but one small stove. Hence there were but few out. Formed a Society—15 joined. The meeting was adjourned to this (Tuesday) eve, to hear an address from Bro. Alvord and appoint the officers. I will let you know the results. Last Sab. eve, I lectured again at Tallmadge on the old Test. Argument. Got into the Meth[odist] Church; tho' some of the members are violently opposed to Abolition.

I have written a note to an Ab. in Massillon, stating that I would be there by Thursday next, and requesting him to get things agoing for me. Probably will have a discussion there. Hope so. Am staying about Middlebury a day or two to take care of John Alvord. He has such a mob-raising tendancy that he needs some guardians. He will tell you his own story here. . . .

Your Affectionate Brother—James A. Thome

My Dear Brother:

I intended to have written in the other letter, but Br. T[home] being in Akron sent it off before I had a chance. Well to begin where I left off. Went from Austinburg to Geneva. Lectured Sab. Eve and all day Monday. It was their annual meeting. A number of additions to the town Soc.—formed also a Ladies Soc. Mrs. Cowles told me she thought they could get 50 names—15 or 20 were given in at the time altho I spoke in regard to it only 5 or 10 min's at the close of one of my lectures. Stopped a few hours for the stage in Unionville—all goes well there. 100 as they told me in each soc. Came on to Willoughby. Soon as I got in town, they insisted upon my stopping to lecture. Found that the cause had made good progress during my absence. By waiting until a Methodist protracted meeting closed, it was supposed we should have no difficulty. Did so, when the Methodist minister (a bitter opposer) declared we should not have the house. A request signed by about 50 of the most respectable inhabitants of the Vill. was then sent up to the Trustees. The majority of them consented and some were anxious for the Lecture, but the minister raved like a mad man declaring as I was told that if I attempted to lecture he would stand in the door with a club. The Trustees cowered before the anathemas of their Preacher and the house was refused. As no other place could be had there they gave me a strong invitation to come and lecture soon as their Presbyterian house is finished. I shall probably go there again on my return in the spring, and perhaps in 4 weeks, at the sitting of the court. The whole Village would have come out if I could have got a place. A number of strong men declared Abo. before I left. I do hope to have a hearing there on [my re]turn, have just written to them about it. Met Br. Thome at Ravenna, since when I have lectured at Cuyahoga Falls once, Tallmadge 3 times, and we have had 5 meetings here. I lectured first. They then challenged to a discussion—arrangements were accordingly made. The 2 lawyers were their champions. The eve. came, when they both backed out and we occupied all the Evening. Next eve, same way—would stop at the end of each 20 min. but all that could be drawn from them was to provoke a few questions. Sabbath, lectured on Bible slavery—a large audience out. Some were converted and some quarrelled. Tuesday Eve we had a meeting in Akron. Br. Thome and I spoke each a short time. They elected officers, etc. and some 10 or 12 joined the soc. I shall lecture there next Monday eve.

Last evening Midd[l]ebury puked. Her stomach had evidently become overloaded by the amount of undiluted Pikery [?] she had taken at the two preceding discussions. The system would not endure it. Spasmodic heavings and retchings were manifest during the whole day. Toward night symptoms more alarming. The com. of arrangements—whom the citizens had chosen to manage their discussion—came to us and affected to be terribly frightened—advised that the meeting be omitted. We told them it was their concern—we had no personal fears—and if the house was unlocked and lighted we should be there. 6 oclock came. Heard no Bell and saw no light. Went down, however, but found the house locked and one of the Trustees had received the key from the Com. and taken it home to his house. Audience soon began to gather. We retired for consultation for a few minutes in an adjoining school Hous[e]. Abolition dander got a little started. Two of the Trustees of the Church with a growl put out and soon we heard the Bell ringing like fire. One of them soon came in and invited us over. Found the door burst in, etc. A goodly number soon gathered in, and Bro. Thome proceeded to lecture. All [was] still until about 8 [o'clock] when in came a broadside of Eggs, Glass, Egg shells, whites and yolks flew on every side. Br. Thom[e']s Fact Book received an egg just in its bowels and I doubt whether one in the House escaped a spattering. I have been trying to clean off this morning, but cant get off the stink. Thome dodged like a stoned gander. He brought up at length against the side of the desk, cocked his eye and stood gazing upward at the flying missiles as they stream[e]d in ropy masses through the house. I fear he'll never stand the *"Goose Egg"* without winking. He apologizes to me this morning by saying he thought the *stove was crackin!!!!* Well to go on. The audience soon got seated again and Br. T. went on. In about 20 minutes, we heard again the yell of the mob outside, and directly another crash told us that another Egg plaster was on its way. They now continued the fire some time like scattering musketry, mingled with their howlings. There was about 40 of them. A Mr. Kent, a merchant of the place, attempted to go out, when a volley was discharged at him and one of them hit him plump in the right Eye. He cam[e] back groaning most piteously. I understand that he says this morning that he is an abolitionist. It being now 9 o'clock, a resolution was passed unanimously to meet in the same place on Friday eve. They then appointed a committee to bring if possible the rioters to justice and the meeting adjourned. The meeting was composed of some of the best men of the village and all appeared firm. The Committee appointed are none of them abolitionists, but are well on the way. I think this will bring the people here to a stand. The mob threaten today dreadfully. Whether the citizens will cower before them or not [we] dont know. There are a few determined men here, but the mob are set on by men of influence most of whom are church members. Abolitionists heretofore in this place have always been mobbed out. We must try to carry the day this time if possible. Have just heard that 26 panes of glass are broken and many eggs smashed without coming through.

I forgot to tell you I am bound to appear as witness at the trial of the Willoughby rioters, and the court sits in about 4 weeks. I think therefore that I shall not go down to Wooster, but take another route and return to Willoughby. I have an urgent invitation from 2 or 3 places I might say 4 or 5 to stop and lecture and in places where they have not heard any thing on the subject. If after I get through there I can overtake Br. Allen I will do so. Dear Bro. we want much to hear from you. Have not heard from the other Brethren this long time.

Yr Bro. Affectionately J. W. Alvord

Weld—What I have to say is that this story of Johns about me "is just as mean as purssly [?]." I was brave as a warrior; but I did really think the stove was exploding with a tremendous force. So soon as I was undeceived, I was bold as a Lion. It was a ludicrous scene though after all. Don't you believe me?

Yours J. A. Thome

NORTHERN WOMEN PETITION CONGRESS

TO ABOLISH SLAVERY IN THE DISTRICT OF COLUMBIA (1834).

THROUGHOUT THE NORTH abolitionists organized women in support of their cause. Since abolition was first and foremost a moral appeal, and since women were widely credited with finer moral sensibilities than men, the abolitionists missed no opportunity to appeal to them in behalf of the slave. Although few of the anti-slavery leaders were prepared to go as far as Garrison in combining abolition and woman's rights, all of them recognized the growing power of feminism and exploited it thoroughly. One of their devices was the "female petition" like the following "Fathers and Rulers" petition, thousands of which deluged Congress until both houses passed a "gag law" in 1836 to shut off the flood. Barnes and Dumond, *Weld-Grimké Letters,* I, 175-176. Reprinted with the permission of Dwight L. Dumond and the American Historical Association.

TO THE HON. THE SENATE AND HOUSE OF REPRESENTATIVES OF THE U. STATES, IN CONGRESS ASSEMBLED:

Petition of the Ladies resident in ——— County, State of Ohio.

FATHERS AND RULERS OF OUR COUNTRY:

Suffer us, we pray you, with the sympathies which we are constrained to feel as wives, as mothers, and as daughters, to plead with you in behalf of a long oppressed and deeply injured class of native Americans residing in that portion of our country which is under your exclusive control. We should poorly estimate the virtues which ought ever to distinguish your honorable body could we anticipate any other than a favorable hearing when our appeal is to men, to philanthropists, to patriots, to the legislators and guardians of a Christian people. We should be less than women, if the nameless and unnumbered wrongs of which the slaves of our sex are made the defenceless victims, did not fill us with horror and constrain us, in earnestness and agony of spirit to pray for their deliverance. By day and by night, their woes and wrongs rise up before us, throwing shades of mournful contrast over the joys of domestic life, and filling our hearts with sadness at the recollection of those whose hearths are desolate.

Nor do we forget, in the contemplation of their other sufferings, the intellectual and moral degradation to which they are doomed; how the soul formed for companionship with angels, is despoiled and brutified, and consigned to ignorance, pollution, and ruin.

Surely then, as the representatives of a people professedly christian, you will bear with us when we express our solemn apprehensions in the language of the patriotic Jefferson "we tremble for our country when we remember that God is just, and that his justice cannot sleep forever," and when in obedience to a divine command "we remember them who are in bonds as bound with them." Impelled by these sentiments, we solemnly purpose, the grace of God assisting, to importunate high Heaven with prayer, and our national Legislature with appeals, until this christian people abjure forever a traffic in the souls of men, and the groans of the oppressed no longer ascend to God from the dust where they now welter.

We do not ask your honorable body to transcend your constitutional powers, by legislating on the subject of slavery within the boundaries of any slaveholding State; but we do conjure you to abolish slavery in the District of Columbia where you exercise exclusive jurisdiction. In the name of humanity, justice, equal rights and impartial law, our country's weal, her honor and her cherished hopes we earnestly implore for this our humble petition, your favorable regard. If both in christian and in heathen lands, Kings have revoked their edicts, at the intercession of woman, surely we may hope that the Legislators of a free, enlightened and christian people will lend their ear to our appeals, when the only boon we crave is the restoration of rights unjustly wrested from the innocent and defenceless.—And as in duty bound your petitioners will ever pray. (T.D.W. 1834)

NAMES NAMES

. . . . .

JOHN GREENLEAF WHITTIER

WRITES "THE SLAVE SHIPS" (1833).

IN ADDITION TO RECRUITING women, the abolitionists sought the support of philanthropists, humanitarians, and literary figures in the North. The Quaker poet John Greenleaf Whittier, first discovered by Garrison in 1826, joined the New England Anti-Slavery Society in 1831 and two years later helped Garrison write the Declaration of Sentiments of the national society. Shy and withdrawn but vigorous and unyielding in his hatred of slavery, Whittier proved an invaluable ally. His early poem "The Slave Ships" (1834) appeared in numerous anti-slavery publications, among them the October 11, 1834 issue of the *Liberator*.

"—— That fatal, that perfidious bark,
Built i' the eclipse, and rigged with curses dark."
Milton's Lycidas

THE FRENCH SHIP LE RODEUR, with a crew of twenty-two men, and with one hundred and sixty negro slaves, sailed from Bonny in Africa, April, 1819. On approaching the line, a terrible malady broke out—an obstinate disease of the eyes—contagious, and altogether beyond the resources of medicine. It was aggravated by the scarcity of water among the slaves, (*only half a wine-glass per day* being allowed to an individual,) and by the extreme impurity of the air in which they breathed. By the advice of the physician, they were brought upon deck occasionally, but some of the poor wretches, locking themselves in each other's arms, leaped overboard, in the hope which so universally prevails among them, of being swiftly transported to their own homes in Africa. To check this, the captain ordered several who were stopped in the attempt, to be shot, or hanged, before their companions. The disease extended to the crew; and one after another were smitten with it, until only *one* remained unaffected. Yet even this dreadful condition did not preclude calculation: to save the expense of supporting slaves rendered unsaleable, and to obtain grounds for a claim against the underwriters, *thirty-six of the negroes, having become blind, were thrown into the sea and drowned!* —(*Speech of M. Benjamin Constant in the Chamber of Deputies, June 17, 1820.*)

In the midst of their dreadful fears, lest the solitary individual, whose sight remained unaffected, should also be seized with the malady, a sail was discovered. It was the Spanish Slaver, Leon. The same disease had been there; and horrible to tell, all the crew had become blind! Unable to assist each other, the vessels parted. The Spanish ship has never since been heard of. The Rodeur reached Guadaloupe on the twenty first of June; the only man who had escaped the disease, and had thus been enabled to steer the slaver into port, caught it in three days after its arrival.—(*Bibliothèque Opthalmologique, for November,* 1819.)

"All ready?" cried the Captain;
"Ay, Ay!" the seamen said—
"Heave up the worthless lubbers,
The dying and the dead."
Up from the slave-ship's prison
Fierce, bearded heads were thrust—
"Now let the sharks look to it—
Toss up the dead ones first!"

Corpse after corpse came up,—
Death had been busy there.
Where every blow is mercy,
Why should the spoiler spare?
Corpse after corpse they cast
Sullenly from the ship,
Yet bloody with the traces
Of fetter-link and whip.

Gloomily stood the captain,
With his arms upon his breast,
With his cold brow sternly knotted,
And his iron lip compress'd.
"Are all the dead dogs over?"
Growl'd through that matted lip—
"The blind ones are no better,
Let's lighten the good ship!"

Hark! from the ship's dark bosom,
The very sounds of hell!—
The ringing clank of iron—
The maniac's short, sharp yell!

The hoarse, low curse, throat-stifled—
  The starving infant's moan—
The horror of a breaking heart
  Pour'd through a mother's groan!

Up from that loathsome prison
  The stricken blind ones came—
Below, had all been darkness—
  Above, was still the same.
Yet the holy breath of Heaven
  Was sweetly breathing there,
And the heated brow of fever
  Cool'd in the soft sea-air.

"Overboard with them, shipmates!"
  Cutlass and dirk were plied:
Fetter'd and blind, one after one,
  Plunged down the vessel's side.
The sabre smote above—
  Beneath, the lean shark lay,
Waiting with wide and bloody jaw
  His quick and human prey.

God of the earth! what cries
  Rang upward unto Thee?
Voices of agony and blood,
  From ship-deck and from sea.
The last dull plunge was heard—
  The last wave caught its stain—
And the unsated sharks look'd up
  For human hearts in vain.

. . . . .

Red glow'd the western waters—
  The setting sun was there,
Scattering alike on wave and cloud
  His fiery mesh of hair.
Amidst a group in blindness,
  A solitary eye
Gazed, from the burden'd slaver's deck,
  Into that burning sky.

"A storm," spoke out the gazer,
  "Is gathering and at hand—
Curse on't—I'd give my other eye
  For one firm rood of land."
And then he laugh'd—but only
  His echoed laugh replied—
For the blinded and the suffering
  Alone were at his side.

Night settled on the waters,
  And on a stormy heaven,
While fiercely on that lone ship's track
  The thunder-gust was driven.
"A sail!—thank God! a sail!"
  And, as the helmsman spoke,
Up through the stormy murmur
  A shout of gladness broke.

Down came the stranger vessel
  Unheeding, on her way,
So near, that on the slaver's deck
  Fell off her driven spray.
"Ho! for the love of mercy—
  We're perishing and blind!"
A wail of utter agony
  Came back upon the wind.

"Help us! for we are stricken
  With blindness every one—
Ten days we've floated fearfully,
  Unnoting star or sun.
Our ship's the slaver Leon—
  We've but a score on board—
Our slaves are all gone over—
  Help—for the love of God!"

On livid brows of agony
  The broad red lightning shone—

But the roar of wind and thunder
  Stifled the answering groan.
Wail'd from the broken waters
  A last despairing cry,
As kindling in the stormy light,
  The stranger ship went by.

. . . . .

In the sunny Guadaloupe
  A dark hull'd vessel lay—
With a crew who noted never
  The night-fall or the day.
The blossom of the orange
  Waved white by every stream,
And tropic leaf, and flower, and bird,
  Were in the warm sun-beam.

And the sky was bright as ever,
  And the moonlight slept as well,
On the palm-trees by the hill-side,
  And the streamlet of the dell.
And the glances of the Creole
  Were still as archly deep,
And her smiles as full as ever
  Of passion and of sleep.

But vain were bird and blossom,
  The green earth and the sky,
And the smile of human faces,
  To the ever-darken'd eye;—
For, amidst a world of beauty,
  The slaver went abroad,
With his ghastly visage written
  By the awful curse of God!

PART III.

THE DEFENSE OF AMERICAN FREEDOMS.

AMOS DRESSER
IS WHIPPED IN NASHVILLE (1835).

THE PUBLIC REACTION against the abolitionists, which set in immediately after they organized in 1833, grew in intensity and rancor as the decade progressed. Southern legislatures offered rewards for the capture of abolitionist leaders, and Northern states yielded to Southern pressures by considering laws to restrict anti-slavery activities. President Jackson lent his support to the forces of repression by recommending a federal law closing the mails to abolitionist literature; and although the matter was finally left to the discretion of local postmasters, the circulation of anti-slavery propaganda was effectively checked. Meanwhile, the right of petition was virtually denied by a succession of Congressional "gag rules" which automatically tabled all incoming petitions. Individual abolitionists found the going rough against Northern hostility and resentment. Their meetings were frequently mobbed and broken up, their property destroyed, and their lives threatened. As a hard-pressed minority they fought back with a vigorous defense of civil liberties, insisting on their right to preach unpopular opinions and pointing to American proscriptive tactics as evidence of a pro-slavery conspiracy to destroy free society.

Amos Dresser, a young seminarian from Lane who was publicly whipped in Nashville for distributing abolitionist tracts, wrote an account of his misadventure which circulated widely in the North. "The Narrative of Amos Dresser" convinced a growing number of Northern liberals who were not necessarily sympathetic to abolitionism that slavery did in fact threaten American civil liberties. *The Narrative of Amos Dresser, with Stone's Letters from Natchez,—An Obituary Notice of the Writer, and Two Letters from Tallahassee, Relating to the Treatment of Slaves* (New York, 1836).

AMOS DRESSER'S OWN NARRATIVE.

. . . ON THE FIRST DAY of last month I left Cincinnati for the purpose of selling the "Cottage Bible," in order, from the profits of the sale, to raise funds sufficient to enable me to complete my education. The largest portion of my books was sent to Nashville by water. I took several copies of the Bible with me, besides a considerable number of the little work entitled "Six Months in a Convent." In packing them into my trunk and the box of my barouche, a number of pamphlets and papers of different descriptions were used to prevent the books from injury by rubbing, intending to distribute them as suitable opportunities should present. Among them were old religious newspapers, anti-slavery publications, numbers of the Missionary Herald, Sunday-school periodicals, temperance almanacs, &c., &c. At Danville, Ky., where a state anti-slavery society had been organized some months before, and where the subject of emancipation seemed to be discussed without restraint, besides selling several copies of my books, I parted with a large share of my anti-slavery publications. In travelling through that state, I distributed most of my temperance almanacs and other papers above mentioned, including a few tracts on slavery, given to those who were willing to receive them. *I gave none of these to any person of color, bond or free, nor had I any intention of doing so.*

Near Gallatin, in Sumner county, Tennessee, I sold a copy of Rankin's Letters on Slavery. I arrived at Nashville on Saturday the 11th of July, and took lodgings at the Nashville Inn. The young man who accompanied me, in bringing into the house my books from the box of the barouche, omitted the anti-slavery tracts and other pamphlets. Their being overlooked did not occupy the attention of either of us, and on Monday morning the barouche was taken to the shop of Mr. Stout to be repaired. In the course of the day Mr. S. remarked to his workmen, as he afterward informed me, that perhaps, as I came from Cincinnati, I was an Abolitionist. On this, one of them commenced rummaging my carriage. In the box he found, among the other pamphlets, a February number of the Anti-Slavery Record, with a cut representing a drove of slaves chained, the two foremost having violins, on which they were playing—the American flag waving in the centre, whilst the slave-driver, with his whip, was urging on the rear. This added considerably to the general excitement, which I afterwards learned, was prevailing in relation to slavery—and in a short time it was noised about that I had been "circulating incendiary periodicals among the free colored people, and trying to excite the slaves to insurrection. . . ." [Dresser is apprehended and brought to the courthouse.]

The meeting being called to order, the mayor stated, that he had caused me to be arrested, and brought before the Committee, in consequence of the excitement produced by the periodicals known to have been in my possession; and that he had also taken into his charge my trunk, which he had delayed opening till my return. The trunk was then produced before the Committee, and a motion made and carried, that I should be interrogated as to its contents before opening it. On being interrogated accordingly, I replied, as the trunk was before them, I preferred that they should make the examination for themselves. It was then resolved, (the whole house voting) that my trunk should be examined. The officer first laid before the Committee a pile of clothing, which was examined very closely—then followed my books, among which was found, one copy of the "Oasis," one of "Rankin's Letters on Slavery," and one of "Bourne's Picture of Slavery in the United States." These, I informed the Committee, I had put in my trunk for my own perusal, as I wished to compare what had been written with the result of my own observation while in the slave states, and that no individual had seen them besides myself. A careful inspection was made of the books also. Then was presented my business and private letters, which were read with eagerness and much interest. Extracts were read aloud. . . .

Great stress was laid on these extracts, and I was questioned very minutely, as to the authors of the letters. They labored much to prove I was sent out by some society, and that I was, under the guise of a religious mission, performing the odious office of an insurrectionary agent.

My journal was next brought in review, but as it had been kept in pencil mark, the memoranda short and hastily written, it served them very little purpose. It was laid down again by the Mayor, who had attempted to read it aloud, with this remark—"It is evidently very hostile to slavery."

A witness was now called forward by whom it was proved, that an anti-slavery periodical of some kind had been left by some individual on the counter of the Nashville Inn. That it was left with a copy of the Cottage Bible, at the time I arrived. On being questioned by me, it turned out to be a number of the Emancipator, used as an envelope, or wrapper to the Bible; other witnesses were called, but this was the substance of all they proved against me. . . .

. . . The trial continued from between four and five o'clock, P.M. till eleven o'clock at night, when I was called upon for my defense. The perplexity I must have felt in making it may well be imagined, when it is recollected that I was charged not with transgressing any law of the state or ordinance of the city, but with conduct to which, if the law had attached the penalty of crime, its forms were totally disregarded, and this too, before an array of persons banded together in contravention of the law, and from whose mandate of execution there was no appeal. However, I took the opportunity thus offered to declare fully my sentiments on the subject of slavery. Whilst I told them I believed slaveholding to be inconsistent with the gospel, and a constant transgression of God's law, I yet said, that in bringing about emancipation, the interests of the master were to be consulted as well as those of the slave. . . . In reference to my demeanor towards the slave, that in the few instances in which I had casually conversed with them, I had recommended quietness, patience, submission; teaching them to "render good for evil," and discountenancing every scheme of emancipation which did not, during its process, look for its success in the good conduct of the slaves whilst they remain such, and to the influence of argument and persuasion addressed to the understandings and consciences of slaveholders, exhorting them to obey God in doing justice and showing mercy to their fellow-men.

After my remarks were ended, the crowd were requested to withdraw whilst the committee deliberated on the case. In company with a friend or two I was directed to a private room near at hand, to await their decision. Up to this period, during the whole proceedings, my mind was composed, my spirits calm and unruffled; nor did I entertain the most distant apprehension there would be so flagrant a violation of my rights as an American citizen, and so deliberate an attempt to dishonor me as a man.

In this confidence I was strengthened by the consideration of all the circumstances of the case. What I had done, I had done openly. *There was no law forbidding what I had done.* . . . In addition to this, too, among my triers, there was a great portion of the respectability of Nashville. Nearly half of the whole number, professors of Christianity, the reputed stay of the church, supporters of the cause of benevolence in the form of Tracts and Missionary Societies and Sabbath-schools, several members, and most of the elders of the Presbyterian church, from whose hands, but a few days before, I had received the emblems of the broken body and shed blood of our blessed Saviour. My expectations, however, were soon shaken by Mr. Braughton's saying on entering the room where I was, that he feared it would go hard with me—that, whilst some of the committee were in favor of thirty-nine, others were for inflicting one hundred lashes, whilst others still thought me worthy of death. My suspense was at last terminated on being summoned to hear the decision; it was prefaced by a few remarks of this kind by the chairman, "that they had acted with great caution and deliberation, and however unsatisfactory their conclusion might be to me, they had acted conscientiously, with a full recognition of their duty to their God"—that they had found me guilty, 1st "of being a member of an Anti-Slavery Society in Ohio;" 2nd, "of having in my possession periodicals published by the American Anti-Slavery Society:" and 3d, "they BELIEVED I had circulated these periodicals and advocated in the community the principles they inculcated." He then pronounced that I was condemned to receive twenty lashes on my bare back, and ordered to leave the place in twenty-four hours. [This was not an hour previous to the commencement of the Sabbath.]

The doors were then thrown open, and the crowd admitted. To them it was once again remarked, that "the committee had been actuated by conscientious motives; and to those who thought the punishment *too severe,* they would only say, that they had done what they, after *mature deliberation,* thought to be right; and to those who thought it *too light,* they must say, that in coming to their decision the committee had regarded not so much the number of stripes, as the disgrace and infamy of being publicly whipped." The sentence being again repeated, it was received with great applause, accompanied by stamping of feet and clapping of hands.

The chairman then called for the sentiments of the spectators in reference to their approbation of the decision of the committee, desiring all who were satisfied with it, and would pledge themselves that I should receive no injury after the execution of the sentence, to signify in the usual way. There was no dissenting voice.

The chairman then expressed, in terms bordering on the extravagant, his high gratification of the sense of propriety that had been manifested in the conduct of the meeting, and that so much confidence was placed in the committee. The crowd was now ordered to proceed to the public square, and form a ring. . . .

I entered the ring that had been formed; the chairman (accompanied by the committee) again called for an expression of sentiment in relation to the sentence passed upon me; again the vote was unanimous in approbation of it, and again did he express his gratification at the good order by which the whole proceeding had been characterized. Whilst some of the company were engaged in stripping me of my garments, a motion was made and seconded that I be exonerated altogether from the punishment. This brought many and furious imprecations on the mover's head, and created a commotion which was appeased only by the sound of the instrument of torture and disgrace upon my naked body.

I knelt to receive the punishment, which was inflicted by Mr. Braughton, the city officer, with a heavy cowskin. When the infliction ceased, an involuntary feeling of thanksgiving to God for the fortitude with which I had been enabled to endure it arose in my soul, to which I began aloud to give utterance. The death-like silence that prevailed for a moment, was suddenly broken with loud exclamations. "G--d d---n him, stop his praying." I was raised to my feet by Mr. Braughton, and conducted by him to my lodging, where it was thought safe for me to remain but for a few moments.

And though most of my *friends* were at the camp-ground, I was introduced into a family of entire strangers, from whom I received a warm reception, and the most kind and tender treatment. They will ever be remembered with grateful emotions.

On the ensuing morning, owing to the great excitement that was still prevailing, I found it necessary to leave the place in disguise, with only what clothing I had about my person; leaving unsold property to the amount of nearly three hundred dollars, and sacrificing at least two hundred on my barouche, horse &c., which I was obliged to sell. Of my effects at Nashville, I have heard nothing since my return, though I have frequently written to my friends concerning them.

Amos Dresser

Cincinnati, August 25, 1835

ELIJAH P. LOVEJOY

ADDRESSES THE CITIZENS OF ST. LOUIS (1835).

ON NOVEMBER 7, 1837 Elijah P. Lovejoy, the Presbyterian minister and abolitionist editor, was killed in Alton, Illinois while defending his press from a mob. The decision which cost him his life, however, was made two years earlier across the river in St. Louis where he first faced irate citizens bent on destroying his newspaper. Through the summer of 1835 St. Louis had seethed with unrest after a particularly brutal lynching of a Negro. At a mass meeting in October resolutions were passed denying the "moral right" of abolitionists to discuss slavery "either orally or through the medium of the press." Although Lovejoy was not mentioned by name, the belief was widespread that he had distributed his paper, the *Observer,* and other anti-slavery materials throughout the state and was therefore guilty of "seditious" practices. Lovejoy published his reply to the charges in the *Observer* on November 5, 1835. As a defense of civil liberties the open letter "To my Fellow-Citizens" was not without its darker side, for the fearless abolitionist was also a zealous anti-Catholic who identified his pro-slavery opponents with the evil of "Popery." Thus his strong statement on civil rights was marred by an equally strong fear of a Catholic conspiracy, seemingly necessary to his concept of himself as a Christian martyr. In his reply he insisted on the right to free discussion with the clear intent of uprooting not only slavery but also the Catholic Church from the Mississippi Valley. "To my Fellow-Citizens," St. Louis *Observer,* November 5, 1835, as quoted in Henry Tanner, *The Martyrdom of Lovejoy* (Chicago, 1881), 57-68.

November 5th, 1835

TO MY FELLOW-CITIZENS:

Recent well-known occurrences in this city, and elsewhere, have, in the opinion of some of my friends, as well as my own, made it my duty to address myself to you personally. And, in so doing, I hope to be pardoned for that apparent egotism which, in such an address, is more or less unavoidable. I hope, also, to write in that spirit of meekness and humility that becomes a follower of the Lamb; and, at the same time, with all that boldness and sincerity of speech which should mark the language of a freeman and a Christian minister. It is not my design or wish to offend any one, but simply to maintain my rights as a republican citizen, free-born, of these United States, and to defend, fearlessly, the cause of truth and righteousness. . . . [Lovejoy denies that he sent anti-slavery publications to Jefferson City, Missouri or anywhere else.]

And now, fellow citizens, having made the above explanation, for the purpose of undeceiving such of you as have honestly supposed me in error; truth and candor require me to add, that had I desired to send a copy of the *Emancipator,* or of any other newspaper, to Jefferson City, I should not have taken the pains to box it up. I am not aware that any law of my country forbids my sending what document I please to a friend or citizen. I know, indeed, that *mob law* has decided otherwise, and that it has become fashionable, in certain parts of this country, to break open the post-office, and take from it such documents as the mob should decide, ought not to pass *unburned.* But I had never imagined there was a sufficiency of respectability attached to the proceeding, to recommend it for adoption to the good citizens of my own State. And grievously and sadly shall I be disappointed to find it otherwise.

In fine, I wish it to be distinctly understood, that I have never, knowingly, to the best of my recollection, sent a single copy of the *Emancipator,* or any other Abolition publication, to a single individual in Missouri, or elsewhere; while yet I claim the *right* to send ten thousand of them if I choose, to as many of my fellow-citizens. Whether I will *exercise* that right or not, is for me, and not for the *mob,* to decide. The right to send publications of any sort to slaves, or in any way to communicate with them, without the *express permission* of their masters, I freely acknowledge that I have not. Nor do I wish to have it. It is with the master alone, that I would have to do, as one freeman with another; and who shall say me nay?

I come now to the proceedings had at the late meetings of our citizens. And in discussing them, I hope not to say a single word that shall wound the feelings of a single individual concerned. It is with principles I have to do, and not with men. And in canvassing them, freely, openly, I do but exercise a right secured by the solemn sanction of the Constitution, to the humblest citizen of this republic—a right that, so long as life lasts, I do not expect to relinquish.

I freely acknowledge the respectability of the citizens who composed the meetings referred to. And were the questions under consideration, to be decided as mere matters of opinion, it would become me, however much I might differ from them to bow in humble silence to the decisions of such a body of my fellow-citizens. But I can not surrender my principles, though the whole world besides should vote them down—I can make no compromise between truth and error, even though my life be the alternative. . . .

The second resolution, [that "the right of free discussion . . . does not imply a moral right on the part of the Abolitionists to freely discuss the question of Slavery . . ."] strictly speaking, neither affirms nor denies anything in reference to the matter in hand. No man has a *moral* right to do any thing improper. Whether, therefore, he has the moral right to discuss the question of slavery, is a point with which human legislation or resolutions have nothing to do. The true issue to be decided is, whether he has the *civil,* the political right, to discuss it or not. And this is a mere question of fact. In Russia, in Turkey, in Austria, nay, even in France, this right most certainly does not exist. But does it exist in Missouri? We decide this question by turning to the Constitution of the State. The Sixteenth Section, Article Thirteenth, of the Constitution of Missouri, reads as follows:

> That the free communication of thoughts and opinions is one of the invaluable rights of man, and that every person may freely speak, write, and print *on any subject,* being responsible for the abuse of that liberty.

Here, then, I find my warrant for using, as Paul did, all freedom of speech.

If I abuse that right, I freely acknowledge myself amenable to the laws.

But it is said, that the right to hold slaves is a constitutional one, and, therefore, not [to] be called in question. I admit the premise, but deny the conclusion. To put a strong case by way of illustration. The Constitution declares that this shall be a perpetual Republic; but has not any citizen the right to discuss under that Constitution, the comparative merits of despotism and liberty? And if he has eloquence and force of argument sufficient, may he not persuade us all to crown him our king? Robert Dale Owen came to this city, and Fanny Wright followed him, openly proclaiming the doctrine that the institution of marriage was a curse to any community, and ought to be abolished. It was, undoubtedly, an abominable doctrine, and one which, if acted out, would speedily reduce society to the level of barbarism and the brutes; yet, who thought of denying Mr. Owen and his disciple the perfect right of avowing such doctrines, or who thought of mobbing them for the exercise of this right? And yet, most surely, the institutions of slavery are not more interwoven with the structure of our society, than those of marriage.

See the danger, and the natural and inevitable result, to which the first step here will lead. To-day, a public meeting declares that you shall not discuss the subject of slavery in any of its bearings, civil or religious. To-morrow, another meeting decides that it is against the peace of society that the principles of Popery shall be discussed, and the edict goes forth to muzzle the press. The next day, it is, in a similar manner, declared that a word must not be said against distilleries, dram-shops, or drunkenness. And so on to the end of the chapter. The truth is, my fellow-citizens, if you give ground a single inch, there is no stopping place. I deem it, therefore, my duty to take my stand upon the Constitution. Here is firm ground—I feel it to be such. And I do most respectfully, yet decidedly, declare to you my fixed determination to maintain this ground. We have slaves, it is true, but *I* am not one. I am a citizen of these United States, a citizen of Missouri, free-born; and having never forfeited the inestimable privileges attached to such a condition, I can not consent to surrender them. But while I maintain them, I hope to do it with all that meekness and humility that become a Christian, and especially a Christian minister. I am ready, not to fight, but to suffer, and if need be, to die for them. Kindred blood to that which flows in my veins, flowed freely to water the tree of Christian liberty, planted by the Puritans on the rugged soil of New England. It flowed as freely on the plains of Lexington, the heights of Bunker Hill, and fields of Saratoga. And freely, too, shall mine flow, yea, as freely as if it were so much water, ere I surrender my right to plead the cause of truth and righteousness before my fellow-citizens, and in the face of all their opposers. . . .

The fifth resolution appoints a committee of vigilance, consisting of seven for each ward, twenty for the suburbs, and seven for each township in the county,—in all, eighty-three persons,—whose duty it shall be to report to the mayor, or the other civil authorities, all persons *suspected* of preaching Abolition doctrines, etc., and should the civil authorities fail to deal with them, on suspicion, why, then, the committee are to call a meeting of the citizens and execute their decrees—in other words, to *lynch* the suspected persons.

Fellow-citizens; where are we, and in what age of the world do we live? Is this the land of freedom or despotism? Is it the ninth or nineteenth century? Have the principles of the *lettres de cachet,* driven from Europe, crossed the Atlantic and taken up their abode in Missouri? Louis the XIV sent men to the Bastile [sic] on suspicion; we, more humane, do but whip them to death, or nearly so. But these things can not last long. A few may be made the innocent victims of lawless violence, yet, be assured, there is a moral sense in the Christendom of the nineteenth century, that will not long endure such odious transactions. A tremendous reaction will take place.

And remember, I pray you, that as Phalaris was the first man roasted in the brazen bull he had constructed for the tyrant of Sicily, so the inventor of the guillotine was by no means the last whose neck had practical experience of the keenness of its edge. I turn, for a moment, to my fellow-Christians of all Protestant denominations.

Respected and beloved Fathers and Brethren: As I address myself to you, my heart is full, well-nigh to bursting, and my eyes overflow. It is indeed a time of trial and rebuke. The enemies of the cross are numerous and bold and malignant in the extreme. From the situation in which the providence of God has placed me, a large portion of their hatred, in this quarter, has concentrated itself on me. You know that now for nearly two years, a constant stream of calumnies and personal abuse of the most viperous kind has been poured upon me, simply because I have been your organ through which—I refer now more especially to my Presbyterian brethren—you have declared your sentiments. You know, also, that I have never, in a single instance, replied to or otherwise noticed these attacks. And now, not only is a fresh attack of ten-fold virulence, made upon my character, but violence is threatened to my person. Think not that it is because I am an Abolitionist that I am so persecuted. They who first started this report knew, and still know, better. In the progress of events, slavery has, doubtless, contributed its share, though a very small one, to the bitterness of hatred with which the *Observer,* and I, as connected with it, are regarded. But the true cause is the open and decided stand which the paper has taken against the encroachments of Popery. This is not my own opinion, but that of others, and indeed of nearly or quite all with whom I have conversed on the subject, and among the rest, as I learn, of a French Catholic. I repeat it, then, the real origin of the cry "Down with the *Observer,*" is to be looked for in its opposition to Popery. The fire that is now blazing and crackling through this city, was kindled on Popish altars, and has been assiduously blown up by Jesuit breath. And now, dear brethren, the question is, shall we flee before it, or stay and abide its fury, even though we perish in the flames? For one, I can not hesitate. The path of duty lies plain before me, and I must walk therein, even though it lead to the whipping-post, the tar-barrel, or even the stake. I was bold and dauntless in the service of sin; it is not fitting that I should be less so in the service of my Redeemer. He sought me out when there was none to help; when I was fast sinking to eternal ruin, he raised me up and placed me on the Rock of Ages; and now, shall I forsake him when he has so few friends and so many enemies in St. Louis? I can not, I dare not, and, his grace sustaining me, *I will not.* . . .

WILLIAM LLOYD GARRISON

PROTECTS THE INTELLECTUAL FREE MARKET (1837).

In his annual message to Congress in December, 1835, President Andrew Jackson recommended a law prohibiting "under severe penalties, the circulation in the Southern States, through the mail, of incendiary publications intended to instigate slaves to insurrection." On the motion of John C. Calhoun, the President's suggestion was referred to a special committee of the Senate, which introduced a bill accompanied by Calhoun's report on February 4, 1836. Calhoun flatly rejected Jackson's recommendation of a federal law on the grounds that the power to preserve their internal peace and security lay with the states themselves "to the entire exclusion of all authority and control on the part of Congress." But Calhoun's bill did not limit state power to suppress abolitionist publications: it provided for the punishment and fine of any postmaster who knowingly transmitted or delivered any "paper" contrary to the laws of any state. Although the bill failed to pass the Senate, it received nineteen votes, including four from the North.

William Lloyd Garrison, in the annual report of the Board of Managers of the Massachusetts Anti-Slavery Society for 1837, reviewed and criticized the Calhoun report with what was not only a scorching denunciation of pro-slavery suppression but one of the most forceful abolitionist statements in defense of civil liberties. *Annual Report of the Board of Managers of the Massachusetts Anti-Slavery Society, 1837* (Boston, 1837) 25-38. Footnotes have been omitted.

. . . The Report, under consideration, bestows the following panegyric upon the "relation" between masters and slaves:

> It is against this relation between the two races, that the blind and criminal zeal of the abolitionists is directed—a relation that now preserves in quiet and security, more than 6,500,000 human beings [!!]—Under this relation, the two races have long lived in peace and prosperity, and, if not disturbed, would long continue so to live [!!]—It may be safely asserted, that there is no example in history, in which a savage people, such as the ancestors of the slaves were when brought into the country, have ever advanced in the same period so rapidly in numbers and *improvement* [!!].

The "relation" which is producing so much happiness, safety, improvement, peace, prosperity, &c. &c. is the relation of one man as a beast, to another man as his absolute owner If such really be its beneficent results, it will certainly bear the test of a most rigid scrutiny; and it is difficult to perceive, why the South should be so angry when we propose to discuss its utility, or why she should require us to preserve unbroken silence!—The solution of this delicate enigma is, that what is affirmed of this "relation" in the Report, is obviously false, in every particular. The slave system is full of the elements of self-destruction: it is a moral Vesuvius—within are raging fires—without is desolation, the awful consequence of successive volcanic eruptions, wherever its lava tide has flowed. And "the end is not yet."

Again:

> The blindness of fanaticism is proverbial. With more zeal than understanding, it constantly misconceives the nature of the object at which it aims, and toward which it rushes with headlong violence, regardless of the means by which it is effected.—Never was its character more fully exemplified than in the present instance. Setting out with the abstract principle that slavery is an evil, the fanatical zealots come at once to the conclusion that it is their duty to abolish it, regardless of the disasters which must follow. Never was conclusion more false or dangerous.

Behold the folly and insanity of the abolitionists! If this be an accurate delineation of their character, it is a poor compliment which Mr. CALHOUN pays to the intelligence, patriotism and piety of the North, to argue that, unless they are put down BY FORCE, the abolitionists can never be vanquished by reason, but will assuredly enlist the people on their side! Fanaticism is quickly consumed by its own fire: its "blindness" ensures its speedy self-destruction. It was one of the best and most popular sentiments ever uttered by Mr. JEFFERSON, that "error of opinion may be safely tolerated, where reason is left free to combat it." "The fanatical zealots" stigmatized by Mr. CALHOUN, do not merely call slavery an "evil," but they brand it as a *sin*—A SYSTEM OF INIQUITIES—one vast aggregation of heaven-daring impieties; and they therefore know that its immediate abandonment is a duty, which wisely and unerringly regards all imaginable consequences, all real interests, whether near or remote, whether appertaining to the few or the many, to the present or the future, to time or to eternity! But they have never been guilty of the folly ascribed to them in the Report,—of asserting that it is "*their* duty" to abolish slavery in the southern States: that "duty" must be performed by the slaveholders themselves.

It is a relief to know wherein the essential wickedness of the abolitionists consists. According to Mr. CALHOUN, it is found alike in the *end* aimed at by them, and in the *means* used to effect that end.

Wicked and cruel as is the end aimed at, it is fully equalled by the criminality of the means by which it is proposed to be accomplished. These consist in organized societies and a powerful press, directed mainly with a view to excite the bitterest animosity and hatred of the people of the non-slaveholding States against the citizens and institutions of the slaveholding States. It is easy to see to what disastrous results such means must tend.—The incessant action of hundreds of societies, and a vast printing establishment, throwing out, daily, thousands of artful and inflammatory publications, must make in time a deep impression on the section of the Union where they freely circulate, and are mainly designed to have effect. The well-informed and thoughtful hold them in contempt, but the young, the inexperienced, the ignorant, and thoughtless, will receive the poison.

Upon the above extract we remark—

1. They who oppose the abolitionists, but argue in favor of the *ultimate* abolition of slavery as a most desirable "end,"—as if such a view of the question would be perfectly agreeable to the holders of slaves,—are thus admonished by Mr. CALHOUN, that such an abolition, at any period however remote, or under any circumstances however favorable, would be "wicked" and "cruel."

2. The organization of societies and the establishment of "a powerful press," are not proofs of "the criminality of the means" adopted by the abolitionists; for they are invariably resorted to by the friends of every benevolent, just and holy enterprise, as essential to its success. Without organized action, and without a press, what progress could be made in the cause of Temperance, of Peace, or of Religion? What could the Bible, or Missionary, or Education Societies do without them?

3. If the abolition press throws out, daily, "thousands of artful and inflammatory publications," this may be a sound reason why the anti-abolition press should throw out, daily, tens of thousands of publications of an opposite tendency—but it cannot justify the plundering of the public mail, nor the destruction of the great palladium of human rights. If infidelity be zealous and daring in the dissemination of its poisonous sentiments, shame upon christianity if it be not as active in its own cause—shame upon it if it demand that infidelity shall be gagged, fettered, and crushed by force, instead of meeting it with those spiritual weapons which are mighty, through God, to the pulling down of strong holds!

4. The assertion, that "the well-informed and thoughtful" hold the anti-slavery publications "in contempt," if true, would voluntarily place Mr. CALHOUN and his associates in the ranks of "the inexperienced, the ignorant and thoughtless"—for they regard these publications with far different feelings: they cannot despise that which excites so much

consternation among themselves. . . . But it is calumnious, and Mr. CALHOUN knows it to be so. If he really believed all that he says in favor of slavery, that it is as beneficent a system as exists under heaven, —and all that he says against the abolitionists, that they are ignorant, unprincipled, insane men,—would he tremble lest they should win over to their side the "wise and prudent," the pious and philanthropic?—Would he confess, that the delusion of a despised band would prove too powerful for the reason of the nation, unless they were put down by the strong arm of the law? Or would he wax hot, and be thrown into a paroxysm of fury, the moment any individual should begin to investigate that system which he says is producing so much happiness and prosperity? His terror—his anger—his dread of examination—his opposition to free discussion—his call for judicial pains and penalties to be inflicted upon the persons of abolitionists on account of their *opinions*—his willingness to shackle the press—his recommendation to make the robbery of the mail of any and every document, whether printed or oral, which merely "touches" the subject of slavery, a lawful and *obligatory* act—all these evince a state of mind ill at ease, a conscience troubled with its own fearful monitions, an understanding filled with guilty confusion. How is the declaration of the Almighty confirmed to the letter!—"For it is written, I will destroy the wisdom of the wise, and will bring to nothing the understanding of the prudent. Where is the wise? where is the disputer of this world? Hath not God made foolish the wisdom of this world?"

Mr. CALHOUN, in the extremity of his argument, holds up the *lex talionis* over the heads of our northern citizens, *in terrorem*. He says, by way of solemn admonition:

> The sober and considerate portion of citizens of non-slaveholding States, who have a deep stake in the existing institutions of the country, would have little forecast not to see that the assaults which are now directed against the institutions of the southern States, may be very easily directed against those which uphold their own property and security [!!].

The effect of this warning must be to relax the muscles and disturb the gravity of our "sober and considerate citizens"—nothing more. Does the Senator from South Carolina credit his own ridiculous assertion, that the same assaults which the abolitionists are making upon the slave system, may be directed against our northern FREE LABOR system? If this could be done, what is there in the temper or disposition of the South toward the North, to make her forbear retaliating in the manner threatened? Why has she descended to the vile and hopeless task of scourging, imprisoning or putting to death, without a trial, such abolitionists as have been identified upon her soil, when she holds such a potent weapon in her hands against the North, and can at any moment throw confusion among us by assailing our own institutions? Is it not strange, that, among the numerous expedients devised by southern task-masters to counteract the efforts of the abolitionists, they have not in a single instance attempted to prove,—by appealing to the Declaration of Independence and the Bible, by reasoning from analogy, by historical facts and arguments, by northern admissions and concessions, by "the relation" of men and things established in nature,—that a New-England farmer has no moral right to hold his farm or his cattle as his property; that a New-England mechanic has no right to receive wages and obtain knowledge; that a New-England merchant commits an aggravated sin against God in buying and selling goods; that it is a violation of the seventh commandment for us to tolerate the marriage institution among our poor and ignorant population; that we are bringing upon this nation the reproach and derision of the world, and rendering it deserving of the judgments of heaven, by possessing houses and lands, rail-roads and manufactories, carriages and horses, ships and steamboats, &c. &c: that we are outraging human rights in making, by law, no distinction between the rich and poor, the high and low, the strong and feeble; that we deserve to be execrated, in that we do not "sell the righteous for silver, and the poor for a pair of shoes," but let every one possess his own body, mind and intellect, for his own benefit!!—Such warnings and remonstrances have never circulated north of the Potomac, nor fallen from the lips of any slaveholder south of Mason & Dixon's line: and if they should be addressed to us by our southern brethren, we pledge ourselves to receive them in good humor—not to get angry—not to threaten to dissolve the Union—not to lynch any of the remonstrants who may happen to sojourn with us—not to rob the U.S. mail—not to offer any rewards for the persons of southern planters—not to organize any vigilance committees—not to call upon the brute force of the nation to stand by us—not to stop our ears, and refuse to hear argument—not to cut out the tongues of those who do not agree with us—not to demand that the South shall go to hanging a few thousands of our opponents, at the peril of losing our trade!! . . .

PART IV.

CONVERTING THE NORTH.

THEODORE WELD
TAKES THE TESTIMONY OF A THOUSAND WITNESSES (1839).

THE MOST DRAMATIC AND IMPRESSIVE abolitionist indictment was Theodore Weld's *Slavery As It Is: The Testimony of a Thousand Witnesses* (New York, 1839) compiled and edited by Weld, his wife Angelina, and her sister Sarah Grimké from newspapers purchased from the New York Commercial Reading Room. "The fact is," Weld admitted, "those dear souls spent six months, averaging more than six hours a day, in searching through thousands upon thousands of Southern newspapers, marking and cutting out facts of slaveholding disclosures. . . . After the work was finished we were curious to know how many newspapers had been examined. So we went up to our attic and took an inventory of bundles, as they were packed heap upon heap. When our count had reached *twenty thousand* newspapers, we said: 'There let that suffice.'" Weld's book was designed, as he explained in the preface, to answer the question: "What is the actual condition of the slaves in the United States?" The selections excerpted are typical of the damaging evidence with which Weld established his Biblical judgment—"Out of thine own mouth do I condemn thee." Within four months the book had sold twenty-two thousand copies. Published by the American Anti-Slavery Society and priced at thirty-seven and one-half cents a copy, it remained the abolitionists' best-seller and reputedly served as a source for Dickens's *American Notes* and Harriet Beecher Stowe's *Uncle Tom's Cabin.* Theodore D. Weld, *Slavery As It Is: Testimony of a Thousand Witnesses* (New York, 1839) 62-63, 77, 125-128.

PUNISHMENTS.

I. *Floggings.*

THE SLAVES ARE terribly lacerated with whips, paddles, &c.; red pepper and salt are rubbed into their mangled flesh; hot brine and turpentine are poured into their gashes; and innumerable other tortures inflicted upon them.

We will in the first place, prove by a cloud of witnesses, that the slaves are whipped with such inhuman severity, as to lacerate and mangle their flesh in the most shocking manner, leaving permanent scars and ridges; after establishing this, we will present a mass of testimony, concerning a great variety of other tortures. The testimony, for the most part, will be that of the slaveholders themselves, and in their own chosen words. A large portion of it will be taken from the advertisements, which they have published in their own newspapers, describing by the scars on their bodies made by the whip, their own runaway slaves. To copy these advertisements *entire* would require a great amount of space, and flood the reader with a vast mass of matter irrelevant to the *point* before us; we shall therefore insert only so much of each, as will intelligibly set forth the precise point under consideration. In the column under the word "witnesses," will be found the name of the individual, who signs the advertisement, or for whom it is signed, with his or her place of residence, and the name and date of the paper, in which it appeared, and generally the name of the place where it is published. Opposite the name of each witness will be an extract, from the advertisement, containing his or her testimony.

WITNESSES.	TESTIMONY.
Mr. D. Judd, jailor, Davidson Co., Tennessee, in the "Nashville Banner," Dec. 10th, 1838.	"Committed to jail as a runaway, a negro woman named Martha, 17 or 18 years of age, has *numerous scars of the whip* on her back."
Mr. Robert Nicoll, Dauphin st. between Emmanuel and Conception st's, Mobile, Alabama, in the "Mobile Commercial Advertiser."	"Ten dollars reward for my woman Siby, *very much scarred about the neck and ears by whipping.*"
Mr. Bryant Johnson, Fort Valley, Houston Co., Georgia, in the "Standard of Union," Milledgeville, Ga. Oct. 2, 1838.	"Ranaway, a negro woman, named Maria, *some scars on her back occasioned by the whip.*"
Mr. James T. De Jarnett, Vernon, Autauga Co., Alabama, in the "Pensacola Gazette," July 14, 1838.	"Stolen a negro woman, named Celia. On examining her back you will find *marks caused by the whip.*"
Maurice Y. Garcia, Sheriff of the County of Jefferson, La., in the "New Orleans Bee," August 14, 1838.	"Lodged in jail, a mulatto boy, *having large marks of the whip,* on his shoulders and other parts of his body."
R. J. Bland, Sheriff of Claiborne Co., Miss. in the "Charleston (S.C.) Courier," August 28, 1838.	"Was committed a negro boy, named Tom, is *much marked with the whip.*

Mr. James Noe, Red River Landing, La., in the "Sentinel," Vicksburg, Miss., August 22, 1837.

"Ranaway, a negro fellow named Dick—has many *scars* on his back from being *whipped.*"

William Craze, jailor, Alexandria, La. in the "Planter's Intelligencer," Sept. 21, 1838.

"Committed to jail, a negro slave—his back is *very badly scarred.*"

James A. Rowland, jailor, Lumberton, North Carolina, in the "Fayetteville (N.C.) Observer," June 20, 1838.

"Committed, a mulatto fellow—his back shows *lasting impressions of the whip,* and leaves no doubt of his being A SLAVE."

J. K. Roberts, sheriff, Blount county Ala., in the "Huntsville Democrat," Dec. 9, 1838.

"Committed to jail, a negro man—his back *much marked* by the whip."

Mr. H. Varillat, No. 23 Girod street, New Orleans—in the "Commercial Bulletin," August 27, 1838.

"Ranaway, the negro slave named Jupiter—has a *fresh mark* of a cowskin on one of his cheeks."

Mr. Cornelius D. Tolin, Augusta, Ga., in the "Chronicle and Sentinel," Oct. 18, 1838.

"Ranaway, a negro man named Johnson—he has a *great many marks of the whip* on his back."

III. BRANDINGS, MAIMINGS, GUN-SHOT WOUNDS, &c.

The slaves are often branded with hot irons, pursued with fire arms and *shot,* hunted with dogs and torn by them, shockingly maimed with knives, dirks, &c; have their ears cut off, their eyes knocked out, their bones dislocated and broken with bludgeons, their fingers and toes cut off, their faces and other parts of their persons disfigured with scars and gashes, *besides* those made with the lash.

We shall adopt, under this head, the same course as that pursued under previous ones,—first give the testimony of the slaveholders themselves, to the mutilations &c. by copying their own graphic descriptions of them, in advertisements published under their own names, and in newspapers published in the slave states, and, generally, in their own immediate vicinity. We shall, as heretofore, insert only so much of each advertisement as will be necessary to make the point intelligible.

WITNESSES. — TESTIMONY.

Mr. Micajah Ricks, Nash County, North Carolina, in the Raleigh "Standard," July 18, 1838.

"Ranaway, a negro woman and two children; a few days before she went off, *I burnt her with a hot iron,* on the left side of her face, *I tried to make the letter M.*"

Mr. Asa B. Metcalf, Kingston, Adams Co. Mi. in the "Natchez Courier," June 15, 1832.

"Ranaway Mary, a black woman, has a *scar* on her back and right arm near the shoulder, *caused by a rifle ball.*"

Mr. William Overstreet, Benton, Yazoo Co., Mi., in the "Lexington (Kentucky) Observer," July 22, 1838.

"Ranaway a negro man named Henry, *his left eye out,* some scars from a *dirk* on and under his left arm, and *much scarred* with the whip."

Mr. R. P. Carney, Clark Co., Ala., in the "Mobile Register," Dec. 22, 1832.

One hundred dollars reward for a negro fellow Pompey, 40 years old, he is *branded* on the *left jaw.*

Mr. J. Guyler, Savannah Georgia, in the "Republican," April 12, 1837.

"Ranaway Laman, an old negro man, grey, has *only one eye.*"

J. A. Brown, jailor, Charleston, South Carolina, in the "Mercury," Jan. 12, 1837.

"Committed to jail a negro man, has *no toes* on his left foot."

Mr. J. Scrivener, Herring Bay, Anne Arundel Co., Maryland, in the "Annapolis Republican," April 18, 1837.

"Ranaway negro man Elijah, has a scar on his left cheek, apparently occasioned by *a shot.*"

Madame Burvant, corner of Chartres and Toulouse streets, New Orleans, in the "Bee," Dec. 21, 1838.

"Ranaway a negro woman named Rachel, has *lost all her toes* except the large one."

Mr. O. W. Lains, in the "Helena (Ark.) Journal," June 1, 1833.

"Ranaway Sam, he was *shot* a short time since, through the hand, and has *several shots in his left arm and side.*"

Mr. R. W. Sizer, in the "Grand Gulf, (Mi.) Advertiser," July 8, 1837.

"Ranaway my negro man Dennis, said negro has been *shot* in the left arm between the shoulders and elbow, which has paralyzed the left hand."

Mr. Nicholas Edmunds, in the "Petersburgh (Va.) Intelligencer," May 22, 1838.

"Ranaway my negro man named Simon, he *has been shot badly* in his back and right arm."

Objection III.–"SLAVEHOLDERS ARE PROVERBIAL FOR THEIR KINDNESS, HOSPITALITY, BENEVOLENCE, AND GENEROSITY."

Multitudes scout as fictions the cruelties inflicted upon slaves, because slaveholders are famed for their courtesy and hospitality. They tell us that their generous and kind attentions to their guests, and their well-known sympathy for the suffering, sufficiently prove the charges of cruelty brought against them to be calumnies, of which their uniform character is a triumphant refutation.

Now that slaveholders are proverbially hospitable to their guests, and spare neither pains nor expense in ministering to their accommodation and pleasure, is freely admitted and easily accounted for. That those who make their inferiors work for them, without pay, should be courteous and hospitable to those of their equals and superiors whose good opinions they desire, is human nature in its every-day dress. The objection consists of a fact and an inference: the fact, that slaveholders have a special care to the accommodation of their *guests;* the inference, that therefore they must seek the comfort of their *slaves*—that as they are bland and obliging to their equals, they must be mild and condescending to their inferiors—that as the wrongs of their own grade excite their indignation, and their woes move their sympathies, they must be touched by those of their chattels—that as they are full of pains-taking toward those whose good opinions and good offices they seek, they will, of course, show special attention to those to whose good opinions they are indifferent, and whose good offices they can *compel*—that as they honor the literary and scientific, they must treat with high consideration those to whom they deny the alphabet—that as they are courteous to certain *persons,* they must be so to "property"—eager to anticipate the wishes of visitors, they cannot but gratify those of their vassals—jealous for the rights of the Texans, quick to feel at the disfranchisement of Canadians and of Irishmen, alive to the oppressions of the Greeks and the Poles, they must feel keenly for their *negroes!* . . .

The fact that slaveholders may be full of benevolence and kindness toward their equals and toward whites generally, even so much so as to attract the esteem and admiration of all, while they treat with the most inhuman neglect their own slaves, is well illustrated by a circumstance mentioned by the Rev. Dr. CHANNING, of Boston, (who once lived in Virginia) in his work on slavery, p. 162, 1st edition:—

"I cannot," says the doctor, "forget my feelings on visiting a hospital belonging to the plantation of a gentleman *highly esteemed for his virtues,* and whose manners and conversation expressed much *benevolence* and *conscientiousness.* When I entered with him the hospital, the first object on which my eye fell was a young woman very ill, probably approaching death. She was stretched on the floor. Her head rested on something like a pillow, but her body and limbs were extended on the hard boards. The owner, I doubt not, had, at least, as much kindness as myself; but he was so used to see the slaves living without common comforts, that the idea of unkindness in the present instance did not enter his mind."

Mr. George A. Avery, an elder of a Presbyterian church in Rochester, N. Y. who resided some years in Virginia, says:—

"On one occasion I was crossing the plantation and approaching the nouse of a friend, when I met him, *rifle in hand,* in pursuit of one of his negroes, declaring he would shoot him in a moment if he got his eye upon him. It appeared that the slave had refused to be flogged, and ran off to avoid the consequences; *and yet the generous hospitality of this man to myself, and white friends generally, scarcely knew any bounds.*

"There were amongst my slaveholding friends and acquaintances, persons who were as *humane* and *conscientious* as men can be, and persist in the impious claim of *property* in a fellow being. Still I can recollect but *one instance* of corporal punishment, whether the subject were male or female, in which the infliction was not on the *bare back* with the *raw hide,* or a similar instrument, the subject being *tied* during the operation to a post or tree. The *exception* was under the following circumstances. I had taken a walk with a friend on his plantation, and approaching his gang of slaves, I sat down whilst he proceeded to the spot where they were at work; and addressing himself somewhat earnestly to a female who was wielding the hoe, in a moment caught up what I supposed a *tobacco stick,* (a stick some three feet in length, on which the tobacco, when cut, is suspended to dry,) about the size of a *man's wrist,* and laid on a number of blows furiously over her head. The woman crouched, and seemed stunned with the blows, but presently recommenced the motion of her hoe."

Dr. David Nelson, a native of Tennessee, and late president of Marion College, Missouri, in a lecture at Northampton, Mass. in January, 1839, made the following statement:—

"I remember a young lady who played well on the piano, and was very ready to weep over any fictitious tale of suffering. I was present when one of her slaves lay on the floor in a high fever, and we feared she might not recover. I saw that young lady *stamp upon her with her feet;* and the only remark her mother made was, 'I am afraid Evelina is too *much* prejudiced against poor Mary.' " . . .

LYDIA MARIA CHILD

EXPLAINS MODERATE ABOLITION (1839).

THE ABOLITIONISTS did not deal solely in denunciation and diatribe. Many of them, noting the animosities stirred by their moral condemnation, softened their tone and altered their appeal to avoid needlessly wounding Southern sensibilities. Lydia Maria Child had already published a successful novel when she married the Whig reformer David Lee Child in 1828. Beginning with Mrs. Child's *An Appeal in Favor of that Class of Americans Called Africans* (1833), both husband and wife wrote numerous articles and pamphlets popularizing the anti-slavery argument. They served briefly as co-editors of the *National Anti-Slavery Standard* in 1843-44, a post which Mrs. Child managed alone for several years after her husband retired.

Mrs. Child was particularly sensitive to the need to correct the image of the abolitionist as an irresponsible and vituperative agitator. Her *Anti-Slavery Catechism,* a thirty-six-page pamphlet written in the form of questions and answers, is conservative in its social philosophy and moderate in its proposals for abolishing slavery. From a low-keyed conversational exchange Mrs. Child's abolitionist emerges as a sensible and humane reformer anxious to help the South reconstruct itself. Ironically, her moderation was just as obnoxious to Southerners bent on strengthening slavery as Weld's relentless probing or Garrison's outraged editorials. Lydia Maria Child, *Anti-Slavery Catechism* (Newburyport, Mass., 1839) 1-36.

• • •

Q. BUT DON'T YOU THINK it would be dangerous to turn the slaves at once loose upon the community?

A. The abolitionists never desired to have them turned loose. They wish to have them governed by salutary laws, so regulated as effectually to protect both master and slave. They merely wish to have the power of punishment transferred from individuals to magistrates; to have the sale of human beings cease; and to have the stimulus of *wages* applied, instead of the stimulus of the *whip.* The relation of master and laborer might still continue; but under circumstances less irksome and degrading to both parties. Even that much abused animal the jackass can be made to travel more expeditiously by suspending a bunch of turnips on a pole and keeping them before his nose, than he can by the continual application of the whip; and even when human beings are brutalized to the last degree, by the soul-destroying system of slavery, they have still sense enough left to be more willing to work two hours for twelve cents than to work one hour for nothing.

Q. I should think this system, in the long run, must be an unprofitable one.

A. It is admitted to be so. Southerners often declare that it takes six slaves to do what is easily performed by half the number of free laborers. . . .

Q. But the masters say the negroes would cut their throats, if they were emancipated.

A. It is safer to judge by uniform experience than by the assertions of the masters, who, even if they have no intention to deceive, are very liable to be blinded by having been educated in the midst of a bad system. Listen to facts on this subject. On the 10th of October, 1811, the Congress of Chili decreed that every child born after that day should be free. In April, 1812, the government of Buenos Ayres ordered that every child born after the 1st of January, 1813, should be free. In 1821, the Congress of Colombia emancipated all slaves who had borne arms in favor of the Republic, and provided for the emancipation, in eighteen years, of the whole slave population of 900,000. In September, 1829, the government of Mexico granted immediate and entire emancipation to every slave. In all these instances, *not one case of insurrection or of bloodshed has ever been heard of, as the result of emancipation.*

In St. Domingo no measures were taken gradually to fit the slaves for freedom. They were suddenly emancipated during a civil war, and armed against British invaders. They at once ceased to be property, and were recognized as human beings. Col. Malefant, who resided on the island, informs us, in his Historical and Political History of the Colonies, that, "after this public act of emancipation, the negroes remained quiet both in the south and west, and they continued to work upon all the plantations. The colony was flourishing. The whites lived happily and in peace upon their estates, and the negroes continued to work for them." General Lacroix, in his Memoirs of St. Domingo, speaking of the same period says: "The colony marched as by enchantment towards its ancient splendor; cultivation prospered; every day produced perceptible proofs of its progress." This prosperous state of things lasted about eight years, and would perhaps have continued to the present day, had not Bonaparte, at the instigation of the old French planters, sent an army to deprive the blacks of the freedom they had used so well. The enemies of abolition are always talking of the horrors of St. Domingo, as an argument to prove that emancipation is dangerous; but historical facts prove that the effort to *restore slavery* occasioned all the bloodshed in that island; while *emancipation produced only the most peaceful and prosperous results.* . . .

Q. But they say the British have had difficulties in their West Indies.

A. The enemies of the cause have tried very hard to get up a "raw-head and bloody-bones" story; but even if you take their own accounts, you will find that they have not been able to adduce any instances of violence in support of their assertions. . . .

Q. Yet people are always saying that free negroes cannot take care of themselves.

A. It is because people are either very much prejudiced or very ignorant on the subject. In the United States, colored persons have scarcely any chance to rise. They are despised, and abused, and discouraged, at every turn. In the slave States they are subject to laws nearly as oppressive as those of the slave. They are whipped or imprisoned, if they try to learn to read or write; they are not allowed to testify in court; and there is a general disposition not to encourage them by giving them employment. In addition to this, the planters are very desirous to expel them from the State, partly because they are jealous of their influence upon the slaves, and partly because those who have slaves to let out, naturally dislike the competition of the free negroes. But if colored people are well treated, and have the same inducements to industry as other people, they work as well and behave as well. A few years ago the Pennsylvanians were very much alarmed at the representations that were made of the increase of pauperism from the ingress of free negroes. A committee was appointed to examine into the subject, and it was ascertained that the colored people not only supported their own poor, but paid a considerable additional sum towards the support of white paupers.

Q. I have heard people say that the slaves would not take their freedom, if it were offered to them.

A. I sincerely wish they would offer it. I should like to see the experiment tried. If the slaves are so well satisfied with their condition, why do they make such severe laws against running away? Why are the patroles [*sic*] on duty all the time to shoot every negro who does not give an account of himself as soon as they call to him? Why, notwithstanding all these pains and penalties, are their newspapers full of advertisements for runaway slaves? If the free negroes are so much worse off than those in bondage, why is it that their laws bestow freedom on any slave, "who saves his master or mistress's life, or performs any meritorious service to the State?" That must be a very bad country where the law stipulates that *meritorious* actions shall be rewarded by making a man more unhappy than he was before! . . .

. . .

Q. Some say that these people are naturally inferior to us; and that the shape of their skulls proves it.

A. If I believed that the colored people were naturally inferior to the whites, I should say that was an additional reason why we ought to protect, instruct, and encourage them. No consistent republican will say that a strong-minded man has a right to oppress those less gifted than himself. Slave-holders do not seem to think the negroes are so stupid as not to acquire knowledge, and make use of it, if they could get a chance. If they do think so, why do their laws impose such heavy penalties on all who attempt to give them any education? Nobody thinks it necessary to forbid the promulgation of knowledge among monkeys. If you believe the colored race are naturally inferior, I wish you would read the history of Toussaint L'Ouverture, the Washington of St. Domingo. Though perfectly black, he was unquestionably one of the greatest and best men of his age. I wish you would hear Mr. Williams of New York, and Mr. Douglass of Philadelphia preach a few times, before you hastily decide concerning the capacity of the colored race for intellectual improvement. As for the shape of their skulls, I shall be well satisfied if our Southern brethren will emancipate all the slaves who have *not* what is called the "African conformation."

. . .

Q. But would you at once give so many ignorant creatures political power, by making them voters?

A. That would be for the wisdom of legislators to decide; and they would probably decide that it would not be judicious to invest emancipated slaves with the elective franchise; for though it is not their fault that they have been kept brutally ignorant, it unfits them for voters. . . .

Q. You know that abolitionists are universally accused of wishing to promote the amalgamation of colored and white people.

A. This is a false charge, got up by the enemies of the cause, and used as a bugbear to increase the prejudices of the community. By the hue and cry that is raised on the subject, one would really suppose that in this free country a certain set of men had power to compel their neighbors to marry contrary to their own inclination. The abolitionists have never, by example, writing, or conversation, endeavored to connect amalgamation with the subject of abolition. When their enemies insist upon urging this silly and unfounded objection, they content themselves with replying, "If there be a natural antipathy between the races, the antipathy will protect itself. If such marriages are contrary to the order of Providence, we certainly may trust Providence to take care of the matter.

It is a poor compliment to the white young men to be so afraid that the moment we allow the colored ones to be educated, the girls will all be running after them." . . .

Q. Is there any truth in the charge that you wish to break down all distinctions of society, and introduce the negroes into our parlors?

A. There is not the slightest truth in this charge. People have pointed to an ignorant shoe-black, and asked me whether I would invite him to visit my house. I answered, "No; I would not do so if he were a white man; and I should not be likely to do it, merely because he was black." An educated person will not naturally like to associate with one who is grossly ignorant. It may be no merit in one that he is well-informed, and no fault of the other that he is ignorant; for these things may be the result of circumstances, over which the individual had no control; but such people will not choose each other's society merely from want of sympathy. For these reasons, I would not select an ignorant man, of any complexion, for my companion; but when you ask me whether that man's children shall have as fair a chance as my own, to obtain an education, and rise in the world, I should be ashamed of myself, both as a Christian and a republican, if I did not say, yes, with all my heart.

Q. But do you believe that prejudice against color ever can be overcome?

A. Yes, I do; because I have faith that all things will pass away, which are not founded in reason and justice. In France and England, this prejudice scarcely exists at all. Their noblemen would never dream of taking offence because a colored gentleman sat beside them in a stage-coach, or at the table of an hotel. Be assured, however, that the abolitionists have not the slightest wish to force you to give up this prejudice. If, after conscientious examination, you believe it to be right, cherish it; but do not adhere to it merely because your neighbors do. Look it in the face—apply the golden rule—and judge for yourself. The Mahometans really think they could not eat at the same table with a Christian, without pollution; but I have no doubt the time will come when this prejudice will be removed. The old feudal nobles of England would not have thought it possible that their descendants could live in a community, where they and their vassals were on a perfect civil equality; yet the apparent impossibility has come to pass, with advantage to many, and injury to none. When we endeavor to conform to the spirit of the gospel, there is never any danger that it will not lead us into paths of peace.

. . .

Q. But if the system works so badly in every respect, why are people so unwilling to give it up?

A. Human nature is willing to endure much, rather than relinquish unbridled licentiousness and despotic control. The emperor of Russia, and the pachas [*sic*] of Egypt would be reluctant to abridge their own power, for the sake of introducing a system of things more conducive to the freedom, virtue and happiness of their subjects. They had rather live in constant fear of the poisoned bowl and the midnight dagger, than to give up the pleasant exercise of tyranny, to which they have so long been accustomed. In addition to this feeling, so common to our nature, there are many conscientious people, who are terrified at the idea of emancipation. It has always been presented to them in the most frightful colors; and bad men are determined, if possible, to prevent the abolitionists from proving to such minds that *the dangers of insurrection all belong to slavery, and would cease when slavery was abolished.*

At the North, the apologists of slavery are numerous and virulent, because their *interests* are closely intertwined with the pernicious system. Inquire into the private history of many of the men, who have called meetings against the abolitionists—you will find that some manufacture negro cloths for the South—some have sons who sell these cloths—some have daughters married to slave-holders—some have plantations and slaves mortgaged to them—some have ships employed in Southern commerce—and some candidates for political offices would bow until their back-bones were broken, to obtain or preserve Southern influence. The Southerners understand all this perfectly well, and despise our servility, even while they condescend to make use of it.

One great reason why the people of this country have not thought and felt right on this subject, is that all our books, newspapers, almanacs and periodicals, have combined to represent the colored race as an inferior and degraded class, who never could be made good and useful citizens. Ridicule and reproach have been abundantly heaped upon them; but their virtues and their sufferings have found few historians. The South has been well satisfied with such a public sentiment. It sends back no echo to disturb their consciences, and it effectually rivets the chain on the necks of their vassals. In this department of service, the Colonization Society has been a most active and zealous agent.

Q. But some people say that all the mobs, and other violent proceedings, are to be attributed to the abolitionists.

A. They might as well charge the same upon St. Paul, when his fearless preaching of the gospel brought him into such imminent peril, that his friends were obliged to "let him down over the wall in a basket," to save his life. As well might St. Stephen have been blamed for the mob that stoned him to death. With the same justice might William Penn have been called the cause of all the violent persecutions against the Quakers.

When principles of truth are sent out in the midst of a perverse generation, they *always* come "not to bring peace, but a sword." The abolitionists have offered violence to no man—they have never attempted to stop the discussions of their opponents; but have, on the contrary, exerted themselves to obtain a candid examination of the subject on all sides. They merely claim the privilege of delivering peaceful addresses at orderly meetings, and of publishing what they believe to be facts, with an honest desire to have them tested by the strictest ordeal of truth.
. . .

Q. But everybody says the discussion of slavery will lead to the dissolution of the Union.
A. There must be something wrong in the Union, if the candid discussion of *any* subject can dissolve it; and for the truth of this remark, I appeal to your own good sense. If the South should be injudicious enough to withdraw from the Union for the sake of preserving a moral pestilence in her borders, it is very certain that slavery cannot long continue after that event. None of the frontier States could long keep their slaves, if we were not obliged by law to deliver up runaways; nor could they any longer rely upon the free States, in cases of emergency, to support slavery by force of arms. The union of these States has been continually disturbed and embittered by the existence of slavery; and the abolitionists would fain convince the whole country that it is best to cast away this apple of discord. Their attachment to the Union is so strong, that they would make any sacrifice of self-interest to preserve it; but they never will consent to sacrifice honor and principle. "Duties are ours; events are God's."

JOSHUA LEAVITT

WARNS OF A SLAVE-POWER CONSPIRACY (1840).

THE ADVERSE NATIONAL REACTION to their campaign forced the abolitionists to challenge the political power of slavery by warning the North of the dangers of a Southern hegemony in the federal government. By 1840 the seeds of the "slave-power conspiracy" had been firmly planted in the Northern mind. Joshua Leavitt, one of the founders of the American Anti-Slavery Society, watched the decline of moral suasion in the Thirties and concluded by the end of the decade that the power of slavery would have to be met by political action. By 1840 Leavitt, along with Elizur Wright, Henry B. Stanton, and Myron Holley, was ready to organize an anti-slavery third party. This shift in abolitionist thinking is clearly illustrated in Leavitt's *Alarming Disclosures! Political Power of Slavery,* a collection of speeches delivered to the Ohio Anti-Slavery Convention in 1840. With the formation of the Liberty Party that same year, Leavitt quit his editorial post on the *Emancipator* and went to Washington, the new nerve-center of anti-slavery, to help direct the legislative lobby supporting John Quincy Adams and Joshua Giddings in the House of Representatives. Joshua Leavitt, *Alarming Disclosures! Political Power of Slavery, Substance of several Speeches by Rev. Joshua Leavitt in the Ohio Anti-Slavery Convention, and other public meetings in that State, in Oct. 1840, and published in the "Emancipator"* (n.d.).

This Political Power is a Property-representation.

BY THE FEDERAL CONSTITUTION, *the representation of the several States is apportioned according to the number of inhabitants, but the slaves are reckoned as equal to three-fifths of their number of free citizens. This was not a concession of political power to the slaves, but to their masters, on account of their being the possessors of slaves as property. Slaves are not inhabitants, in the eyes of the southern laws. They do not enjoy the privileges, exercise the functions, or sustain the character of inhabitants. They neither vote nor pay taxes, nor bear arms, nor do they exert any personal influence upon those who do. The representation of slaves is a mere property representation.*

The extent and bearing of this Political Power aggravates its injustice.

By the last apportionment, based upon the census of 1830, (*when the slaves were less than two millions,*) *the number of representatives in Congress is 242 of which the free States have 142, and the slave States 100. But by their number of inhabitants, in the legal sense, i.e., of* free *persons, the slave States are only entitled to seventy-five representatives. Twenty-five southern representatives, therefore, represent mere property, a monopoly, a part of that single interest which makes the whole hundred a* unit. *What would be thought should the bank monopoly claim* one *representative in Congress, or should the North claim a representative for every forty eight millions of property invested in banks, and the same for the like amount in manufactories? These 25 representatives of slave property, skillfully managed, are sufficient to decide nearly all closely contested questions that arise. Very few debatable measures have been carried these 30 years by a greater majority than 25.*

The census and apportionment of 1840, will doubtless, show a still greater disparity. Let it be borne in mind that the calculations which follow are based on the census of 1830.

The free inhabitants of Ohio were 937,877, and she has 19 representatives; while Virginia, with fewer free *inhabitants by almost two hundred thousand, has 21, being equitably entitled to only 16. This is a specimen of the injustice. But for her* property *representation, Virginia would have 5 members of Congress less than she now has, and 3 less than Ohio. . . .*

The Electoral vote is compounded of both the others, and of course combines the inequalities of both. Thus, Pennsylvania with 1,348,233 inhabitants, chooses 30 electors of President. The six States, of South Carolina, Georgia, Alabama, Mississippi, Louisiana and Kentucky, with a free population of 200,000 less, choose 52. The whole North choose 168, and the whole South 126, total 294; whereas, by free inhabitants, the North is entitled to 178 and the South only to 101. These 45 electors, thus conceded to the slaveholders, may generally decide the election, and, in fact, determine who shall and who shall not be the President of the United States.

The injustice which the North suffers from its position as a "conquered province," is still aggravated by a comparison of the number of voters in the two sections. True republicanism requires that every man of full age, actually and fully a resident of the country, should have an equal voice in the election of rulers. This is the theory of republicanism; it is the theory of the Constitution, and of our naturalization laws. Con-

sequently, political power ought to be apportioned according to the number of voters, as they alone constitute the political as well as physical strength of a State, and every one of them has, according to republican doctrine, "equal rights," and the main object of government is to protect those rights. Now, the actual apportionment is very different. At the Presidential election in 1836, the whole number of votes given was about one and a half million, of which the free states gave considerably over a million. Each elector of the free states represented 6,334 voters, while each Southern elector represented only 3,130—less than half as many. The state of New York gave about three hundred thousand votes, and chose 42 electors. Ten of the slave States, being all excepting Kentucky, Tennessee, and Arkansas, gave only about the same number, and chose 93 electors! Five votes at the South have as much weight in the choice of President, as eleven in the state of New York. New Jersey, with 52,000 votes, chose eight electors; Virginia with 53,000 votes, chose 23, or nearly three to one! A Virginia member of Congress represents, on an average, 2,554 slaveholders; a New Jersey member 8,874 freemen. By a rule of apportionment adopted in Virginia, among the several districts of the State, this disparity is rendered still greater. The Federal Ratio, being the standard, the districts where there are the most slaves have but a mere handful of voters. Six members of the present Congress, were elected by less than six thousand votes, i.e. less than 1000 votes apiece. The six New Jersey members received over 26,000 votes, or 4,300 each if divided. A voter in one of these districts has more than four times the power in Congress that is held by a freeman of New Jersey. And yet New Jersey complains of being disfranchised, without ever tracing her wrong to its cause. Two districts in New York, having 49,000 voters, elect five representatives; a number of districts in Virginia having the same number of voters, elect twenty. Ohio, with 202,000 choose 21 electors; Virginia, North and South Carolina, Alabama and Mississippi, with 211,000 choose 76. How is it possible that a government can be administered with impartiality, and a just regard to the interests of the different sections, when the power of election is so shamefully divided? . . .

This Political Power has been continually encroaching upon the Government, and now holds the Union as a Conquered Province.

Let us look first at the appointments to office.—Of the fifty two years since the Constitution went into operation, the President has been from the slaveholding section forty years; and of the remaining twelve years, four were occupied by Mr. J. Q. Adams, who had for his prime minister,

Henry Clay, to whom he was indebted for his election, and four more by Mr. Van Buren, who glories in the cognomen of "the northern man with southern principles." And now, the same Slave Power is again assaying to occupy the chair with a native Virginian, on the alleged ground that even Martin Van Buren is not subservient enough. For the last four terms, the Vice President, who is President of the Senate and has the casting vote between the two sections, has been a slaveholder, and now, neither party thinks of nominating any but a slaveholder. Whichever party prevails, we believe there has never been a case in which any other than a slaveholder was elected by the Senate President, pro tem. *During the last 35 years, the free States have been allowed a Speaker of the House for seven years; but since the Missouri compromise, only two years; and now no party thinks of nominating a northern man as Speaker. Yet the South is a small minority of the whole nation—pays but a small part of the public revenue—has never made any superior sacrifices for the common welfare,—in short, has no claims whatever to this remarkable assumption of pre-eminence, except solely on the original ground—they are slaveholders, and will have it so, or ———!*

A majority of the judges in the Supreme Court are from the Slave States, and so have been for a whole generation, although the great mass of trade and of law business is confined to the North. But the slaveocracy says, it is necessary for the security of that institution, to have the control of the Judiciary, and so it must be. It is the opinion of many, however, that the actual strength of slavery in the Supreme Court does not lie in its majority of southern men, but that, whenever any question of law shall arise between liberty and slavery, the majority of the Court will go quite as far in favor of old Saxon doctrines, as our northern Judges, Story and Thompson of the East, McLean and Baldwin of the West—will let them. . . .

Look now at the composition of the President's Cabinet. At the head stands Mr. Forsyth, of Georgia, Secretary of State, and the instigator, as it is understood, of the infamous course pursued towards the unfortunate captives of the Amistad. The Secretary of War is Mr. Poinsett, of S. C. signalized by the arduous endeavors to procure the annexation of Texas to the United States. Then, Mr. Paulding, of N. Y., Secretary of the Navy, whose sole claim to the office, so far as the newspapers ever alleged, is his having written a book in defence of slavery, and falsified another book of his own to favor the same system. The Secretary of the Treasury, so far as I know, has neither merits nor demerits on this question, unless his advocacy of the Sub-Treasury is a merit, as Senator Walker supposed that this would be a great benefit to the planters, by making free labor cheap, without lowering the price of cotton. The Attorney General, Gilpin, I believe, took a leading part in the pro-slavery proceedings of the citizens of Philadelphia against abolition, in 1835—6. The P. M. G. Niles, of Connecticut, while a member of the U. S. Senate, omitted no opportunity of testifying his fidelity to his slave masters, and his malignity towards the abolitionists.

And all this is so, because the people choose to have it so. It is because slavery has blinded the eyes of the people, as well as corrupted the hearts of politicians of all parties. In this way, the slaveholders hold the Union to their hands as a conquered province—too strong, indeed, to be trifled with, but by a little management kept in as abject submission to this invincible usurped power, as Canada is to the British crown.

Incompatibility of Free and Slave institutions.

The government of the United States, thus constituted, has now been employed for fifty years in searching after an impracticability, an inherent absurdity, as undiscoverable as the Philosopher's Stone, or Perpetual Motion. The wisdom of our statesmen has been occupied, parties have been formed, administrations put up and put down, laws and plans of policy adopted and rescinded, with a view to devise a course of measures which should, by one operation, work favorably to the industry and enterprise of the free, and to the lash-extorted labor of the slave. For this, our policy has been kept continually in a state of change; and what is very remarkable, each successive change originated by the Slave Power. We challenge an instance, in forty-years, where a change has been made in the general policy of the government, except at the dictation of the slaveholders. They established the embargo, declared the war, brought in the manufacturing system, destroyed the old United States Bank, introduced the tariff system and the late U. S. Bank, turned against both and destroyed them, produced the specie circular, brought in the sub-treasury, and are now turning against the hard currency and sub-treasury, and all coming round again in favor of the credit system, and it would not be strange to find, in less than five years, the whole South, with Mr. Calhoun at their head, coming out again, fully in favor of a protective tariff. Thus the South is constantly in changes. . . .

The great evil now complained of is, that our government, being under the control of the Slave Power, has undertaken to make slave labor and free labor prosper under the same policy, which is just as absurd as perpetual motion. Nay, it has undertaken to produce a specific, as visionary as the philosopher's stone, by which slave labor can be made to prosper at all. No course of policy has ever yet been devised, under which slavery can be made profitable, or can support itself without draining, in some way, the resources of the free. Yet southern men cling to slavery, because it gratifies their love of domination at home, and because it gives them political power to control the nation. And having nothing to lose by change, they are willing to keep the country continually under experiments, to see if it is possible to devise a way in which this grand monopoly can support itself. . . .

PART V.

SCHISM.

WILLIAM LLOYD GARRISON
REPUDIATES THE GOVERNMENT OF THE UNITED STATES (1837).

WHILE ABOLITIONISTS LIKE Joshua Leavitt, Elizur Wright, and Henry B. Stanton were turning to political action by 1840, other moral suasionists, led by Garrison, interpreted the conservative political and clerical reaction against them as proof of the complete corruption of American church and state. If the American people would not heed God's word and free the slave, then true Christians must "come out from among them"—refuse to vote, hold office, or in any way recognize a government contaminated by slavery. This total Christian solution the Garrisonians interpreted as the final realization of the original promise of the American Anti-Slavery Society to cleanse the conscience of the nation. The philosophy of perfectionism, which also embraced woman's rights and nonresistance, is explained by Garrison in his editorial prospectus in the *Liberator* for 1838. The secessionist logic of perfectionism pointed immediately to a rift in the anti-slavery ranks and ultimately, after the schism of 1840, to the doctrine of "No Union with Slaveholders." *Liberator,* December 15, 1837.

THE TERMINATION OF the present year will complete the seventh volume of the *Liberator:* we have served, therefore, a regular apprenticeship in the cause of LIBERTY, and are now prepared to advocate it upon a more extended scale. . . .

In entering upon our eighth volume, the abolition of slavery will still be the grand object of our labors, though, not, perhaps, so exclusively as heretofore. There are other topics which, in our opinion, are intimately connected with the great doctrine of inalienable human rights; and which, while they conflict with no religious sect, or political party, as such, are pregnant with momentous consequences to the freedom, equality, and happiness of mankind. These we shall discuss as time and opportunity may permit.

The motto upon our banner has been, from the commencement of our moral warfare, "OUR COUNTRY IS THE WORLD—OUR COUNTRYMEN ARE ALL MANKIND." We trust that it will be our only epitaph. Another motto we have chosen is, UNIVERSAL EMANCIPATION. Up to this time we have limited its application to those who are held in this country, by Southern taskmasters, as marketable commodities, goods and chattels, and implements of husbandry. Henceforth we shall use it in its widest latitude: the emancipation of our whole race from the dominion of man, from the thraldom of self, from the government of brute force, from the bondage of sin—and bringing them under the dominion of God, the control of an inward spirit, the government of the law of love, and into the obedience and liberty of Christ, who is "*the* same, yesterday, TO-DAY, and forever."

It has never been our design, in conducting the *Liberator*, to require of the friends of emancipation any political or sectarian shibboleth; though, in consequence of the general corruption of all political parties and religious sects, and of the obstacles which they have thrown into the path of emancipation, we have been necessitated to reprove them all. Nor have we any intention,—at least, not while ours professes to be an anti-slavery publication, dictinctively and eminently,—to assail or give the preference to any sect or party. We are bound by no denominational trammels; we are not political partisans; we have taken upon our lips no human creed; we are guided by no human authority; we cannot consent to wear the livery of any fallible body. The abolition of American slavery we hold to be COMMON GROUND, upon which men of all creeds, complexions and parties, if they have true humanity in their hearts, may meet on amicable and equal terms to effect a common object. But whoever marches on to that ground, loving his creed, or sect, or party, or any wordly interest, or personal reputation or property, or friends, or wife, or children, or life itself, more than the cause of bleeding humanity,—or expecting to promote his political designs, or to enforce his sectarian dogmas, or to drive others from the ranks on account of their modes of faith,—will assuredly prove himself to be unworthy of his abolition profession, and his real character will be made manifest to all, for severe and unerring tests will be applied frequently: it will not be possible for him to make those sacrifices, or to endure those trials, which unbending integrity to the cause will require. . . .

Next to the overthrow of slavery, the cause of PEACE will command our attention. . . .

Now the doctrine we shall endeavor to inculate is, that the kingdoms of this world are to become the kingdoms of our Lord and of his Christ; consequently, that they are all to be supplanted, whether they are called despotic, monarchical, or republican, and he only who is King of kings, and Lord of lords, is to rule in righteousness. The kingdom of God is to be established IN ALL THE EARTH, and it shall never be destroyed, but it shall "BREAK IN PIECES AND CONSUME ALL OTHERS:" its elements are righteousness and peace, and joy in the Holy Ghost: without are dogs, and sorcerers, and whoremongers, and murderers, and idolators, and whatsoever loveth and maketh a lie. . . .

As to the governments of this world, whatever their titles or forms, we shall endeavor to prove that, in their essential elements, and as at present administered, they are all Anti-Christ; that they can never, by human wisdom, be brought into conformity to the will of God; that they cannot be maintained except by naval and military power; that all their penal enactments, being a dead letter without an army to carry them into effect, are virtually written in human blood; and that the followers of Jesus should instinctively shun their stations of honor, power, and emolument—at the same time "submitting to every ordinance of man, for the Lord's sake," and offering no *physical* resistance to any of their mandates, however unjust or tyrannical. The language of Jesus is, "My kingdom is not of this world, else would my servants fight." . . .

Human governments are to be viewed as judicial punishments. If a people turn the grace of God into lasciviousness, or make their liberty an occasion for anarchy,—or if they refuse to belong to the "one fold and one Shepherd,"—they shall be scourged by governments of their own choosing, and burdened with taxation, and subjected to physical control, and torn by factions, and made to eat the fruits of their evil doings, until they are prepared to receive the liberty and the rest which remain on earth as well as in heaven, for THE PEOPLE OF GOD. This is in strict accordance with the arrangement of Divine Providence.

So long as men contemn the perfect government of the Most High, and will not fill up the measure of Christ's sufferings in their own persons, just so long will they desire to usurp authority over each other—just so long will they pertinaciously cling to human governments, *fashioned in the likeness and administered in the spirit of their own disobedience.* Now, if the prayer of our Lord be not a mockery; if the Kingdom of God is to come universally, and his will to be done ON EARTH AS IT IS IN HEAVEN; and if, in that kingdom, no carnal weapon can be wielded, and swords are beaten into ploughshares, and spears into pruning-hooks, and there is none to molest or make afraid, and no statute-book but the Bible, and no judge but Christ; then why are not Christians obligated to come out NOW, and be separate from "the kingdoms of this world," which are all based upon THE PRINCIPLE OF VIOLENCE, and which require their officers and servants to govern and be governed by that principle? . . .

. . . We regret, indeed, that the principles of abolitionists seem to be quite unsettled upon a question of such vast importance, and so vitally connected with the bloodless overthrow of slavery. It is time for all our friends to know where they stand. If those whose yokes they are endeavoring to break by the fire and hammer of God's word, would not, in their opinion, be justified in appealing to physical force, how can they justify others of a different complexion in doing the same thing? And if they conscientiously believe that the slaves would be guiltless in shedding the blood of their merciless oppressors, let them say so unequivocally—for there is no neutral ground in this matter, and the time is near when they will be compelled to take sides.

As our object is *universal* emancipation,—to redeem woman as well as man from a servile to an equal condition,—we shall go for the RIGHTS OF WOMAN to their utmost extent.

JAMES G. BIRNEY
ACCEPTS THE NOMINATION OF THE LIBERTY PARTY (1840).

THE TASK OF REFUTING Garrison's Old Testament authoritarianism fell to James G. Birney, an Alabama slaveholder turned abolitionist and after 1837 the leading figure in the American Anti-Slavery Society. Birney reasoned that since the political power of slavery blocked the spread of moral suasion, abolitionists would have to use their votes and their political talents to win Northern support. In his "A Letter on the Political Obligations of Abolitionists," published in the *Emancipator* on May 2, 1839, he rejected the "no government" theory of reform as a dangerous fallacy and argued that political action was consonant with the aims of those who founded the national society.

However, the duty of abolitionists to vote was one question, their obligation to organize a third party another. Although a few of the rank-and-file abolitionists were ready to make "independent nominations," their leaders were slow to declare themselves. Reluctant to cast off their Whig affiliations in an election year, they studied the political terrain carefully before going ahead with their plans to form an anti-slavery party. But when in April, 1840 seventy-six delegates, chiefly from western New York, assembled at Albany at the call of Myron Holley and proceeded to nominate Birney for president on the Liberty Party ticket, Birney "cheerfully acceded" after giving his reasons for challenging the two major parties. Dwight L. Dumond, ed., *Letters of James Gillespie Birney, 1831-1857* (New York, 1938) 2 vols., I, 562-574. Reprinted with the permission of Dwight L. Dumond and the American Historical Association.

James G. Birney to Myron Holley, Joshua Leavitt, and Elizur Wright, Jr.

New York
May 11th, 1840.

GENTLEMEN: Your note of April 2nd, informing me that the National Convention of the friends of immediate emancipation, then in session in the city of Albany, with a view to concentrate their votes at the coming Presidential election, had selected me as their candidate for the office of President of the same, was duly received. . . .

So far as the Presidential question is concerned, this is the lamentable presentation made before the world;—of a Republic, professing in the most solemn manner, before the nations, that all men are created equal—that they are equally entitled to liberty and to the pursuit of happiness—having two candidates for her highest office—citizens of the free States—pledging their honor not themselves to disturb, and the official power with which they seek to be clothed, not to permit the National Legislature to disturb a system which wrests from ONE-SIXTH of our native countrymen their personal liberty—robs them of the rewards of their labor,—scoffs at *their* right to the pursuit of happiness, and sells them as beasts in the market. Mr. Van Buren declares that liberty for all inhabitants of this country is so *inexpedient* as to be equivalent to a constitutional inhibition to grant it—and pledges himself to interpose the Presidential *veto,* should Congress do even what it constitutionally can, to grant it. General Harrison declares it *unconstitutional* for Congress to grant and secure their liberty to the enslaved in the District of Columbia,—a territory over which the Constitution has conferred on Congress the powers of "exclusive legislation." . . .

These are the candidates between whom abolitionists are called to discriminate. . . .

To what extent the democratic abolitionists intend supporting Mr. Van Buren, I have not the means of knowing. The fact, that but little is said about it, is some proof that his abolition supporters will be few. How far the *rush* of the Whig Abolitionists to the Harrison standard may influence them to rejoin their former political associates, it is not for me to say.

That a large proportion of the Whig Abolitionists have decided to support General Harrison may be considered certain. They will do so, not because his "bowing the knee to the dark spirit of Slavery" is altogether unobjectionable to them. Not at all: they sincerely dislike *this* presentation of Gen. H.—but they think, there are *other interests* of the country of primer importance than the immediate abolition of slavery—interests that have already been injuriously affected under the administration of Mr. Van Buren, which they have persuaded themselves will be wholly destroyed if his administration be continued through another term, but revived and cherished if General H. should be elected.

The "other interests" here meant are such as relate to the pecuniary, commercial, agricultural and manufacturing conditions of the country. It is not denied, that these are important interests well meriting the protection of the government. But they are not the *highest* concerns of a government. The security of life—of liberty—of civil and religious privileges—of the rights of conscience—of the right to use our own faculties for the promotion of our own happiness—of free locomotion,—all these.

together with the defence of the barriers and outposts thrown around them by the laws, constitute the highest concerns of a government. . . .

Is not the hope vain and groundless which would persuade us to look for security, or respect even for the rights of a free people, when their government is controlled by slaveholders, whose daily use and occupation it is through life, to trample on *all rights?* Is Mr. Van Buren to be blamed for aiding in the overthrow of the rights of his fellow citizens? He is only fulfilling the contract by which he secured his election—he is only redeeming, according to equitable construction, his pledge to the slave power, a pledge openly given and known beforehand, to all people. . . . Mr. Van Buren's administration—whatever may have been its disregard of the Constitution, not only in its spirit but its letter—has been, in the largest and most comprehensive sense, coincident with his covenant engagements with the slaveholder.

It is not denied that Mr. Van Buren, in keeping faith with the Slave Power, has disregarded and trampled under foot the inherent and constitutional rights of the people. Nor is it intended by anything that has been said to plead for his re-election. Far from it. His administration has been decidedly the most pernicious with which this republic has been cursed. But the fact that it has been so, only proves the greater ascendancy of the Slave Power in the control of the government. A power whose chief interest (the slave system) is in direct antagonism to the free institutions everywhere—whose Agriculture is desolation—whose Commerce is mainly confined to a crazy wagon and half-fed team of oxen or mules as the means of carrying it on—whose manufacturing "Machinery" is limited to the bones and sinews of reluctant slaves—whose currency is individual notes always *to be* paid, (it may be at some broken bank,) and mortgages on men and women and children who may run away or die, and on land, which without them, is of little value: such a power is certainly not the most competent to manage the affairs of a government based on the everlasting truth, that all men are created free and entitled to their liberty, and to whose prosperity no bounds could be assigned if the elements of it were but left free and unfettered. . . .

But the Whig abolitionists say, Mr. Van Buren ought to be put out of office. They are right—I fully agree with them. . . . But to turn out Mr. Van Buren is one thing—to supply his place with one who has sworn a stricter fealty to the same power, is quite another. . . .

Whatever of hope trained party leaders may succeed in exciting in the credulous and sanguine, of better times, on the substitution of Mr. Van Buren with Gen. Harrison, I see no solid ground for expecting any material change in the condition of the country, so far as that change depends on the administration of the government. An administration directed by the Slave Power has brought us into our present plight, and the remedy proposed, is, another administration equally subservient, to say the least, to the same Power! This may well consist with the objects of the *servile* leaders of the North—with the aims of expectants of office,—but it is death to the dearest rights of the people. These rights can never be placed out of imminent danger, till the influence of the Slave Power in the administration of affairs is utterly overthrown, and the government confided to men, brought up under the influence of the republican institutions and habits of the North, *and who are known to have imbibed the spirit of these institutions.* Is Gen. Harrison such a man? . . . If any suppose so, I ask them where are the proofs? Are they to be found in the fact that he has placed himself under the care and *surveillance* of a pro-slavery committee in a free State? Or in the fact, that his claims to be a candidate for the Presidency have been submitted to the slaveholders for their examination and approbation, and that the result of the test has been that he is pronounced "SOUND TO THE CORE?" Are these the proofs of his qualification for being *such* a successor of Mr. Van Buren as the cause of equal rights and the honor and prosperity of the country call for? They prove in my view anything but his qualifications to redeem our republicanism from contempt,—the country from swift-coming ruin. . . .

The conclusion of the whole matter is, that, as a people, we are trying an experiment as unphilosophical in theory as it has been, and ever will be, found impossible in practice: to make a harmonious whole out of parts that are, in principle and essence, discordant. It is in vain to think of a sincere union between the North and the South, if the first remains true to her republican principles and habits, and the latter persist in her slaveholding despotism. They are incapable, from their natures, of being made *one*. They can no more be welded together into one body of uniform strength and consistency, than clay and brass. They may, it is true, be pressed together and made to cohere by extraneous appliances; and the line of contact may be daubed over and varnished and concealed; but the first shock will make them fall asunder and disclose the fact, that there never was any real incorporation of the substance. A huge oligarchy, as the South is, made up of a multitude of petty despotisms, acting on the principle that men are *not* created equal—that a favored *few* are born, ready booted and spurred, to leap into the saddles with which the backs of the *many* are furnished by nature—such a government, I say, when brought by circumstances into close juxtaposition and incessant intercourse with republics acting on principles diametrically opposite, must soon be brought to modify and eventually to relinquish its principles and practices,—or *vice versa*, the republics must undergo a similar change, and assimilate themselves to the practices of the despotisms. One or the other must, in the end, gain the entire ascendancy. . . .

I have thus given the reasons which satisfy my mind, that abolitionists ought not to aid in the election of any one to office who is but the pliant minister of the Slave Power. The election of such only gives fresh strength to that Power, and aggravates the national malady. . . .

Fully convinced that the plan of "independent nominations" is the most effectual for the rescue of the country from the domination of the Slave Power, and for the emancipation of the slaves, I cheerfully accede to the nomination made by the Albany Convention, and consent that my name may be used as a means of concentrating the votes of abolitionists at the next Presidential election.

To Messrs. Myron Holley
Joshua Leavitt *Committee* Your obedient servant,
E. Wright, Jr. James G. Birney

LEWIS TAPPAN

INTERPRETS THE SCHISM OF 1840.

THE YEAR 1840 saw the disruption of the American Anti-Slavery Society. While the political abolitionists were shifting their allegiance to the newly formed Liberty Party, the Executive Committee of the society prepared to dismantle their organization, which was without funds and riddled with dissension. It was a nearly moribund society which Garrison set out to capture at the annual meeting in May, 1840. He had already gained almost complete ascendancy over New England anti-slavery, a command which he now used to seize control of the national society. Importing a boatload of women delegates from Lynn, he arrived in New York determined to force recognition of their right to membership. The crisis came early in the meetings over the nomination and election of Abby Kelley, a Garrisonian lieutenant and militant feminist, to the Executive Committee. When she was elected with the votes of the female contingent from Massachusetts, Lewis Tappan led over four hundred moderate opponents of Garrison's perfectionism out of the hall and into a basement room, where they formed the American and Foreign Anti-Slavery Society which excluded women. Tappan gave a highly personal but essentially accurate account of the schism in a letter written to Theodore Weld soon after the secession. Lewis Tappan to Theodore Weld, May 26, 1840. Tappan Manuscripts, *Weld-Grimké Letters,* II, 836. Reprinted with the permission of Dwight L. Dumond and the American Historical Association.

[New York] May 26/40

BROTHER WELD:

I want you to consider the following things—

1. The *split* was not *solely* on account of the claim that women shall vote, speak, be on committees, be officers, etc.
2. It was not [at] all because [of] opposition to their being *members* of the Society.
3. But it was chiefly because Garrison and his party (for although he and a few others profess *not* to speak the sentiments of the major part of the old M[assachusett]s Soc. yet it is evident they follow W. L. G's beck in everything) foisted upon the Amer. Anti Soc. the woman question, no government question, etc., and the bad spirit shown by the Liberator, etc.
4. When the Constitution of the A. Anti S. Soc. was formed in 1833, and

the word "person" introduced, *all concerned* considered that it was to be understood as it is usually understood in our benevolent Societies. All have a right to be *members,* but the *business* to be conducted by the men. This understanding continued for 6 years. W. L. G. so understood it. See Phelp's remark in M's Abolitionist.

5. W. L. G. introduced the question into the Anti S. Soc. to make an experiment upon the public. He had avowed before that there were subjects paramount to the Anti S. cause. And he was using the Society as an instrument to establish these notions. Since he introduced this question the slave has been lost sight of mainly. I add no more. See the Reporter.

L. T.

Women have equal rights with men, and therefore they have a right to form societies of women only. Men have the same right. *Men* formed the Amer. Anti S. Society.

THE MASSACHUSETTS ANTI-SLAVERY SOCIETY
DENOUNCES THE UNION (1844).

After the schism of 1840 the Garrisonians, secure in their Massachusetts stronghold, continued down to the eve of the Civil War to repudiate the federal government and demand the peaceful dissolution of the Union. The resolutions and debates of the Twelfth Annual Meeting of the Massachusetts Anti-Slavery Society were typical of the disunionist sentiments and aversion to political action of the die-hard moral suasionists, who throughout the late Forties and Fifties demanded "No Union with Slaveholders." *The Twelfth Annual Meeting of the Massachusetts Anti-Slavery Society* (1844), in *Twelfth Annual Report, presented to the Massachusetts Anti-Slavery Society by its Board of Managers* (Boston, 1844).

WEDNESDAY AFTERNOON.

. . .

The following resolutions were introduced by Mr. Garrison, chairman of the Business Committee; and, on motion, it was voted, that the first be now considered.

Resolved, That the Church of Christ, like its Head, has never held a slave—has never apologized for slavery—has never known a slaveholder as one of its members—has never stopped its ear to the cry of the poor—has never received the plunder of the poor with which to spread the gospel, circulate the Bible, publish tracts, or to establish Sunday schools; and has never held within its embrace dumb dogs which will not bark against the wrongs which crush humanity; therefore, the American Church, which perpetrates all these enormous crimes, is not the Church of Christ, but the synagogue of Satan.

Resolved, That the ballot-box is not an anti-slavery, but a pro-slavery argument, so long as it is surrounded by the United States Constitution, which forbids all approach to it, except on condition that the voter shall surrender fugitive slaves—suppress negro insurrections—sustain a piratical representation in Congress—and regard man-stealers as equally eligible with the truest friends of human freedom and equality to any or all the offices under the United States Government.

Previous to the discussion, the following resolutions were introduced by Mr. Quincy, in behalf of the members of the Business Committee; and the sixth was placed for consideration with the resolution already under discussion:

1. Resolved, That, until the leading organs and influences of the Whig and Democratic parties, instead of being pro-slavery shall become anti-slavery, we strongly repudiate the idea that an abolitionist can consistently sustain either.

2. Resolved, That our sense of the inherent fallacy, as well as danger to our cause, of a distinct anti-slavery political party, impels us to utter a strong and solemn warning against joining or sustaining one, to all who are beginning to consider how they can help to abolish slavery.

3. Resolved, That the hostile origin and progress of the existing political organization, and the unworthy character of its leading influences, compel us, in justice to the anti-slavery enterprise, to repudiate strongly the idea that any enlightened abolitionist can consistently sustain the Third party, or accord to it the name of a Liberty party, until, instead of being pro-slavery, it shall become anti-slavery.

4. Resolved, That we welcome to our platform the honest abolitionist, of whatever political party, while, at the same time, we refuse to give that party the credit of his honesty, so long as it shall refuse to be guided by it, and deny the anti-slavery consistency of sustaining either of the three as at present constituted.

5. Resolved, That while we give great comparative approbation to the scattering of votes, or to independent temporary nomination for the more effectually influencing the existing parties to act for our cause, we deem it the only true and consistent position, to withhold support and sanction from the Constitution of the U. States; and to present to the consciences of our countrymen the duty of dissolving their connection with the government, until it shall have abolished slavery.

6. Resolved, That since we are bound by a sense of duty and consistency to refuse our support to pro-slavery political arrangements, we cannot but be doubly solicitous to withdraw our sanction from all those religious institutions which are constantly forming the character of the people, and by the influence of which the political institutions are moulded, and do, therefore, as a measure of the plainest expediency in the conduct of our cause, as well as of the highest duty to enslaved humanity, recommend withdrawal from all churches which do not place slavery in the same category with crime.

7. Resolved, That we entreat all those members of churches who have separated from their respective pro-slavery bodies, that they may not be partakers of their sins, not to stop here, but to be instant in season and out of season in anti-slavery labors, and to unite with us as they did at first, now that they have found our principle of coming out and being separate from ecclesiastical pro-slavery to be a just one, and not (as they once thought it) a reason for leaving us.

The resolutions were commented on by Charles C. Burleigh, of Philadelphia; and after an enlivening song by the Hutchinsons, the discussion was continued by Messrs. Jewett, of Providence, R. I., Samuel J. May, of Lexington, who moved to amend the first resolution by substituting the word "permits" for the word "perpetrates," and by striking out all after the words "Church of Christ" in the last sentence; Edmund Quincy of Dedham, who moved to amend the amendment, by striking out the whole of the resolution introduced by the Business Committee. This amendment was opposed by Wm. A. White of Watertown, and Stephen S. Foster of New Hampshire; advocated by Addison Davis of Lynn, Charles L. Remond of Salem, Frederick Douglass of Lynn, Edmund Quincy of Dedham, and Abby Kelley; and, on motion, the Society voted to adjourn, after a song by the Hutchinsons.

After a spirited song, the vote to adjourn was reconsidered, and the question on the amendment, striking out the first resolution, was put, and lost; after which, on motion of James Boyle, the Society adjourned. . . .

THURSDAY EVENING.

The Society met, pursuant to adjournment, in Faneuil Hall; and its session was opened by a most inspiring song from the Hutchinsons.

Stephen S. Foster presented a "Protest against the Constitution of the United States"—as follows:

PROTEST

Of the Massachusetts Anti-Slavery Society against the Constitution of the United States and the Union.

We, the officers and members of the Massachusetts Anti-Slavery Society, assembled in the city of Boston, this 25th day of January, A. D. 1844, do hereby publicly record our solemn PROTEST against the Constitution of the United States, and the Union between the Northern and Southern States of this Confederacy, for the following reasons:—

1. Because the Constitution prohibits us from giving succor and protection to fugitive slaves, when pursued by their masters, and requires that such "shall be given up" to be returned into slavery; thereby imposing upon us, as citizens of a non-slaveholding State, the menial and degrading duty of guarding the plantations of Southern slave-masters—a duty more vile and infamous, in the eyes of the civilized world, than that of the miscreant slave-driver, who is stimulated to his loathsome task by the hope of pecuniary reward.

2. Because, in the event of an attempt by the slaves to throw off their chains, and assert their freedom by a resort to arms, in imitation of the example of the founders of this republic, the Constitution requires us to aid in furnishing a sufficient military and naval force to compel their submission—which requisition makes us, emphatically, SLAVEHOLDERS, and compels us, contrary to our own convictions of duty and high sense of honor, to trample on the glorious sentiments of the Declaration of Independence, dishonor the memories of our fathers, who fought and bled in their defence, and render ourselves base and despicable hypocrites, who, while prating of liberty and man's inalienable rights, stand pledged before the world to fight the battles of slavery.

3. Because the Constitution, contrary to the principles of natural justice and republican equality, grants to the slaveholding States a property representation in Congress, and thereby greatly enhances the power and temptation to hold slaves, by paying a bonus to the master in the shape of an increase of political power in the councils of the nation.

4. Because, through the power of Southern influence, slavery, and that most execrable species of piracy, the slave-trade, are legalized in our national capital; and we, in common with other citizens of the North, are taxed for the erection of prisons for the accomodation of slave-traders.

5. Because we regard a political union and alliance with slave-holders, (man-stealers,) under all circumstances, as a curse and crime—a sin against God, and a foul blot upon our characters, for which no conceivable advantages could compensate.

6. Because slavery, throughout the entire South, depends upon the Union for its existence; or, in the words of Mr. Underwood of Kentucky, on the floor of Congress, "The dissolution of the Union is the dissolution of slavery"—and to sanction and sustain a Union thus "gloated and cemented with the blood and marrow" of millions of our countrymen, would be to draw down upon ourselves and our common country the righteous indignation and just judgments of our Creator, who has given to all an equal right to freedom.

7. Because our colored fellow-citizens are utterly denied the rights of citizenship throughout the slave-claiming States, and in many cases are thrown into loathsome prisons, and finally sold into perpetual slavery, to defray the expense of their imprisonment.

8. Because, under the existing compact, according to a recent decision of the Supreme Court, any northern freeman may be seized by a vagrant southerner, and claimed as his property; if so claimed, he is denied the right of trial by jury, and must be sent into slavery—provided the person claiming him, can satisfy one of the Judges of the Supreme, or the Circuit Court of the United States, that he has previously robbed him of his liberty.

9. Because, if known to be abolitionists, we can have no protection for our persons or property in any of the slave-claiming States, but are virtually outlawed and exposed to the halter and faggot throughout the entire South, and that, too, with the connivance of the civil authorities of those States.

10. Because large rewards have been offered by the Legislatures and people of several of the southern States, for the abduction of some of our most valued citizens; and these rewards still remain uncancelled. . . .

For the reasons here enumerated, and others of similar import to which we might refer, we now publicly ABJURE OUR ALLEGIANCE TO THE CONSTITUTION OF THE UNITED STATES AND THE UNION, and place the broad seal of our reprobation on this unnatural and unholy alliance between Liberty and Slavery. The Union, in our judgment, is not only at war with the law and government of God, and destructive of the peace, the honor, and prosperity of the North, but of no *real* benefit to the South, since it serves to delay the "day of her visitation," only to plunge her the deeper into infamy and ruin. We therefore declare its obligations, so far as they relate to ourselves, utterly *null* and *void;* and we now publicly pledge ourselves to seek, in all suitable ways, its peaceful dissolution.

We shall accept of no office under the Constitution of the United States, as long as slavery remains an element of the government; nor shall we aid in electing others to fill such offices. But throwing ourselves back upon our natural rights, and the legitimate principles of revolution, we (or such of us as may think proper to go to the polls,) shall hereafter employ the ballot-box to make known our opposition to the Union, and break up this iniquitous alliance, to which we are still compelled to give support.

For the purity of our motives in thus seeking to dissolve a connection [*sic*], which, from our childhood, we have been taught to hallow and revere, we appeal to the Almighty Ruler of the universe, on whom we mainly depend for the success of our enterprise. And while we invoke His blessings on our efforts to emancipate our countrymen from their chains, and free ourselves from guilt, by breaking the fatal league on which their enthrallment mainly depends, we earnestly invite the friends of freedom throughout the North to unite with us in this measure; and hereafter to vote for REPEAL, instead of casting their ballots for abolitionists for office, which they cannot fill without first taking an oath to support and defend the slave power.

Henceforth, let REPEAL be our watchword and rallying cry; and to this point let our efforts be especially directed, till slavery shall be abolished, or the league which now binds us to that execrable institution, and unites our destinies, in peace and in war, with the destinies of the guilty slavemaster, shall be finally broken.

In behalf of the Society.

Mr. Foster was followed by W. L. Garrison, who presented the following resolution, embodying in a brief form the same propositions, which he supported in a forcible speech:

Whereas, no political union can possibly exist between freemen and slaveholders, nor can they possibly agree to form any such union, on the basis of equal rights; and

Whereas, the Constitution of the United States was conceived in sin and brought forth in iniquity—was adopted by a bloody compromise, involving the sacrifice of the bodies and souls of millions of the people, and the loss of universal liberty—and enforces obligations and duties which are incompatible with the enjoyment of freedom and equal rights; and

Whereas, the natural consequences of such an unholy compact have followed its adoption in swift and frightful succession—to wit, the wide extension and vigorous perpetuity of the slave system and the slave market—the multiplication of the victims of slavery from half a million to nearly three millions—the robbery of the North of a vast amount of its hard-earned wealth, and the degradation and impoverishment of Northern laborers—the imprisonment and enslavement of Northern seamen on account of their complexion—the denial of the right of petition, of speech and of representation, in Congress, to freemen—the utter corruption of the morals and religion of the land—and, finally, the outlawry, from one half of the republic, of all those who really embrace and practically carry out the self-evident truths of the Declaration of Independence, in regard to inalienable rights; therefore,

Resolved, That the national compact, being in principle and practice an insupportable despotism, and from its inception before God null and void, it is the right, it is the duty of all the friends of impartial liberty and a righteous government to withdraw their allegiance from this compact, and by a moral and peaceful revolution to effect its overthrow.

. . . The discussion of the resolutions was then continued by David Lee Child, of New York; Thomas Earle, of Philadelphia; and Stephen S. Foster; and after a song by the Hutchinsons, the Society adjourned.

THE LIBERTY PARTY
HOLDS A NATIONAL CONVENTION (1843).

WHILE THE GARRISONIANS elaborated their doctrine of "No Union with Slaveholders," political abolitionists were strengthening the Liberty Party and preparing for the presidential election of 1844. The party, whose total vote numbered only 7,100 in 1840, reached a high-water mark of 65,000 votes in the elections of 1843, and a year later won enough presidential votes in New York (15,000) to defeat Clay and throw the election to Polk. Resolutions passed in 1843 at the Buffalo convention denying the power of the federal government to establish or continue slavery anywhere, and declaring the fugitive slave clause of the Constitution "absolutely void," spelled out the political alternatives to Garrisonian disunionism before the Mexican War. "The National Liberty Convention," *Emancipator Extra,* Tract No. 1 (September 1843).

. . . *The following resolutions* were adopted by the Convention, at its several sittings:

RESOLUTIONS.

PREAMBLE: Being assembled in general Convention, as the representatives of the Liberty party in the United States, and feeling it incumbent on us to set forth, clearly and fully, the principles which govern us, and the purposes which we seek to accomplish, and this, the rather because these principles and purposes have been much misunderstood, and either ignorantly or maliciously much misrepresented: be it therefore

1. *Resolved,* That human brotherhood is a cardinal doctrine of true Democracy, as well as of pure Christianity, which spurns all inconsistent limitations; and neither the political party which repudiates it, nor the political system which is not based upon it, nor controlled in its practical workings, by it, can be truly Democratic or permanent.

2. *Resolved,* That the Liberty party, placing itself upon this broad principle, will demand the absolute and unqualified divorce of the General Government from Slavery, and also the restoration of equality of rights, among men, in every State where the party exists, or may exist.

3. *Resolved,* That the Liberty party has not been organized for any temporary purpose, by interested politicians, but has arisen from among the people, in consequence of a conviction, hourly gaining ground, that no other party in the country represents the true principles of American Liberty, or the true spirit of the Constitution of the United States.

4. *Resolved,* That the Liberty party has not been organized merely for the overthrow of Slavery. Its first decided effort must indeed be directed against slave-holding, as the grossest form and most revolting manifestation of Despotism; but it will also carry out the principles of Equal Rights, into all their practical consequences and applications, and support every just measure conducive to individual and social freedom.

5. *Resolved,* That the Liberty party is not a Sectional party, but a National party—has not originated in a desire to accomplish a single object, but in a comprehensive regard to the great interests of the whole country—is not a new party, or a third party, but is the party of 1776, reviving the principles of that memorable era, and striving to carry them into practical application.

6. *Resolved,* That it was understood in the times of the Declaration and the Constitution, that the existence of slavery in some of the States, was in derogation of the principles of American Liberty, and a deep stain upon the character of the country, and the implied faith of the States and the Nation was pledged, that slavery should never be extended beyond its then existing limits; but should be gradually, and, yet, at do [*sic*] distant day, wholly abolished by State authority.

7. *Resolved,* That the faith of the States, and the nation they pledged, was most nobly redeemed by the voluntary abolition of slavery in several of the States, and by the adoption of the ordinance of 1787, for the government of the Territory North West of the river Ohio, then the only Territory in the United States, and consequently the only Territory subject in this respect to the control of Congress, by which ordinance slavery was forever excluded from the vast regions which now compose the States of Ohio, Indiana, Illinois, Michigan, and the Territory of Wiskonsan, and an incapacity to bear up any other than freemen, was impressed on the soil itself.

8. *Resolved,* That the faith of the States and Nation thus pledged, has been shamefully violated by the omission, on the part of many of the States, to take any measures whatever for the abolition of slavery in the District of Columbia, and in the Territories of Louisiana and Florida; by the legislation of Congress; by the protection afforded by national legislation and negotiation to slaveholding in American vessels,

on the high seas, employed in the coastwise slave traffic; and by the extension of slavery far beyond its original limits, by acts of Congress, admitting new slave States into the Union.

9. *Resolved,* That the fundamental truths of the Declaration of Independence, that all men are endowed by their Creator with certain inalienable rights, among which are life, liberty, and the pursuit of happiness, was made the fundamental law of our National Government, by that amendment of the constitution which declares that no person shall be deprived of life, liberty or property, without due process of law. . . .

10. *Resolved,* That we recognize as sound, the doctrine maintained by slaveholding Jurists, that slavery is against natural rights, and strictly local, and that its existence and continuance rests on no other support than State legislation, and not on any Authority of Congress.

11. *Resolved,* That the General Government has, under the Constitution, no power to establish or continue slavery any where, and therefore that all treaties and acts of Congress establishing, continuing or favoring slavery in the District of Columbia, in the Territory of Florida, or on the high seas, are unconstitutional, and all attempts to hold men as property within the limits of exclusive natural jurisdiction, ought to be prohibited by law.

12. *Resolved,* That the plea sometimes urged, in behalf of the constitutionality of slaveholding under the sanction of national legislation, that the continuance of slavery was secured in the District of Columbia, by stipulations in the Deeds of cession by Virginia and Maryland, and in Florida by the provisions of the Treaty with Spain is false in fact; and the other plea, sometimes urged to the same purpose, that Congress might constitutionally authorize slaveholding in the District, under the power to legislate for the same in all cases whatsoever, and in Florida under the power to make needful rules and regulations for the government of national territories, and in American vessels on the seas under the power to regulate commerce, cannot be sound in law, so long as the great interdict of the People against depriving *any person* of life, liberty, or property, without due process of law, remains unaltered.

13. *Resolved,* That the provision of the Constitution of the United States, which confers extraordinary political powers on the owners of slaves, and thereby constituting the two hundred and fifty thousand slave-holders in the slave States a privileged aristocracy; and the provision for the reclamation of fugitive slaves from service, are anti-republican in their character, dangerous to the liberties of the people, and ought to be abrogated. . . .

16. *Resolved,* That the peculiar patronage and support hitherto ex-

tended to slavery and slave-holding, by the General Government, ought to be immediately withdrawn, and the example and influence of national authority ought to be arrayed on the side of Liberty and free labor. . . .

24. *Resolved,* That we believe intelligence, religion, and morality, to be the indispensable supports of good government, and are therefore in favor of general education; we believe, also, that good government itself is necessary to the welfare of society, and are therefore in favor of rigid public economy, and strict adherence to the principles of justice in every department of its administration.

25. *Resolved,* That freedom of speech and of the press, and the right of petition, and the right of trial by jury, are sacred and inviolable; and that all rules, regulations and laws, in derogation of either are oppressive, unconstitutional, and not to be endured by a free people.

26. *Resolved,* That we regard voting in an eminent degree, as a moral and religious duty, which when exercised, should be by voting for those who will do all in their power for immediate emancipation. . . .

29. *Resolved,* That we especially entreat the friends of Liberty in the slave States to reflect on the vast importance of voting openly for Liberty, and Liberty men; and to remember and adopt the words of the illustrious Washington, who said, "There is but one proper and effectual mode by which the abolition of slavery can be accomplished, and that is by legislative authority; and this, as far as my suffrage will go, shall not be wanting." . . .

37. *Whereas,* The Constitution of these United States is a series of agreements, covenants, or contracts between the people of the United States, each with all, and all with each; and

Whereas, It is a principle of universal morality, that the moral laws of the Creator are paramount to all human laws; or, in the language of an apostle, that "we ought to obey God, rather than men;"—and

Whereas, The principle of Common Law—that any contract, covenant, or agreement, to do an act derogatory to natural right, is vitiated and annulled by its inherent immorality—has been recognized by one of the Justices of the Supreme Court of the United States, who, in a recent case, expressly holds that "*any* contract that rests upon such a basis, is *void;*—and

Whereas, The third clause of the second section of the fourth article of the Constitution of the United States—when construed as providing for the surrender of a fugitive slave—*does* "rest upon such a basis," in that it is a contract to rob a man of a natural right—namely, his natural right to his own liberty; and is, therefore, absolutely *void,*

Therefore, Resolved, That we hereby give it to be distinctly understood, by this nation and the world, that, as abolitionists, considering that the strength of our cause lies in its righteousness—and our hope for it in our conformity to the LAWS OF GOD, and our respect for the RIGHTS OF MAN, we owe it to the Sovereign Ruler of the Universe, as a proof of our allegiance to Him, in all our civil relations and offices, whether as private citizens, or as public functionaries sworn to support the Constitution of the United States, to regard and to treat the third clause of the second section of the fourth article of that instrument, whenever applied to the case of a fugitive slave, as utterly null and void, and consequently as forming no part of the Constitution of the United States, whenever we are called upon, or sworn, to support it.

38. *Resolved,* That the power given to Congress by the Constitution, to provide for calling out the militia to suppress insurrection, does not make it the duty of the Government to maintain slavery by military force, much less does it make it the duty of the citizens to form a part of such military force. When freemen unsheath the sword it should be to strike for *Liberty,* not for Despotism.

39. *Resolved,* That to preserve the peace of the citizens, and secure the blessings of freedom, the Legislature of each of the free States, ought to keep in force suitable statutes, rendering it penal for any of its inhabitants to transport, or aid in transporting from such State, any person sought, to be thus transported, merely because subject to the slave laws of any other State; this remnant of independence being accorded to the free States, by the decision of the Supreme Court, in the case of Prigg, *vs.* the State of Pennsylvania. . . .

PART VI.

THE ANTI-SLAVERY ENTERPRISE.

HENRY HIGHLAND GARNET

CALLS ON THE SLAVES TO RESIST (1843).

IN THE TWO DECADES after 1840 the free Negro played an increasingly important role in the anti-slavery movement. While many of the free Negroes in the North were abolitionists of long standing and had been instrumental in converting white reformers to abolition, by the Forties there appeared a younger generation, many of them escaped slaves, who supplied a new tone of urgency to the abolitionist argument. One of these militant free Negro agitators was Henry Highland Garnet, a slave who had escaped with his family as a child, settled in New York City, graduated from Oneida, and trained himself first for the teaching profession and then for the ministry. At the National Convention of Colored Citizens held in Buffalo in 1843 Garnet presented "An Address to the Slaves of the United States of America," which he proposed to print and distribute to the slaves. Although the Convention rejected his proposal as too radical, six years later John Brown had the "Address" printed at his own expense. "An Address to the Slaves of the United States of America" by Henry Highland Garnet, in *Negro Orators and Their Orations* (Washington, D. C., 1925), Carter G. Woodson, ed. Reprinted with the permission of Associated Publishers.

BRETHREN AND FELLOW CITIZENS: Your brethren of the North, East, and West have been accustomed to meet together in National Conventions, to sympathize with each other, and to weep over your unhappy condition. In these meetings we have addressed all classes of the free, but we have never, until this time, sent a word of consolation and advice to you. . . .

Many of you are bound to us, not only by the ties of a common humanity, but we are connected by the more tender relations of parents, wives, husbands, and sisters, and friends. As such we most affectionately address you.

Slavery has fixed a deep gulf between you and us, and while it shuts out from you the relief and consolation which your friends would willingly render, it afflicts and persecutes you with a fierceness which we might not expect to see in the fiends of hell. But still the Almighty Father of mercies has left to us a glimmering ray of hope, which shines out like a lone star in a cloudy sky. Mankind are becoming wiser, and better—the oppressor's power is fading, and you, every day, are becoming better informed, and more numerous. Your grievances, brethren, are many. We shall not attempt, in this short address, to present to the world all the dark catalogue of the nation's sins, which have been committed upon an innocent people. Nor is it indeed necessary, for you feel them from day to day, and all the civilized world looks upon them with amazement. . . .

Nearly three millions of your fellow-citizens are prohibited by law and public opinion (which in this country is stronger than law) from reading the Book of Life. Your intellect has been destroyed as much as possible, and every ray of light they have attempted to shut out from your minds. The oppressors themselves have become involved in the ruin. They have become weak, sensual, and rapacious—they have cursed you—they have cursed themselves—they have cursed the earth which they have trod. . . .

SLAVERY! How much misery is comprehended in that single word. What mind is there that does not shrink from its direful effects? Unless the image of God be obliterated from the soul, all men cherish the love of liberty. The nice discerning political economist does not regard the sacred right more than the untutored African who roams in the wilds of Congo. Nor has the one more right to the full enjoyment of his freedom than the other. In every man's mind the good seeds of liberty are planted, and he who brings his fellow down so low, as to make him contented with a condition of slavery, commits the highest crime against God and man. Brethren, your oppressors aim to do this. They endeavor to make you as much like brutes as possible. When they have blinded the eyes of your mind—when they have embittered the sweet waters of life—when they have shut out the light which shines from the word of God—then, and not till then, has American slavery done its perfect work.

TO SUCH DEGRADATION IT IS SINFUL IN THE EXTREME FOR YOU TO MAKE VOLUNTARY SUBMISSION. The divine commandments you are in duty bound to reverence and obey. If you do not obey them, you will surely meet with the displeasure of the Almighty. He requires you to love Him supremely, and your neighbor as yourself—to keep the Sabbath day holy—to search the Scriptures—and bring up your children with respect for His laws, and to worship no other God but Him. But slavery sets all these at nought, and hurls defiance in the face of Jehovah. The forlorn condition in which you are placed does not destroy your obligation to God. You are not certain of heaven, because you allow yourselves to remain in a state of slavery, where you cannot obey the commandments of the

Sovereign of the universe. If the ignorance of slavery is a passport to heaven, then it is a blessing, and no curse, and you should rather desire its perpetuity than its abolition. God will not receive slavery, nor ignorance, nor any other state of mind, for love and obedience to Him. Your condition does not absolve you from your moral obligation. The diabolical injustice by which your liberties are cloven down, NEITHER GOD NOR ANGELS, OR JUST MEN, COMMAND YOU TO SUFFER FOR A SINGLE MOMENT. THEREFORE IT IS YOUR SOLEMN AND IMPERATIVE DUTY TO USE EVERY MEANS, BOTH MORAL, INTELLECTUAL, AND PHYSICAL, THAT PROMISES SUCCESS. . . .

Brethren, it is as wrong for your lordly oppressors to keep you in slavery as it was for the man thief to steal our ancestors from the coast of Africa. You should therefore now use the same manner of resistance as would have been just in our ancestors when the bloody foot-prints of the first remorseless soul-thief was placed upon the shores of our fatherland. The humblest peasant is as free in the sight of God as the proudest monarch that ever swayed a sceptre. Liberty is a spirit sent out from God, and like its great Author, is no respecter of persons.

Brethren, the time has come when you must act for yourselves. It is an old and true saying that, "if hereditary bondmen would be free, they must themselves strike the blow." You can plead your own cause, and do the work of emancipation better than any others. The nations of the Old World are moving in the great cause of universal freedom, and some of them at least will, ere long, do you justice. The combined powers of Europe have placed their broad seal of disapprobation upon the African slave-trade. But in the slaveholding parts of the United States the trade is as brisk as ever. They buy and sell you as though you were brute beasts. The North has done much—her opinion of slavery in the abstract is known. But in regard to the South, we adopt the opinion of the *New York Evangelist*—"We have advanced so far, that the cause apparently waits for a more effectual door to be thrown open than has been yet." We are about to point you to that more effectual door. Look around you, and behold the bosoms of your loving wives heaving with untold agonies! Here [sic] the cries of your poor children! Remember the stripes your fathers bore. Think of the torture and disgrace of your noble mothers. Think of your wretched sisters, loving virtue and purity, as they are driven into concubinage and are exposed to the unbridled lusts of incarnate devils. Think of the undying glory that hangs around the ancient name of Africa—and forget not that you are native-born American citizens, and as such you are justly entitled to all the rights that are granted to the freest. Think how many tears you have poured out upon the soil which you have cultivated with unrequited toil and enriched with your blood; and then go to your lordly enslavers and tell them plainly, that you *are determined to be free.* Appeal to their sense of justice, and tell them that they have no more right to oppress you than you have to enslave them. Entreat them to remove the grievous burdens which they have imposed upon you, and to remunerate you for your labor. Promise them renewed diligence in the cultivation of the soil, if they will render to you an equivalent for your services. Point them to the increase of happiness and prosperity in the British West Indies since the Act of Emancipation. Tell them in language which they cannot misunderstand of the exceeding sinfulness of slavery, and of a future judgment, and of the righteous retributions of an indignant God. Inform them that all you desire is FREEDOM, and that nothing else will suffice. Do this, and forever after cease to toil for the heartless tyrants, who give you no other reward but stripes and abuse. If they then commence work of death, they, and not you, will be responsible for the consequences. You had far better all die—*die immediately,* than live slaves, and entail your wretchedness upon your posterity. If you would be free in this generation, here is your only hope. However much you and all of us may desire it, there is not much hope of redemption without the shedding of blood. If you must bleed, let it all come at once—rather *die freemen than live to be the slaves.* It is impossible, like the children of Israel, to make a grand exodus from the land of bondage. The Pharaohs are on both sides of the blood-red waters! You cannot move *en masse* to the dominions of the British Queen—nor can you pass through Florida and overrun Texas, and at last find peace in Mexico. . . .

You will not be compelled to spend much time in order to become inured to hardships. From the first movement that you breathed the air of heaven, you have been accustomed to nothing else but hardships. The heroes of the American Revolution were never put upon harder fare than a peck of corn and few herrings per week. You have not become enervated by the luxuries of life. Your sternest energies have been beaten out upon the anvil of severe trial. Slavery has done this to make you subservient to its own purposes; but it has done more than this, it has prepared you for any emergency. If you receive good treatment, it is what you can hardly expect; if you meet with pain, sorrow, and even death, these are the common lot of the slaves. . . .

In 1822, Denmark Veazie, of South Carolina, formed a plan for the liberation of his fellowmen. In the whole history of human efforts to overthrow slavery, a more complicated and tremendous plan was never formed. He was betrayed by the treachery of his own people, and died a martyr to freedom. Many a brave hero fell, but history, faithful to her high trust, will transcribe his name on the same monument with Moses, Hampden, Tell, Bruce, and Wallace, Toussaint L'Ouverture, Lafayette, and Washington. That tremendous movement shook the whole empire of slavery. The guilty soul-thieves were overwhelmed with fear. It is a matter of fact that at this time, and in consequence of the threatened revolution, the slave States talked strongly of emancipation. But they blew but one blast of the trumpet of freedom, and then laid it aside. As these men became quiet, the slaveholders ceased to talk about emancipation: and now behold your condition to-day! Angels sigh over it, and humanity has long since exhausted her tears in weeping on your account!

The patriotic Nathaniel Turner followed Denmark Veazie. He was goaded to desperation by wrong and injustice. By despotism, his name has been recorded on the list of infamy, and future generations will remember him among the noble and brave.

Next arose the immortal Joseph Cinque, the hero of the Amistad. He was a native African, and by the help of God he emancipated a whole ship-load of his fellowmen on the high seas. And he now sings of liberty on the sunny hills of Africa and beneath his native palm-trees, where he hears the lion roar and feels himself as free as the king of the forest.

Next arose Madison Washington, that bright star of freedom, and took his station in the constellation of true heroism. He was a slave on board the brig *Creole,* of Richmond, bound to New Orleans, that great slave mart, with a hundred and four others. Nineteen struck for liberty or death. But one life was taken, and the whole were emancipated, and the vessel was carried into Nassau, New Providence.

Noble men! Those who have fallen in freedom's conflict, their memories will be cherished by the true-hearted and the God-fearing in all future generations; those who are living, their names are surrounded by a halo of glory.

Brethren, arise, arise! Strike for your lives and liberties. Now is the day and the hour. Let every slave throughout the land do this, and the days of slavery are numbered. You cannot be more oppressed than you have been—you cannot suffer greater cruelties than you have already. *Rather die freemen than live to be slaves.* Remember that you are FOUR MILLIONS!

It is in your power so to torment the God-cursed slaveholders that they will be glad to let you go free. If the scale was turned, and black men were the masters and white men the slaves, every destructive agent and element would be employed to lay the oppressor low. Danger and death would hang over their heads day and night. Yes, the tyrants would meet with plagues more terrible than those of Pharaoh. But you are a patient people. You act as though you were made for the special use of these devils. You act as though your daughters were born to pamper the lusts of your masters and overseers. And worse than all, you tamely submit while your lords tear your wives from your embraces and defile them before your eyes. In the name of God, we ask, are you men? Where is the blood of your fathers? Has it all run out of your veins? Awake, awake; millions of voices are calling you! Your dead fathers speak to you from their graves. Heaven, as with a voice of thunder, calls on you to arise from the dust.

Let your motto be resistance! *resistance!* RESISTANCE! No oppressed people have ever secured their liberty without resistance. What kind of resistance you had better make you must decide by the circumstances that surround you, and according to the suggestion of expediency. Brethren, adieu! Trust in the living God. Labor for the peace of the human race, and remember that you are FOUR MILLIONS!

NEW ENGLAND ABOLITIONISTS
ENLIST THE CONSCIENCE WHIGS (1845).

THE CENTER OF OPPOSITION to Manifest Destiny, to the annexation of Texas, and to the Mexican War lay in New England, where abolitionists joined with Conscience Whigs in fighting a last-ditch stand against the forces of expansion. The pamphlet-petition *How to Settle the Texas Question* (1845), a product of this effort at cooperation, contained instructions for circulation along with an "Address" signed by thirty-nine prominent New Englanders including Charles Francis Adams, Charles Sumner, George S. Hillard, Henry Wilson, and Rockwell Hoar as well as the abolitionists Garrison, Wendell Phillips, Whittier, and Stanton. The fact that the Garrisonians, despite their disunionist principles, were willing to cooperate with politicians who had not yet officially declared themselves "Conscience Whigs" was an indication that anti-slavery sentiment in New England could now unite men with radically different programs. *How to Settle the Texas Question* (Boston, 1845).

DIRECTIONS.

1. To ALL. Read this tract carefully.

2. Cut off the last leaf; attach the petition on it by paste or wafers to one or more sheets of paper, and then get as many signatures as you can to it; men and women on separate petitions.

3. Send the petitions, when signed, under cover, directed to any trusty member of Congress, at Washington, D. C., so as to reach there, if possible, by the first Monday of December, 1845, or to Elizur Wright, Jr., 10 Court Street, Boston.

4. Get the tract, or some part of it, printed in any religious or political newspapers you can.

5. If you can write, put something on the subject of Texas and slavery into any newspaper you can.

6. *To Every Reader.* Appoint yourself a committee *to see to it,* that the remonstrance is carried from house to house, and presented prominently at the Town meeting on the 10th of November, so that every adult inhabitant of your town may have an opportunity to sign.

7. *To Editors of Newspapers.* You are respectfully requested to copy the following address, or some part of it, and lend your aid to its object.

8. *To County and Town Committees.* Have public meetings in your counties and towns against the admission of Texas as a slave State, and let every man speak against it as the spirit moves him; and get signatures to the petitions at these meetings. Publish the number of signatures in the newspapers.

9. *To Clergymen.* You are entreated in the name of God and Christ to pray for the slave; and preach at least one sermon against the admission of Texas as a slave State, as soon as may be.

10. *To Women.* Circulate the petitions, and get as many signatures among your own sex as possible.

At a meeting of citizens *without distinction of party,* held at Cambridge, Oct. 21st, 1845, a large Committee was appointed to act against the admission of Texas as a Slave State. That Committee, composed of men from different parties, issues the following

ADDRESS:
TO THE FRIENDS OF FREE INSTITUTIONS IN MASSACHUSETTS AND OTHER FREE STATES.

Fellow Citizens,

The Texas question is yet UNDECIDED. That question, so far as it is of any importance to the United States, or Mexico, or mankind, is not whether the people who are to inhabit that vast territory are to be connected with this or that country, or to stand independent, but whether they are to consist of slaves and slaveholders; whether those fertile plains shall in all coming time rejoice under the plough of free labor, or groan under the unwilling and unblessed toil of slaves,—slaves so rapidly consumed by their toil, that more than half our present republic shall be turned into a mere Guinea coast, to keep up the supply. The question is, whether, in order to fortify the present most unrighteous power of our slaveholders, both over their slaves and the people of the free States, slavery shall be created anew,—and we ourselves do it,—over a vast country, where Mexico had abolished it.

Whether this or that mode of annexation is constitutional or not,—will violate our treaties with Mexico or not,—will lead us into war or not,—though these are important questions, and perhaps not yet irrevocably decided in the wrong, they are comparatively insignificant. They have been deeply discussed. The slaveholders have carried many of the opponents of slavery with them on these questions, acting with apparent success on their old principle of *divide and conquer*. Let these questions pass for settled. Still, the all important one remains, that to which we have referred above. The slaveholders,—whose, from first to last, the scheme of annexation is,—have thus far cunningly kept the discussion almost wholly away from that issue. They will use the utmost address to complete their nefarious project without raising it. But it is the real question, not at all forestalled by any thing yet done, which, silently or vocally, for weal or for woe, we, by our representatives at Washington, must soon decide. Shall what nine tenths of the slaveholders themselves acknowledge to be an almost intolerable curse to our thirteen Southern States, and what we *know* to be such to the whole country, be branded upon the virgin soil of which thirteen more States are to be made? Thank God, this is a question which the people of the free States have yet the power to decide! . . .

Hitherto slavery has bound the Southern States so strongly together that they have contrived by union and concert, vigilance and political sagacity, always to defeat the North. But they fear lest new States to be formed from the northwest territory should overturn the balance in the Senate, and add to the strength of the free States in the House. If Texas can be annexed, the balance in the Senate will turn in favor of slavery, and the free majority in the House will be diminished. Half a dozen slave States can easily be formed out of Texas in a few years. This will give slavery an overwhelming majority in the Senate.

Are the free States ready to deliver themselves up, bound hand and foot, to the South? Will slaveholders use their power so gently and benevolently towards the North that we have nothing to fear? The slaveholders hate the free labor of the North. They are jealous of our agricultural, commercial, and manufacturing prosperity, our increasing wealth, our free institutions. With all their bluster of chivalry, they are neither honest nor just. If Texas be annexed we need expect no more justice or mercy at their hands than they have shown to the slaves and Indians.

The most momentous question which has ever been brought before the nation since the declaration of independence, is now presented. Shall the voice of the United States be given for liberty or slavery? Early in the next session of Congress the Texan Constitution will be presented for ratification or rejection. Whether it shall be ratified or rejected depends on the votes of members from the free States. What those votes will be, will be decided by the course pursued by their constituents. If the people of the North raise a strong and clear voice of remonstrance, their representatives must obey.

In the subsequent pages of this tract an attempt is made to show what indeed admits of no dispute, that Texas is not annexed, much less its slavery, and that the true way to defeat the wicked design of the slaveholders is to lay immediately before Congress an overwhelming expression of the will of the people. Every one into whose hands these pages may fall is earnestly requested to give all the aid in his power by signing, circulating and forwarding remonstrances.

Fellow citizens! now is the time for action. The North can send to Congress the names of more than a million voters against the annexation of any more slavery. Use all your efforts, and doubt not they will be successful. Have confidence in the country—Have faith in God. . . .

But before inquiring what should be done, it may be well to consider the precise situation in which Texas now stands to this Union. The Democratic papers shout exultingly that annexation is completed, and nothing but mere forms remain to make Texas, as well in name as in fact, one of the United States. Most of the other papers seem, though with more or less reluctance, to acquiesce in the same conclusion. Indeed, a very general feeling pervades the community, that we must reconcile ourselves as we best can, to Texas, with her Slavery, as an inevitable evil.

The real fact, however, is, that Texas is no part of the American Union, and no possible act of hers can make her so. Nothing but the deliberate legislative action of Congress can consummate the annexation. All, therefore, which now prevents effectual resistance to the measure, arises from the state of public opinion. To enlighten and animate public opinion is the great difficulty remaining. Let us examine the resolution for annexing Texas: It provides "that Congress doth consent that the territory properly included within and rightfully belonging to the Republic of Texas, may be erected into a new State, to be called the State of Texas, with a republican form of government to be adopted by the people," "in order that the same may be admitted as one of the States of the Union." This section clearly does not admit Texas, but merely gives the consent of Congress to Texas forming a State Constitution as a mode of preparing for its admission. . . .

It does not admit of question, that if Congress does not accept the constitution of Texas, it will remain a foreign nation. . . .

But some persons, who have hitherto opposed annexation, now say that further resistance is hopeless; therefore let us now submit with becoming resignation to the new order of things. With this unworthy and pusillanimous suggestion, we have no sympathy. Why should we yield before the battle is fully fought? Are we to take it for granted that the new Congress will be as mean spirited as the last? That all the northern

Democratic representatives will prove traitors, before they have been tried?

Congress will always echo the will of the people, when distinctly and strongly pronounced. Shall we assume that the great majority of the people of the free States acquiesce in annexation, before they have expressed an opinion on the subject? Man can never know beforehand the result of his efforts; that depends on an all-wise Providence. But the path of duty is plainly marked out to him, and he must never cease to contend for right and justice, because he fears his efforts will prove unavailing. . . .

The means are obvious. Let every one feel it his own personal duty to do something in this cause. Let every town and village be roused by lectures—let remonstrances to Congress against the admission of Texas as a slave State be everywhere circulated—let the clergy be prompt to preach resistance to annexation and slavery as a religious duty. Let conventions of the people be called in every State, to give expression to popular opinion. Let every man who reads this address be sure that he does something himself to defeat the nefarious plot to sustain slavery. Many can address popular assemblies; many can write for the public; all can converse with their friends—all can sign their names to a protest. If every man who thinks right on this subject will only do his duty, annexation may yet be defeated; and the North be for the first time triumphant in the great warfare between liberty and slavery. . . .

TO THE HONORABLE SENATE AND HOUSE OF REPRESENTATIVES OF THE UNITED STATES IN CONGRESS ASSEMBLED.

The undersigned, citizens of the State of
solemnly remonstrate and protest against the admission of Texas as a State of this Union, for various reasons, but this especially, because its constitution, as far as it can, supports and perpetuates slavery.

JAMES RUSSELL LOWELL
ASSAILS THE MEXICAN WAR (1846).

As an abolitionist, pacifist, and strong supporter of Garrison, James Russell Lowell wrote his *Biglow Papers* with the conviction that the Mexican War was "a national crime committed in behoof of Slavery, our common sin." Hosea Biglow, the unlettered but shrewd New England farmer from Jaalam and mouthpiece of Lowell's anti-slavery humanitarianism, refuses to join in the "pullin' o' triggers to extend the aree of abusin' the niggers" and remains at home to keep a sharp eye on political trimmers and professional patriots. In No. I of the First Series, "A Letter from Mr. Ezekiel Biglow of Jaalam to the Hon. Joseph T. Buckingham, Editor of the Boston Courier, Inclosing a Poem of his Son, Mr. Hosea Biglow," Hosea recounts his experiences with the recruiting sergeant in Boston. The introductory letter has been omitted. *The Writings of James Russell Lowell* (Boston, 1890: Riverside edition), 11 vols., VIII, 43-50.

Thrash away, you'll *hev* to rattle
  On them kittle-drums o' yourn,—
'T aint a knowin' kind o' cattle
  Thet is ketched with moldy corn;
Put in stiff, you fifer feller,
  Let folks see how spry you be,—
Guess you'll toot till you are yeller
  'Fore you git ahold o' me!

Thet air flag 's a leetle rotten,
  Hope it aint your Sunday's best;—
Fact! it takes a sight o' cotton
  To stuff out a soger's chest:
Sence we farmers hev to pay fer 't,
  Ef you must wear humps like these,
S'posin' you should try salt hay fer 't,
  It would du ez slick ez grease.

'T would n't suit them Southun fellers,
  They 're a dreffle graspin' set,
We must ollers blow the bellers
  Wen they want their irons het;

May be it 's all right ez preachin',
  But *my* narves it kind o' grates,
Wen I see the overreachin'
  O' them nigger-drivin' States.

Them thet rule us, them slave-traders,
  Haint they cut a thunderin' swarth
(Helped by Yankee renegaders),
  Thru the vartu o' the North!
We begin to think it 's nater
  To take sarse an' not be riled;—
Who 'd expect to see a tater
  All on eend at bein' biled?

Ez fer war, I call it murder,—
  There you hev it plain an' flat;
I don't want to go no furder
  Than my Testyment fer that;
God hez sed so plump an' fairly,
  It 's ez long ez it is broad,
An' you 've gut to git up airly
  Ef you want to take in God.

'T aint your eppyletts an' feathers
  Make the thing a grain more right;
'T aint afollerin' your bell-wethers
  Will excuse ye in His sight;
Ef you take a sword an' dror it,
  An' go stick a feller thru,
Guv'ment aint to answer for it,
  God 'll send the bill to you.

Wut 's the use o' meetin'-goin'
  Every Sabbath, wet or dry,
Ef it 's right to go amowin'
  Feller-men like oats an' rye?
I dunno but wut it 's pooty
  Trainin' round in bobtail coats,—
But it 's curus Christian dooty
  This 'ere cuttin' folks's throats.

They may talk o' Freedom's airy
  Tell they 're pupple in the face,—
It 's a grand gret cemetary

Fer the barthrights of our race;
They jest want this Californy
So 's to lug new slave-States in
To abuse ye, an' to scorn ye,
An' to plunder ye like sin.

Aint it cute to see a Yankee
Take sech everlastin' pains,
All to get the Devil's thankee
Helpin' on 'em weld their chains?
Wy, it 's jest ez clear ez figgers,
Clear ez one an' one make two,
Chaps thet make black slaves o' niggers
Want to make wite slaves o' you.

Tell ye jest the eend I 've come to
Arter cipherin' plaguy smart,
An' it makes a handy sum, tu,
Any gump could larn by heart;
Laborin' man an' laborin' woman
Hev one glory an' one shame.
Ev'y thin' thet 's done inhuman
Injers all on 'em the same.

'T aint by turnin' out to hack folks
You 're agoin' to git your right,
Nor by lookin' down on black folks
Coz you 're put upon by wite;
Slavery aint o' nary color,
'T aint the hide thet makes it wus,
All it keers fer in a feller
'S jest to make him fill its pus.

Want to tackle *me* in, du ye?
I expect you 'll hev to wait;
Wen cold lead puts daylight thru ye
You 'll begin to kal'late;
S'pose the crows wun't fall to pickin'
All the carkiss from your bones,
Coz you helped to give a lickin'
To them poor half-Spanish drones?

Jest go home an' ask our Nancy
Wether I 'd be sech a goose

Ez to jine ye,—guess you 'd fancy
  The etarnal bung wuz loose!
She wants me fer home consumption,
  Let alone the hay 's to mow,—
Ef you 're arter folks o' gumption,
  You 've a darned long row to hoe.

Take them editors thet 's crowin'
  Like a cockerel three months old,—
Don't ketch any on 'em goin',
  Though they *be* so blasted bold;
Aint they a prime lot o' fellers?
  'Fore they think on 't guess they 'll sprout
(Like a peach thet 's got the yellers),
  With the meanness bustin' out.

Wal, go 'long to help 'em stealin'
  Bigger pens to cram with slaves,
Help the men thet 's ollers dealin'
  Insults on your fathers' graves;
Help the strong to grind the feeble,
  Help the many agin the few,
Help the men thet call your people
  Witewashed slaves an' peddlin' crew!

Massachusetts, God forgive her,
  She 's akneelin' with the rest,
She, thet ough' to ha' clung ferever
  In her grand old eagle-nest;
She thet ough' to stand so fearless
  W'ile the wracks are round her hurled,
Holdin' up a beacon peerless
  To the oppressed of all the world!

Ha'n't they sold your colored seamen?
  Ha'n't they made your env'ys w'iz?
Wut 'll make ye act like freemen?
  Wut 'll git your dander riz?
Come, I 'll tell ye wut I 'm thinkin'
  Is our dooty in this fix,
They 'd ha' done 't ez quick ez winkin'
  In the days o' seventy-six.

Clang the bells in every steeple,
  Call all true men to disown
The tradoocers of our people,
  The enslavers o' their own;
Let our dear old Bay State proudly
  Put the trumpet to her mouth,
Let her ring this messidge loudly
  In the ears of all the South:—

"I 'll return ye good fer evil
  Much ez we frail mortils can,
But I wun't go help the Devil
  Makin' man the cus o' man;
Call me coward, call me traiter,
  Jest ez suits your mean idees,—
Here I stand a tyrant-hater,
  An' the friend o' God an' Peace!"

Ef I 'd *my* way I hed ruther
  We should go to work an' part,
They take one way, we take t' other,
  Guess it would n't break my heart;
Man hed ough' to put asunder
  Them thet God has noways jined;
An' I should n't gretly wonder
  Ef there 's thousands o' my mind.

June 17, 1846

LYSANDER SPOONER AND HENRY BOWDITCH DEBATE THE CONSTITUTION (1845-1849).

AFTER THE MEXICAN WAR the question of the constitutional status of slavery increasingly occupied the attention of both the North and the South. Generally, political abolitionists tended to interpret the Constitution as an anti-slavery instrument, Garrisonians as a pro-slavery "covenant with death." Lysander Spooner, a self-made Massachusetts lawyer and political abolitionist, was the most thorough and tenacious of those constitutional theorists who attempted to prove that slavery had no legal existence in the United States. His ponderous argument, *The Unconstitutionality of Slavery,* (*a*) published in 1845 and reissued with a second part in 1847, 1853, 1856, and 1860, served as campaign literature for anti-slavery politicians bent on capturing the Constitution. Insisting that the Constitution did not create slavery as a new institution, Spooner returned to the Declaration of Independence, the state constitutions, and the Articles of Confederation for confirmation of his argument that slavery "had always been a mere abuse sustained by the common consent of the strongest party," an assumption which rested on a narrow and extremely legalistic interpretation of the word "freeman" as it was used in English law in the eighteenth century.

The pro-slavery interpretation of the Constitution as "an agreement with Hell" was espoused by most of the Garrisonians, most notably by Wendell Phillips and Henry Ingersoll Bowditch, a member of the famous family of scientists and a humanitarian reformer who joined the Massachusetts Anti-Slavery Society. As a trained lawyer, Bowditch was not impressed by Spooner's cranky and seemingly factitious argument. His own *Slavery and the Constitution* (1849), (*b*) was intended as a rebuttal to Spooner's book based on an examination of the Constitution "according to the common meaning of its terms" and establishing the "incontrovertible conclusion" that it legalized and upheld slavery. Lysander Spooner, *The Unconstitutionality of Slavery* (Boston, 1853), 36-56; William I. Bowditch, *Slavery and the Constitution* (Boston, 1849), ch. XII. Footnotes and citations have been omitted.

(*a*)

CHAPTER V. THE DECLARATION OF INDEPENDENCE.

. . . THE DECLARATION WAS certainly the constitutional law of this country for certain purposes. For example, it absolved the people from their allegiance to the English crown. It would have been so declared by the judicial tribunals of this country, if an American, during the revolutionary war, or since, had been tried for treason to the crown. If, then, the declaration were the constitutional law of the country for that purpose, was it not also constitutional law for the purpose of recognizing and establishing, as law, the natural and inalienable right of individuals to life, liberty, and the pursuit of happiness? The lawfulness of the act of absolving themselves from their allegiance to the crown, was avowed by the people of the country—and that too in the same instrument that declared the absolution—to rest entirely upon, and to be only a consequence of the natural right of all men to life, liberty, and the pursuit of happiness. If, then, the act of absolution was lawful, does it not necessarily follow that the principles that legalized the act, were also law? And if the country ratified the act of absolution, did they not also necessarily ratify and acknowledge the principles which they declared legalized the act?

It is sufficient for our purpose, if it be admitted that this principle was the law of the country at that particular time, (1776)—even though it had continued to be the law for only a year, or even a day. For if it were the law of the country even for a day, it freed every slave in the country—(if there were, as we say there were not, any legal slaves then in the country.) And the burden would then be upon the slaveholder to show that slavery had *since* been *constitutionally* established. And to show this, he must show an express *constitutional* designation of the particular individuals, who have since been made slaves. Without such particular designation of the individuals to be made slaves, (and not even the present constitutions of the slave States make any such designation,) all constitutional provisions, purporting to authorize slavery, are indefinite, and uncertain in their application, and for that reason void. . . .

CHAPTER VI.
THE STATE CONSTITUTIONS OF 1789.

. . . The eleven constitutions formed, were all democratic in their general character. The most of them eminently so. They generally recognized, in some form or other, the natural rights of men, as one of the fundamental principles of the government. Several of them asserted these rights in the most emphatic and authoritative manner. Most or all of them had also specific provisions incompatible with slavery. Not one of them has any specific recognition of the existence of slavery. Not one of them granted any specific authority for its continuance. . . .

Several of the constitutions, to wit, those of Georgia, South Carolina, North Carolina, Maryland, Delaware, Pennsylvania, New York—but not Virginia, New Jersey, Massachusetts or New Hampshire—repeatedly use the word "freeman" or "freemen," when describing the electors, or other members of the state.

The only question that can arise from the use of these words "free" and "freeman," are these, viz.: Are they used as the correlatives, or opposites of slaves? Or are they used in that political sense, in which they are used in the common law of England, and in which they had been used in the colonial charters, viz., to describe those persons possessed of the privilege of citizenship, or some corporate franchise, as distinguished from aliens, and those not enjoying franchises, although free from personal slavery? . . .

Up to the time of our revolution, the *only* meaning which the words "free" and "freemen" had, in the English law, in the *charters granted to the colonies,* and in the important documents of a political character, was when used to designate a person enjoying some franchise or privilege, as distinguished from aliens or persons not enjoying a similar franchise. They were never used to designate a free person as distinguished from a slave—for the very sufficient reason that all these *fundamental* laws presumed that there were no slaves. . . .

The legal rule of interpretation before mentioned, viz., that an innocent meaning must be given to all words that are susceptible of it—would compel us to give the words this meaning, instead of a meaning merely correlative with slavery, even if we had no other ground than the rule, for so doing. But we have other grounds. For instance:—Several of these constitutions have themselves explicitly given to the words this meaning. While not one of them has given them a meaning correlative with slaves, inasmuch as none of them purport either to establish, authorize, or even to know of the existence of slavery. . . .

(*b*) CHAPTER XII.
THE CONSTITUTION ACCORDING TO THE COMMON MEANING OF ITS TERMS.

The people made it, the people adopted it, the people must be supposed to read it with the help of common sense, and cannot be presumed to admit in it any hidden or extraordinary meaning.

At the time of the adoption of the Constitution, slavery existed in all the States except Massachusetts. How far, if at all, does this instrument support or countenance the institution?

Art. 1, sec. 2: "Representatives and direct taxes shall be apportioned among the several States which may be included within this union, according to their respective numbers, which shall be determined by adding to the whole number of free persons, including those bound to service for a term of years, and excluding Indians not taxed, three-fifths of all other persons."

By this section, persons are divided into those who are free and those who are slaves; for to the whole number of *free* persons are to be added three-fifths of *all other* persons, that is, persons not free, or *slaves*. If we adopt the plain, obvious, and common meaning of the words as their true meaning, this conclusion is incontrovertible.

It is sometimes urged, that by "free person" is meant "citizen." But the expression cannot be taken in any such technical sense. Under the expression "free persons" are included those bound to service for a term of years, and therefore from it are excluded those bound to service for life, or slaves.

This article, therefore, recognizes slavery as explicitly as if the word *slave* itself had been used, and gives to the free persons in a Slave State, solely because they are slaveholders, a larger representation, and consequently greater political power, than the same number of free persons in a Free State. A BOUNTY ON SLAVEHOLDING!

Art. 1, sec. 9: "The *migration or importation* of such persons as any of the States now existing shall think proper to admit, shall not be prohibited by the Congress prior to the year one thousand eight hundred and eight; but a tax or duty may be imposed on such *importation,* not exceeding ten dollars for each person."

It is clear that this section recognizes a difference between the meaning of *migration* and *importation,* since, if both words mean the same thing, no reason whatever can be assigned why a tax is not permitted in both cases. . . . The true meaning of the section seems obvious. A person who migrates does so of his own accord: he cannot be said to be migrated by any other person. He is wholly a free agent. A person who is imported does not import himself, but is imported by some other person. He is passive. The importer is the free agent; the person imported is not a free agent. . . . On our construction, Congress had power to lay a tax on persons imported as property or slaves, but had no right to tax free persons migrating.

By this clause, therefore, Congress was prevented, during twenty years, from prohibiting the foreign slave-trade with any States that pleased to allow it. But, by Art. 1, sec. 8, Congress had the general power "to regulate commerce with foreign nations." Consequently, *the slave-trade was exempted from the operation of the general power, with a view to place the slave-trade, during twenty years, solely under the control of the Slave States.* It could not be wholly stopped, so long as one State wished to continue it. It is a clear compromise in favor of slavery. True, the compromise was a temporary one; but it will be noticed, that Congress, even after 1808, was not obliged to prohibit the trade; and, in point of fact, until 1819 the laws of Congress authorized the States to sell into slavery, for their own benefit, negroes imported contrary to the laws of the United States! So unmixed should be our satisfaction at the oft-repeated boast, that ours was the first nation to prohibit the African slave-trade! . . .

CHARLES SUMNER
ATTACKS SEGREGATION IN BOSTON (1849).

ALTHOUGH THE RECORD OF the abolitionists in improving the condition of the Northern free Negro was not uniformly impressive, many of them nevertheless were deeply committed to equal rights. As a result of anti-slavery pressure, Massachusetts in 1843 repealed a law prohibiting intermarriage and a few years later abolished Jim Crow railroad cars. The culmination of abolitionist efforts to establish equal opportunity came in 1849 with the attempt to end segregation in Boston schools. Despite successful integration in other cities and towns, Boston's Smith School, founded as a private school for Negro children, remained segregated even though it had been incorporated into the public school system as early as 1820. In 1849, after several years of abolitionist agitation, Benjamin Roberts, a Negro suing in the name of his five-year-old daughter, succeeded in bringing a case before the Supreme Judicial Court of Massachusetts. Roberts was represented by Charles Sumner, who employed a brilliant and strikingly modern argument in demolishing the separate-but-equal theory. Chief Justice Shaw, speaking for the court, upheld the power of the Boston School Committee to exclude Negro children from white schools, but in 1855 the legislature vindicated Sumner by abolishing segregation throughout the commonwealth. *Argument of Charles Sumner, esq., against the constitutionality of separate schools, in the case of Sarah C. Roberts* vs *the city of Boston. Before the Supreme Court of Mass., Dec. 4, 1849* (Boston, 1849).

MAY IT PLEASE YOUR HONORS:

CAN any discrimination, on account of color or race, be made, under the Constitution and Laws of Massachusetts, among the children entitled to the benefit of our public schools? This is the question which the Court is now to hear, to consider, and to decide.

Or, stating the question with more detail, and with a more particular application to the facts of the present case, are the Committee, having the superintendence of the public schools of Boston, entrusted with the *power*, under the constitution and laws of Massachusetts, to exclude colored children from these schools, and to compel them to resort for their education to separate schools, set apart for colored children only, at distances from their homes less convenient than those open to white children? . . .

I begin with the principle, that, according to the spirit of American institutions, and especially of the Constitution of Massachusetts, *all men, without distinction of color or race, are equal before the law.* . . .

. . . The fact that a child is black, or that he is white, cannot of itself be considered a qualification, or a disqualification. It is not to the skin that we can look for the criterion of fitness for our Public Schools.

But it is said that the Committee are intrusted with a discretion, in the exercise of their power, and that, in this discretion, they may distribute, assign, and classify all children belonging to the schools of the city, *according to their best judgment,* making, if they think proper, a discrimination of color or race. Without questioning that they are intrusted with a discretion, it is outrageous to suppose that it can go to this extent. The Committee can have no discretion which is not in harmony with the Constitution and laws. Surely, they cannot, in their mere discretion, nullify a sacred and dear-bought principle of Human Rights, which is expressly guaranteed by the Constitution.

Still further,—and here I approach a more technical view of the subject,—it is an admitted principle, that the regulations and bylaws of municipal corporations must be *reasonable,* or they are inoperative and void. . . .

And here we are brought once more, in another form, to the question of the validity of the discrimination on account of color by the School Committee of Boston. Is this *legally reasonable?* Is it reasonable, in the exercise of their discretion, to separate the descendants of the African race from the white children, in consequence of their descent merely? . . .

It is clear that the Committee may classify scholars, according to their age and sex; for the obvious reasons that these distinctions are inoffensive, and especially recognized as *legal* in the law relating to schools. (Revised Statutes, c. 23, § 63.) They may also classify scholars according to their moral and intellectual qualifications, because such a power is necessary to the government of schools. But the Committee cannot assume, *a priori,* and without individual examination, that an *entire race* possess certain moral or intellectual qualities, which shall render it proper to place them all in a class by themselves. Such an exercise of the discretion with which the Committee are intrusted, must be unreasonable, and therefore illegal.

But it is said that the Committee, in thus classifying the children, have not violated any principle of Equality, inasmuch as they have provided a school with competent instructors for the colored children, where they have equal advantages of instruction with those enjoyed by the white children. It is said that in excluding the colored children from the Public Schools open to white children, they furnish them an equivalent.

To this there are several answers. I shall touch upon them only briefly, as the discussion, through which we have now travelled, substantially covers the whole ground. . . .

2d. The second is, that, in point of fact, it is not an equivalent. We have already seen that it is the occasion of inconveniences to the colored children and their parents, to which they would not be exposed, if they had access to the nearest public schools, besides inflicting upon them the stigma of Caste. Still further, and this consideration cannot be neglected, the matters taught in the two schools may be precisely the same; but a school, exclusively devoted to one class, must differ essentially, in its spirit and character, from that public school known to the law, where all classes meet together in equality. It is a mockery to call it an equivalent.

3d. But there is yet another answer. Admitting that it is an equivalent, still the colored children cannot be compelled to take it. Their rights are Equality before the law; nor can they be called upon to renounce one jot of this. They have an equal right with white children to the general public schools. A separate school, though well endowed, would not secure to them that precise Equality, which they would enjoy in the general public schools. The Jews in Rome are confined to a particular district, called the Ghetto. In Frankfort they are condemned to a separate quarter, known as the Jewish quarter. It is possible that the accommodations allotted to them are as good as they would be able to occupy, if left free to choose throughout Rome and Frankfort; but this compulsory segregation from the mass of citizens is of itself an *inequality* which we condemn with our whole souls. It is a vestige of ancient intolerance directed against a despised people. It is of the same character with the separate schools in Boston.

Thus much for the doctrine of equivalents, as a substitute for equality.

In determining that the Committee have no *power* to make a discrimination of color or race, we are strengthened by yet another consideration. If the power exists in the present case, it must exist in many others. It cannot be restrained to this alone. The Committee may distribute all the children into classes—merely according to their discretion. They may establish a separate school for the Irish or the Germans, where each may nurse an exclusive spirit of nationality alien to our institutions. They may separate Catholics from Protestants, or, pursuing their discretion still further, they may separate the different sects of Protestants, and establish one school for Unitarians, another for Presbyterians, another for Baptists, and another for Methodists. They may establish a separate school for the rich, that the delicate taste of this favored class may not be offended by the humble garments of the poor. They may exclude the children of mechanics from the Public Schools, and send them to separate schools by themselves. All this, and much more, can be done by the exercise of the high-handed power which can make a discrimination on account of color or race. The grand fabric of our Public Schools, the pride of Massachusetts—where, at the feet of the teacher, innocent childhood should meet, unconscious of all distinctions of birth—where the Equality of the Constitution and of Christianity should be inculcated by constant precept and example—may be converted into a heathen system of proscription and Caste. We may then have many different schools, the representatives of as many different classes, opinions, and prejudices; but we shall look in vain for the true Public School of Massachusetts. Let it not be said that there is little danger that any Committee will exercise their discretion to this extent. They must not be entrusted with the power. In this is the only safety worthy of a free people. . . .

There are some other matters not strictly belonging to the juridical aspect of the case, and yet of importance to its clear comprehension, upon which I shall touch briefly before I close.

It is sometimes said in extenuation of the present system in Boston, that the separation of the white and black children was originally made at the request of the colored parents. This is substantially true. . . .

These facts are interesting in the history of the Boston Schools, but they cannot in any way affect the rights of the colored people, or the powers of the Committee. These rights and these powers stand on the Constitution and laws of the Commonwealth. . . .

It is clear that the sentiments of the colored people have now changed. The present case, and the deep interest which they manifest in it, thronging the court to hang on this discussion, attest the change. With increasing knowledge, they have learned to know their rights, and to feel the degradation to which they have been doomed. Their present effort is the token of a manly character which this court will cherish and respect. The spirit of Paul now revives in them, even as when he said, "I am a Roman citizen."

But it is said that these separate schools are for the mutual benefit of children of both colors, and of the Public Schools. In similar spirit, slavery is sometimes said to be for the mutual benefit of master and slave, and of the country where it exists. In one case there is a mistake as great as in the other. This is clear. Nothing unjust, nothing ungenerous can be for the benefit of any person, or any thing. Shortsighted mortals may hope to draw from some seeming selfish superiority, or from a gratified vanity of class, a permanent good; but even-handed justice rebukes these efforts, and with certain power redresses the wrong. The whites themselves are injured by the separation. Who can doubt this? With the law as their monitor, they are taught to regard a portion of the human family, children of God, created in his image, co-equals in his love, as a separate and degraded class—they are taught practically to deny that grand revelation of Christianity—the Brotherhood of Mankind. Their hearts, while yet tender with childhood, are necessarily hardened by this conduct, and their subsequent lives, perhaps, bear enduring testimony to this legalized uncharitableness. Nursed in the sentiment of Caste, receiving it with the earliest food of knowledge, they are unable to eradicate it from their natures, and then weakly and impiously charge upon their Heavenly Father the prejudice which they have derived from an unchristian school, and which they continue to embody and perpetuate in their institutions. Their characters are debased, and they become less fit for the magnanimous duties of a good citizen. . . .

Who can say, that this does not injure the blacks? Theirs, in its best estate, is an unhappy lot. Shut out by a still lingering prejudice from many social advantages, a despised class, they feel this proscription from the Public Schools as a peculiar brand. Beyond this, it deprives them of those healthful animating influences which would come from a participation in the studies of their white brethren. It adds to their discouragements. It widens their separation from the rest of the community, and postpones that great day of reconciliation which is sure to come.

The whole system of public schools suffers also. It is a narrow perception of their high aim which teaches that they are merely to furnish to all the scholars an equal amount in knowledge, and that, therefore, provided all be taught, it is of little consequence where, and in what company it be done. The law contemplates not only that they shall all be taught, but that they shall be taught *all together*. They are not only to receive equal quantities of knowledge, but all are to receive it in the same way. All are to approach together the same common fountain; nor can there be any exclusive source for any individual or any class. The school is the little world in which the child is trained for the larger world of life. It must, therefore, cherish and develop the virtues and the sympathies which are employed in the larger world. And since, according to our institutions, all classes meet, without distinction of color, in the performance of civil duties, so should they all meet, without distinction of color, in the school, beginning there those relations of equality which our Constitution and laws promise to all.

As the State receives strength from the unity and solidarity of its citizens, without distinction of class, so the school receives new strength from the unity and solidarity of all classes beneath its roof. In this way, the poor, the humble, and the neglected, share not only the companionship of their more favored brethren, but enjoy also the protection of their presence, in drawing towards the school a more watchful superintendence. A degraded or neglected class, if left to themselves, will become more degraded or neglected. To him that hath shall be given; and the world, true to these words, turns from the poor and outcast to the rich and fortunate. It is the aim of our system of Public Schools, by the blending of all classes, to draw upon the whole school the attention which is too apt to be given only to the favored few, and thus secure to the poor their portion of the fruitful sunshine. But the colored children, placed apart by themselves, are deprived of this blessing.

Nothing is more clear than that the welfare of classes, as well as of individuals, is promoted by mutual acquaintance. The French and English, for a long time regarded as natural enemies, have at last, from a more intimate communion, found themselves to be natural friends. Prejudice is the child of ignorance. It is sure to prevail where people do not know each other. Society and intercourse are means established by Providence for human improvement. They remove antipathies, promote mutual adaptation and conciliation, and establish relations of reciprocal regard. Whoso sets up barriers to these, thwarts the ways of Providence, crosses the tendencies of human nature, and directly interferes with the laws of God.

May it please your Honors: Such are some of the things which it has occurred to me to say in this important cause. I have occupied much of your time, but I have not yet exhausted the topics. Still, which way soever we turn, we are brought back to one single proposition—*the equality of men before the law*. This stands as the mighty guardian of the rights of the colored children in this case. It is the constant, ever-present, tutelary genius of this Commonwealth, frowning upon every privilege of birth, upon every distinction of race, upon every institution of Caste. You cannot slight it, or avoid it. You cannot restrain it. It remains that you should welcome it. Do this, and your words will be a "charter and freehold of rejoicing" to a race which has earned by much suffering a title to much regard. Your judgment will become a sacred landmark, not in jurisprudence only, but in the history of Freedom, giving precious encouragement to all the weary and heavy-laden wayfarers in this great cause. Massachusetts will then, through you, have a fresh title to regard, and be once more, as in times past, an example to the whole land. . . .

FREDERICK DOUGLASS
REVIEWS THE PROGRESS OF ABOLITION (1855).

THE BEST KNOWN and probably the ablest of the Negro abolitionists was Frederick Douglass. An escaped slave, Douglass joined the Garrisonians in 1841 but gradually became disillusioned by the inadequacies of the "No Union with Slaveholders" doctrine. He broke with Garrison, became a constitutionalist, founded his own newspaper in Rochester, New York, and hopefully supported the political abolitionists. But political abolitionism too, he soon realized, presented its problems: the Free Soilers "promised much and performed little," and the Liberty Party continued to represent a hopelessly small minority of anti-slavery advocates. In a lecture entitled "The Anti-Slavery Movement" and given before the Rochester Ladies Anti-Slavery Society in 1855, Douglass summarized the history and assessed the accomplishments of the various anti-slavery groups since 1840, noting paradoxically the effect of political controversy in dividing the abolitionists into rival parties and at the same time uniting the North in opposition to slavery. "The Anti-Slavery Movement. A lecture by Frederick Douglass, before the Rochester ladies' anti-slavery society, Rochester, 1855," collected in Philip S. Foner, *The Life and Writings of Frederick Douglass* (New York, 1950) 4 vols., II, 333-359. Reprinted with the permission of International Publishers, Inc.

. . . BUT I PROPOSE to speak of the different anti-slavery sects and parties, and to give my view of them very briefly. There are four principal divisions.

1st. The Garrisonians, or the American Anti-Slavery Society.

2d. The Anti-Garrisonians, or the American and Foreign Anti-Slavery Society.

3d. The Free Soil Party, or Political Abolitionists.

4th. The Liberty Party, or Gerrit Smith School of Abolitionists. . . .

I shall consider, first, the Garrisonian Anti-Slavery Society. I call this the Garrisonian Society, because Mr. Garrison is, confessedly, its leader. This Society is the oldest of modern Anti-Slavery Societies. It has, strictly speaking, two weekly papers, or organs—employs five or six lecturers—and holds numerous public meetings for the dissemination of its views. Its peculiar and distinctive feature is, its doctrine of *"no union with slaveholders."* This doctrine has, of late, become its bond of union, and the condition of good fellowship among its members. Of this Society,

I have to say, its logical result is but negatively, anti-slavery. Its doctrine, of "no union with slaveholders," carried out, dissolves the Union, and leaves the slaves and their masters to fight their own battles, in their own way. This I hold to be an abandonment of the great idea with which that Society started. It started to free the slave. It ends by leaving the slave to free himself. It started with the purpose to imbue the heart of the nation with sentiments favorable to the abolition of slavery, and ends by seeking to free the North from all responsibility of slavery, other than if slavery were in Great Britain, or under some other nationality. This, I say, is the practical abandonment of the idea, with which that Society started. It has given up the faith, that the slave can be freed short of the overthrow of the Government; and then, as I understand that Society, it leaves the slaves, as it must needs leave them, just where it leaves the slaves of Cuba, or those of Brazil. The nation, as such, is given up as beyond the power of salvation by the foolishness of preaching; and hence, the aim is now to save the North; so that the American Anti-Slavery Society, which was inaugurated to convert the nation, after ten years' struggle, parts with its faith, and aims now to save the North. One of the most eloquent of all the members of that Society, and the man who is only second to Mr. Garrison himself, defines the Garrisonian doctrine thus:

> All the slave asks of us, is to stand out of his way, withdraw our pledge to keep the peace on the plantation; withdraw our pledge to return him; withdraw that representation which the Constitution gives in proportion to the number of slaves, and without any agitation here, without any individual virtue, which the times have eaten out of us, God will vindicate the oppressed, by the laws of justice which he has founded. Trample under foot your own unjust pledges, break to pieces your compact with hell by which you become the abettors of oppression. Stand alone, and let no cement of the Union bind the slave, and he will right himself.

That is it. "Stand alone;" the slave is to "right himself." I dissent entirely from this reasoning. It assumes to be true what is plainly absurd, and that is, that a population of slaves, without arms, without means of concert, and without leisure, is more than a match for double its number, educated, accustomed to rule, and in every way prepared for warfare, offensive or defensive. This Society, therefore, consents to leave the slave's freedom to a most uncertain and improbable, if not an impossible, contingency.

But, *"no union with slaveholders."*

As a mere expression of abhorrence of slavery, the sentiment is a good one; but it expresses no intelligible principle of action, and throws no light on the pathway of duty. Defined, as its authors define it, it leads to false doctrines, and mischievous results. It condemns Gerrit Smith for sitting in Congress, and our Savior for eating with publicans and sinners. Dr. Spring uttered a shocking sentiment, when he said, if one prayer of his would emancipate every slave, he would not offer that prayer. No less shocking is the sentiment of the leader of the disunion forces, when he says, that if one vote of his would emancipate every slave in this country, he would not cast that vote. Here, on a bare theory, and for a theory which, if consistently adhered to, would drive a man out of the world—a theory which can never be made intelligible to common sense—the freedom of the whole slave population would be sacrificed.

But again: "no union with slaveholders." I dislike the morality of this sentiment, in its application to the point at issue. For instance: A. unites with B. in stealing my property, and carrying it away to California, or to Australia, and, while there, Mr. A. becomes convinced that he did wrong in stealing my property, and says to Mr. B., "no union with property stealers," and abandons him, leaving the property in his hands. Now, I put it to this audience, has Mr. A., in this transaction, met the requirements of stringent morality? He, certainly, has not. It is not only his duty to separate from the thief, but to restore the stolen property to its rightful owner. And I hold that in the Union, this very thing of restoring to the slave his long-lost rights, can better be accomplished than it can possibly be accomplished outside of the Union. This, then, is my answer to the motto, "No union with slaveholders." . . .

But to the second branch of the anti-slavery movement. The American and Foreign Anti-Slavery Society has not yet departed from the original ground, but stands where the American Anti-Slavery Society stood at the beginning. The energies of this association are mainly directed to the revival of anti-slavery in the Church. It is active in the collection, and in the circulation of facts, exposing the character of slavery, and in noting the evidences of progress in the Church on the subject. It does not aim to abolish the Union, but aims to avail itself of the means afforded by the Union to abolish slavery. The Annual Report of this Society affords the amplest and truest account of the anti-slavery movement, from year to year. Nevertheless, I am somewhat against this Society, as well as against the American Anti-Slavery Society. It has almost dropped the main and most potent weapon with which slavery is to be assailed and overthrown, and that is speech. At this moment, when every nerve should be strained to prevent a reaction, that Society has not a single lecturing agent in the field.

The next recognized anti-slavery body is the Free Soil party, *alias*—the Free Democratic party, *alias*—the Republican party. It aims to limit and denationalize slavery, and to relieve the Federal Government from all responsibility for slavery. Its motto is, *"Slavery Local—Liberty National."* The objection to this movement is the same as that against the American Anti-Slavery Society. It leaves the slaves in his [*sic*] fetters—in the undisturbed possession of his master, and does not grapple with the question of emancipation in the States.

The fourth division of the anti-slavery movement is, the *"Liberty Party"*—a small body of citizens, chiefly in the State of New York, but having sympathizers all over the North. It is the radical, and to my thinking, the *only* abolition organization in the country, except a few local associations. It makes a clean sweep of slavery everywhere. It denies that slavery is, or *can* be legalized. It denies that the Constitution of the United States is a pro-slavery instrument, and asserts the power and duty of the Federal Government to abolish slavery in every State of the Union. Strictly speaking, I say this is the only party in the country which is an abolition party. The mission of the Garrisonians ends with the dissolution of the Union—that of the Free Soil party ends with the relief of the Federal Government from all responsibility for slavery; but the Liberty Party, by its position and doctrines, and by its antecedents, is pledged to continue the struggle while a bondman in his chains remains to weep. Upon its platform must the great battle of freedom be fought out—if upon any short of the bloody field. It must be under no partial cry of "no union with slaveholders;" nor selfish cry of "no more slavery extension;" but it must be, "no slavery for man under the whole heavens." The slave as a man and a brother, must be the vital and animating thought and impulse of any movement, which is to effect the abolition of slavery in this country. Our anti-slavery organizations must be brought back to this doctrine, or they will be scattered and left to wander, and to die in the wilderness, like God's ancient people, till another generation shall come up, more worthy to go up and possess the land.

One anti-slavery movement nearly died out fifty years ago, and I am not prepared to deny the possibility of a like fate for this one. The elements of discord and deterioration are already in it, and working their legitimate results. And yet I am not gloomy. Present organizations may perish, but the cause will go on. That cause has a life, distinct and independent of the organizations patched up from time to time to carry it forward. . . .

In conclusion, I have taken a sober view of the present anti-slavery movement. I am sober, but not hopeless. There is no denying, for it is everywhere admitted, that the anti-slavery question is the great moral and social question now before the American people. A state of things has gradually been developed, by which that question has become the first thing in order. It has got to be met. Herein is my hope. The great idea of impartial liberty is now fairly before the American people. Anti-slavery is no longer a thing to be prevented. The time for prevention is past. This is great gain. When the movement was younger and weaker—when it wrought in a Boston garret to human apprehension, it might have been silently put out of the way. Things are different now. It has grown too abundant—its ramifications too extended—its power too omnipotent, to be snuffed out by the contingencies of infancy. . . .

Another source of congratulation is the fact that, amid all the efforts made by the Church, the Government, and the people at large, to stay the onward progress of this movement, its course has been onward, steady, straight, unshaken, and unchecked from the beginning. Slavery has gained victories, large and numerous; but never, as against this movement—against a temporizing policy, and against Northern timidity, the slave power has been victorious; but against the spread and prevalence in the country, of a spirit of resistance to its aggression, and of sentiments favorable to its entire overthrow, it has yet accomplished nothing. Every measure, yet devised and executed, having for its object the suppression of anti-slavery, has been as idle and fruitless as pouring oil to extinguish fire. A general rejoicing took place, on the passage of "the Compromise Measures" of 1850. Those measures were called peace measures, and were afterwards termed by both the great parties of the country, as well as by leading statesmen, a final settlement of the whole question of slavery; but experience has laughed to scorn the wisdom of pro-slavery statesmen; and their final settlement of agitation seems to be the final revival, on a broader and grander scale than ever before, of the question which they vainly attempted to suppress forever. The Fugitive Slave Bill has especially been of positive service to the anti-slavery movement. It has illustrated before all the people the horrible character of slavery toward the slave, in hunting him down in a free State, and tearing him away from wife and children, thus setting its claims higher than marriage or parental claims. It has revealed the arrogant and overbearing spirit of the slave States towards the free States; despising their principles—shocking their feelings of humanity, not only by bringing before them the abominations of slavery, but by attempting to make them parties to the crime. It has called into exercise among the colored people, the hunted ones, a spirit of manly resistance well calculated to surround them with a bulwark of sympathy and respect hitherto unknown. For men are always disposed to respect and defend rights, when the victims of oppression stand up manfully for themselves.

There is another element of power added to the anti-slavery movement of great importance; it is the conviction, becoming every day more general and universal, that slavery must be abolished in the South, or it will demoralize and destroy liberty in the North. It is the nature of slavery to beget a state of things all around it, favorable to its own continuance. This fact connected with the system of bondage, is beginning to be more fully realized. The slave-holder is not satisfied to associate with men in the Church or in the State, unless he can thereby stain them with the blood of his slaves. To be a slave-holder, is to be a propagandist from necessity; for slavery can only live by keeping down the undergrowth morality which nature supplies. Every new-born white babe comes armed from the Eternal presence, to make war on slavery. The heart of pity, which would melt in due time over the brutal chastisements it sees inflicted on the helpless, must be hardened. And this work goes on every day in the year, and every hour in the day.

What is done at home, is being done also abroad here in the North. And even now the question may be asked, have we at this moment a single free State in the Union? The alarm at this point will become more general. The slave power must go on in its career of exactions. Give, give, will be its cry, till the timidity which concedes shall give place to courage, which shall resist. Such is the voice of experience, such has been the past, such is the present, and such will be that future, which, so sure as man is man, will come. Here I leave the subject; and I leave off where I began, consoling myself and congratulating the friends of freedom upon the fact that the anti-slavery cause is not a new thing under the sun; not some moral delusion which a few years' experience may dispel. It has appeared among men in all ages, and summoned its advocates from all ranks. Its foundations are laid in the deepest and holiest convictions, and from whatever soul the demon, selfishness, is expelled, there will this cause take up its abode. Old as the everlasting hills; immovable as the throne of God; and certain as the purposes of eternal power against all hindrances, and against all delays, and despite all the mutations of human instrumentalities, it is the faith of my soul that this Anti-Slavery cause will triumph.

PART VII.

THE GATHERING CRISIS.

HARRIET BEECHER STOWE

DEFENDS THE ALTAR OF LIBERTY (1852).

THE COMPROMISE OF 1850 signaled the beginning of the ten-year sectional struggle which ended in civil war. The reaction of the North to the new Fugitive Slave Law was swift and drastic: a rash of personal liberty laws and a series of dramatic slave rescues testified to a growing anti-slavery strength in New England and the Old Northwest. Harriet Beecher Stowe was already famous in the North and notorious in the South as the author of *Uncle Tom's Cabin* when she agreed to contribute the first of a projected series of Liberty Tracts to encourage Northern defiance of the hated law. *The Two Altars,* subtitled *Two Pictures in One,* contrasts the "Altar of Liberty, 1776" with the political altar of 1850. In the first vignette the wife of a Revolutionary soldier welcomes the commissioners of the Continental Congress, who are collecting supplies for the army, and gives them blankets and clothing. Her children dutifully add their warm woolen stockings to the growing pile.

Soon the old sleigh drove off from the brown house tightly packed and heavily loaded. And Gracie and Dicky were creeping up to their little beds.

"There's been something put on the altar of Liberty to-night, hasn't there, Dick?"

"Yes, indeed," said Dick; and, looking up to his mother, he said, "But, mother, what did you give?"

"I?" said the mother musingly.

"Yes, you, mother; what have you given to the country?"

"All that I have, dears," said she, laying her hands gently on their heads,—"my husband and my children!"

The following is the second part of Mrs. Stowe's tract. Harriet Beecher Stowe, *The Two Altars; or, Two Pictures in One,* Liberty Tracts.—No. 1 (Boston, 1852).

II.—THE ALTAR OF ———, OR 1850.

THE SETTING SUN OF chill December lighted up the solitary front window of a small tenement on ——— street, which we now have occasion to visit. As we push gently aside the open door, we gain sight of a small room, clean as busy hands can make it, where a neat, cheerful young mulatto woman is busy at an ironing-table. A basket full of glossy-bosomed shirts, and faultless collars and wristbands, is beside her, into which she is placing the last few items with evident pride and satisfaction. A bright, black-eyed boy, just come in from school, with his satchel of books over his shoulder, stands, cap in hand, relating to his mother how he has been at the head of his class, and showing his school-tickets, which his mother, with untiring admiration, deposits in the little real china tea-pot,—which, as being their most reliable article of gentility, is made the deposit of all the money and most especial valuables of the family.

"Now, Henry," says the mother, "look out and see if father is coming along the street;" and she begins filling the little black tea kettle, which is soon set singing on the stove.

From the inner room now daughter Mary, a well-grown girl of thirteen, brings the baby, just roused from a nap, and very impatient to renew his acquaintance with his mamma.

"Bless his bright eyes!—mother will take him," ejaculates the busy little woman, whose hands are by this time in a very floury condition, in the incipient stages of wetting up biscuit,—"in a minute;" and she quickly frees herself from the flour and paste, and, deputing Mary to roll out her biscuit, proceeds to the consolation and succor of young master.

"Now, Henry," says the mother, "you'll have time, before supper, to take that basket of clothes up to Mr. Sheldin's;—put in that nice bill, that you made out last night. I shall give you a cent for every bill you write out for me. What a comfort it is, now, for one's children to be gettin' learnin' so!"

Henry shouldered the basket, and passed out the door, just as a neatly-dressed colored man walked up, with his pail and white-wash brushes.

"O, you've come, father, have you?—Mary, are the biscuits in?—you may as well set the table, now. Well, George, what's the news?"

"Nothing, only a pretty smart day's work. I've brought home five dollars, and shall have as much as I can do, these two weeks;" and the man, having washed his hands, proceeded to count out his change on the ironing-table.

"Well, it takes you to bring in the money," said the delighted wife; "nobody but you could turn off that much in a day!"

"Well, they do say—those that's had me once—that they never want any other hand to take hold in their rooms. I s'pose its a kinder practice I've got, and kinder natural!"

"Tell ye what," said the little woman, taking down the family strong box,—to wit, the china tea-pot, aforenamed,—and pouring the contents on the table, "we're getting mighty rich, now! We can afford to get Henry his new Sunday-cap, and Mary her muslin-de-laine dress;—take care, baby, you rogue!" she hastily interposed, as young master made a dive at a dollar bill, for his share in the proceeds.

"He wants something, too, I suppose," said the father; "let him get his hand in while he's young."

The baby gazed, with round, astonished eyes, while mother, with some difficulty, rescued the bill from his grasp; but, before any one could at all anticipate his purpose, he dashed in among the small change with such zeal as to send it flying all over the table.

"Hurra!—Bub's a smasher!" said the father, delighted; "he'll make it fly, he thinks;" and, taking the baby on his knee, he laughed merrily, as Mary and her mother pursued the rolling coin all over the room.

"He knows now, as well as can be, that he's been doing mischief," said the delighted mother, as the baby kicked and crowed uproariously;—"he's such a forward child, now, to be only six months old!—O, you've no idea, father, how mischievous he grows," and therewith the little woman began to roll and tumble the little mischief-maker about, uttering divers frightful threats, which appeared to contribute, in no small degree, to the general hilarity.

"Come, come, Mary," said the mother, at last, with a sudden burst of recollection; "you mustn't be always on your knees fooling with this child!—Look in the oven at them biscuits."

"They're done exactly, mother,—just the brown!"—and, with the word, the mother dumped baby on to his father's knee, where he sat contentedly munching a very ancient crust of bread, occasionally improving the flavor thereof by rubbing it on his father's coat-sleeve.

"What have you got in that blue dish, there?" said George, when the whole little circle were seated around the table.

"Well, now, what *do* you suppose?" said the little woman, delighted;—"a quart of nice oysters,—just for a treat, you know. I wouldn't tell you till this minute," said she, raising the cover.

"Well," said George, "we both work hard for our money, and we don't owe anybody a cent; and why shouldn't we have our treats, now and then, as well as rich folks?"

And gayly passed the supper hour; the tea-kettle sung, the baby crowed, and all chatted and laughed abundantly.

"I'll tell you," said George, wiping his mouth, "wife, these times are quite another thing from what it used to be down in Georgia. I remember then old Mas'r used to hire me out by the year; and one time, I remember, I came and paid him in two hundred dollars,—every cent I'd taken. He just looked it over, counted it, and put it in his pocket-book, and said, 'You are a good boy, George,'—and he gave me *half-a-dollar!*"

"I want to know, now!" said his wife.

"Yes, he did, and that was every cent I ever got of it; and, I tell you, I was mighty bad off for clothes, them times."

"Well, well, the Lord be praised, they're over, and you are in a free country now!" said the wife, as she rose thoughtfully from the table, and brought her husband the great Bible. The little circle were ranged around the stove for evening prayers.

"Henry, my boy, you must read,—you are a better reader than your father,—thank God, that let you learn early!"

The boy, with a cheerful readiness, read, "The Lord is my shepherd," and the mother gently stilled the noisy baby, to listen to the holy words. Then all kneeled, while the father, with simple earnestness, poured out his soul to God.

They had but just risen,—the words of Christian hope and trust scarce died on their lips,—when lo! the door was burst open, and two men entered; and one of them, advancing, laid his hand on the father's shoulder. "This is the fellow," said he.

"You are arrested in the name of the United States!" said the other.

"Gentlemen, what is this?" said the poor man, trembling.

"Are you not the property of *Mr. B.*, of Georgia?" said the officer.

"Gentlemen, I've been a free, hard-working man, these ten years."

"Yes, but you are arrested, on suit of Mr. B., as his slave."

Shall we describe the leave-taking?—the sorrowing wife, the dismayed children, the tears, the anguish,—that simple, honest, kindly home, in a moment so desolated! Ah, ye who defend this because it is law, think, for one hour, what if this that happens to your poor brother should happen to you! . . .

It was a crowded court-room, and the man stood there to be tried—for life?—no; but for the life of life—for liberty!

Lawyers hurried to and fro, buzzing, consulting, bringing authorities,—all anxious, zealous, engaged,—for what?—to save a fellow-man from bondage?—no; anxious and zealous lest he might escape,—full of zeal to deliver him over to slavery. The poor man's anxious eyes follow vainly the busy course of affairs, from which he dimly learns that he is to be sacrificed—on the altar of the Union; and that his heart-break and anguish, and the tears of his wife, and the desolation of his children, are, in the eyes of these well-informed men, only the bleat of a sacrifice, bound to the horns of the glorious American altar! . . .

Again it is a bright day, and business walks brisk in this market. Senator and statesman, the learned and patriotic, are out, this day, to give their countenance to an edifying and impressive, and truly American spectacle,—the sale of a man! All the preliminaries of the scene are there: dusky-browed mothers, looking with sad eyes while speculators are turning round their children,—looking at their teeth, and feeling of their arms; a poor, old, trembling woman, helpless, half-blind, whose last child is to be sold, holds on to her bright boy with trembling hands. Husbands and wives, sisters and friends, all soon to be scattered like the chaff of the threshing-floor, look sadly on each other with poor nature's last tears; and among them walk briskly glib, oily politicians, and thriving men of law, letters and religion, exceedingly sprightly and in good spirits,—for why?—it isn't *they* that are going to be sold; it's only somebody else. And so they are very comfortable, and look on the whole thing as quite a matter-of-course affair; and, as it is to be conducted to-day, a decidedly valuable and judicious exhibition.

And now, after so many hearts and souls have been knocked and thumped this way and that way by the auctioneer's hammer, comes the *instructive* part of the whole; and the husband and father, whom we saw in his simple home, reading and praying with his children, and rejoicing, in the joy of his poor ignorant heart, that he lived in a free country, is now set up to be admonished of his mistake.

Now there is great excitement, and pressing to see, and exultation and approbation; for it is important and interesting to see a man put down that has tried to be a *free man.*

"That's he, is it?—Couldn't come it, could he?" says one.

"No, and he will never come it, that's more," says another, triumphantly.

"I don't generally take much interest in scenes of this nature," says a grave representative;—"but I came here to-day for the sake of the *principle!*"

"Gentlemen," says the auctioneer, "we've got a specimen here that some of your northern abolitionists would give any price for; but they shan't have him!—no! we've looked out for that. The man that buys him must give bonds never to sell him to go north again!"

"Go it!" shout the crowd, "good!—good!—hurra!" "An impressive idea!" says a senator; "a noble maintaining of principle!" and the man is bid off, and the hammer falls with a last crash on his hearth, and hopes, and manhood, and he lies a bleeding wreck on the altar of Liberty!

Such was the altar in 1776;—such is the altar in 1850!

GERRIT SMITH

CHARGES A UNITED STATES MARSHAL WITH KIDNAPPING (1852).

Abolitionists were not content to agitate against the Fugitive Slave Law; they defied it by rescuing recaptured fugitives. On October 1, 1851 in Syracuse, New York, a fugitive slave from Missouri, William Henry, known in the city as Jerry, was arrested by United States Marshal Henry Allen and brought before a commissioner of the United States District Court. Before a hearing could be held Jerry was rescued, recaptured, rescued once more, and hustled off to Canada. Eventually thirteen of Jerry's rescuers, among them the Liberty Party leader Gerrit Smith, were charged with obstructing justice. At the trials held in January, 1853, one of the men was found guilty, one innocent, while two more prosecutions ended in hung juries and the rest of the cases were dropped. In the meantime the abolitionists countered with a strategy of their own by indicting Marshal Allen for kidnapping. Allen was tried and acquitted in June, 1852; but the very fact of indictment by a grand jury was proof of a militant anti-slavery public opinion in Syracuse. Gerrit Smith's argument at the kidnapping trial was printed and circulated throughout the Northeast. *Abstract of the Argument on the Fugitive Slave Law Made by Gerrit Smith in Syracuse, June, 1852 on the Trial of Henry W. Allen, U.S. Marshal, for Kidnapping* (Syracuse, n.d.).

. . . It is admitted in the pleadings, that the prisoner had a part in this undertaking to sink his fellow-man into slavery. It is true, that these admissions do not make that part as extensive, as it really was, and as extensive as we should have shown it to be, had we been allowed to produce witnesses. It nevertheless, answers my purpose in the argument, which I am, now, to make, that the prisoner had a confessedly clear and responsible part in this undertaking.

And, now, what is the prisoner's excuse for this high crime against his brother man? It is, that he acted under law, and according to law. Well, if he did, then he is innocent. If not, then he is guilty. I admit, that this is the hinge, on which this case turns. If that is a Constitutional, valid law, under which the prisoner acted, and if he rightly interpreted its scope and claims, then he should be acquitted—and, otherwise, convicted.

It is sometimes said, that it is unreasonable to require a merely ministerial officer to know what is law. But every man is required, and most reasonably, too, to know what is the law. . . .

I will, now, proceed to show, that the law, under which the prisoner acted, is Unconstitutional, and that he is, therefore, a kidnapper. I will regard the law as intended to apply to slaves, whether it does, or does not, apply to any other class of persons.

My first position is, that the law is Unconstitutional, because it withholds trial by jury.

The Constitution requires trial by jury in all criminal prosecutions. Why does it? Because, in such prosecutions, the highest interests of the accused—character, liberty, life—are in peril. Hence, he is entitled to the advantage of a jury trial.

Now, I admit, that the prosecution for the recovery of a fugitive slave is but a civil prosecution. Nevertheless, it is a prosecution, which perils the liberty of the defendant—ay, his liberty for life. . . . The convict in the State Prison is deprived of his liberty; but not of his manhood. His manhood survives; and is under the full protection of the laws. . . . But the prosecution for the recovery of a slave, if it goes against the defendant, sinks him into a chattel, and leaves him not a shred of his manhood, nor the least protection of the law. . . .

But it may be said, that the enactors of this law intended to deny the jury trial to the black race only. Alas, what an outraged race it is! In the words of the prophet Isaiah, "This is a people robbed and spoiled. They are all of them snared in holes, and they are hid in prison houses. They are for a prey, and none delivereth for a spoil, and none saith, restore"—Such, doubtless, was the intention. Indeed, had the intention been to deny it to the white race also, scarcely would the lives of the enactors have been safe from the fury of that haughty race. This distinction between one portion of the American people and the other, although a stupendous crime, at which all should stand aghast, is, nevertheless, acquiesced in, and approved, by this superlatively guilty nation.

This law does, in its terms, apply to both whites and blacks, and exposes both to its penalties. What, however, if the public sentiment is such, as to confine its operation, for the present, to the blacks?—will not the denial of the right of trial by jury to one race of our citizens prepare the way for denying it to every other race of our citizens?—and will it not hasten the day, when this right shall be cloven down in every part of our land, and denied to every class of our people?

My second position is, that the law is Unconstitutional, because the

Commissioner is not authorized by the Constitution to do what the law requires of him.

The law invests him with a judicial office—a judicial office in the eye, and in the meaning, of the Constitution. It requires him "to hear and determine the case." . . .

It is, nevertheless, held, that the trial of the fugitive servant in the State to which he has fled, is but a preliminary trial, and that his decisive trial is, according to the theory of the case, to be in a State Court, in the State from which he escaped. Our answer to this, is—First, that we see no propriety in calling that a preliminary trial, which is a comprehensive and conclusive one—a comprehensive and conclusive one so far as investigating and passing upon all the questions on the whole case can make it such. Second, that the trial under the Federal and paramount government, would operate as an estoppel to the institution of a suit in the State Court. . . . Third, that the law of 1850, claiming, as it does, that the Federal Government has exclusive jurisdiction of this case, does not presume, and could not presume, on any auxiliary or supplementary action, at the hands of another sovereignty. It must itself make a complete provision for the demands of the case. . . .

The fact, that the commissioner is appointed by a judge proves, that he is not a judge. Surely, surely, the Constitution recognizes no such monstrous doctrine, as that one judge can appoint another judge. . . .

The fact, that the commissioner is paid in fees for his services does also, and does conclusively, prove that he is not a Constitutional judge. The Constitutional judge receives a salary for his services. . . .

But it may be said, that the Constitution authorizes Congress to "vest the appointment of such inferior offices, as they think proper, in the courts of law." For the reasons already given, however, the commissioner cannot be one of these "inferior officers." The services of a judge are required of him; and no person can be a Constitutional judge, who receives his judgeship from a judge, or who receives his compensation in fees. . . .

My third position is, that the law is Unconstitutional, because it offers a bribe.

To say, that a law, which offers a bribe is Constitutional, is to cast great reproach and insult upon the Constitution. . . .

My fourth position is, that the law is Unconstitutional, because it allows the suits under it to be decided solely on affidavits.

These are suits at the common law: affidavits are unknown to the common law: and, yet, these suits are to be decided solely on affidavits! . . .

My fifth position is, that the law is Unconstitutional, because it provides for disposing of the cases under it by exparte testimony.

The law provides for admitting testimony on the plaintiff's side only. It makes no provision whatever—not even by the slightest implication—for the reception of testimony, even rebutting testimony, from the defendant's side. . . .

This Unconstitutional feature of the law is all the more glaring from the fact, that the exparte testimony, for which the law provides, and which the law pronounces sufficient, is of the weakest kind—being mere affidavits. . ..

My seventh position is, that the law is Unconstitutional, because of its interference of the legislative with the judicial department of the Government. . . .

The legislature is to make the laws: but it does not follow, that it is authorized to control the judicial administration of them. What if the legislature has, hitherto, been allowed to encroach upon the judicial? It is not, therefore, to be allowed to continue its encroachments. Prescription cannot be justly claimed for them.

In no respect should the legislative be allowed to override the judicial—least of all, in respect to the kind and amount of evidence—the evidence being so vital a part of the lawsuit. Again, if in one class of cases, the legislature may dictate to the judiciary to receive testimony on one side only, why may it not do so in cases of every class? And, if it may dictate so far, why may it not forbid all testimony? . . .

My twelfth position is, that the law is Unconstitutional, because it recognizes the Constitutionality of slavery in the Territories.

There cannot be slavery in the Territories—for the Territories are under the exclusive control of Congress; and Congress is under the exclusive control of the Constitution; and the Constitution is such, that slavery can neither be set up, nor suffered, under it. The institutions of a Territory must harmonize with the Constitution. So far as they are repugnant to it, they are destitute of legal force. . . .

My fourteenth position is, that the law is Unconstitutional, because it undertakes to suspend the writ of Habeas Corpus. . . .

What mean the two lines, at the close of the sixth section of this law—"And shall prevent all molestation of said person or persons by any process issued by any court, judge, magistrate, or other person whomsoever?" If they do not mean to shut out the writ of Habeas Corpus, then what do they mean? . . . If they do not, then they are mere surplusage: and the imputation of surplusage to a law must be avoided, if possible. . . .

My argument is ended. How came this grossly Unconstitutional law to be enacted? How came such able lawyers as Clay and Webster to favor its enactment? The solution is, that they acted in the case, not as lawyers, but as politicians. They had a compromise to make; and make it they must, and make it they did, at whatever expense to an oppressed and outraged race, and at whatever expense to their reputation as lawyers. Even a very great lawyer, when he has consented to merge the lawyer in the politician, can make sad havoc of law. . . .

It may be too late for America to learn the lesson—nevertheless, it is a lesson of truth, and of unspeakably important truth, that no people can be secure in their rights any further than they believe, that their rights are derived from God; nor any further than they believe, that laws to be valid and obligatory, must be laws for the protection, instead of the destruction, of rights.

WENDELL PHILLIPS

VINDICATES THE ABOLITIONISTS (1853).

IF ANTI-SLAVERY SENTIMENT spread rapidly through the North after 1850, the abolitionists remained an unpopular minority. Even as Free Soil convictions hardened and politicians became more determined to check the growth of slavery, the abolitionists—and particularly the Garrisonians—were everywhere repudiated. No one was more keenly aware of their precarious position as a minority than Wendell Phillips, the Boston Brahmin and greatest of the anti-slavery orators. In a speech delivered at the Melodeon, January 27, 1853, he made an impassioned defense of the abolitionist agitator as playing an essential role in a society where the majority ruled. "Philosophy of the Abolition Movement," as he subsequently entitled his speech, is still the best single statement of the abolitionist theory of reform. Wendell Phillips, "Philosophy of the Abolition Movement." Speech before the Massachusetts Anti-Slavery Society, at the Melodeon, Boston, January 27, 1853. *Speeches, Lectures, and Letters by Wendell Phillips* (Boston, 1863), 98-153.

. . . I WISH, MR. CHAIRMAN, to notice some objections that have been made to our course ever since Mr. Garrison began his career, and which have been lately urged again, with considerable force and emphasis, in the columns of the London Leader, the able organ of a very respectable and influential class in England. . . .

The charges to which I refer are these: that, in dealing with slaveholders and their apologists, we indulge in fierce denunciations, instead of appealing to their reason and common sense by plain statements and fair argument;—that we might have won the sympathies and support of the nation, if we would have submitted to argue this question with a manly patience; but, instead of this, we have outraged the feelings of the community by attacks, unjust and unnecessarily severe, on its most valued institutions, and gratified our spleen by indiscriminate abuse of leading men, who were often honest in their intentions, however mistaken in their views;—that we have utterly neglected the ample means that lay around us to convert the nation, submitted to no discipline, formed no plan, been guided by no foresight, but hurried on in childish, reckless, blind, and hot-headed zeal,—bigots in the narrowness of our views, and fanatics in our blind fury of invective and malignant judgment of other men's motives. . . .

What is the denunciation with which we are charged? It is endeavoring, in our faltering human speech, to declare the enormity of the sin of making merchandise of men,—of separating husband and wife,—taking the infant from its mother, and selling the daughter to prostitution,—of a professedly Christian nation denying, by statute, the Bible to every sixth man and woman of its population, and making it illegal for "two or three" to meet together, except a white man be present! What is this harsh criticism of motives with which we are charged? It is simply holding the intelligent and deliberate actor responsible for the character and consequences of his acts. Is there any thing inherently wrong in such denunciation or such criticism? This we may claim—we have never judged a man but out of his own mouth. We have seldom, if ever, held him to account, except for acts of which he and his own friends were proud. All that we ask the world and thoughtful men to note are the principles and deeds on which the American pulpit and American public men plume themselves. We always allow our opponents to paint their own pictures. Our humble duty is to stand by and assure the spectators, that what they would take for a knave or a hypocrite is really, in American estimation, a Doctor of Divinity or Secretary of State. . . .

So far, however you distrust my philosophy, you will not doubt my statements. That we have denounced and rebuked with unsparing fidelity will not be denied. Have we not also addressed ourselves to that other duty, of arguing our question thoroughly?—of using due discretion and fair sagacity in endeavoring to promote our cause? Yes, we have. Every statement we have made has been doubted. Every principle we have laid down has been denied by overwhelming majorities against us. No one step has ever been gained but by the most laborious research and the most exhausting argument. And no question has ever, since Revolutionary days, been so thoroughly investigated or argued here, as that of slavery. Of that research and that argument, of the whole of it, the old-fashioned, fanatical, crazy Garrisonian antislavery movement has been the author. From this band of men has proceeded every important argument or idea which has been broached on the antislavery question from 1830 to the present time. . . .

. . . How shall a feeble minority, without weight or influence in the country, with no jury of millions to appeal to,—denounced, vilified, and contemned,—how shall we make way against the overwhelming weight of some colossal reputation, if we do not turn from the idolatrous present, and appeal to the human race? saying to your idols of to-day, "Here we are defeated; but we will write our judgment with the iron pen of a century to come, and it shall never be forgotten, if we can help it, that you were false in your generation to the claims of the slave!"

At present, our leading men, strong in the support of large majorities, and counting safely on the prejudices of the community, can afford to despise us. They know they can overawe or cajole the Present; their only fear is the judgment of the Future. Strange fear, perhaps, considering how short and local their fame! But however little, it is their all. Our only hold upon them is the thought of that bar of posterity, before which we are all to stand. . . . We are weak here—out-talked, out-voted. You load our names with infamy, and shout us down. But our words bide their time. We warn the living that we have terrible memories, and that their sins are never to be forgotten. We will gibbet the name of every apostate so black and high that his children's children shall blush to bear it. Yet we bear no malice,—cherish no resentment. . . .

So far from the antislavery cause having lacked a manly and able discussion, I think it will be acknowledged hereafter that this discussion has been one of the noblest contributions to a literature really American. Heretofore, not only has our tone been but an echo of foreign culture, but the very topics discussed and the views maintained have been too often pale reflections of European politics and European philosophy. No matter what dress we assumed, the voice was ever "the voice of Jacob." At last we have stirred a question thoroughly American; the subject has been looked at from a point of view entirely American; and it is of such deep interest, that it has called out all the intellectual strength of the nation. For once, the nation speaks its own thoughts in its own language, and the tone also is all its own. It will hardly do for the defeated party to claim that, in this discussion, all the ability is on their side. . . .

Sir, when a nation sets itself to do evil, and all its leading forces, wealth, party, and piety, join in the career, it is impossible but that those who offer a constant opposition should be hated and maligned, no matter how wise, cautious, and well planned their course may be. We are peculiar sufferers in this way. The community has come to hate its reproving Nathan so bitterly, that even those whom the relenting part is beginning to regard as standard-bearers of the antislavery host think it unwise to avow any connection or sympathy with him. I refer to some of the leaders of the political movement against slavery. They feel it to be their mission to marshal and use as effectively as possible the present convictions of the people. They cannot afford to encumber themselves with the odium which twenty years of angry agitation have engendered in great sects sore from unsparing rebuke, parties galled by constant defeat, and leading men provoked by unexpected exposure. They are willing to confess, privately, that our movement produced theirs, and that its continued existence is the very breath of their life. But, at the same time, they would fain walk on the road without being soiled by too close contact with the rough pioneers who threw it up. They are wise and honorable, and their silence is very expressive.

When I speak of their eminent position and acknowledged ability, another thought strikes me. Who converted these men and their distinguished associates? It is said we have shown neither sagacity in plans, nor candor in discussion, nor ability. Who, then, or what, converted Burlingame and Wilson, Sumner and Adams, Palfrey and Mann, Chase and Hale, and Phillips and Giddings? Who taught the Christian Register, the Daily Advertiser, and that class of prints, that there were such things as a slave and a slaveholder in the land, and so gave them some more intelligent basis than their mere instincts to hate William Lloyd Garrison? What magic wand was it whose touch made the toadying servility of the land start up the real demon that it was, and at the same time gathered into the slave's service the professional ability, ripe culture, and personal integrity that grace the Free Soil ranks? We never argue! These men, then, were converted by simple denunciation! They were all converted by the "hot," "reckless," "ranting," "bigoted," "fanatic" Garrison, who never troubled himself about facts, nor stopped to argue with an opponent, but straightway knocked him down! . . . Do not criticise too much the agency by which such men were converted. That blade has a double edge. Our reckless course, our empty rant, our fanaticism, has made Abolitionists of some of the best and ablest men in the land. We are inclined to go on, and see if even with such poor tools we cannot make some more. . . .

We are perfectly willing—I am for one—to be the dead lumber that shall make a path for these men into the light and love of the people. . . . After all, Mr. Chairman, this is no hard task. We know very well, that, notwithstanding this loud clamor about our harsh judgment of men and things, our opinions differ very little from those of our Free Soil friends, or of intelligent men generally, when you really get at them. . . .

Caution is not always good policy in a cause like ours. It is said that, when Napoleon saw the day going against him, he used to throw away all the rules of war, and trust himself to the hot impetuosity of his soldiers. The masses are governed more by impulse than conviction; and even were it not so, the convictions of most men are on our side, and this will surely appear, if we can only pierce the crust of their prejudice or indifference. I observe that our Free Soil friends never stir their audience so deeply as when some individual leaps beyond the platform, and strikes upon the very heart of the people. Men listen to discussions of laws and tactics with ominous patience. It is when Mr. Sumner, in Faneuil Hall, avows his determination to disobey the Fugitive Slave Law, and cries out, "I was a man before I was a Commissioner,"—when Mr. Giddings says of the fall of slavery, quoting Adams, "Let it come; if it must come in *blood*, yet I say, LET IT COME!"—that their associates on the platform are sure they are wrecking the party—while many a heart beneath beats its first pulse of antislavery life. . . .

It would be superfluous to say that we grant the entire sincerity and true-heartedness of these men. But in critical times, when a wrong step entails most disastrous consequences, to "mean well" is not enough. Sincerity is no shield for any man from the criticism of his fellow-laborers. I do not fear that such men as these will take offence at our discussion of their views and conduct. Long years of hard labor, in which we have borne at least our share, have resulted in a golden opportunity. How to use it, friends differ. Shall we stand courteously silent, and let these men play out the play, when, to our thinking, their plan will slacken the zeal, balk the hopes, and waste the efforts of the slave's friends? No! . . .

Every thoughtful and unprejudiced mind must see that such an evil as slavery will yield only to the most radical treatment. If you consider the work we have to do, you will not think us needlessly aggressive, or that we dig down unnecessarily deep in laying the foundations of our enterprise. A money power of two thousand millions of dollars, as the prices of slaves now range, held by a small body of able and desperate men; that body raised into a political aristocracy by special constitutional provisions; cotton, the product of slave labor, forming the basis of our whole foreign commerce, and the commercial class thus subsidized; the press bought up, the pulpit reduced to vassalage, the heart of the common people chilled by a bitter prejudice against the black race; our leading men bribed, by ambition, either to silence or open hostility;—in such a land, on what shall an Abolitionist rely? On a few cold prayers, mere lip-service, and never from the heart? On a church resolution, hidden often in its records, and meant only as a decent cover for servility in daily practice? On political parties, with their superficial influence at best, and seeking ordinarily only to use existing prejudices to the best advantage? Slavery has deeper root here than any aristocratic institution has in Europe; and politics is but the common pulse-beat, of which revolution is the fever-spasm. Yet we have seen European aristocracy survive storms which seemed to reach down to the primal strata of

European life. Shall we, then, trust to mere politics, where even revolution has failed? How shall the stream rise above its fountain? Where shall our church organizations or parties get strength to attack their great parent and moulder, the Slave Power? Shall the thing formed say to him that formed it, Why hast thou made me thus? The old jest of one who tried to lift himself in his own basket, is but a tame picture of the man who imagines that, by working solely through existing sects and parties, he can destroy slavery. Mechanics say nothing but an earthquake, strong enough to move all Egypt, can bring down the Pyramids.

Experience has confirmed these views. The Abolitionists who have acted on them have a "short method" with all unbelievers. They have but to point to their own success, in contrast with every other man's failure. To waken the nation to its real state, and chain it to the consideration of this one duty, is half the work. So much we have done. Slavery has been made the question of this generation. To startle the South to madness, so that every step she takes, in her blindness, is one step more toward ruin, is much. This we have done. Witness Texas and the Fugitive Slave Law. To have elaborated for the nation the only plan of redemption, pointed out the only exodus from this "sea of troubles," is much. This we claim to have done in our motto of IMMEDIATE, UNCONDITIONAL EMANCIPATION ON THE SOIL. The closer any statesmanlike mind looks into the question, the more favor our plan finds with it. The Christian asks fairly of the infidel, "If this Religion be not from God, how do you explain its triumph, and the history of the first three centuries?" Our question is similar. If our agitation has not been wisely planned and conducted, explain for us the history of the last twenty years! Experience is a safe light to walk by, and he is not a rash man who expects success in future from the same means which have secured it in times past.

THEODORE PARKER
PROPHESIES A REVOLUTION (1854).

THE PASSAGE OF the Kansas-Nebraska Act on May 30, 1854 stirred the North to immediate protest. Stephen Douglas, the author of the law which established the principle of "squatter sovereignty," admitted that he could have traveled from Boston to Chicago by the light of his burning effigies. Certainly the flames of resentment in Boston, fanned by the popular preacher Theodore Parker, flared high. As pastor of the Twenty-eighth Congregational Society, Parker preached anti-slavery to thousands of Bostonians, first at the Melodeon and then at the Music Hall. Parker did more than preach: he led the Boston vigilance committee in daring rescues of the fugitives Ellen and William Craft and Shadrach, and then organized protests when equally bold plots to rescue Sims and Anthony Burns miscarried. But Parker's chief contributions to abolition were his vigorous, topical sermons, which more than almost any other anti-slavery productions popularized the abolitionist argument in New England. The following is taken from a sermon on the Nebraska Act. Identifying slavery with the "money power" as a "retrogressive" force in American life, Parker calls for a "progressive" revolution in American thought which will ensure the "development of mankind." *The Nebraska Question. Some Thoughts on the New Assault upon Freedom in America, and the General State of the Country in Relation Thereunto, set forth in a Discourse Preached at the Music Hall, in Boston, on Monday, February 12, 1854 by Theodore Parker, Minister of the XVIII Congregational Society in Boston* (Boston, 1854), 50-65.

. . . THE SLAVE POWER has long been seeking to extend its jurisdiction. It has eminently succeeded. It fills all the chief offices of the nation; the Presidents are Slave Presidents; the Supreme Court is of Slave Judges, every one; the district Judges,—you all know Judge Sprague, Judge Grier, Judge Kane. In all that depends on the political action of America, the Slave power carries the day. In what depends on industry, population, education, it is the North. The Slave power seeks to extend its institutions at the expense of humanity. The North works with it. In this century, the South has been foiled in only two efforts: to extend Slavery to California and Oregon: nine times it has succeeded.

Now see why the South wishes to establish Slavery in Nebraska.

1. She wishes to gain a direct power in Congress. So she wants new

Slave States, that she may have new Slave Senators to give her the uttermost power in the Senate of the United States.

2. Next, she wishes indirectly to gain power by directly checking the rapid growth of the free States of the North. If Nebraska is free, the tide of immigration will set thither, as once to Ohio, Michigan, Illinois, as now to Wisconsin, Iowa, Minnesota. There will be a rapid increase of free men, with their consequent wealth, education, ideas, democratic institutions, free States, with consequent political power.

All this the South wishes to avoid; for the South—I must say it—is the enemy of the North. She is the foe to Northern Industry—to our mines, our manufactures, and our commerce. Thrice, in my day, has she sought to ruin all three. She is the foe to our institutions—to our Democratic politics in the State, our Democratic culture in the school, our Democratic work in the community, our Democratic equality in the family, and our Democratic religion in the Church. . . .

Such are the two general reasons why the South wishes Slavery in this new territory. But here is a third reason quite special.

3. There must be communication with the West. Three railroads are possible; one lies through Mexican territory, but we have not got it, for the Gadsden treaty is not yet a fact accomplished:—two others lie through Nebraska territory. One or the other of them must be built. If Nebraska is free soil, the Slave master cannot take his Slave across, for the law of the free soil makes the black man free. But if Nebraska is a Slave State, then the master can go there and carry his "chattels personal" through,—coffles of men, droves of women, herds of children, attended by the "missionary from Boston," and the bloodhounds of the kidnapper. She wants right of way for her institution; a Slave railroad from the Mississippi to the Pacific. Such are the reasons why she wants to establish Slavery there. . . .

So the question is, shall we let Slavery into the two great territories of Kanzas and Nebraska? That is a question of economy. Here it is. Shall men work with poor industrial tools, or with good ones? Shall they have the varied industry of New England and the North, or the Slave labor of Virginia and Carolina? Shall their land be worth five dollars and eight cents an acre, as in South Carolina, or thirty dollars and a half as in Connecticut? Shall the people all be comfortable, engaged in honest work, which enriches while it elevates; or shall a part be the poorest of the world that a few may be idle and rich?

It is a question of political morality. Shall the Government be a commonwealth where all are citizens, or an aristocracy where man owns his brother man? Shall there be the schools of Ohio, or the ignorance of Tennessee? Shall it be a virtue and a dignity to teach, as it is in the public schools of Boston; a great charity, as some of you are administering in private schools for the ignorant and poor; or shall it be a crime, as in Virginia, where Mrs. Douglas, by sentence of Court, is now serving out her time in the House of Correction, for teaching a black child its letters? Shall there be the public libraries, newspapers, lectures, lyceums, of Massachusetts; or the ignorance, the ignoble sloth of Mississippi and Alabama? Aye! it is a question of domestic morality. Shall a man have a right to his own limbs, his liberty, his life? Shall the mother own the babe that is born from her bosom? Shall she be a maid, and keep her innocence and her honor? Shall she be a wife, faithful to him that she loves, or shall she be the instrument of a master's lust, who has the law to enforce rape and violence? That is the question.

It is a great religious question. Shall the passions and ambition of base men have rule in Nebraska, or the natural law of the most High God? . . .

I know Northern politicians say, "Slavery will never go there!" Do they believe their own word? They believe it! In 1820, they said it could not go to Missouri; then, there were but 10,222 therein; now, 87,422! more than a quarter of all the Slaves in the United States are North of 36° 30′. Desperate men from the Slave States of the Atlantic and the Mississippi, too miserable to reach California, will find their El Dorado in Nebraska, take Slaves there and work their lives out! It will be a better breeding State than Virginia herself.

Congress, it is said, has no right to legislate for the people of the territory against Slavery. It must be left to the inhabitants thereof. There are 485,000 square miles,—not 1,000 men, not two hundred voters. Shall two hundred squatters entail Slavery on a country as large as all Germany, Switzerland, France, Belgium, and Holland? Is it "democratic" for Congress to allow two hundred stragglers in the wilderness, cheating the Indians, swearing, violent, half of them unable to write or read. . . ?

Suppose we grant this,—will that be the end? Suppose Slavery flows into Nebraska,—is that all? . . . Our great enemy demands sacrifices, not of interest but of principle; the sacred principle of natural right, allegiance to the Eternal God. "Grant it," say they, "or we will dissolve the Union." Presently that cry will be raised again, "Save the Union! Oh! save the Union." "The Union is in danger—this hour!" will be rung again in our deceived ears. Suppose it is granted. Only once in seventy years has the Southern demand been rejected,—when she asked to put Slavery into Oregon. But the conscience of the North,—there is not much of it,—not enough to act, only to grumble, or perchance to swear. The conscience of the North complains. "Stop that agitation, or I will dissolve the Union at once," says the South. Then the North says again, "Hush! Save the Union!" and there will not be a whisper from Whig or Democrat. The Church has got its mean mouth sewed up with an iron thread.

Then the South will demand again, "Grant us this demand, or we will dissolve the Union!"—and the same thing goes over and over again. Do you think the North fears a dissolution of the Union? As much as I fear that this handful of flowers shall rise and strike the life out of my soul. *No! No!* Think not of that. Is it love of Country which prompts the Northern sacrifice of conscience? No! never! Never, no! It is love of the dollar. It is love of the power of the majority, of the Slaveholder's power, not love of man, but love of money. While the North can make money by the Union, there is no danger of dissolution!

Grant this, and see what follows. I omit the probable acts of individual States, over which Congress has no direct control.

I. The South will claim that the master has a right to take his Slaves into a free State—spite of its laws to the contrary—and hold them there —first, for a definite time, say seven years; next, for an indefinite period in perpetuity. That will restore Slavery to the North and enable the sons of New England to return to their native land with their "chattels personal." Perhaps it will require no Act of Congress to do this—and "supersede" the Ordinance of 1787, or declare it "inoperative and void." The whole may be done any day by the Supreme Court of the United States; any day when the President shall say, "Down with you, Judges. Do as you are bid." Whigs and Democrats can do all things through money, which stengtheneth them! will the North consent? Why not, nothing is so supple as the Northern neck.

II. Then the South will seek more Slave territory. Here is what is wanted:—a part of Mexico,—the Gadsden treaty stipulates for about 39,000,000 acres, eight States as large as Massachusetts; Cuba, which the Slave power has long coveted; Porto Rico; Hayti, which the Democratic Christians hate with such bitterness; Jamaica and the other West Indies; the Sandwich Islands; other parts of the Northern and Southern continent. Slavery must be put in all these places. Will the North consent? Why not? habit makes all things easy. What an excellent "field for religious enterprise" Hayti would be, if this Republic should restore Slavery to St. Domingo! Conquer your prejudices!

III. Then she will seek to restore the African Slave trade. Here are the steps. 1, to authorize any State to import Slaves; 2, to authorize any individual to do so in spite of the adverse laws of any State which will be declared "inoperative and void," or "superseded." . . .

Who is to blame? The South? Well, look and see! In the House of Representatives there are 88 Southern men; there are 144 from the North. In the Senate, the South has 30, the North 32. But out of the two and thirty Northern Senators, not twelve men can be found to protest against this wicked Bill. The President is a Northern man; the Cabinet has a majority from the North; the Committee of Senators who reported this Bill has a majority of Northern men; its Chairman is a Northern man. . . .

The Northern conscience, the Northern religion, the Northern faith in God—where is it? Is it in the midst of the people—the young men and the young women; in your hearts and in my heart? Let us see. Let our actions speak. Now is the time; a month hence may be too late; aye, a week, and the deed may be done. Let us, at least, be manly, and do our part. . . .

But we shall not toil in vain. Slavery is nothing. It exists only by a whim. Theocracy is nothing, Monarchy is nothing, Aristocracy nothing. America has no "Pope," no "King," no "Noble;" a breath unmakes them as a breath once made. Slavery is no more if we say it; the monster dies. In one day the North could annihilate all the Slavery which depends on the Federal Government—abolish it on the Federal soil, the Capital, and the Territories; abolish the American Slave Trade, declare it piracy, or other felony. That would be only common legislation. The next day we could abolish it in the Slave States. That would be Revolution.

THOMAS W. HIGGINSON

TAKES A RIDE THROUGH KANSAS (1857).

In April, 1854, a month before the passage of the Kansas-Nebraska Act, the Free Soil partisan Eli Thayer founded the Massachusetts Emigrant Aid Society. During the next two years its successor, the New England Emigrant Aid Society, sent nearly thirteen hundred settlers to Kansas, where they fought with "border ruffians" from Missouri for control of the territory. In 1856 Thomas W. Higginson, an energetic Unitarian minister and member of Boston's vigilance committee, made a trip to Kansas to judge for himself the success of the various Kansas aid societies in holding the territory as free soil. His report, a series of letters signed "Worcester," first appeared in Horace Greeley's *Tribune* and subsequently were collected and published by the American Anti-Slavery Society as *A Ride Through Kanzas.* An abolitionist faith in the just use of force which later led Higginson to accept a colonelcy in the Union Army here dictates the conclusion that "the sooner the people of Kanzas have a revolution the better." *A Ride Through Kanzas* (New York, 1857), 14-24.

V.—THE PEOPLE.

Lawrence, October 4, 1856.

Ever since the rendition of Anthony Burns, in Boston, I have been looking for *men.* I have found them in Kanzas. The virtue of courage (for although these two words originally meant the same thing, they have become separated now) has not died out of the Anglo-American race, as some have hastily supposed. It needs only circumstances to bring it out. A single day in Kanzas makes the American Revolution more intelligible than all Sparks or Hildreth can do. The same event is still in progress here.

I have always wondered whether, in the midst of war, tumult, and death, the same daily current of life went on, and men's hearts accommodated themselves to the occasion. In heroic races, I now see that it is so. In Kanzas, nobody talks of courage, for every one is expected to exhibit it.

Take, for instance, the Sunday attack on Lawrence, a fortnight ago. The army which approached it consisted of 2,800 by the estimate here—

3,000 by Governor Geary's estimate, and 3,200 by the statement of *The Missouri Republican,* in a singular article, which described the capture of the town, although it never happened. This force was in sight the greater part of the day, and though Governor Geary's aid was invoked, it was known that it could not arrive till evening; thus allowing time for the destruction of everything.

Against this force, the number at first counted upon was *one hundred;* that being the supposed number of fighting men left, after the arrest of the hundred about whom I wrote to you, as prisoners. To the surprise of all, however, more than two hundred rallied to the fort. The lame came on crutches, and the sick in blankets.

Two hundred men against fourteen times their number! And the fort a mere earthen redoubt, of no pretensions—for the only fort worth the name is on the hill above the town, and was at this time useless. And yet (here comes the point) I was assured by Governor Robinson and a dozen others, that among this devoted handful the highest spirits prevailed; they were laughing and joking as usual, and only intent on selling their lives as dearly as possible.

They had no regular commander, any more than at Bunker Hill; but the famous "Old Captain Brown" moved about among them, saying, "Fire low, boys; be sure to bring down your eye to the hinder sight of your rifle, and aim at the feet rather than the head."

A few women were in the fort that day—all who could be armed. Others spent the whole Sunday making cartridges. I asked one of these how she felt: "Well, I can't remember that I felt any way different from usual," answered the quiet housekeeper, after due reflection. So they all say. One young girl sat at her door, reading, a mile or so from the scene of action. "Once in a while I looked up," she said, "when there was a louder shot than usual."

The chief fighting was among skirmishers, and there was no actual attack on the fort. The newspapers have had the particulars before, and I only mention the affair to show the spirit of buoyant courage which almost universally prevails. It must be remembered, also, that even now these people are poorly armed, and still worse off for ammunition. On this occasion they had but a few rounds apiece.

Persons at the North who grudge their small subscriptions to Kanzas, should remember that a few dollars may sometimes save a thousand. Osawatamie was sacrificed, after one of the most heroic defences in history, for want of ammunition. Brown and twenty-seven others resisted two hundred, killing thirty-three and wounding forty-nine, (eighty-two in all, by the Pro-Slavery statement) and then retreated through these, with the loss of but one man, shot as he was swimming the creek. A hundred dollars worth of ammunition would have prevented, on that occasion, the destruction of $60,000 worth of property. . . .

As for Lawrence, it has one of the most beautiful situations I every looked upon. It stands on a bank above a bend in the river; across the river are miles of woods, while behind the town rise two beautiful hills, which *are* hills, and not merely the endless swells of rolling prairie of which my Eastern eyes have grown so tired. Indeed, this whole region far surpasses, in respect to hills and forest, both Iowa and Nebraska, and even Northern Kanzas, while the prairies are richer, and coal and stone are interspersed. Give it freedom, and a few years will make Kanzas the garden of America. This year the Missourians have almost ruined the corn; but never have I seen such luxuriance of melons, squashes, and pumpkins. I have seen some fine stock, too, on the more favored farms; but that kind of riches soon takes to itself legs, more dangerous, in the present state of Kanzas, than the proverbial wings.

Lawrence is three times as large as Topeka, and at present much more busy. It has, however, suffered much more from want of food. For instance, I have just talked with a man whom I knew at the East. "I came out here," said he, "with $1,500 in money. I have served through the whole war. My wife and nine children have lived more than two weeks on green corn and squash. I have in my house no meat, no flour, no meal, no potatoes, no money to buy them, no prospect of a dollar; but *I'll live or die in Kanzas!*"

Afterwards this man's wife wrote to me in almost the same words.

Such is the spirit of multitudes, many of whom are as badly off as this man. There is the greatest generosity, and men share with each other while anything is left; but after that, what then?

The State Committee works with energy and system to relieve distress, and may be entirely relied upon, but its funds are also exhausted. The expense of sending emigrants, arms, and ammunition, through Iowa and Nebraska, has been so enormous, that but little has yet reached Kanzas in any other form; and the cost of supporting the army here has been also enormous—some $300 per day. At the very time when farm labor was most needed, all the able-bodied men have been obliged to live for weeks in camp, at the public expense—they themselves being the principal public.

This discourages and drives out the timid and lukewarm, and educates the remainder to endurance. People in Kanzas are like Indians—they eat what they can, and sleep where they can; and when they have no house and no food they wait awhile till something turns up. I can see that this state of things brings out some bad qualities, but far more good ones. . . .

VIII.—THE FUTURE.

WORCESTER, Mass., October 20, 1856.

. . . I have observed for many years that the more thorough an Abolitionist any man is, the more correct are his prophecies as to American affairs; and in this respect, at least, the present writer is pretty well qualified. I will therefore give the reasons which lead me to think, contrary to the opinions of many at the East, that the present comparative quiet of Kanzas is only the prelude to a severer struggle than any she has yet seen; that this struggle will occur soon after the Presidential election; and that it will be almost equally certain to occur, whether Fremont or Buchanan be elected.

The foundation for these opinions can be made very intelligible.

1. The real question at issue is, not the invasions of Missourians, nor the blockading of the river, but the enforcing of the bogus laws. The laws still exist, the Courts are still controlled by Missouri, and this is the real root of the difficulty, over which neither Governor Geary nor any one else (except Congress) has any legitimate control. The essential trouble, therefore, must either remain unsettled till Congress meets again, or be settled by force.

2. There is not the slightest increase of harmony between the parties, but the contrary. Both sides expect to see the contest renewed. I did not hear of a single man, on either side, except Governor Geary and his satellites, who thought otherwise.

3. Both sides are making actual preparations for a renewal. The settlers are collecting arms, ammunition, and fresh men. The Missourians are doing the same. True, men from both sides are leaving the country; but they are going, either with the design to return soon after the election, or else from personal dissatisfaction—not because they expect permanent peace.

4. Neither party *desires* peace, under the present auspices. The Missourians do not desire it, until they see that it involves the speedy introduction of Slavery. And the settlers do not desire it, when it means submission to the laws which a foreign State imposed upon them, and the daily arrest of their own men while Pro-Slavery men go free.

5. War always educates men to itself, disciplines them, teaches them

to bear its fatigue, anxiety, and danger, and actually to enjoy them. I saw abundant instances of this on the Free State side; and I believe it to be so with the Missourians. Everybody testified that the army of two thousand eight hundred, which last besieged Lawrence, was better armed and better drilled than any previous invading force; and all agreed that at the battle of Hickory Point the Missourians showed more courage than ever before. . . .

7. The reason why the strife is postponed, by tacit agreement, is easily told. The Missourians are waiting, in stronger and stronger hopes that Geary will do their work. The Free State men submit to his aggressions, *only* because the election is coming. That, and that only, gives them patience; precisely as the hope of flight to Canada keeps slaves from insurrection. They cling to the hope, not of escaping the contest, but of placing it on a more favorable footing. Take away the dream of Fremont, and no power could make these injured men endure a week longer the combined oppression of the Administration and of Missouri. Besides, every letter that comes to them from the East, exhorts them to "endure till November, and all will be well." Is it strange, then, if they seem almost too submissive, with such a prospect? . . .

9. Look out, therefore, for trouble in Kanzas, in November. Elect Fremont, and there will be a last desperate effort of Missouri to obtain possession of Kanzas. In this they will rely on the aid of the United States Courts and troops, and will have it, whatever Gov. Geary says. The policy of the Administration will be unchanged. It is absurd to suppose that Pierce, Cushing, and Douglass will not still bid for Southern favor, after the election of Fremont. *They will have nothing else left to do.* They will look out for a Pro-Slavery reaction four years afterward, (and it will come then, if not sooner) and steer for that wave. Still, the Kanzas men will have a great advantage, for the United States troops will not in that case act against them *with a will,* and they have nothing else to fear.

In case of Buchanan's election, the whole power of Missouri, backed by the whole power of the Administration, will be directed upon Kanzas. The two forces will be identified. They will be brought to bear as one; and, thank God, *resisted as one.* The defenders of Freedom will fight, at last, as they never yet have fought. Heretofore, they have submitted to injuries from the weakest United States official, which they would never have borne from whole armies of Missourians. They will not make this nice distinction much longer. Oppression is oppression, wherever it comes from, they will say. "If that is treason, make the most of it."

We must have a new dictionary, and the definition of this much abused word must be: "Treason, the rope by which the real traitors seek to hang those who resist them."

Such treason as this is fast ripening in Kanzas. Call it revolution if you please.

If the United States Government and Border-Ruffianism are to mean the same thing, the sooner the people of Kanzas have revolution the better. So they will say, and who shall gainsay it? They have borne to the utmost. Another ounce of weight, and they will bear it no longer; and a less thing than the dispersion of their Legislature, or the destruction of their hotel, will be the signal.

Before I went to Kanzas I feared that her children would gradually scatter and flee, rather than meet a final, *desperate* struggle. I stand corrected. They will stay and meet it. They will meet it, if need be, unaided.

Will they be unaided? Ask Governor Grimes and the thousands of freemen of Iowa. Ask every man who has a heart left in his bosom.

Kanzas may be crushed, but not without a final struggle more fearful than that of Hungary; a struggle which will convulse a continent before it is ended, and separate forever those two nations of North and South, which neither Union nor Constitution has yet welded into one.

HINTON HELPER
INCITES CLASS WAR
IN THE SOUTH (1857).

IN 1857 HINTON R. HELPER, a nonslaveholder from North Carolina, published *The Impending Crisis,* a combination diatribe and statistical analysis proving slavery the cause of all the "shame, poverty, ignorance, tyranny and imbecility of the South." Helper's book was one of the comparatively few Southern abolitionist works, chiefly economic in emphasis and in no sense a humanitarian plea for the slave. In fact, he later explained that it "was *not* written in behalf of the negroes—as has been erroneously stated—but in behalf of the *whites.*" If he lacked sympathy for the Negro, Helper was driven by a compulsive hatred of his "depraved" master. The only hope for the South lay with the nonslaveholding yeoman farmers who must "strike for freedom" by destroying the political power of the planter oligarchy. *The Impending Crisis* was ignored by Helper's yeomanry and burned as insurrectionary by the planters. In the North, however, the book was welcomed by the abolitionists as a major contribution to their cause. Sixty-eight Republican congressmen endorsed a fund to distribute one hundred thousand copies as campaign propaganda. The impact of the book was attributable in part to its appearance in the same year as John Brown's raid, in part to its statistical evidence proving slavery a retrogressive force opposing America's economic development. *The Impending Crisis: How to Meet It* (Baltimore, 1857), Ch. II.

CHAPTER II.

INSCRIBED ON THE BANNER, which we herewith unfurl to the world, with the full and fixed determination to stand by it or die by it, unless one of more virtuous efficacy shall be presented, are the mottoes which, in substance, embody the principles, as we conceive, that should govern us in our patriotic warfare against the most subtle and insidious foe that ever menaced the inalienable rights and liberties and dearest interests of America:

1st. Thorough Organization and Independent Political Action on the part of the Non-Slaveholding whites of the South.

2nd. Ineligibility of Slaveholders—Never another vote to the Trafficker in Human Flesh.

3rd. No Co-operation with Slaveholders in Politics—No Fellowship with them in Religion—No Affiliation with them in Society.

4th. No Patronage to Slaveholding Merchants—No Guestship in Slave-waiting Hotels—No Fees to Slaveholding Lawyers—No Employment of Slaveholding Physicians—No Audience to Slaveholding Parsons.

5th. No Recognition of Pro-slavery Men, except as Ruffians, Outlaws, and Criminals.

6th. Abrupt Discontinuance of Subscription to Pro-slavery Newspapers.

7th. The Greatest Possible Encouragement to Free White Labor.

8th. No more Hiring of Slaves by Non-slaveholders.

9th. Immediate Death to Slavery, or if not immediate, unqualified Proscription of its Advocates during the Period of its Existence.

10th. A Tax of Sixty Dollars on every Slaveholder for each and every Negro in his Possession at the present time, or at any intermediate time between now and the 4th of July, 1863—said Money to be Applied to the transportation of the Blacks to Liberia, to their Colonization in Central or South America, or to their Comfortable Settlement within the Boundaries of the United States.

11th. An additional Tax of Forty Dollars per annum to be levied annually, on every Slaveholder for each and every Negro found in his possession after the 4th of July, 1863—said Money to be paid into the hands of the Negroes so held in Slavery, or, in cases of death, to their next of kin, and to be used by them at their own option.

This, then, is the outline of our scheme for the abolition of slavery in the Southern States. Let it be acted upon with due promptitude, and, as certain as truth is mightier than error, fifteen years will not elapse before every foot of territory, from the mouth of the Delaware to the emboguing of the Rio Grande, will glitter with the jewels of freedom. Some time during this year, next, or the year following, let there be a general convention of non-slaveholders from every slave State in the Union, to deliberate on the momentous issues now pending. First, let them adopt measures for holding in restraint the diabolical excesses of the oligarchy; secondly, in order to cast off the thraldom which the infamous slave-power has fastened upon them, and, as the first step necessary to be taken to regain the inalienable rights and liberties with which they were invested by Nature, but of which they have been divested by the accursed dealers in human flesh, let them devise ways and means for the complete annihilation of slavery; thirdly, let them put forth an equitable and comprehensive platform, fully defining their position, and inviting the active sympathy and co-operation of the millions of down-trodden non-slaveholders throughout the Southern and Southwestern States. Let all these things be done, not too hastily, but with calmness, deliberation, prudence, and circumspection; if need be, let the delegates to the convention continue in session one or two weeks; only let their labors be wisely and thoroughly performed; let them, on Wednesday morning, present to the poor whites of the South, a well-digested scheme for the reclamation of their ancient rights and prerogatives, and, on the Thursday following, slavery in the United States will be worth absolutely less than nothing; for then, besides being so vile and precarious that nobody will want it, it will be a lasting reproach to those in whose hands it is lodged.

. . . . .

From the abstract of our plan for the abolition of slavery, it will be perceived that, so far from allowing slaveholders any compensation for their slaves, we are, and we think justly, in favor of imposing on them a tax of sixty dollars for each and every negro now in their possession, as also for each and every one that shall be born to them between now and the 4th of July, 1863; after which time, we propose that they shall be taxed forty dollars per annum, annually, for every person by them held in slavery, without regard to age, sex, color, or condition—the money, in both instances, to be used for the sole advantage of the slaves. As an addendum to this proposition, we would say that, in our opinion, if slavery is not totally abolished by the year 1869, the annual tax ought to be increased from forty to one hundred dollars; and furthermore, that if the institution does not then almost immediately disappear under the onus of this increased taxation, the tax ought in the course of one or two years thereafter, to be augmented to such a degree as will, in harmony with other measures, prove an infallible deathblow to slavery on or before the 4th of July, 1876.

At once let the good and true men of this country, the patriot sons of the patriot fathers, determine that the sun which rises to celebrate the centennial anniversary of our national independence, shall not set on the head of any slave within the limits of our Republic. Will not the non-slaveholders of the North, of the South, of the East, and of the West, heartily, unanimously sanction this proposition? Will it not be cheerfully indorsed by many of the slaveholders themselves? Will any *respectable* man enter a protest against it? On the 4th of July, 1876—sooner, if we can—let us make good, at least so far as we are concerned, the Declaration of Independence, which was proclaimed in Philadelphia on the 4th of July, 1776—that "all men are endowed by their Creator with certain inalienable rights; that among these, are life, liberty, and the pursuit of happiness; that to secure these rights, governments are instituted among men, deriving their just powers from the consent of the governed; that whenever any form of government becomes destructive of these ends, it is the right of the people to alter or to abolish it, and to institute a new government, laying its foundation on such principles, and organizing its powers in such form, as to them shall seem most likely to effect their safety and happiness." In purging our land of the iniquity of negro slavery, we will only be carrying on the great work that was so successfully commenced by our noble sires of the Revolution; some future generation may possibly complete the work by annulling the last and least form of oppression.

To turn the slaves away from their present homes—away from all the property and means of support which their labor has mainly produced, would be unpardonably cruel—exceedingly unjust. Still more cruel and unjust would it be, however, to the non-slaveholding whites no less than to the negroes, to grant further toleration to the existence of slavery. In any event, come what will, transpire what may, the institution must be abolished. The evils, if any, which are to result from its abolition, cannot, by any manner of means, be half as great as the evils which are certain to overtake us in case of its continuance. The perpetuation of slavery is the climax of iniquity.

. . . .

HENRY THOREAU

PLEADS FOR CAPTAIN JOHN BROWN (1859).

THOREAU WAS NOT AN abolitionist and had scant respect for reformers to whom he recommended more mountain-climbing and fewer conventions. Yet John Brown seemed to him not an agitator or reformer merely but at once a Puritan and transcendentalist—a true man of principle. He had heard Brown speak in Concord just before he left for Virginia and the raid on Harper's Ferry; and while Brown awaited execution, Thoreau addressed his unsympathetic fellow-townsmen in his behalf "to correct the tone and the statements of my countrymen generally respecting his character and actions." *A Plea for Captain John Brown,* perhaps the greatest of nineteenth century American public addresses, went further in justifying violence than most abolitionists were willing to go in October 1859. In combining the abolitionist doctrine of higher law and his own belief in the majority of one, Thoreau naturally concluded that "a man has a perfect right to interfere with the slaveholder in order to rescue the slave." The *Plea,* with its call for direct intervention, returned the moral issue to the center of the territorial question and anticipated the abolitionist acceptance of force as the solution to the slavery problem. "A Plea for Captain John Brown," *The Writings of Henry David Thoreau* (Boston, 1893: Riverside edition), 11 vols., X, 197-236.

I TRUST THAT YOU will pardon me for being here. I do not wish to force my thoughts upon you, but I feel forced myself. Little as I know of Captain Brown, I would fain do my part to correct the tone and the statements of the newspapers, and of my countrymen generally, respecting his character and actions. It costs us nothing to be just. We can at least express our sympathy with, and admiration of, him and his companions, and that is what I now propose to do. . . .

He was one of that class of whom we hear a great deal, but, for the most part, see nothing at all,—the Puritans. It would be in vain to kill him. He died lately in the time of Cromwell, but he reappeared here. Why should he not? Some of the Puritan stock are said to have come over and settled in New England. They were a class that did something else than celebrate their forefathers' day, and eat parched corn in remembrance of that time. They were neither Democrats nor Republicans, but men of simple habits, straightforward, prayerful; not thinking much of rulers who did not fear God, not making many compromises, nor seeking after available candidates. . . .

He was a man of Spartan habits, and at sixty was scrupulous about his diet at your table, excusing himself by saying that he must eat sparingly and fare hard, as became a soldier, or one who was fitting himself for difficult enterprises, a life of exposure.

A man of rare common sense and directness of speech, as of action; a transcendentalist above all, a man of ideas and principles,—that was what distinguished him. . . . He was not in the least a rhetorician, was not talking to Buncombe or his constituents anywhere, had no need to invent anything but to tell the simple truth, and communicate his own resolution; therefore he appeared incomparably strong, and eloquence in Congress and elsewhere seemed to me at a discount. It was like the speeches of Cromwell compared with those of an ordinary king. . . .

But to make haste to *his* last act, and its effects.

The newspapers seem to ignore, or perhaps are really ignorant, of the fact that there are at least as many as two or three individuals to a town throughout the North who think much as the present speaker does about him and his enterprise. I do not hesitate to say that they are an important and growing party. We aspire to be something more than stupid and timid chattels, pretending to read history and our Bibles, but desecrating every house and every day we breathe in. Perhaps anxious politicians may prove that only seventeen white men and five negroes were concerned in the late enterprise; but their very anxiety to prove this might suggest to themselves that all is not told. Why do they still dodge the truth? They are so anxious because of a dim consciousness of the fact, which they do not distinctly face, that at least a million of the free inhabitants of the United States would have rejoiced if it had succeeded. They at most only criticise the tactics. Though we wear no crape, the thought of that man's position and probable fate is spoiling many a man's day here at the North for other thinking. If any one who has seen him here can pursue successfully any other train of thought, I do not know what he is made of. . . .

On the whole, my respect for my fellow-men, except as one may outweigh a million, is not being increased these days. I have noticed the cold-blooded way in which newspaper writers and men generally speak of this event, as if an ordinary malefactor, though one of unusual "pluck,"—as the Governor of Virginia is reported to have said, using the language of the cock-pit, "the gamest man he ever saw,"—had been caught, and were about to be hung. He was not dreaming of his foes when the governor thought he looked so brave. It turns what sweetness I have to gall, to hear, or hear of, the remarks of some of my neighbors. When we heard at first that he was dead, one of my townsmen observed that "he died as the fool dieth;" which, pardon me, for an instant suggested a likeness in him dying to my neighbor living. Others, craven-hearted, said, disparagingly, that "he threw his life away," because he resisted the government. Which way have they thrown *their* lives, pray?—such as would praise a man for attacking singly an ordinary band of thieves or murderers. I hear another ask, Yankee-like, "What will he gain by it?" as if he expected to fill his pockets by this enterprise. Such a one has no idea of gain but in this worldly sense. If it does not lead to a "surprise" party, if he does not get a new pair of boots, or a vote of thanks, it must be a failure. "But he won't gain anything by it." Well, no, I don't suppose he could get four-and-sixpence a day for being hung, take the year round; but then he stands a chance to save a considerable part of his soul—and *such* a soul!—when *you* do not. No doubt you can get more in your market for a quart of milk than for a quart of blood, but that is not the market that heroes carry their blood to. . . .

A man does a brave and humane deed, and at once, on all sides, we hear people and parties declaring, "I didn't do it, nor countenance *him* to do it, in any conceivable way. It can't be fairly inferred from my past career." I, for one, am not interested to hear you define your position. I don't know that I ever was or ever shall be. I think it is mere egotism, or impertinent at this time. Ye needn't take so much pains to wash your skirts of him. No intelligent man will ever be convinced that he was any creature of yours. He went and came, as he informs us, "under the auspices of John Brown and nobody else." The Republican party does not perceive how many his *failure* will make to vote more correctly than they would have them. They have counted the votes of Pennsylvania & Co., but they have not correctly counted Captain Brown's vote. He has taken the wind out of their sails,—the little wind they had,—and they may as well lie to and repair. . . .

Insane! A father and six sons, and one son-in-law, and several more men besides,—as many at least as twelve disciples,—all struck with insanity at once; while the same tyrant holds with a firmer gripe than ever his four millions of slaves, and a thousand sane editors, his abettors, are saving the country and their bacon! Just as insane were his efforts in Kansas. Ask the tyrant who is his most dangerous foe, the sane man or the insane? Do the thousands who know him best, who have rejoiced at his deeds in Kansas, and have afforded him material aid there, think him insane? Such a use of this word is a mere trope with most who persist in using it, and I have no doubt that many of the rest have already in silence retracted their words.

Read his admirable answers to Mason and others. How they are dwarfed and defeated by the contrast! On the one side, half-brutish, half-timid questioning; on the other, truth, clear as lightning, crashing into their obscene temples. They are made to stand with Pilate, and Gessler, and the Inquisition. How ineffectual their speech and action! and what a void their silence! They are but helpless tools in this great work. It was no human power that gathered about this preacher. . . .

I have no respect for the penetration of any man who can read the report of that conversation and still call the principal in it insane. It has the ring of a saner sanity than an ordinary discipline and habits of life, than an ordinary organization, secure. Take any sentence of it,—"Any questions that I can honorably answer, I will; not otherwise. So far as I am myself concerned, I have told everything truthfully. I value my word, sir." The few who talk about his vindictive spirit, while they really admire his heroism, have no test by which to detect a noble man, no amalgam to combine with his pure gold. They mix their own dross with it. . . .

"All is quiet at Harper's Ferry," say the journals. What is the character of that calm which follows when the law and the slaveholder prevail? I regard this event as a touchstone designed to bring out, with glaring distinctness, the character of this government. We needed to be thus assisted to see it by the light of history. It needed to see itself. When a government puts forth its strength on the side of injustice, as ours to maintain slavery and kill the liberators of the slave, it reveals itself a merely brutal force, or worse, a demoniacal force. It is the head of the Plug-Uglies. It is more manifest than ever that tyranny rules. I see this government to be effectually allied with France and Austria in oppressing mankind. There sits a tyrant holding fettered four millions of slaves; here comes their heroic liberator. This most hypocritical and diabolical government looks up from its seat on the gasping four millions, and inquires with an assumption of innocence: "What do you assault me for? Am I not an honest man? Cease agitation on this subject, or I will make a slave of you, too, or else hang you."

We talk about a *representative* government; but what a monster of a government is that where the noblest faculties of the mind, and the *whole* heart, are not *represented*. . . .

The only government that I recognize—and it matters not how few are at the head of it, or how small its army—is that power that establishes justice in the land, never that which establishes injustice. What shall we think of a government to which all the truly brave and just men in the land are enemies, standing between it and those whom it oppresses? A government that pretends to be Christian and crucifies a million Christs every day!

Treason! Where does such treason take its rise? I cannot help thinking of you as you deserve, ye governments. Can you dry up the fountains of thought? High treason, when it is resistance to tyranny here below, has its origin in, and is first committed by, the power that makes and forever recreates man. When you have caught and hung all these human rebels, you have accomplished nothing but your own guilt, for you have not struck at the fountain-head. . . .

I hear many condemn these men because they were so few. When were the good and the brave ever in a majority? Would you have had him wait till that time came?—till you and I came over to him? The very fact that he had no rabble or troop of hirelings about him would alone distinguish him from ordinary heroes. His company was small indeed, because few could be found worthy to pass muster. Each one who there laid down his life for the poor and oppressed was a picked man, culled out of many thousands, if not millions; apparently a man of principle, of rare courage, and devoted humanity; ready to sacrifice his life at any moment for the benefit of his fellow-man. It may be doubted if there were as many more their equals in these respects in all the country, —I speak of his followers only,—for their leader, no doubt, scoured the land far and wide, seeking to swell his troop. These alone were ready to step between the oppressor and the oppressed. Surely they were the very best men you could select to be hung. That was the greatest compliment which this country could pay them. They were ripe for her gallows. She has tried a long time, she has hung a good many, but never the right one before. . . .

It was his peculiar doctrine that a man has a perfect right to interfere by force with the slaveholder, in order to rescue the slave. I agree with him. They who are continually shocked by slavery have some right to be shocked by the violent death of the slaveholder, but no others. Such will be more shocked by his life than by his death. I shall not be forward to think him mistaken in his method who quickest succeeds to liberate the slave. I speak for the slave when I say that I prefer the philanthropy of Captain Brown to that philanthropy which neither shoots me nor liberates me. . . .

Who is it whose safety requires that Captain Brown be hung? Is it indispensable to any Northern man? Is there no resource but to cast this man also to the Minotaur? If you do not wish it, say so distinctly. While these things are being done, beauty stands veiled and music is a screeching lie. Think of him,—of his rare qualities!—such a man as it takes ages to make, and ages to understand; no mock hero, nor the representative of any party. A man such as the sun may not rise upon again in this benighted land. To whose making went the costliest material, the finest adamant; sent to be the redeemer of those in captivity; and the only use to which you can put him is to hang him at the end of a rope! You who pretend to care for Christ crucified, consider what you are about to do to him who offered himself to be the saviour of four millions of men. . . .

I am here to plead his cause with you. I plead not for his life, but for his character,—his immortal life; and so it becomes your cause wholly, and is not his in the least. Some eighteen hundred years ago Christ was crucified; this morning, perchance, Captain Brown was hung. These are the two ends of a chain which is not without its links. He is not Old Brown any longer; he is an angel of light. . . .

MONCURE CONWAY

JOINS THE SECOND AMERICAN REVOLUTION (1861).

WHEN SOUTH CAROLINA SECEDED in December, 1860, supporting its action with the right of revolution in the Declaration of Independence, the abolitionists were forced to reconsider the principle and the document on which their crusade was based. Could secession be justified on the ground of national self-determination and the rights of a whole people, or did individual rights control and determine the right to revolt? Were there both good and bad revolutions? Moncure Conway, the Virginia abolitionist, wrestled with these questions only to conclude that loyal Northerners were the true revolutionists against their own wrong. The son of a slaveholder, Conway had been converted to transcendentalism and abolition by Emerson and had preached against slavery in Washington and Cincinnati before settling in New England. When the war broke out he was living in Concord and editing the anti-slavery *Commonwealth* in Boston. Reluctantly he accepted the Civil War as "not absolutely, only relatively necessary," but defended the Union cause by distinguishing between rebellion and revolution. *The Rejected Stone,* a pamphlet of one hundred and thirty-two pages, is a lengthy and conditional defense of the war as the product of a humanitarian revolution. *The Rejected Stone: or Insurrection* vs. *Resurrection in America.* By a Native of Virginia (Boston, 1861) Ch. IV, "A Rebellion *vs.* A Revolution," 75-84.

THERE HAS BEEN A general confusion in the minds of both parties as to their historical and moral position in this conflict. They of the South have claimed that they are revolutionists, and justify themselves under the right of revolution. Many of the North have accepted the terms, justly reasoning that the right of revolution implies an interest, and possibly, as now, a duty pledged to prevent it. Revolution depends for its dignity and heroism purely upon the worth and justice of its cause; for, as all would applaud a child's resistance to his father when that father demanded of it some dishonorable act, so all would cry shame on the violent rebellion against a kind and good parent. Had our American Revolution been for the purpose of forming our Colonies into a band of robbers and pirates, no Pitt would have been found to plead our cause, no Lafayette to fight our battles. Revolution, in an unjust cause, is only an inauguration of bloodshed and assassination.

Therefore it is wrongly called Revolution. Revolution is a word nearly related to Evolution, and indicates the normal and healthy progression of the world on the prescribed orbit of civilization; pangs it may have, but they are the precious pangs of birth into life; it may wring tears, but each tear falls in blessed light, and gives some tint to the bow that halos the world. Revolution has marched on with the advancing world, and with it the fire of war and the cloud of sorrow; but its fire and cloud have been pillars leading on to Humanity's Promised Lands. . . .

We are the Revolutionists. It was the revolution of the American nation that made this war necessary; the South stands relatively where it always stood, and where the tyrant has stood since the world began. This is true, not in any fanciful or strained sense, but in the simplest and most direct sense. Slavery has always ruled this country. As soon as a seat of power was reared, Slavery assumed it. Its rod was extended over the lot of the righteous, and they put forth their hands to iniquity. It ruled commerce, it expunged the truth of history, it brought its Index Expurgatorius on the page of school-book and prayer-book. Scholars wrote for it, divines preached for it; it clasped the Bible with handcuffs and festooned the Cross of Christ with chains.

Against this Tyrant America at last inaugurated a revolution. Slowly and with many disparagements the feeble cause of Liberty prepared for a final struggle. Her pulses beat low, her heart-throbs are faint; she is only not crushed because purblind oppression imagines the life already, or nearly, ebbed out. But an old fire that was in deep alliance with the central heats of the earth, and under which old Wrong had again and again shrivelled like a burnt scroll, yet lingered in her heart. Anon the flame leapt out at eye and tongue; and despite the play of the engines, despite the cold water-jets sent from pulpit and press and society and office, the winds of Heaven fanned that flame until the parties were consumed, the political elements melted with fervent heat, and Slavery compelled to begin the world over again, and rebuild its throne over those ashes if it could!

It was the noblest revolution the world ever saw that placed Abraham Lincoln in the White House at Washington; the noblest, because the first ever known upon this planet where the legitimate weapons of Truth were alone used. These mighty strongholds yielded to the voices, the persuasions, the reasons, of earnest and just men; they were besieged with arrows of light, shelled with the bombs of Free School and Free Thought. . . .

And thus the revolution, without the firing of a gun from the side of the revolutionists, had gone on, until the steps of Freedom were on the threshold of a liberated and redeemed New World. The dayspring from on high had already visited us; the banner which had fallen out of the sky to blazon itself only in the scars and stripes on the slave's back, or on some weaker nation beside us, once more floated up, and promised to symbolize, as of old, the streaks of Humanity's advancing day.

The Southern movement is, then, not a revolution, but a rebellion against the noblest of revolutions. It is a league of confederates against the peaceful and legal evolution of Liberty on this continent. It is an Insurrection against a Resurrection. It is Slavery, hoary tyrant of the ages, standing before Humanity's morning, lifting its bars against the day-streaks, and crying, "Back! back, accursed Dawn, into the chambers of Night!" . . .

Shall we now spend our blood, our time, our strength, fighting with Slavery for the treasures dragged from the waves,—wrecker against wrecker? In that they will be ahead of us; their drags and nets of spoil are longer and better, their eagerness for their prey greater. Shall we rekindle those extinguished light-houses? shall we see that, all along the Atlantic and the Pacific and the Gulf, the rays of Freedom and Justice to all shine out clear and beautiful, marking for every struggling bark—for Germany, Hungary, Poland, for all—a path of light to a haven of safety and rest? Then we save the wrecker and the wrecked. We kindle lights that shine not only outward upon those ready to perish in the stormy waves of Old World oppression, but inward upon our more pitiable fellow-men, wandering in the darkness of crime, morally wrecked on the rocks of barbarism, because America has hitherto failed to provide with the light-houses of trade and power those of national righteousness and honor.

Thus and thus alone we cease to be in the seat of George the Third, fighting against the bud that by normal growth would grow from our side and climb to its fruitage. We ourselves become revolutionists against our own wrong. We emege from the ancient kingdom of Oppression, and make this a holy war,—a second Revolution achieving for the nations of the world what our first achieved for thirteen colonies.

PART VIII.

ARMAGEDDON AND AFTER.

THE REVEREND GILBERT HAVEN GLIMPSES THE MILLENNIUM (1863).

ONCE LINCOLN SIGNED the Emancipation Proclamation, the abolitionists saw their goal in sight. National atonement had created the possibility of national salvation. The war for the slave, though not yet ended, was passing through fiery destruction into a final redemptive phase which would usher in the millennium. Such was the confident prediction of the Methodist clergyman and abolitionist Gilbert Haven in a sermon preached to his Boston congregation on November 26, 1863, two days after the battle of Missionary Ridge. "The War and the Millennium," in forecasting the imminent arrival of Christian equality and brotherhood, summarizes the faith which had sustained the abolitionist crusade for thirty years. "The War and the Millennium," *National Sermons, Speeches and Letters on Slavery and its War: From the Passage of the Fugitive Slave Bill to the Election of President Grant* (Boston, 1869), 378-386.

. . . TO GAIN THIS VICTORY we are now contending.

1. The separation of man by artificial social barriers is one of the earliest and deepest expressions of our rebellious nature. . . .

All governments based on the few, by the few, and for the few, are hostile to the government of Christ, and must be abolished before His glory fully comes. They were conceived in sin and shapen in iniquity. They breed pride, licentiousness, violence in the ruler,—poverty, cowardice, sycophancy, ignorance, lawlessness in the ruled. . . . The government of man and of the Church must correspond. Both must be a brotherhood of equals.

2. Then comes the unification of Man. Unless he is one, Church nor State can ever be one. Christ cannot be the Head of our household. Whatever opposes this consummation,—blood, language, color, caste,—must give way, that Christ may be all and in all.

These vital principles are involved in our struggle. The first we saw at the first. So the whole world, kings and peoples, instinctively saw that the struggle was over that idea, over both ideas. The nation hailed the first with unbounded fervor—Union for the sake of Union. But thoughtful men hailed the grander idea that rose behind and above it,—

"Another sun risen on mid noon,"—

the Equality and Fraternity of Man. Union, not for ourselves alone, but for all men, was our strongest, our most general feeling. It carried us safely over the disastrous days of our first defeats, through that first winter of fearful idleness, when the riotous rebels built their camp-fires and boiled the bones of our slain heroes in sight of our capital. It carried us through the still more terrible calamities of the Peninsula defeats, and the yet severer defeat of our confidence in the commander of that campaign.

But the people clung with increasing devotion to their idea, and its embodiment in American nationality. Three hundred thousand men hastened to cast themselves into the gulf, that Union and democracy might be preserved. . . .

3. But a greater truth than all the rest was born of the exigencies of this hour. We found we as yet had known nothing, as it were, of the scope and fullness of that word Democracy. It was with us, at the worst, equality of white people, and the slavery of all other complexions; at the best, equality of the whites, and the liberty, but not fraternity, of the blacks. Not the oneness of man as man,—never, never. We fell into spasms at the thought of that divine truth, as a mushroom lord of England might at his equality with his servant.

But the wisdom of God is wiser than men. You did not create the doctrine of human fraternity. You may have fancied that you did; that it was your patent, and could be limited and controlled at your pleasure. So did the Athenian democrats. Where are they? So have the Southern slavemongers. Where are they? God, my friends, not you, made man, of one father, that all might be brethren, that each should in honor prefer one another, esteeming others better than themselves. He is pushing us forward to His, not our, Millennium. He is using and blessing us if we choose to work with Him. If not, He is none the less using us, while also chastising, for the advancement of mankind to the same goal. He maketh our wrath or righteousness alike to praise and prosper Him. Whether gradually, and by the operation of laws that have been molding and transforming man for ages, or suddenly, and by the breaking up of the present order and institution of a new earth and new man, as some devout students of the Bible believe, whichever be the way, the end is sure and the same. The Millennium is a world of men, equal, brotherly, united, and holy. Every approach to that state now renders its violent introduction less necessary. If it can be effected by natural causes there will be no need of the supernatural. It is being effected. The divine doctrine of democracy has become choked with weeds and stones. We said "It is true and grand, but it is only for white folks. Do you dare to say that that negro and I are of one blood, and should be one in social and civil life? that it is as much his duty to ignore my complexion as it is mine to ignore his? Horrible!" And so we stone the prophets who simply preach to us our own doctrine of democracy, rationally and divinely developed.

But God is taking vengeance on us for destroying His servants, and is compelling us to rise to the heights [*sic*] of our own principles at the threat of losing all its lower developments, which we see to be our essential life. We listen, refuse, yield, and most reluctantly obey. . . .

Thus shall the millennial day break upon the world. It may be in a day. Events are hastening it forward. Every step in Europe is to emancipation, equalization, unification. There is no possibility of peace there on any other basis. Nor is there here.

Christendom thus unified, heathendom and Islamdom will soon be regenerated. Social vices will abate their violence. Liberty and unity will prevent wars and armaments, royal houses, and luxurious absorption by a few families of the people's wealth. Legitimate industry will pay the old debts of kings and crimes, and easily supply the slight demands of a popular and peaceful government. Intemperance, Sabbath-breaking, infidelity, all the fruits of crowned and Catholic Europe, will be replaced with the graces of Christianity. The Lord Jesus will be the real and recognized, if not visible, sovereign of the world. . . .

WILLIAM LLOYD GARRISON AND WENDELL PHILLIPS

RESOLVE THE FATE OF THE AMERICAN ANTI-SLAVERY SOCIETY (1865).

WITH THE END of the war and the coming of Reconstruction the abolitionists faced the question of whether to continue their work in behalf of the freedmen or to disband. This was the issue confronting the American Anti-Slavery Society at its meeting in May, 1865. Declaring that the work of the Society was now done, Garrison, his radicalism tempered by victory and accolades, called for dissolution. His speech in support of the motion summarized his own version of the meaning and purpose of the abolitionist crusade and at the same time betrayed his essentially conservative social philosophy. Wendell Phillips, rejecting outright the reasoning of his old friend and arguing for the continuance of the Society, insisted that the real work of creating racial democracy had only begun. When his resolution to dissolve the society was decisively beaten, Garrison refused to accept the presidency and Phillips was elected in his place. The American Anti-Slavery Society continued to exist without the support of the old leaders until 1870 when, with the passage of the Fifteenth Amendment, Phillips announced that at last "our long work is sealed." *Liberator,* May 26, 1865.

MR. GARRISON: . . . This Society is "The American *Anti-Slavery* Society." That was the object. The thought never entered my mind then [i.e., when composing the Declaration of Sentiments of the American Anti-Slavery Society in 1833], nor has it at any time since, that when slavery had received its death wound, there would be any disposition or occasion to continue the Anti-Slavery Society a moment longer. But, of course, in looking over the country, we saw the free colored people more or less laboring under disabilities, and suffering from injustice, and we declared that, incidentally, we did not mean to overlook them, but should vindicate their rights, and endeavor to get justice done to them. The point is here. We organized expressly for the abolition of slavery; we called our Society an *Anti-Slavery* Society. The other work was incidental. Now, I believe slavery is abolished in this country; abolished constitutionally; abolished by a decree of this nation, never, never to be

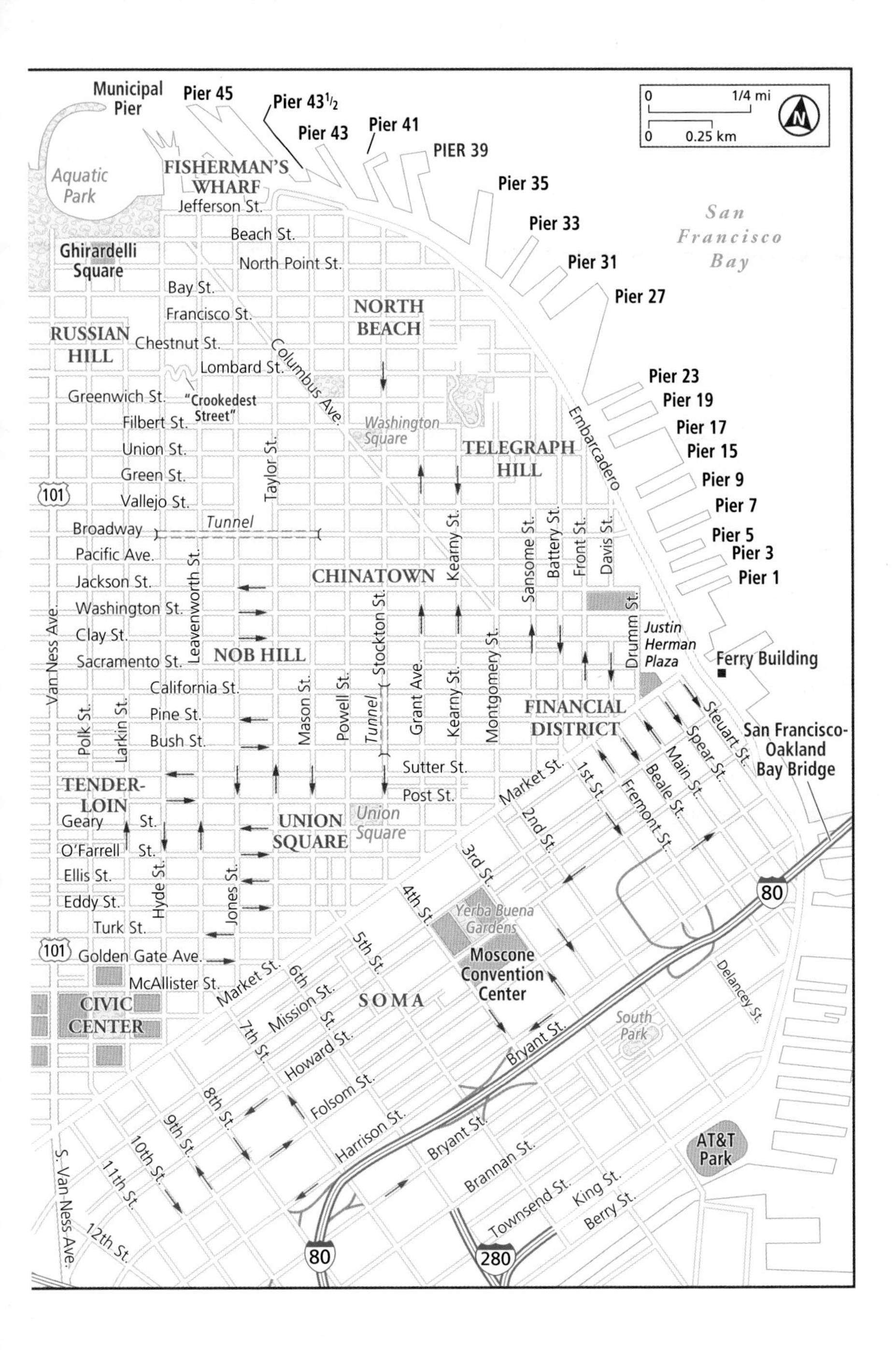
Municipal Pier
Pier 45
Pier 43½
Pier 43
Pier 41
PIER 39
Pier 35
Pier 33
Pier 31
Pier 27
Pier 23
Pier 19
Pier 17
Pier 15
Pier 9
Pier 7
Pier 5
Pier 3
Pier 1
0 1/4 mi
0 0.25 km
N
San Francisco Bay
Aquatic Park
FISHERMAN'S WHARF
Jefferson St.
Beach St.
North Point St.
Ghirardelli Square
Bay St.
Francisco St.
NORTH BEACH
RUSSIAN HILL
Chestnut St.
Lombard St.
Columbus Ave.
Greenwich St.
"Crookedest Street"
Filbert St.
Washington Square
Union St.
Green St.
Vallejo St.
Broadway
Tunnel
Pacific Ave.
Jackson St.
Washington St.
Clay St.
Sacramento St.
California St.
Pine St.
Bush St.
Sutter St.
Post St.
Geary St.
O'Farrell St.
Ellis St.
Eddy St.
Turk St.
Golden Gate Ave.
McAllister St.
101
TELEGRAPH HILL
Embarcadero
Taylor St.
Kearny St.
Sansome St.
Battery St.
Front St.
Davis St.
Drumm St.
CHINATOWN
Leavenworth St.
Stockton St.
Montgomery St.
Justin Herman Plaza
Ferry Building
NOB HILL
Van Ness Ave.
Mason St.
Powell St.
Grant Ave.
FINANCIAL DISTRICT
Steuart St.
Spear St.
Main St.
Beale St.
Fremont St.
1st St.
2nd St.
Market St.
San Francisco-Oakland Bay Bridge
Polk St.
Larkin St.
TENDER-LOIN
Hyde St.
Jones St.
UNION SQUARE
Union Square
3rd St.
4th St.
5th St.
6th St.
7th St.
8th St.
9th St.
10th St.
11th St.
12th St.
80
Yerba Buena Gardens
Moscone Convention Center
Delancey St.
CIVIC CENTER
Mission St.
SOMA
Howard St.
Folsom St.
Harrison St.
Bryant St.
South Park
Brannan St.
Townsend St.
King St.
Berry St.
AT&T Park
S. Van Ness Ave.
280

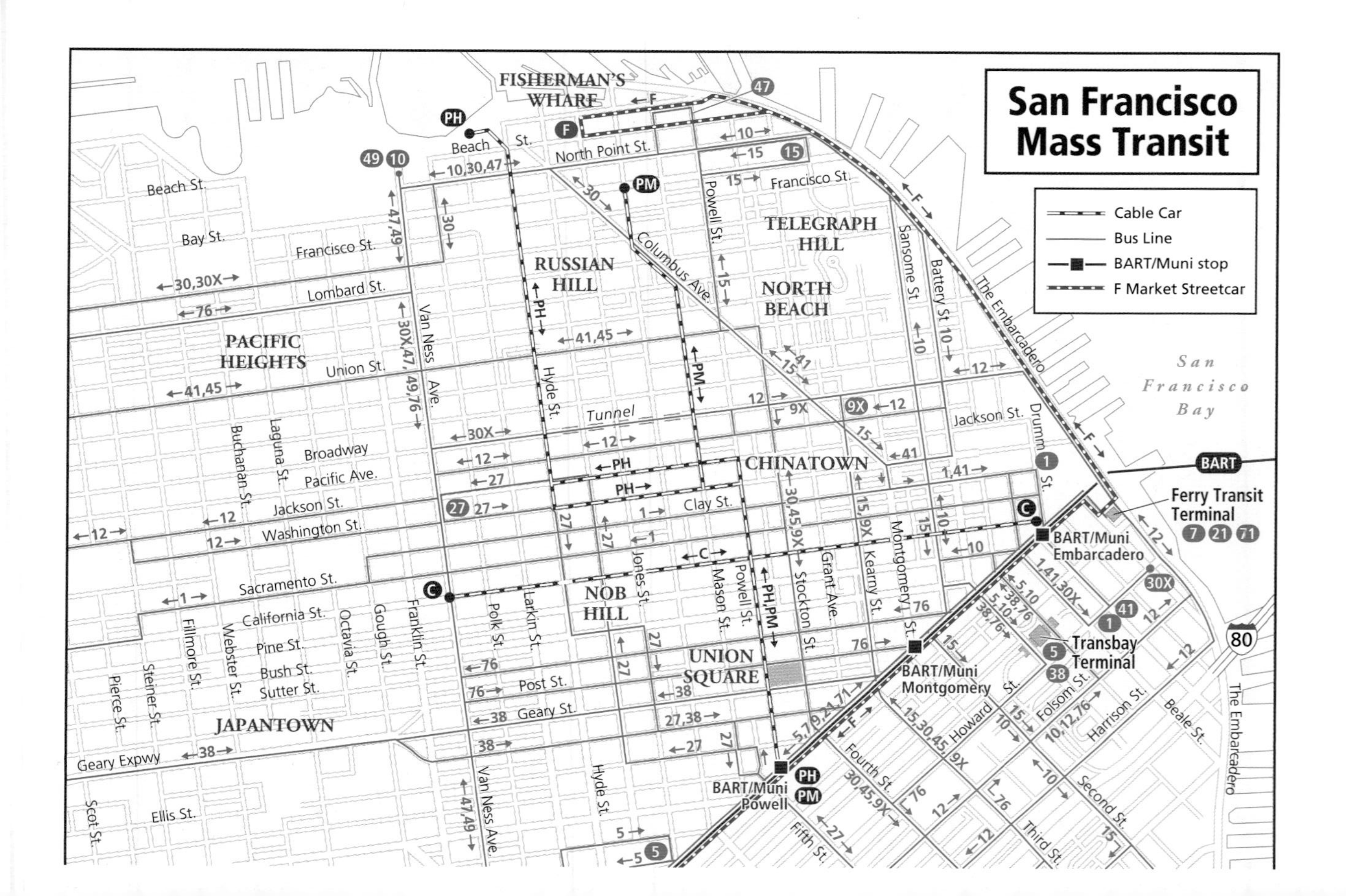
San Francisco Mass Transit
Cable Car
Bus Line
BART/Muni stop
F Market Streetcar
San Francisco Bay
BART
Ferry Transit Terminal
BART/Muni Embarcadero
Transbay Terminal
BART/Muni Montgomery
BART/Muni Powell
FISHERMAN'S WHARF
TELEGRAPH HILL
NORTH BEACH
RUSSIAN HILL
CHINATOWN
NOB HILL
UNION SQUARE
PACIFIC HEIGHTS
JAPANTOWN
The Embarcadero
Battery St
Sansome St
Montgomery St.
Kearny St.
Grant Ave.
Stockton St.
Powell St.
Mason St.
Jones St.
Hyde St.
Larkin St.
Polk St.
Van Ness Ave.
Franklin St.
Gough St.
Octavia St.
Laguna St.
Buchanan St.
Webster St.
Fillmore St.
Steiner St.
Pierce St.
Scot St.
Drumm St.
Jackson St.
Clay St.
Washington St.
Sacramento St.
California St.
Pine St.
Bush St.
Sutter St.
Post St.
Geary St.
Geary Expwy
Ellis St.
Union St.
Broadway
Pacific Ave.
Lombard St.
Francisco St.
Bay St.
Beach St.
North Point St.
Columbus Ave.
Tunnel
Beale St.
Harrison St.
Folsom St.
Howard St.
Second St.
Third St.
Fourth St.
Fifth St.
80

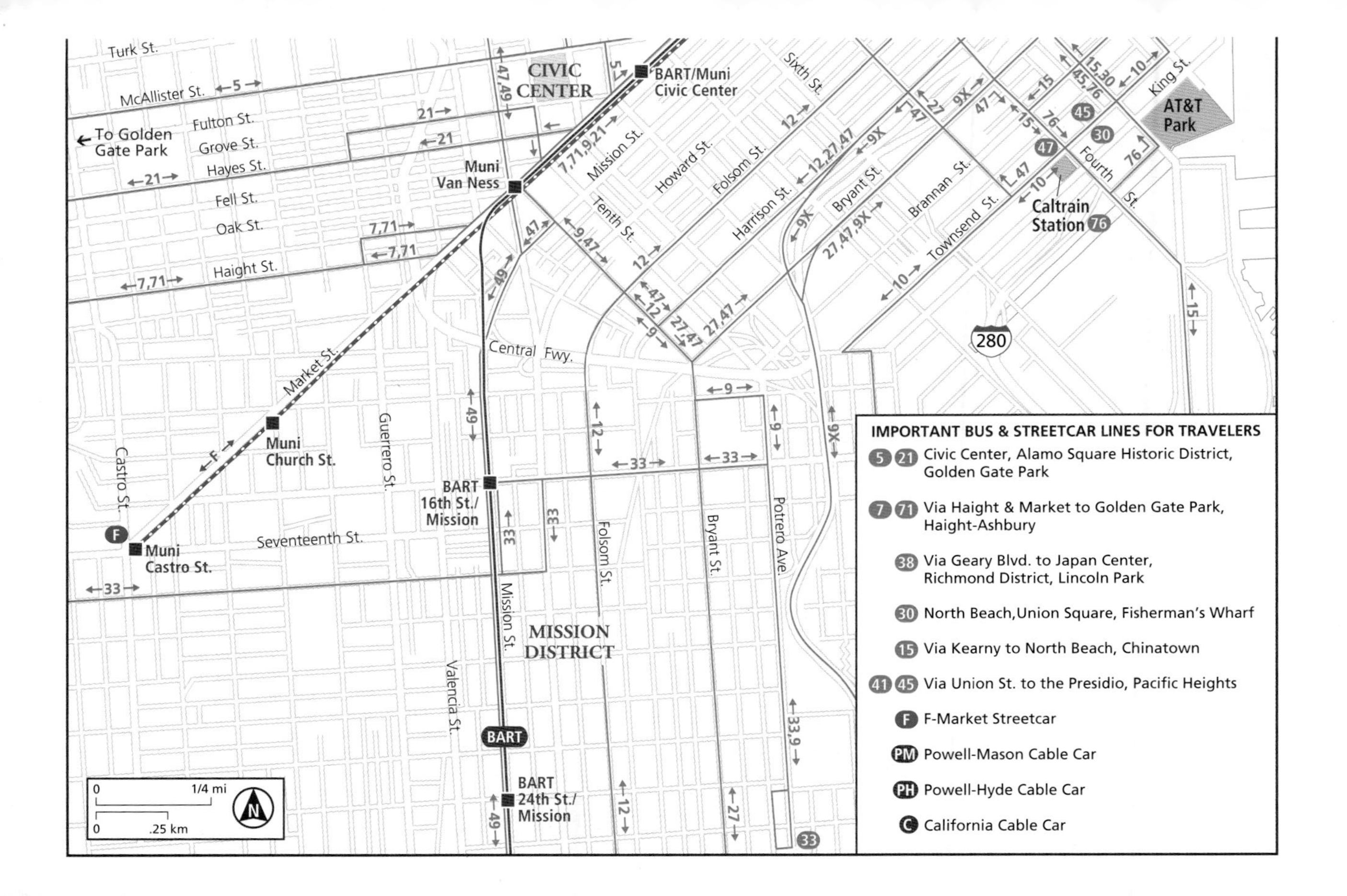
IMPORTANT BUS & STREETCAR LINES FOR TRAVELERS
5 21 Civic Center, Alamo Square Historic District, Golden Gate Park
7 71 Via Haight & Market to Golden Gate Park, Haight-Ashbury
38 Via Geary Blvd. to Japan Center, Richmond District, Lincoln Park
30 North Beach,Union Square, Fisherman's Wharf
15 Via Kearny to North Beach, Chinatown
41 45 Via Union St. to the Presidio, Pacific Heights
F F-Market Streetcar
PM Powell-Mason Cable Car
PH Powell-Hyde Cable Car
C California Cable Car
CIVIC CENTER
MISSION DISTRICT
AT&T Park
Caltrain Station
BART/Muni Civic Center
Muni Van Ness
Muni Church St.
Muni Castro St.
BART 16th St./Mission
BART 24th St./Mission
To Golden Gate Park
Turk St.
McAllister St.
Fulton St.
Grove St.
Hayes St.
Fell St.
Oak St.
Haight St.
Market St.
Castro St.
Seventeenth St.
Guerrero St.
Valencia St.
Mission St.
Folsom St.
Bryant St.
Potrero Ave.
Central Fwy.
Tenth St.
Howard St.
Harrison St.
Brannan St.
Townsend St.
Sixth St.
Fourth St.
King St.
280
0 1/4 mi
0 .25 km

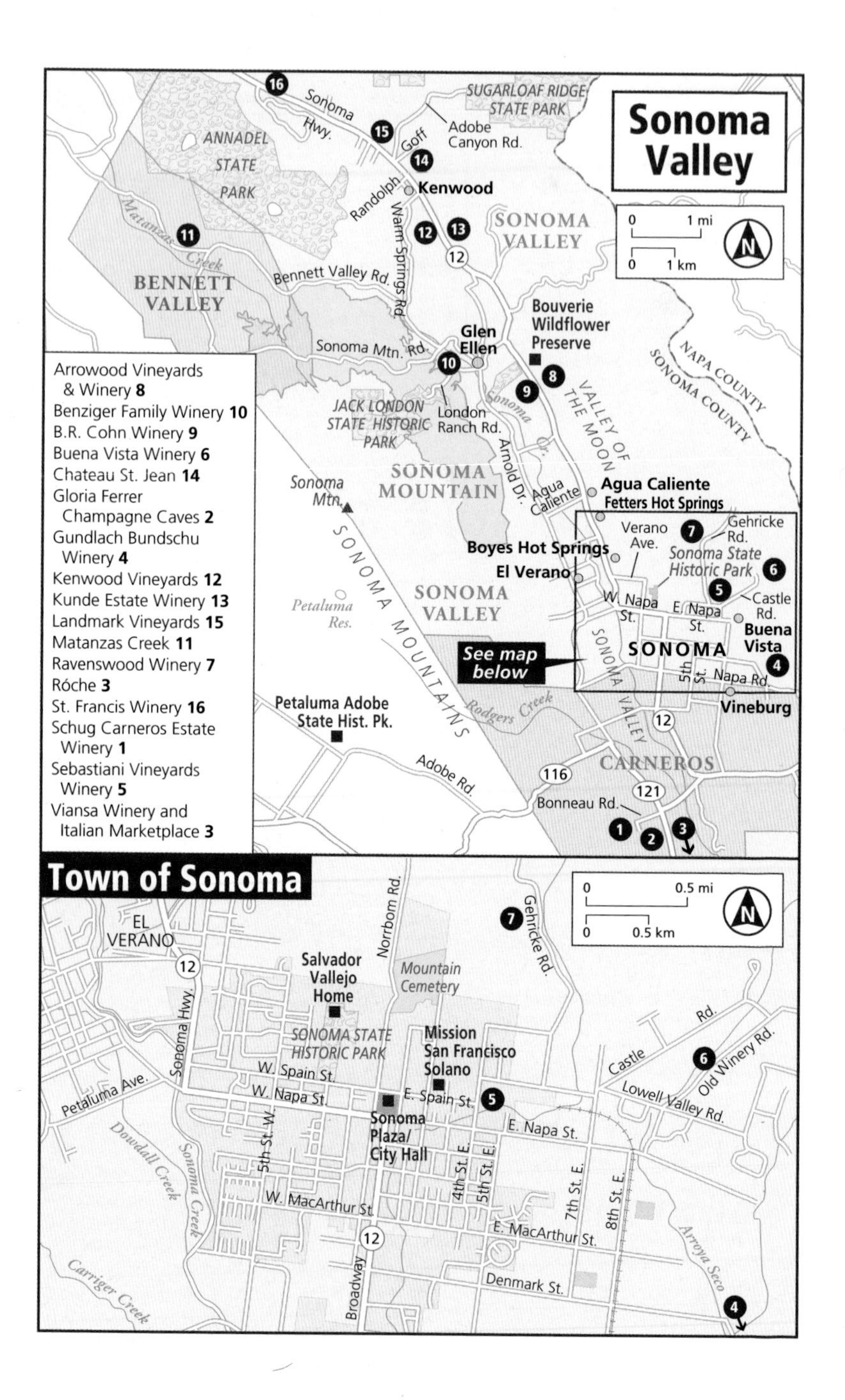

Sonoma Valley
0 1 mi
0 1 km
N
Arrowood Vineyards & Winery 8
Benziger Family Winery 10
B.R. Cohn Winery 9
Buena Vista Winery 6
Chateau St. Jean 14
Gloria Ferrer Champagne Caves 2
Gundlach Bundschu Winery 4
Kenwood Vineyards 12
Kunde Estate Winery 13
Landmark Vineyards 15
Matanzas Creek 11
Ravenswood Winery 7
Róche 3
St. Francis Winery 16
Schug Carneros Estate Winery 1
Sebastiani Vineyards Winery 5
Viansa Winery and Italian Marketplace 3
SUGARLOAF RIDGE STATE PARK
Sonoma Hwy.
Adobe Canyon Rd.
Goff
ANNADEL STATE PARK
Kenwood
Randolph
Warm Springs Rd.
SONOMA VALLEY
Matanzas Creek
BENNETT VALLEY
Bennett Valley Rd.
Bouverie Wildflower Preserve
Glen Ellen
Sonoma Mtn. Rd.
NAPA COUNTY
SONOMA COUNTY
JACK LONDON STATE HISTORIC PARK
London Ranch Rd.
Sonoma Cr.
VALLEY OF THE MOON
Arnold Dr.
SONOMA MOUNTAIN
Sonoma Mtn.
Agua Caliente
Agua Caliente
Fetters Hot Springs
Verano Ave.
Gehricke Rd.
Boyes Hot Springs
Sonoma State Historic Park
El Verano
SONOMA MOUNTAINS
Petaluma Res.
SONOMA VALLEY
W. Napa St.
E. Napa St.
Castle Rd.
Buena Vista
SONOMA
See map below
5th St.
Napa Rd.
Vineburg
Rodgers Creek
Petaluma Adobe State Hist. Pk.
CARNEROS
Adobe Rd.
Bonneau Rd.
Town of Sonoma
0 0.5 mi
0 0.5 km
EL VERANO
Norrbom Rd.
Gehricke Rd.
Salvador Vallejo Home
Mountain Cemetery
Sonoma Hwy.
SONOMA STATE HISTORIC PARK
Mission San Francisco Solano
Castle Rd.
Old Winery Rd.
W. Spain St.
Petaluma Ave.
W. Napa St.
E. Spain St.
Lowell Valley Rd.
Sonoma Plaza/ City Hall
E. Napa St.
Dowdall Creek
Sonoma Creek
5th St. W.
4th St. E.
5th St. E.
7th St. E.
8th St. E.
W. MacArthur St.
E. MacArthur St.
Arroya Seco
Broadway
Denmark St.
Carriger Creek

Frommer's®

San Francisco

2008

by Matthew Richard Poole
and Erika Lenkert

Here's what the critics say about Frommer's:

"Amazingly easy to use. Very portable, very complete."

—*Booklist*

"Detailed, accurate, and easy-to-read information for all price ranges."

—*Glamour Magazine*

"Hotel information is close to encyclopedic."

—*Des Moines Sunday Register*

BICENTENNIAL 1807 WILEY 2007 BICENTENNIAL

Wiley Publishing, Inc.

Published by:

Wiley Publishing, Inc.

111 River St.
Hoboken, NJ 07030-5774

ISBN: 978-0-470-14437-4

Editor: Marc Nadeau
Production Editor: Katie Robinson
Cartographer: Guy Ruggiero
Photo Editor: Richard Fox
Anniversary Logo Design: Richard Pacifico
Production by Wiley Indianapolis Composition Services

For information on our other products and services or to obtain technical support, please contact our Customer Care Department within the U.S. at 800/762-2974, outside the U.S. at 317/572-3993 or fax 317/572-4002.

Wiley also publishes its books in a variety of electronic formats. Some content that appears in print may not be available in electronic formats.

Manufactured in the United States of America

5 4 3 2 1

Contents

5 Where to Stay 57

6 Where to Dine 98

7 Exploring San Francisco 148

8 City Strolls 192

9 Shopping 205

10 San Francisco After Dark 223

11 Side Trips from San Francisco 245

12 The Wine Country 272

by Erika Lenkert

Index 327

List of Maps

An Invitation to the Reader

In researching this book, we discovered many wonderful places—hotels, restaurants, shops, and more. We're sure you'll find others. Please tell us about them, so we can share the information with your fellow travelers in upcoming editions. If you were disappointed with a recommendation, we'd love to know that, too. Please write to:

Frommer's San Francisco 2008
Wiley Publishing, Inc. • 111 River St. • Hoboken, NJ 07030-5774

An Additional Note

Please be advised that travel information is subject to change at any time—and this is especially true of prices. We therefore suggest that you write or call ahead for confirmation when making your travel plans. The authors, editors, and publisher cannot be held responsible for the experiences of readers while traveling. Your safety is important to us, however, so we encourage you to stay alert and be aware of your surroundings. Keep a close eye on cameras, purses, and wallets, all favorite targets of thieves and pickpockets.

About the Authors

Matthew Richard Poole, a native Californian, has authored more than two dozen travel guides to California, Hawaii, and abroad, and is a regular contributor to radio and television travel programs, including numerous guest appearances on the award-winning *Bay Area Backroads* television show. Before becoming a full-time travel writer and photographer, he worked as an English tutor in Prague, a ski instructor in the Swiss Alps, and a scuba instructor in Maui and Thailand. He currently lives in San Francisco but spends most of his time on the road searching for new adventures. His other Frommer's titles include *California, San Francisco,* the *Irreverent Guide to San Francisco,* and *Portable Disneyland.*

A native San Franciscan, **Erika Lenkert** divides her time between San Francisco and Napa Valley where she is forever seeking the next best restaurant, hotel room, and fun way to savor the region. She frequently writes *InStyle* magazine's party guides and offers up tasty tips on the region for *Food & Wine* magazine. In her spare time she pays visits to local and national television news programs where she gives entertaining and cooking tips based on her book *The Last-Minute Party Girl: Fashionable, Fearless, and Foolishly Simple Entertaining.*

Frommer's Star Ratings, Icons & Abbreviations

Every hotel, restaurant, and attraction listing in this guide has been ranked for quality, value, service, amenities, and special features using a **star-rating system.** In country, state, and regional guides, we also rate towns and regions to help you narrow down your choices and budget your time accordingly. Hotels and restaurants are rated on a scale of zero (recommended) to three stars (exceptional). Attractions, shopping, nightlife, towns, and regions are rated according to the following scale: zero stars (recommended), one star (highly recommended), two stars (very highly recommended), and three stars (must-see).

In addition to the star-rating system, we also use **seven feature icons** that point you to the great deals, in-the-know advice, and unique experiences that separate travelers from tourists. Throughout the book, look for:

Finds	Special finds—those places only insiders know about
Fun Fact	Fun facts—details that make travelers more informed and their trips more fun
Kids	Best bets for kids and advice for the whole family
Moments	Special moments—those experiences that memories are made of
Overrated	Places or experiences not worth your time or money
Tips	Insider tips—great ways to save time and money
Value	Great values—where to get the best deals

The following **abbreviations** are used for credit cards:

AE American Express
DC Diners Club
DISC Discover
MC MasterCard
V Visa

Frommers.com

Now that you have this guidebook, to help you plan a great trip, visit our website at **www.frommers.com** for additional travel information on more than 3,600 destinations. We update features regularly, to give you instant access to the most current trip-planning information available. At Frommers.com, you'll find scoops on the best airfares, lodging rates, and car rental bargains. You can even book your travel online through our reliable travel booking partners. Other popular features include:

- Online updates of our most popular guidebooks
- Vacation sweepstakes and contest giveaways
- Newsletters highlighting the hottest travel trends
- Online travel message boards with featured travel discussions

What's New in San Francisco

What's new in San Francisco is that the city has become obsessed with going green. Never a city to just follow environmental issues, San Francisco is aggressively spearheading America's movement to reduce greenhouse gasses by showing its citizens and corporations how even little changes can, in the long run, make a difference to the environment. And because tourism is the world's largest industry, even you can contribute to the environmentally conscious campaign by being a carbon-neutral vacationer. Here's how:

PLAN GREEN First, let's save you some other kind of green—money. If you plan on seeing a lot of attractions in the city, you might want to purchase the new **Go San Francisco Card,** a sort of money-saving E-Ticket that gets you pre-paid entry to about 45 of the most popular attractions in the city, Bay Area, and Wine Country, including museums, walking tours, bike rentals, wine tastings, and sightseeing tours.

Another option is the **San Francisco CityPass,** which focuses more on the city-wide sights and costs slightly less. I suggest researching both via their websites to decide which is better for you. By the way, both the Go Card and CityPass offer unlimited public transportation—including cable cars, Metro streetcars, and the entire bus system—throughout the city, so you'll increase your carbon-neutral karma just by purchasing one. See p. 11 for details.

EXPLORE GREEN In the previous edition there was a suggested itinerary that involved driving to and around the Wine Country—not a very eco-friendly way to spend the day. So I've replaced it with my favorite thing to do in the entire Bay Area: ride a bike from Fisherman's Wharf to Tiburon (a small town just across the bay). It's a beautiful, exhilarating, and environmentally conscious way to spend the day. The route takes you over the Golden Gate Bridge, through the heart of Sausalito, and finally to Tiburon, where you can have a frosty beer and lunch at the best outdoor cafe in the Bay Area. And here's the best part: You don't have to bike back. After lunch, you and your bike can take the passenger ferry across the bay to Fisherman's Wharf—right back to where you started. See p. 188.

SLEEP GREEN Yes, even the hotel you stay in can make a difference to the environment. For example, the city's new $25-million-dollar **Orchard Garden Hotel** (p. 67) is part of California's first generation of truly "green" hotels and the only hotel in the state built to the nationally accepted standards for green buildings developed by the U.S. Green Building Council (USGBC). Just about every aspect of the vanguard accommodations is geared towards creating a healthy environment for guests and staff, from the eco-friendly construction materials to an in-room recycling system.

Numerous other hotels within the city are joining the green bandwagon as well, from using citrus-based cleaning products to installing low-flow toilets and fluorescent or LED lighting.

You can do your part as well by asking about a hotel's commitment to environmental preservation before you make a reservation, and by leaving a note for housekeeping stating that you don't need the towels or sheets changed daily (thereby saving water and energy).

DINE GREEN Even what and where you eat can make a difference. Transportation accounts for 14% of the energy used for food in the U.S. (an estimated 100 billion gallons of oil per year). By eating at restaurants that obtain their ingredients within the Bay Area "food shed"—the region within 100 miles of the city—you can help cut down the amount of carbon dioxide produced by long-haul trucks, ships, trains, and planes.

You'll help save even more energy by patronizing sustainable restaurants that only purchase organically grown foods (processing foods and manufacturing fertilizers and pesticides consume significant amounts of energy).

I've added 23 more restaurants to this edition, almost all of which use locally harvested organic foods, steroid-free meats from Northern California ranchers, and fresh coastal seafood as often as possible—much of it purchased by local chefs directly from our amazing **Farmers' Market** (p. 216). Some of my favorite supporters include **A16, Ame, Chez Panisse** (of course), **Delfina, Kokkari, The Slanted Door,** and **Zuni Café,** but there are dozens more throughout the city.

By the way, bottled water is a huge waste of resources and energy—it has to be processed, bottled, and transported from as far away as Asia and Europe. San Francisco's tap water comes from the Yosemite mountains. It's both safe to drink and clean tasting, so next time tell your waiter you want Hetch Hetchy Reservoir's finest.

PLAY GREEN Who thought going green could be so much fun? A new tour run by the **San Francisco Electric Tour Company** (p. 154) lets you ride around on Segway Human Transporters, those weird-looking, upright, battery-powered scooters you've probably seen on TV. After a 40-minute lesson, you tool around Fisherman's Wharf on a fun and informative guided tour (*way* better than a stinky, polluting bus tour).

But wait, there's more. Be sure to check out the new talking **GoCars** (p. 158). I see them all over town now—the tiny yellow three-wheeled convertible vehicles that are cleverly guided by a talking GPS (Global Positioning System) and give a computer-guided tour of the city's highlights. As you drive, the talking car tells you where to turn and what landmarks you're passing. It's both fun and far more energy efficient than a car or tour bus.

In other news, the magnificent **de Young Museum** (p. 161) in Golden Gate Park is the city's new must-see site. The museum's collection includes American paintings, African arts, sculptural and decorative arts, and textiles, but it's the building itself that will amaze you—a striking facade consisting of 950,000 pounds of textured and perforated copper and a 144-foot tower that slowly spirals toward the sky.

Over at Fisherman's Wharf is the gargantuan new **Boudin at the Wharf** (p. 152), a 26,000-square-foot baking emporium that's nearly half a block longand houses not only their signature demonstration bakery (strangely mesmerizing) but also a museum, gourmet marketplace, cafe, espresso bar, and restaurant.

And since we're on the green theme, I can't help but mention my favorite museum: **The Exploratorium** (p. 162). *Scientific American* magazine calls it "the best science museum in the world" and I couldn't agree more. Inside you'll find dozens of mind-blowing interactive exhibits, including ones that study how human activity affects the earth's climate (and how you can help make a difference). It's like a mad scientist's penny arcade, an educational fun house, and an experimental laboratory all rolled into one.

GIVE BACK GREEN Simple changes in the way you travel: That's all it takes to go from being just another tourist to becoming part of the growing community of proactive vacationers who find satisfaction in giving back to the environment as much as they're taking—if not more.

And what better way to say thank you to the city than to plant a few trees before you leave? About 40 trees are planted every Saturday on the streets of San Francisco with the help of residents and volunteers. The planting finishes around noon with a potluck lunch hosted by the neighbors to thank volunteers for their time. Call **Friends of the Urban Forest** (© **415/561-6890;** www.fuf.net) before you arrive to see how you can help make a difference.

1

The Best of San Francisco

In a city where parade themes include "Weapons of Ass Destruction" and starting your holiday with an Irish coffee at the Buena Vista Café is de rigueur, it's pretty much guaranteed that you'll have a fun time vacationing in San Francisco. Where else in the world will you find a restaurant whose servers are all gorgeous transvestites? Where it's considered good, clean fun to get airborne in your car? Or where locals don't even pause for earthquakes under 5.0 on the Richter scale?

And it's always been this way: San Francisco's reputation as a rollicking city where almost anything goes dates back to the boom-or-bust days of the California Gold Rush. The result is a wee bit o' heaven for everyone: In a city that is so beautiful, exciting, and cosmopolitan there's always something enjoyable to see and do no matter how long you're staying. I've lived here for 14 years and I'm still discovering new things about this city almost every day.

There are, however, three things you should know before coming to San Francisco that will help you blend in with the locals. First, don't call it 'Frisco. (You wouldn't call New York just "York," would you?) Second, please don't call our beloved cable cars "trolleys." A trolley is a British shopping cart. Third, always dress warmly. Bob Hope once remarked that San Francisco is the city of four seasons—every day. Temperatures can drop darn quick when the fog rolls in, so be prepared.

But the best advice I can give you about San Francisco is to just *go.* Enjoy the cool blast of salty air as you stroll across the Golden Gate. Stuff yourself with dim sum in Chinatown. Browse the secondhand shops along Haight Street. Recite poetry in a North Beach coffeehouse. Walk along the beach, skate through Golden Gate Park, ride the cable cars, tour a Victorian mansion, explore Alcatraz Island, go to a Giants ballgame: Like an eternal world's fair, it's all happening in San Francisco, and everyone's invited. All you have to do is arrive with an open mind, this guidebook, and a sense of adventure—the rest is waiting for you.

Right then. Let's get this vacation started.

1 The Best Only-in-San Francisco Experiences

- **A Powell-Hyde Cable-Car Ride:** Skip the less-scenic California line and take the Powell-Hyde cable car down to Fisherman's Wharf—the ride is worth the wait. When you reach the top of Nob Hill, grab the rail with one hand and hold your camera with the other, because you're about to see a view of the bay that'll make you all weepy. See p. 152.
- **An Adventure at Alcatraz:** Even if you loathe tourist attractions, you'll dig Alcatraz. Just looking at The Rock from across the bay is enough to give you the heebie-jeebies—and the park rangers have put together an

excellent audio tour. Heck, even the boat ride across the bay is worth the price. See p. 148.

- **A Walk across the Golden Gate Bridge:** Don your windbreaker and walking shoes and prepare for a wind-blasted, exhilarating journey across San Francisco's most famous landmark. It's simply one of those things you have to do at least once in your life. See p. 158.
- **A Stroll through Chinatown:** Chinatown is a trip. I've been through it at least 100 times, and it has never failed to entertain me. Skip the ersatz camera and luggage stores and head straight for the food markets, where a cornucopia of critters that you'll never see at Safeway sit in boxes waiting for the wok. (Is that an armadillo?) Better yet, take one of Shirley Fong-Torres's Wok Wiz Tours of Chinatown (p. 186).
- **Watching the San Francisco Giants play at AT&T Park:** If it's baseball season, then you *must* spend an afternoon or evening watching the National League's Giants lose at one of the finest ballparks in America. For only $10 you can buy a bleacher-seat ticket on the day of a game. Even if the season's over, you can still take a guided tour of the stadium. See p. 149.

2 The Best Splurge Hotels

- **The Ritz-Carlton,** 600 Stockton St., Nob Hill (✆ **800/241-3333** or 415/296-7465; www.ritzcarlton.com), is the sine qua non of luxury hotels, offering near-perfect service and every possible amenity. Even if you can't afford a guest room, come for the mind-blowing Sunday brunch. See p. 76.
- **Four Seasons Hotel San Francisco,** 757 Market St., SoMa (✆ **800/819-5053** or 415/633-3000; www.fourseasons.com), is the perfect combination of opulence, hipness, and class. I can't afford it either, but I sure love to hang out at the bar and pretend. See p. 78.
- **The Mandarin Oriental,** 222 Sansome St., Financial District (✆ **800/622-0404** or 415/276-9888; www.mandarinoriental.com/sanfrancisco), is perched so high above the city that the fog rolls in *below* you. It's surreal. Maybe I really did die and go to heaven? See p. 85.
- **The St. Regis Hotel,** 125 Third St., SoMa (✆ **877/787-3447** or 415/284-4000; www.stregis.com/sanfrancisco), has these touch-screen remote controls that let you operate everything in your room—without leaving your bed. Add a destination restaurant and a fabulous two-floor spa, and why would you ever want to leave? See p. 79.

3 The Best Moderately Priced Hotels

- **Laurel Inn,** 444 Presidio Ave., Pacific Heights (✆ **800/552-8735** or 415/567-8467; www.thelaurelinn.com), may be off the beaten track, but it's one of the best affordable, fashionable hotels in the city. Just outside of the southern entrance to the Presidio in the midst of residential Presidio Heights, it's a chic motel with soothing, contemporary decor and equally calming prices. See p. 91.
- **Hotel Bohème,** 444 Columbus Ave. (✆ **415/433-9111;** www.hotelboheme.com), is the perfect mixture of art, style, class, romance, and location—just steps from the sidewalk

cafes of North Beach. If Bette Davis were alive today, this is where she'd stay. See p. 88.

- **The Warwick Regis,** 490 Geary St., Union Square (✆ **800/203-3232** or 415/928-7900; www.warwicksf.com), is for travelers who prefer stately old-world style over floral fun. Extremely well cared for and beautifully decorated, it's one of my favorite midrange picks. See p. 70.
- **Hotel Adagio,** 550 Geary St., Union Square (✆ **800/228-8830** or 415/775-5000; www.thehoteladagio.com), is far more chic and hip than its category counterparts. The 1929 Spanish Revival building has sexy streamlined rooms swathed in rich shades of brown, and a very chic restaurant and bar on the ground level. See p. 65.
- **The Golden Gate Hotel,** 775 Bush St. (✆ **800/835-1118;** www.goldengatehotel.com), receives nothing but kudos from satisfied guests. Just 2 blocks from Union Square, this 1913 Edwardian hotel is a real charmer and a fantastic value. See p. 72.

4 The Best Dining Experiences

- **The Best of the City's Fine Dining:** Restaurant **Michael Mina,** 335 Powell St., Union Square (✆ **415/397-9222**), is the place to go for Union Square fine dining. Dozens of fancifully presented small portions add up to a delightfully long, lavish meal. And then there's **Restaurant Gary Danko,** 800 North Point St., Fisherman's Wharf (✆ **415/749-2060**), always a sure bet for a perfect contemporary French meal complete with polished service and flambéed finales. See p. 102 and p. 127, respectively.
- **Best Classic San Francisco Dining Experience:** The lovable loudmouths working behind the narrow counter of the **Swan Oyster Depot,** 1517 Polk St. (✆ **415/673-1101**), have been satisfying patrons with fresh crab, shrimp, oysters, and clam chowder since 1912. My dad doesn't care much for visiting San Francisco ("Too crowded!") but he loves having lunch at this beloved seafood institution. See p. 117.
- **Best Dining on Dungeness Crab:** Eating fresh Dungeness crabmeat straight from Fisherman's Wharf seafood vendors' boiling pots at the corner of Jefferson and Taylor streets is the quintessential San Francisco experience. See p. 155.
- **Best Dim Sum Feast:** If you like Chinese food and the current small-plates craze, you'll love to "do dim sum." At the city's best dim sum house, **Ton Kiang,** 5821 Geary Blvd., the Richmond (✆ **415/387-8273**), p. 147, you'll be wowed by the variety of dumplings and mysterious dishes. For downtown dim sum, the venerable **Yank Sing,** 101 Spear St. (✆ **415/957-9300**), p. 110, offers an exotic edible surprise on every cart that's wheeled to your table.
- **Best Breakfast:** We have a tie: **Dottie's True Blue Café,** 522 Jones St. (✆ **415/885-2767**), p. 106, has taken the classic American breakfast to a new level—maybe the best I've ever had. Crummy neighborhood, superb food. **Ella's,** 500 Presidio Ave. (✆ **415/441-5669**), is far more yuppie, equally as divine, and in a much better neighborhood, but it's so popular that the wait on weekend mornings is brutal. See p. 132.
- **Best Funky Atmosphere:** That's an easy one: **Tommy's Joynt,** 1101 Geary Blvd. (✆ **415/775-4216**). The interior looks like a Buffalo Bill museum that imploded, the exterior

paint job looks like a circus tent on acid, and the huge trays of *hofbrau* classics will make your arteries harden just by looking at them. See p. 140.

- **Best Family-Style Restaurant:** Giant platters of classic Italian food and carafes filled with table wine are placed on long wooden tables by motherly waitresses while Sinatra classics play to the festive crowd of contented diners. Welcome to North Beach–style family dining at **Capp's Corner,** 1600 Powell St. (© **415/989-2589**). See p. 123.
- **Best Surreal Dining Experience:** This has to be sitting cross-legged on a pillow, shoes off, smoking apricot tobacco out of a hookah, eating baba ghanouj, and drinking spiced wine in an exotic Middle Eastern setting while beautiful, sensuous belly dancers glide across the dining room. Unwind your mind at **Kan Zaman,** 1793 Haight St. (© **415/751-9656**). See p. 145.
- **Best Wine Country Dining:** If you're a foodie, you already know that one of the top restaurants in the world, **French Laundry,** 6640 Washington St. (© **707/944-2380**), p. 301, is about 1½ hours north of the city in Wine Country's tiny town of Yountville. Only die-hard diners need apply: You'll need to fight for a reservation 2 months in advance. A more relaxed alternative is **Terra,** 1345 Railroad Ave., St. Helena (© **707/963-8931**), where award-winning chef Hiro Sone shows his culinary creativity and mastery of French, Italian, and Japanese cuisine within a historic fieldstone split dining room. See p. 305.

5 The Best Things to Do for Free (or Almost)

- **Meander along the Marina's Golden Gate Promenade and Crissy Field.** There's something about strolling the promenade that just feels right. The combination of beach, bay, boats, Golden Gate views, and clean cool breezes is good for the soul. See p. 178.
- **Wake up with North Beach coffee.** One of the most pleasurable smells of San Francisco is the aroma of roasted coffee beans wafting down Columbus Avenue in the early morning. Start the day with a cup of Viennese on a sidewalk table at **Caffè Grecco** (423 Columbus Ave.; © 415/397-6261), followed by a walk down Columbus Avenue to the bay.
- **Browse the Haight.** Though the power of the flower has wilted, the Haight is still, more or less, the Haight: a sort of resting home for aging hippies, ex-Deadheads, skate punks, and an eclectic assortment of young panhandlers. Think of it as a people zoo as you walk down the rows of used-clothing stores, hip boutiques, and leather shops, trying hard not to stare at that girl (at least I *think* it's a girl) with the pierced eyebrows and shaved head. End the mystery tour with a pitcher of sangria and a plate of mussels at **Cha Cha Cha** (p. 144), one of my favorite restaurants that's a bargain to boot.
- **Pretend to be a guest at the Palace or Fairmont hotels.** You may not be staying the night, but you can certainly feel like a million bucks in the public spaces at **The Palace Hotel** (p. 79). The extravagant creation of banker "Bonanza King" Will Ralston in 1875, The Palace Hotel has one of the grandest rooms in the city: the **Garden Court.** Running a close second is the magnificent lobby at Nob Hill's **Fairmont Hotel & Tower** (p. 74).

- **Sip a cocktail in the clouds.** Some of the greatest ways to view the city are from top-floor lounges in fine hotels such as the Sir Francis Drake, Union Square (p. 234), the Grand Hyatt San Francisco (p. 240), and The Mark Hopkins InterContinental, Nob Hill (p. 240). Drinks aren't cheap, but it beats paying for a dinner. Besides, if you nurse your drink (or order something like tea or coffee), the combo of atmosphere, surroundings, and view is a bargain.

6 The Best Outdoor Activities

- **A Day in Golden Gate Park:** Exploring Golden Gate Park is a crucial part of the San Francisco experience. Its arboreal paths stretch from the Haight all the way to Ocean Beach, offering dozens of fun things to do along the way. Top sights are the Conservatory of Flowers, the Japanese Tea Garden, and the fabulous new de Young Museum (p. 161). The best time to go is Sunday, when portions of the park are closed to traffic (rent a bike for the full effect). Toward the end of the day, head west to the beach and watch the sunset. See p. 173.

The Best Activities for Families

For a list of San Francisco attractions that appeal to kids of all ages, see the "Especially for Kids" box on p. 182 of chapter 7.

- **A Walk along the Coastal Trail:** Stroll the forested Coastal Trail from Cliff House to the Golden Gate Bridge, and you'll see why San Franciscans put up with living on a fault line. Start at the parking lot just above Cliff House and head north. On a clear day, you'll have incredible views of the Marin Headlands, but even on foggy days, it's worth the trek to scamper over old bunkers and relish the cool, salty air (dress warmly). See "The Presidio & Golden Gate National Recreation Area," beginning on p. 176, for more on this area.
- **A Wine Country Excursion:** It'll take you about an hour to get there, but once you arrive you'll want to hopscotch from one winery to the next, perhaps picnic in the vineyards, or have an alfresco lunch at someplace atmospheric like Tra Vigne. And consider this: When the city is fogged in and cold, Napa and Sonoma are almost always sunny and warm. See chapter 12 for more information.
- **A Climb up or down the Filbert Street Steps:** San Francisco is a city of stairs, and the crème de la crème of steps is on Filbert Street between Sansome Street and the east side of Telegraph Hill. The terrain is so steep here that Filbert Street becomes Filbert Steps, a 377-step descent that wends its way through flower gardens and some of the city's oldest and most varied housing. It's a beautiful walk down, and great exercise going up.
- **A Visit to Muir Woods, Stinson Beach, and Point Reyes:** If you have wheels, reserve a day for a trip across the Golden Gate Bridge. Take the Stinson Beach exit off Highway 101, and spend a few hours gawking at the monolithic redwoods at Muir Woods (this place is amazing). Next, head up the coast to the spectacular Point Reyes National Seashore. Rain or shine, it's a day trip you'll never forget. See "Muir Woods & Mount Tamalpais" and "Point Reyes National Seashore," beginning on p. 266 and p. 267, respectively.

7 The Best Places to Hang with the Locals

- **A Feast at the Ferry Building:** During Farmers' Market days, this bayfront alfresco market is packed with local shoppers vying for the freshest in local produce, breads, and flowers—or just mingling during their lunch breaks. But the building itself has become a mecca for food lovers who browse the outstanding artisan food shops and restaurants daily and then linger over glasses of wine at the festive wine bar. See p. 155.
- **Cafe-Hopping in North Beach:** It's a classic San Francisco experience: lingering at a sidewalk cafe on Columbus Avenue, watching people from all over the world walk by. Start the day with a latte at Café Greco, then wander over to Caffè Trieste, a haven for true San Francisco characters. See "Walking Tour 2: Getting to Know North Beach," beginning on p. 198, for a walking tour of the area.

8 The Best Offbeat Travel Experiences

- **A Soul-Stirring Sunday Morning Service at Glide Memorial Church:** Every city has churches, but only San Francisco has the Glide. An hour or so with Reverend Cecil Williams and his exuberant gospel choir will surely shake your soul and let the glory out, no matter what your religious beliefs may be—everybody leaves this Tenderloin church spiritually uplifted and slightly misty-eyed. See p. 180.
- **A Cruise through the Castro:** The most populated and festive street in the city is not just for gays and lesbians (although the best cruising in town *is* right here). Although there are some great shops and cafes, it's the people-watching here that makes the trip a must. If you have time, catch a flick at the beautiful 1930s Spanish colonial movie palace, the Castro Theatre (p. 244). See "Neighborhoods Worth a Visit," beginning on p. 168, for more on the Castro.
- **Skating through Golden Gate Park on a Weekend:** C'mon! When's the last time you've been skating? And if you've never tried skating before, there's no better place to learn than on the wide, flat main street through Golden Gate Park, which is closed to vehicles on weekends.
- **Catching Big Air in Your Car:** Relive *Bullitt* or *The Streets of San Francisco* as you careen down the center lane of Gough Street between Ellis and Eddy streets, screaming out "Woooeee!" as you feel the pull of gravity leave you momentarily, followed by the thump of the car suspension bottoming out. Wimpier folk can settle for driving down the steepest street in San Francisco: Filbert Street, between Leavenworth and Hyde streets.
- **AsiaSF:** The gender-bending waitresses—mostly Asian men dressed *very* convincingly as hot-to-trot women—will blow your mind with their lip-synched show tunes, which take place every night. Bring the parents—they'll love it. See p. 115.

2

Planning Your Trip to San Francisco

1 Visitor Information

The **San Francisco Visitor Information Center,** on the lower level of Hallidie Plaza, 900 Market St., at Powell Street (© **415/391-2000;** www.onlyinsan francisco.com), is the best source of specialized information about the city. Even if you don't have a specific question, you might want to request the free *Visitors Planning Guide* and the *San Francisco Visitors* kit. The kit includes a 6-month calendar of events; a city history; shopping and dining information; and several good, clear maps; plus lodging information. The bureau highlights only its members' establishments, so if it doesn't have what you're looking for, that doesn't mean it's nonexistent.

You can also get the latest on San Francisco at the following online addresses:

- The *Bay Guardian,* the city's free weekly paper: **www.sfbg.com**
- *SF Gate,* the city's *Chronicle* newspaper: **www.sfgate.com**
- CitySearch: **sanfrancisco.citysearch.com**

2 Entry Requirements

PASSPORTS

For information on how to get a passport, go to **"Passports"** in the **"Fast Facts"** section of this chapter—the websites listed provide downloadable passport applications as well as the current fees for processing passport applications. For an up-to-date, country-by-country listing of passport requirements around the world, go to the "Foreign Entry Requirements" Web page of the U.S. State Department at **http://travel.state.gov**. International visitors can obtain a visa application at the same website. ***Note:*** Children are required to present a passport when entering the United States at airports. More information on obtaining a passport for a minor can be found at http://travel.state.gov.

VISAS

For specifics on how to get a visa, go to **"Visas"** in the **"Fast Facts"** section of this chapter.

The U.S. State Department has a **Visa Waiver Program (VWP)** allowing citizens of the following countries (at press time) to enter the United States without a visa for stays of up to 90 days: Andorra, Australia, Austria, Belgium, Brunei, Denmark, Finland, France, Germany, Iceland, Ireland, Italy, Japan, Liechtenstein, Luxembourg, Monaco, the Netherlands, New Zealand, Norway, Portugal, San Marino, Singapore, Slovenia, Spain, Sweden, Switzerland, and the United Kingdom. Canadian citizens may enter the United States without visas; they will

Value Money-Saving Tourist Passes

If you're the type who loves to cram as many tourist attractions as possible in one trip, then you might want to consider purchasing a **San Francisco CityPass** or **GO San Francisco Card.** The **CityPass** includes 7 days of unlimited public transportation (including cable cars, Metro streetcars, and the entire bus system), and access to six of the city's major attractions: the California Palace of the Legion of Honor and de Young museums, the Asian Art Museum, the San Francisco Museum of Modern Art, the Exploratorium, and a Blue & Gold Fleet bay cruise. You can buy a CityPass at any of the above attractions or online at www.citypass.net. Current rates are $54 for adults and $39 for kids 5 to 17. For more information, visit the CityPass website at **www.citypass.net** or send an e-mail to info@citypass.com. For recorded information, call ✆ **888/330-5008.**

I think the better deal, however, is the **GO San Francisco Card** (✆ **800/887-9103;** www.gosanfranciscocard.com). It offers free or discounted admission to more than 45 of the most popular attractions, activities, and tours throughout the Bay Area and Wine Country; has far more flexibility (available in 1-, 2-, 3-, 5-, and 7-day increments over a 14-day period); and comes with a nifty little full-color guidebook that fits in your back pocket. In addition, some stores and restaurants offer discounts of up to 20% to Go San Francisco Card holders. The Go Cards are smart-technology enabled, which means they operate by calendar day and are activated the first time they are swiped, so you'll want to start your touring early in the morning to get the most value. The 2-day card costs $65 for adults ($39 for kids 3–13), and doesn't need to be used on consecutive days. You can purchase the GO Cards via their website or at the San Francisco Visitor Information Center (p. 47), Red & White Fleet Ticket Booth (p. 185), or Wax Museum (p. 156).

need to show passports and proof of residence, however. ***Note:*** Any passport issued on or after October 26, 2006, by a VWP country must be an **e-Passport** for VWP travelers to be eligible to enter the U.S. without a visa. Citizens of these nations also need to present a round-trip air or cruise ticket upon arrival. E-Passports contain computer chips capable of storing biometric information, such as the required digital photograph of the holder. (You can identify an e-Passport by the symbol on the bottom center cover of your passport.) If your passport doesn't have this feature, you can still travel without a visa if it is a valid passport issued before October 26, 2005, and includes a machine-readable zone, or between October 26, 2005, and October 25, 2006, and includes a digital photograph. For more information, go to **www.travel.state.gov/visa**.

Citizens of all other countries must have (1) a valid passport that expires at least 6 months later than the scheduled end of their visit to the United States, and (2) a tourist visa, which may be obtained without charge from any U.S. consulate.

As of January 2004, many international visitors traveling on visas to the United States will be photographed and fingerprinted on arrival at Customs in

Tips **Dear Visa: I'm Off to San Francisco!**

Some credit card companies recommend that you notify them of any impending trip abroad so that they don't become suspicious when the card is used numerous times in a foreign destination and block your charges. Even if you don't call your credit card company in advance, you can always call the card's toll-free emergency number (see "Fast Facts," p. 32) if a charge is refused—a good reason to carry the phone number with you. And try to bring more than one card with you on your trip; a card might not work for any number of reasons, so having a backup is the smart way to go.

airports and on cruise ships in a program created by the Department of Homeland Security called **US-VISIT.** Exempt from the extra scrutiny are visitors entering by land or those (mostly in Europe; see p. 10) who don't require a visa for short-term visits. For more information, go to the Homeland Security website at **www.dhs.gov/dhspublic**.

MEDICAL REQUIREMENTS

Unless you're arriving from an area known to be suffering from an epidemic (particularly cholera or yellow fever), inoculations or vaccinations are not required for entry into the United States. If you have a medical condition that requires **syringe-administered medications,** carry a valid signed prescription from your physician; syringes in carry-on baggage will be inspected. Insulin in any form should have the proper pharmaceutical documentation. If you have a disease that requires treatment with **narcotics,** you should also carry documented proof with you—smuggling narcotics aboard a plane carries severe penalties in the U.S.

For **HIV-positive visitors,** requirements for entering the United States are somewhat vague and change frequently. For up-to-the-minute information, contact **AIDSinfo** (✆ **800/448-0440** or 301/519-6616 outside the U.S.; www.aidsinfo.nih.gov) or the **Gay Men's Health Crisis** (✆ **212/367-1000;** www.gmhc.org).

CUSTOMS

For information on what you can bring into and take out of San Francisco, go to **"Customs"** in the **"Fast Facts"** section of this chapter.

3 When to Go

If you're dreaming of convertibles, Frisbee on the beach, and tank-topped evenings, change your reservations and head to Los Angeles. Contrary to California's sunshine-and-bikini image, San Francisco's weather is "mild" (to put it nicely) and can often be downright bone-chilling because of the wet, foggy air and cool winds—it's nothing like that of Southern California. Summer, the most popular time to visit, is often characterized by damp, foggy days; cold, windy nights; and crowded tourist destinations. A good bet is to visit in spring or, better yet, autumn. Every September, right about the time San Franciscans mourn being cheated (or fogged) out of another summer, something wonderful happens: The thermometer rises, the skies clear, and the locals call in sick to work and head for the beach. It's what residents call "Indian summer." The city is also delightful during winter, when the opera and ballet seasons are in full swing; there are fewer tourists, many hotel prices are lower, and downtown bustles with holiday cheer.

CLIMATE

San Francisco's temperate, marine climate usually means relatively mild weather year-round. In summer, chilling fog rolls in most mornings and evenings, and if temperatures top 70°F (21°C), the city is ready to throw a celebration. Even when autumn's heat occasionally stretches into the 80s (upper 20s Celsius) and 90s (lower 30s Celsius), you should still dress in layers, or by early evening you'll learn firsthand why sweatshirt sales are a great business at Fisherman's Wharf. In winter, the mercury seldom falls below freezing and snow is almost unheard of, but that doesn't mean you won't be whimpering if you forget your coat. Still, compared to most of the states' weather conditions, San Francisco's are consistently pleasant.

It's that beautifully fluffy, chilly, wet, heavy, sweeping fog that makes the city's weather so precarious. A rare combination of water, wind, and topography creates Northern California's summer fog bank. It lies off the coast, and rising air currents pull it in when the land heats up. Held back by coastal mountains along a 600-mile front, the low clouds seek out any passage they can find. The easiest access is the slot where the Pacific Ocean penetrates the continental wall—the Golden Gate.

San Francisco's Average Temperatures & Rainfall

	Jan	Feb	Mar	Apr	May	June	July	Aug	Sept	Oct	Nov	Dec
High °F	56	59	61	64	67	70	71	72	73	70	62	56
Low °F	43	46	47	48	51	53	55	56	55	52	48	43
High °C	13	15	16	18	19	21	22	22	23	21	17	13
Low °C	6	8	8	9	11	12	13	13	13	11	9	6
Rain (in.)	4.5	4.0	3.3	1.2	0.4	0.1	0.1	0.1	0.2	1.0	2.5	2.9
Rain (mm)	113.0	101.9	82.8	30.0	9.7	2.8	0.8	1.8	5.1	26.4	63.2	73.4

SAN FRANCISCO CALENDAR OF EVENTS

For more information, visit www.sfvisitor.org for an annual calendar of local events.

February

Chinese New Year, Chinatown. In 2008, public celebrations will again spill onto every street in Chinatown. Festivities begin with the "Miss Chinatown USA" pageant parade, and climax a week later with a celebratory parade of marching bands, rolling floats, barrages of fireworks, and a block-long dragon writhing in and out of the crowds. The revelry runs for several weeks and wraps up with a memorable parade through Chinatown that starts at Market and Second streets and ends at Kearny Street. Arrive early for a good viewing spot on Kearny Street. You can purchase bleacher seats online starting in December. Make your hotel reservations early. For dates and information, call ✆ **415/982-3000** or visit www.chineseparade.com.

Tips **Travel Attire**

Even if it's sunny out, don't forget to bring a jacket; the weather can change almost instantly from sunny and warm to windy and cold in San Francisco.

March

St. Patrick's Day Parade, Union Square and Civic Center. Everyone's an honorary Irish person at this festive affair, which starts at 11:30am at Market and Second streets and continues to City Hall. But the party doesn't stop there. Head down to the Civic Center for the post-party, or venture to The Embarcadero's Harrington's bar (245 Front St.) and celebrate with hundreds of the Irish-for-a-day yuppies as they gallivant around the closed-off streets and numerous pubs. For information, call ✆ **415/675-9885;** www.sfstpatricksdayparade.com. Sunday before March 17.

April

Cherry Blossom Festival, Japantown. Meander through the arts-and-crafts and food booths lining the blocked-off streets around Japan Center and watch traditional drumming, flower arranging, origami making, or a parade celebrating the cherry blossom and Japanese culture. Call ✆ **415/563-2313** for information. Mid- to late April.

San Francisco International Film Festival, around San Francisco with screenings at the AMC Kabuki 8 Cinemas (Fillmore and Post sts.), and at many other locations. Begun in 1957, this is America's oldest film festival. It features close to 200 films and videos from more than 50 countries. Tickets are relatively inexpensive, and screenings are accessible to the public. Entries include new films by beginning and established directors. For a schedule or information, call ✆ **415/561-5000** or visit www.sffs.org. Mid-April to early May.

May

Cinco de Mayo Festival, Mission District. This is when the Latino community celebrates the victory of the Mexicans over the French at Puebla in 1862; mariachi bands, dancers, food, and a parade fill the streets of the Mission. The parade starts at 10am at 24th and Bryant streets and ends at the Civic Center, though rumor has it that in 2007 the Festival will be held on 24th Street. Contact the Mission Neighborhood Center for more information at ✆ **415/206-0577.** First Sunday in May.

Bay to Breakers Foot Race, The Embarcadero through Golden Gate Park to Ocean Beach. Even if you don't participate, you can't avoid this run from downtown to Ocean Beach, which stops morning traffic throughout the city. More than 75,000 entrants gather—many dressed in wacky, innovative, and sometimes X-rated costumes—for the approximately 7.5-mile run. If you don't want to run, join the throng of spectators who line the route. Sidewalk parties, bands, and cheerleaders of all ages provide a good dose of true San Francisco fun. For recorded information, call ✆ **415/359-2800,** or check their website www.baytobreakers.com. Third Sunday of May.

Carnaval Festival, Harrison Street between 16th and 23rd streets. The Mission District's largest annual event, held from 9:30am to 6pm, is a day of festivities that includes food, music, dance, arts and crafts, and a parade that's as sultry and energetic as the Latin American and Caribbean people behind it. For one of San Franciscans' favorite events, more than half a million spectators line the parade route, and samba musicians and dancers continue to entertain on 14th Street, near Harrison, at the end of the march where you'll find food and craft booths, music, and more revelry. Call the hot line at ✆ **415/920-0125** for information. Celebrations are held

Saturday and Sunday of Memorial Day weekend, but the parade is on Sunday morning only. See www.carnavalsf.com for more information.

June

Union Street Art Festival, Pacific Heights, along Union Street from Steiner to Gough streets. This outdoor fair celebrates San Francisco with themes, gourmet food booths, music, entertainment, and a juried art show featuring works by more than 250 artists. It's a great time and a chance to see the city's young well-to-dos partying it up. Call the **Union Street Association** (✆ **415/441-7055**) for more information or see www.unionstreetfestival.com. First weekend of June.

Haight-Ashbury Street Fair, Haight-Ashbury. A far cry from the froufrou Union Street Fair, this grittier fair features alternative crafts, ethnic foods, rock bands, and a healthy number of hippies and street kids whooping it up and slamming beers in front of the blaring rock-'n'-roll stage. The fair usually extends along Haight between Stanyan and Ashbury streets. For details and the exact date, call ✆ **415/863-3489** or visit www.haightstreetfair.org.

North Beach Festival, Grant Avenue, North Beach. In 2006, this party celebrated its 52nd anniversary; organizers claim it's the oldest urban street fair in the country. Close to 100,000 city folk meander along Grant Avenue, between Vallejo and Union streets, to eat, drink, and browse the arts-and-crafts booths, poetry readings, swing-dancing venue, and *arte di gesso* (sidewalk chalk art). But the most enjoyable parts of the event are listening to music and people-watching. Call ✆ **415/989-2220** or visit www.northbeachfestival.com for details. Usually Father's Day weekend, but call to confirm.

Stern Grove Music Festival, Sunset District. Pack a picnic and head out early to join the thousands who come here to lie in the grass and enjoy classical, jazz, and ethnic music and dance in the grove, at 19th Avenue and Sloat Boulevard. The Festival's 70th year will be marked in 2007. The free concerts take place every Sunday at 2pm between mid-June and August. Show up with a lawn chair or blanket. There are food booths if you forget snacks, but you'll be dying to leave if you don't bring warm clothes—the Sunset District can be one of the coldest parts of the city. Call ✆ **415/252-6252** for listings; www.sterngrove.org. Sundays, mid-June through August.

San Francisco Lesbian, Gay, Bisexual, Transgender Pride Parade & Celebration, downtown's Market Street. This prideful event draws up to one million participants who celebrate all of the above—and then some. The parade proceeds west on Market Street until it gets to the Civic Center, where hundreds of food, art, and information booths are set up around several soundstages. Call ✆ **415/864-3733** or visit www.sfpride.org for information. Usually the third or last weekend of June.

July

Fillmore Jazz Festival, Pacific Heights. July starts with a bang, when the upscale portion of Fillmore closes to traffic and the blocks between Jackson and Eddy are filled with arts and crafts, gourmet food, and live jazz from 10am to 6pm. Call ✆ **510/970-3217** for more information; www.fillmorejazzfestival.com. First weekend in July.

Fourth of July Celebration & Fireworks, Fisherman's Wharf. This event can be something of a joke—more often than not, fog comes into the city, like everyone else, to join in the festivities. Sometimes it's almost impossible to view the million-dollar pyrotechnics from Pier 39 on the northern waterfront. Still, it's a party, and if the skies are clear, it's a darn good show. Visit www.4thofjulysf.com for more info.

San Francisco Marathon, San Francisco and beyond. This is one of the largest marathons in the world. It starts and ends at the Ferry Building at the base of Market Street, winds 26-plus miles through virtually every neighborhood in the City, and crosses the Golden Gate Bridge. For entry information, visit www.runsfm.com. Usually the last weekend in July.

September

Sausalito Art Festival, Sausalito. A juried exhibit of more than 20,000 original works of art, this festival includes music—provided by jazz, rock, and blues performers from the Bay Area and beyond—and international cuisine, enhanced by wines from some 50 Napa and Sonoma producers. Parking is impossible; take the **Blue & Gold Fleet ferry** (✆ **415/705-5555**) from Fisherman's Wharf to the festival site. For more information, call ✆ **415/332-3555** or log on to www.sausalitoartfestival.org. Labor Day weekend.

Opera in the Park, usually in Sharon Meadow, Golden Gate Park. Each year the San Francisco Opera launches its season with a free concert featuring a selection of arias. Call ✆ **415/861-4008** to confirm the location and date. Usually the Sunday after Labor Day.

San Francisco Blues Festival, on the grounds of Fort Mason, the Marina. The largest outdoor blues music event on the West Coast will be 35 years old in 2007 and continues to feature local and national musicians performing back-to-back during the 3-day extravaganza. You can charge tickets by phone at ✆ **415/421-8497** or online at www.ticketmaster.com. For information, call ✆ **415/979-5588** or visit www.sfblues.com. Usually in late September.

Folsom Street Fair, along Folsom Street between 7th and 12th streets, SoMa, from 11am to 6pm. This is a local favorite for its kinky, outrageous, leather-and-skin gay-centric blowout celebration. It's hard-core, so only open-minded and adventurous types need head into the leather-clad and partially dressed crowds. For info call ✆ **415/861-3247** or visit www.folsomstreetfair.org. Last Sunday of September.

October

Fleet Week, Marina and Fisherman's Wharf. Residents gather along the Marina Green, The Embarcadero, Fisherman's Wharf, and other vantage points to watch incredible (and loud!) aerial performances by the Blue Angels, flown in tribute to our nation's marines. Call ✆ **650/599-5057** or visit www.fleetweek.us/fleetweek for details and dates.

Artspan Open Studios, various San Francisco locations. Find an original piece of art to commemorate your trip, or just see what local artists are up to by grabbing a map to over 800 artists' studios that are open to the public during weekends in October. Call ✆ **415/861-9838** or visit www.artspan.org for more information.

Castro Street Fair, the Castro. Celebrate life in the city's most famous gay neighborhood. Call ✆ **415/841-1824** or visit www.castrostreetfair.org for information. First Sunday in October, from 11am to 6pm.

Italian Heritage Parade, North Beach and Fisherman's Wharf. The city's Italian community leads the festivities around Fisherman's Wharf, celebrating Columbus's landing in America. The year 2008 marks the festival's 140th, and as usual includes a parade along

Columbus Avenue. But for the most part, it's a great excuse to hang out in North Beach and people-watch. For information, call ✆ **415/587-8282** or visit www.sfcolumbusday.org. Observed the Sunday before Columbus Day.

Exotic Erotic Halloween Ball, The Cow Palace, on the southern outskirts of San Francisco. Thousands come here dressed in costume, lingerie, and sometimes even less than that. It's a wild fantasy affair with bands, dancing, and costume contests. ***Beware:*** It can be somewhat cheesy. Advance tickets range from $60 to $125 per person. For information, call ✆ **415/567-BALL** or visit www.exoticeroticball.com. One or two Friday or Saturday nights before Halloween.

Halloween, the Castro. This is a huge night in San Francisco, especially in the flamboyant gay community of the Castro. Drop by for music, costume contests, and all-around revelry when streets are shut down and filled with a mixed crowd reveling in costumes of extraordinary imagination. For info visit www.halloweeninthecastro.com. October 31.

San Francisco Jazz Festival, various San Francisco locations. This festival presents eclectic programming in an array of fabulous jazz venues throughout the city. With close to 3 weeks of nightly entertainment and dozens of performers, the jazz festival is a hot ticket. Past events have featured Herbie Hancock, Dave Brubeck, the Modern Jazz Quartet, Wayne Shorter, and Bill Frisell. For information, call ✆ **800/850-SFJF** or 415/788-7353; or visit www.sfjazz.org. Also check the website for other events throughout the year. Late October and early November.

December

The Nutcracker, War Memorial Opera House, Civic Center. The **San Francisco Ballet** (✆ **415/865-2000**) performs this Tchaikovsky classic annually. Order tickets to this holiday tradition well in advance. Visit www.sfballet.org for information.

4 Getting There

BY PLANE

The northern Bay Area has two major airports: San Francisco International and Oakland International.

SAN FRANCISCO INTERNATIONAL AIRPORT Almost four dozen major scheduled carriers serve **San Francisco International Airport** (✆ **650/821-8211;** www.flysfo.com), 14 miles directly south of downtown on U.S. 101. Travel time to downtown during commuter rush hour is about 40 minutes; at other times, it's about 20 to 25 minutes.

You can also call **511** or visit www.511.org for up-to-the-minute information about public transportation and traffic.

FLYING FOR LESS: TIPS FOR GETTING THE BEST AIRFARE

- Passengers who can book their tickets either **long in advance or at the last minute,** or who **fly midweek** or **at less-trafficked hours,** may pay a fraction of the full fare. If your schedule is flexible, say so, and ask if you can secure a cheaper fare by changing your flight plans.
- Search **the Internet** for cheap fares. The most popular online travel agencies are **Travelocity.com** (www.travelocity.co.uk); **Expedia.com** (www.expedia.co.uk and www.expedia.ca); and **Orbitz.com**. In the U.K., go to **Travelsupermarket** (✆ **0845/**

345-5708; www.travelsupermarket.com), a flight search engine that offers flight comparisons for the budget airlines whose seats often end up in bucket-shop sales. Other websites for booking airline tickets online include **Cheapflights.com, SmarterTravel.com, Priceline.com,** and **Opodo** (www.opodo.co.uk). Meta search sites (which find and then direct you to airline and hotel websites for booking) include **Sidestep-com** and **Kayak.com**—the latter includes fares for budget carriers like Jet Blue and Spirit as well as the major airlines. **Site59.com** is a great source for last-minute flights and getaways. In addition, most **airlines** offer online-only fares that even their phone agents know nothing about. British travelers should check **Flights International** (✆ **0800/0187050;** www.flights-international.com) for deals on flights all over the world.

- Watch local newspapers for **promotional specials** or **fare wars,** when airlines lower prices on their most popular routes. Also keep an eye on price fluctuations and deals at websites such as **Airfarewatchdog.com** and **Farecast.com.**
- Try to book a ticket **in its country of origin.** If you're planning a one-way flight from Johannesburg to New York, a South Africa–based travel agent will probably have the lowest fares. For foreign travelers on multileg trips, book in the country of the first leg; for example, book San Francisco–Chicago–Montréal–San Francisco in the U.S.
- **Consolidators,** also known as bucket shops, are wholesale brokers in the airline-ticket game. Consolidators buy deeply discounted tickets ("distressed" inventories of unsold seats) from airlines and sell them to online ticket agencies, travel agents, tour operators, corporations, and, to a lesser degree, the general public. Consolidators advertise in Sunday newspaper travel sections (often in small ads with tiny type), both in the U.S. and the U.K. They can be great sources for cheap international tickets. On the down side, bucket shop tickets are often rigged with restrictions, such as stiff cancellation penalties (as high as 50% to 75% of the ticket price). And keep in mind that most of what you see advertised is of limited availability. Several reliable consolidators are worldwide and available online. **STA Travel** (www.statravel.com) has been the world's leading consolidator for students since purchasing Council Travel, but their fares are competitive for travelers of all ages. **Flights.com** (✆ **800/TRAV-800;** www.flights.com) has excellent fares worldwide, particularly to Europe. They also have "local" websites in 12 countries. **FlyCheap** (✆ **800/FLY-CHEAP;** www.1800flycheap.com) has especially good fares to sunny destinations. **Air Tickets Direct** (✆ **800/778-3447;** www.airticketsdirect.com) is based in Montréal and leverages the currently weak Canadian dollar for low fares; they also book trips to places that U.S. travel agents won't touch, such as Cuba.
- Join **frequent-flier clubs.** Frequent-flier membership doesn't cost a cent, but it does entitle you to free tickets or upgrades when you amass the airline's required number of frequent-flier points. You don't even have to fly to earn points; **frequent-flier credit cards** can earn you thousands of miles for doing your everyday shopping. But keep in mind that award seats are limited, seats on popular routes are hard to snag, and more and

more major airlines are cutting their expiration periods for mileage points—so check your airline's frequent-flier program so you don't lose your miles before you use them. ***Inside tip:*** Award seats are offered almost a year in advance, but seats also open up at the last minute, so if your travel plans are flexible, you may strike gold. To play the frequent-flier game to your best advantage, consult the community bulletin boards on **FlyerTalk** (www.flyertalk.com) or go to Randy Petersen's **Inside Flyer** (www.insideflyer.com). Petersen and friends review all the programs in detail and post regular updates on changes in policies and trends.

ARRIVING AT THE AIRPORT

IMMIGRATION & CUSTOMS CLEARANCE Foreign visitors arriving by air, no matter what the port of entry, should cultivate patience and resignation before setting foot on U.S. soil. U.S. airports have considerably beefed up security clearances in the years since the terrorist attacks of 9/11, and clearing Customs and Immigration can take as long as 2 hours.

People traveling by air from Canada, Bermuda, and certain Caribbean countries can sometimes clear Customs and Immigration at the point of departure, which is much faster.

GETTING INTO TOWN FROM SAN FRANCISCO INTERNATIONAL AIRPORT

The fastest and cheapest way to get from SFO to the city is to take **BART** (Bay Area Rapid Transit; ✆ **415/989-2278;** www.bart.gov), which offers numerous stops within downtown San Francisco. This route, which takes about 35 minutes, avoids traffic on the way and costs a heck of a lot less than taxis or shuttles (about $6 each way, depending on exactly where you're going). Just jump on the airport's free shuttle bus to the International terminal, enter the BART station there, and you're on your way to San Francisco. Trains leave approximately every 15 minutes.

A **cab** from the airport to downtown costs $35 to $40, plus tip, and takes about 30 minutes, traffic permitting.

SuperShuttle (✆ **800/BLUE-VAN** or 415/558-8500; www.supershuttle.com) is a private shuttle company that offers door-to-door airport service, in which you share a van with a few other passengers. They will take you anywhere in the city, charging $15 per person to a residence or business. On the return trip, add $8 to $15 for each additional person depending on whether you're traveling from a hotel or a residence. The shuttle stops at least every 20 minutes, sometimes sooner, and picks up passengers from the marked areas outside the terminals' upper levels. Reservations are required for the return trip to the airport only and should be made 1 day before departure. These shuttles often demand they pick you up 2 hours before your domestic flight and 3 hours before international flights and during holidays. Keep in mind that you could be the first one on and the last one off, so this trip could take a while; you might want to ask before getting in. For $65, you can either charter the entire van for up to seven people or an Execucar private sedan for up to four people. For more info on the Execucar, call ✆ **800/410-4444.**

The San Mateo County Transit system, **SamTrans** (✆ **800/660-4287** in Northern California, or 650/508-6200; www.samtrans.com), runs two buses between the San Francisco Airport and the Transbay Terminal at First and Mission streets. Bus no. 292 costs $1.50 and makes the trip in about 55 minutes. The KX bus costs $4 and takes just 35 minutes but permits only one carry-on bag. Both buses run daily. The no. 292 starts at

5:25am Monday through Friday and 5:30am on weekends; both run until 1am and run every half-hour until 7:30pm, when they run hourly. The KX starts at 5:53am and ends at 10:37pm Monday through Friday. On weekends, service runs from 7:19am to 9:30pm, runs every half-hour until 6:30pm, and then changes to an hourly schedule.

OAKLAND INTERNATIONAL AIRPORT About 5 miles south of downtown Oakland, at the Hegenberger Road exit of Calif. 17 (U.S. 880; if coming from south, take 98th Ave.), **Oakland International Airport** (© **800/247-6255** or 510/563-3300; www.oaklandairport.com) primarily serves passengers with East Bay destinations. Some San Franciscans prefer this less-crowded, accessible airport during busy periods—especially because by car it takes around half an hour to get there from downtown San Francisco (traffic permitting). The airport is also accessible by BART, which is not influenced by traffic because it travels on its own tracks (see below for more information).

GETTING INTO TOWN FROM OAKLAND INTERNATIONAL AIRPORT

Taxis from the Oakland Airport to downtown San Francisco are expensive—approximately $50, plus tip.

Bayporter Express (© **877/467-1800** in the Bay Area, or 415/467-1800 elsewhere; www.bayporter.com) is a shuttle service that charges $26 for the first person and $12 for each additional person for the ride from the Oakland Airport to downtown San Francisco. Children under 12 pay $7. The fare for outer areas of San Francisco is higher. The service accepts advance reservations. To the right of the Oakland Airport exit, there are usually shuttles that take you to San Francisco for around $20 per person. The shuttles in this fleet are independently owned, and prices vary.

The cheapest way to reach downtown San Francisco is to take the shuttle bus from the Oakland Airport to **BART** (Bay Area Rapid Transit; © **510/464-6000;** www.bart.gov). The AirBART shuttle bus runs about every 15 minutes Monday

---

Tips Coping with Jet Lag

Jet lag is a pitfall of traveling across time zones. If you're flying north–south and you feel sluggish when you touch down, your symptoms will be the result of dehydration and the general stress of air travel. When you travel east–west or vice-versa, however, your body becomes thoroughly confused about what time it is, and everything from your digestive system to your brain is knocked for a loop. Traveling east, say from San Francisco to Boston, is more difficult on your internal clock than traveling west, say from Atlanta to Hawaii, because most peoples' bodies are more inclined to stay up late than fall asleep early.

Here are some tips for combating jet lag:

- **Reset your watch** to your destination time before you board the plane.
- **Drink lots of water** before, during, and after your flight. Avoid alcohol.
- **Exercise and sleep well** for a few days before your trip.
- If you have trouble sleeping on planes, **fly eastward on morning flights.**
- **Daylight** is the key to resetting your body clock. At the website for **Outside In** (www.bodyclock.com), you can get a customized plan of when to seek and avoid light.

---

through Saturday from 5am to 12:05am and Sunday from 8am to 12:05am. It makes pickups in front of terminals 1 and 2 near the ground transportation signs. Tickets must be purchased at the Oakland Airport's vending machines prior to boarding. The cost is $2 for the 10-minute ride to BART's Coliseum station in Oakland. BART fares vary, depending on your destination; the trip to downtown San Francisco costs $3.15 and takes 15 minutes once you're on board. The entire excursion should take around 45 minutes.

BY CAR

San Francisco is easily accessible by major highways: **Interstate 5,** from the north, and **U.S. 101,** which cuts south–north through the peninsula from San Jose and across the Golden Gate Bridge to points north. If you drive from Los Angeles, you can take the longer coastal route (437 miles and 11 hr.) or the inland route (389 miles and 8 hr.). From Mendocino, it's 156 miles and 4 hours; from Sacramento, 88 miles and 1½ hours; from Yosemite, 210 miles and 4 hours.

If you are driving and aren't already a member, it's worth joining the **American Automobile Association (AAA; ✆ 800/922-8228;** www.csaa.com). It charges $49 to $79 per year (with an additional one-time joining fee), depending on where you join, and provides roadside and other services to motorists. **Amoco Motor Club** (**✆ 800/334-3300;** www.bpmotorclub.com) is another recommended choice.

For information about renting a car, see the "Car Rentals" section (beginning on p. 54) of chapter 4, "Getting to Know San Francisco."

BY TRAIN

Traveling by train takes a long time and usually costs as much as, or more than, flying. Still, if you want to take a leisurely ride across America, rail may be a good option.

San Francisco–bound **Amtrak** (**✆ 800/872-7245** or 800/USA-RAIL; www.amtrak.com) trains leave from New York and cross the country via Chicago. The journey takes about 3½ days, and seats sell quickly. At this writing, the lowest round-trip fare costs about $300 from New York and $270 from Chicago. Round-trip tickets from Los Angeles range from $120 to as much as $200. Trains arrive in Emeryville, just north of Oakland, and connect with regularly scheduled buses to San Francisco's Ferry Building and the Caltrain station in downtown San Francisco.

Caltrain (**✆ 800/660-4287** or 415/546-4461; www.caltrain.com) operates train service between San Francisco and the towns of the peninsula. The city depot is at 700 Fourth St., at Townsend Street.

5 Money & Costs

It's always advisable to bring money in a variety of forms on a vacation: a mix of cash, credit cards, and ATM cards. You should also have enough petty cash upon arrival to cover airport incidentals, tipping, and transportation to your hotel before you leave home. You can always withdraw money upon arrival at an airport ATM, but you'll still need to make smaller change for tipping.

ATMs

In San Francisco and nationwide, the easiest and best way to get cash away from home is from an ATM (automated teller machine), sometimes referred to as a "cash machine," or "cashpoint." The **Cirrus** (**✆ 800/424-7787;** www.mastercard.com) and **PLUS** (**✆ 800/843-7587;** www.visa.com) networks span the country; you can find them even in remote regions. Go to your bank card's website to find ATM locations at your destination. Be sure you know your daily withdrawal limit before you depart.

Note: Many banks impose a fee every time you use a card at another bank's ATM, and that fee is often higher for international transactions (up to $5 or more) than for domestic ones (where they're rarely more than $2). In addition, the bank from which you withdraw cash may charge its own fee. To compare banks' ATM fees within the U.S., use **www.bankrate.com**. Visitors from outside the U.S. should also find out whether their bank assesses a 1% to 3% fee on charges incurred abroad.

Tip: One way around these fees is to ask for cash back at grocery, drug, and convenience stores that accept ATM cards and don't charge usage fees (be sure to ask). Of course, you'll have to purchase something first.

CREDIT CARDS & DEBIT CARDS

Credit cards are the most widely used form of payment in the United States: **Visa** (Barclaycard in Britain), **MasterCard** (Eurocard in Europe, Access in Britain, Chargex in Canada), **American Express, Diners Club,** and **Discover.** They also provide a convenient record of all your expenses, and offer relatively good exchange rates. You can withdraw cash advances from your credit cards at banks or ATMs, but high fees make credit-card cash advances a pricey way to get cash.

It's highly recommended that you travel with at least one major credit card. You must have a credit card to rent a car, and hotels and airlines usually require a credit card imprint as a deposit against expenses.

TRAVELER'S CHECKS

Traveler's checks are something of an anachronism from the days before the ATM made cash accessible at any time. Traveler's checks used to be the only sound alternative to traveling with dangerously large amounts of cash. They were as reliable as currency, but, unlike cash, could be replaced if lost or stolen.

These days, traveler's checks are less necessary because most cities have 24-hour ATMs that allow you to withdraw small amounts of cash as needed. However, keep in mind that you will likely be charged an ATM withdrawal fee if the bank is not your own, so if you're withdrawing money every day, you might be better off with traveler's checks—provided that you don't mind showing identification every time you want to cash one. Visitors should make sure that traveler's checks are denominated in U.S. dollars; foreign-currency checks are often difficult to exchange.

You can buy traveler's checks at most banks. Most are offered in denominations of $20, $50, $100, $500, and sometimes $1,000. Generally, you'll pay a service charge ranging from 1% to 4%.

The most popular traveler's checks are offered by **American Express** (**© 800/807-6233; © 800/221-7282** for cardholders—this number accepts collect calls, offers service in several foreign languages, and exempts Amex gold and platinum cardholders from the 1% fee.); **Visa** (**© 800/732-1322**)—AAA members can obtain Visa checks for a $9.95 fee (for checks up to $1,500) at most AAA offices or by calling **© 866/339-3378;** and **MasterCard** (**© 800/223-9920**).

Be sure to keep a copy of the traveler's checks' serial numbers separate from your checks in the event that they are stolen or lost. You'll get a refund faster if you know the numbers.

Another option is the new **prepaid traveler's check cards,** reloadable cards that work much like debit cards but aren't linked to your checking account. The **American Express Travelers Cheque Card,** for example, requires a minimum deposit ($300), sets a maximum balance ($2,750), and has a one-time issuance fee of $15. You can withdraw money from an ATM ($2.50 per transaction, not including bank fees), and the funds can be purchased in dollars, euros, or pounds. If you lose the card, your available funds will be refunded within 24 hours.

6 Travel Insurance

The cost of travel insurance varies widely, depending on the cost and length of your trip, your age and health, and the type of trip you're taking, but expect to pay between 5% and 8% of the vacation itself. You can get estimates from various providers through **InsureMyTrip.com**. Enter your trip cost and dates, your age, and other information, for prices from more than a dozen companies.

For **U.K. citizens,** insurance is always advisable when traveling in the States. Travelers or families who make more than one trip abroad per year may find that an annual travel insurance policy works out cheaper. Check **www.moneysupermarket.com**, which compares prices across a wide range of providers for single- and multi-trip policies.

Most big travel agents offer their own insurance and will probably try to sell you their package when you book a holiday. Think before you sign. **Britain's Consumers' Association** recommends that you insist on seeing the policy and reading the fine print before you buy travel insurance. **The Association of British Insurers** (**© 020/7600-3333;** www.abi.org.uk) gives advice by phone and publishes *Holiday Insurance,* a free guide to policy provisions and prices. You might also shop around for better deals: Try **Columbus Direct** (**© 0870/033- 9988;** www.columbusdirect.net).

TRIP-CANCELLATION INSURANCE

Trip-cancellation insurance will help you retrieve your money if you have to back out of a trip or depart early, or if your travel supplier goes bankrupt. Trip cancellation traditionally covers such events as sickness, natural disasters, and State Department advisories. The latest news in trip-cancellation insurance is the availability of **expanded hurricane coverage** and the **"any-reason"** cancellation coverage—which costs more but covers cancellations made for any reason. You won't get back 100% of your prepaid trip cost, but you'll be refunded a substantial portion. **TravelSafe** (**© 888/885-7233;** www.travelsafe.com) offers both types of coverage. Expedia also offers any-reason cancellation coverage for its air-hotel packages.

For details, contact one of the following recommended insurers: **Access America** (© 866/807-3982; www.accessamerica.com); **Travel Guard International** (© 800/826-4919; www.travelguard.com); **Travel Insured International** (© 800/243-3174; www.travelinsured.com); and **Travelex Insurance Services** (© 888/457-4602; www.travelex-insurance.com).

MEDICAL INSURANCE

Although it's not required of travelers, health insurance is highly recommended. Most health insurance policies cover you if you get sick away from home—but check your coverage before you leave.

International visitors should note that unlike many European countries, the United States does not usually offer free or low-cost medical care to its citizens or visitors. Doctors and hospitals are expensive, and in most cases will require advance payment or proof of coverage before they render their services. Good policies will cover the costs of an accident, repatriation, or death. Packages such as **Europ Assistance's "Worldwide Healthcare Plan"** are sold by European automobile clubs and travel agencies at attractive rates. **Worldwide Assistance Services, Inc.** (✆ **800/777-8710;** www.worldwideassistance.com) is the agent for Europ Assistance in the United States.

Though lack of health insurance may prevent you from being admitted to a hospital in nonemergencies, don't worry about being left on a street corner to die: The American way is to fix you now and bill the living daylights out of you later.

If you're ever hospitalized more than 150 miles from home, **MedjetAssist** (✆ **800/527-7478;** www.medjetassistance.com) will pick you up and fly you to the hospital of your choice in a medically equipped and staffed aircraft 24 hours day, 7 days a week. Annual memberships are $225 individual, $350 family; you can also purchase short-term memberships.

Canadians should check with their provincial health plan offices or call **Health Canada** (✆ 866/225-0709; www.hc-sc.gc.ca) to find out the extent of their coverage and what documentation and receipts they must take home in case they are treated in the United States.

LOST-LUGGAGE INSURANCE

On flights within the U.S., checked baggage is covered up to $2,500 per ticketed passenger. On flights outside the U.S. (and on U.S. portions of international trips), baggage coverage is limited to approximately $9.07 per pound, up to approximately $635 per checked bag. If you plan to check items more valuable than what's covered by the standard liability, see if your homeowner's policy covers your valuables, get baggage insurance as part of your comprehensive travel-insurance package, or buy Travel Guard's "BagTrak" product.

If your luggage is lost, immediately file a lost-luggage claim at the airport, detailing the luggage contents. Most airlines require that you report delayed, damaged, or lost baggage within 4 hours of arrival. The airlines are required to deliver luggage, once found, directly to your house or destination free of charge.

7 Health

STAYING HEALTHY

Yes, the water's okay to drink in San Francisco, but you can spend your vacation in your hotel room if you wear shoes impractical for hiking the city's hills, or catch a cold because you didn't dress for winter weather in mid-July.

The United States **Centers for Disease Control and Prevention** (✆ **800/311-3435;** www.cdc.gov) provides up-to-date information on health hazards by region or country and offers tips on food safety. The website **www.tripprep.com**, sponsored by a consortium of travel medicine practitioners, **Travel Health Online,** may also offer helpful advice on traveling abroad. You can find listings of reliable clinics overseas at the **International Society of Travel Medicine** (www.istm.org).

WHAT TO DO IF YOU GET SICK AWAY FROM HOME

If you worry about getting sick away from home, you may want to consider **medical travel insurance** (see above). In most cases, however, your existing health plan will provide all the coverage you need, but be sure to carry your identification card with you at all times. I list **hospitals** and **emergency numbers** under "Fast Facts" later in this chapter.

If you suffer from a chronic illness, consult your doctor before your departure. Pack **prescription medications** in your carry-on luggage, and carry them in their original containers, with pharmacy labels—otherwise they won't make it through airport security. Visitors from outside the U.S. should carry generic names of prescription drugs. For U.S.

Avoiding "Economy Class Syndrome"

Deep vein thrombosis, or as it's know in the world of flying, "economy-class syndrome," is a blood clot that develops in a deep vein. It's a potentially deadly condition that can be caused by sitting in cramped conditions—such as an airplane cabin—for too long. During a flight (especially a long-haul flight), get up, walk around, and stretch your legs every 60 to 90 minutes to keep your blood flowing. Other preventative measures include frequent flexing of the legs while sitting, drinking lots of water, and avoiding alcohol and sleeping pills. If you have a history of deep vein thrombosis, heart disease, or another condition that puts you at high risk, some experts recommend wearing compression stockings or taking anticoagulants when you fly; always ask your physician about the best course for you. Symptoms of deep vein thrombosis include leg pain or swelling, or even shortness of breath.

travelers, most reliable health-care plans provide coverage if you get sick away from home. Foreign visitors may have to pay all medical costs upfront and be reimbursed later. See "Medical Insurance," under "Travel Insurance," above.

8 Safety

STAYING SAFE

For a big city, San Francisco is relatively safe, and requires only that you use common sense (for example, don't leave your new video camera on the seat of your parked car). However, in neighborhoods such as Lower Haight, the Mission, the Tenderloin (a few blocks west of Union Sq.), and Fisherman's Wharf (at night especially), it's a good idea to pay attention to yourself and your surroundings.

Avoid carrying valuables with you on the street, and don't display expensive cameras or electronic equipment. Hold on to your pocketbook, and place your billfold in an inside pocket. In theaters, restaurants, and other public places, keep your possessions in sight.

Remember also that hotels are open to the public, and in a large hotel, security may not be able to screen everyone entering. Always lock your room door—don't assume that inside your hotel you are automatically safe.

Driving safety is important, too. Ask your rental agency about personal safety, and ask for a traveler-safety brochure when you pick up your car. Ask for written directions to your destination or a map with the route clearly marked. (Many agencies offer the option of renting a cellphone for the duration of your car rental; check with the rental agent when you pick up the car.) Try to arrive and depart during daylight hours.

Recently, more crime has involved cars and drivers. If you drive off a highway into a doubtful neighborhood, leave the area as quickly as possible. If you have an accident, even on the highway, stay in your car with the doors locked until you assess the situation or until the police arrive. If you're bumped from behind on the street or are involved in a minor accident with no injuries, and the situation appears to be suspicious, motion to the other driver to follow you. Never get out of your car in such situations. Go directly to the nearest police precinct, well-lit service station, or 24-hour store.

Always try to park in well-lit and well-traveled areas. Never leave any packages or valuables in sight. If someone attempts to rob you or steal your car, don't try to resist the thief or carjacker. Report the incident to the police department immediately by calling ✆ **911.** This is a free call, even from pay phones.

9 Specialized Travel Resources

TRAVELERS WITH DISABILITIES

Most disabilities shouldn't stop anyone from traveling. There are more options and resources out there than ever before.

Most of San Francisco's major museums and tourist attractions have wheelchair ramps. Many hotels offer special accommodations and services for wheelchair users and other visitors with disabilities. As well as the ramps, they include extra-large bathrooms and telecommunication devices for hearing-impaired travelers. The San Francisco Convention and Visitors Bureau (p. 47) should have the most up-to-date information.

Travelers in wheelchairs can request special ramped taxis by calling **Yellow Cab** (✆ **415/626-2345**), which charges regular rates for the service. Travelers with disabilities can also get a free copy of the ***Muni Access Guide,*** published by the San Francisco Municipal Transportation Agency, Accessible Services Program, One South Van Ness, third floor (✆ **415/923-6142**), which is staffed weekdays from 8am to 5pm. Many of the major car-rental companies offer hand-controlled cars for drivers with disabilities. **Alamo** (✆ **800/651-1223**), **Avis** (✆ **800/331-1212,** ext. 7305), and **Budget** (✆ **800/314-3932**) have special hot lines that help provide such a vehicle at any of their U.S. locations with 48 hours' advance notice; **Hertz** (✆ **800/654-3131**) requires between 24 and 72 hours' advance notice at most locations.

Organizations that offer a vast range of resources and assistance to disabled travelers include **MossRehab** (✆ **800/CALL-MOSS;** www.mossresourcenet.org); the **American Foundation for the Blind (AFB)** (✆ **800/232-5463;** www.afb.org); and **SATH (Society for Accessible Travel & Hospitality)** (✆ **212/447-7284;** www.sath.org). **AirAmbulanceCard.com** is now partnered with SATH and allows you to preselect top-notch hospitals in case of an emergency.

Access-Able Travel Source (✆ **303/232-2979;** www.access-able.com) offers a comprehensive database on travel agents from around the world with experience in accessible travel; destination-specific access information; and links to such resources as service animals, equipment rentals, and access guides.

Many travel agencies offer customized tours and itineraries for travelers with disabilities. Among them are **Flying Wheels Travel** (✆ **507/451-5005;** www.flyingwheelstravel.com); and **Accessible Journeys** (✆ **800/846-4537** or 610/521-0339; www.disabilitytravel.com).

Flying with Disability (www.flying-with-disability.org) is a comprehensive information source on airplane travel. **Avis Rent a Car** (✆ **888/879-4273**) has an "Avis Access" program that offers services for customers with special travel needs. These include specially outfitted vehicles with swivel seats, spinner knobs, and hand controls; mobility scooter rentals; and accessible bus service. Be sure to reserve well in advance.

Also check out the quarterly magazine ***Emerging Horizons*** (www.emerginghorizons.com), available by subscription ($16.95 year U.S.; $21.95 outside U.S.).

The "Accessible Travel" link at **Mobility-Advisor.com** (www.mobility-advisor.com) offers a variety of travel resources to disabled persons.

British travelers should contact **Holiday Care** (✆ **0845-124-9971** in U.K.

only; www.holidaycare.org.uk) to access a wide range of travel information and resources for disabled and elderly people.

GAY & LESBIAN TRAVELERS

If you head down to the Castro—an area surrounding Castro Street near Market Street—you'll understand why the city is a mecca for gay and lesbian travelers. Since the 1970s, this unique part of town has remained a colorfully festive neighborhood, teeming with "out" city folk who meander the streets shopping, eating, partying, or cruising. If anyone feels like an outsider in this part of town, it's heterosexuals, who, although warmly welcomed in the community, may feel uncomfortable or downright threatened if they harbor any homophobia or aversion to being checked out. For many San Franciscans, it's just a fun area (especially on Halloween) with some wonderful shops.

Gays and lesbians make up a good deal of San Francisco's population, so it's no surprise that clubs and bars all over town cater to them. Although lesbian interests are concentrated primarily in the East Bay (especially Oakland), a significant community resides in the Mission District, around 16th and Valencia streets.

Several local publications concentrate on in-depth coverage of news, information, and listings of goings-on around town for gays and lesbians. The *Bay Area Reporter* (www.ebar.com) has the most comprehensive listings, including a weekly calendar of events. Distributed free on Thursday, it can be found stacked at the corner of 18th and Castro streets and at Ninth and Harrison streets, as well as in bars, bookshops, and stores around town. It may also be available in gay and lesbian bookstores elsewhere in the country.

GUIDES & PUBLICATIONS For a good book selection, contact **Giovanni's Room,** 345 S. 12th St., Philadelphia, PA 19107 (© **215/923-2960;** www.giovannisroom.com); and **A Different Light Bookstore,** 489 Castro St., San Francisco, CA 94114 (© **415/431-0891;** www.adlbooks.com).

The **International Gay and Lesbian Travel Association (IGLTA)** (© **800/448-8550** or 954/776-2626; www.iglta.org) is the trade association for the gay and lesbian travel industry, and offers an online directory of gay- and lesbian-friendly travel businesses and tour operators.

Many agencies offer tours and travel itineraries specifically for gay and lesbian travelers. **Above and Beyond Tours** (© **800/397-2681;** www.abovebeyondtours.com) are gay Australia tour specialists. San Francisco–based **Now, Voyager** (© **800/255-6951;** www.nowvoyager.com) offers worldwide trips and cruises; and **Olivia** (© **800/631-6277;** www.olivia.com) offers lesbian cruises and resort vacations.

Gay.com Travel (© **800/929-2268** or 415/644-8044; www.gay.com/travel or www.outandabout.com) is an excellent online successor to the popular ***Out & About*** print magazine. It provides regularly updated information about gay-owned, gay-oriented, and gay-friendly lodging, dining, sightseeing, nightlife, and shopping establishments in every important destination worldwide. British travelers should click on the "Travel" link at **www.uk.gay.com** for advice and gay-friendly trip ideas.

The Canadian website **GayTraveler (gaytraveler.ca)** offers ideas and advice for gay travel all over the world.

The following travel guides are available at many bookstores, or you can order them from any online bookseller: ***Spartacus International Gay Guide, 35th Edition*** (Bruno Gmünder Verlag; www.spartacusworld.com/gayguide) and ***Odysseus: The International Gay Travel Planner, 17th Edition*** (www.odyusa.com); and the ***Damron*** guides (www.damron.com), with separate, annual books for gay men and lesbians.

SENIOR TRAVEL

Nearly every attraction in San Francisco offers a senior discount; age requirements vary, and specific prices are listed in chapter 7. Public transportation and movie theaters also have reduced rates. Don't be shy about asking for discounts, but always carry some kind of identification, such as a driver's license, that shows your date of birth.

Members of **AARP,** 601 E St. NW, Washington, DC 20049 (✆ **888/687-2277;** www.aarp.org), get discounts on hotels, airfares, and car rentals. AARP offers members a wide range of benefits, including *AARP: The Magazine* and a monthly newsletter. Anyone over 50 can join.

Recommended publications offering travel resources and discounts for seniors include: the quarterly magazine ***Travel 50 & Beyond*** (www.travel50andbeyond.com) and the bestselling paperback ***Unbelievably Good Deals and Great Adventures That You Absolutely Can't Get Unless You're Over 50 2005–2006, 16th Edition*** (McGraw-Hill), by Joann Rattner Heilman.

FAMILY TRAVEL

If you have enough trouble getting your kids out of the house in the morning, dragging them thousands of miles away may seem like an insurmountable challenge. But family travel can be immensely rewarding, giving you new ways of seeing the world through smaller pairs of eyes.

San Francisco is full of sightseeing opportunities and special activities geared toward children. See "Especially for Kids," in chapter 7, beginning on p. 182, for information and ideas for families. Also watch for the "Kids" icon throughout this guide.

Recommended family travel websites include **Family Travel Forum** (www.familytravelforum.com), a comprehensive site that offers customized trip planning; **Family Travel Network** (www.familytravelnetwork.com), an online magazine providing travel tips; and **TravelWithYourKids.com** (www.travelwithyourkids.com), a comprehensive site written by parents for parents offering sound advice for long-distance and international travel with children.

PUBLICATIONS ***Frommer's San Francisco with Kids*** (Wiley Publishing, Inc.) is a good source of kid-specific information for your trip. The ***Unofficial Guide to California with Kids*** is also a useful resource if you plan to travel throughout the state.

AFRICAN-AMERICAN TRAVELERS

Black Travel Online (www.blacktravelonline.com) posts news on upcoming events and includes links to articles and travel-booking sites. **Soul of America** (www.soulofamerica.com) is a comprehensive website, with travel tips, event and family-reunion postings, and sections on historically black beach resorts and active vacations.

Agencies and organizations that provide resources for black travelers include: **Rodgers Travel** (✆ **800/825-1775;** www.rodgerstravel.com); the **African American Association of Innkeepers International** (✆ **877/422-5777;** www.africanamericaninns.com); and **Henderson Travel & Tours** (✆ **800/327-2309** or 301/650-5700; www.hendersontravel.com), which has specialized in trips to Africa since 1957.

Go Girl: The Black Woman's Guide to Travel & Adventure (Eighth Mountain Press) is a compilation of travel essays by writers including Jill Nelson and Audre Lorde. ***Travel and Enjoy Magazine***

(© **866/266-6211;** www.travelandenjoy.com) is a travel magazine and guide. The well-done ***Pathfinders Magazine*** (© **877/977-PATH;** www.pathfinderstravel.com) includes articles on everything from Rio de Janeiro to Ghana to upcoming ski, diving, golf, and tennis trips.

STUDENT TRAVEL

A valid student ID will often qualify students for discounts on airfare, accommodations, entry to museums, cultural events, movies, and more. The **International Student Travel Confederation (ISTC)** (www.istc.org) was formed in 1949 to make travel around the world more affordable for students. Check out its website for comprehensive travel services information and details on how to get an **International Student Identity Card (ISIC),** which qualifies students for substantial savings on rail passes, plane tickets, entrance fees, and more. It also provides students with basic health and life insurance and a 24-hour helpline. The card is valid for a maximum of 18 months. You can apply for the card online or in person at **STA Travel** (© **800/781-4040** in North America; www.statravel.com), the biggest student travel agency in the world; check out the website to locate STA Travel offices worldwide. If you're no longer a student but are still under 26, you can get an **International Youth Travel Card (IYTC)** from the same people, which entitles you to some discounts. **Travel CUTS** (© **800/592-2887;** www.travelcuts.com) offers similar services for both Canadians and U.S. residents. Irish students may prefer to turn to **USIT** (© **01/602-1904;** www.usit.ie), an Ireland-based specialist in student, youth, and independent travel.

TRAVELING WITH PETS

If you're thinking of taking your pet along with you to romp on a California beach, make sure you do a little research. For one thing, dogs are restricted from running free on most public beaches in the San Francisco area (though the law is often ignored). To find out where you can bring man's best friend, check out the online **Pets Welcome** service (www.petswelcome.com), which lists accommodations that allow pets. The site also lists pet-related publications, medical travel tips, and links to other pet-related websites.

A good book to carry along is ***The California Dog Lover's Companion: The Insider's Scoop on Where to Take Your Dog*** (Avalon Travel Publishing), a 900-page source for complete statewide listings of fenced dog parks, dog-friendly beaches, and other indispensable information.

Also note that San Francisco has strict leash laws (including stiff penalties for failing to pick up waste). In the event that your pet requires medical care while you're visiting, call or visit the **SF/SPCA Animal Hospital,** 2500 16th St. at Harrison Street (© **415/554-3030;** www.sfspca.org). The **San Francisco Veterinary Specialists,** located at 600 Alabama St. at 18th Street (© **415/401-9200;** www.sfvs.net), is open 24 hours, 7 days a week.

10 Sustainable Tourism/Ecotourism

Each time you take a flight or drive a car, CO_2 is released into the atmosphere. You can help neutralize this danger to our planet through "carbon offsetting"—paying someone to reduce your CO_2 emissions by the same amount you've added. Carbon offsets can be purchased in the U.S. from companies such as **Carbonfund.org** (www.carbonfund.org) and **TerraPass** (www.terrapass.org); and, in

Frommers.com: The Complete Travel Resource

It should go without saying, but we highly recommend **Frommers.com,** voted Best Travel Site by *PC Magazine.* We think you'll find our expert advice and tips; independent reviews of hotels, restaurants, attractions, and preferred shopping and nightlife venues; vacation giveaways; and an online booking tool indispensable before, during, and after your travels. We publish the complete contents of over 128 travel guides in our **Destinations** section covering nearly 3,600 places worldwide to help you plan your trip. Each weekday, we publish original articles reporting on **Deals and News** via our free **Frommers.com Newsletter** to help you save time and money and travel smarter. We're betting you'll find our new **Events** listings (http://events.frommers.com) an invaluable resource; it's an up-to-the-minute roster of what's happening in cities everywhere—including concerts, festivals, lectures and more. We've also added weekly **Podcasts, interactive maps,** and hundreds of new images across the site. Check out our **Travel Talk** area featuring **Message Boards** where you can join in conversations with thousands of fellow Frommer's travelers and post your trip report once you return.

the U.K., from **Climate Care** (www.climatecare.org).

Although one could argue that any vacation that includes an airplane flight can't be truly "green," you can go on holiday and still contribute positively to the environment. In addition to purchasing carbon offsets from the companies mentioned above, you can take other steps towards responsible travel. Choose forward-looking companies who embrace responsible development practices, helping preserve destinations for the future by working alongside local people. An increasing number of sustainable tourism initiatives can help you plan a family trip and leave as small a "footprint" as possible on the places you visit.

Responsible Travel (www.responsibletravel.com), run by a spokesperson for responsible tourism in the travel industry, contains a great source of sustainable travel ideas.

You can find eco-friendly travel tips, statistics, and touring companies and associations—listed by destination under "Travel Choice"—at the TIES website, **www.ecotourism.org**. Also check out **Conservation International** (www.conservation.org)—which, with *National Geographic Traveler,* annually presents **World Legacy Awards** (www.wlaward.org) to those travel tour operators, businesses, organizations, and places that have made a significant contribution to sustainable tourism.

11 Staying Connected

TELEPHONES

Generally, hotel surcharges on long-distance and local calls are astronomical, so you're better off using your **cellphone** or a **public pay telephone.** Many convenience groceries and packaging services sell **prepaid calling cards** in denominations up to $50; for international visitors these can be the least expensive way to call home. Many public pay phones at airports now accept American Express, MasterCard, and Visa credit cards. **Local**

calls made from pay phones in most locales cost either 25¢ or 35¢ (no pennies, please).

Most long-distance and international calls can be dialed directly from any phone. **For calls within the United States and to Canada,** dial 1 followed by the area code and the seven-digit number. **For other international calls,** dial 011 followed by the country code, city code, and the number you are calling.

Calls to area codes **800, 888, 877,** and **866** are toll-free. However, calls to area codes **700** and **900** (chat lines, bulletin boards, "dating" services, and so on) can be very expensive—usually a charge of 95¢ to $3 or more per minute, and they sometimes have minimum charges that can run as high as $15 or more.

For **reversed-charge** or **collect calls,** and for **person-to-person** calls, dial the number 0, then the area code and number; an operator will come on the line, and you should specify whether you are calling collect, person-to-person, or both. If your operator-assisted call is international, ask for the overseas operator.

For **local directory assistance** ("information"), dial 411; for long-distance information, dial 1, then the appropriate area code and 555-1212.

INTERNET/E-MAIL

WITHOUT YOUR OWN COMPUTER

San Francisco is totally wired. You'll find that many cafes have wireless access, as do many hotels. Check www.wifi411.com for a huge list of Wi-Fi hotspots—including every Starbucks coffee shop, Kinko's copy store, or McDonald's—or stop by one of the following locations around town where you can get online access, perhaps with a sandwich and a cup o' joe.

You can do your laundry, listen to music, dine, and check your stocks online at SoMa's **Brainwash,** 1122 Folsom St., between Seventh and Eighth streets (© **415/861-FOOD;** www.brainwash.com). It's open Monday through Thursday from 7am to 11pm, Friday and Saturday from 7am to midnight, and Sunday from 8am to 11pm; rates are $3 for 20 minutes.

You can't wash your clothes at **Quetzal,** 1234 Polk St., at Bush Street (© **415/673-4181**), but you can get a cup of coffee and a nosh while you're online for 16¢ a minute. They're open Monday through Saturday from 6:45am to 9pm and Sunday from 7:30am to 8pm.

For access without the ambience, try **Copy Central,** 110 Sutter St., at Montgomery Street (© **415/392-6470;** www.copycentral.com), which provides access cards costing 20¢ per minute. It's open Monday through Thursday from 8am to 8pm and Friday from 8am to 7pm. Ditto **Kinko's,** 1967 Market St., near Gough Street (© **415/252-0864;** www.kinkos.com), which charges 25¢ per minute. Both of these companies have numerous locations around town.

WITH YOUR OWN COMPUTER

More and more hotels, resorts, airports, cafes, and retailers are going Wi-Fi (wireless fidelity), becoming "hotspots" that offer free high-speed Wi-Fi access or charge a small fee for usage. Wi-Fi is even found in campgrounds, RV parks, and entire towns. Most laptops sold today have built-in wireless capability. To find public Wi-Fi hotspots at your destination, go to **www.jiwire.com;** its Hotspot Finder holds the world's largest directory of public wireless hotspots.

For dial-up access, most business-class hotels in the U.S. offer dataports for laptop modems, and a few thousand hotels in the U.S. and Europe now offer free high-speed Internet access—though you might have to pay a one-time connection fee that's good for 24 hours.

Wherever you go, bring a **connection kit** of the right power and phone adapters, a spare phone cord, and a spare Ethernet network cable—or find out whether your hotel supplies them to guests.

For information on electrical currency conversions, see "Electricity," in the "Fast Facts" section at the end of this chapter.

12 Packages for the Independent Traveler

Package tours are simply a way to buy the airfare, accommodations, and other elements of your trip (such as car rentals, airport transfers, and sometimes even activities) at the same time and often at discounted prices.

One good source of package deals is the airlines themselves. Most major airlines offer air/land packages, including **American Airlines Vacations** (✆ 800/321-2121; www.aavacations.com), **Delta Vacations** (✆ 800/654-6559; www.deltavacations.com), **Continental Airlines Vacations** (✆ 800/301-3800; www.covacations.com), and **United Vacations** (✆ 888/854-3899; www.unitedvacations.com). Several big **online travel agencies**—Expedia, Travelocity, Orbitz, Site59, and Lastminute.com—also do a brisk business in packages.

Travel packages are also listed in the travel section of your local Sunday newspaper. Or check ads in the national travel magazines such as *Arthur Frommer's Budget Travel Magazine, Travel + Leisure, National Geographic Traveler,* and *Condé Nast Traveler.*

FAST FACTS: San Francisco

American Express For travel arrangements, traveler's checks, currency exchange, and other member services, there's an office at 455 Market St., at First Street (✆ **415/536-2600**), in the Financial District, open Monday through Friday from 9am to 5:30pm and Saturday from 10am to 2pm. To report lost or stolen traveler's checks, call ✆ **800/221-7282.** For American Express Global Assist, call ✆ **800/554-2639.**

Area Code The area code for San Francisco is **415;** for Oakland, Berkeley, and much of the East Bay, **510;** for the peninsula, generally **650.** Napa and Sonoma are **707.** Most phone numbers in this book are in San Francisco's 415 area code, but there's no need to dial it if you're within city limits.

ATM Networks See "Money & Costs," p. 21.

Automobile Organizations Auto clubs will supply maps, suggested routes, guidebooks, accident and bail-bond insurance, and emergency road service. The **American Automobile Association (AAA)** is the major auto club in the United States. If you belong to an auto club in your home country, inquire about AAA reciprocity before you leave. You may be able to join AAA even if you're not a member of a reciprocal club; to inquire, call AAA (✆ **800/222-4357**). AAA is actually an organization of regional auto clubs, so look under "AAA Automobile Club" in the White Pages of the telephone directory. AAA has a nationwide emergency road service telephone number (✆ 800/AAA-HELP).

Babysitters If you're staying at one of the larger hotels, the concierge can usually recommend a reliable babysitter. If not, contact **Bay Supersitters** at ✆ 415/221-9716.

Business Hours Most banks are open Monday through Friday from 9am to 5pm as well as Saturday mornings. Many banks also have ATMs for 24-hour banking. (See the "Money & Costs" section beginning on p. 21.)

Most stores are open Monday through Saturday from 10 or 11am to at least 6pm, with shorter hours on Sunday. But there are exceptions: Stores in Chinatown, Ghirardelli Square, and Pier 39 stay open much later during the tourist season, and large department stores, including Macy's and Nordstrom, keep late hours.

Most restaurants serve lunch from about 11:30am to 2:30pm and dinner from about 5:30 to 10pm. They sometimes serve later on weekends. Nightclubs and bars are usually open daily until 2am, when they are legally bound to stop serving alcohol.

Car Rentals See "Getting Around," p. 51.

Cashpoints See "Money & Costs," p. 21.

Currency The most common bills are the $1 (a "buck"), $5, $10, and $20 denominations. There are also $2 bills (seldom encountered), $50 bills, and $100 bills (the last two are usually not welcome as payment for small purchases).

Coins come in seven denominations: 1¢ (1 cent, or a penny); 5¢ (5 cents, or a nickel); 10¢ (10 cents, or a dime); 25¢ (25 cents, or a quarter); 50¢ (50 cents, or a half dollar); the gold-colored Sacagawea coin, worth $1; and the rare silver dollar.

For additional information see "Money & Costs," p. 21.

Customs **What You Can Bring Into San Francisco:** Every visitor more than 21 years of age may bring in, free of duty, the following: (1) 1 liter of wine or hard liquor; (2) 200 cigarettes, 100 cigars (but not from Cuba), or 3 pounds of smoking tobacco; and (3) $100 worth of gifts. These exemptions are offered to travelers who spend at least 72 hours in the United States and who have not claimed them within the preceding 6 months. It is altogether forbidden to bring into the country foodstuffs (particularly fruit, cooked meats, and canned goods) and plants (vegetables, seeds, tropical plants, and the like). Foreign tourists may carry in or out up to $10,000 in U.S. or foreign currency with no formalities; larger sums must be declared to U.S. Customs on entering or leaving, which includes filing form CM 4790. For details regarding U.S. Customs and Border Protection, consult your nearest U.S. embassy or consulate, or **U.S. Customs** (✆ **202/927-1770;** www.customs.ustreas.gov).

What You Can Take Home from San Francisco:

Canadian Citizens: For a clear summary of Canadian rules, write for the booklet *I Declare,* issued by the **Canada Border Services Agency** (✆ **800/461-9999** in Canada, or 204/983-3500; **www.cbsa-asfc.gc.ca**).

U.K. Citizens: For information, contact **HM Customs & Excise** at ✆ **0845/010-9000** (from outside the U.K., 020/8929-0152), or consult their website at **www.hmce.gov.uk**.

Australian Citizens: A helpful brochure available from Australian consulates or Customs offices is *Know Before You Go.* For more information, call the **Australian Customs Service** at ✆ **1300/363-263,** or log on to **www.customs.gov.au**.

New Zealand Citizens: Most questions are answered in a free pamphlet available at New Zealand consulates and Customs offices: *New Zealand Customs Guide for Travellers, Notice no. 4.* For more information, contact **New Zealand Customs,** The Customhouse, 17–21 Whitmore St., Box 2218, Wellington (✆ **04/473-6099** or 0800/428-786; **www.customs.govt.nz**).

Dentists In the event of a dental emergency, see your hotel concierge or contact the **San Francisco Dental Office,** 131 Steuart St., Suite 323 (✆ **415/777-5115**), between Mission and Howard streets, which offers emergency service and comprehensive dental care Monday, Tuesday, and Friday from 7:30am to 4:30pm, Wednesday and Thursday from 10:30am to 6:30pm.

Drinking Laws The legal age for purchase and consumption of alcoholic beverages is 21; proof of age is required and often requested at bars, nightclubs, and restaurants, so it's always a good idea to bring ID when you go out. Supermarkets and convenience stores in California sell beer, wine, and liquor.

Most restaurants serve alcohol, but some only serve beer and wine—it depends on the type of liquor license they own. By law all bars, clubs, restaurants, and stores cannot sell or serve alcohol after 2am, and "last call" tends to start at 1:30am. There are no county or calendar alcohol restrictions in California.

Do not carry open containers of alcohol in your car or any public area that isn't zoned for alcohol consumption. The police can fine you on the spot. And nothing will ruin your trip faster than getting a citation for DUI ("driving under the influence"), so don't even think about driving while intoxicated.

Drugstores **Walgreens** pharmacies are all over town, including one at 135 Powell St. (✆ **415/391-4433**). The store is open Monday through Friday from 7am to midnight and Saturday and Sunday from 8am to midnight; the pharmacy is open Monday through Friday from 8am to 9pm, Saturday from 9am to 5pm; it's closed on Sunday. The branch on Divisadero Street at Lombard (✆ **415/931-6415**) has a 24-hour pharmacy.

Earthquakes There will always be earthquakes in California, most of which you'll never notice. However, in case of a significant shaker, there are a few basic precautionary measures you should know. When you are inside a building, seek cover; do not run outside. Stand under a doorway or against a wall, and stay away from windows. If you exit a building after a substantial quake, use stairwells, not elevators. If you are in your car, pull over to the side of the road and stop—but not until you are away from bridges, overpasses, telephone poles, and power lines. Stay in your car. If you're out walking, stay outside and away from trees, power lines, and the sides of buildings. If you're in an area with tall buildings, find a doorway in which to stand.

Electricity Like Canada, the United States uses 110–120 volts AC (60 cycles), compared to 220–240 volts AC (50 cycles) in most of Europe, Australia, and New Zealand. If your small appliances use 220–240 volts, you'll need a 110-volt transformer and a plug adapter with two flat parallel pins to operate them here. Downward converters that change 220–240 volts to 110–120 volts are difficult to find in the United States, so bring one with you.

Embassies & Consulates All embassies are located in the nation's capital, Washington, D.C. Some consulates are located in major U.S. cities, and most nations have a mission to the United Nations in New York City. If your country isn't listed below, call for directory information in Washington, D.C. (✆ **202/555-1212**) or log on to **www.embassy.org/embassies**.

The embassy of **Australia** is at 1601 Massachusetts Ave. NW, Washington, D.C. 20036 (✆ **202/797-3000;** www.austemb.org). There are consulates in New York, Honolulu, Houston, Los Angeles, and San Francisco.

The embassy of **Canada** is at 501 Pennsylvania Ave. NW, Washington, D.C. 20001 (✆ **202/682-1740;** www.canadianembassy.org). Other Canadian consulates are in Buffalo (New York), Detroit, Los Angeles, New York, and Seattle.

The embassy of **Ireland** is at 2234 Massachusetts Ave. NW, Washington, D.C. 20008 (✆ **202/462-3939;** www.irelandemb.org). Irish consulates are in Boston, Chicago, New York, San Francisco, and other cities. See website for complete listing.

The embassy of **New Zealand** is at 37 Observatory Circle NW, Washington, D.C. 20008 (✆ **202/328-4800;** www.nzemb.org). New Zealand consulates are in Los Angeles, Salt Lake City, San Francisco, and Seattle.

The embassy of the **United Kingdom** is at 3100 Massachusetts Ave. NW, Washington, D.C. 20008 (✆ **202/588-7800;** www.britainusa.com). Other British consulates are in Atlanta, Boston, Chicago, Cleveland, Houston, Los Angeles, New York, San Francisco, and Seattle.

Emergencies Call ✆ **911** to report a fire, call the police, or get an ambulance anywhere in the United States. This is a toll-free call (no coins are required at public telephones).

Gasoline (Petrol) At press time, in the U.S., the cost of gasoline (also known as gas, but never petrol), is abnormally high (about $3.30 per gallon at press time). Taxes are already included in the printed price. One U.S. gallon equals 3.8 liters or .85 imperial gallons. Fill-up locations are known as gas or service stations.

Holidays Banks, government offices, post offices, and many stores, restaurants, and museums are closed on the following legal national holidays: January 1 (New Year's Day), the third Monday in January (Martin Luther King, Jr., Day), the third Monday in February (Presidents' Day), the last Monday in May (Memorial Day), July 4 (Independence Day), the first Monday in September (Labor Day), the second Monday in October (Columbus Day), November 11 (Veterans' Day/Armistice Day), the fourth Thursday in November (Thanksgiving Day), and December 25 (Christmas). The Tuesday after the first Monday in November is Election Day, a federal government holiday in presidential-election years (held every 4 years, and next in 2008).

For more information on holidays see "Calendar of Events," earlier in this chapter.

Hospitals **Saint Francis Memorial Hospital,** 900 Hyde St., between Bush and Pine streets on Nob Hill (✆ **415/353-6000**), provides emergency service 24 hours a day; no appointment is necessary. The hospital also operates a **physician-referral service** (✆ **800/333-1355** or 415/353-6566).

Internet Access See "Internet/E-mail," p. 31.

Legal Aid If you are "pulled over" for a minor infraction (such as speeding), never attempt to pay the fine directly to a police officer; this could be construed as attempted bribery, a much more serious crime. Pay fines by mail, or directly into the hands of the clerk of the court. If accused of a more serious offense, say and do nothing before consulting a lawyer. Here the burden is on the state to prove a person's guilt beyond a reasonable doubt, and everyone has the right to remain silent, whether he or she is suspected of a crime or actually arrested. Once arrested, a person can make one telephone call to a party of his or her choice. International visitors should call their embassy or consulate.

Lost & Found Be sure to tell all of your credit card companies the minute you discover your wallet has been lost or stolen and file a report at the nearest police precinct. Your credit card company or insurer may require a police report number or record of the loss. Most credit card companies have an emergency toll-free number to call if your card is lost or stolen; they may be able to wire you a cash advance immediately or deliver an emergency credit card in a day or two. Visa's U.S. emergency number is ✆ **800/847-2911** or 410/581-9994. American Express card holders and traveler's check holders should call ✆ **800/221-7282.** MasterCard holders should call ✆ **800/307-7309** or 636/722-7111. For other credit cards, call the toll-free number directory at ✆ **800/555-1212.**

If you need emergency cash over the weekend when all banks and American Express offices are closed, you can have money wired to you via **Western Union** (✆ **800/325-6000;** www.westernunion.com).

Laundry Most hotels offer laundry service. But if you want to save money you can easily tote your gear to a local laundromat or dry cleaner. Ask your hotel for the nearest location—they're all over town. Or for a scene with your suds, go to SoMa's **Brainwash,** 1122 Folsom St., between Seventh and Eighth streets (✆ **415/861-FOOD**). See above for hours.

Newspapers & Magazines The city's main daily is the *San Francisco Chronicle,* which is distributed throughout the city. Check out the *Chronicle*'s massive Sunday edition that includes a pink "Datebook" section—an excellent preview of the week's upcoming events. The free weekly *San Francisco Bay Guardian* (www.sfbg.com) and *San Francisco Weekly* (www.sfweekly.com), tabloids of news and listings, are indispensable for nightlife information; they're widely distributed through street-corner kiosks and at city cafes and restaurants.

Of the many free tourist-oriented publications, the most widely read are *San Francisco Guide* (www.sfguide.com), a handbook-size weekly containing maps and information on current events, and *Where San Francisco* (www.wheremagazine.com), a glossy regular format monthly magazine. You can find them in most hotels, shops, and restaurants in the major tourist areas.

Passports **For Residents of Australia:** You can pick up an application from your local post office or any branch of Passports Australia, but you must schedule an interview at the passport office to present your application materials. Call the **Australian Passport Information Service** at ✆ **131-232,** or visit the government website at www.passports.gov.au.

For Residents of Canada: Passport applications are available at travel agencies throughout Canada or from the central **Passport Office,** Department of Foreign Affairs and International Trade, Ottawa, ON K1A 0G3 (✆ **800/567-6868;** www.ppt.gc.ca). ***Note:*** Canadian children who travel must have their own passports. However, if you hold a valid Canadian passport issued before December 11, 2001, that bears the name of your child, the passport remains valid for you and your child until it expires.

For Residents of Ireland: You can apply for a 10-year passport at the **Passport Office,** Setanta Centre, Molesworth Street, Dublin 2 (✆ **01/671-1633;** www.irlgov.ie/iveagh). Those under age 18 and over 65 must apply for a 3-year passport. You can also apply at 1A South Mall, Cork (✆ **021/272-525**) or at most main post offices.

For Residents of New Zealand: You can pick up a passport application at any New Zealand Passports Office or download it from their website. Contact the **Passports Office** at ✆ **0800/225-050** in New Zealand or 04/474-8100, or log on to www.passports.govt.nz.

For Residents of the United Kingdom: To pick up an application for a standard 10-year passport (5-yr. passport for children under 16), visit your nearest passport office, major post office, or travel agency; or contact the **United Kingdom Passport Service** at ✆ **0870/521-0410** or search its website at www.ukpa.gov.uk.

Police For emergencies, dial ✆ **911** from any phone; no coins are needed. For other matters, call ✆ **415/553-0123.**

Post Office Dozens of post offices are located around the city. The closest to Union Square is inside the Macy's department store at 170 O'Farrell St. (✆ **800/275-8777** or 415/956-0131; www.usps.gov). You can pick up mail addressed to you and marked "General Delivery" (Poste Restante) at the **Civic Center Post Office Box Unit,** General Delivery, San Francisco, CA 94142-9991 (✆ **800/275-8777** or 415/563-7284). The street address is 101 Hyde St.

Safety See "Safety," earlier in this chapter.

Smoking If San Francisco is California's most European city in looks and style, the comparison stops when it comes to smoking in public. Each year, smoking laws in the city become stricter. Since 1998, smoking has been prohibited in restaurants and bars. Hotels are also offering more nonsmoking rooms, which often leaves those who like to puff out in the cold—sometimes literally.

Taxes In the United States, there is no value-added tax (VAT) or other indirect tax at the national level. Every state, county, and city has the right to levy its own local tax on all purchases, including hotel and restaurant checks, airline tickets, and so on, and is not included in the price tags you'll see on merchandise. This tax is not refundable. Sales tax in San Francisco is 8.5%. Hotel tax is charged on the room tariff only (which is not subject to sales tax) and is set by the city, ranging from 12% to 17% around Northern California.

Telephone, Telegraph, Telex & Fax Generally, hotel surcharges on long-distance and local calls are astronomical, so you're better off using your **cellphone** or a **public pay telephone.** Many convenience groceries and packaging services sell

prepaid calling cards in denominations up to $50; for international visitors these can be the least expensive way to call home. Many public phones at airports now accept American Express, MasterCard, and Visa credit cards. **Local calls** made from public pay phones in most locales cost either 25¢ or 35¢. Pay phones do not accept pennies, and few will take anything larger than a quarter.

Most long-distance and international calls can be dialed directly from any phone. **For calls within the United States and to Canada,** dial 1 followed by the area code and the seven-digit number. **For other international calls,** dial 011 followed by the country code, city code, and the number you are calling.

Calls to area codes **800, 888, 877,** and **866** are toll-free. However, calls to area codes **700** and **900** (chat lines, bulletin boards, "dating" services, and so on) can be very expensive—usually a charge of 95¢ to $3 or more per minute, and they sometimes have minimum charges that can run as high as $15 or more.

For **reversed-charge or collect calls,** and for person-to-person calls, dial the number 0, then the area code and number; an operator will come on the line, and you should specify whether you are calling collect, person-to-person, or both. If your operator-assisted call is international, ask for the overseas operator.

For **local directory assistance** ("information"), dial 411; for long-distance information, dial 1, then the appropriate area code and 555-1212.

Telegraph and telex services are provided primarily by Western Union. You can telegraph money, or have it telegraphed to you, very quickly over the Western Union system, but this service can cost as much as 15% to 20% of the amount sent.

Most hotels have **fax machines** available for guest use (be sure to ask about the charge to use it). Many hotel rooms are even wired for guests' fax machines. A less expensive way to send and receive faxes may be at stores such as **The UPS Store** (formerly Mail Boxes Etc.).

Time San Francisco is in the Pacific Standard Time zone, which is 8 hours behind Greenwich Mean Time and 3 hours behind Eastern Standard Time. The continental United States is divided into **four time zones:** Eastern Standard Time (EST), Central Standard Time (CST), Mountain Standard Time (MST), and Pacific Standard Time (PST). Alaska and Hawaii have their own zones. For example, when it's 9am in San Francisco (PST), it's 7am in Honolulu (HST),10am in Denver (MST), 11am in Chicago (CST), noon in New York City (EST), 5pm in London (GMT), and 2am the next day in Sydney.

Daylight saving time is in effect from 2am on the second Sunday in March until 2am on the first Sunday in November, except in Arizona, Hawaii, the U.S. Virgin Islands, and Puerto Rico. Daylight saving moves the clock 1 hour ahead of standard time.

Tipping Tips are a very important part of certain workers' income, and gratuities are the standard way of showing appreciation for services provided. (Tipping is certainly not compulsory if the service is poor!) In hotels, tip **bellhops** at least $1 per bag ($2–$3 if you have a lot of luggage) and tip the **chamber staff** $1 to $2 per day (more if you've left a disaster area for him or her to clean up). Tip the **doorman** or **concierge** only if he or she has provided you with some specific service (for example, calling a cab for you or obtaining difficult-to-get theater tickets). Tip the **valet-parking attendant** $2 every time you get your car.

In restaurants, bars, and nightclubs, tip **service staff** 15% to 20% of the check, tip **bartenders** no less than $1 per drink, tip **checkroom attendants** $1 per garment, and tip **valet-parking attendants** $1 per vehicle.

As for other service personnel, tip **cab drivers** 15% of the fare; tip **skycaps** at airports at least $1 per bag ($2–$3 if you have a lot of luggage); and tip **hairdressers** and **barbers** 15% to 20%.

Toilets Those weird, oval-shaped, olive-green kiosks on the sidewalks throughout San Francisco are high-tech self-cleaning public toilets. They've been placed on high-volume streets to provide relief for pedestrians. French potty-maker JCDecaux gave them to the city for free—advertising covers the cost. It costs 25¢ to enter, with no time limit, but I don't recommend using the ones in the sketchier neighborhoods such as the Mission because they're mostly used by crackheads and prostitutes. Large hotels are often the best bet for clean facilities.

Visas For information about U.S. Visas go to **http://travel.state.gov** and click on "Visas." Or go to one of the following websites:

Australian citizens can obtain up-to-date visa information from the **U.S. Embassy Canberra,** Moonah Place, Yarralumla, ACT 2600 (✆ **02/6214-5600**); or by checking the U.S. Diplomatic Mission's website at **http://usembassy-australia.state.gov/consular.**

British subjects can obtain up-to-date visa information by calling the **U.S. Embassy Visa Information Line** (✆ **0891/200-290**) or by visiting the "Visas to the U.S." section of the American Embassy London's website at **www.usembassy.org.uk.**

Irish citizens can obtain up-to-date visa information through the **Embassy of the USA Dublin,** 42 Elgin Rd., Dublin 4, Ireland (✆ **353/1-668-8777;** or by checking the "Consular Services" section of the website at **http://dublin.usembassy.gov.**

Citizens of **New Zealand** can obtain up-to-date visa information by contacting the **U.S. Embassy New Zealand,** 29 Fitzherbert Terrace, Thorndon, Wellington (✆ **644/472-2068**), or get the information directly from the website at **http://wellington.usembassy.gov.**

3

Suggested San Francisco Itineraries

If you've left your brain at the office and want someone else to make all the tough decisions during your vacation, you'll love this chapter. It's where I tell you what *I* think you should see and do during your vacation in San Francisco. It's broken down into One Day, Two Day, and Three Day sections, depending on how long you're in town. If you've already made your way through "The Best in One Day," the Two Day tour starts where the One Day schedule left off, and so on. But if you really want to enjoy even a fraction of what San Francisco has to offer, you should plan on staying at least three days, preferably a week. And because renting a car in the city is an expensive hassle (and driving in the city is insane), we're going to do all our transportation via foot, bus, and bike. Right, then: Let's get started.

1 The Best of San Francisco in 1 Day

If you've got only one day to explore the city, put on your walking shoes and start early. You've got a lot of ground to cover just to get to the must-sees, but luckily, condensed geography (and hopefully weather) are in your favor. The whirlwind tour starts with a scenic ride on a cable car followed by a tour of Alcatraz Island. Next you'll hoof it up to two of the city's most colorful neighborhoods—Chinatown and North Beach—for lunch, shopping, browsing, cocktails, dinner, and cappuccino. Get an early start, because you're about to have a long yet wonderful day in the city by the bay. ***Start:*** *Bus no. 2, 3, 4, 30, 45, or 76 to Union Square.*

❶ Union Square

Union Square—which was named for a series of pro-union mass demonstrations staged here on the eve of the Civil War—isn't an attraction in itself, but it's the epicenter of the city's shopping district. Macy's, Saks, Tiffany's, Victoria's Secret, and company are located here, and are surrounded by blocks crammed with hundreds of other high-end boutiques. There are very few shopping bargains here, but it's fun to play lookey-loo. Just 3 blocks down, at Powell and Market streets, is the cable car turnaround where you'll embark on a ride on the nation's only moving National Historic Landmark. See p. 152.

❷ Cable Cars & Lombard Street ★★★

Don't be intimidated by the line of people at the cable car turnaround at Market and Powell streets—the ride is worth the wait. The $5 thrill ride starts with a steep climb up Nob Hill, then passes through Chinatown and Russian Hill before plummeting down Hyde Street to Fisherman's Wharf. It's an experience

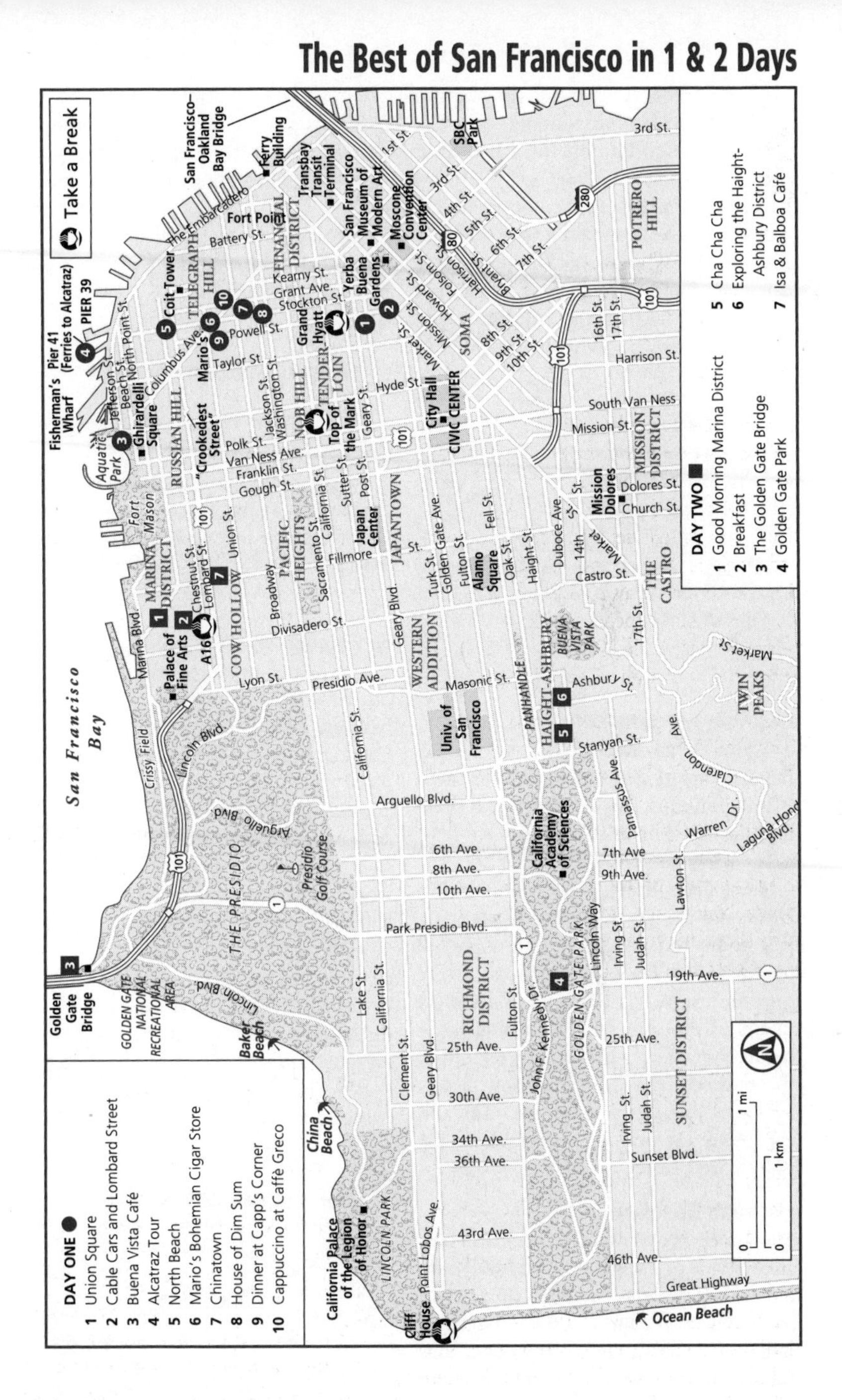
DAY ONE
1 Union Square
2 Cable Cars and Lombard Street
3 Buena Vista Café
4 Alcatraz Tour
5 North Beach
6 Mario's Bohemian Cigar Store
7 Chinatown
8 House of Dim Sum
9 Dinner at Capp's Corner
10 Cappuccino at Caffè Greco
DAY TWO
1 Good Morning Marina District
2 Breakfast
3 The Golden Gate Bridge
4 Golden Gate Park
5 Cha Cha Cha
6 Exploring the Haight-Ashbury District
7 Isa & Balboa Café
Take a Break
San Francisco Bay
Golden Gate Bridge
GOLDEN GATE NATIONAL RECREATIONAL AREA
Baker Beach
China Beach
Cliff House
California Palace of the Legion of Honor
LINCOLN PARK
Ocean Beach
Great Highway
THE PRESIDIO
Presidio Golf Course
Crissy Field
Palace of Fine Arts
MARINA DISTRICT
Fort Mason
Aquatic Park
Ghirardelli Square
Fisherman's Wharf
Pier 41 (Ferries to Alcatraz)
PIER 39
Coit Tower
TELEGRAPH HILL
RUSSIAN HILL
"Crookedest Street"
NOB HILL
TENDER-LOIN
FINANCIAL DISTRICT
Ferry Building
San Francisco–Oakland Bay Bridge
Transbay Transit Terminal
San Francisco Museum of Modern Art
Yerba Buena Gardens
Moscone Convention Center
SBC Park
Grand Hyatt
Top of the Mark
Mario's
Fort Point
COW HOLLOW
PACIFIC HEIGHTS
JAPANTOWN
Japan Center
WESTERN ADDITION
City Hall
CIVIC CENTER
SOMA
Alamo Square
Univ. of San Francisco
PANHANDLE
HAIGHT-ASHBURY
BUENA VISTA PARK
Mission Dolores
MISSION DISTRICT
THE CASTRO
POTRERO HILL
TWIN PEAKS
California Academy of Sciences
GOLDEN GATE PARK
RICHMOND DISTRICT
SUNSET DISTRICT
0 1 mi
0 1 km

you'll never forget. (***Note:*** If you want to check out the famous winding stretch of Lombard Street, hop off the cable car at the intersection of Hyde and Lombard streets and, when you've seen enough, either walk the rest of the way down to Fisherman's Wharf or take the next cable car that comes along.) For maximum thrill, stand during the ride and hold onto the brass rail. See p. 159.

3 BUENA VISTA CAFÉ
After you've completed your first Powell-Hyde cable car ride, it's a San Francisco tradition to celebrate with an Irish coffee at the Buena Vista Café, located at 2765 Hyde St. across from the cable car turnaround (© **415/474-5044**). The first Irish coffees served in America were mixed here in 1952, and they're still the best in the Bay Area. See p. 236.

4 Alcatraz Tour ★★★
To tour "The Rock," the Bay Area's famous abandoned prison on its own island, you must first get there, and that's half the fun. The brief but beautiful ferry ride offers captivating views of the Golden Gate Bridge, the Marin Headlands, and the city. Once inside, an excellent audio tour guides you through cell blocks and offers a colorful look at the prison's historic past as well as its most infamous inmates. Book well in advance because these tours consistently sell out in the summer. Bring snacks and beverages—the ferry's pickings are slim and expensive, and nothing is available on the island. See p. 148.

5 North Beach ★★★
One of the best ways to get the San Francisco vibe is to mingle with the locals, and one of my favorite places to do so is in San Francisco's "Little Italy." Dozens of Italian restaurants and coffeehouses continue to flourish in what is still the center of the city's Italian community. A stroll along Columbus Avenue will take you past eclectic little cafes, delis, bookstores, bakeries, and coffee shops that give North Beach its Italian-bohemian character. See p. 169.

Tip: Be sure to see chapter 8, "City Strolls," for highlights of North Beach and Chinatown.

6 MARIO'S BOHEMIAN CIGAR STORE
Okay, so the menu's limited to coffee drinks and a few sandwiches (the meatball is my favorite), but the convivial atmosphere and large windows that are perfect for people-watching make this tiny, pie-shaped cafe a favorite even with locals. 566 Columbus Ave.; © **415/362-0536.** See p. 124.

7 Chinatown ★★
One block from North Beach is a whole other world: Chinatown. San Francisco has one of the largest communities of Chinese people in the United States, with more than 80,000 people condensed around Grant Avenue and Stockton Street. Although frequented by tourists, the area caters mostly to the Chinese community, who crowd the vegetable and herb markets, restaurants, and shops carrying those ubiquitous pink plastic bags. It's worth a peek if only to see the Stockton Street markets hawking live frogs, armadillos, turtles, and odd sea creatures destined for tonight's dinner table. ***Tip:*** The dozens of knickknack shops are a great source of cheap souvenirs. See p. 170.

8 HOUSE OF DIM SUM
You can't visit Chinatown and not sample dim sum. Walk to 735 Jackson St. to the House of Dim Sum (© 415/399-0888) and order shrimp dumplings, pork dumplings, sweet buns, turnip cake, and the sweet rice with chicken wrapped in a lotus leaf. Find an empty table, pour a side of soy sauce, and dig in.

9 Dinner at Capp's Corner ★

What I love about North Beach are its old-school restaurants—those dusty, frumpy, loud, and over-sauced bastions of bacchanal. **Capp's Corner** (1600 Powell St; ✆ **415/989-2589**) is one of my favorites, where patrons sit at long tables and dine family-style via huge platters of Italian comfort food served by brusque waitresses while Frank croons his classics on the jukebox. See p. 123.

10 Cappuccino at Caffè Greco ★

By now you should be stuffed and exhausted. Good. End the night with a cappuccino at **Caffè Greco** (423 Columbus Ave.; ✆ **415/397-6261**). Sit at one of the sidewalk tables and reminisce on what a great day you had in San Francisco.

2 The Best of San Francisco in 2 Days

On your second day, get familiar with other famous landmarks around the city. Start with breakfast, a science lesson, and a pleasant bayside stroll in the Marina District. Next, cross the famed Golden Gate Bridge on foot, then take a bus to Golden Gate Park. After a stroll through the city's beloved park, it's time for lunch and power shopping on Haight Street, followed by dinner and cocktails back in the Marina District. Smashing. ***Start:*** *Bus no. 22, 28, 30, 30X, 43, 76, or 82X.*

1 Good Morning Marina District

The area that became famous for its destruction during the 1989 earthquake has long been one of the most picturesque and coveted patches of local real estate. Here, along the northern edge of the city, multimillion-dollar homes back up against the bayfront Marina, where a flotilla of sailboats and the mighty Golden Gate Bridge make for a magnificent backdrop for a morning stroll.

Start the day with good cup of coffee on Chestnut Street (see "Take a Break" below), then walk to the Palace of Fine Arts building, built for the Panama-Pacific Exhibition of 1915 and home of the Exploratorium (p. 162). Spend a few hours being thoroughly entertained at the "best science museum in the world" (kids *love* this place), then walk over to Crissy Field (p. 178), where restored wetlands and a beachfront path lead to historic Fort Point (p. 178) and the footpath that will take you up to the southern end of the Golden Gate Bridge.

2 BREAKFAST

If you can't jumpstart your brain properly without a good cup of coffee, then begin your day at **The Grove** (2016 Fillmore St.; tel] **415/474-1419;** p. 134), located in the Marina District—it's as cozy as an old leather couch. If you want a more substantial breakfast, walk over to **Home Plate** (2274 Lombard St.; ✆ **415/922-HOME;** p. 135) for a hefty omelet and freshly baked scones. It's one of my favorite breakfast places in the city.

3 The Golden Gate Bridge ★★★

It's one of those things you have to do at least once in you life—walk across the fabled Golden Gate Bridge, the most photographed man-made structure in the world (p. 158). As you would expect, the views along the span are spectacular and the wind a wee bit chilly, so bring a light jacket. It takes at least an hour to walk northward to the vista point and back. When you return to the southern end, board either Muni bus no. 28 or no. 29

(be sure to ask the driver if the bus is headed toward Golden Gate Park).

4 Golden Gate Park ★★★

Stretching from the middle of the city to the Pacific Ocean and comprising 1,017 acres, Golden Gate Park is one of the city's greatest attributes. Since its development in the late 1880s, it has provided San Franciscans with urban respite via dozens of well-tended gardens, museums, and great grassy expanses prime for picnicking, lounging, or tossing a Frisbee.

Have the bus driver drop you off near John F. Kennedy Drive. Walking eastward on JFK Drive, you'll pass three of the park's most popular attractions: Stow Lake, the newly renovated de Young Museum, and the wonderful Conservatory of Flowers (a must-visit). See p. 173.

5 CHA CHA CHA ★★
By now you're probably starving, so walk out of the park and into the Haight to Cha Cha Cha (1801 Haight St.; ✆ **415/386-7670**; p. 144.), one of my favorite restaurants in the city. Order plenty of dishes from the tapas-style menu and dine family-style. Oh, and don't forget a pitcher of sangria—you've earned it.

6 Exploring the Haight-Ashbury District ★★★

Ah, the Haight. Birthplace of the Summer of Love and Flower Power, shrine to the Grateful Dead, and the place where America's nonconformists still congregate over beers, bongos, and buds. Spend at least an hour strolling up Haight Street (p. 172), browsing the cornucopia of used clothes stores, leather shops, head shops, and poster stores. There are some great bargains to be found here, especially for vintage clothing. When you get to the intersection of Haight and Masonic streets, catch the Muni no. 43 bus heading north, which will take you through the Presidio and back to the Marina District.

7 Dinner & Drinks

You've had a full day, my friend, so rest your weary bones at the back patio at **Isa** (3324 Steiner St.; ✆ **415/567-9588;** p. 133), a fantastic and surprisingly affordable French restaurant in the Marina. If there's still gas in your tank after dinner, walk over to the **Balboa Café** (3199 Fillmore St.; ✆ **415/921-3944**) and practice your pick-up lines among the young-and-restless, who practically live here.

3 The Best of San Francisco in 3 Days

If we weren't on a tight budget I'd have you rent a car and head to the Wine Country for a day of wine tasting, but that would probably blow your budget (if not, skip to the Wine Country chapter; see p. 272). Instead, we're going to do one of my all-time favorite things to do on my day off—ride a bike from Fisherman's Wharf to Sam's Anchor Cafe in Tiburon (that small peninsula just north of Alcatraz Island). The beautiful and exhilarating ride takes you over the Golden Gate Bridge, through the heart of Sausalito, and along the scenic North Bay bike path, ending with a frosty beer and lunch at the best outdoor cafe in the Bay Area. And here's the best part: You don't have to bike back. After lunch, you can take the passenger ferry across the bay to Fisherman's Wharf—right to your starting point. Brilliant. ***Start:*** *Powell-Hyde cable-car line. Bus no. 10, 19, 30, or 47.*

---

1 Rent a Bicycle

Walk, take a bus, or ride the Powell-Hyde cable car (which goes right by it) to **Blazing Saddles** bicycle rental shop at 2715 Hyde St, between Beach and North Point streets near Ghirardelli Square

(✆ **415/202-8888;** p. 188). Rent a single or tandem bike for a full day, and be sure to ask for: 1) a free map pointing out the route to Sam's in Tiburon, 2) ferry tickets, 3) a bicycle lock, and 4) a bottle of water. Bring your own sunscreen, a hat (for the deck at Sam's), and a light jacket—no matter how warm it is right now, the weather can change in minutes. Each bike has a small pouch hooked to the handlebars where you can stuff your stuff.

Fun Tip: While you're here, ask about the GoCar rentals—they're a blast to drive and a great way to explore the city. (See the GoCar sidebar on p. 158 for more info.)

❷ The Warming Hut

Start pedaling along the map route to Golden Gate Bridge. You'll encounter one short, steep hill right from the start at Aquatic Park, but it's okay to walk your bike (hey, you haven't had your coffee fix yet). Keeping riding westward through Fort Point and the Marina Green to Crissy Field. At the west end of Crissy Field, alongside the bike path, is The Warming Hut, a white, barnlike building where you can fuel up with a light snack and coffee drinks. (Don't eat too much.) Several picnic tables nearby offer beautiful views of the bay.

❸ Biking the Golden Gate

After your break, there's one more steep hill up to the bridge. Follow the bike path to the west side of the bridge (pedestrians must stay on the east side), cross the bridge, and take the road to your left heading downhill and crossing underneath

Highway 101. Coast all the way to Sausalito.

❹ Exploring Sausalito

You'll love Sausalito. Coasting your bike onto Bridgeway is like being transported to one of those seaside towns on the French Riviera (p. 262). Lock the bikes and mosey around on foot for a while.

> **5 HORIZONS**
> If you're thirsty, ask for a table on the bayside deck at **Horizons** (558 Bridgeway; ✆ **415/331-3232**) and order a Bloody Mary, but don't eat yet. See p. 264.

❻ North Bay Tour

Back on the bike, head north again on the bike path as it winds along the bay. When you reach the Mill Valley Car Wash at the end of the bike path, turn right onto East Blithedale Avenue, which will cross Highway 101 and turn into Tiburon Boulevard. (This is the only sucky part of the ride where you'll encounter traffic.) About a mile past Highway 101 you'll enter a small park called Blackie's Pasture. (Look for the life-size bronze statue erected in 1995 to honor Tiburon's beloved "mascot" Blackie.) Now it's an easy cruise on the bike path all the way to Sam's.

❼ Lunch at Sam's Anchor Cafe

Ride your bike all the way to the south end of Tiburon and lock your bike at the bike rack near the ferry dock. Walk over to the ferry loading dock and check the ferry departure schedule for "Tiburon to Pier 39/Fisherman's Wharf." Then walk over to **Sam's Anchor Cafe** (27 Main St.; ✆ **415/435-4527;** p. 262), request a table on the back patio overlooking the harbor, and relax with a cool drink—you've earned it.

❽ Ferry Ride Back to San Francisco

When it's time to leave, board the ferry with your bike (bike riders board first, so don't stand in line) and enjoy the ride from Tiburon to San Francisco, with a short stop at Angel Island State Park. From Pier 39 it's a short ride back to the rental shop.

After all this adventuring, it's time to reenergize your body and soul with an Irish whiskey at the **Buena Vista Cafe** (2765 Hyde St.; ✆ **415/474-5044,** across from the cable car turnaround), a short walk from the bike rental shop. After libations, take the cable car back to your hotel for some rest and a shower, then spend the rest of the evening enjoying dinner.

If this isn't one of the best days you've had on your vacation, send me this book and I'll eat it.

4

Getting to Know San Francisco

This chapter offers useful information on how to become better acquainted with San Francisco, even though half the fun of becoming familiar with this city is wandering around and haphazardly stumbling upon great shops, restaurants, and vistas that even locals might not know about. You'll find that although the city is metropolitan, San Francisco is still a small town—one where you won't feel like a stranger for long.

If you get disoriented, just remember that downtown is east and the Golden Gate Bridge is north—and even if you do get lost, you probably won't go too far, since water surrounds three sides of the city. The most difficult challenge you'll have, if you're traveling by car (which I suggest you avoid), is mastering the maze of one-way streets.

1 Orientation

VISITOR INFORMATION

The **San Francisco Visitor Information Center,** on the lower level of Hallidie Plaza, 900 Market St., at Powell Street (© **415/391-2000;** www.onlyinsanfrancisco.com), has brochures, discount coupons, and advice on restaurants, sights, and events in the city; their website offers a incredible amount of information as well. The on-site staff can provide answers in German, Japanese, French, Italian, and Spanish. To find the office, descend the escalator at the cable car turnaround. The office is open Monday through Friday from 9am to 5pm, and Saturday and Sunday from 9am to 3pm, May through October. However, it is closed on Sundays during winter and Easter, Thanksgiving Day, and Christmas Day. Phones are answered in person Monday through Friday only. Otherwise, dial © **415/391-2001** any time, day or night, for a recorded message about current cultural events, theater, music, sports, and other special happenings.

Pick up a copy of the ***Bay Guardian*** **(www.sfbg.com)** or the ***S.F. Weekly*** **(www.sfweekly.com),** the city's free alternative papers, to get listings of all city happenings. You'll find them in kiosks throughout the city and in most cafes.

For specialized information on Chinatown's shops and services, and on the city's Chinese community in general, contact the **Chinese Chamber of Commerce,** 730 Sacramento St. (© **415/982-3000**), open daily from 9am to 5pm.

CITY LAYOUT

San Francisco occupies the tip of a 32-mile peninsula between San Francisco Bay and the Pacific Ocean. Its land area measures about 46 square miles, although the city is often referred to as being 7 square miles. At more than 900 feet high, towering Twin Peaks (which are, in fact, two neighboring peaks), marks the geographic center of the city and is a great place to take in a vista of San Francisco.

Tips **Finding Your Way**

For a full-color map of San Francisco and its public transportation, see the "San Francisco Neighborhoods" and "San Francisco Mass Transit" maps in the color insert at the beginning of this book.

With lots of one-way streets, San Francisco might seem confusing at first, but it will quickly become easy to negotiate. The city's downtown streets are arranged in a simple grid pattern, with the exceptions of Market Street and Columbus Avenue, which cut across the grid at right angles to each other. Hills appear to distort this pattern, however, and can disorient you. As you learn your way around, the hills will become your landmarks and reference points.

MAIN ARTERIES & STREETS **Market Street** is San Francisco's main thoroughfare. Most of the city's buses travel this route on their way to the Financial District from the outer neighborhoods to the west and south. The tall office buildings clustered downtown are at the northeast end of Market; 1 block beyond lies The Embarcadero and the bay.

The Embarcadero ★—an excellent strolling, skating, and biking route (thanks to recent renovations)—curves along San Francisco Bay from south of the Bay Bridge to the northeast perimeter of the city. It terminates at Fisherman's Wharf, the famous tourist-oriented pier. Aquatic Park, Fort Mason, and Golden Gate National Recreation Area are on the northernmost point of the peninsula.

From the eastern perimeter of Fort Mason, **Van Ness Avenue** runs due south, back to Market Street. The area just described forms a rough triangle, with Market Street as its southeastern boundary, the waterfront as its northern boundary, and Van Ness Avenue as its western boundary. Within this triangle lie most of the city's main tourist sights.

FINDING AN ADDRESS Since most of the city's streets are laid out in a grid pattern, finding an address is easy when you know the nearest cross street. Numbers start with 1 at the beginning of the street and proceed at the rate of 100 per block. When asking for directions, find out the nearest cross street and your destination's neighborhood, but be careful not to confuse numerical avenues with numerical streets. Numerical avenues (Third Ave. and so on) are in the Richmond and Sunset districts in the western part of the city. Numerical streets (Third St. and so on) are south of Market Street in the east and south parts of town.

NEIGHBORHOODS IN BRIEF

For further discussion of some of the neighborhoods below, see the "Neighborhoods Worth a Visit" section of chapter 7, beginning on p. 168. For a color map of the city, see the "San Francisco Neighborhoods" map in the color insert of this book.

Union Square Union Square is the commercial hub of San Francisco. Most major hotels and department stores are crammed into the area surrounding the actual square, which was named for a series of violent pro-union mass demonstrations staged here on the eve of the Civil War. A plethora of upscale boutiques, restaurants, and galleries occupy the spaces tucked between the larger buildings. A few blocks west is the **Tenderloin** neighborhood, a patch of poverty and blight where you should keep your wits about you. The **Theater District** is 3 blocks west of Union Square.

The Financial District East of Union Square, this area, bordered by The Embarcadero and by Market, Third, Kearny, and Washington streets, is the city's business district and the stamping grounds for many major corporations. The pointy Transamerica Pyramid, at Montgomery and Clay streets, is one of the district's most conspicuous architectural features. To its east sprawls The Embarcadero Center, an 8½-acre complex housing offices, shops, and restaurants. Farther east still is the old Ferry Building, the city's pre-bridge transportation hub. Ferries to Sausalito and Larkspur still leave from this point. However, in 2003, the building became an attraction in itself when it was completely renovated, jampacked with outstanding restaurant and gourmet food- and wine-related shops, and surrounded by a farmers' market a few days a week, making it a favorite place of San Francisco's residents seeking to stock their kitchens.

Nob Hill & Russian Hill Bounded by Bush, Larkin, Pacific, and Stockton streets, Nob Hill is a genteel, well-heeled district still occupied by the city's major power brokers and the neighborhood businesses they frequent. Russian Hill extends from Pacific to Bay and from Polk to Mason. It contains steep streets, lush gardens, and high-rises occupied by both the moneyed and the bohemian.

Chinatown A large red-and-green gate on Grant Avenue at Bush Street marks the official entrance to Chinatown. Beyond lies a 24-block labyrinth, bordered by Broadway, Bush, Kearny, and Stockton streets, filled with restaurants, markets, temples, shops, and, of course, a substantial percentage of San Francisco's Chinese residents. Chinatown is a great place for exploration all along Stockton and Grant streets, Portsmouth Square, and the alleys that lead off them, like Ross and Waverly. This district has a maddening combination of incessant traffic and horrible drivers, so don't even think about driving around here.

North Beach This Italian neighborhood, which stretches from Montgomery and Jackson to Bay Street, is one of the best places in the city to grab a coffee, pull up a cafe chair, and do some serious people-watching. Nightlife is equally happening in North Beach; restaurants, bars, and clubs along Columbus and Grant avenues attract folks from all over the Bay Area, who fight for a parking place and romp through the festive neighborhood. Down Columbus toward the Financial District are the remains of the city's Beat Generation landmarks, including Ferlinghetti's City Lights Bookstore and Vesuvio's Bar. Broadway—a short strip of sex joints—cuts through the heart of the district. **Telegraph Hill** looms over the east side of North Beach, topped by Coit Tower, one of San Francisco's best vantage points.

Fisherman's Wharf North Beach runs into Fisherman's Wharf, which was once the busy heart of the city's great harbor and waterfront industries. Today it's a kitschy and mildly entertaining tourist area with little, if any, authentic waterfront life, except for a small fleet of fishing boats and some lethargic sea lions. What it does have going for it are activities for the whole family, with attractions, restaurants, trinket shops, and beautiful views and walkways everywhere you look.

The Marina District Created on landfill for the Pan Pacific Exposition of 1915, the Marina District boasts some of the best views of the Golden Gate, as well as plenty of grassy fields alongside San Francisco Bay. Elegant Mediterranean-style homes and apartments, inhabited by the city's well-to-do singles and wealthy families, line the streets. Here, too, are the Palace of Fine Arts, the Exploratorium, and Fort Mason Center. The main street is Chestnut, between Franklin and Lyon, which abounds with shops, cafes, and boutiques. Because of its landfill foundation, the Marina was one of the hardest-hit districts in the 1989 quake.

Cow Hollow Located west of Van Ness Avenue, between Russian Hill and the Presidio, this flat, grazable area supported 30 dairy farms in 1861. Today, Cow Hollow is largely residential and largely yuppie. Its two primary commercial thoroughfares are Lombard Street, known for its many relatively inexpensive motels, and Union Street, a flourishing shopping sector filled with restaurants, pubs, cafes, and shops.

Pacific Heights The ultra-elite, such as the Gettys and Danielle Steel—and those lucky enough to buy before the real-estate boom—reside in the mansions and homes in this neighborhood. When the rich meander out of their fortresses, they wander down to Union Street and join the pretty people who frequent the street's long stretch of chic boutiques and lively neighborhood restaurants, cafes, and bars.

Japantown Bounded by Octavia, Fillmore, California, and Geary, Japantown shelters only a small percentage of the city's Japanese population, but exploring these few square blocks and the shops and restaurants within them is still a cultural experience.

Civic Center Although millions of dollars have gone toward brick sidewalks, ornate lampposts, and elaborate street plantings, the southwestern section of Market Street can still feel a little sketchy due to the large number of homeless who wander the area. The Civic Center at the "bottom" of Market Street, however, is a stunning beacon of culture and refinement. This large complex of buildings includes the domed and dapper City Hall, the Opera House, Davies Symphony Hall, and the Asian Art Museum. The landscaped plaza connecting the buildings is the staging area for San Francisco's frequent demonstrations for or against just about everything.

SoMa No part of San Francisco has been more affected by recent development than the area south of Market Street (dubbed "SoMa"), the area within the triangle of The Embarcadero, Highway 101, and Market Street. Until a decade ago it was a district of old warehouses and industrial spaces, with a few scattered underground nightclubs, restaurants, and shoddy residential areas. But when it became the hub of dot-commercialization and half-million-dollar-plus lofts, its fate changed forever. Today, though dot-coms don't occupy much of the commercial space, the area is jumping thanks to fancy loft residents, the baseball stadium, and surrounding businesses, restaurants, and nightclubs in addition to urban entertainment such as the Museum of Modern Art, Yerba Buena Gardens, Metreon, and a slew of big-bucks hotels that make tons of money from businesspeople. Though still gritty in some areas, it's growing more glittery by the year.

Mission District This is another area that was greatly affected by the city's new wealth. The Mexican and Latin American populations here, with their cuisine, traditions, and art, make the

Mission District a vibrant area to visit. Some parts of the neighborhood are still poor and sprinkled with the homeless, gangs, and drug addicts, but young urbanites have also settled in the area, attracted by its "reasonably" (a relative term) priced rentals and endless oh-so-hot restaurants and bars that stretch from 16th and Valencia streets to 25th and Mission streets. Less adventurous tourists may just want to duck into Mission Dolores, cruise by a few of the 200-plus amazing murals, and head back downtown. But anyone who's interested in hanging with the hipsters and experiencing the hottest restaurant and bar nightlife should definitely beeline it here. Don't be afraid to visit this area, but do use caution at night.

The Castro One of the liveliest streets in town, the Castro is practically synonymous with San Francisco's gay community (even though it is technically a street in the Noe Valley District). Located at the very end of Market Street, between 17th and 18th streets, the Castro has dozens of shops, restaurants, and bars catering to the gay community. Open-minded straight people are welcome, too.

Haight-Ashbury Part trendy, part nostalgic, part funky, the Haight, as it's most commonly known, was the soul of the psychedelic, free-loving 1960s and the center of the counterculture movement. Today, the gritty neighborhood straddling upper Haight Street on the eastern border of Golden Gate Park is more gentrified, but the commercial area still harbors all walks of life. Leftover aging hippies mingle with grungy, begging street kids outside Ben & Jerry's Ice Cream Store (where they might still be talking about Jerry Garcia), nondescript marijuana dealers whisper "Buds" as shoppers pass, and many people walking down the street have Day-Glo hair. But you don't need to be a freak or wear tie-dye to enjoy the Haight—the ethnic food, trendy shops, and bars cover all tastes. From Haight Street, walk south on Cole Street for a more peaceful and quaint neighborhood experience.

Richmond & Sunset Districts San Francisco's suburbs of sorts, these are the city's largest and most populous neighborhoods, consisting mainly of small (but expensive) homes, shops, and neighborhood restaurants. Although they border Golden Gate Park and Ocean Beach, few tourists venture into "The Avenues," as these areas are referred to locally, unless they're on their way to the Cliff House, zoo, or Palace of the Legion of Honor.

2 Getting Around

For a map of San Francisco's public transportation options, see the "San Francisco Mass Transit" color map in the insert of this book. You can also call 511 for current transportation and traffic information or check www.511.org.

BY PUBLIC TRANSPORTATION

The **San Francisco Municipal Transportation Agency,** 1 S. Van Ness Ave., better known as "Muni" (© **415/673-6864;** www.sfmuni.com), operates the city's cable cars, buses, and streetcars. Together, these three services crisscross the entire city. Fares for buses and streetcars are $1.50 for adults; 50¢ for seniors over 65, children 5 to 17, and riders with disabilities. Cable cars, which run from 6:30am to 12:50am, cost a whopping $5 for all people over 5 ($1 for seniors and riders with disabilities 9pm–7am). Needless to say, they're packed primarily with tourists. Exact change is required on all

Value Muni Discounts

Muni discount passes, called **Passports,** entitle holders to unlimited rides on buses, streetcars, and cable cars. A Passport costs $11 for 1 day, $18 for 3 days, and $24 for 7 consecutive days. Another option is buying a **CityPass,** which entitles you to unlimited Muni rides for 7 days, plus admission to the numerous attractions (p. 11). Passports are also sold every day from 8am to midnight at the information booths in the baggage claim areas at San Francisco International Airport. You can also buy a Passport or CityPass at the San Francisco Visitor Information Center, Powell/Market cable car booth, Holiday Inn Civic Center, and TIX Bay Area booth at Union Square, among other outlets.

vehicles except cable cars. Fares are subject to change. If you're standing waiting for Muni and have wireless Web access (or from any computer), check www.nextmuni.com to get up-to-the-minute information about when the next bus or streetcar is coming. Muni's NextBus uses satellite technology and advanced computer modeling to track vehicles on their routes. Each vehicle is fitted with a satellite tracking system so the information is constantly updated.

For detailed route information, phone Muni or consult the Muni map at the front of the San Francisco Yellow Pages. If you plan to use public transportation extensively, you might want to invest in a comprehensive transit and city map ($2), sold at the San Francisco Visitor Information Center (p. 47), Powell/Market cable car booth, and many downtown retail outlets. Also, see the "Muni Discounts" box for more information.

CABLE CAR San Francisco's cable cars might not be the most practical means of transport, but the rolling historic landmarks are a fun ride. The three lines are concentrated in the downtown area. The most scenic, and exciting, is the **Powell-Hyde line,** which follows a zigzag route from the corner of Powell and Market streets, over both Nob Hill and Russian Hill, to a turntable at gaslit Victorian Square in front of Aquatic Park. The **Powell-Mason line** starts at the same intersection and climbs Nob Hill before descending to Bay Street, just 3 blocks from Fisherman's Wharf. The least scenic is the **California Street line,** which begins at the foot of Market Street and runs a straight course through Chinatown and over Nob Hill to Van Ness Avenue. All riders must exit at the last stop and wait in line for the return trip. The cable car system operates from approximately 6:30am to 12:50am, and each ride costs $5.

BUS Buses reach almost every corner of San Francisco and beyond—they even travel over the bridges to Marin County and Oakland. Overhead electric cables power some buses; others use conventional gas engines. All are numbered and display their destinations on the front. Signs, curb markings, and yellow bands on adjacent utility poles designate stops, and most bus shelters exhibit Muni's transportation map and schedule. Many buses travel along Market Street or pass near Union Square and run from about 6am to midnight. After midnight, there is infrequent all-night "Owl" service. For safety, avoid taking buses late at night.

Popular tourist routes include bus nos. 5, 7, and 71, all of which run to Golden Gate Park; 41 and 45, which travel along Union Street; and 30, which runs between Union Square and Ghirardelli Square. A bus ride costs $1.50 for adults and 50¢ for seniors over 65, children 5 to 17, and riders with disabilities.

STREETCAR Five of Muni's six streetcar lines, designated J, K, L, M, and N, run underground downtown and on the streets in the outer neighborhoods. The sleek rail cars make the same stops as BART (see below) along Market Street, including Embarcadero Station (in the Financial District), Montgomery and Powell streets (both near Union Square), and the Civic Center (near City Hall). Past the Civic Center, the routes branch off: The J line takes you to Mission Dolores; the K, L, and M lines run to Castro Street; and the N line parallels Golden Gate Park and extends all the way to The Embarcadero and AT&T Park. Streetcars run about every 15 minutes, more frequently during rush hours. They operate Monday through Friday from 5am to 12:15am, Saturday from 6am to approximately 12:15am, and Sunday from approximately 8am to 12:20am. The L and N lines operate 24 hours a day, 7 days a week, but late at night, regular buses trace the L and N routes, which are normally underground, from atop the city streets. Because the operation is part of Muni, the fares are the same as for buses, and passes are accepted.

The most recent new line to this system is not a newcomer at all, but is, in fact, an encore performance of San Francisco's beloved rejuvenated 1930s streetcar. The beautiful, retro multicolored F-Market streetcar runs from 17th and Castro streets to Beach and Jones streets; every other streetcar continues to Jones and Beach streets in Fisherman's Wharf. This is a quick and charming way to get up- and downtown without any hassle.

BART BART, an acronym for **Bay Area Rapid Transit** (✆ **415/989-2278;** www.bart.gov), is a futuristic-looking, high-speed rail network that connects San Francisco with the East Bay—Oakland, Richmond, Concord, and Fremont. Four stations are on Market Street (see "Streetcar," above). Fares range from $1.45 to $7.35, depending on how far you go. Machines in the stations dispense tickets that are magnetically encoded with a dollar amount. Computerized exits automatically deduct the correct fare. Children 4 and under ride free. Trains run every 15 to 20 minutes, Monday through Friday from 4am to midnight, Saturday from 6am to midnight, and Sunday from 8am to midnight. In keeping with its futuristic look, BART now offers online trip planners that you can download to your PDA, iPod, or phone.

The 33-mile BART extension, which extends all the way to San Francisco International Airport, opened in June 2003. See the "Getting There" section in chapter 2, beginning on p. 17, for information on getting into town from the airport.

BY TAXI

This isn't New York, so don't expect a taxi to appear whenever you need one—if at all. If you're downtown during rush hour or leaving a major hotel, it won't be hard to hail a cab; just look for the lighted sign on the roof that indicates the vehicle is free. Otherwise, it's a good idea to call one of the following companies to arrange a ride; even then, there's been more than one time when the cab never came for me. What to do? Call back if your cab is late and insist on attention, but don't expect prompt results on weekends, no matter how nicely you ask. The companies are: **Veteran's Cab** (✆ **415/552-1300**), **Luxor Cabs** (✆ **415/282-4141**), and **Yellow Cab** (✆ **415/626-2345**). Rates are approximately $2.85 for the first mile and 45¢ each fifth of a mile thereafter.

BY CAR

You don't need a car to explore downtown San Francisco. In fact, with the city becoming more crowded by the minute, a car can be your worst nightmare—you're likely to end up stuck in traffic with lots of aggressive and frustrated drivers, pay upwards of

$30 a day to park (plus a whopping new 14% parking lot tax), and spend a good portion of your vacation looking for a parking space. Don't bother. However, if you want to venture outside the city, driving is the best way to go.

Before heading outside the city, especially in winter, call ✆ **800/427-7623** for California **road conditions.** You can also call 511 for current traffic information.

CAR RENTALS All the major rental companies operate in the city and have desks at the airports. When we last checked, you could get a compact car for a week for anywhere from $165 to $315, including all taxes and other charges, but prices change dramatically on a daily basis and depend on which company you rent from.

Some of the national car-rental companies operating in San Francisco include **Alamo** (✆ 800/327-9633; www.alamo.com), **Avis** (✆ 800/331-1212; www.avis.com), **Budget** (✆ 800/527-0700; www.budget.com), **Dollar** (✆ 800/800-4000; www.dollar.com), **Enterprise** (✆ 800/325-8007; www.enterprise.com), **Hertz** (✆ 800/654-3131; www.hertz.com), **National** (✆ 800/227-7368; www.nationalcar.com), and **Thrifty** (✆ 800/367-2277; www.thrifty.com).

Car-rental rates vary even more than airline fares. Prices depend on the size of the car, where and when you pick it up and drop it off, the length of the rental period, where and how far you drive it, whether you buy insurance, and a host of other factors. A few key questions can save you hundreds of dollars, but you have to ask—reservations agents don't often volunteer money-saving information:

- Are weekend rates lower than weekday rates? Ask if the rate is the same for pickup Friday morning, for instance, as it is for Thursday night. Reservations agents won't volunteer this information, so don't be shy about asking.
- Does the agency assess a drop-off charge if you don't return the car to the same location where you picked it up?
- Are special promotional rates available? If you see an advertised price in your local newspaper, be sure to ask for that specific rate; otherwise, you could be charged the standard rate. Terms change constantly.
- Are discounts available for members of AARP, AAA, frequent-flier programs, or trade unions? If you belong to any of these organizations, you may be entitled to discounts of up to 30%.
- How much tax will be added to the rental bill? Will there be local tax and state tax?
- How much does the rental company charge to refill your gas tank if you return with the tank less than full? Most rental companies claim their prices are "competitive," but fuel is almost always cheaper in town, so you should try to allow enough time to refuel the car before returning it.

Some companies offer "refueling packages," in which you pay for an entire tank of gas upfront. The cost is usually fairly competitive with local prices, but you don't get credit for any gas remaining in the tank. If a stop at a gas station on the way to the airport will make you miss your plane, then by all means take advantage of the fuel purchase option. Otherwise, skip it.

Most agencies enforce a minimum-age requirement—usually 25. Some also have a maximum-age limit. If you're concerned that these limits might affect you, ask about rental requirements at the time of booking to avoid problems later.

Make sure you're insured. Hasty assumptions about your personal auto insurance or a rental agency's additional coverage could end up costing you tens of thousands of dollars, even if you are involved in an accident that is clearly the fault of another driver.

Tips Safe Driving

Keep in mind the following handy driving tips:

- California law requires that both drivers and passengers wear seat belts.
- You can turn right at a red light (unless otherwise indicated), after yielding to traffic and pedestrians, and after coming to a complete stop.
- Cable cars always have the right of way, as do pedestrians at intersections and crosswalks.
- Pay attention to signs and arrows on the streets and roadways, or you might suddenly find yourself in a lane that requires exiting or turning when you want to go straight. What's more, San Francisco's many one-way streets can drive you in circles, but most road maps of the city indicate which way traffic flows.

If you already have your own car insurance, you are most likely covered in the United States for loss of or damage to a rental car and liability in case of injury to any other party involved in an accident. Be sure to check your policy before you spend extra money (around $10 or more per day) on the **collision damage waiver (CDW)** offered by all agencies.

Most major credit cards (especially gold and platinum cards) provide some degree of coverage as well—if they were used to pay for the rental. Terms vary widely, however, so be sure to call your credit card company directly before you rent and rely on the card for coverage. If you are uninsured, your credit card may provide primary coverage as long as you decline the rental agency's insurance. If you already have insurance, your credit card may provide secondary coverage, which basically covers your deductible. However, note that *credit cards will not cover liability,* which is the cost of injury to an outside party and/or damage to an outside party's vehicle. If you do not hold an insurance policy, you should seriously consider buying additional liability insurance from your rental company, even if you decline the CDW.

PARKING If you want to have a relaxing vacation, don't even attempt to find street parking on Nob Hill, in North Beach, in Chinatown, by Fisherman's Wharf, or on Telegraph Hill. Park in a garage or take a cab or a bus. If you do find street parking, pay attention to street signs that explain when you can park and for how long. Be especially careful not to park in zones that are tow areas during rush hours. And be forewarned, San Francisco has instituted a 14% parking tax, so don't be surprised by that garage fee!

Curb colors also indicate parking regulations. *Red* means no stopping or parking; *blue* is reserved for drivers with disabilities who have a disabled plate or placard; *white* means there's a 5-minute limit; *green* indicates a 10-minute limit; and *yellow* and *yellow-and-black* curbs are for stopping to load or unload passengers or luggage only. Also, don't park at a bus stop or in front of a fire hydrant, and watch out for street-cleaning signs. If you violate the law, you might get a hefty ticket or your car might be towed; to get your car back, you'll have to get a release from the nearest district police department and then go to the towing company to pick up the vehicle.

When parking on a hill, apply the hand brake, put the car in gear, and *curb your wheels*—toward the curb when facing downhill, away from the curb when facing uphill. Curbing your wheels not only prevents a possible "runaway" but also keeps you from getting a ticket—an expensive fine that is aggressively enforced.

BY FERRY

TO/FROM SAUSALITO, TIBURON, OR LARKSPUR The **Golden Gate Ferry Service** fleet (✆ **415/455-2000;** www.goldengateferry.org) shuttles passengers daily between the San Francisco Ferry Building, at the foot of Market Street, and downtown Sausalito and Larkspur. Service is frequent, departing at reasonable intervals every day of the year except January 1, Thanksgiving Day, and December 25. Phone or check the website for an exact schedule. The ride takes half an hour, and one-way fares are $6.45 for adults; $3.35 for seniors, passengers with disabilities, and youth 6 to 18. Children 5 and under travel free when accompanied by a full-fare paying adult (limit two children per adult). Family rates are available on weekends.

Ferries of the **Blue & Gold Fleet** (✆ **415/773-1188** for recorded info, or 415/705-5555 for tickets; www.blueandgoldfleet.com) also provide round-trip service to downtown Sausalito and Tiburon, leaving from Fisherman's Wharf at Pier 41. The one-way cost is $8.50 for adults, $4.50 for kids 5 to 11. Boats run on a seasonal schedule; phone for departure information. Tickets can be purchased at Pier 41.

5

Where to Stay

Whether you want a room with a view or just a room, San Francisco is more than accommodating to its 15.7 million annual guests. Most of the city's 200-plus hotels cluster near Union Square, but some smaller independent gems are scattered around town.

When reading over your options, keep in mind that prices listed are "rack" (published) rates. At big, upscale hotels, almost no one actually pays them, and there are always deals to be had. Therefore, you should always ask for special discounts or, even better, vacation packages. It's often possible to get the room you want for $100 less than what is quoted here, except when the hotels are packed (usually during summer and due to conventions) and bargaining is close to impossible. Use the rates listed here for the big hotels as guidelines for comparison only; prices for inexpensive choices and smaller B&Bs are closer to reality, however.

Hunting for hotels in San Francisco can be a tricky business, particularly if you're not a seasoned traveler. What you don't know—and the reservations agent may not tell you—could very well ruin your vacation, so keep the following pointers in mind when it comes time to book a room:

- Prices listed below do not include state and city taxes, which total 14%. Other hidden extras include parking fees, which can be up to $45 per day (also subject to 14% tax!), and hefty surcharges—up to $1 per local call—for telephone use.
- San Francisco is Convention City, so if you want a room at a particular hotel during high season (summer, for example), book well in advance.
- Be sure to have a credit card in hand when making a reservation, and know that you may be asked to pay for at least 1 night in advance. (This doesn't happen often, though.)
- Hotels usually hold reservations until 6pm. If you don't tell the staff you're arriving late, you might lose your room.
- Almost every hotel in San Francisco requires a credit card imprint for "incidentals" (and to prevent walkouts). If you don't have a credit card, be sure to make special arrangements with the management before you hang up the phone, and make a note of the name of the person with whom you spoke.

Pricing Categories

The accommodations listed below are classified first by area, and then by price, using the following categories: **Very Expensive,** more than $250 per night; **Expensive,** $200 to $250 per night; **Moderate,** $150 to $200 per night; and **Inexpensive,** less than $150 per night. These categories reflect the rack rates for an average double room during the high season, which runs approximately from April to September.

- When you check in, if your room isn't up to snuff, politely inform the front desk of your dissatisfaction and ask for another. If the hotel can accommodate you, they almost always will—and sometimes will even upgrade you!

Read the following entries carefully: Many hotels also offer rooms at rates above and below the price category that applies to most of the units. If you like the sound of a place that's a bit over your budget, it never hurts to call and ask a few questions. Also note that we do not list single rates. Some hotels, particularly more affordable choices, do charge lower rates for singles, so inquire about them if you are traveling alone.

San Francisco is a popular destination year-round, so although there are bargains available, rooms here will still seem expensive compared to those in many other U.S. destinations. Still, you should always ask about weekend discounts, corporate rates, and family plans. Most larger hotels, and many smaller ones, offer them, but many reservations agents don't mention them unless you ask about them specifically.

You'll find nonsmoking rooms available in all larger hotels and many smaller hotels; reviews indicate establishments that are entirely nonsmoking. Nowadays, the best advice for smokers is to confirm a smoking-permitted room in advance, and if there's a special cleaning charge per night.

Although you'll find that most accommodations have an abundance of amenities (including phones, unless otherwise noted), don't be alarmed by the lack of air-conditioned guest rooms. San Francisco's weather is so mild, you'll hardly ever need it.

Most larger hotels can accommodate guests who use wheelchairs and those who have other special needs. Ask when you make a reservation to ensure that your hotel can accommodate your needs, especially if you are interested in a bed-and-breakfast.

HELPING HANDS Having reservations about your reservations? Leave it up to the pros:

San Francisco Reservations, 360 22nd St., Suite 300, Oakland, CA 94612 (© **800/677-1500** or 510/628-4450; www.hotelres.com), arranges reservations for more than 150 of San Francisco's hotels and often offers discounted rates. Their nifty website allows Internet users to make reservations online.

Other good online sites with discounted rates include **www.hotels.com** and **www.placestostay.com.**

1 The Best Hotel Bets

- **Best for Families:** Kids like the **Westin St. Francis,** 335 Powell St. (© **866/500-0038** or 415/397-7000), because upon arrival, children under 12 get the travel-themed Westin Kids Club backpack filled with a make-your-own postcard kit,

---

Value **Dial Direct**

When booking a room in a chain hotel, call the hotel's local line and the toll-free number and see where you get the best deal. A hotel makes nothing on a room that stays empty. The clerk who runs the place is more likely to know about vacancies than someone from the toll-free number and will often grant deep discounts in order to fill up rooms.

Tips Get the Latest on Hotels

Whenever I'm booking a room somewhere I haven't stayed before, I always check out www.TripAdvisor.com. Its unsolicited traveler reviews paint a full picture, provide a broad range of opinions, and give what I've found to be an excellent and trustworthy consensus.

colored pencils, a travelogue, a map of the world, and a safari hat. Parents with babies get a rubber duck, a night light, and an emergency kit. At the nautically themed **Argonaut,** 495 Jefferson St. (© **866/415-0704** or 415/563-0800), kids get to pick a toy out of the "treasure chest," and parents will appreciate the free cribs and strollers. But the place kids will probably love the most is the **Hotel del Sol,** 3100 Webster St. (© **877/433-5765** or 415/921-5520), with its "Kids are VIPs" program that includes a lending library of books, toys, and videos; evening cookies and milk; and a plethora of toys to use by the heated outdoor pool. Parents will love the bonded babysitting services and the three baby-proofed rooms, among many other perks for families. See p. 62, 87, and 90, respectively.

- **Best for Romance:** Oozing with bohemian romance is **The Hotel Bohème,** 444 Columbus Ave. (© **415/433-9111**). See p. 88.
- **Best Public Space in a Historic Hotel: The Palace Hotel,** 2 New Montgomery St. (© **888/625-5144** or 415/512-1111), the extravagant creation of banker "Bonanza King" Will Ralston in 1875, has one of the grandest rooms in the city: the Garden Court. Equally eye-catching is the magnificent lobby at Nob Hill's **The Fairmont Hotel & Tower,** 950 Mason St. (© **866/540-4491** or 415/772-5000). See p. 79 and 74, respectively.
- **Best Trendy Scene:** If you want to shack up with the tragically hip, head to **Clift Hotel,** 495 Geary St. (© **800/697-1791** or 415/775-4700), which promises upscale flirting at its bar, the Redwood Room. See p. 238. Less chichi and funkier in style and location is **The Phoenix Hotel,** 601 Eddy St. (© **800/248-9466** or 415/776-1380), where guests lounge poolside or hang at the too-cool Bambuddha Lounge. See p. 60 and 93, respectively.
- **Best Service and Amenities:** As usual, **The Ritz-Carlton,** 600 Stockton St. (© **800/241-3333** or 415/296-7465), corners the market in ultimate luxury, from its stunning ground-floor bathrooms to its fabulous restaurant to everything in between. Of course such pampering comes at a cost, but if you can afford it, it's worth the splurge. See p. 76. While it doesn't have quite the number of perks that the Ritz has, the **St. Regis Hotel,** 125 Third St. (© **877/787-3447** or 415/284-4000), is a fabulous place to stay. From its state-of-the-art rooms swathed in browns and creams to its huge spa, gym, hopping bar scene, and destination-restaurant Ame—not to mention its location next to the Museum of Modern Art—it's one of my favorite hotels in the city. See p. 79.

2 Union Square

VERY EXPENSIVE

Campton Place Hotel ★★ This luxury boutique hotel offers some of the best accommodations in town—not to mention the most expensive. Rooms are compact but comfy, with limestone, pear wood, and Italian-modern decor. The two executive suites and one luxury suite push the haute envelope to even more luxurious heights. Discriminating returning guests will still find superlative service, California king-size beds, exquisite bathrooms, bathrobes, top-notch toiletries, slippers, and every other necessity and extra that's made Campton Place a favored temporary address. Alas, Campton Place Restaurant lost its award-winning chef Daniel Humm in 2005, but the restaurant still offers a respectable French/California menu. The jury's still out on whether it's a destination in its own right.

340 Stockton St. (between Post and Sutter sts.), San Francisco, CA 94108. ✆ **866/332-1670** or 415/781-5555. Fax 415/955-5536. www.camptonplace.com. 110 units. $350–$485 double; $585–$2,000 suite. American breakfast $18. AE, DC, MC, V. Valet parking $38. Bus: 2, 3, 4, 30, 38, or 45. Cable car: Powell–Hyde or Powell–Mason lines (1 block west). BART: Market St. **Amenities:** Restaurant; outdoor fitness terrace; concierge; secretarial services; room service; laundry service; same-day dry cleaning. *In room:* A/C, TV w/pay movies, dataport, minibar, hair dryer, iron, safe, T1 line.

Clift Hotel ★ Ian Schrager, king of such ultrahip hotels as New York's Royalton and Paramount, L.A.'s Mondrian, and Miami's Delano, renovated this classic old luxury property a few years back. Young trendsetters now flock here for overpriced monochrome lavender streamlined rooms with often-minuscule bathrooms, glamorous atmosphere, and a heavy dose of attitude. Its best attribute is the renovated historic Redwood Room, complete with sexy redwood walls (all made from one tree!) and Deco lighting from 1933 and a luxurious and rather uncomfortable interior designed by Philippe Starck. The equally trendy, expensive, and mediocre Asia de Cuba restaurant adjoins the swank lounge. If you ask me, the only reason to pay the high prices here is if you're interested in being surrounded by the young and hip. Otherwise, there are far better rooms around town at a similar or lower price.

Fun Fact **Inflation at the Clift**

When it first opened in 1915 the Clift Hotel charged a mere $2 per night.

495 Geary St. (at Taylor St.), San Francisco, CA 94102. ✆ **800/697-1791** or 415/775-4700. Fax 415/441-4621. www.clifthotel.com. 363 units. $325–$460 double; from $455 studio suite; from $950 deluxe suite. AE, DC, DISC, MC, V. Valet parking $45. Bus: 2, 3, 4, 30, 38, or 45. Cable car: Powell–Hyde or Powell–Mason lines (2 blocks east). **Amenities:** Restaurant; bar; exercise room; concierge; room service; same-day laundry service/dry cleaning. *In room:* TV/DVD, minibar, hair dryer, Wi-Fi ($10/day).

Grand Hyatt San Francisco ★ If the thought of a 10-second walk to Saks Fifth Avenue makes your pulse race, this high-rise luxury hotel is the place for you. The Grand Hyatt sits amid all the downtown shopping while also boasting some of the best views in the area. The lobby is indeed grand, with Chinese artifacts and enormous ceramic vases. Thankfully, the well-kept rooms were recently renovated; they're swankier than they used to be, and now feature the Hyatt's signature Grand Bed with pillow top mattresses, ultra-plush pillows and down (or down alternative) duvets. Each room has a lounge chair as well as a small desk and sitting area. Views from most of the 36 floors are truly spectacular.

Rates for concierge-level Regency Club rooms ($50 extra) include access to the lounge, honor bar, continental breakfast, and evening hors d'oeuvres. Three floors hold business-plan guest rooms, which for $25 extra get you 24-hour access to a printer, a photocopier, and office supplies; free local calls and credit card phone access; and a daily newspaper.

Accommodations Near Union Square & Nob Hill

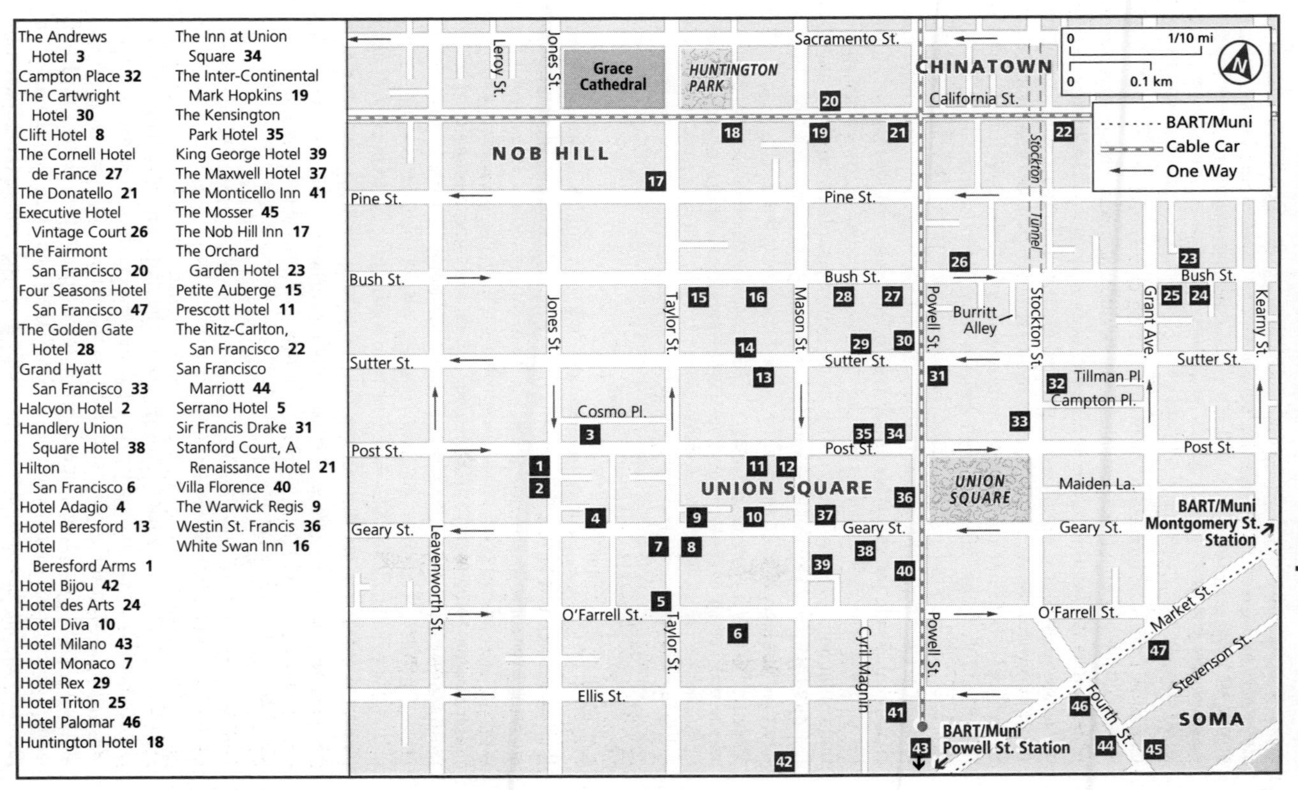

345 Stockton St. (between Post and Sutter sts.), San Francisco, CA 94108. ✆ **888/591-1234** or 415/398-1234. Fax 415/391-1780. www.sanfrancisco.grand.hyatt.com. 685 units. $199–$329 double; Regency Club $50 additional. AE, DC, DISC, MC, V. Valet parking $41. Bus: 2, 3, 4, 30, 38, or 45. Cable car: Powell–Hyde or Powell–Mason lines (2 blocks west). **Amenities:** Restaurant; bar; health club; concierge; business center; secretarial services; limited room service; laundry service; same-day dry cleaning, Wi-Fi in public areas. *In room:* A/C, TV w/pay movies, dataport, minibar, coffeemaker, hair dryer, iron, safe, high-speed Internet access ($9.95/day), 2 phone lines with speaker capability.

Hotel Monaco ★★ This remodeled 1910 Beaux Arts building has plenty of atmosphere thanks to a whimsically ethereal lobby with a two-story French inglenook fireplace. The guest rooms, which were upgraded in 2006, follow suit, with canopy beds, Asian-inspired armoires, bamboo writing desks, lively stripes, and vibrant color. Everything is bold but tasteful, and as playful as it is serious, with nifty extras like flatscreen TVs, complimentary high-speed wireless Internet access and Wi-Fi, and two-line cordless phones. The decor, combined with the truly grand neighboring Grand Café restaurant that's ideal for cocktails and mingling (but also serves breakfast and lunch), would put this place on my top-10 list if it weren't for rooms that tend to be too small (especially for the price) and the lack of a sizable gym. That said, it's a fine Union Square option, which happens to include complimentary wine and cheese tasting accompanied by shoulder and neck massages. ***Tip:*** If you were/are a big fan of Jefferson Airplane, inquire about their Grace Slick Shrine Suite.

501 Geary St. (at Taylor St.), San Francisco, CA 94102. ✆ **866/622-5284** or 415/292-0100. Fax 415/292-0111. www.monaco-sf.com. 201 units. $229–$409 double; $279–$619 suite. Rates include evening wine and cheese tasting. Call for discounted rates. AE, DC, DISC, MC, V. Valet parking $39. Bus: 2, 3, 4, 27, or 38. Pets accepted. **Amenities:** Restaurant; exercise room; spa; Jacuzzi; sauna; steam room; concierge; courtesy car; business center; room service; in-room massage; laundry service; dry cleaning. *In room:* A/C, TV, dataport, minibar, coffeemaker w/Starbucks coffee, hair dryer, iron, safe, wireless high-speed Internet access, CD player.

Prescott Hotel ★★ It may be small and lack common areas, but the boutique Prescott Hotel has some big things going for it. The staff treats you like royalty, rooms are attractively unfrilly and masculine, the location (just a block from Union Square) is perfect, and limited room service is provided by Wolfgang Puck's restaurant Postrio. Ralph Lauren fabrics in dark tones of green, plum, and burgundy and crisp white Italian linens blend well with the cherrywood furnishings in each of the soundproof rooms; the view, alas, isn't so pleasant. The very small bathrooms contain terry robes and Aveda products, and the suites have Jacuzzi bathtubs. Concierge-level guests are pampered with a free continental breakfast and evening cocktails and hors d'oeuvres.

545 Post St. (between Mason and Taylor sts.), San Francisco, CA 94102. ✆ **866/271-3632** or 415/563-0303. Fax 415/563-6831. www.prescotthotel.com. 164 units. $245–$350 double; $280 concierge-level double (including breakfast and evening cocktail reception); from $365 suite. AE, DC, DISC, MC, V. Valet parking $40. Bus: 2, 3, 4, 30, 38, or 45. Cable car: Powell–Hyde or Powell–Mason lines (1 block east). **Amenities:** Restaurant; bar; small exercise room; concierge; limited courtesy car; limited room service. *In room:* TV w/pay movies, dataport, minibar, hair dryer, iron, safe, high-speed wireless Internet access, video games.

Westin St. Francis ★★ *Kids* At the turn of the 20th century, Charles T. Crocker and a few of his wealthy buddies decided that San Francisco needed a world-class hotel, and up went the St. Francis. Since then, hordes of VIPs have hung their hats and hosiery here, including Emperor Hirohito of Japan, Queen Elizabeth II of England, Mother Teresa, King Juan Carlos of Spain, the shah of Iran, and all the U.S. presidents from Taft through Clinton. In 1972, the hotel gained the 32-story Tower, doubling its capacity and adding banquet and conference centers. The older rooms of the main building vary in size and have more old-world charm than the newer rooms, but the Tower is remarkable for its great views of the city (including from the glass elevators) from above the 18th floor.

Although the St. Francis is too massive to offer the personal service you get at the smaller deluxe hotels on Nob Hill, few other hotels in San Francisco can match its majestic aura. Stroll through the vast, ornate lobby, and you can feel 100 years of history oozing from its hand-carved redwood paneling. The hotel has done massive renovations costing $185 million over the past decade, replacing the carpeting, furniture, and bedding in every main-building guest room; gussying up the lobby; restoring the facade; and adding one of the hottest downtown dining spots, the very expensive and fancy Michael Mina (p. 102).

The Westin makes kids feel right at home, too, with a goody bag upon check-in. The tower's Grandview Rooms evoke a contemporary design along the lines of the W Hotel. The historic main building accentuates its history with traditional, more elegant ambience, high ceilings, and crown molding. Alas, the venerable Compass Rose tearoom is no longer.

335 Powell St. (between Geary and Post sts.), San Francisco, CA 94102. ✆ **866/500-0038** or 415/397-7000. Fax 415/774-0124. www.westinstfrancis.com. 1,195 units. Main building: $229–$529 double; Tower (Grand View): $219–$559 double; from $650 suite (in either building). Extra person $30. Continental breakfast $15–$18. AE, DC, DISC, MC, V. Valet parking $42. Bus: 2, 3, 4, 30, 38, 45, or 76. Cable car: Powell–Hyde or Powell–Mason lines (direct stop). Pets under 40 lb. accepted (dog beds available on request). **Amenities:** 2 restaurants; elaborate health club and spa; concierge; car-rental desk; business center; room service. *In room:* A/C, TV, dataport, minibar, fridge available upon request, hair dryer, iron, high-speed Internet access ($15), Wi-Fi ($9.95/day), cordless phones.

EXPENSIVE

The Cartwright Hotel ★ Diametrically opposed to the hip-hop, happenin' Hotel Triton down the street, The Cartwright Hotel is geared toward the more mature traveler. Management takes pride in its reputation for offering comfortable rooms at fair prices, which explains why most guests have been repeat customers for a long time. Remarkably quiet, despite its convenient location near one of the busiest downtown corners, the eight-story hotel looks not unlike it did when it opened some 80 years ago. Antiques collected during its decades of faithful service furnish the lobby and the individually decorated (and sometimes very small) rooms. A nice perk usually reserved for fancier hotels is the fully equipped bathrooms, all of which have tubs, rainfall shower heads, Aveda products, terry robes (in deluxe rooms), and thick fluffy towels. Complimentary wine is served in the small library each night, and afternoon tea and fresh-baked cookies are a daily treat, as are the apples and hot beverages in the lobby 'round the clock. A breakfast room serves a complimentary expanded continental breakfast with a make-your-own-waffle station.

524 Sutter St. (at Powell St.), San Francisco, CA 94102. ✆ **800/919-9779** or 415/421-2865. Fax 415/398-6345. www.cartwrighthotel.com. 114 units. $199–$259 double. Rates include 24-hr. tea, coffee, and apples in the lobby, continental breakfast, nightly wine hour, weekday newspapers, and afternoon cookies. AE, DC, DISC, MC, V. Valet parking $35; self-parking $25. Bus: 2, 3, 4, 30, or 45. Cable car: Powell–Hyde or Powell–Mason lines (direct stop). **Amenities:** Access to nearby health club for $15; concierge; free wireless Internet access. *In room:* TV, dataport, fridge upon request, hair dryer, iron, free wireless Internet access.

The Donatello ★ *Value* If you're not looking for trendy lodgings or an anonymous business hotel but want old-world elegance, book a room here. The Donatello is, in a word, dignified. The lobby is classy, with Italian marble and a serious staff. The airy, contemporary Art Nouveau rooms, which are some of the largest in the city (an average of 400 sq. ft.), were overhauled in 2006 with new bedding, carpet, and furniture and feature original art, king-size mattresses, and textiles. Unfortunately, most of the extra-large windows lack great views, but if it's fresh air you're after, the fifth floor has seven terrace rooms.

501 Post St. (at Mason St.), San Francisco, CA 94102. ✆ **800/227-3184** or 415/441-7100. Fax 415/885-8842. www.thedonatellosf.com. 94 units. $139–$295 double. Children under 12 stay free in parent's room. AE, DC, DISC, MC, V. Valet parking $28. Bus: 2, 3, 4, 30, 38, or 45. Cable car: Powell–Hyde or Powell–Mason lines (1 block west). **Amenities:** Restaurant; bar; exercise room; concierge; limited room service; same-day laundry service/dry cleaning; 2 meeting spaces. *In room:* A/C, TV w/pay movies, dataport, fridge, microwave, toaster, coffeemaker, hair dryer, iron, free Wi-Fi, CD player.

Executive Hotel Vintage Court ★ *Value* Consistent personal service and great value attract a loyal clientele at this European-style hotel 2 blocks north of Union Square. The chocolate-brown lobby, accented with comfy couches, is welcoming enough to actually spend a little time in, especially when California wines are being poured each evening from 5 to 6pm free of charge (each week a local vintner is on hand to do the pouring).

But the varietals don't stop at ground level. Each tidy, quiet, and comfortable room is named after a winery and boasts a modern country look (think Pottery Barn meets Napa Valley), where greens and earth tones reign supreme, with cream duvets and lovely mahogany-slat blinds. Niebaum-Coppola Penthouse Suite (named after the winery owned by the movie maverick), the deluxe two-room penthouse suite, has an original 1912 stained-glass skylight, wood-burning fireplace, whirlpool tub, complete entertainment center, and panoramic views of the city. Smokers, book a room elsewhere because puffing is prohibited in all rooms here. On the bright side, pets are welcome.

Masa's, one of the city's more upscale restaurants, serves very expensive contemporary French dinners here.

650 Bush St. (between Powell and Stockton sts.), San Francisco, CA 94108. ✆ **888/388-3932** or 415/392-4666. Fax 415/433-4065. www.vintagecourt.com. 107 units. $159–$229 double; $325–$395 penthouse suite. Rates include continental breakfast and evening wine reception. AE, DC, DISC, MC, V. Valet parking $37; self-parking $27. Bus: 2, 3, 4, 30, 45, or 76. Cable car: Powell–Hyde or Powell–Mason lines (direct stop). **Amenities:** Restaurant; access to off-premises health club ($14/day); concierge; in-room massage; same-day laundry service/dry cleaning. *In room:* A/C, TV, dataport, minibar, coffeemaker, hair dryer, iron, video games, wireless Internet.

Handlery Union Square Hotel ★ *Kids* A mere half-block from Union Square, the Handlery was already a good deal frequented by European travelers before the 1908 building underwent a complete overhaul a few years ago. Now you'll find every amenity you could possibly need, plus lots of extras, in the extremely tasteful and modern (although sedate and a little dark) rooms. Rooms range from coral and gray in the historic building to taupe and tan in the newer club-level building. In between is a heated outdoor pool. Literally everything was replaced in the rooms: mattresses, alarm radios, refrigerators, light fixtures, paint, carpets, and furnishings. Perks include adjoining L.A.-based chain restaurant The Daily Grill (which is unfortunately not as good as its sister restaurants down south) and club-level options (all in the newer building) that include larger rooms, a complimentary morning newspaper, a bathroom scale, robes, two two-line phones, and adjoining doors that make the units great choices for families. Downsides? Not a lot of direct light, no grand feeling in the lobby, and lots of trekking if you want to go to and from the adjoining buildings that make up the hotel. All in all, it's a good value for downtown, but, personally, this would be a choice second to the less expensive Warwick Regis or Savoy.

351 Geary St. (between Mason and Powell sts.), San Francisco, CA 94102. ✆ **800/843-4343** or 415/781-7800. Fax 415/781-0269. www.handlery.com. 377 units. $249–$269 double; Club section $249–$289 double; Owner's Suite $600. Extra person $10. AE, DC, DISC, MC, V. Parking $32. Bus: 2, 3, 4, 30, 38, or 45. Cable car: Powell–Hyde or Powell–Mason lines (direct stop). **Amenities:** Restaurant; heated outdoor swimming pool; access to nearby health club ($10/day); sauna; barbershop; room service; babysitting; same-day laundry. *In room:* Central air, TV w/Nintendo and pay movies, dataport, fridge, free coffee/tea-making facilities, hair dryer, iron, safe, wireless Internet access, voice mail.

Hilton San Francisco Complete with bustling conventioneers and a line to register that resembles airport check-in, the Hilton's lobby is so enormous and busy that it feels more like a convention hall than a hotel. The three connecting buildings (the original 19-story main structure, a 46-story tower topped by a panoramic restaurant, and a 23-story landmark with 386 luxurious rooms and suites) bring swarms of visitors. Even during quieter times, the sheer enormity of the place makes the Hilton somewhat overwhelming.

After you get past the sweeping grand lobby, jump on an elevator, and wind through endless corridors to your room, you're likely to find the mystique ends with clean but run-of-the-mill standard-size corporate accommodations. That said, some of the views from the floor-to-ceiling windows in the main tower's rooms are memorable. All rooms have flatscreen TVs, bathrooms with walk-in showers (no tubs), Serta Suite Dreams beds, and a pillow menu that ensures you get a pillow that suits your firmness preference.

Still, the overall feel and decor of the hotel are impersonal and plain—perfect for conventioneers, but not for a romantic weekend. One bonus is the 13,000-square-foot health club and day spa. The Hilton has four restaurants: Cityscape, on the 46th floor, offers classic California cuisine and a breathtaking 360-degree view; Intermezzo serves Mediterranean-style food; The Café offers a buffet; and Kiku of Tokyo offers—you guessed it—Japanese food. The Lobby Bar also offers bar snacks.

333 O'Farrell St. (between Mason and Taylor sts.), San Francisco, CA 94102. ✆ **800/445-8667** or 415/771-1400. Fax 415/771-6807. www.sanfrancisco.hilton.com. 1,908 units. $195–$409 double; $315–$3,700 junior suite. Children stay free in parent's room. AE, DC, DISC, MC, V. Parking $47 (some oversize vehicles cannot be accommodated, depending on height). Bus: 2, 3, 4, 7, 9, 21, 27, 30, 38, 45, or 71. Cable car: Powell–Hyde or Powell–Mason lines (1 block east). **Amenities:** 4 restaurants; bar; outdoor pool; outdoor whirlpool, health club; spa; sauna; concierge; tour desk; car-rental desk; business center; secretarial services; room service; laundry service; dry cleaning; wireless Internet access in public spaces. *In room:* A/C, 27-in. flatscreen TV, dataport, minibar, coffeemaker, hair dryer, iron, high-speed Internet access.

Hotel Adagio ★★ *Value* Our local hip-hotel company, Joie de Vivre, revamped every one of this 1929 Spanish Revival hotel's 171 large, bright guest rooms in gorgeous modern style. They're real lookers, each with a walnut brown and mocha color palette and dark wood furnishings. Other plusses include firm mattresses, double-paned windows that open, quiet surroundings, voice mail, and plenty of elbowroom. Executive floors (7–16) also come with robes, upscale amenities, makeup mirrors, and stereos with iPod ports. Bathrooms are old but spotless, and have resurfaced tubs. Feel like splurging? Go for one of the two penthouse-level suites; one has lovely terraces with a New York vibe. Another good reason to stay here is the restaurant/bar **Cortez,** which draws a lively crowd of locals who meet here after work to nosh on small plates in the groovy lounge. ***Tip:*** Rooms above the eighth floor have good, but not great, views of the city.

550 Geary St., San Francisco, CA 94102. ✆ **800/228-8830** or 415/775-5000. Fax 415/775-9388. www.thehoteladagio.com. 171 units. $189–$279 double. AE, DISC, MC, V. Valet parking $35. **Amenities:** Restaurant; bar; fitness

center; concierge; business center w/free wireless Internet; room service; laundry service; dry cleaning; luggage storage room. *In room:* TV w/Nintendo and pay movies, dataport, minibar, fridge, hair dryer, iron, safe, free high-speed Internet access, CD player.

Hotel Diva ★ A showbiz darling when it opened in 1985, the sleek, ultramodern Diva won "Best Hotel Design" from *Interiors* magazine. A profusion of curvaceous glass, marble, and steel marks the Euro-tech lobby; and the minimalist rooms are spotless and neat, with fashionable "Italian modern" furnishings of monochromatic colors, silver, and wood. Enormous headboards are made of polished stainless steel meant to evoke the bow of a ship. Personally, I find the hotel a little on the cold side (figuratively speaking). But toys and services abound, and fitness and business centers complete the package. The downside is that these rooms have views that make you want to keep the chic curtains closed. Pets aren't just welcome, they have their own hotel package deal, which includes a daily dog walk, "Diva Dog Tag," and sheepskin throw rug to insure a restful night. (Now that's ruffing it!) ***Insider tip:*** Reserve one of the rooms ending in 09, which have extra-large bathrooms with vanity mirrors and makeup tables.

440 Geary St. (between Mason and Taylor sts.), San Francisco, CA 94102. ✆ **800/553-1900** or 415/885-0200. Fax 415/346-6613. www.hoteldiva.com. 115 units. $129–$299 double; $159–$329 junior suite; from $470 suite. Extra person $10. AE, DC, DISC, MC, V. Valet parking $35. Bus: 38 or 38L. Cable car: Powell–Mason line. **Amenities:** Coffee/tea service 6:30–10am; exercise room; concierge; laundry service; dry cleaning; free wireless Internet access (in rooms, too). *In room:* A/C, TV/DVD/CD, dataport, hair dryer, iron, safe.

Hotel Rex ★ Joie de Vivre, the most creative hotel group in the city, is the brains behind this cleverly restored historic building, a restoration that was inspired by the San Francisco art and literary salons of the 1920s and '30s. JDV kept some of the imported furnishings and the European boutique hotel ambience, but gave the lobby and rooms a major face-lift, adding the decorative flair that makes its hotels among the most popular in town. The clublike lobby lounge is modeled after a 1920s literary salon and is, like all the group's properties, cleverly stylish. (They even host jazz artists Fri 6–8pm.) The guest rooms are above average in size, decorated with custom wall coverings, hand-painted lampshades, and works by local artists. If you have one of the rooms in the back, you'll look out over a shady, peaceful courtyard. It's also in a great location, situated near several fine galleries, theaters, and restaurants.

562 Sutter St. (between Powell and Mason sts.), San Francisco, CA 94102. ✆ **800/433-4434** or 415/433-4434. Fax 415/433-3695. www.thehotelrex.com. 94 units. $159–$269 double; $400 suite. AE, DC, DISC, MC, V. Valet parking $34. Bus: 2, 3, 4, 30, 38, or 45. Cable car: Powell–Hyde or Powell–Mason lines (1 block east). **Amenities:** Access to nearby health club; concierge; business center; room service (7am–11pm); same-day laundry service/dry cleaning. *In room:* TV w/pay movies, dataport, minibar, hair dryer, iron, free high-speed Internet access and Wi-Fi throughout, CD player.

Hotel Triton ★ Described as vogue, chic, retrofuturistic, and even neo-baroque, this Kimpton Group property is whimsy at its boutique-hotel best. The completely renovated lobby features a 360-degree mural by emerging artist Kari Pei (yes, from *that* Pei family–she's I. M. Pei's daughter-in-law) that relates the history of San Francisco and Triton. The funky-fun (if not a wee bit too small) designer suites named after musicians and artists like Jerry Garcia, Wyland (the ocean artist), and Santana, along with all the other rooms, are eco-friendly, featuring filtered water and air, all-natural linens, recycle trash cans, and water conservation fixtures. Even the cleaning products used in the hotel are environmentally sensitive to please the tree-hugger in all of us. All the rooms include modern touches like armoires hiding Sony flatscreen TVs and iPod iH5 docking stations that double as a clock radios. Not to be outdone, the fitness center touts DirecTV in the cardio machines.

The hotel serves coffee and tea each morning, freshly baked cookies at 3pm and 8pm. Wine, tarot readings, and chair massages are available each evening (included in the room rate) in the lobby. The bustling and casual Café de la Presse has a cool French cafe vibe but overpriced food.

342 Grant Ave. (at Bush St.), San Francisco, CA 94108. ✆ **800/800-1299** or 415/394-0500. Fax 415/394-0555. www.hoteltriton.com. 140 units. $179–$239 double; $279–$379 suite. AE, DC, DISC, MC, V. Parking $37, oversize vehicles an additional $2. Cable car: Powell–Hyde or Powell–Mason lines (2 blocks west). Pets stay free with conditional agreement. **Amenities:** Cafe; fitness center; business center (fee); room service; same-day laundry service/dry cleaning. *In room:* A/C, flatscreen TV, dataport, minibar, coffeemaker on request, hair dryer, iron, Web TV, free Wi-Fi.

The Inn at Union Square ★★ As narrow as an Amsterdam canal house, The Inn at Union Square is the antithesis of the big, impersonal hotels that surround Union Square. If you need plenty of elbowroom, skip this one. But if you're looking for an inn whose staff knows each guest's name, read on. One-half block west of the square, this six-story inn makes up for its small stature by spoiling guests with a pile of perks. Mornings start with a continental breakfast served in lounges stocked with daily newspapers, and evening emerges with appetizers of wine, cheese, fruit, and chocolates served in sweet little fireplace lounges at the end of each hall. There's also unlimited use of a nearby full-service health club with heated lap pool. The handsome rooms are individually decorated with Georgian reproductions, goose-down pillows, and floral fabrics, and they are smaller than average but infinitely more appreciated than the cookie-cutter rooms of most larger hotels. Smoking is not allowed anywhere in the hotel.

440 Post St. (between Mason and Powell sts.), San Francisco, CA 94102. ✆ **800/288-4346** or 415/397-3510. Fax 415/989-0529. www.unionsquare.com. 30 units. $169–$219 double; from $370 suite. Rates include continental breakfast; all-day tea and cider, afternoon wine and hors d'oeuvres; and evening cookies. AE, DC, DISC, MC, V. Valet parking $36. Bus: 2, 3, 4, 30, 38, or 45; all Market St. buses. Cable car: Powell–Hyde or Powell–Mason lines. **Amenities:** Access to nearby health club (for a nominal fee); concierge; secretarial services; laundry service; dry cleaning. *In room:* TV, dataport, hair dryer, iron, free wireless high-speed Internet access.

The Kensington Park Hotel ★ The Kensington is a spiffed-up fairly old hotel with a cheery, eager-to-please (albeit sometimes short-handed) staff, tasteful accommodations, and extra efforts—like afternoon tea and sherry—that show the hotel cares about its guests. Large guest rooms on the 5th through 12th floors have handsome Queen Anne–style furnishings, and the bathrooms, though small, are sweetly appointed in brass and marble. As for the views, ask for an upper corner room, and you'll get postcard views of Nob Hill or Union Square. If you want the full treatment, book the Royal Suite, which contains a canopy bed, fireplace, Jacuzzi, and wet bar. The hotel adjoins a popular fantasy—and fancy—seafood restaurant called Farallon (p. 100); hotel guests are given preferred seating.

450 Post St. (between Powell and Mason sts.), San Francisco, CA 94102. ✆ **800/553-1900** or 415/788-6400. Fax 415/399-9484. www.kensingtonparkhotel.com. 92 units. $129–$299 double; $159–$329 Royal Court Rooms; from $399 suite. Extra person $10. Rates include afternoon tea and sherry. AE, DC, DISC, MC, V. Valet parking $35; extra charge for oversize cars. Cable car: Powell–Hyde or Powell–Mason lines (½ block east). **Amenities:** Restaurant; coffee/tea service 7–10am; concierge; business center; same-day dry cleaning. *In room:* TV w/pay movies, dataport, hair dryer, iron, free Wi-Fi.

The Orchard Garden Hotel ★★ If Al Gore was a hotelier, this would be his hotel. The new $25-million-dollar Orchard Garden Hotel is California's first generation of truly "green" hotels and the only hotel in the state that was built to the nationally accepted standards for green buildings developed by the U.S. Green Building Council (USGBC). From the eco-friendly construction materials to an in-room recycling system and the use of organic, citrus-based cleaning products, just about every aspect of this vanguard property is geared toward creating a healthy environment for guests and staff. It's also the first hotel in the city to use the European-style keycard system that turns power off to the entire room each time you leave, thereby saving about 20% in energy consumption. But going green doesn't mean you have to cut back on comfort—yes, that's Egyptian cotton linen on the king-size bed, real feather down in the pillows, and plush spa-style robes in the closet. The 86 guest rooms are super-insulated (and very quiet), and decorated in natural wood tones with soothing light colors. Spacious bathrooms come with Aveda bath products (organic, of course). High-tech toys include HD LCD TVs, DVD/CD players, iPod docking stations, and dual-line cordless telephones on large work desks. The hotel also has a pleasant rooftop garden, a small fitness center (and $15 passes to Club One), and the lobby-level **Roots Restaurant,** which serves contemporary American cuisine made from locally sourced organic products for breakfast, lunch, and dinner. The hotel's location at Bush and Grant streets is ideal, with Chinatown, Union Square, and the Financial District all just a short walk away. ***Note:*** If the hotel is fully booked, inquire about their sister property—The Orchard Hotel—up the street.

466 Bush St. (at Grant St.), San Francisco, CA 94108. ✆ **888/717-2881** or 415/399-9807. Fax 415/393-9917. www.theorchardgardenhotel.com. 82 units. $169–$499 double. AE, DC, DISC, MC, V. Valet parking $24. Cable car: Powell–Hyde or Powell–Mason lines. **Amenities:** Restaurant; fitness center; concierge; morning car service to Financial District; bicycle storage; business center; evening turndown; free DVD library. *In room:* A/C, flatscreen HD TV, minibar, cordless phone, iPod docking station, coffeemaker, DVD/CD player dataport, Wi-Fi, hair dryer, robes, iron, safe.

Petite Auberge ★★ Nobody does French provincial like the Petite Auberge: handcrafted armoires, delicate sheer curtains, cozy little fireplaces in most rooms, and an adorable array of antiques and knickknacks. Honeymooners should splurge on the petite suite, which has a private entrance, deck, and spa tub. The breakfast room, with its mural of a country market scene, terra-cotta tile floors, and gold-yellow tablecloths, opens onto a small garden. California wines, tea, and hors d'oeuvres (included in the room rates) are served each afternoon, and guests have free rein of the fridge stocked with soft drinks. Bathers take note: Eight rooms have showers only, while others have tubs.

863 Bush St. (between Taylor and Mason sts.), San Francisco, CA 94102. ✆ **800/365-3004** or 415/928-6000. Fax 415/673-7214. www.petiteaubergesf.com. 26 units. $199–$239 double; $269 petite suite. Rates include full breakfast and afternoon reception. AE, DC, DISC, MC, V. Parking $32. Bus: 2, 3, 4, 30, 38, or 45. Cable car: Powell–Hyde or Powell–Mason lines. **Amenities:** Access to small exercise room next door; concierge; babysitting; same-day laundry service/dry cleaning. *In room:* TV, dataport, hair dryer, robes; Wi-Fi ($7.95/day); high-speed Internet available at sister hotel next door, the **White Swan Inn,** see p. 70.

Serrano Hotel ★ Los Angeles designer Cheryl Rowley (who also designed the Hotel Monaco; p. 71) swathed this 17-story 1920s hotel in her trademark vibrant color and added a playful dash of Moroccan flair while preserving the building's Spanish Revival integrity. Original architectural elements dot the colorful lobby, with its whimsically painted beams, high ceilings, large ornate fireplace, and dramatic colonnade. Equally vibrant guest rooms (sometimes small) have oversize windows and high ceilings, cherrywood headboards, terry robes, and theater-themed artwork. The hotel is in the heart of the Theater District, right off Union Square, and is pet-friendly.

405 Taylor St. (at O'Farrell St.), San Francisco, CA 94102. ✆ **866/289-6561** or 415/885-2500. Fax 415/474-4879. www.serranohotel.com. 236 units. From $199 double; from $329 suite. Rates include morning coffee and tea service and afternoon beverages. AE, DC, DISC, MC, V. Valet parking $39. Bus: 2, 3, 4, 27, or 38. Cable car: Powell or Market. Pets accepted. **Amenities:** Restaurant/bar; exercise room; sauna; concierge; courtesy car; business center w/fax; limited room

Fun Fact **A Living Legend**

Tom Sweeny, the head doorman at the Sir Francis Drake hotel, is a living San Francisco historical monument. Dressed in traditional Beefeater's attire (you can't miss those $1,400 duds), he's been the subject of countless snapshots—an average 200 per day for the past 25 years—and has shaken hands with every president since Jerry Ford.

service; babysitting by referral; same-day laundry service/dry cleaning; Wi-Fi in meeting rooms and public spaces. *In room:* A/C, TV w/pay movies, dataport, minibar, hair dryer, iron, safe, free high-speed Internet access.

Sir Francis Drake ★★ This landmark hotel is one of San Francisco's grand dames, operating continuously since 1928 in the heart of Union Square. The Kimpton Hotel company has done a wonderful job renovating the hotel (which was sorely needed since I was a kid), giving this elegant lady a much-needed makeover. I've always been a fan of the Hotel Monaco's modern, slightly offbeat interiors with bold patterns and custom furnishings, and they've incorporated a similar style at this property, though with a cream and sage green color scheme. It's always a pleasure to have Tom Sweeny, the ebullient (and legendary) Beefeater doorman, handle your bags as you enter the elegant, captivating lobby with its gilded high ceilings, glittering crystal chandeliers, and massive curved marble staircase that leads to a mezzanine overlooking bustling Powell Street. It's a grand entrance experience you won't soon forget.

Scala's Bistro (p. 105), one of the most festive restaurants downtown, serves good Italian cuisine in a stylish setting on the first floor; the Italian-style Caffe Espresso does an equally commendable job serving coffees, pastries, and sandwiches daily in its spot adjacent to the hotel. Harry Denton's Starlight Room (p. 234), on the 21st floor, offers cocktails, entertainment, and dancing nightly with a panoramic view of the city.

450 Powell St. (at Sutter St.), San Francisco, CA 94102. ✆ **800/795-7129** or 415/392-7755. Fax 415/391-8719. www.sirfrancisdrake.com. 417 units. $239–$289 double; from $5,200 suite. AE, DC, DISC, MC, V. Valet parking $38. Bus: 2, 3, 4, 45, or 76. Cable car: Powell–Hyde or Powell–Mason lines (direct stop). Pets welcome. **Amenities:** 2 restaurants; bar; exercise room; concierge; limited room service; same-day laundry service/dry cleaning; Wi-Fi. *In room:* A/C, TV w/movies on demand, dataport, minibar, hair dryer, iron, free Wi-Fi.

Villa Florence ★ Located ½ block south of Union Square, fronting the Powell Street cable car line, the seven-story Villa Florence is in one of the liveliest sections of the city (no need to drive, 'cause you're already here). The Villa Florence provides guests a taste of contemporary Italian decor—designed by Cheryl Rowley of Beverly Hills—with cherrywood furniture, plantation shutters, windows that actually open, and perks such as 27-inch flatscreen TVs with DVD players and CD players. You'll like the large, comfortable beds draped in down comforters with Frette duvets, as well as such luxury touches as Aveda bath products and Frette bathrobes. Worth noting, however, is that the hotel itself is old and the structure looks it, despite freshly applied lipstick and powder. It shouldn't worry you, though, since everything here is nice enough. The hotel's ground-floor restaurant, Kuleto's (p. 104) (one of downtown's most bustling and stylish Italian restaurants), helps make it a worthy contender among Union Square's medium-priced inns—as if the location alone weren't reason enough to book a room.

225 Powell St. (between Geary and O'Farrell sts.), San Francisco, CA 94102. ✆ **866/823-4669** or 415/397-7700. Fax 415/397-1006. www.villaflorence.com. 183 units. $199–$249 double; $249–$299 studio suites. Rates include

evening wine. AE, DC, DISC, MC, V. Valet parking $35, plus an extra $10–$15 per day for oversize vehicles and SUVs. Bus: 2, 3, 4, 30, 38, or 45. Cable car: Powell–Hyde or Powell–Mason lines (direct stop). **Amenities:** Access to nearby health club ($15/day); concierge; courtesy car; business center; secretarial services; babysitting on request; same-day laundry service/dry cleaning; in-room spa services. *In room:* A/C, ceiling fan, flatscreen TV w/pay movies, dataport, minibar, fridge, coffeemaker, hair dryer, iron, free Wi-Fi, CD player.

The Warwick Regis ★★ *Value* Louis XVI might have been a rotten monarch, but he certainly had taste. Fashioned in the style of pre-Revolutionary France, the Warwick is awash with pristine French and English antiques, Italian marble, chandeliers, four-poster beds, hand-carved headboards, and the like. The result is an expensive-looking hotel that, for all its pleasantries and perks, is surprisingly affordable when compared to its Union Square contemporaries. Rooms can be on the small side; nonetheless, they're some of the city's most charming. Honeymooners should splurge on the fireplace rooms with four-poster beds—ooh la la! Adjoining the lobby is La Scene Restaurant and Bar, a beautiful place to start your day with a latte and end it with a nightcap.

490 Geary St. (between Mason and Taylor sts.), San Francisco, CA 94102. ✆ **800/203-3232** or 415/928-7900. Fax 415/441-8788. www.warwicksf.com. 74 units. $199–$299 double; $299–$399 suite. AE, DC, DISC, MC, V. Parking $29. Bus: 2, 3, 4, 27, or 38. Cable car: Powell–Hyde or Powell–Mason lines. **Amenities:** Restaurant; access to nearby health club ($15/day); concierge; business center; secretarial services; 24-hr. room service; babysitting; laundry service; dry cleaning. *In room:* TV, dataport, minibar, hair dryer, iron, safe, wireless Internet access.

White Swan Inn ★★ From the moment you're buzzed into this well-secured inn, you'll know you're not in a generic bed-and-breakfast. The romantically homey rooms are warm and cozy—the perfect place to snuggle up with a good book. They're also quite big, with hardwood entryways, rich dark-wood furniture, working fireplaces, and an assortment of books tucked in nooks. The decor is English elegance at its best, if not to excess (floral prints and ceramic bric-a-brac abound). The luxury king suites are not much better than regular rooms, just a wee bit bigger, and feature perks like evening turndown, bathrobes, and a wet bar stocked with complimentary beverages. Each morning, a breakfast buffet is served in a common room just off a tiny garden. Afternoon reception, consisting of hors d'oeuvres, sherry, wine, and home-baked pastries, can be enjoyed in front of the fireplace while you browse through the books in the library or in the parlor.

The inn's location—2½ blocks from Union Square—makes this nonsmoking 1900s building a charming and serene choice, with service and style that will please travelers of all ages.

845 Bush St. (between Taylor and Mason sts.), San Francisco, CA 94108. ✆ **800/999-9570** or 415/775-1755. Fax 415/775-5717. www.whiteswaninnsf.com. 26 units. $229–$319 double; $269 luxury king suite; $319 2-room suite. Extra person $20. Rates include breakfast and afternoon wine and hors d'oeuvres. AE, DC, DISC, MC, V. Valet parking $32. Bus: 1, 2, 3, 4, 27, or 45. Cable car: Powell St. line (1 block north). **Amenities:** Small exercise room; concierge; same-day laundry service; Internet station in conference room (20¢/min.). *In room:* Dataport, fridge w/free beverages, coffeemaker, hair dryer, iron, Wi-Fi ($7.95/day).

MODERATE

Hotel Beresford Arms *Value* The bargain prices are the main reason I recommend this dependable, if unfashionable, hotel. On the plus side, suites have bidets, whirlpool bathtubs, and a wet bar or fully equipped kitchenette—an advantage for families—and a continental breakfast is included in the price of all rooms. All accommodations include plenty of in-room perks, including an afternoon "Social Hour" with wine, tea, and snacks. The location, between the Theater District and Union Square, in a quieter section of San Francisco, is ideal for visitors without cars, and the price for what you get is hard to beat. The on-site **White Horse Tavern,** a quaint replica of an old English pub, serves dinner Tuesday through Saturday. ***Tip:*** Rooms that face Post Street might be a bit noisier than others, but they're also larger and sunnier, and some have window seats.

701 Post St. (at Jones St.), San Francisco, CA 94109. ✆ **800/533-6533** or 415/673-2600. Fax 415/929-1535. www.beresford.com. 95 units. $99–$279 double. Extra person $10. Children under 12 stay free in parent's room. Rates include pastry, coffee, afternoon wine and tea. Senior and AAA discounts available. AE, DC, DISC, MC, V. Valet parking $20. Bus: 2, 3, 4, 27, or 38. Cable car: Powell–Hyde line (3 blocks east). **Amenities:** Access to nearby health club ($10/day); laundry service; free Internet access in lobby. *In room:* TV, dataport, minibar, hair dryer upon request, iron.

Hotel Milano ★ Neoclassical Italian design patterned after Giorgio Armani's villa in Milan, elegantly streamlined rooms (with double-paned soundproof windows), moderate prices, and a central location next to the San Francisco Centre make Hotel Milano a popular choice for tourists and businesspeople alike. The hotel also has a film-production facility and private screening room to entice media types. Corporate travelers come for the spacious guest rooms, which feature everything an executive could want, from wireless Internet to video game systems and work desks. Suites have spa tubs and bidets.

55 Fifth St. (between Market and Mission sts.), San Francisco, CA 94103. ✆ **800/398-7555** or 415/543-8555. Fax 415/543-5885. www.hotelmilanosf.com. 108 units. $109–$199 double. Extra person $20. AE, DC, DISC, MC, V. Valet parking $33. Bus: All Market St. buses. **Amenities:** Fitness room; spa; steam room and sauna; concierge; laundry; valet. *In room:* A/C, TV w/video games, fax, dataport, fridge, hair dryer, iron, safe, Wi-Fi ($9.95/day).

King George Hotel ★ *Value* Built in 1914 for the Panama–Pacific Exhibition (when rooms went for $1 per night), the boutique King George has fared well over the years with its mostly European clientele. The location—surrounded by cable car lines, the Theater District, Union Square, and dozens of restaurants—is superb, and the rooms are surprisingly quiet for such a busy spot (sadly, the interior noise is definitely audible through thin, old walls). The guest rooms can be very small (in the smallest rooms it can be difficult for two people to maneuver at the same time), but they still manage to find room for writing desks, private bathrooms, and king or queen pillow-top beds with down comforters. A big hit since it started a few years back is the hotel's English afternoon tea, served in the Windsor Tea Room Saturday, Sunday, and holidays from 1 to 4pm. Recent additions include a pub, a 24-hour business center, and an upgraded "executive" level.

334 Mason St. (between Geary and O'Farrell sts.), San Francisco, CA 94102. ✆ **800/288-6005** or 415/781-5050. Fax 415/835-5991. www.kinggeorge.com. 153 units. $175 double; $195 suite. Breakfast $9.95–$13. Special-value packages available seasonally. AE, DC, DISC, MC, V. Valet parking $26; self-parking $23. Bus: 1, 2, 3, 4, 5, 7, 30, 38, 45, 70, or 71. Cable car: Powell–Hyde or Powell–Mason lines (1 block west). **Amenities:** Tearoom; evening lounge/bar; $12 access to health club ½ block away; concierge; 24-hr. business center; secretarial services; room service; same-day laundry service/dry cleaning; wireless Internet access in lobby. *In room:* TV w/video games and pay movies, dataport, hair dryer, iron, safe, free Wi-Fi.

The Monticello Inn ★ Federal-style decor, Chippendale furnishings, grandfather clocks, Revolutionary War paintings, two fireplaces, and other period props throughout the lobby attempt to create a Colonial milieu. Although it makes for a pleasant entrance, the effect doesn't follow through to the modern guest rooms which, though comfortable and spacious, aren't winning any design awards with their striped white and light blue wallpaper and color-coordinated bedspreads. Despite the homely air conditioners in the walls, you could be quite content here, especially considering the extras—umbrellas, voice mail, a morning ride to the Financial District, complimentary coffee from 6:30 to 9am, and evening wine hour from 5 to 6pm. The service is wonderful and the downtown location is *primo.* The adjoining Puccini & Pinetti restaurant features modern Italian cuisine.

127 Ellis St. (at Powell St.), San Francisco, CA 94102. ✆ **866/778-6169** or 415/392-8800. Fax 415/398-2650. www.monticelloinn.com. 91 units. $149–$229 double; $199–$249 suite. Extra person $20. Rates include coffee and tea in the lobby and evening wine; continental breakfast $6. AE, DC, DISC, MC, V. Valet parking $37. Bus: All Market St. buses. Streetcar: All Market St. streetcars. Cable car: Powell–Hyde or Powell–Mason lines (direct stop). Pets accepted. **Amenities:** Access to great nearby health club ($15/day); concierge; limited room service; laundry service; dry cleaning; Internet access. *In room:* A/C, TV w/video games and pay movies, dataport, minibar, fridge, hair dryer, iron, free Wi-Fi.

INEXPENSIVE

The Andrews Hotel For the location, price, and service, the Andrews is a safe bet for an enjoyable stay in San Francisco. Two blocks west of Union Square, the Andrews was a Turkish bath before its conversion in 1981. As is typical in Euro-style hotels, the rooms are small but well maintained and comfortable, with nice touches like white lace curtains and fresh flowers. Continued upgrades help keep things fresh, but large bathroom lovers beware—the facilities here are tiny. A bonus is the adjoining Fino Bar and Ristorante, which offers respectable Italian fare and free wine to hotel guests in the evening.

624 Post St. (between Jones and Taylor sts.), San Francisco, CA 94109. ✆ **800/926-3739** or 415/563-6877. Fax 415/928-6919. www.andrewshotel.com. 48 units, some with shower only. $92–$142 double; $139–$179 superior rooms. Rates include continental breakfast, coffee in lobby, and evening wine. AE, DC, MC, V. Valet parking $25. Bus: 2, 3, 4, 30, 38, or 45. Cable car: Powell–Hyde or Powell–Mason lines (3 blocks east). **Amenities:** Restaurant; access to nearby health club; concierge; room service (5:30–10pm); babysitting; nearby self-service laundromat; laundry service; dry cleaning. *In room:* TV/VCR w/video library, dataport, fridge, hair dryer on request, iron, free Wi-Fi, CD player in suites only.

The Cornell Hotel de France Its quirks make this small French-style hotel more charming than many others in its price range. Pass the office, where a few faces will glance in your direction and smile, and embark on a ride in the old-fashioned elevator (we're talking seriously old-school here) to get to your basic room. Each floor is dedicated to a French painter and decorated with reproductions. Rooms are all plain and comfortable, with desks and chairs, and are individually and simply decorated. Smoking is not allowed. The full American breakfast included in the rate is served in the cool cavernlike provincial basement restaurant, Jeanne d'Arc. Union Square is just a few blocks away.

715 Bush St. (between Powell and Mason sts.), San Francisco, CA 94108. ✆ **800/232-9698** or 415/421-3154. Fax 415/399-1442. www.cornellhotel.com. 55 units. $85–$155 double. Rates include full American breakfast. AE, DC, DISC, MC, V. Parking across the street $17. Bus: 2, 3, 4, 30, or 45. Cable car: Powell–Hyde or Powell–Mason lines. **Amenities:** Restaurant; computer w/Internet in lobby. *In room:* TV, dataport, hair dryer, Wi-Fi (for a fee).

The Golden Gate Hotel ★ *Value* San Francisco's stock of small hotels in historic turn-of-the-20th-century buildings includes some real gems, and The Golden Gate Hotel is one of them. It's 2 blocks north of Union Square and 2 blocks down (literally) from the crest of Nob Hill, with cable car stops at the corner for easy access to Fisherman's Wharf and Chinatown. The city's theaters and best restaurants are also within walking distance. But the best thing about the 1913 Edwardian hotel—which definitely has a B&B feel—is that it's family run: John and Renate Kenaston and daughter Gabriele are hospitable innkeepers who take obvious pleasure in making their guests comfortable. Each individually decorated room has recently been repainted and carpeted and has handsome antique furnishings (plenty of wicker) from the early 1900s, quilted bedspreads, and fresh flowers. Request a room with a claw-foot tub if you enjoy a good, hot soak. Afternoon tea is served daily from 4 to 7pm, and guests are welcome to use the house fax and computer with wireless Internet free of charge.

775 Bush St. (between Powell and Mason sts.), San Francisco, CA 94108. ✆ **800/835-1118** or 415/392-3702. Fax 415/392-6202. www.goldengatehotel.com. 25 units, 14 with bathroom. $85–$105 double without bathroom; $150 double with bathroom. Rates include continental breakfast and afternoon tea. AE, DC, MC, V. Self-parking $20. Bus: 2, 4, 30, 38, or 45. Cable car: Powell–Hyde or Powell–Mason lines (1 block east). BART: Powell and Market. **Amenities:** Access to health club 1 block away; activities desk; laundry service/dry cleaning next door. *In room:* TV, dataport, hair dryer and iron upon request, free Wi-Fi.

Halcyon Hotel *Value* Inside this small, four-story brick building is a penny-pincher's dream come true, the kind of place where you'll find everything you need yet won't have to pay through the nose to get it. The small but clean studio guest rooms are equipped with microwave ovens, refrigerators, flatware and utensils, toasters, alarm clocks, coffeemakers and coffee, phones with free local calls, mail delivery, and voice mail—all the comforts of home in the heart of Union Square (you can even bring your pet!). A coin-operated washer and dryer are located in the basement, along with free laundry soap and irons. The managers are usually on hand to offer friendly, personal service, making this option all in all an unbeatable deal. Be sure to ask about special rates for weekly stays.

649 Jones St. (between Geary and Post sts.), San Francisco, CA 94102. ✆ **800/627-2396** or 415/929-8033. Fax 415/441-8033. www.halcyonsf.com. 25 units. $79–$99 double year-round; $450–$600 weekly. AE, DC, DISC, MC, V. Parking garage nearby $14–$16 per day. Bus: 2, 3, 4, 9, 27, or 38. Pets accepted. **Amenities:** Access to nearby health club; concierge; tour desk; laundry facilities; free fax available in lobby. *In room:* TV, dataport, kitchen, fridge, coffeemaker, hair dryer, iron, voice mail.

Hotel Beresford The small, less expensive sister property of the Hotel Beresford Arms (see above), the seven-floor Hotel Beresford is another good, moderately priced choice near Union Square. Perks are the same: satellite TV, phone, radio, private bathrooms with either a tub or shower, and stocked fridges. The guest rooms are decorated in Victorian style and very well kept, with plenty of personal touches you don't often find in a budget hotel. Rates even include continental breakfast. The on-site **White Horse Tavern,** a quaint replica of an old English pub, serves dinner Tuesday through Saturday and is a favorite for folks who like less trendy hullabaloo with their meal.

635 Sutter St. (near Mason St.), San Francisco, CA 94102. ✆ **800/533-6533** or 415/673-9900. Fax 415/474-0449. www.beresford.com. 114 units. $89–$165 double. Extra person $10. Rates include continental breakfast. Children under 12 stay free in parent's room. AE, DC, DISC, MC, V. Valet parking $20. Bus: 2, 3, 4, 30, 38, or 45. Cable car: Powell–Hyde line (1 block east). **Amenities:** Restaurant/pub; access to nearby health club ($10/day); laundry service; free high-speed Internet access in kiosk in lobby. *In room:* TV, dataport, minibar, hair dryer upon request, iron.

Hotel Bijou ★ *Value* Three words sum up this hotel: clean, colorful, and cheap. Although it's on the periphery of the gritty Tenderloin (just 3 blocks off Union Sq.), once inside this gussied-up 1911 hotel, all's cheery, bright, and perfect for budget travelers who want a little style with their savings. Joie de Vivre hotel group disguised the hotel's age with lively decor, a Deco theater theme, and a heck of a lot of vibrant paint. To the left of the small lobby is a "theater" where guests can watch San Francisco–based double features nightly (it has cute old-fashioned theater seating, though it's just a basic TV showing videos). Upstairs, rooms named after locally made films are small, clean, and colorful (think buttercup, burgundy, and purple), and have all the basics from clock radios, dressers, and small desks to tiny bathrooms (one of which is so small you have to close the door to access the toilet). Alas, a few mattresses could be firmer, and there's only one small and slow elevator. But considering the price, and perks like the continental breakfast and friendly service, you can't go wrong here.

111 Mason St., San Francisco, CA 94102. ✆ **800/771-1022** or 415/771-1200. Fax 415/346-3196. www.hotelbijou.com. 65 units. $99–$159 double. Rates include continental breakfast. AE, DC, DISC, MC, V. Valet parking $27. Bus: All Market St. buses. Streetcar: Powell St. station. **Amenities:** Concierge; limited room service; same-day laundry service/dry cleaning; DSL access in lobby ($4/20 min). *In room:* TV, dataport, hair dryer, iron, high-speed Internet, Wi-Fi ($7.95/day).

Hotel Carlton ★ *Value* If you're looking for wonderfully cheap, attractive, and clean accommodations and don't mind being in the gritty center of the city, book a room here. The Joie de Vivre hotel group is behind this 163-room hotel that was built in 1927 and revamped in May 2004 in "global vintage" decor. The interior design is globally eclectic, with travel photographs from the American Himalayan Foundation, tribal figurines, Oriental rugs, a vibrant sari-like color scheme, imported hand-painted Moroccan tables, and cool Lucite-beaded table lamps in the guest rooms. Outside, the neighborhood is drab, but it's only a 7-block walk to Union Square, and with doubles starting at a mere $93, you can splurge for a taxi with the money saved. Or stick nearby and try **Saha,** their Arabian-fusion restaurant (think hummus, pizza, Yemenese meatballs, and seared scallops), which serves breakfast and dinner. Heck, they even throw in a complimentary evening wine hour in the lobby.

1075 Sutter St. (between Larkin and Hyde sts.), San Francisco, CA 94109. ✆ **800/922-7586** or 415/673-0242. Fax 415/673-4904. www.jdvhospitality.com. 163 units. $93–$199 double. Rates include evening wine reception. AE, MC, V. Valet parking $30; self parking $25. Bus: 2, 3, 4, 19, or 76. **Amenities:** Restaurant; concierge; laundry; dry cleaning. *In room:* TV, coffeemaker, hair dryer, iron, safe, free Wi-Fi.

Hotel des Arts ★★ *Value* While this bargain find has the same floor plan as San Francisco's numerous other Euro-style hotels—small lobby, narrow hallways, cramped rooms—the owners of the des Arts have made an obvious effort to distance themselves from the competition by including a visually stimulating dose of artistic license throughout the hotel. The lobby, for example, hosts a rotating art gallery featuring contemporary works by emerging local artists and is outfitted with groovy furnishings, while the guest rooms are soothingly situated with quality furnishings and tasteful accouterments. There's one suite that can sleep up to four persons at no additional charge. You'll love the lively location as well: right across the street from the entrance to Chinatown and 2 blocks from Union Square. There's even a French brasserie right downstairs. Considering the price (rooms with a very clean shared bathroom start at $59), quality, and location, it's quite possibly the best budget hotel in the city. ***Tip:*** Log onto the hotel's website to check out the "Painted Rooms" designed by local artists, then call the hotel directly to book your favorite.

447 Bush St. (at Grant St.), San Francisco, CA 94108. ✆ **800/956-4322** or 415/956-3232. Fax 415/956-0399. www.sfhoteldesarts.com. 51 units, 26 with private bathroom. $79–$159 with bathroom; $59–$79 double without bathroom. Rates include continental breakfast. AE, DC, MC, V. Nearby parking $18. Cable car: Powell–Hyde and Powell–Mason lines. **Amenities:** 24-hr. concierge, fax, and copy services; laundry and valet service. *In room:* TV, 2-line direct-dial telephone w/dataport and voice mail, minifridge and microwave in many rooms, hair dryer, iron and board.

3 Nob Hill

VERY EXPENSIVE

The Fairmont San Francisco ★★★ *Kids* The granddaddy of Nob Hill's elite cadre of ritzy hotels—and the only spot in San Francisco where each of the city's cable car lines meet—the century-old Fairmont is a must-visit if only to marvel at the incredibly glamorous lobby with its vaulted ceilings, Corinthian columns, a spectacular spiral staircase, and rococo furniture (it's easy to feel underdressed in such opulent surroundings). And yes, such decadence carries to the guest rooms where luxuries abound: oversized marble bathrooms, thick down blankets, goose-down king pillows, extra-long mattresses, and large walk-in closets. Because it's perched at the top of Nob Hill, there are spectacular city views from every guest room, but nuances such as a health club & spa, a 24-hour concierge, twice-daily maid service, babysitting services, and a business center enhance every guest's stay. Within the lobby is the ornate **Laurel Court** restaurant and lounge, which serves as the hotel's centerpiece. (It's fun to indulge in afternoon tea here, served daily 2:30–4:30pm.) A local institution that's been around since I was a kid is the hotel's **Tonga Room,** a fantastically kitsch Disneyland-like tropical bar and restaurant where happy hour hops and "rain" falls every 30 minutes.

950 Mason St. (at California St.), San Francisco, CA 94108. ✆ **866/540-4491** or 415/772-5000. Fax 415/772-5086. www.fairmont.com. 591 units. Main building $229–$349 double; from $500 suite. Tower $289–$469 double; from $750 suite. Penthouse $12,500. Extra person $30. AE, DC, DISC, MC, V. Parking $43. Cable car: California St. line (direct stop). **Amenities:** 2 restaurants/bars; health club (free for Fairmont President's Club members; $15/day or $20/2 days, non-members); concierge; tour desk; car-rental desk; business center; shopping arcade; salon; room service; massage; babysitting; same-day laundry service/dry cleaning; wireless Internet in lobby. *In room:* A/C, TV w/pay movies and video games available, dataport, kitchenette in some units, minibar, hair dryer, iron, safe, high-speed Internet access.

The Huntington Hotel ★★ One of the kings of Nob Hill, the stately Huntington Hotel has long been a favorite retreat for Hollywood stars and political VIPs who desire privacy and security. Family-owned since 1924—an extreme rarity among large hotels—the Huntington eschews pomp and circumstance; absolute privacy and unobtrusive service are its mainstays. Although the lobby, decorated in grand 19th-century style, is rather petite compared to its Nob Hill neighbors, the guest rooms are like spacious apartments; they feature Brunschwig & Fils fabrics and bed coverings, antique French furnishings, and dreamy views of the city. Be warned, however, that they are also quirky and sprinkled with downscale items; one room where I recently stayed had motel-quality doorknobs and a tiny, plain bathroom. Where they make up for the room deficiencies is a genuinely gracious staff and the celestial **Nob Hill Spa** (the best in the city). The lavish suites, so opulent that they've been featured in *Architectural Digest,* are individually decorated with custom-made furnishings. Prices are steep, as you would expect, but special offers such as the Romance Package, which includes champagne, specialty teas, limousine service, and two 50-minute massages from their spa, make the Huntington worth considering for a special occasion. **The Big Four** restaurant offers expensive contemporary American cuisine, including the best $16 chicken pot pie I've ever had. Live piano music is played nightly in the lounge.

1075 California St. (between Mason and Taylor sts.), San Francisco, CA 94108. ✆ **800/227-4683** or 415/474-5400. Fax 415/474-6227. www.huntingtonhotel.com. 135 units. $350–$500 single or double; $600–$1,350 suite. Continental breakfast $14. Special packages available. AE, DC, DISC, MC, V. Valet parking $29. Bus: 1. Cable car: California St. line (direct stop). **Amenities:** Restaurant; lounge; indoor heated pool (ages 16 and up); health club; spa; steam room; sauna; yoga and Pilates room; Jacuzzi; concierge; massage; babysitting; same-day laundry service/dry cleaning. *In room:* A/C, TV w/pay movies, dataport, kitchenettes in some units, minibar, fridges in some units, hair dryer, iron, safe, Wi-Fi ($9.95/day).

InterContinental Mark Hopkins ★★★ Built in 1926 on the spot where railroad millionaire Mark Hopkins's turreted mansion once stood, the 19-story Mark Hopkins gained global fame during World War II when it was de rigueur for Pacific-bound servicemen to toast their goodbye to the States in the Top of the Mark cocktail lounge.

Nowadays, this grand hotel caters mostly to convention-bound corporate executives, since its prices often require corporate charge accounts. Each neoclassical room is exceedingly comfortable and comes with all the fancy amenities you'd expect from a world-class hotel, including custom furniture, plush fabrics, sumptuous bathrooms, Frette bathrobes, and extraordinary views of the city. The luxury suites are twice the size of most San Francisco apartments and cost close to a month's rent per night. A minor caveat: The hotel has only three guest elevators, making a quick trip to your room difficult during busy periods.

The **Top of the Mark** (p. 240), a fantastic bar/lounge (open daily), offers dancing to live jazz or swing, Sunday brunch, and cocktails in swank, old-fashioned style. (Romantics, this place is for you, but keep in mind that there's a $10 cover fee Fri–Sat after 8:30pm for the live nightly entertainment.) The Nob Hill Restaurant offers California cuisine nightly and breakfast on Sunday.

1 Nob Hill (at California and Mason sts.), San Francisco, CA 94108. ✆ **800/972-3124** or 415/392-3434. Fax 415/421-3302. www.markhopkins.net. 380 units. $399–$599 double; from $650 suite; from $3,000 luxury suite. Breakfast $17 for juice, coffee, and pastry to $23 for full buffet. AE, DC, DISC, MC, V. Valet parking $44, some oversize vehicles prohibited. Bus: 1. Cable car: California St. or Powell lines (direct stop). **Amenities:** 2 restaurants; bar; exercise room; concierge; business center; secretarial services; room service; babysitting; laundry service/dry cleaning; concierge-level floors. *In room:* A/C, TV w/pay movies, VCR/DVD in suites only, dataport, minibar, coffeemaker, hair dryer, iron, safe, Wi-Fi in all rooms for nominal fee.

The Ritz-Carlton, San Francisco ★★★ Ranked among the top hotels in the world, The Ritz-Carlton San Francisco has been the benchmark for the city's luxury hotels since it opened in 1991. A Nob Hill landmark, the former Metropolitan Insurance headquarters stood vacant for years until The Ritz-Carlton company acquired it and embarked on a $100-million, 4-year renovation. The interior was completely gutted and restored with fine furnishings, fabrics, and artwork, including a pair of Louis XVI blue marble urns with gilt mountings, and 19th-century Waterford candelabras. And just to make sure they stay on top, the rooms were completely upgraded last year to the tune of $12.5 million, and now include 32-inch LCD TVs, DVD/CD players, Wi-Fi, and two cordless phones. The Italian marble bathrooms offer every possible amenity: double sinks, telephone, name-brand toiletries, and plush terry robes. The more expensive rooms take advantage of the hotel's location—the south slope of Nob Hill—and have good views of the city. Clubrooms, on the top floors, have a dedicated concierge, separate elevator-key access, and complimentary small plates throughout the day. No restaurant in town has more formal service than this hotel's **Dining Room,** which serves modern French cuisine with a Japanese influence. The less formal **Terrace Restaurant** offers contemporary Mediterranean cuisine and the city's best Sunday brunch. The Lobby lounge serves classic afternoon tea and cocktails with low-key live entertainment daily, and sushi Wednesday through Saturday.

600 Stockton St. (between Pine and California sts.), San Francisco, CA 94108. ✆ **800/241-3333** or 415/296-7465. Fax 415/986-1268. www.ritzcarlton.com. 336 units. $445–$480 double; $600–$850 club-level double; from $750–$850 executive suite. Buffet breakfast $32; Sun champagne brunch $65. Weekend discounts and packages available. AE, DC, DISC, MC, V. Parking $55. Cable car: California St. cable car line (direct stop). **Amenities:** 2 restaurants; 3 bars; indoor pool; outstanding fitness center; Jacuzzi; steam room; concierge; courtesy car; business center; secretarial services; room service; in-room massage and manicure; same-day laundry service/dry cleaning. *In room:* A/C, TV w/pay movies, dataport, minibar, hair dryer, iron, safe, high-speed Internet access and Wi-Fi ($13/day).

Stanford Court, A Renaissance Hotel ★★ The Stanford Court has maintained a long and discreet reputation as one of San Francisco's most exclusive hotels. Keeping company with the Ritz, Fairmont, Mark Hopkins, and Huntington hotels atop

Value Accommodations with Free Parking

Despite my exhortations to leave the driving to locals and use the public transportation system to get around, I know that some of you will still want to drive the crazy streets of San Francisco, or at least arrive by car. But with parking fees averaging $30 to $40 a night at most hotels, the extra charges can add up for visitors with wheels. So if you're going to rent a car or bring your own, you might want to consider staying at one of these hotels that offers free parking:

- Beck's Motor Lodge, the Castro, p. 94
- Cow Hollow Motor Inn & Suites, Marina District/Cow Hollow, p. 91
- Hostelling International San Francisco—Fisherman's Wharf, p. 92
- Hotel Del Sol, Marina District/Cow Hollow, p. 90
- Laurel Inn, Marina District/Cow Hollow, p. 91
- Marina Motel, Marina District/Cow Hollow, p. 92
- Phoenix Hotel, Civic Center, p. 93
- San Francisco Airport North Travelodge, Near the Airport, p. 97
- Seal Rock Inn, Richmond District, p. 87
- The Wharf Inn, North Beach/Fisherman's Wharf, p. 89

Nob Hill, it's frequented mostly by corporate execs. The foundation was originally the mansion of Leland Stanford, whose legacy lives on in the many portraits and biographies that adorn the rooms. At first, the guest rooms come across as austere and antiquated compared to those at most other top-dollar business hotels, but the quality and comfort of the furnishings are so superior that you're forced to admit there's little room for improvement. The Stanford Court also prides itself on its impeccable service. The lobby, furnished in 19th-century style with Baccarat chandeliers, French antiques, and a gorgeous stained-glass dome, makes for a grand entrance.

Many of the guest rooms have partially canopied beds; all have writing desks and feature the new signature Renaissance bedding with new linens and down duvets and oak armoires that conceal the television sets. Bathrooms contain robes, telephones, and heated towel racks. Deluxe rooms have Frette linens. A thoughtful perk: There is no charge for toll-free or credit card calls made from your room, and complimentary coffee and tea are available with a wake-up call request.

905 California St. (at Powell St.), San Francisco, CA 94108. ✆ **800/HOTELS** or 415/989-3500. Fax 415/391-0513. www.stanfordcourt.com. 393 units. $299 double; from $550 suite. Continental breakfast $17–$22; American breakfast $21–$26. AE, DC, DISC, MC, V. Valet parking $41. Bus: 1. Cable car: Powell–Hyde, Powell–Mason, or California–Van Ness lines (direct stop). **Amenities:** Restaurant; lounge; 24-hr. fitness center; concierge; free car to downtown destinations; business center; room service; same-day laundry service/dry cleaning. *In room:* A/C, TV w/pay movies and Web TV, dataport, hair dryer, iron, $9.95 high-speed Internet access and local call package.

MODERATE

The Nob Hill Inn ★★ Built in 1907 as a private home, this four-story inn has been masterfully refurbished with Victorian-style antiques, expensive fabrics, reproduction artwork, and a magnificent etched-glass European-style lift. Even the low-priced Gramercy rooms receive equal attention: with good-size bathrooms (with claw-foot tubs), antique furnishings, faux-antique phones, discreetly placed televisions, and comfortable full-size beds. Granted, the cheaper rooms are quite small, but they're so utterly charming that it's tough to complain, especially when you consider that rates include continental breakfast, afternoon tea and sherry, and the distinction of staying in one of the city's most prestigious neighborhoods. ***Tip:*** Ideal for families of four are the inn's one-bedroom apartment-style suites, which include a stocked kitchenette, a private master bedroom, and a parlor with a sofa sleeper.

1000 Pine St. (at Taylor St.), San Francisco, CA 94109. ✆ **415/673-6080.** Fax 415/673-6098. www.nobhillinn.com. 21 units. $125–$195 double; $245–$275 suite. Rates include continental breakfast, afternoon tea, and sherry. AE, DC, DISC, MC, V. Parking $25–$35 per day in nearby garages. Bus: 1. Cable car: California St. line. **Amenities:** Concierge. *In room:* TV, kitchenette in some, hair dryer, iron.

4 SoMa

VERY EXPENSIVE

Four Seasons Hotel San Francisco ★★★ What makes this überluxury hotel that opened in late 2001 one of my favorites in the city is its perfect combination of elegance, trendiness, and modern luxury. The entrance, either off Market or through a narrow alley off Third Street, is deceptively underwhelming, although it does tip you off to the hotel's overall discreetness. Take the elevators up to the lobby and you're instantly surrounded by calm, cool, and collected hotel perfection. After all, what's not to love about dark mood lighting, comfy leather chairs, bottomless bowls of olives and spicy wasabi-covered peanuts, a tempting cocktail list, and a pianist playing jazz standards intermingled with No Doubt and Cold Play? Many of the oversize rooms (starting at 460 sq. ft. and including 46 suites) overlook Yerba Buena Gardens. Not too trendy, not too traditional, they're just right, with custom-made mattresses and pillows that guarantee the all-time best night's sleep, beautiful works of art, and huge luxury marble bathrooms with deep tubs and L'Occitane toiletries. Hues of taupe, beige, and green are almost as soothing as the impeccable service. Adding to the perks are free access to the building's huge Sports Club L.A. (the best hotel gym in the city), round-the-clock business services, a 2-block walk to Union Square and the Moscone Convention Center, and a vibe that combines sophistication with a hipness far more refined than the W or the Clift. Its only contender in that department is the St. Regis.

757 Market St. (between Third and Fourth sts.), San Francisco, CA 94103. ✆ **800/819-5053** or 415/633-3000. Fax 415/633-3001. www.fourseasons.com/sanfrancisco. 277 units. $450–$855 double; $825 executive suite. AE, DC, DISC, MC, V. Parking $39. Bus: All Market St. buses. Streetcar: F, and all underground streetcars. BART: All trains. **Amenities:** Restaurant; bar; huge fitness center; spa; concierge; high-tech business center; secretarial services; salon; room service; in-room massage; overnight laundry service/dry cleaning, wireless Internet access in lobby. *In room:* A/C, TV w/pay movies, fax, dataport, minibar, hair dryer, safe, high-speed Internet access ($13/day).

Hotel Palomar ★★ The Kimpton Boutique Hotels' most luxurious downtown property occupies the top five floors of a refurbished 1907 landmark office building. As the group's most refined boutique property, the Art Deco–inspired interior designed by Cheryl Rowley features rooms with an updated twist on 1930s modern design—artful, understated textural elements such as emerald-tone velvets, fine woods, and raffia. Tailored lines and rich textures throughout lend a sophisticated, fresh aspect to the overall air of elegance. Rooms, however, can range from very cozy (read: small) to soothingly spacious (try for a corner room overlooking Market St.); they're also bound to be in mint condition thanks to soft-goods upgrades in 2007. There's not much in the way of public spaces, but the hotel makes up for it with its rooms' fab-factor, homey luxuries like DVD/CD players and flatscreen TVs, and its dining room, the **Fifth Floor Restaurant** (p. 114), which is one of the most expensive and upscale restaurants in town. That said, if you want the full-blown luxury hotel experience—with every hotel amenity under the sun—you're better off with one of the Nob Hill or Union Square big boys.

12 Fourth St. (at Market St.), San Francisco, CA 94103. ✆ **866/373-4941** or 415/348-1111. Fax 415/348-0302. www.hotelpalomar.com. 198 units. From $369 double; from $569 suite. Continental breakfast $22. AE, DC, DISC, MC, V. Parking $44. Streetcar: F, and all underground streetcars. BART: All trains. Pets welcome. **Amenities:** Restaurant; fitness center; concierge; courtesy car; business center; secretarial services; room service; in-room massage; babysitting; same-day laundry service/dry cleaning. *In room:* A/C, TV, dataport, minibar, fridge, hair dryer, iron, safe, free high-speed Internet and Wi-Fi, CD player.

The Palace Hotel ★ The original 1875 Palace was one of the world's largest and most luxurious hotels, and every time you walk through the doors here, you'll be reminded how incredibly majestic old luxury really is. Rebuilt after the 1906 quake, its most spectacular attributes remain the regal lobby and the Garden Court, a San Francisco landmark restaurant that was restored to its original 1909 grandeur. A double row of massive Italian-marble Ionic columns flank the court, and 10 huge chandeliers dangle above. The real heart-stopper, however, is the 80,000-pane stained-glass ceiling (good special effects made Mike Douglas look like he fell through it in the movie *The Game*). Regrettably, the rooms aren't *quite* as grand. But they're vastly improved and emulate yesteryear's refinement with mahogany beds, warm gold paint and upholstery, and tasteful artwork.

The **Garden Court** is famous for its elaborate brunch on special holidays and a scaled-down version on regular weekends. Maxfield's Restaurant, a traditional San Francisco grill, serves lunch and dinner. Kyo-ya, an authentic Japanese restaurant, is highly regarded; and The Pied Piper Bar is named after the $2.5-million Maxfield Parrish mural that dominates the room.

2 New Montgomery St. (at Market St.), San Francisco, CA 94105. ✆ **888/625-5144** or 415/512-1111. Fax 415/543-0671. www.sfpalace.com. 552 units. $550–$650 double; from $775 suite. Extra person $40. Children under 18 sharing existing bedding stay free in parent's room. Weekend rates and packages available. AE, DC, DISC, MC, V. Parking $40. Bus: All Market St. buses. Streetcar: All Market St. streetcars. **Amenities:** 4 restaurants; bar; health club w/skylight-covered, heated lap pool; spa; Jacuzzi; sauna; concierge; 24-hr. business center; room service; laundry service; dry cleaning; wireless Internet in lobby, conference rooms w/wireless Internet access. *In room:* A/C, TV w/pay movies, dataport, minibar, hair dryer, iron, safe, high-speed Internet access ($16/day).

St. Regis Hotel ★★★ The latest in full-blown high-tech luxury is yours at this überchic 40-story SoMa tower, which debuted in late 2005. Strategically located near the Museum of Modern Art and Yerba Buena Gardens, this shrine to urban luxury welcomes guests (and residents willing to pay upwards of $2 million for an apartment) with a 16-foot-long gas fireplace and streamlined lobby bar that's frequented by city socialites. A "personal butler" will take you to your room and show you how to use its coolest feature: a touch-screen control panel that works everything, from the phone to the drapes to the temperature to the lights. Decor is minimalist, with dark woods, cream, taupes, and sexy touches like Barcelona benches, 42-inch plasma TVs, and leather paneling (at least in the suites). Bathrooms beckon with deep soaking tubs, 13-inch LCD TVs, rainforest showerheads, and fancy toiletries. You may want to lounge on a chaise and can peek into the happenings of downtown bustle or the green patch of grass that marks Yerba Buena Gardens, but definitely leave your room for an afternoon at the posh two-floor **Remède Spa,** the huge pool and fitness center, and restaurant **Ame,** where chef Hiro Sone, who also owns Terra in Napa Valley, presides over

Accommodations around Town

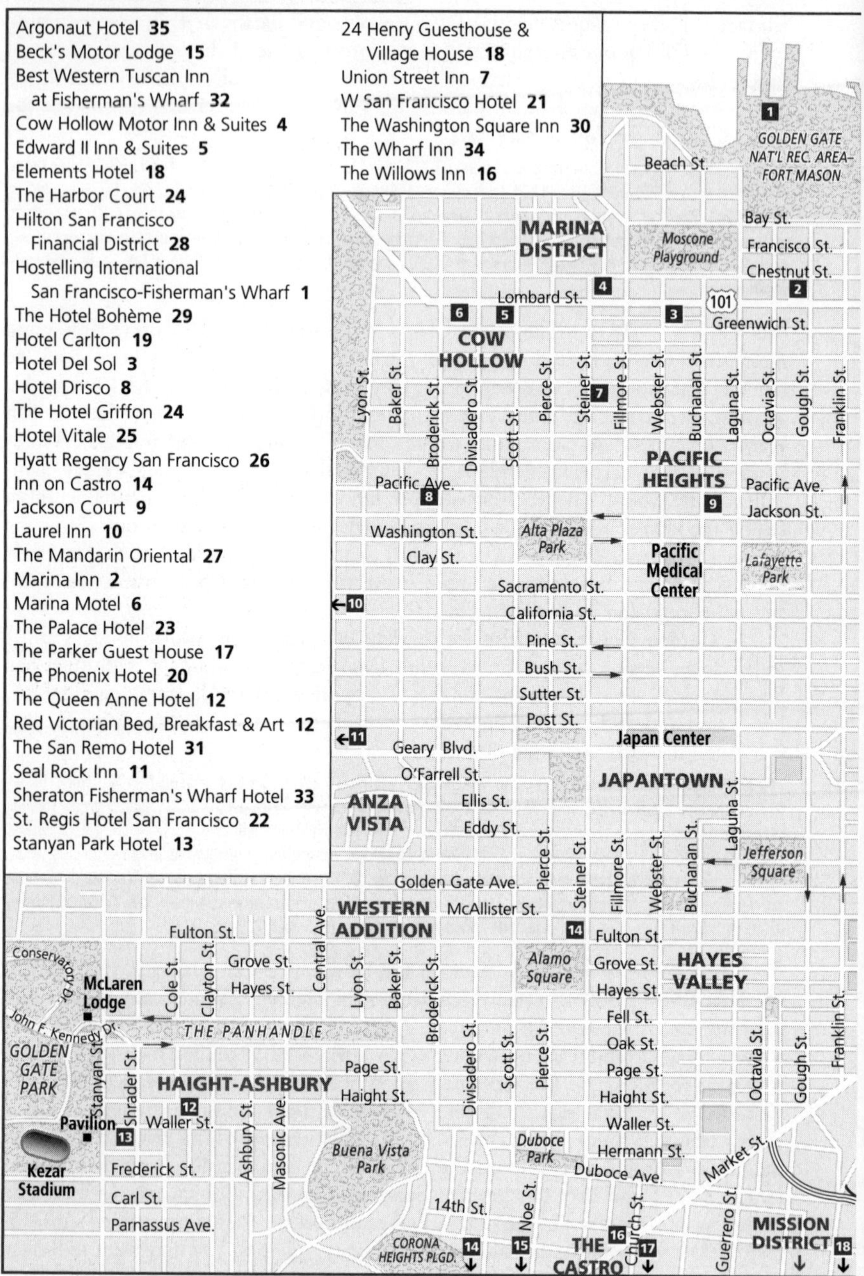

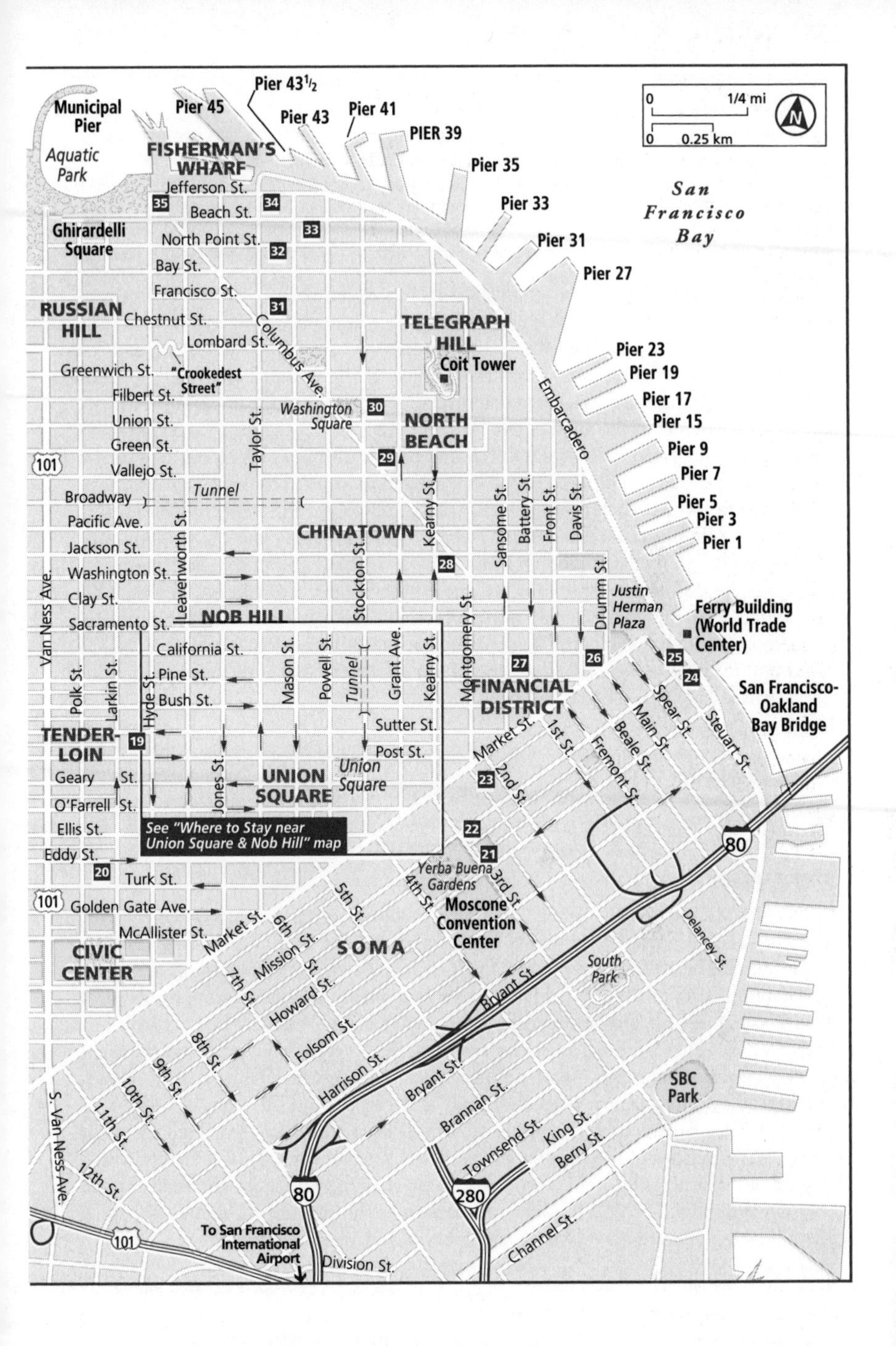
Municipal Pier
Aquatic Park
Pier 45
Pier 43½
Pier 43
Pier 41
PIER 39
Pier 35
Pier 33
Pier 31
Pier 27
Pier 23
Pier 19
Pier 17
Pier 15
Pier 9
Pier 7
Pier 5
Pier 3
Pier 1
San Francisco Bay
0 1/4 mi
0 0.25 km
FISHERMAN'S WHARF
Ghirardelli Square
RUSSIAN HILL
TELEGRAPH HILL
Coit Tower
"Crookedest Street"
Washington Square
NORTH BEACH
CHINATOWN
NOB HILL
FINANCIAL DISTRICT
Justin Herman Plaza
Ferry Building (World Trade Center)
San Francisco-Oakland Bay Bridge
TENDER-LOIN
UNION SQUARE
Union Square
See "Where to Stay near Union Square & Nob Hill" map
Yerba Buena Gardens
Moscone Convention Center
SOMA
South Park
CIVIC CENTER
SBC Park
To San Francisco International Airport
Tunnel
Jefferson St.
Beach St.
North Point St.
Bay St.
Francisco St.
Chestnut St.
Lombard St.
Greenwich St.
Filbert St.
Union St.
Green St.
Vallejo St.
Broadway
Pacific Ave.
Jackson St.
Washington St.
Clay St.
Sacramento St.
California St.
Pine St.
Bush St.
Sutter St.
Post St.
Geary St.
O'Farrell St.
Ellis St.
Eddy St.
Turk St.
Golden Gate Ave.
McAllister St.
Columbus Ave.
Embarcadero
Van Ness Ave.
Polk St.
Larkin St.
Hyde St.
Leavenworth St.
Jones St.
Taylor St.
Mason St.
Powell St.
Stockton St.
Grant Ave.
Kearny St.
Montgomery St.
Sansome St.
Battery St.
Front St.
Davis St.
Drumm St.
Market St.
1st St.
2nd St.
3rd St.
4th St.
5th St.
6th St.
7th St.
8th St.
9th St.
10th St.
11th St.
12th St.
Fremont St.
Beale St.
Main St.
Spear St.
Steuart St.
Delancey St.
Mission St.
Howard St.
Folsom St.
Harrison St.
Bryant St.
Brannan St.
Townsend St.
King St.
Berry St.
Channel St.
Division St.
S. Van Ness Ave.
101
80
280
19
20
21
22
23
24
25
26
27
28
29
30
31
32
33
34
35

an Asian-influenced menu that includes delicacies such as hamachi sashimi and decadences like foie gras and unagi (eel) over mushroom risotto.

125 Third St. (at Mission St.), San Francisco, CA 94103. ✆ **877/787-3447** or 415/284-4000. Fax 415/284-4100. www.stregis.com/sanfrancisco. 260 units. Double from $529–$679; suites from $1,050–$8,500. AE, DC, DISC, MC, V. Parking $45 per day. Bus: 15, 30, or 45. Streetcar: J, K, L, or M to Montgomery. **Amenities:** 2 restaurants; bar; health club w/heated lap pool; giant spa; steam room; sauna; whirlpool; 24-hr. concierge; 24-hr. business center; room service; laundry service; dry cleaning; wireless Internet ($15/day), conference rooms. *In room:* A/C, 2 TVs w/pay movies, fax, dataport, minibar, hair dryer, iron upon request, safe, high-speed Internet access ($15/day), printer, scanner, copier.

W San Francisco Hotel ★★ Starwood Hotels & Resorts' 31-story property is as modern and hip as its fashionable clientele. Sophisticated, slick, and stylish, it suits its neighbors, which include the Museum of Modern Art, the Moscone Center, and the Metreon entertainment center. The striking gray granite facade, piped with polished black stone, complements the octagonal three-story glass entrance and lobby. The hip, urban style extends to the guest rooms, which have a residential feel. Each contains a feather bed with a goose-down comforter and pillows, Waterworks linens, an oversize dark-wood desk, an upholstered chaise longue, and louvered blinds that open to (usually) great city views. Each room also contains a compact media wall complete with a Sony CD/DVD player, an extensive CD library, and a 27-inch color TV with optional high-speed Internet service (and an infrared keyboard) at $15 per day. Bathrooms are super-sleek and stocked with Bliss products. Furthering the cool vibe is a bi-level **XYZ** bar and restaurant, which serves wonderful Californian cuisine within a beautiful modern interior. In 2005, the W welcomed a 5,000-square-foot outpost of NYC's **Bliss Spa** to the premises. All in all, this is one of the top places to stay in San Francisco, particularly if you enjoy the nightlife scene.

181 Third St. (between Mission and Howard sts.), San Francisco, CA 94103. ✆ **877/WHOTELS** or 415/777-5300. Fax 415/817-7823. www.whotels.com/sanfrancisco. 410 units. From $359 double; $1,800–$2,500 suite. AE, DC, DISC, MC, V. Valet parking $40. Bus: 15, 30, or 45. Streetcar: J, K, L, or M to Montgomery. **Amenities:** Restaurant; 2 bars; heated atrium pool and Jacuzzi; fitness center; spa; concierge; business center; secretarial services; 24-hr. room service; same-day laundry service/dry cleaning; Wi-Fi in public spaces. *In room:* A/C, TV w/pay movies, fax (in some rooms), dataport, minibar, coffeemaker, hair dryer, iron, safe, high-speed Internet access, CD/DVD player.

EXPENSIVE

The Harbor Court ★★ When The Embarcadero Freeway was torn down after the Big One in 1989, one of the major benefactors was the "wellness-themed" Harbor Court hotel: The 1926 landmark building's backyard view went from a wall of cement to a dazzling vista of the Bay Bridge (be sure to request a bay-view room, for an extra fee). Located just off The Embarcadero at the edge of the Financial District, this former YMCA books a lot of corporate travelers, but anyone who seeks stylish, high-quality accommodations—half-canopy beds, large armoires, writing desks, soundproof windows, new beds, bedding, and carpet, and 27-inch LCD TVs in 2005—with a superb view and lively scene will be perfectly content here. A major bonus is the free use of the adjoining fitness club, a top-quality YMCA facility with a giant indoor swimming pool. Two more reasons to stay here are the daily hosted evening wine reception and the adjacent **Ozumo Sushi Bar and Robata Grill,** which has a hugely popular happy hour, a cool vibe, and wonderful cuisine.

165 Steuart St. (between Mission and Howard sts.), San Francisco, CA 94105. ✆ **866/792-6283** or 415/882-1300. Fax 415/882-1313. www.harborcourthotel.com. 131 units. $195–$425 double. Continental breakfast $10. AE, DC, DISC, MC, V. Parking $35. Bus: 14 or 80X. Streetcar: Embarcadero. Pets accepted. **Amenities:** Access to adjoining health club and large, heated indoor pool; courtesy car weekday mornings; room service (breakfast only); same-day laundry service/dry cleaning; safe. *In room:* A/C, TV, dataport, minibar, hair dryer, iron, free Wi-Fi.

The Hotel Griffon ★★ Among San Francisco's small boutique hotels, this is a top contender. Ideally situated on the historic waterfront and steps from the heart of the Financial District and Ferry Building Marketplace (p. 155), the Griffon is impeccably outfitted with a soothing design sensibility. Completely renovated in 2007, it boasts contemporary features such as 32-inch flatscreen TVs, lofty ceilings, marble vanities, Aveda bath products, cozy window seats, and plush bedding (really, this place is smooth). Be sure to request a bay-view room overlooking the Bay Bridge—the added perks and view make it well worth the extra cost. Smokers, book a room elsewhere—there's no puffing allowed here.

155 Steuart St. (between Mission and Howard sts.), San Francisco, CA 94105. ✆ **800/321-2201** or 415/495-2100. Fax 415/495-3522. www.hotelgriffon.com. 62 units. $189–$295 double; $385–$445 suite. Rates include extended continental breakfast and newspaper and free Mon–Fri morning town car service within the Financial District. AE, DC, DISC, MC, V. Parking $28. All Market St. buses and streetcars, BART, and ferries. **Amenities:** Restaurant; access to large health club and pool next door (for a fee); concierge; morning car service to downtown; secretarial services; limited room service; in-room massage; laundry service; dry cleaning; free wireless Internet access in lobby and restaurant. *In room:* TV, dataport, minibar, coffeemaker, hair dryer, iron, safe, free high-speed Internet access.

Hotel Vitale ★★ Perched at the foot of The Embarcadero with outstanding waterfront and Bay Bridge views from east-facing rooms, this 199-unit hotel opened in early 2005 to instant popularity. In addition to its prime location across from the Ferry Building Marketplace (p. 155), Hotel Vitale looks pretty darned chic, from the clean-lined lobby, lounge, and decent but not destination-worthy **Americano** restaurant (with a hopping after-work bar scene), to the modern and masculine rooms awash in earth tones and armed with contemporary perks like flatscreen TVs, CD players with groovy compilations, gourmet minibars and for-sale bath products, huge bathrooms with walk-in showers, and nature-themed pop art. Despite excellent service from the well-trained staff, there are a few subtleties that separate Vitale from true luxury hotel status: For example, my fancy flatscreen TV didn't face the bed or the couch and wasn't on hinges that allowed it to be adjusted—very annoying—and the fitness room is flat-out lame with three cardio machines and a few weights. However, they're now offering complimentary access to the nearby YMCA health club, which has all the workout essentials. So, if you can live with a few quirks, it's a very attractive place

---

Finds Elements: A Hip Mission District Hotel

Bad credit? No problem. There's finally a place for the perpetually young and broke to stay and play in the heart of the Mission District. The **Elements Hotel** is sort of a cross between a boutique hotel and a hostel, offering both private rooms and shared dorms, all with private bathrooms. Add to that Wi-Fi Internet access throughout the hotel, a free Internet lounge, rooftop parties, free movie nights, lockers, free continental breakfast, luggage storage and laundry facilities, free linens, TVs (in private rooms), a lively restaurant and lounge called Medjool, and a plethora of inexpensive ethnic cafes in the neighborhood, and baby, you've got it made. The hotel is at 2524 Mission St., between 21st and 22nd streets (✆ **866/327-8407** or 415/647-4100; www.elementssf.com). Rates per person are between $25 and $30; expect higher rates and minimum stays during holidays.

Kids The Best Family-Friendly Hotels

Argonaut Hotel (p. 87) Not only is it near all the funky kid fun of Fisherman's Wharf and the National Maritime Museum, but this bayside hotel, a winner for the whole family, also has kid-friendly perks like the opportunity for each child to grab a gift from the hotel's "treasure chest."

Comfort Suites (p. 96) Enough pay cable channels to keep you and your kids glued to the TV set for an entire day, and a pull-out sleeper sofa in addition to a king-size bed, make this an attractive option for families.

Cow Hollow Motor Inn & Suites (p. 91) Two-bedroom suites allow kids to shack up in style instead of camping on the pull-out couch.

The Fairmont San Francisco (p. 74) While the glamorous lobby and spectacular city views will please parents, kids will be thrilled by the hotel's **Tonga Room,** a fantastically kitsch Disneyland-like tropical bar and restaurant where "rain" falls every 30 minutes.

Handlery Union Square Hotel (p. 64) Never mind that it's been completely renovated. The real kid-friendly kickers here are the adjoining rooms in the "newer" addition; a heated, clean, outdoor pool; and the adjoining restaurant, The Daily Grill, which offers the gamut of American favorites.

Hotel Del Sol (p. 90) It's colorful enough to represent a Crayola selection, but tots are more likely to be impressed by the "Kids are VIPs" program that includes a lending library, toys and videos, evening cookies and milk, and accouterments for the heated pool (think sunglasses, visors, beach balls). Parental perks include access to a bonded babysitting service and three baby-proofed rooms and family suite (three adjoining rooms).

San Francisco Airport North Travelodge (p. 97) It's nothing fancy, but if you've got an early flight out, want to stay near the airport, and don't want to rent an extra room to accommodate the little ones, this place (with pull-out couches in 20 out of the 199 rooms) is a good bet.

Stanyan Park Hotel (p. 96) Plenty of elbowroom and a half-block walk to Golden Gate Park's Children's Playground make this a prime spot for crashing family style. But the biggest bonuses are the suites, which come with one or two bedrooms, a full kitchen, and a dining area.

Westin St. Francis (p. 62) A classic San Francisco hotel down to its hospitality, the Westin welcomes the little ones with fun gifts and free drink refills at its restaurants.

to stay—my NYC friend loves this hotel—especially if you book one of the suites with 270-degree San Francisco views.

8 Mission St. (at Embarcadero), San Francisco, CA 94105. ✆ **888/890-8868** or 415/278-3700. Fax 415/278-3750. www.hotelvitale.com. 199 units. $269–$399 double; from $699 suite. Rates include morning paper, free morning yoga, and free courtesy car to downtown locations on weekdays. AE, DC, DISC, MC, V. Valet parking $42. Bus: 2, 7, 14, 21, 71, or 71L. **Amenities:** Restaurant; exercise room; spa; concierge; business center; room service; laundry service; dry

cleaning; free Internet salon; free Wi-Fi. *In room:* A/C, TV w/pay movies, dataport, minibar, hair dryer, iron, safe, high-speed Internet access, Wi-Fi, CD player.

San Francisco Marriott ★★ Some call it a masterpiece; others liken it to the world's biggest parking meter. In either case, the Marriott is one of the largest buildings in the city, making it a popular stop for convention-goers and those looking for a room with a view. Fortunately, the controversy does not extend to the rooms, which are pleasant, vibrant, and contemporary with large bathrooms and exceptional city vistas. ***Tip:*** Upon arrival, enter from Fourth Street, between Market and Mission, to avoid a long trek to the registration area.

55 Fourth St. (between Market and Mission sts.), San Francisco, CA 94103. ✆ **800/228-9290** or 415/896-1600. Fax 415/486-8101. www.Marriott.com/sfodt. 1,598 units. $199–$349 double; $499–$3,250 suite. AE, DC, DISC, MC, V. Parking $46. Bus: All Market St. buses. Streetcar: All Market St. streetcars. Cable car: Powell–Hyde or Powell–Mason lines (3 blocks west). **Amenities:** 2 restaurants; 2 bars; indoor pool; health club; tour desk; car rental; business center; dry cleaning; Wi-Fi in select areas. *In room:* A/C, TV w/pay movies, dataport, hair dryer, iron, high-speed Internet ($13/day).

MODERATE

The Mosser ★ *Value* "Hip on the Cheap" might best sum up The Mosser, a highly atypical budget hotel that incorporates Victorian architecture with modern interior design. It originally opened in 1913 as a luxury hotel only to be dwarfed by the far more modern sky-rise hotels that surround it. But a major multimillion-dollar renovation a few years back transformed this aging charmer into a sophisticated, stylish, and surprisingly affordable SoMa lodging. Guest rooms are replete with original Victorian flourishes—bay windows and hand-carved moldings—that juxtapose well with the contemporary custom-designed furnishings, granite showers, stainless steel fixtures, ceiling fans, Frette linens, double-paned windows, and modern electronics. The least expensive rooms are quite small and share a bathroom, but are an incredible deal for such a central location. The hotel's restaurant, Annabelle's Bar & Bistro, serves lunch and dinner, and The Mosser even houses Studio Paradiso, a state-of-the-art recording studio. The location is excellent as well—3 blocks from Union Square, 2 blocks from the MOMA and Moscone Convention Center, and half a block from the cable car turnaround. It also borders on a "sketchy" street, but then again, so do most hotels a few blocks west of Union Square.

54 Fourth St. (at Market St.), San Francisco, CA 94103. ✆ **800/227-3804** or 415/986-4400. Fax 415/495-7653. www.themosser.com. 166 units, 112 with bathroom. $169–$259 double with bathroom; $79–$99 double without bathroom. Rates include safe-deposit boxes at front desk. AE, DC, DISC, MC, V. Parking $30, plus $10 for oversize vehicles. Streetcar: F, and all underground Muni and BART. **Amenities:** Restaurant; bar; 24-hr. concierge; same-day laundry service/dry cleaning. *In room:* Ceiling fan, TV, dataport, hair dryer, iron/ironing board, AM/FM stereo w/CD player, voice mail, Wi-Fi ($9.95/day).

5 The Financial District

VERY EXPENSIVE

The Mandarin Oriental ★★★ No hotel combines better ultra-luxury digs with incredible views than this gem. The only reason to pause in the lobby or mezzanine is for the traditional tea service or cocktails. Otherwise, heaven begins after a rocketing ride on the elevators to the rooms, all of which are located between the 38th and 48th floors of a high-rise. The opulent rooms also feature contemporary Asian-influenced decor, but the best details by far are the huge windows with superb city views, particularly when the fog rolls in below you. Not all rooms have tub-side views (incredible and standard with the signature rooms), but every one does have a luxurious marble bathroom stocked with terry and cotton cloth robes, a makeup mirror, and silk slippers. An added bonus: The restaurant, **Silks,** has a kitchen crew working wonders with the Asian-influenced menu. If the dining room weren't so awkwardly empty, it'd be a recommended destination. That said, even without the whole package, it's an excellent place to dine.

222 Sansome St. (between Pine and California sts.), San Francisco, CA 94104. ✆ **800/622-0404** or 415/276-9888. Fax 415/433-0289. www.mandarinoriental.com. 158 units. $375–$725 double; $645–$695 signature rooms; from $1,450 suite. Continental breakfast $21; American breakfast $32. AE, DC, DISC, MC, V. Valet parking $36. Bus: All Market St. buses. Streetcar: J, K, L, or M to Montgomery. **Amenities:** Restaurant; bar; fitness center; concierge; car rental; business center; room service; in-room massage; laundry service; same-day dry cleaning; wireless Internet access. *In room:* A/C, TV w/pay movies, fax on request, dataport, minibar, hair dryer, iron, safe, Wi-Fi ($13/day), CD player.

EXPENSIVE

Hilton San Francisco Financial District ★ Finally there's a good reason to stay in Chinatown! Reopened in 2006 after a $40-million renovation, this upscale hotel geared toward the needs of the business traveler is a good choice for anyone seeking a convenient downtown location perfect for forays into Chinatown, North Beach, and beyond. All of the comfortably modern rooms feature either city or bay views, so you really can't go wrong. The panoramic bay views of Coit Tower, Telegraph Hill, and Alcatraz are wholly unobstructed as you look straight down the Columbus Avenue thoroughfare to Ghirardelli Square. The in-room contemporary decor includes dark muted earth-tone carpets; warm honey-colored wood; and lush, pristine palette beds with crisp white linens and featherbeds swathed in masculine dusty blue, tan, and slate-gray pillows and accents. All units boast modern goodies such as MP3-compatible alarm clocks and flatscreen TVs. All signature-floor accommodations have balconies. The seven suites have bamboo floors, fireplaces, balconies, and large luxurious bathrooms, some with nice touches like sleek yours-and-mine sinks. For concierge-floor guests, a complimentary breakfast is served in a private lounge. A coffee bar in the lobby is perfect for getting your morning fix on the fly, and the renowned day spa, trū, offers world-class treatments, a variety of them in their one-of-a-kind rainforest room with walk-through waterfall. The restaurant, Seven Fifty, blends Mediterranean and Californian cuisine, while the high-backed *Star Trek*–esque chairs in the lounge make you feel like you are commander of the fleet.

750 Kearny St., at Washington St., San Francisco, CA 94108. ✆ **800/HILTONS** or 415/433-6660. Fax 415/765-7891. www.sanfranciscofinancialdistrict.hilton.com. 549 units. $199–$429 double; $989–$1,200 suite. AE, DC, DISC, MC, V. Valet parking $42. Bus: 1, 9AX, 9BX, or 15. Cable car: California. **Amenities:** Restaurant; bar; coffee bar; spa; fitness room; concierge; 24-hr. business center; secretarial services; free car service to downtown; room service; laundry service; same-day dry cleaning; foreign currency exchange; notary public. *In room:* A/C, TV w/pay movies, dataport, minibar, hair dryer, iron, safe, Wi-Fi ($9.95).

Hyatt Regency San Francisco ★ The Hyatt Regency, a convention favorite, rises from the edge of The Embarcadero Center at the foot of Market Street. The gray concrete structure, with a 1970s, bunkerlike facade, is shaped like a vertical triangle, serrated with long rows of jutting balconies. The 17-story atrium lobby, illuminated by museum-quality theater lighting, has a waterway flowing through it.

Rooms are furnished in "contemporary decor" à la corporate hotel fashion. Bonuses include ergonomic workstation chairs; textiles in shades of gold, charcoal gray, and celadon; and coffeemakers. Definitely not a standout choice for shacking up.

The Eclipse Café serves breakfast and lunch daily; during evenings it becomes A Cut Above steakhouse. The 13-Views Lounge serves cocktails and bar food for dinner.

Finds Sleeping Seaside

You would think that a city surrounded on three sides by water would have a slew of seaside hotels. Oddly enough, it has very few, one of which is the **Seal Rock Inn.** It's about as far from Union Square and Fisherman's Wharf as you can place a hotel in San Francisco, but that just makes it all the more unique. The motel fronts Sutro Heights Park, which faces Ocean Beach. Most rooms in the four-story structure have at least partial views of the ocean; at night, the sounds of the surf and distant foghorns lull guests to sleep. The rooms, although large and spotless, are old and basic, with rose and teal floral accents. Only some rooms have kitchenettes, but phones, TVs, fridges, covered parking, and use of the enclosed patio and pool area are standard. On the ground floor of the inn is a small old-fashioned restaurant serving breakfast and lunch. Golden Gate Park and the Presidio are both nearby, and the Geary bus—which snails its way to Union Square and Market Street—stops right out front and takes at least a half-hour to get downtown.

The Seal Rock Inn (✆ **888/732-5762** or 415/752-8000; fax 415/752-6034; www.sealrockinn.com) is at 545 Point Lobos Ave. (at 48th Ave.), San Francisco, CA 94121. Double rooms range from $105 to $143.

The Equinox, a revolving rooftop restaurant and bar that's open for cocktails and dinner, has 360-degree city views.

5 Embarcadero Center, San Francisco, CA 94111. ✆ **888/591-1234** or 415/788-1234. Fax 415/398-2567. www.sanfranciscoregency.hyatt.com. 802 units. $189–$349 double; extra $50 for executive suite. Continental breakfast $18. AE, DC, DISC, MC, V. Valet parking $41. Bus: All Market St. buses. Streetcar: All Market St. streetcars. **Amenities:** Restaurant; cafe; bar; fitness center; concierge; car rental; business center; dry cleaning. *In room:* A/C, TV w/pay movies, dataport, minibar, hair dryer, safe, Wi-Fi ($9.95/day).

6 North Beach/Fisherman's Wharf

EXPENSIVE

Argonaut Hotel ★★ *Kids* The Kimpton Hotel Group is behind Fisherman's Wharf's best hotel, a true boutique gem that's ideally located at San Francisco Maritime National Historical Park (p. 163) near Fisherman's Wharf and half a block from the bay. The four-story timber and brick landmark building was originally built in 1908 as a warehouse for the California Fruit Canners Association, and later used by William Randolph Hearst to store items that eventually ended up inside his Hearst Castle in San Simeon. Its 239 rooms and 13 suites are whimsically decorated to emulate a luxury cruise ship in cheerful nautical colors of blue, white, red, and yellow (though evidence of its modest past appears in original brick walls, large timbers, and steel warehouse doors). Along with all the standard hotel amenities are special touches such as flatscreen TVs, DVD/CD players, Aveda toiletries, and—get this—leopard-spotted bathrobes. All guests are welcome at weekday evening wine receptions and can use the lobby's two popular (and free) Internet terminals. Suites have wonderful views and come fully loaded with telescopes and spa tubs. If possible, try to book a "view" room, which overlooks the wharf or bay (some rooms offer fabulous views of Alcatraz and the Golden Gate Bridge). If you're bringing the kids, know that the Argonaut's friendly staff goes out of their way to make little ones feel at home and allows each pint-size guest to pick a new plaything from the hotel's "treasure chest." With so many offerings it's no surprise the hotel was awarded a Four Diamond rating from AAA. ***Tip:*** The concierge seems to be able to work wonders when you need tickets to Alcatraz—even when the trips are officially sold out.

495 Jefferson St (at Hyde St.), San Francisco, CA 94109. ✆ **866/415-0704** or 415/563-0800. Fax 415/563-2800. www.argonauthotel.com. 252 units. $189–$389 double; $489–$1,089 suite. Rates include evening wine in the lobby, daily newspaper, and kid-friendly perks like cribs and strollers. AE, DC, DISC, MC, V. Parking $39. Bus: 10, 30, or 47. Streetcar: F. Cable car: Powell–Hyde line. **Amenities:** Restaurant; bar; fitness center; concierge; laundry service; dry cleaning; yoga video and mats; Wi-Fi in public areas. *In room:* A/C, flatscreen TV w/Nintendo and pay movies, minibar, coffeemaker, hair dryer, iron, safe, free high-speed Internet access, DVD and CD players, Web TV.

Sheraton Fisherman's Wharf Hotel Built in the mid-1970s, this contemporary, four-story hotel offers the reliable comforts of a Sheraton in San Francisco's most popular tourist area. In other words, the clean, modern rooms are comfortable and well equipped but nothing unique to the city. On the bright side, they have a heated outdoor pool (a rarity in San Francisco). A corporate floor caters exclusively to business travelers.

2500 Mason St. (between Beach and North Point sts.), San Francisco, CA 94133. ✆ **800/325-3535** or 415/362-5500. Fax 415/956-5275. www.sheratonatthewharf.com. 529 units. $199–$299 double; $550–$1,000 suite. Extra person $20. Continental breakfast $13. AE, DC, DISC, MC, V. Valet parking $36. Bus: 10 or 49. Streetcar: F. Cable car: Powell–Mason line (1 block east, 2 blocks south). **Amenities:** Restaurant; bar; outdoor heated pool; exercise room; concierge; car-rental desk; business center; limited room service; laundry; dry cleaning. *In room:* A/C, TV, fax (in suites only), dataport, coffeemaker, hair dryer, high-speed Internet ($9.95/day).

MODERATE

Best Western Tuscan Inn at Fisherman's Wharf ★★ Like an island of respectability in a sea of touristy schlock, this boutique Best Western is one of the best midrange hotels at Fisherman's Wharf. It continues to exude a level of style and comfort far beyond that of its neighboring competitors. For example, every evening in the plush lobby warmed by a grand fireplace, a wine reception is hosted by the manager, and the adjoining **Café Pescatore** serves wonderful pizzas and grilled meats from their wood-burning oven. The rooms are a definite cut above competing Fisherman's Wharf hotels: all are handsomely decorated and have writing desks and armchairs. The only caveat is the lack of scenic views—a small price to pay for a good hotel in a great location.

425 North Point St. (at Mason St.), San Francisco, CA 94133. ✆ **800/648-4626** or 415/561-1100. Fax 415/561-1199. www.tuscaninn.com. 221 units. $129–$369. Rates include coffee, tea, and evening wine reception. AE, DC, DISC, MC, V. Parking $36. Bus: 10, 15, or 47. Cable car: Powell–Mason line. Pets welcome for $50 fee. **Amenities:** Access to nearby gym; concierge; courtesy car; secretarial services; limited room service; same-day laundry service/dry cleaning. *In room:* A/C, TV w/video games and pay movies, dataport, minibar, coffeemaker, hair dryer, iron, free Wi-Fi.

The Hotel Bohème ★★ *Finds* Romance awaits at the intimate Hotel Bohème. Although it's located on the busiest avenue in the neighborhood, once you climb the staircase to this narrow second-floor boutique hotel, you'll discover a style and demeanor reminiscent of a home in upscale Nob Hill. Alas, there are no common areas other than a little booth for check-in and concierge, but rooms, though small, are truly sweet, with gauze-draped canopies, stylish decor such as ornate parasols shading ceiling lights, and walls dramatically colored with lavender, sage green, black, and pumpkin. The staff is ultra-hospitable, and bonuses include sherry in the lobby each afternoon. Some fabulous cafes, restaurants, bars, and shops along Columbus Avenue are just a few steps away, and Chinatown and Union Square are within easy walking distance. ***Note:*** Although the bathrooms are spiffy, they're also tiny and have showers only. Also, request a room off the street side, which is quieter.

444 Columbus Ave. (between Vallejo and Green sts.), San Francisco, CA 94133. ✆ **415/433-9111**. Fax 415/362-6292. www.hotelboheme.com. 15 units. $164–$184 double. Rates include afternoon sherry. AE, DC, DISC, MC, V. Parking $12–$31 at nearby public garages. Bus: 12, 15, 30, 41, 45, or 83. Cable car: Powell–Mason line. **Amenities:** Concierge. *In room:* TV, dataport, hair dryer, iron, free Wi-Fi.

The Washington Square Inn ★ This small, comely, European-style bed-and-breakfast is ideal for older couples who prefer a quieter, more subdued environment than the commotion of downtown San Francisco. It's across from Washington Square in North Beach—a coffee-craver's haven—and within walking distance of Fisherman's Wharf and Chinatown. All rooms feature European antiques, ceiling fans, flatscreen TVs, and private bathrooms, while some have fireplaces or sitting areas in bay windows. A light breakfast is served in your room or the lobby, and in the evening hors d'oeuvres are served with wine.

1660 Stockton St. (between Filbert and Union sts.), San Francisco, CA 94133. ✆ **800/388-0220** or 415/981-4220. Fax 415/397-7242. www.wsisf.com. 15 units. $149–$289 double. Rates include continental breakfast and afternoon tea, wine, and hors d'oeuvres. AE, DISC, MC, V. Valet parking $35; self parking $15. Bus: 15, 30, 41, or 45. **Amenities:** Limited room service. *In room:* Flatscreen TV, dataport, hair dryer, iron on request, free Wi-Fi, CD player.

INEXPENSIVE

The San Remo Hotel ★ *Value* This small, European-style *pensione* is one of the best budget hotels in San Francisco. In a quiet North Beach neighborhood, within walking distance of Fisherman's Wharf, the Italianate Victorian structure originally served as a boardinghouse for dockworkers displaced by the great fire of 1906. As a result, the rooms are small and bathrooms are shared, but all is forgiven when it comes time to pay the bill. Rooms are decorated in cozy country style, with brass and iron beds; oak, maple, or pine armoires; and wicker furnishings. The immaculate shared bathrooms feature tubs and brass pull-chain toilets with oak tanks and brass fixtures. If the penthouse—which has its own bathroom, TV, fridge, and patio—is available, book it: You won't find a more romantic place to stay in San Francisco for so little money.

2237 Mason St. (at Chestnut St.), San Francisco, CA 94133. ✆ **800/352-7366** or 415/776-8688. Fax 415/776-2811. www.sanremohotel.com. 62 units, 61 with shared bathroom. $65–$90 double; $175–$185 penthouse suite. AE, DC, MC, V. Self-parking $13–$14. Bus: 10, 15, 30, or 47. Streetcar: F. Cable car: Powell–Mason line. **Amenities:** Access to nearby health club; 2 massage chairs; self-service laundry; TV room; Internet kiosk in lobby. *In room:* Ceiling fan.

The Wharf Inn ★ *Value* My top choice for good-value/great-location lodging at Fisherman's Wharf, The Wharf Inn offers above-average accommodations at one of the most popular tourist attractions in the world. The well-stocked rooms are done in handsome tones of earth, muted greens, and burnt orange, but more importantly, they are situated smack-dab in the middle of the wharf, a mere two blocks from Pier 39 and the cable car turnaround, and within walking distance of The Embarcadero and North Beach. The inn is ideal for car-bound families because parking is free (that saves at least $25 a day right off the bat).

2601 Mason St. (at Beach St.), San Francisco, CA 94133. ✆ **877/275-7889** or 415/673-7411. Fax 415/776-2181. www.wharfinn.com. 51 units. $99–$209 double; $299–$439 penthouse. AE, DC, DISC, MC, V. Free parking. Bus: 10, 15, 39, or 47. Streetcar: F. Cable car: Powell–Mason or Powell–Hyde lines. **Amenities:** Access to nearby health club ($10/day); concierge; tour desk; free coffee/tea, and newspapers. *In room:* TV, dataport, hair dryer on request, iron on request, free Wi-Fi.

7 The Marina/Pacific Heights/Cow Hollow

EXPENSIVE

Hotel Drisco ★★ *Finds* Located on one of the most sought-after blocks of residential property in all of San Francisco, the Drisco, built in 1903, is one of the city's best small hotels. Refinements by interior designer Glenn Texeira (who also did the Ritz-Carlton in Manila) are evident from the very small lobby and sitting areas to the calming atmosphere of the cream, yellow, and green guest rooms. As in the neighboring mansions, traditional antique furnishings and thick, luxurious fabrics abound here. The hotel's comfy beds will make you want to loll late into the morning before primping in the large marble bathrooms, complete with robes and slippers. Each suite has a couch that unfolds into a bed (although you would never guess from the looks of it), an additional phone and TV, and superior views. A 24-hour coffee and tea service is available on the ground floor, in the same comfy rooms where breakfast is served. If you're arriving by car, however, you may not want to stay here as there is no hotel parking.

2901 Pacific Ave. (at Broderick St.), San Francisco, CA 94115. ✆ **800/634-7277** or 415/346-2880. Fax 415/567-5537. www.hoteldrisco.com. 48 units. $249 double; $369–$399 suite. Rates include buffet breakfast and evening wine hour. AE, DC, DISC, MC, V. No parking available. Bus: 3 or 24. **Amenities:** Exercise room and free pass to YMCA; concierge; business center; limited room service; same-day laundry service/dry cleaning. *In room:* TV/VCR, dataport, minibar, fridge, hair dryer, iron, safe, free high-speed Internet access, CD player.

MODERATE

Hotel Del Sol ★★ *Kids* *Value* The cheeriest motel in town is located just 2 blocks off the Marina District's bustling section of Lombard. Three-level Hotel del Sol is all about festive flair and luxury touches. The sunshine theme extends from the Miami Beach–style use of vibrant color, as in the yellow, red, orange, and blue exterior, to the heated courtyard pool, which beckons the youngish clientele as they head for their cars parked (for free!) in cabana-like spaces. This is also one of the most family-friendly places to stay, with a "Kids are VIPs" program, including a family suite (three adjoining rooms with bunks and toys); a lending library of kids' books, toys, and videos; childproofing kits; three rooms that have been professionally baby-proofed; bonded babysitting services; evening cookies and milk; and pool toys; and sunglasses and visors for the young ones. Fair-weather fun doesn't stop at the front door of the hotel, which boasts 57 spacious rooms (updated with all new bedding, paint, carpets, drapes, and sofas in 2006) with equally perky interior decor (read: loud and colorful) as well as unexpected extras like CD players, Aveda products, and tips on the town's happenings and shopping meccas. Suites also include minifridges and DVD players.

3100 Webster St. (at Greenwich St.), San Francisco, CA 94123. ✆ **877/433-5765** or 415/921-5520. Fax 415/931-4137. www.thehoteldelsol.com. 57 units. $139–$199 double; $179–$239 suite. Rates include continental breakfast and free newspapers in the lobby. AE, DC, DISC, MC, V. Free parking. Bus: 22, 28, 41, 43, 45, or 76. **Amenities:** Heated outdoor pool; same-day dry cleaning. *In room:* TV/VCR, dataport, kitchenettes in 3 units, fridge and DVD in suites only, iron, Wi-Fi ($7.95/day), CD player.

Jackson Court ★★ The Jackson Court, a stately three-story brownstone Victorian mansion, is in one of San Francisco's most exclusive neighborhoods, Pacific Heights. Its only fault—that it's far from the action—is also its blessing: If you crave a blissfully quiet vacation in elegant surroundings, this is the place. The rooms are individually furnished with superior-quality antique furnishings; two have wood-burning fireplaces (whose use is de rigueur in the winter) and two have gas fireplaces. The Blue Room features an inviting window seat; the Garden Court Suite has handcrafted wood paneling, a king bed, and a large picture window looking onto the private garden patio. After a continental breakfast of muffins, scones, croissants, oatmeal, juice, and fruit, spend the day browsing the shops along nearby Union and Fillmore streets and return in time for afternoon tea.

2198 Jackson St. (at Buchanan St.), San Francisco, CA 94115. ✆ **415/929-7670.** Fax 415/929-1405. www.jacksoncourt.com. 10 units. $160–$225 double. Rates include continental breakfast and afternoon tea. AE, MC, V. Parking on street only. Bus: 1, 3, 12, or 22. **Amenities:** Concierge; dry cleaning; guests allowed to use high-speed Internet in office. *In room:* TV, dataport, hair dryer, iron available on request.

Laurel Inn ★★ *Value* If you don't mind being out of the downtown area, this hip hotel is one of the most tranquil and affordably high-style places to rest your head. Tucked just beyond the southernmost tip of the Presidio and Pacific Heights, the outside is nothing impressive—just another motor inn. And that's what it was until the Joie de Vivre hotel company breathed new life into the place. Now decor is *très* chic and modern, with Zen-like influences (think W Hotel at half the price). The rooms, some of which have excellent city views, are smartly designed and decorated in the style of a contemporary studio apartment. The continental breakfast is fine, but why bother when you're across the street from **Ella's** (p. 132), which serves San Francisco's best breakfast? Other thoughtful touches: 24-hour coffee and tea service, pet-friendly rooms, a CD and video lending library, and indoor parking. There's also great shopping a block away at Sacramento Street; and the new and hip **G Bar,** which serves libations and a surprisingly active slice of glamorous young Pacific Heights–style revelry.

444 Presidio Ave. (at California Ave.), San Francisco, CA 94115. ✆ **800/552-8735** or 415/567-8467. Fax 415/928-1866. www.thelaurelinn.com. 49 units. $169–$209 double. Rates include continental breakfast and afternoon lemonade and cookies. AE, DC, DISC, MC, V. Free parking. Bus: 1, 3, 4, or 43. Pets accepted. **Amenities:** Adjoining bar; access to the mind-blowing JCC gym across the street at $10 per day; concierge; same-day laundry/dry cleaning. *In room:* TV/VCR, dataport, kitchenette in some units, hair dryer, iron, wired and wireless Internet access ($8/day), CD player.

Union Street Inn ★★ Who would have guessed that one of the most delightful B&Bs in California would be in San Francisco? This two-story 1903 Edwardian fronts perpetually busy (and trendy shopping and bar-hopping stop) Union Street, but is as quiet as a church on the inside. The individually decorated rooms are furnished with down comforters, fresh flowers, fruit baskets, and bay windows (beg for one with a view of the garden). A few even have Jacuzzi tubs for two. An extended full breakfast is served in the parlor, in your room, or on an outdoor terrace overlooking a lovely English garden. The ultimate honeymoon retreat is the private carriage house behind the inn, but any room at this warm, friendly inn is guaranteed to please.

2229 Union St. (between Fillmore and Steiner sts.), San Francisco, CA 94123. ✆ **415/346-0424.** Fax 415/922-8046. www.unionstreetinn.com. 5 units, 1 cottage. $179–$289 double. Rates include breakfast, hors d'oeuvres, and evening beverages. AE, DISC, MC, V. Nearby parking $15. Bus: 22, 28, 41, or 45. *In room:* TV, free wireless Internet access, CD/DVD player.

INEXPENSIVE

Cow Hollow Motor Inn & Suites *Kids* If you're less interested in being downtown than in playing in and around the beautiful bayfront Marina, check out this modest brick hotel on busy Lombard Street. There's no fancy theme, but each room has cable TV, free local phone calls, free covered parking, and a coffeemaker. Families will appreciate the one- and two-bedroom suites, which have full kitchens and dining areas as well as antique furnishings and surprisingly tasteful decor.

2190 Lombard St. (between Steiner and Fillmore sts.), San Francisco, CA 94123. ✆ **415/921-5800.** Fax 415/922-8515. www.cowhollowmotorinn.com. 129 units. $72–$125 double. Extra person $10. AE, DC, MC, V. Free parking. Bus: 28, 30, 43, or 76. **Amenities:** Laundry and dry cleaning within a block. *In room:* A/C, TV, dataport, full kitchens in suites only, coffeemaker, hair dryer, free high-speed DSL and Wi-Fi.

Edward II Inn & Suites ★ This three-story "English country" inn has a room for almost anyone's budget, ranging from *pensione* units with shared bathrooms to luxuriously appointed suites and cottages with whirlpool bathtubs and fireplaces. Originally built to house guests who attended the 1915 Pan-Pacific Exposition, it's still a good place to stay in spotless and comfortably appointed rooms with cozy antique furnishings. They've recently added a small fitness center and the Café Maritime, a seafood restaurant open for dinner. Room prices even include a full continental breakfast. Nearby Chestnut and Union streets offer some of the best shopping and dining in the city. The adjoining pub serves drinks nightly. The only caveat is that the hotel's Lombard Street location is usually congested with traffic.

3155 Scott St. (at Lombard St.), San Francisco, CA 94123. ✆ **800/473-2846** or 415/922-3000. Fax 415/931-5784. www.edwardii.com. 29 units, 21 with bathroom. $69–$99 double with shared bathroom; $115–$139 double with private bathroom; $179–$199 junior suite. Extra person $25. Rates include continental breakfast and evening sherry. AE, DISC, MC, V. Self-parking $12 1 block away. Bus: 28, 30, 43, or 76. **Amenities:** Pub; fitness center ($10/day); computer station (for nominal fee). *In room:* TV, hair dryer and iron available on request, free high-speed and wireless Internet access.

Hostelling International San Francisco—Fisherman's Wharf *Finds* Unbelievable but true—you can get front-row bay views for a mere $23 a night. This hostel, on national park property, provides dorm-style accommodations and offers easy access to the Marina's shops and restaurants. Rooms sleep 2 to 12 people and there are 10 private rooms available; communal space includes a fireplace, kitchen, dining room, coffee bar, pool table, and foosball. The breakfast alone practically makes it worth the price. Make reservations well in advance.

Fort Mason, Building 240, San Francisco, CA 94123. ✆ **415/771-7277.** Fax 415/771-1468. http://sfhostel.com. 150 beds. $23–$29 per person per night; kids $15–$17 per night. Rates include breakfast. MC, V. Free limited parking. Bus: 28, 30, 47, or 49. **Amenities:** Self-service laundry and kitchen; meeting room; baggage storage; secure lockers; free Wi-Fi; computer kiosks for small fee.

Marina Inn ★ *Value* Marina Inn is one of the best low-priced hotels in San Francisco. How it offers so much for so little is mystifying. Each guest room in the 1924 four-story Victorian looks like something from a country furnishings catalog, complete with rustic pinewood furniture, a four-poster bed with silky-soft comforter, pretty wallpaper, and soothing tones of rose, hunter green, and pale yellow. You also get remote-control televisions discreetly hidden in pine cabinetry—all for as little as $75 a night. Combine that with continental breakfast, friendly service, a business center in the lobby with an Internet kiosk, free Wi-Fi, and an armada of shops and restaurants within easy walking distance, and there you have it: one of my top choices for best overall value. ***Note:*** Traffic can be a bit noisy here, so the hotel added double panes on windows facing the street. Still, if you're a light sleeper you might want to stay at the Union Street Inn (see earlier in this chapter).

3110 Octavia St. (at Lombard St.), San Francisco, CA 94123. ✆ **800/274-1420** or 415/928-1000. Fax 415/928-5909. www.marinainn.com. 40 units. Nov–Feb $75–$115 double; Mar–May $85–$135 double; June–Oct $95–$145 double. Rates include continental breakfast. AE, DC, DISC, MC, V. Bus: 28, 30, 43, or 76. *In room:* TV, hair dryer and iron on request, free Wi-Fi.

Marina Motel Established in 1939, the Marina Motel is one of San Francisco's first motels, built for the opening of the Golden Gate Bridge. The same family has owned this peach-colored, Spanish-style stucco building for three generations, and they've taken exquisite care of it. All rooms look out onto an inner courtyard, which is awash with beautiful flowering plants and wall paintings by local artists. Though the rooms show minor signs of wear and tear, they're all quite clean, bright, quiet, and pleasantly decorated with framed lithographs of old San Francisco—a thoughtful touch that adds to the motel's old-fashioned character and which makes these budget accommodations stand out from all the rest along busy Lombard Street. Two-bedroom suites with fully equipped kitchens are also available. Location-wise, the Presidio and Marina Green are mere blocks away, and you can easily catch a bus downtown. The only downside is the street noise, which is likely to burden light sleepers. ***Bonus:*** All rooms include a breakfast coupon valid for two entrees for the price of one at **Judy's Restaurant,** a short walk from the motel.

2576 Lombard St. (between Divisadero and Broderick sts.), San Francisco, CA 94123. ✆ **800/346-6118** or 415/921-9406. Fax 415/921-0364. www.marinamotel.com. 38 units. $89–$159 double; $199 suite. Lower rates in winter. Rates include 2-for-1 breakfast coupon at nearby cafe. AE, DISC, MC, V. Free covered parking. Bus: 28, 29, 30, 43, or 45. Dogs accepted with $10 nightly fee. *In room:* Dataport, fridge, coffeemaker, hair dryer, iron.

8 Japantown & Environs

The Queen Anne Hotel ★★ *Value* This majestic 1890 Victorian charmer was once a grooming school for upper-class young women. Restored in 1980 and renovated in early 2006, the four-story building recalls San Francisco's golden days. Walk under rich red draperies to the lavish "grand salon" lobby replete with English oak wainscoting and period antiques and it's not hard to imagine that you've been transported to a different era. Guest rooms also contain a profusion of antiques—armoires, marble-top dressers, and other Victorian-era pieces. Some have corner turret bay windows that look out on tree-lined streets, as well as separate parlor areas and wet bars; others have cozy reading nooks and fireplaces. All rooms have phones and nice bath amenities in their marble-tiled bathrooms. Guests can relax in the parlor, with two fireplaces, or in the hotel library. If you don't mind staying outside the downtown area, this hotel is highly recommended and very classic San Francisco.

1590 Sutter St. (between Gough and Octavia sts.), San Francisco, CA 94109. ✆ **800/227-3970** or 415/441-2828. Fax 415/775-5212. www.queenanne.com. 48 units. $110–$199 double; $169–$350 suite. Extra person $10. Rates include continental breakfast on weekday mornings, local free limousine service (weekday mornings), afternoon tea and sherry, and morning newspaper. AE, DC, DISC, MC, V. Parking $14. Bus: 2, 3, or 4. **Amenities:** Access to nearby health club for $10; 24-hr. concierge; business center; same-day dry cleaning; front desk safe. *In room:* TV, dataport, hair dryer, iron, free wired Internet access in some rooms and Wi-Fi throughout.

9 Civic Center

MODERATE

The Phoenix Hotel ★★ If you'd like to tell your friends back home that you stayed in the same hotel as Linda Ronstadt, David Bowie, Keanu Reeves, Moby, Franz Ferdinand, and Interpol, this is the place to go. On the fringes of San Francisco's less-than-pleasant Tenderloin District, which is rife with the homeless and crack addicts, this well-sheltered retro 1950s-style hotel is a gathering place for visiting rock musicians, writers, and filmmakers who crave a dose of Southern California—hence the palm trees and pastel colors. The focal point of the Palm Springs–style hotel is a small, heated outdoor pool adorned with a mural by artist Francis Forlenza and ensconced in a modern-sculpture garden.

The rooms are more pop than plush, with bright island-inspired furnishings and original local art; every room faces the pool. In addition to the usual amenities, the hotel offers movies on request and a party vibe that's not part of the package at most city hotels. Some big bonuses: free parking and the hotel's restaurant and club, the groovy and very hip **Bambuddha Lounge** (✆ **415/885-5088**), which serves Southeast Asian cuisine with cocktail-lounge flair. If you want luxury and quiet, stay elsewhere, but if you're looking for a great scene and fun vibe, head to The Phoenix.

601 Eddy St. (at Larkin St.), San Francisco, CA 94109. ✆ **800/248-9466** or 415/776-1380. Fax 415/885-3109. www.thephoenixhotel.com. 44 units. $149–$169 double; $219–$399 suite. Rates include continental breakfast. AE, DC, MC, V. Free parking. Bus: 19, 31, 38, or 47. **Amenities:** Bar; heated outdoor pool; concierge; tour desk; in-room massage; same-day laundry service/dry cleaning. *In room:* TV, VCR on request, dataport, fridge and microwave in some rooms, hair dryer, iron, high-speed Internet and Wi-Fi ($7.95/day).

10 The Castro

Though most accommodations (usually converted homes) in the Castro cater to a gay and lesbian clientele, everyone is welcome. Unfortunately, there are few choices, and their amenities don't really compare to those at most of the better (and much larger) hotels throughout San Francisco.

MODERATE

The Parker Guest House ★★ This is the best B&B option in the Castro, and one of the best in the entire city. In fact, even some of the better hotels could learn a thing or two from this fashionable, gay-friendly, 5,000-square-foot, 1909 beautifully restored Edwardian home and adjacent annex a few blocks from the heart of the Castro's action. Within the bright, cheery urban compound, period antiques abound. But thankfully, the spacious guest rooms are wonderfully updated with smart patterned furnishings, voice mail, robes, and spotless private bathrooms (plus amenities) en suite or, in two cases, across the hall. A fire burns nightly in the cozy living room, and guests are also welcome to make themselves at home in the wood-paneled common library (with fireplace and piano), sunny breakfast room overlooking the garden, and spacious garden with fountains and a steam room. Animal lovers will appreciate the companionship of the house pugs Porter and Pasty.

520 Church St. (between 17th and 18th sts.), San Francisco, CA 94114. ✆ **888/520-7275** or 415/621-3222. Fax 415/621-4139. www.parkerguesthouse.com. 21 units. $129–$199 double; $219 junior suite. Rates include extended continental breakfast and evening wine and cheese. AE, DISC, MC, V. Self-parking $17. Bus: 22 or 33. Streetcar: J Church. **Amenities:** Access to nearby health club; steam room; concierge. *In room:* TV, dataport, hair dryer, iron, free Wi-Fi.

INEXPENSIVE

Beck's Motor Lodge In a town where DINK (double income, no kids) tourists happily spend fistfuls of money, you'd think someone would create a gay luxury hotel—or even a moderate hotel, for that matter. But absurdly, the most commercial and modern accommodations in the touristy Castro is this run-of-the-mill motel. Standard but contemporary, the ultra-tidy rooms include low-Levitz furnishings, a sun deck overlooking upper Market Street's action, and free parking. Unless you're into homey B&Bs, this is really your only choice in the area—fortunately, it's very well maintained. But be warned that this is a party spot; party people stay here, and the staff can be brusque.

2222 Market St. (at 15th St.), San Francisco, CA 94114. ✆ **800/227-4360** in the U.S., except CA, 800/955-2325 within CA or 415/621-8212. Fax 415/241-0435. www.becksmotorlodgesf.com. 58 units. $93–$151 double. AE, DC, DISC, MC, V. Free parking. Bus: 8 or 37. Streetcar: F. **Amenities:** Coin-operated washing machines. *In room:* TV, dataport, fridge, coffeemaker, free Wi-Fi.

Inn on Castro ★ One of the better choices in the Castro, half a block from all the action, is this Edwardian-style inn decorated with contemporary furnishings, original modern art, and fresh flowers throughout. It definitely feels more like a home than an inn, so if you like less commercial abodes, this place is for you. Most rooms share a small back patio, and the suite has a private entrance and outdoor sitting area. The inn also offers access to six individual nearby apartments ($125–$190) with complete kitchens. Note that rates include a full breakfast, and that the least expensive rooms share a bathroom.

321 Castro St. (at Market St.), San Francisco, CA 94114. ✆ **415/861-0321.** Fax 415/861-0321. www.innoncastro.com. 8 units, 2 with bathroom across the hall; 6 apts. $105–$165 double. Rates include full breakfast and evening brandy. AE, DC, MC, V. Streetcar: F, K, L, or M. **Amenities:** Hall fridges stocked w/free sodas and water. *In room:* Flatscreen TV, dataport, hair dryer, free Wi-Fi, DVD/CD.

24 Henry Guesthouse & Village House Its central Castro location is not the only thing that makes 24 Henry a good choice for gay travelers. The 24 Henry building, an 1870s Victorian on a serene side street, is quite charming, as is the Village House sister property 4 blocks away. All of the individually decorated guest rooms have high ceilings and period furniture; most have shared bathrooms. A continental breakfast is served each morning in the parlor. All rooms are nonsmoking.

24 Henry St. (near Sanchez St.), San Francisco, CA 94114. ✆ **800/900-5686** or 415/864-5686. Fax 415/864-0406. www.24henry.com. 10 units, 3 with bathroom. $75–$100 double with shared bathroom; $119–$139 double with private bathroom. Extra person $20. Rates include continental breakfast. AE, MC, V. Bus: 8, 22, 24, or 37. Streetcar: F, J, K, L, M, or N. **Amenities:** Wi-Fi throughout.

The Willows Inn ★ Right in the heart of the Castro, the all-nonsmoking Willows Inn employs a staff eager to greet and attend to visitors. The country and antique willow furnishings don't strictly suit a 1903 Edwardian home, but everything's quite comfortable—especially considering the extras, which include an expanded continental breakfast (fresh fruit, yogurt, baked goods, gourmet coffee, eggs, assorted teas, and orange juice), the morning paper, nightly cocktails, a sitting room (with a DVD player), and a pantry with limited kitchen facilities. The homey rooms vary in size from large (queen-size bed) to smaller (double bed) and are priced accordingly. Each room has a vanity sink, and all the rooms share eight water closets and shower rooms.

710 14th St. (near Church and Market sts.), San Francisco, CA 94114. ✆ **800/431-0277** or 415/431-4770. Fax 415/431-5295. www.willowssf.com. 12 units, none with bathroom. $105–$135 double; $145 suite. Rates include continental breakfast. AE, DC, DISC, MC, V. Bus: 22 or 37. Streetcar: Church St. station (across the street) or F. *In room:* TV/VCR, fridge, free Wi-Fi.

11 Haight-Ashbury

MODERATE

Red Victorian Bed, Breakfast & Art ★ *Finds* Still having flashbacks from the 1960s? Or want to? No problem. A room at the Red Vic, in the heart of the Haight, will throw you right back into the Summer of Love (minus, of course, the free-flowing LSD). Owner Sami Sunchild has re-created this historic hotel and "Peace Center" as a living museum honoring the bygone era. The rooms are inspired by San Francisco's sights and history, and are decorated accordingly. The Flower Child Room has a sun on the ceiling and a rainbow on the wall, while the bed sports a hand-crocheted shawl headboard. The Peacock Suite, though pricey, is one funky room, with red beads, a canopy bed, and multicolored patterns throughout. The clincher is its bedroom bathtub, which has a circular pass-through looking into the sitting area. Four guest rooms have private bathrooms; the rest share four bathrooms down the hall. In general, the rooms and bathrooms are clean and the furnishings lighthearted. Rates for longer stays are a great deal. A family-style continental breakfast is a gathering place for a worldly array of guests, and there's a gift shop called the Meditation Room and Peace Center. Be sure to check out Sami's website to get a sneak peek at the weird and wonderful guest rooms.

1665 Haight St. (between Cole and Belvedere sts.), San Francisco, CA 94117. ✆ **415/864-1978.** Fax 415/863-3293. www.redvic.com. 18 units, 4 with private bathroom. $89–$110 double with shared bathroom, $129–$149 double with private bathroom; $229 suite. Rates include continental breakfast and afternoon tea. Lower rates for stays of 3 days or more. AE, DISC, MC, V. Guarded parking lot nearby. Metro: N line. Bus: 7, 66, 71, or 73.

Stanyan Park Hotel ★★ *Kids* *Value* The only real hotel on the east end of Golden Gate Park and the west end of funky-chic Haight Street, this small inn offers classic San Francisco–style living at a very affordable price. The Victorian structure, which has operated as a hotel under a variety of names since the turn of the 20th century and is on the National Register of Historic Places, offers good-size rooms all done in period decor. Its three stories are decorated with antique furnishings; Victorian wallpaper; and pastel quilts, curtains, and carpets. Families will appreciate the six one- and two-bedroom suites, each of which has a full kitchen and formal dining and living rooms and can sleep up to six comfortably. Tea is served each afternoon from 4 to 6pm. Continental breakfast is served in the dining room off the lobby from 6 to 10am. All rooms are nonsmoking.

750 Stanyan St. (at Waller St.), San Francisco, CA 94117. ✆ **415/751-1000.** Fax 415/668-5454. www.stanyanpark.com. 36 units. $135–$209 double; $265–$335 suite. Rates include continental breakfast and afternoon and evening tea service. Rollaway $20; cribs free. AE, DISC, MC, V. Off-site parking $14. Bus: 7, 33, 43, 66, or 71. Streetcar: N. *In room:* TV, dataport, kitchen (in suites only), hair dryer, iron in suites or on request, free Wi-Fi.

12 Near San Francisco International Airport

MODERATE

Embassy Suites ★ If you've stayed at an Embassy Suites before, you know the drill. But this hotel is one of the best airport options, if only for the fact that every room is a suite. But there is more: The property has an indoor pool, whirlpool, courtyard with fountain, palm trees, and bar/restaurant. Plus, each tastefully decorated two-room suite was updated in 2006 with all new linens and mattresses and has nice additions such as two TVs. The all-new lobby debuted in early 2006. Additionally, a complimentary breakfast of your choice is available before you're whisked to the airport on the free shuttle—all that and the price is still right.

250 Gateway Blvd., South San Francisco, CA 94080. ✆ **800/EMBASSY** or 650/589-3400. Fax 650/589-1183. www.embassysuites.com. 312 units. $139–$199 double. Rates include breakfast and free evening beverages. AE, DC, MC, V. **Amenities:** Restaurant; bar; indoor pool; Jacuzzi; airport shuttle. *In room:* A/C, TV, fridge, coffeemaker, hair dryer, iron, microwave, Wi-Fi ($9.95/day).

INEXPENSIVE

Comfort Suites *Kids* Two miles north of the airport, well outside the heart of the city, Comfort Suites is a well-appointed option for travelers on the way into or out of town. Each studio-suite has a king-size bed, queen-size sleeper sofa (great for the kids), and all the basic amenities for weary travelers. There are also enough pay cable channels to keep you glued to your TV set for an entire day. Rooms are fine—and slated for an upgrade in 2007—but the freebies are the most attractive part of this hotel: a deluxe breakfast of waffles, eggs, sausage, and the like; an airport shuttle; and use of the outdoor hot tub.

121 E. Grand Ave., South San Francisco, CA 94080. ✆ **866/764-1377.** Fax 650/589-7796. www.sfosuites.com. 168 units. $119 double. Rates include continental breakfast. AE, DC, DISC, MC, V. **Amenities:** Outdoor Jacuzzi; airport shuttle. *In room:* A/C, TV, fridge, microwave, coffeemaker, hair dryer, iron, free high-speed Internet access in some rooms and Wi-Fi in all rooms.

San Francisco Airport North Travelodge *Kids* The Travelodge is a good choice for families, mainly because of the hotel's large heated pool. The rooms are as ordinary as you'd expect from a Travelodge. Still, they're comfortable and come with plenty of perks like Showtime and free toll-free and credit card calls. Each junior suite has a microwave and refrigerator. The clincher is the 24-hour complimentary shuttle, which makes the 2-mile trip to the airport in 5 minutes.

326 S. Airport Blvd. (off Hwy. 101), South San Francisco, CA 94080. ✆ **800/578-7878** or 650/583-9600. Fax 650/873-9392. www.sfotravelodge.com. 199 units. $89–$139 double. AE, DC, DISC, MC, V. Free parking. **Amenities:** Restaurant; heated outdoor pool; courtesy shuttle to airport; dry cleaning; fax and copier services; high-speed Internet access at computer station (for fee). *In room:* A/C, TV w/pay movies, microwave available, coffeemaker, hair dryer, iron, safe.

6

Where to Dine

For more than a decade the readers of *Bon Appétit* magazine have named San Francisco their top city for dining out. And for good reason—with more than 3,500 restaurants offering cuisines from around the globe, San Francisco has more restaurants per capita than any other city in the United States.

San Francisco also attracts some of the world's most talented chefs, drawn not only to the creative freedom that has always defined San Francisco's culinary scene, but also to the year-round access to Northern California's unparalleled abundance of organic produce, seafood, free-range meats, and wine.

Afghan, Cajun, Burmese, Moroccan, Persian, Cambodian, Basque, vegan—whatever you're in the mood for, this town has it covered, which is why more San Franciscans eat out than any other city's residents in the U.S. And all you need to join America's largest dinner party is an adventurous palate, because half the fun of visiting San Francisco is the opportunity to sample the flavors of the world in one fell swoop.

Although dining in San Francisco is almost always a hassle-free experience, you should keep a few things in mind:

- If you want a table at the restaurants with the best reputations, you probably need to book 6 to 8 weeks in advance for weekends, and a couple of weeks ahead for weekdays.
- If there's a long wait for a table, ask if you can order at the bar, which is often faster and more fun.
- Don't leave *anything* valuable in your car while dining, particularly in or near high-crime areas such as the Mission, downtown, or—believe it or not—Fisherman's Wharf. (Thieves know tourists with nice cameras and a trunkful of mementos are headed there.) Also, it's best to give the parking valet only the key to your car, *not* your hotel room or house key.
- ***Remember:*** It is against the law to smoke in any restaurant in San Francisco, even if it has a separate bar or lounge area. You're welcome to smoke outside, however.
- This ain't New York: Plan on dining early. Most restaurants close their kitchens around 10pm.
- If you're driving to a restaurant, add extra time to your itinerary for parking, which can be an especially infuriating exercise in areas like the

---

Pricing Categories

The restaurants listed below are classified first by area, then by price, using the following categories: **Very Expensive,** dinner from $75 per person; **Expensive,** dinner from $50 per person; **Moderate,** dinner from $35 per person; and **Inexpensive,** dinner less than $35 per person. These categories reflect prices for an appetizer, main course, dessert, and glass of wine.

Tips **E-Reservations**

Want to book your reservations online? Go to **www.opentable.com,** where you can save seats in San Francisco and the rest of the Bay Area in real time.

Mission, Downtown, the Marina, and, well, pretty much everywhere. And expect to pay at least $10 to $13 for valet service, *if* the restaurant offers it.

1 The Best Dining Bets

- **Best Hotel Restaurant: Ame,** 689 Mission St. (© **415/284-4040**), located in the swank St. Regis Hotel, means "rain" in Japanese. But the only drops you'll see coming down here are tears of joy from local foodies who no longer have to drive to St. Helena to enjoy a meal by Hiro Sone, James Beard Award winner and master of Japanese, French, and Italian cuisine.
- **Best for Impressing Clients:** Show your business associates you've got class—and deep pockets—by reserving a table at the Financial District's **Aqua,** 252 California St. (© **415/956-9662**). See p. 107.
- **Best Romantic Spot:** Anyone who loves classic French cooking will be seduced at **Fleur de Lys,** 777 Sutter St. (© **415/673-7779**), under the rich burgundy-tented canopy that swathes the elegant room in romance. There's lots of question-popping here, too. See p. 100.
- **Best for a Celebration:** Great food, a full bar, and a lively atmosphere are the key ingredients that make **Boulevard,** 1 Mission St. (© **415/543-6084**), the place to celebrate. See p. 114. Or celebrate Latino-style with pitchers of sangria at the Haight's **Cha Cha Cha,** 1801 Haight St. (© **415/386-7670**). See p. 144.
- **Best Decor:** Celeb restaurant designer Pat Kuleto spent a week sketching sea life at the Monterey Bay Aquarium before applying his genius to whimsical **Farallon,** 450 Post St. (© **415/956-6969**). See p. 100. Another fantastic design feat is within the **Grand Café,** 501 Geary St. (© **415/292-0101**), where the old-world European ballroom meets Art Nouveau glamour. See p. 102.
- **Best Wine List:** Renowned sommelier Rajat Parr, at **Michael Mina,** 335 Powell St. (© **415/397-9222**), will pour liquid heaven provided you can swallow the steep prices. See p. 102. Another sip-worthy spot is **bacar,** 448 Brannan St. (© **415/904-4100**), which offers 60 wines by the glass.
- **Best Pizza: Pauline's,** 260 Valencia St. (© **415/552-2050**), p. 141, does two things—pizzas and salads—but does them both better than any other restaurant in the city.
- **Best Brunch:** The Sunday spread at the **Terrace Restaurant** in the **Ritz-Carlton,** 600 Stockton St. (© **415/773-6198**), offers the city's most lavish buffet, featuring sushi, caviar, freshly made blinis, and endless oysters on the half-shell. See chapter 5, p. 76.
- **Best Dim Sum:** Downtown and Chinatown dim sum restaurants may be more centrally located, but that's all they've got on **Ton Kiang,** 5821 Geary Blvd. (© **415/387-8273**), where carts bring the best Chinese dumplings and other dim sum delicacies to your table. See p. 147.

Tips Multicourse Dining

Ordering a "fixed-price," "prix-fixe," or "tasting" menu can be a good bargain as well as a great way to sample lots of dishes at one sitting. Many dining rooms in town offer these multicourse menus, which tend to cost around $75 for four courses, including dessert.

- **Best Vegetarian Food:** For excellent farm-fresh food and an equally stunning view of the Golden Gate, go to **Greens Restaurant,** Building A, Fort Mason Center (✆ **415/771-6222**). See p. 133. Also check out **Millennium,** 580 Geary St. (✆ **415/345-3900**).
- **Best Cafe:** If you want to know what life was like before Starbucks, spend some time at North Beach's beloved **Mario's Bohemian Cigar Store,** 566 Columbus Ave. (✆ **415/362-0536**); and **Caffè Trieste,** 601 Vallejo St. (✆ **415/392-6739**). See chapter 10, p. 240.
- **Best Dive:** Anyone who's a connoisseur of funky little ethnic eateries will love **Sam Wo,** 813 Washington St. (✆ **415/982-0596**), my favorite Chinatown dive. See p. 121.

2 Union Square

VERY EXPENSIVE

Farallon ★ SEAFOOD While this seafood restaurant is hands-down the most whimsical with its stunning oceanic decor, the high price tag and fine, but not mind-blowing, food make it a better cocktail-and-appetizer stop than dinner choice. The multimillion-dollar attraction's outrageous decor follows the "coastal" cuisine theme; hand-blown jellyfish lamps, kelp bed–like backlit columns, glass clamshells, sea-urchin light fixtures, a sea-life mosaic floor, and a tentacle-encircled bar set the scene. (Thankfully, designer Pat Kuleto's impressive renovation of the 1924 building left the original Gothic arches intact.)

Executive chef Mark Franz, who opened the once-famous restaurant Stars with Jeremiah Tower, orchestrates the cuisine. He offers starters ranging from the expected (a variety of very expensive oysters) to the more ambitious (seared breast of squab with roasted foie gras, leg confit raviolo, and rhubarb chutney)—with a few meat and game items stuck in for good measure. The whimsy-meets-sophistication extends only as far as the food—the service and wine lists (more than 400 by the bottle; 30 by the glass) are seriously professional. Personally, I prefer stopping in for appetizers at the bar. The scene may be swank, but for seafood, Aqua (p. 107) is worlds better.

450 Post St. (between Mason and Powell sts., adjoining the Kensington Park Hotel). ✆ **415/956-6969.** www.farallonrestaurant.com. Reservations recommended. Pre-theater 3-course prix-fixe dinner menu $45; main courses $30–$39 dinner. AE, DC, DISC, MC, V. Mon 5:30–10pm; Tues–Wed 5:30–10:30pm; Fri–Sat 5:30–11pm; Sun 5–10pm. Valet parking $12. Bus: 2, 3, 4, or 38.

Fleur de Lys ★★ FRENCH Fleur de Lys is the city's most traditional and formal classic French affair. Draped in 900 yards of rich patterned fabric mood-lit with dim French candelabras, and accented with an extraordinary sculptural floral centerpiece, this restaurant is a romantic spot, so long as your way of wooing includes donning a dinner jacket, which is "appreciated" but not required. Equally formal is the cuisine of chef Hubert Keller (former President Clinton's first guest chef at the White House),

Dining in Union Square & the Financial District

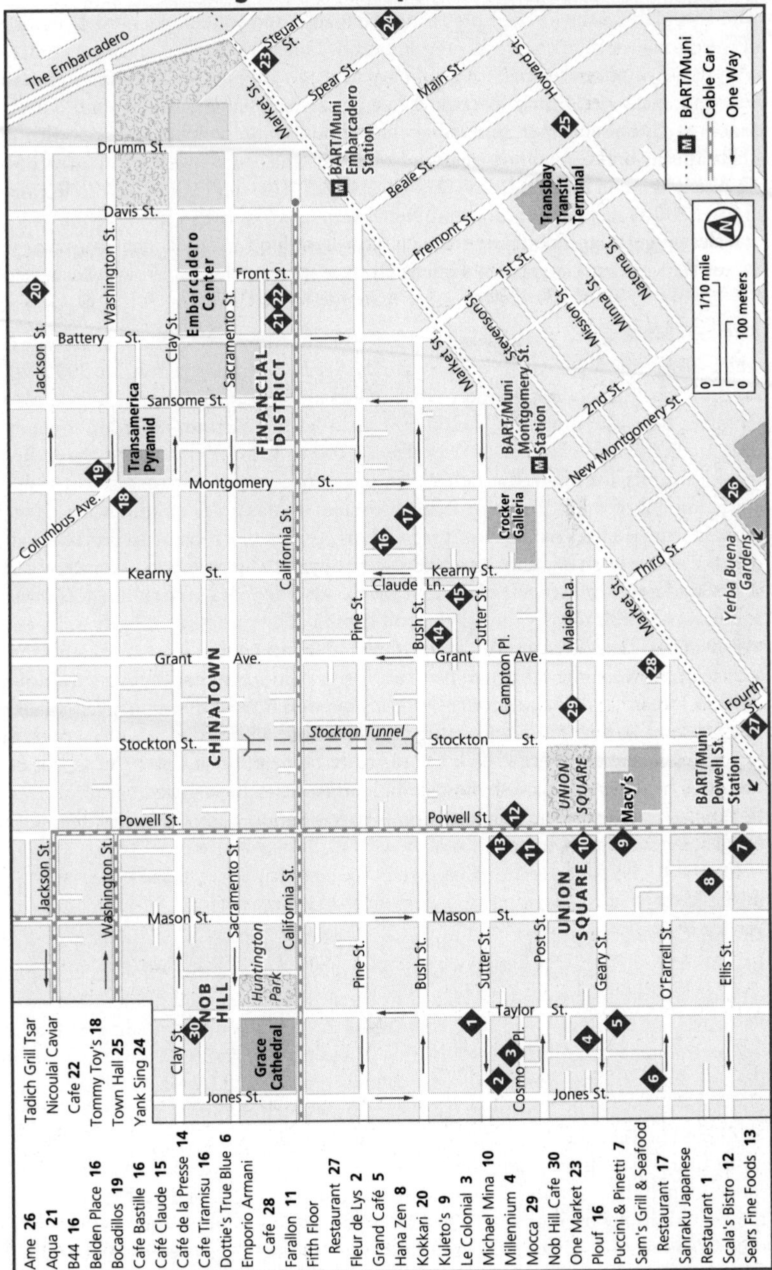

who is usually in the kitchen preparing the menus and watching a closed-circuit TV of the dining room to ensure all goes smoothly. Diners in favor of grazing should start with the "Symphony" appetizer, a culinary medley with bite-size samplings of roasted beet and anchovies, pistachio-crusted foie gras, Maine lobster tartare, and butternut squash vichyssoise. Other sure things include radicchio-wrapped salmon with cannellini beans and Banyuls vinegar and olive oil; and lamb loin with roasted potato stew, whole-grain mustard, and honey and red-wine reduction. The selection of around 700 French, California, and Northwestern wines is also impressive.

777 Sutter St. (at Jones St.). ✆ **415/673-7779.** www.fleurdelyssf.com. Reservations required. 3-course menu $70; 4-course $77; 5-course $88; vegetarian tasting menu $68. Vegan option available with advance notice. AE, DC, MC, V. Mon–Thurs 6–9:30pm; Fri 5:30–10:30pm; Sat 5–10:30pm. Valet parking $13. Bus: 2, 3, 4, 27, or 38.

Michael Mina ★★★ AMERICAN Chef Michael Mina, who became a celebrity chef while overseeing Aqua (p. 107) and was *Bon Appétit* Chef of the Year for 2005–2006, takes the small-plate dining concept to extremes at this sexy, swank spot. Previously the Compass Rose tearoom in the Westin St. Francis hotel, the cream-on-cream room, with deep leather lounge chairs and tables that are too wide for romance, sets the scene for this formal prix-fixe affair. But rather than three dishes, courses arrive as a trio of different renditions of the same theme (plus three sides to match) on custom Mina-designed modular china. That's six different preparations per dish or a total of 18 different flavors over the course of an evening. It's a bit fussy for anyone who prefers to order a few things that sound good and eat lots of bites of them, but if the idea of sampling lots of styles and flavors appeals to you, this edible food-combination case study is likely to be a culinary wonder. Take diver scallops for example. One preparation is accented with lemon Osetra caviar while the other two pair them with yellow corn and summer truffles and smoked tomato and Maine lobster—not to mention three different "chilled salads" in tiny glasses. You might also find crispy pork loin done with risotto, as pulled pork with apple ravioli, and as barbecue with a corn fritter. Some dishes hit, some miss, but in all cases this is a swank affair with an incredible wine list by Rajat Parr.

335 Powell St. (at Geary St.). ✆ **415/397-9222.** www.michaelmina.net. Reservations recommended. 3-course tasting menu $98; seasonal classic tasting menu $135. AE, DC, DISC, MC, V. Dinner Mon–Sat 5:30–10pm; Sun 5:30–9:30pm. Valet parking $17. Bus: 2, 3, 4, 30, 38, 45, or 76.

EXPENSIVE

Grand Café ★ FRENCH If you aren't interested in exploring restaurants beyond those in Union Square and want a huge dose of atmosphere with your seared salmon, Grand Café is your best bet. Its claims to fame? The most grand dining room in San Francisco, an enormous 156-seat, turn-of-the-20th-century grand-ballroom-like dining oasis that's a magnificent combination of old Europe and Art Nouveau. To match the surroundings, chef Ron Boyd, a San Francisco native and Domaine Chandon alum, serves dressed-up French-inspired California dishes such as sautéed salmon with French lentils and house-cured bacon or salade niçoise. You can also drop by for a lighter meal in the more casual front room, the Petit Café, which offers a raw bar and similar dishes for about half the price. In fact, I prefer to hang out in the cafe and nosh on pizzas from the wood-burning oven or a big bowl full of mussels swimming in broth with a side of sourdough bread—it's twice the atmosphere at half the price. There's also a wonderful selection of small-batch American whiskeys and single-malt Scotches.

501 Geary St. (at Taylor St., adjacent to the Hotel Monaco). ✆ **415/292-0101.** www.grandcafe-sf.com. Reservations recommended. Main courses $18–$28. AE, DC, DISC, MC, V. Mon–Fri 7–10:30am; Sat 8am–2:30pm; Sun

9am–2:30pm; Mon–Fri 11:30am–2:30pm; Sun–Thurs 5:30–10pm; Fri–Sat 5:30–11pm. Valet parking free at brunch, $15 for 3 hr. at dinner, $3 each additional half-hour. Bus: 2, 3, 4, 27, or 38.

Le Colonial ★ *Finds* VIETNAMESE Viet-chic environs—picture slowly spinning ceiling fans, tropical plants, rattan furniture, and French Colonial decor—and quality French Vietnamese food make this an excellent choice for folks who want to nosh at one of the sexiest restaurants in town. The upstairs lounge (which opens at 4:30pm) is where romance reigns, with cozy couches, seductive surroundings, and a well-dressed cocktail crowd of post-work professionals who nosh on coconut-crusted crab cakes and Vietnamese spring rolls. In the tiled downstairs dining room and along the stunning heated front patio, guests savor the vibrant flavors of coconut curry with black tiger prawns, mangos, eggplant, and Asian basil and tender wok-seared beef tenderloin with watercress onion salad.

20 Cosmo Place (off Taylor St., between Post and Sutter sts.). ✆ **415/931-3600.** www.lecolonialsf.com. Reservations recommended. Main courses $20–$38. AE, DC, MC, V. Sun–Wed 5:30–10pm; Thurs–Sat 5:30–11pm. Public valet parking $6 1st hr., $2 each additional half-hr. Bus: 2, 3, 4, or 27.

MODERATE

Bocadillos ★★ *Finds* SPANISH/BASQUE TAPAS The sister to Piperade (p. 122) is flat-out fabulous if you're in the mood for tapas or Spanish-influenced small plates. Executive chef Gerald Hirigoyen celebrates his Basque roots with outstanding calamari with creamy tomato-and-garlic romesco sauce, scallops "mole cortado" with sherry and orange, sautéed hot peppers, tuna carpaccio, decadent foie gras sushi rolls, and astoundingly tasty warm chocolate cake with sautéed bananas. Just watch your budget—at up to $12 per plate the tab can creep up on you. You might also want to check out their breakfast, which includes baked eggs with chorizo and manchego cheese. But don't come anticipating a formal dining environment or a cocktail: This small Financial District space is cafe-casual and beer-and-wine only.

710 Montgomery St. (at Washington St.). ✆ **415/982-2622.** www.bocasf.com. Breakfast items $2–$6; lunch and dinner small items $3–$12. AE, DC, DISC, MC, V. Mon–Fri 7am–11pm; Sat 5–11pm. Closed Sun. Bus: 15, 30X, or 41.

Café Claude ★ FRENCH Euro transplants love Café Claude, a crowded and lively restaurant tucked into a narrow (and very European feeling) side street near Union Square. Seemingly everything—every table, spoon, saltshaker, and waiter—is imported from France. With prices topping out at about $22 on the menu featuring classics like steak tartare, steamed mussels, duck confit, escargot, steak with spinach gratin and crisp potatoes, and quail stuffed with pine nuts, sausage, and wild rice, Café Claude offers an affordable slice of Paris without leaving the city. But beware: My last visit the service was rather . . . er . . . French as well. There's live jazz on Thursdays, Fridays, and Saturdays from 7:30 to 10:30pm, and atmospheric sidewalk seating is available when the weather permits.

7 Claude Lane (off Sutter St.). ✆ **415/392-3515.** www.cafeclaude.com. Reservations recommended. Main courses $8–$12 lunch, $14–$22 dinner. AE, DC, DISC, MC, V. Mon–Sat 11:30am–10:30pm; Sun 5:30–10:30pm. Bus: 30. Cable car: Powell–Mason.

Hana Zen ★ *Finds* JAPANESE Even most locals don't know about this Japanese restaurant, mistaking it for just another touristy sushi bar. Sure, they serve good sushi, but what makes this place special is the yakitori bar, which cranks out savory skewered and grilled meats and veggies that we can never seem to get enough of. It's all prepared Benihana style, with acrobatic chefs whirling knives around and making lots of *"Hai!"*

"ahhh," and "ooohh" sounds. My favorites are the asparagus spears wrapped in thinly sliced pork, and the grilled marinated shiitake mushrooms. A few tables are perched beside windows overlooking downtown San Francisco, but the best seats are at the long, arched yakitori bar, where the deft chefs spear together nearly 30 versions of the meal-on-a-stick. You can order either one pair at a time if you like the show, or all at once for a feast; about a half dozen make a meal. The terminally indecisive can opt for the Yakitori Dinner Set for $20, which makes an interesting light meal for two.

115 Cyril Magnin St. (at Ellis St.). ✆ **415/421-2101.** Sushi/yakitori items $4–$6. AE, DC, MC, V. Lunch daily 11:30am–5pm; dinner Sun–Thurs 5pm–midnight and Fri–Sat 5pm–1am. Bus: 27 or 38.

Kuleto's ★ ITALIAN Kuleto's is one of downtown's Italian darlings. Muscle your way into a seat at the antipasto bar or at the chef's counter overlooking the kitchen, and fill up on Italian specialties and selections from the wine list featuring 30 by-the-glass options. Or partake in the likes of penne pasta drenched in tangy lamb-sausage marinara sauce, clam linguine (generously overloaded with fresh clams), or any of the grilled fresh-fish specials in the casually refined dining room. If you don't arrive by 6pm, expect to wait—this place fills up fast. Not to worry though, you can always cross the hotel lobby to the wine bar, which also serves the full menu and is open from 6 to 10pm daily. Don't have time to sit down? Try Cafe Kuleto's, which is located just outside and serves panini, pastries, salads, and espresso to go, open daily from 7am to 8pm.

In the Villa Florence Hotel, 221 Powell St. (between Geary and O'Farrell sts.). ✆ **415/397-7720.** www.kuletos.com. Reservations recommended. Breakfast $5–$15; main courses $12–$25. AE, DC, DISC, MC, V. Mon–Fri 7–10:30am; Sat–Sun 8–10:30am; daily 11:30am–11pm. Bus: 2, 3, 4, or 38. Streetcar: All streetcars. Cable car: Powell–Mason or Powell–Hyde lines.

Millennium ★★ VEGAN Banking on the trend toward lighter, healthier cooking, chef Eric Tucker and his band of merry waiters set out to prove that a meatless menu doesn't mean you have to sacrifice taste. In a narrow, handsome, Parisian-style dining room with checkered tile flooring, French windows, and sponge-painted walls, Millennium has had nothing but favorable reviews for its egg-, butter-, and dairy-free creations since the day it opened. Favorites include Balinese-style salt and pepper-crusted oyster mushrooms with blood orange chile jam, and main courses such as truffled potato Wellington stuffed with shiitake mushroom duxelles served with spring onion and lentil sugo, seared asparagus, blood orange, and capers; or *masala dosa,* a lentil rice crepe with South Indian chickpea and red chard curry, sweet and spicy papaya chutney, and mint raita. No need to divert from PC dining with your wine choice—all the selections here are organic.

In the Savoy Hotel, 580 Geary St. (at Jones St.). ✆ **415/345-3900.** www.millenniumrestaurant.com. Reservations recommended. Main courses $18–$22. AE, DC, DISC, MC, V. Sun–Thurs 5:30–9:30pm; Fri–Sat 5:30–10pm. Bus: 38. Streetcar: All Muni lines. BART: Powell St.

Puccini & Pinetti ★ *Kids* ITALIAN It takes some *buco bravado* to open yet another Italian restaurant in San Francisco, but partners Bob Puccini and Steve Pinetti obviously did their homework—this trendy little trattoria has been packed since the day it opened. The formula isn't exactly unique: large portions of good food at fair prices. What really makes it work, though, is the upbeat yet casual ambience, colorful decor, busy exhibition kitchen, and convenient corner location near Union Square. The menu doesn't take any chances either: Italian standbys—pastas, salads, thin-crust wood-fired–oven pizzas, pastas, grilled meats—dominate the menu. The fresh-baked focaccia sandwiches do well during lunch, as do the grilled portobello mushrooms with fresh mozzarella, roasted peppers, and mixed baby greens. The creamy tiramisu and devil's food cake both make for a proper finish. ***Tip:*** This is one of the few places in the Union Square area that actually welcomes kids—in fact, they get to make their own pizza.

129 Ellis St. (at Cyril Magnin St.). ✆ **415/392-5500.** www.pucciniandpinetti.com. Reservations recommended. Main courses $8–$20. AE, DC, DISC, MC, V. Mon–Thurs 11:30am–10pm; Fri–Sat 11:30am–11pm; Sun 5–10pm. Cable car: Powell-Mason line. Bus: 27 or 38.

Scala's Bistro ★★ FRENCH/ITALIAN Firmly entrenched at the base of the refurbished Sir Francis Drake hotel, this downtown favorite blends Italian-bistro and old-world atmosphere with jovial and bustling results. With just the right balance of elegance and informality, this is a perfect place to have some fun (and apparently most people do). Of the tempting array of Italian and French dishes, it's de rigueur to start with the "Earth and Surf" calamari appetizer or grilled portobello mushrooms. Golden beet salad and garlic cream mussels are also good bets. Generous portions of moist, rich duck-leg confit will satisfy hungry appetites, but if you can order only one thing, make it Scala's signature dish: seared salmon. Resting on a bed of creamy buttermilk mashed potatoes and accented with a tomato, chive, and white-wine sauce, it's downright delicious. Finish with Bostini cream pie, a dreamy combo of vanilla custard and orange chiffon cake with a warm chocolate glaze.

In the Sir Francis Drake hotel, 432 Powell St. (at Sutter St.). ✆ **415/395-8555.** www.scalasbistro.com. Reservations recommended. Breakfast $7–$10; main courses $12–$24 lunch and dinner. AE, DC, DISC, MC, V. Daily 8–10:30am and 11:30am–midnight. Bus: 2, 3, 4, 30, 45, or 76. Cable car: Powell–Hyde line.

Straits Restaurant ★ SINGAPOREAN Straits is the place to go if you're in the mood for some adventurous Asian-inspired dining. I'm a huge fan of Chef Chris Yeo's spicy Malaysian-Indian-Chinese offerings, such as *murtabak* (stuffed Indian bread), chile crab, basil chicken, *nonya daging rendang* (beef simmered in lime leaves), *ikan pangang* (banana leaf-wrapped barbecued salmon with chile paste), and, hottest of all, his green curry (prawns, scallops, and mussels simmered in a jalapeño-based curry). The stylish restaurant—practically glowing with its profusion of polished woods, stainless steel accents, and gleaming open kitchen—is located on the fourth floor of the fancy new San Francisco Centre (right above Bloomingdale's in fact), so you can squeeze in an afternoon of power shopping before your culinary adventure begins.

San Francisco Centre, 845 Market St., Suite 597. ✆ **415/668-1783.** www.straitsrestaurants.com. Reservations recommended. Main courses $10–$27. AE, DC, MC, V. Daily 11am–2am. Bus: 2, 3, 4, or 38.

INEXPENSIVE

Café de la Presse FRENCH/AMERICAN Parisians will find this 1930s-style French bistro and international newsstand familiarly comforting. But you needn't hail from across the pond to enjoy freshly baked pastries, coffee drinks, sidewalk seating, and French-speaking staff. Its location, directly across from the Chinatown gates, makes it one of the best places in the Union Square area to sit and enjoy the busy downtown vibe. The menu offers light fare for breakfast—at somewhat inflated prices—and meatier bistro-style entrees such as duck leg confit and braised beef stew for lunch and dinner. But the main reason to come here isn't to indulge your appetite, it's to browse the foreign magazine and newspaper racks for a bit, then rest your weary feet, nurse a cappuccino, nibble on a pastry, and soak up the street-side scene.

352 Grant Ave. (at Bush St.). ✆ **415/398-2680.** Breakfast $6.25–$10; lunch and dinner main courses (other than fish and meat) $9–$13; fish and meat main courses $15–$20. AE, DC, DISC, MC, V. Breakfast Mon–Fri 7:30–10am,

Sat–Sun 8–11:30am; lunch Mon–Fri 11:30am–2:30pm; dinner Mon–Thurs 5:30–9:30pm, Fri–Sun 5:30–10pm; brunch Sat–Sun 11:30am–4pm. Bus: 9X, 15, 30, or 45.

Dottie's True Blue Café ★ *Kids* AMERICAN/BREAKFAST This family-owned breakfast restaurant is one of my favorite downtown diners. This is the kind of place you'd expect to see off Route 66, where most customers are on a first-name basis with the staff and everyone is welcomed with a hearty hello and steaming mug of coffee. Dottie's serves far-above-average American morning fare (big portions of French toast, pancakes, bacon and eggs, omelets, and the like), delivered to tables laminated with old movie star photos on rugged, diner-quality plates. Whatever you order arrives with delicious homemade bread, muffins, or scones, as well as house-made jelly. There are also daily specials and vegetarian dishes.

In the Pacific Bay Inn, 522 Jones St. (at O'Farrell St.). ✆ **415/885-2767.** Reservations not accepted. Breakfast $5–$11. DISC, MC, V. Wed–Mon 7:30am–3pm (lunch 11:30am–3pm). Bus: 2, 3, 4, 27, or 38. Cable car: Powell–Mason line.

Emporio Armani Cafe ★ ITALIAN All the hobnobbing of an elite luncheon comes at a moderate price at the Armani Cafe. This upscale-casual cafe consists of a circular counter in the middle of Armani's ever-fashionable (and expensive) clothing store, a few tables on a mezzanine, and some crowded sidewalk seats when the weather's agreeable. Yes, it's a bit unusual to be eating amongst the racks of clothes, but that's what makes this cafe such a great place to take a break from Union Square shopping. Local favorites include the antipasto *misto,* panini, salads, and daily pizza specials. And just in case you need a stiff drink after seeing the prices of their designer suits, the bar stays open until 7pm.

1 Grant Ave. (at O'Farrell St., off Market St.). ✆ **415/677-9010.** Reservations accepted. Main courses $9–$17. AE, DC, DISC, MC, V. Winter Mon–Sat 11am–4pm, Sun noon–4pm; summer Mon–Sat 11am–4pm, Sun noon–4pm. Bus: All Union Sq. buses.

Mocca ★ ITALIAN If you're like me and can't be bothered with a long lunch when there's serious shopping to be done, head to this classic Italian deli on foot-traffic-only Maiden Lane. Here it's counter service and cash only for sandwiches, caprese (Italian tomato and mozzarella salad), and big leafy salads. You can enjoy them at the few indoor tables or the umbrella-shaded tables on the pedestrian-only street-front which look onto Union Square.

175 Maiden Lane (at Stockton St.). ✆ **415/956-1188.** Reservations not accepted. Main courses $7–$13. No credit cards. Pastry and coffee daily 10:30am–5:30pm; lunch daily 11am–5:30pm. Bus: All Union Sq. buses.

Sanraku Japanese Restaurant ★ *Value* JAPANESE/SUSHI A perfect combination of great cooked dishes and sushi at bargain prices makes this straightforward, bright, and busy restaurant the best choice in the area for Japanese food. The friendly, hardworking staff does its best to keep up with diners' demands, but the restaurant gets quite busy during lunch, when a special box lunch of the likes of California roll, soup, salad, deep-fried salmon roll, and beef with noodles with steamed rice comes at a very digestible $9.50. The main menu, which is always available, features great sesame chicken with teriyaki sauce and rice; tempura; a vast selection of *nigiri* (raw fish sushi) and rolls; and delicious combination plates of sushi, sashimi, and teriyaki. Dinner sees brisk business, too, but there always seems to be an available table.

704 Sutter St. (at Taylor St.). ✆ **415/771-0803.** www.sanraku.com. Main courses $7–$13 lunch, $10–$26 dinner; 7-course fixed-price dinner $55. AE, DC, DISC, MC, V. Mon–Sat lunch 11am–4pm and dinner 4–10pm; Sun dinner 4–10pm. Bus: 2, 3, 4, 27, or 38. Cable car: Powell–Mason line.

Sears Fine Foods ★ *Kids* AMERICAN Sears is not just another downtown diner—it's an old-fashioned institution, famous for its crispy, dark-brown waffles, light sourdough French toast served with house-made strawberry preserves, and silver dollar–size Swedish pancakes (18 per serving!). As the story goes, Ben Sears, a retired clown, founded the diner in 1938. His Swedish wife, Hilbur, was responsible for the legendary pancakes, which, although the restaurant is under new ownership, are still whipped up according to her family's secret recipe. Sears also offers classic lunch and dinner fare—try the Reuben for lunch and cod fish and chips for dinner, followed by a big slice of pie for dessert. Breakfast is served until 3pm every day, and plan on a brief wait to be seated on weekends.

439 Powell St. (between Post and Sutter sts.). ✆ **415/986-0700.** www.searsfinefood.com. Reservations accepted for parties of 6 or more. Breakfast $3–$8; salads and soups $3–$8; main courses $6–$10. AE, DC, MC, V. Daily 6:30am–10pm (breakfast until 3pm). Cable car: Powell-Mason and Powell-Hyde lines. Bus: 2, 3, 4, or 38.

3 Financial District

VERY EXPENSIVE

Aqua ★★ SEAFOOD At San Francisco's finest seafood restaurant, heralded chef Laurent Manrique dazzles customers with a bewildering juxtaposition of earth and sea. Under his care, the artfully composed dishes are delicately decadent: the ahi tartare with fresh herbs, Moroccan spices, and lemon confit is divine and one of the best I've ever had. Other favorites are the celery root soup with black truffle flan, frogs' legs, and rock shrimp; the Alaskan black cod wrapped in smoked bacon and accompanied by tomato and date chutney and glazed carrots; and the braised veal cheeks with smoked foie gras and beef consommé—all perfectly paired with wines chosen by the sommelier. The large dining room with high ceilings, elaborate floral displays, and oversized mirrors is pleasing to the eye if not to the ear. (It can get quite loud on busy nights.) Steep prices prevent most people from making a regular appearance, but for special occasions or billable lunches, Aqua is highly recommended.

252 California St. (near Battery). ✆ **415/956-9662.** www.aqua-sf.com. Reservations recommended. Main courses $29–$39; 3-course menu $68; 6-course tasting menu $95; vegetarian tasting menu $65. AE, DC, DISC, MC, V. Mon–Fri 11:30am–2pm; Mon–Sat 5:30–10:30pm; Sun 5:30–9:30pm. Valet parking (dinner only) $10. Bus: All Market St. buses.

EXPENSIVE

One Market ★★ CALIFORNIA Some of the city's best food has been served at this popular Embarcadero restaurant since 1993. Amid the airy main dining room with its open exhibition kitchen, cozy banquettes, mahogany trim, and slate flooring is a sea of diners feasting from a farm-fresh menu put together by Chef Mark Dommen, who has a passion for using only the freshest local ingredients—they helped establish the Ferry Plaza Farmers' Market across the street and now support it by shopping there—to create highly original dishes. During my last visit, my table was wowed by the truly divine beet carpaccio, shellfish, and seafood sampler (*not* your everyday platter), and a superb crispy skin pork saddle with fava beans and chorizo broth. Whatever you choose, you're bound to find a perfectly accompanying wine from the "cellar," which has over 500 selections of American vintages. Arrive early to mingle with the spirited corporate crowd that convenes from 4:30 to 7pm for happy hour at the bar—it's a fun scene.

1 Market St. (at Stuart St., across from Justin Herman Plaza). ✆ **415/777-5577.** www.onemarket.com. Reservations recommended. Lunch $16–$23; dinner $20–$33. AE, DC, DISC, MC, V. Mon–Fri 11:30am–2pm and 5:30–9pm; Sat 5:30–10pm. Valet parking $10. All Market St. buses; all BART trains.

Finds The Sun on Your Face at Belden Place

San Francisco has always been woefully lacking in the alfresco dining department. One exception is **Belden Place,** an adorable little brick alley in the heart of the Financial District that is open only to foot traffic. When the weather is agreeable, the restaurants that line the alley break out the big umbrellas, tables, and chairs, and *voilà*—a bit of Paris just off Pine Street.

A handful of adorable cafes line Belden Place and offer a variety of cuisines all at moderate prices. There's **Cafe Bastille,** 22 Belden Place (✆ **415/986-5673**), a classic French bistro and fun speak-easy basement serving excellent crepes, mussels, and French onion soup; it schedules live jazz on Fridays. **Cafe Tiramisu,** 28 Belden Place (✆ **415/421-7044**), is a stylish Italian hot spot serving addictive risottos and gnocchi. **Plouf,** 40 Belden Place (✆ **415/986-6491**), specializes in big bowls of mussels slathered in your choice of seven sauces, as well as fresh seafood. **B44,** 44 Belden Place (✆ **415/986-6287**), serves up a side order of Spain alongside its revered paella and other seriously zesty Spanish dishes.

Conversely, come at night for a Euro-speak-easy vibe with your dinner.

The Slanted Door ★★ VIETNAMESE What started in 1995 as an obscure little family-run restaurant in the Mission District has become one of the most popular and written-about restaurants in the city. Due to its meteoric rise—helped along by celebrity fans such as Mick Jagger, Keith Richards, and Quentin Tarantino—it's been relocated within a beautiful bay-inspired, custom-designed space at the Ferry Building Marketplace. What hasn't changed is a menu filled with incredibly fresh and flavorful Vietnamese dishes such as catfish clay-pot flavored with cilantro, ginger, and Thai chilies; an amazing green papaya salad with roasted peanuts; and fragrant peppercorn duck served with apples and watercress. If the cellophane noodles with fresh Dungeness crab meat are on the menu, *definitely* order them. Be sure to start the feast with a pot of tea from their eclectic collection.

1 Ferry Plaza (at The Embarcadero and Market). ✆ **415/861-8032.** www.slanteddoor.com. Reservations recommended. Lunch main courses $8.50–$17; most dinner dishes $15–$27; 7-item fixed-price dinner $45 (parties of 7 or more only). AE, MC, V. Daily 11am–2:30pm; Sun–Thurs 5:30–10pm; Fri–Sat 5:30–10:30pm. Bus: All Market Street buses. Streetcar: F, N-Judah line.

Tommy Toy's ★ CHINESE If you want romantic, extravagant Chinese, come to Tommy's. Fashioned after the 19th-century quarters of the Empress Dowager's sitting room and replete with mood-lit candelabras and antique paintings, it's perhaps the only Chinese restaurant in the city where dressing up is apropos. Most evenings, the dining room is filled mostly with tourists and traveling business types, while locals are more likely to come for the fixed-price lunches (the multi-course "Executive Luncheon" is a bargain at $23). Not much changes on the expensive, French-influenced Chinese menu, but that's fine with the loyalists who return year after year for such beautifully presented dishes as minced squab in leaves of lettuce; sautéed lobster with mushrooms, chives, and angel-hair crystal noodles; and puff-pastry–topped creamy lobster bisque. During my visits, the food has varied from fine to very good, but the portions are always substantial and the decor is definitely memorable.

655 Montgomery St. (at Clay and Washington sts.). ✆ **415/397-4888.** www.tommytoys.com. Reservations recommended. Main courses $17–$23; fixed-price lunch $23; fixed-price dinner $58–$65. AE, DC, DISC, MC, V. Mon–Fri 11:30am–2:30pm; daily 5:30–9:30pm. Valet parking (dinner only) $8. Bus: 9AX, 9BX, 12, 15, or 41.

Waterfront Restaurant CALIFORNIA Bay Bridge views, a sunny patio, a sleek industrial-chic dining room, and great food made The Waterfront an instant hit after its renovation and reopening in late 1997. Unfortunately, the parade of chefs in and out of the kitchen has made what was a sure thing now more of an interesting gamble. Still, the atmosphere alone can induce idyllic San Francisco memories—especially when you're seated outdoors on a sunny day. Fortunately, the menu's now trying to stick with safe classics such as Dungeness crab cakes; sautéed chicken breast with herbed polenta, spinach, and truffle rosemary pan sauce; and salads, pizzas, and wood-fired grill items. The wine list includes many selections starting at just $27.

Pier 7 (on The Embarcadero near Broadway). ✆ **415/391-2696.** www.waterfrontsf.com. Reservations recommended. Main courses $18–$30. AE, DC, DISC, MC, V. Daily 11:30am–10:30pm. Valet parking $7. Streetcar: F.

MODERATE

Kokkari ★★ GREEK/MEDITERRANEAN The funny thing is, I've been to Athens, and the food there wasn't nearly as good as what they're serving at Kokkari (Ko-*kar*-ee), one of my favorite restaurants in the city. My love affair starts with the setting: a beautifully rustic dining area with a commanding fireplace and oversize furnishings. Past the tiny bar, the other main room is pure rustic revelry with exposed wood beams, pretty standing lamps, and a view of the glass-enclosed private dining room. Then there are the wonderful, traditional Aegean dishes. A must-order appetizer is the *Marithes Tiganites,* a beautiful platter of whole crispy smelts enhanced with garlic-potato *skordalia* (a traditional Greek dip) and lemon. Other favorites are the *pikilia* (a sampling of traditional Greek spreads served with dolmades and house-made pitas) and the fabulous mesquite-grilled octopus salad. Try not to overindulge before the main courses, which include grilled whole petrale sole with lemon, olive oil, and braised greens; to-die-for moussaka (eggplant, lamb, potato, and béchamel); and lamb chops with oven-roasted lemon-oregano potatoes. Also consider the rotisserie specialties such as a rotisserie-roasted pork loin.

200 Jackson St. (at Front St.). ✆ **415/981-0983.** www.kokkari.com. Reservations recommended. Main courses $14–$23 lunch, $19–$35 dinner. AE, DC, DISC, MC, V. Lunch Mon–Fri 11:30am–2:30pm; bar menu 2:30–5:30pm; dinner Mon–Thurs 5:30–10pm, Fri 5:30–11pm, Sat 5–11pm. Valet parking (dinner only) $8. Bus: 12, 15, 41, or 83.

Sam's Grill & Seafood Restaurant ★ *Finds* SEAFOOD Power-lunching at Sam's is a San Francisco tradition, and Sam's has done a brisk business with Financial District suits since—get this—1867. Even if you're not carrying a briefcase, this is the place to come for time-capsule dining at its most classically San Francisco. Pass the crowded entrance and small bar to get to the main dining room—packed with virtually all men—kick back, and watch yesteryear happen today. (Or conversely, slide into a curtained booth and see nothing but your dining companion.) Tuxedo-clad waiters race around, doling out big crusty cuts of sourdough bread and distributing salads overflowing with fresh crab and Roquefort vinaigrette, towering plates of seafood pasta with marinara, charbroiled fish, roasted chicken, and old-school standbys like calves' liver with bacon and onions or Salisbury steak. Don't worry—they didn't forget classic creamed spinach. The restaurant's mildly salty service and good old-fashioned character make everything on the menu taste that much better.

Tips Fast Food from Around the World

Catering to the dense population of downtown white-collar workers, the **Rincon Center's Food Court** at the corner of Spear and Mission streets has about a dozen to-go places serving cheap, respectable fare running the gastronomic gamut: Korean, American, Mexican, pizza, coffee and cookies, Indian, Thai, sandwiches, Middle Eastern, and Chinese. Seat-yourself tables are dispersed throughout the indoor courtyard. Most of the restaurants are open Monday through Friday from 11am to 3pm, but some remain open until early evening.

Similar inexpensive eats can be found at the **Ferry Building Marketplace** (p. 155) and **Justin Herman Plaza,** both at the foot of Market Street at the Embarcadero.

374 Bush St. (between Montgomery and Kearny sts.). ✆ **415/421-0594.** Reservations recommended for dinner and for 6 or more at lunch. Main courses $12–$24. AE, DC, DISC, MC, V. Mon–Fri 11am–9pm. Bus: 15, 45, or 76.

Tadich Grill ★ SEAFOOD Not that the veteran restaurant needed more reason to be beloved, but the city's ongoing loss of local institutions makes 158-year-old Tadich the last of a long-revered dying breed. This business began as a coffee stand during the 1849 gold rush and claims to be the very first to broil seafood over mesquite charcoal back in the early 1920s. An old-fashioned power-dining restaurant to its core, Tadich boasts its original mahogany bar, which extends the length of the restaurant, and seven booths for private powwows. Big plates of sourdough bread top the tables.

You won't find fancy California cuisine here. The novella-like menu features a slew of classic salads such as sliced tomato with Dungeness crab or prawn Louis, meats and fish from the charcoal broiler, and even casseroles. The seafood cioppino is a specialty, as is the baked casserole of stuffed turbot with crab and shrimp à la Newburg, and the petrale sole with butter sauce. Everything comes with a heaping side of fries, but if you crave something green, order the creamed spinach.

240 California St. (between Battery and Front sts.). ✆ **415/391-1849.** Reservations not accepted. Main courses $14–$20. MC, V. Mon–Fri 11am–9:30pm; Sat 11:30am–9:30pm. Bus: All Market St. buses. Streetcar: All Market St. streetcars. BART: Embarcadero.

Tsar Nicoulai Caviar Cafe ★ CAVIAR Tsar Nicoulai is a wonderful little U-shaped 15-seat counter within the Ferry Building Marketplace where all sorts of caviar, champagne by the glass, and roe-related snacks are served to fans of fish roe. Drop by without reservations for the best American and imported caviars (served by the taste or the ounce), blinis hot off the griddle, caviar and champagne samplers, and specials like seafood salads and truffled scrambled eggs. If you haven't yet done so elsewhere, try the fun, colorful varieties of whitefish roe, which come in flavors of beet and saffron, ginger, wasabi, and truffle.

Ferry Building Marketplace, 1 Ferry Building no. 12 (at The Embarcadero and Market St.). ✆ **415/288-8630.** www.tsarnicoulai.com. Reservations not accepted. Caviar $10–$76 for samplers or 1-gram portions. Salads and such $10–$18. AE, MC, V. Mon–Fri 11am–7pm; Sat 9am–6pm; Sun 11am–5pm. Bus: All Market St. buses. Streetcar: F or N-Judah line.

Yank Sing ★★ CHINESE/DIM SUM Loosely translated as "a delight of the heart," Yank Sing is widely regarded as the best dim sum restaurant in the downtown area. The servers are good at guessing your gastric threshold as they wheel stainless steel carts carrying small plates of exotic dishes around the vast dining room; if they whiz right by your table there's probably a good reason. If you're new to dim sum (which, translated, means "to touch the heart"), stick with the safe, recognizable classics such as spareribs, stuffed crab claws, scallion pancakes, shrimp balls, pork buns, and steamed dumplings filled with delicious concoctions of pork, beef, fish, or vegetables. A second location, open Monday through Friday from 11am to 3pm, is at 49 Stevenson St., off First Street (✆ **415/541-4949**) in SoMa, and has outdoor seating for fair-weather dining.

101 Spear St. (at Mission St. at Rincon Center). ✆ **415/957-9300.** www.yanksing.com. Dim sum $3.65–$9.30 for 2–6 pieces. AE, DC, MC, V. Mon–Fri 11am–3pm; Sat–Sun and holidays 10am–4pm. Validated parking in Rincon Center Garage. Bus: 1, 12, 14, or 41. Streetcar: F. Cable car: California St. line. BART: Embarcadero.

4 SoMa

For a map of restaurants in this section, see the "Dining around Town" map on p. 112.

VERY EXPENSIVE

Ame ★★★ NEW AMERICAN Restaurateurs Hiro Sone and Lissa Doumani, the owners of the sensational Napa Valley restaurant Terra, have blessed us foodies with an equally fantastic restaurant in the city. Located on the ground level of the new and *très* chic St. Regis Hotel, the L-shaped dining room with its mesquite flooring, red accents, and long striped curtains fits right in with the hotel's minimalist theme. Sone, a master of Japanese, French, and Italian cuisines, offers an array of exotic selections that are utterly tempting: ragout of sweetbreads with salsify and forest mushrooms; Japanese egg custard with lobster and urchin; mushroom risotto topped with foie gras; grilled Wagyu beef with fried Miyagi oysters and rémoulade sauce. If you can't figure out where to start on a menu where everything looks wonderful, opt for Sone's A Taste of Ame, an $81 five-course tasting menu that, for an additional $60, is paired with a bevy of wines by the glass. After dinner, be sure to enjoy an aperitif at the hotel's swank bar where the city's elite congregate nightly

689 Mission St. (at Third St.). ✆ **415/284-4040.** www.amerestaurant.com. Reservations recommended. Main courses $19–$25 lunch, $22–$35 dinner. AE, DC, DISC, MC, V. Daily 5:30–10pm. Valet parking $12 for the 1st 3 hr. Bus: 15, 30, or 45. Streetcar: J, K, L, or M to Montgomery.

bacar ★★ AMERICAN BRASSERIE No other dining room makes wine as integral to the meal as popular bacar. Up to 250 eclectic, fashionable diners pack into this warehouse-restaurant's three distinct areas—the casual (loud) downstairs salon; the bustling lounge, bar, and main dining room; or the more quiet upstairs mezzanine, which looks down on the lounge and bar's action—for the creamy salt-cod and crab *brandade* (purée) and zesty roasted mussels with a chile-and-garlic sauce that begs to be soaked up by the accompanying grilled bread. Ditto the grilled mesquite pork chop with mashed yams and pineapple-mango chutney. Just as much fun is the wine selection, which gives you more than 1,400 choices. Around 65 wines are served by the glass, 2-ounce pour, or 250- or 500-milliliter decanter. If you want a festive night out, this is the place to come—especially when jazz is playing Monday through Saturday evenings. ***Note:*** bacar is open only 1 day per week (Fri) for lunch.

448 Brannan St. (at Third St.). ✆ **415/904-4100.** www.bacarsf.com. Reservations recommended. Lunch 3-course fixed-price menu $22; main courses dinner $22–$38. AE, DC, DISC, MC, V. Sun 5:30–10pm; Mon–Thurs 5:30–11pm; Fri 11:30am–2:30pm and 6:30pm–midnight; Sat 5:30pm–midnight. Valet parking (Mon–Sat from 5:30pm) $10. Bus: 15, 30, 45, 76, or 81.

Dining around Town

A. Sabella's **56**
A16 **8**
Absinthe **43**
Ace Wasabi's Rock 'n' Roll Sushi **4**
Alioto's **55**
Ana Mandara **53**
Andalé Taqueria **5**
AsiaSF **68**
Aziza **21**
bacar **71**
Barney's Gourmet Hamburgers **2**
Beach Chalet Brewery & Restaurant **23**
Betelnut **13**
Boudin at the Wharf **56**
Boulevard **65**
Burma Superstar **19**
Café Flore **33**
Cafe Pescatore **58**
Cha Cha Cha **26**
Chez Nous **16**
Chow **35**
Citrus Club **29**
Cliff House **21**
Delfina **38**
E'Angelo Restaurant **7**
Eliza's **19**
Ella's **19**
Firewood Cafe **34**
Fog City Diner **61**
Forbes Island **59**
Foreign Cinema **40**
Frjtz Fries **42**
Gordon Biersch Brewery Restaurant **66**
Greens Restaurant **1**
The Grove **6**
Hard Rock Cafe **60**
Harris' **49**
Hayes Street Grill **44**
Home Plate **10**
House of Prime Rib **48**
Isa **3**
Jardinière **45**
Kan Zaman **28**
Khan Toke Thai House **21**
La Folie **51**
La Méditerranée **15**
Little Star Pizza **22**
Lou's Pier 47 **57**
Manora's **69**
Mecca **36**
Mel's Drive-In **12**
MoMo's **72**
Pane e Vino **14**
Park Chow **24**
Pauline's **39**
Piperade **62**
PlumpJack Café **11**
Pluto's **9**
Quince **17**
The Ramp **73**
Restaurant Gary Danko **53**
RNM **30**
San Francisco Art Institute Café **52**
Scoma's **54**
The Slanted Door **64**
Straits Restaurant **67**
Swan Oyster Depot **47**
Tablespoon **50**
Takara **18**
Taquerias La Cumbre **37**
Thanh Long **25**
Thep Phanom **31**
Ti Couz **39**
Tommy's Joynt **46**
Ton Kiang **20**
Tsar Nicoulai Caviar Cafe **64**
2223 Restaurant & Bar **32**
Waterfront Restaurant **63**
Zuni Café **41**
Zuppa **70**

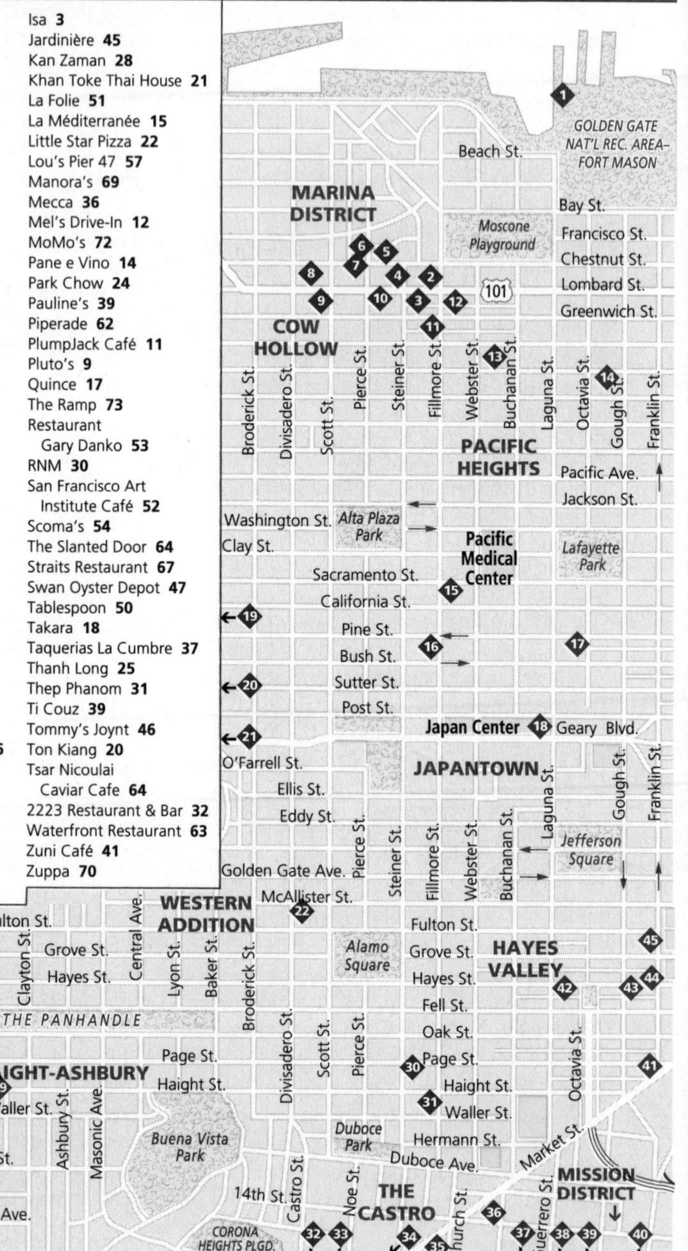

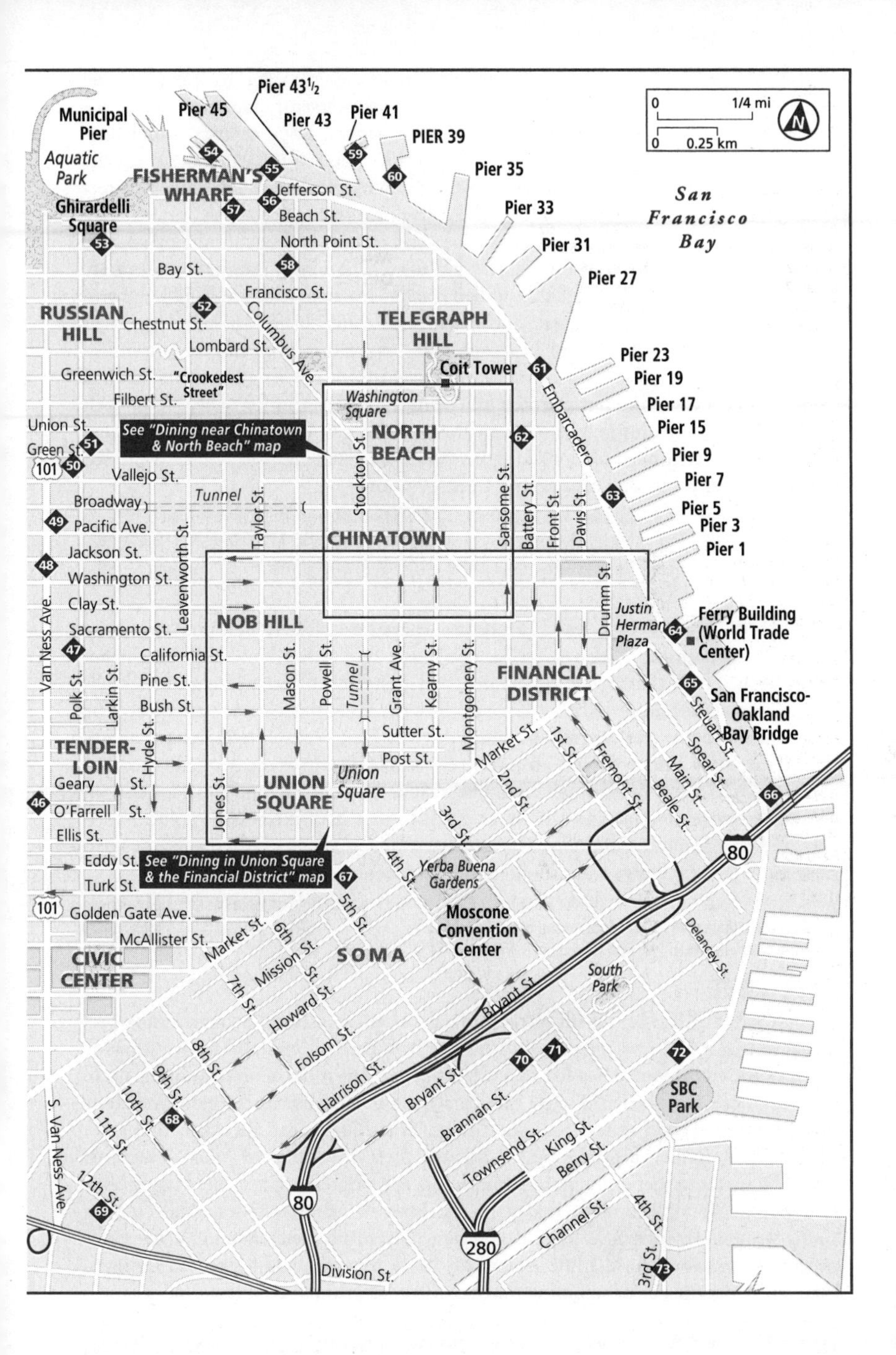

Municipal Pier
Aquatic Park
Pier 45
Pier 43½
Pier 43
Pier 41
PIER 39
Pier 35
Pier 33
Pier 31
Pier 27
Pier 23
Pier 19
Pier 17
Pier 15
Pier 9
Pier 7
Pier 5
Pier 3
Pier 1
0 1/4 mi
0 0.25 km
N
San Francisco Bay
FISHERMAN'S WHARF
Ghirardelli Square
Jefferson St.
Beach St.
North Point St.
Bay St.
Francisco St.
RUSSIAN HILL
Chestnut St.
Lombard St.
Columbus Ave.
TELEGRAPH HILL
Coit Tower
Greenwich St.
"Crookedest Street"
Filbert St.
Washington Square
NORTH BEACH
Embarcadero
Union St.
Green St.
See "Dining near Chinatown & North Beach" map
Vallejo St.
Broadway
Tunnel
Pacific Ave.
Jackson St.
Washington St.
Clay St.
Sacramento St.
California St.
Pine St.
Bush St.
Sutter St.
Post St.
Geary St.
O'Farrell St.
Ellis St.
Eddy St.
Turk St.
Golden Gate Ave.
McAllister St.
Van Ness Ave.
Polk St.
Larkin St.
Hyde St.
Leavenworth St.
Jones St.
Taylor St.
Mason St.
Powell St.
Stockton St.
Grant Ave.
Kearny St.
Montgomery St.
Sansome St.
Battery St.
Front St.
Davis St.
Drumm St.
CHINATOWN
NOB HILL
FINANCIAL DISTRICT
Justin Herman Plaza
Ferry Building (World Trade Center)
San Francisco-Oakland Bay Bridge
Steuart St.
Spear St.
Main St.
Beale St.
Fremont St.
1st St.
2nd St.
3rd St.
4th St.
5th St.
6th St.
7th St.
8th St.
9th St.
10th St.
11th St.
12th St.
Market St.
TENDER-LOIN
UNION SQUARE
Union Square
See "Dining in Union Square & the Financial District" map
Yerba Buena Gardens
Moscone Convention Center
CIVIC CENTER
SOMA
Mission St.
Howard St.
Folsom St.
Harrison St.
Bryant St.
Brannan St.
Townsend St.
King St.
Berry St.
Channel St.
Division St.
Delancey St.
South Park
SBC Park
S. Van Ness Ave.
101
80
280
46 47 48 49 50 51 52 53 54 55 56 57 58 59 60 61 62 63 64 65 66 67 68 69 70 71 72 73

Boulevard ★★ AMERICAN Master restaurant designer Pat Kuleto and chef Nancy Oakes are behind one of San Francisco's most beloved restaurants. Inside, the dramatically artistic Belle Epoque interior, with vaulted brick ceilings, floral banquettes, a mosaic floor, and tulip-shaped lamps, is the setting for Oakes's equally impressive sculptural and mouthwatering dishes. Starters alone could make a perfect meal, especially if you indulge in pan-seared day boat sea scallops with sautéed fresh hearts of palm, pomelo, basil, toasted shallots, and macadamia nuts, or the pan-seared foie gras with rhubarb syrup on whole grain toast. The nine or so main courses are equally creative and might include grilled Pacific sea bass with fresh gulf prawns, grilled artichoke, spring asparagus, and green garlic purée; or fire-roasted Angus filet with crispy Yukon gold potatoes, béarnaise sauce, sautéed spinach and crimini mushrooms, and red wine *jus*. Finish with warm chocolate cake with a chocolate caramel center, caramel corn, and butterscotch ice cream. Three levels of formality—bar, open kitchen, and main dining room—keep things from getting too snobby. Although steep prices prevent most from making Boulevard a regular gig, you'd be hard-pressed to find a better place for a special, fun-filled occasion.

1 Mission St. (between The Embarcadero and Steuart sts.). ✆ **415/543-6084.** www.boulevardrestaurant.com. Reservations recommended. Main courses $14–$22 lunch, $28–$39 dinner. AE, DC, DISC, MC, V. Mon–Fri 11:30am–2pm; Sun–Thurs 5:30–10pm; Fri–Sat 5:30–10:30pm. Valet parking $12 lunch, $10 dinner. Bus: 12, 15, 30, 32, or 41. BART: Embarcadero.

Fifth Floor Restaurant ★★ FRENCH Fantastic executive chef and two-time James Beard nominee Melissa Perello, previously of Charles Nob Hill, sommelier Emily Wines (yes, that is her last name), and pastry chef Leena Hung are the all-female culinary dream team behind one of the city's finest restaurant experiences. The decor—rich colors and fabrics, burgundy velvet banquettes, Frette linens, zebra-striped carpeting, and a clublike atmosphere—is as luxurious as the perfectly executed and wonderfully fresh menu, which might include Alaskan halibut "en cocotte" with asparagus, spring onions, and lemon; or veal rib-eye with wilted baby spinach, apricots, and chanterelle mushrooms. The wine program also reigns, with one of the most prestigious and expensive lists around and a professional team to serve it.

In the Hotel Palomar, 12 Fourth St. (at Market St.). ✆ **415/348-1555.** www.fifthfloorrestaurant.com. Reservations recommended. Main courses $26–$45; tasting menu $75–$115. AE, DC, DISC, MC, V. Mon–Thurs 5:30–10pm; Fri–Sat 5:30–11pm. Valet parking $12 with validation. Bus: All Market St. buses.

EXPENSIVE

MoMo's AMERICAN With an abundance of patio seating, a huge swank-yet-casual dining room, and proximity to AT&T Park baseball stadium, festive MoMo's hits a home run if you're headed to a Giants game, but is not a destination in itself. Crowds of upscale sports fans make this a place fun to hang out on the patio and chow down on greasy-good thin-sliced onion rings, refreshing seared ahi salad, thin-crust pizza, and awesome burgers. Come sundown, there are dozens of other restaurants where I'd prefer to spend my money, but singles appreciate the bar scene. Happy hour is hopping Monday through Friday in the baseball off season—especially during sunny weather. If you're headed here on a game day, make a reservation or arrive early, because party people form a line around the block to get in, and it's no fun trying to eat standing at the bar or wrestling for one of the coveted patio tables.

760 Second St. (at King St.). ✆ **415/227-8660.** www.sfmomos.com. Reservations recommended. Main courses $12–$39. AE, DC, DISC, MC, V. Sun–Wed 11:30am–9pm; Thurs–Sat 11:30am–10pm. Valet parking $8 lunch, $11 dinner, $20 game hours. Bus: 15, 30, 45, or 80x. Streetcar: F or N.

Town Hall ★ AMERICAN Mitchell and Steven Rosenthal (Postrio) and front man Doug Washington (Vertigo, Jardinière, and Postrio) are behind this SoMa warehouse hot spot featuring an attractive and rustically glitzy interior and huge portions of hearty American regional cuisine. The homey food's good, and might include the likes of ale-batter fish and chips, duck confit enchiladas, and slow-braised lamb shank with creamy polenta and natural *jus.*

342 Howard St. (at Fremont St.). ✆ **415/908-3900.** www.townhallsf.com. Reservations recommended. Main courses $10–$17 lunch, $18–$26 dinner. AE, MC, V. Lunch Mon–Fri 11:30am–2:30pm; dinner Sun–Thurs 5:30–10pm, Fri–Sat 5:30–11pm. Bus: 10, 14, or 76.

MODERATE

Gordon Biersch Brewery Restaurant ★ CALIFORNIA Popular with the young Republican crowd (loose ties and tight skirts predominate), this modern, two-tiered brewery and restaurant eschews traditional brewpub fare—no cheesy nachos on this menu—in an attempt to attract a more upscale clientele. And it works. Goat cheese ravioli is a bestseller, followed by the pecan-crusted half-chicken with garlic mashed potatoes. Start with the delicate and crunchy fried calamari appetizer or, if you're a garlic hound, the tangy Caesar salad. Most dishes can be paired with one of the brewery's lagers or ales. Couples bent on a quiet, romantic dinner can skip this place; when the lower-level bar fills up, you practically have to shout to be heard. Beer-lovers who want to pair their suds with decent grub, however, will be quite content.

2 Harrison St. (on The Embarcadero). ✆ **415/243-8246.** www.gordonbiersch.com. Reservations recommended. Main courses $10–$23. AE, DC, DISC, MC, V. Sun–Thurs 11:30am–midnight; Fri–Sat 11:30am–2am. Bus: 32.

Zuppa ★★ ITALIAN If you're looking for a casual-chic dinner spot with good affordable food, lively ambience, and a somewhat hip crowd, Zuppa is it. Located among the warehouses of SoMa, this warmed industrial room awash with dark wood tables features a back-wall bar orchestrated by on-site owners Joseph and Mary (yes, really). Joe, whose career launched from Spago Hollywood more than 2 decades ago, oversees the menu while Mary works the front of the house. With a menu of items that don't top $20, this is the way San Francisco dining used to be—if you can't decide between the antipasti of lemon-cured tuna with veggies, pizza with clams and garlic, or bone-in rib-eye, you can order all of them and not break the bank. A selection of cured meats, pizzas, and antipasti make it easy to snack through a meal, but don't. The pastas—particularly the pork ragu—are fantastic and shouldn't be missed, and the entrees are great as well—especially when paired with an Italian wine. ***Take note:*** Parking in local lots around here costs more on game days (the Giants ballpark is nearby)—expect to pay around $15. Otherwise, it's very affordable.

564 Fourth St. (between Brannan and Bryant sts.). ✆ **415/777-5900.** www.zuppa-sf.com. Reservations recommended. Main courses $16–$19. AE, DC, DISC, MC, V. Lunch Mon–Fri 11:30am–2:30pm; dinner Mon–Thurs 5:30–10pm, Fri–Sat 5:30–11pm, Sun 5–9pm. Street parking or pay at nearby lots. Bus: 9X, 12, 30, 45, or 76.

INEXPENSIVE

AsiaSF ★ ASIAN/CALIFORNIA Part restaurant, part gender-illusionist musical revue, AsiaSF manages to be both entertaining and satisfying. As you're entertained by mostly Asian men dressed as women (who lip-sync show tunes when they're not waiting on tables), you can nibble on superb grilled shrimp and herb salad; baby back pork ribs with honey tamarind glaze, pickled carrots, and sweet-potato crisps; or filet mignon with Korean dipping sauce, miso eggplant, and fried potato stars. The full bar, *Wine Spectator* award–winning wine list, and sake list add to the festivities. Fortunately, the food and the atmosphere are as colorful as the staff, which means a night here is more than a meal—it's a very happening event.

201 Ninth St. (at Howard St.). ✆ **415/255-2742.** www.asiasf.com. Reservations recommended. Main courses $9–$20. AE, DISC, MC, V (Mon–Wed $25 minimum). Sun–Thurs 6–10pm; Fri 6:45–10pm; Sat 5–10pm; cocktails and dancing until 2am on weekends. Bus: 9, 12, or 47. Streetcar: Civic Center on underground streetcar. BART: Civic Center.

Manora's ★ THAI Manora's cranks out some of the best Thai food in town and is well worth a jaunt to SoMa. But this is no relaxed affair: It's perpetually packed (unless you come early), and you'll be seated sardinelike at one of the cramped but well-appointed tables. During the dinner rush, the noise level can make conversation among larger parties almost impossible, but the food is so darned good, you'll probably prefer to turn toward your plate and stuff your face anyway. Start with a Thai iced tea or coffee and tangy soup or chicken satay, which comes with decadent peanut sauce. Follow these with any of the wonderful dinner dishes—which should be shared—and a side of rice. There are endless options, including a vast array of vegetarian plates. Every remarkably flavorful dish arrives seemingly seconds after you order it, which is great if you're hungry, a bummer if you were planning a long, leisurely dinner. ***Tip:*** Come before 7pm or after 9pm if you don't want a loud, rushed meal.

1600 Folsom St. (at 12th St.). ✆ **415/861-6224.** www.manorathai.com. Reservations recommended for 4 or more. Main courses $7–$12. MC, V. Mon–Fri 11:30am–2:30pm; Mon–Sat 5:30–10:30pm; Sun 5–10pm. Bus: 9, 12, or 47.

5 Nob Hill/Russian Hill

For a map of restaurants in this section, see the "Dining around Town" map on p. 112.

VERY EXPENSIVE

La Folie ★★★ *Finds* FRENCH I call this unintimidating, cozy, intimate French restaurant "the house of foie gras." Why? Because on my first visit, virtually every dish overflowed with the ultrarich delicacy. Subsequent visits proved that foie gras still reigns here, but more than that, it reconfirmed La Folie's long-standing reputation as one of the city's very best fine dining experiences—and without any stuffiness to boot. Chef/owner Roland Passot, who unlike many celebrity chefs is actually in the kitchen each night, offers melt-in-your-mouth starters such as seared foie gras with caramelized pineapple and star anise vanilla muscat broth. Generous main courses include rôti of quail and squab stuffed with wild mushrooms and wrapped in crispy potato strings; butter-poached lobster with glazed blood oranges and shiso, scallion, carrot, and toasted almond salad; and roast venison with vegetables, quince, and huckleberry sauce. The staff is extremely approachable and knowledgeable, and the new surroundings (think deep wood paneling, mirrors, long, rust-colored curtains, and gold-hued Venetian plaster) are now as elegant as the food. Best of all, the environment is relaxed, comfortable, and intimate. Finish with any of the delectable desserts. If you're not into the three-, four-, or five-course tasting menu, don't be deterred; the restaurant tells me they'll happily price out individual items.

2316 Polk St. (between Green and Union sts.). ✆ **415/776-5577.** www.lafolie.com. Reservations recommended. 3-course tasting menu $65; 4-course tasting menu $75; 5-course chef's tasting menu $85; vegetarian tasting menu $65. AE, DC, DISC, MC, V. Mon–Sat 5:30–10:30pm. Valet parking $15. Bus: 19, 41, 45, 47, 49, or 76.

EXPENSIVE

House of Prime Rib ★★ STEAKHOUSE Anyone who loves a huge slab of meat and old-school–style dining will feel right at home at this shrine to prime (rib). It's a fun and ever-packed affair within the men's clublike dining rooms (fireplaces included), where drinks are stiff, waiters are loose, and all the beef is roasted in rock salt, sliced tableside, and served with salad dramatically tossed tableside followed by creamed spinach and either mashed potatoes or a baked potato and Yorkshire pudding, which accompany the entree. To placate the occasional non-meat eater, they offer a fish-of-the-day special.

1906 Van Ness Ave. (near Washington St.). ✆ **415/885-4605.** Reservations recommended. Complete dinners $28–$33. AE, MC, V. Mon–Thurs 5:30–10pm; Fri 5–10pm; Sat 4:30–10pm; Sun 4–10pm. Valet parking $7. Bus: 47 or 49.

Tablespoon ★★ AMERICAN This crowded neighborhood restaurant ladles out such wonderful and well-priced New American cuisine that no one seems to mind the narrow dining room, its rather loud acoustics, or the wait for a table—sometimes despite having a reservation. The winning recipe is a savvy mix of casually sophisticated food and semiswank surroundings by co-owners chef Robert Riescher (previously of Central California's renowned Erna's Elderberry House) and front man John Jasso, who worked the crowds at destination restaurants Gary Danko and Fifth Floor. Like most hot spots these days, the menu highlights small plates (as well as entrees), but its selections are seasoned with uncommon panache, such as Riescher's roasted Jerusalem artichoke soup with braised short rib ravioli, delicate ahi tuna carpaccio with fennel salad and Meyer lemon vinaigrette, and hearty oven-roasted pork tenderloin with roasted Brussels sprouts and root vegetables. If you're looking to taste your way through an affordable meal surrounded by locals, this is one of the best places to do it. ***Note:*** Parking is nearly impossible to find in the neighborhood after 6pm.

2209 Polk St. (between Vallejo and Green sts.). ✆ **415/268-0140.** www.tablespoonsf.com. Reservations recommended. Main courses $17–$23. AE, MC, V. Mon–Sat 6–midnight; Sun 5–10pm. Bus: 19, 36, 41, or 45.

MODERATE

Nob Hill Cafe ★ *Finds* ITALIAN/PIZZA Considering the steep cost and formality of most Nob Hill restaurants, it's no wonder that residents don't mind waiting around for a table to open up at this cozy neighborhood bistro. This is the kind of place where you can come wearing jeans and sneakers, tuck into a large plate of linguine with clams and a glass of pinot, and leave fulfilled without blowing a wad of dough (pastas are in the humble $9–$12 range). The dining room is split into two small, simple rooms, with windows looking onto Taylor Street and bright local art on the walls. Service is friendly, and one of the owners is almost always on hand to make sure everyone's content. When the kitchen is "on," expect hearty Northern Italian comfort fare worth at least twice its price; even on off days, it's still a bargain. Start with a salad or the decadent polenta with pesto and parmigiano, then fill up on the veal piccata, any of the pastas or pizzas, or petrale sole. ***Tip:*** Parking can be difficult in Nob Hill; fortunately, they offer valet parking a block away at the corner of Washington and Taylor streets.

1152 Taylor St. (between Sacramento and Clay sts.). ✆ **415/776-6500.** www.nobhillcafe.com. Reservations not accepted. Main courses $7–$16. DC, MC, V. Daily 11:30am–3pm and 5–10pm. Bus: 1.

Swan Oyster Depot ★★ *Finds* SEAFOOD Turning 96 years old in 2008, Swan Oyster Depot is a classic San Francisco dining experience you shouldn't miss. Opened in 1912, this tiny hole in the wall, run by the city's friendliest servers, is little more than a narrow fish market that decided to slap down some bar stools. There are only 20 or so stools here, jammed cheek-by-jowl along a long marble bar. Most patrons come for a quick cup of chowder or a plate of oysters on the half shell that arrive chilling on crushed ice. The menu is limited to fresh crab, shrimp, oyster, clam cocktails, a few types of smoked fish, Maine lobster, and Boston-style clam chowder, all of which are exceedingly fresh. ***Note:*** Don't let the lunchtime line dissuade you—it moves fast.

1517 Polk St. (between California and Sacramento sts.). ✆ **415/673-1101.** Reservations not accepted. Seafood cocktails $7–$15; clams and oysters on the half-shell $7.95 per half-dozen. No credit cards. Mon–Sat 8am–5:30pm. Bus: 1, 19, 47, or 49.

6 Chinatown

For a map of restaurants in this section, see the "Dining near Chinatown & North Beach" map on p. 119.

INEXPENSIVE

Brandy Ho's Hunan Food ★ CHINESE Fancy black-and-white granite tabletops and a large, open kitchen give you the first clue that the food at this casual restaurant is a cut above the usual Hunan fare. Take my advice and start immediately with fried dumplings (in sweet-and-sour sauce) or cold chicken salad and then move on to fish-ball soup with spinach, bamboo shoots, noodles, and other goodies. The best main course is Three Delicacies, a combination of scallops, shrimp, and chicken with onion, bell pepper, and bamboo shoots, seasoned with ginger, garlic, and wine, and served with black-bean sauce. Most dishes are quite hot and spicy, but the kitchen will adjust the level to meet your specifications. A full bar includes Asian-food–friendly libations like plum wine and sake from 11:30am to 11pm.

217 Columbus Ave. (at Pacific Ave.). ✆ **415/788-7527.** www.brandyhos.com. Reservations recommended. Main courses $8–$13. AE, DISC, MC, V. Sun–Thurs 11:30am–11pm; Fri–Sat 11:30am–midnight. Paid parking available at 170 Columbus Ave. Bus: 15 or 41.

Gold Mountain ★ *Finds* *Kids* CHINESE/DIM SUM This gymnasium-size restaurant is a must-visit for anyone who's never experienced what it's like to dine with hundreds of Chinese-speaking patrons conversing loudly at enormous round tables among glittering chandeliers and gilded dragons while dozens of white-shirted waitstaff push around stainless steel carts filled with small plates of exotic-looking edible adventures (Was that sentence long enough for you?). Chicken feet, pork buns, shrimp dumplings, honey-walnut prawns (yum), the ubiquitous chicken-in-foil, and a myriad of other quasi-recognizable concoctions that range from appealing to revolting (never ate beef tripe, never will) whiz about at eye-level. I remember coming here as a little kid on late Saturday mornings and being infatuated with the entire cacophonous event. And even if you eat until you're ill, you'll never put down more than $20 worth of food, making Gold Mountain a real bargain as well, especially for large groups. Don't even bother with the regular menu: it's the dim sum service from 8am and 3pm on weekends and 10:30am to 3pm on weekdays that you want.

664 Broadway (between Grant Ave. and Stockton St.). ✆ **415/296-7733.** Main courses $3–$9. AE, MC, V. Mon–Fri 10:30am-3pm and 5–9:30pm; Sat–Sun 8am–3pm and 5–9:30pm. Bus: 12, 15, 30, or 83.

Great Eastern ★ *Finds* CHINESE If you like seafood and Chinese food and have an adventurous palate, you're going to love Great Eastern, which is well known among serious foodies for serving hard-to-find seafood pulled straight from the myriad of tanks that line the walls. Rock cod, steelhead, sea conch, sea bass, shrimp, frogs, soft-shell turtle, abalone—if it's even remotely aquatic and edible, it's on the menu at this popular Hong Kong–style dinner house that's mostly frequented by Chinese locals (so you know its good). The day's catch, sold by the pound, is listed on a board. Both

CLOSED
due to
accidental demolition
WEGEN BISSIGEN
EICHHÖRNCHEN GESCHLOSSEN
CERRADO
CABRAS
Κλειστό
Μετεωρίτες
POOL CLOSED
ELECTRIC EELS
プールも
閉鎖中
FERMÉ POUR
RAISON
DE GRÈVE
DES BONNES
Hotel
closed for
facelifting
FECHADO!
POR CAUSA DE
ATAQUES DOS CROCODILOS
I don't speak
sign language.
©2007 Travelocity.com LP. CST# 2056372-50.

travelocity
You'll never roam alone.

Dining near Chinatown & North Beach

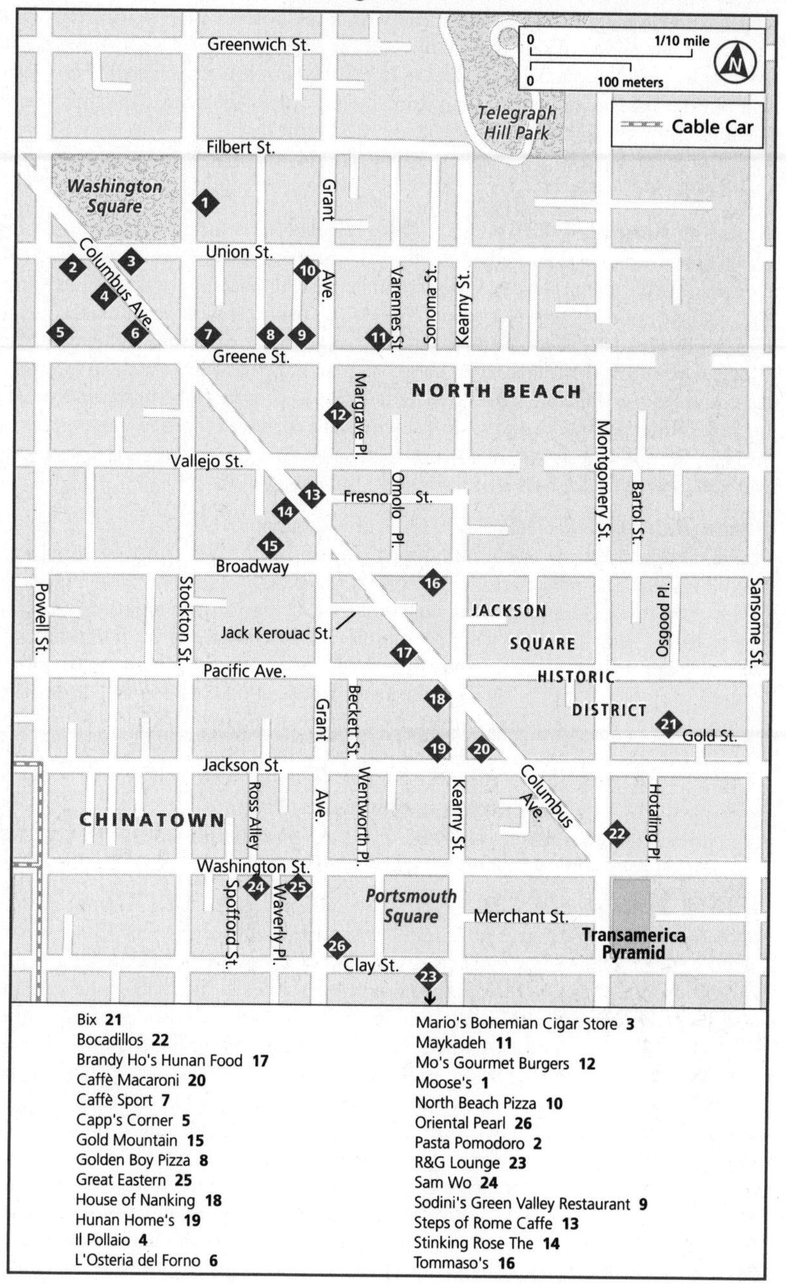

upper- and lower-level dining rooms are stylish in a Chinatown sort of way, with shiny black and emerald furnishings. The dim sum is excellent here as well—some say it's even better than the venerable Yank Sing (p. 110)—so give it a try as well. ***Tip:*** Unless you can translate an authentic Hong Kong menu, order a set dinner (the crab version is fantastic) or point to another table and say, "I want that."

649 Jackson St. (between Kearny St. and Grant Ave.). ✆ **415/986-2500.** Most main courses $8–$13. AE, MC, V. Daily 10am–1am. Bus: 15, 30, 41, or 45.

House of Nanking ★ CHINESE This place would be strictly a tourist joint if it weren't for the die-hard fans who happily wait—sometimes up to an hour—for a coveted seat at this inconspicuous little restaurant serving Shanghai-style cuisine. Order the requisite pot stickers, green-onion-and-shrimp pancakes with peanut sauce, or any number of pork, rice, beef, seafood, chicken, or vegetable dishes from the menu, but I suggest you trust the waiter when he recommends a special. Even with an expansion that doubled the available space, seating is tight, so prepare to be bumped around a bit and don't expect perky or attentive service—it's all part of the Nanking experience.

919 Kearny St. (at Columbus Ave.). ✆ **415/421-1429.** Reservations accepted for groups of 8 or more. Main courses $6–$12. MC, V. Mon–Fri 11am–10pm; Sat–Sun noon–10pm. Bus: 9, 12, 15, or 30.

Hunan Home's ★★ CHINESE One of Chinatown's best restaurants, Hunan Home's is a feast for the eyes—ubiquitous pink-and-white walls lined with big wall-to-wall mirrors that reflect armies of fish tanks and tacky chandeliers—as well as the palate. The rule of thumb here is not to put anything in your mouth until you're armed with a glass of water, because most every dish is *ooooweeeee* hot! Start with Home's excellent hot-and-sour soup (the acid test of every Chinese restaurant) or wonton soup (chock-full of shrimp, chicken, barbecued pork, squid, and vegetables), followed by the succulent bread appetizer, a platter of prawns with honeyed walnuts, and the scallops à la Hunan (sautéed along with snow peas, baby corn, celery, and mushrooms). Photographs of the more popular dishes are posted out front, though it's hard to tell which ones will singe your nose hairs.

622 Jackson St. (between Kearny St. and Grant Ave.). ✆ **415/982-2844.** Main courses $7.95–$12. AE, DC, DISC, MC, V. Daily 11:30am–2:30pm and 5–9:30pm. Bus: 15, 30, 41, or 45.

Oriental Pearl ★ CHINESE/DIM SUM Wherever the Chiu Chow region in southern China is, one thing's for sure: They're eating well there! Oriental Pearl specializes in regional Chiu Chow cuisine, a variation of Cantonese that's unlike anything you've ever seen or tasted, such as the house special chicken meatball—a delicate mix of shrimp, chicken, water chestnuts, and ham wrapped in a thin veneer of egg whites. Other recommended choices are the *pei pa* tofu with shrimp, seafood chow mein, and spicy braised prawns, all served by spiffy waiters wearing white shirts and black bow ties. The roomy, spotless restaurant is so obscurely located on the second floor of a business complex that it must rely almost exclusively on repeat and word-of-mouth clientele; but the word must be spreading, because it's usually packed. Unlike most other restaurants in Chinatown, dim sum is ordered via a menu, which isn't as fun but guarantees freshness (the steaming baskets of shrimp and scallop dumplings are excellent). Prices are slightly higher than average, but most definitely worth the extra money.

760 Clay St. (between Kearny St. and Grant Ave.). ✆ **415/433-1817.** Main courses $8.25–$9.50. AE, DC, DISC, MC, V. Daily 11am–3pm and 5–9:30pm. Bus: 15, 30, 41, or 45.

R&G Lounge ★ CHINESE It's tempting to take your chances and duck into any of the exotic restaurants in Chinatown, but if you want a sure thing, go directly to the three-story R&G Lounge. During lunch, all three floors are packed with hungry neighborhood workers who go straight for the $5.50 rice-plate specials. Even then, you can order from the dinner menu, which features legendary deep-fried salt-and-pepper crab (a little greasy for my taste); and wonderful chicken with black-bean sauce. A personal favorite is melt-in-your-mouth R&G Special Beef, which explodes with the tangy flavor of the accompanying sauce. I was less excited by the tired chicken salad, house specialty noodles, and bland spring rolls. But that was just fine since I saved room for generous and savory seafood in a clay pot and classic roast duck.

631 Kearny St. (at Clay St.). ✆ **415/982-7877.** www.rnglounge.com. Reservations recommended. Main courses $9.50–$30. AE, DC, DISC, MC, V. Daily 11am–9:30pm. Parking validated across the street at Portsmouth Sq. garage 24 hr. or Holiday Inn after 5pm. Bus: 1, 9AX, 9BX, or 15. Cable Car: California.

Sam Wo CHINESE Very handy for late-nighters, Sam's is a total dive that's usually packed at one in the morning with party people trying to sober up (I've been pulling all-nighters here since I was a teen). The century-old restaurant's two pocket-size dining rooms are located on top of each other, on the second and third floors—take the stairs past the grimy first-floor kitchen. You'll probably have to share a table, but this place is for mingling almost as much as for eating (the bossy waitresses are pure comedy). The house specialty is *jook,* known as *congee* in its native Hong Kong—a thick rice gruel flavored with fish, shrimp, chicken, beef, or pork; the best is Sampan, made with rice and seafood. Try sweet-and-sour pork rice, wonton soup with duck, or a roast-pork/rice-noodle roll. More traditional fried noodles and rice plates are available, too, but I always end up ordering the same thing: tomato beef with noodles and house special chow mein.

813 Washington St. (by Grant Ave.). ✆ **415/982-0596.** Reservations not accepted. Main courses $3.50–$6. No credit cards. Mon–Sat 11am–3am; Sun 11am–9:30pm in summer and on holidays. Bus: 9x, 15, 30, or 45.

7 North Beach/Telegraph Hill

For a map of restaurants in this section, see the "Dining near Chinatown & North Beach" map on p. 119.

EXPENSIVE

Bix ★★ *Moments* AMERICAN/CALIFORNIA The martini lifestyle may now be *en vogue,* but it was never out of style in this glamorous retro '30s-era supper club. Bix is utterly stylish, with curving mahogany paneling, giant silver pillars, and dramatic lighting, all of which sets the stage for live music and plenty of hobnobbing. Though the sleek setting has overshadowed the food in the past, the legions of diners entranced by the Bix experience don't seem to care—and it seems as of late Bix is "on" again. Chicken hash has been a menu favorite for the past 19 years, but newer luxury comfort-food dishes—such as caviar service, marrowbones with toast and shallot confit, steak tartare, and pan-roasted seasonal fish dishes—are developing their own fan clubs. ***Bargain tip:*** At lunch a three-course prix-fixe menu goes for $25.

56 Gold St. (between Sansome and Montgomery sts.). ✆ **415/433-6300.** www.bixrestaurant.com. Reservations recommended. Main courses $12–$15 lunch, $16–$32 dinner. AE, DC, DISC, MC, V. Mon–Thurs 4:30–11pm; Fri 11:30am–2pm and 5:30pm–midnight; Sat 5:30pm–midnight; Sun 6–10pm. Valet parking $10. Bus: 15, 30, 41, or 45.

Moose's ★ NEW AMERICAN A big blue neon moose marks your arrival at North Beach's most schmoozy restaurant, where Nob Hill socialites and local politicians gather nightly over cocktails and cioppino. But convivial Moose's is not just an image. On recent visits, the food—which highlights seasonal local small farm organic ingredients—has been quite good. Appetizers are innovative, fresh, and well balanced (thank goodness for a truly good Caesar salad and steamed Prince Edward Island mussels). Main courses (especially meats) are always expertly prepared and beautifully presented. Try the Massachusetts striped bass with broccoli, cauliflower, cipollini onions, and lemon; garlic pan-seared duck with shaved Brussels sprouts, black lentils, onions, and duck *jus;* or grilled Niman Ranch rib-eye. Another reason to love Moose's: They make a darned good Mooseburger.

The bar, separated from the main dining room by a low, frosted-glass partition, remains busy long after the kitchen closes. There's jazz piano nightly and during Sunday brunch.

1652 Stockton St. (between Filbert and Union sts.). ✆ **800/28-MOOSE** or 415/989-7800. www.mooses.com. Reservations recommended. Main courses $11–$34. AE, DC, DISC, MC, V. Daily 5–10pm; brunch Sat–Sun 10am–2:30pm. 3-hr. valet parking $6 lunch, $9 dinner. Bus: 15, 30, 41, or 45.

MODERATE

Maykadeh PERSIAN/MIDDLE EASTERN If you're looking to add a little exotic adventure to your North Beach dinner plans, this is the place to go. Surrounded by a sea of Italian bistros, Maykadeh is one of San Francisco's best and most elegant Persian restaurants. The Middle East may no longer be the culinary capital of the world, but at Maykadeh you can still sample the exotic flavors that characterize Persian cuisine. Of the dozen or so appetizers, some of the best are eggplant with mint garlic sauce; stuffed grape leaves; and lamb tongue with lime juice, sour cream, and saffron (c'mon, live a little). About eight mesquite-grilled items are on the menu, including filet of lamb marinated in lime, homemade yogurt, saffron, and onions. House specialties include half a dozen vegetarian dishes, among them eggplant braised with saffron, fresh tomato, and dried lime.

470 Green St. (between Kearny St. and Grant Ave.). ✆ **415/362-8286.** www.maykadehrestaurant.com. Reservations recommended. Main courses $13–$27. MC, V. Mon–Thurs 11:45am–10:30pm; Fri–Sat 11:45am–11pm; Sun 11:45am–10pm. Valet parking $7 lunch, $8 dinner. Bus: 15, 30, or 41.

Piperade ★★ BASQUE Chef Gerald Hirigoyen takes diners on a Basque adventure in this charming, small restaurant. Surrounded by a low wood-beam–lined ceiling, oak floors, and soft sconce lighting, it's a casual affair where diners indulge in small and large plates of Hirigoyen's superbly flavorful West Coast Basque cuisine. Your edible odyssey starts with small plates—or plates to be shared—like my personal favorites: piquillo peppers stuffed with goat cheese; and a bright and simple salad of garbanzo beans with calamari, chorizo, and piquillo peppers. Share entrees, too. Indulge in New York steak with braised shallots and french fries or sop up every drop of the sweet and savory red-pepper sauce with the braised seafood and shellfish stew. Save room for orange blossom beignets: Light and airy with a delicate and moist web of dough within and a kiss of orange essence, the beignet is dessert at its finest. There's a communal table for drop-in diners and front patio seating during warmer weather.

1015 Battery St. (at Green St.). ✆ **415/391-2555.** www.piperade.com. Reservations recommended. Main courses $17–$24. AE, DC, DISC, MC, V. Mon–Fri 11:30am–3pm and 5:30–10:30pm; Sat 5:30–10:30pm; closed Sun. Bus: 10, 12, 30, or 82x.

The Stinking Rose ITALIAN Garlic is the "flower" from which this restaurant gets its name. From soup to ice cream, the supposedly healthful herb is a star ingredient in almost every dish. ("We season our garlic with food," exclaims the menu.) From a gourmet point of view, The Stinking Rose is unremarkable. Pizzas, pastas, and meats smothered in simple, overpowering sauces are tasty, but they're memorable only for their singular garlicky intensity. That said, this is a fun place; the restaurant's lively atmosphere and odoriferous aroma combine for good entertainment. The best dishes include iron-skillet–roasted mussels, shrimp, and crab with garlic sauce; smoked mozzarella, garlic, and tomato pizza; salt-roasted tiger prawns with garlic parsley glaze; and 40-clove garlic chicken (served with garlic mashed potatoes, of course). ***Note:*** For those who are not garlic-inclined, they offer garlic-free "Vampire Fare."

325 Columbus Ave. (between Vallejo and Broadway). ✆ **415/781-7673.** www.thestinkingrose.com. Reservations recommended. Main courses $13–$30. AE, DC, DISC, MC, V. Daily 11am–11pm. Bus: 15, 30, 41, or 45.

INEXPENSIVE

Caffè Macaroni ★ *Finds* ITALIAN You wouldn't know it from the looks (or name) of it, but this tiny, funky restaurant on busy Columbus Avenue is one of the best southern Italian restaurants in the city. It looks as though it can hold only two customers at a time, and if you don't duck your head when entering the upstairs dining room, you might as well ask for one lump or two. Fortunately, the kitchen also packs a wallop, dishing out a large variety of antipasti and excellent pastas. The spinach-and-cheese ravioli with wild-mushroom sauce and the gnocchi are outstanding. The owners and staff are always vivacious and friendly, and young ladies in particular will enjoy the attentions of the charming Italian men manning the counter. If you're still pondering whether you should eat here, consider that most entrees are under $15.

124 Columbus Ave. (at Jackson St.). ✆ **415/956-9737.** www.caffemacaroni.com. Reservations accepted. Main courses $9–$15. AE, MC, V. Mon–Sat 11am–2:30pm and 5:30–11pm; Sun noon–10pm. Bus: 15 or 41.

Caffè Sport ★ ITALIAN People either love or hate this stodgy, garlic-smelling Sicilian eatery. Every square inch is cluttered with hanging hams, fishnets, decorative plates, dolls, mirrors, and over 2 decades' worth of dust, Caffè Sport was once a culinary landmark. Now it's better known for its surly staff and eclectic ambience than for its good—though cream- and butter-heavy—food. Still, the fare is served up with hearty portions of tongue-in-cheek attitude along with huge garlic-laden pasta dishes. Lunch is tame in comparison to dinner, when the Sport is mobbed and lively, and strangers might be packed together family style. Disregard the menu and just accept the waiter's "suggestions." Whatever arrives—whether calamari, mussels, or shrimp in tomato-garlic sauce, or pasta in pesto sauce—it's bound to be *bene.* Bring a huge appetite and plenty of cash (they don't take credit cards), but above all, don't be late if you have a reservation.

574 Green St. (between Grant and Columbus aves.). ✆ **415/981-1251.** Reservations recommended. Main courses $15–$30. No credit cards. Tues–Sat noon–2pm and 5–10:30pm. Bus: 15, 30, 41, or 45.

Capp's Corner ★ *Value* ITALIAN Capp's is a place of givens: It's a given that high-spirited regulars are hunched over the bar and that you'll be served huge portions of straightforward Italian fare at low prices in a raucous atmosphere that prevails until closing. The waitresses are usually brusque and bossy, but always with a wink. Long tables are set up for family-style dining: bread, soup, salad, and choice of around 20 classic main dishes (herb-roasted leg of lamb, spaghetti with meatballs, *osso buco* with polenta, fettuccine with prawns and white-wine sauce)—all for $15 or $17 or so per person, around $10 for kids. You might have to wait awhile for a table, but if you want fun and authentic old-school dining without pomp or huge prices, you'll find the wait worthwhile.

1600 Powell St. (at Green St.). ✆ **415/989-2589.** www.cappscorner.com. Reservations accepted. Complete dinners $15–$17. AE, DC, MC, V. Daily 11:30am–2:30pm; Mon–Fri 4:30–10:30pm; Sat–Sun 4–11pm. Bus: 15, 30, or 41.

Golden Boy Pizza ★ *Value* ITALIAN/PIZZA Pass by Golden Boy when the bars are hopping in North Beach and you'll find a crowd of inebriated sots savoring steamy slices of wondrously gooey pizza. But you don't have to be on a red wine buzz to enjoy the big, doughy squares of Italian-style pizzas, each enticingly placed in the front windows (the aroma alone is deadly). Locals have flocked here for years to fill up on one of the cheapest and cheesiest meals in town. Expect to take your feast to go on busy nights, as there are only a few bar seats inside.

542 Green St. (between Stockton St. and Grant Ave.). ✆ **415/982-9738.** Pizza slice $2.50–$3.50. No credit cards. Sun–Thurs 11:30am–11pm; Fri–Sat 11:30am–2am. Bus: 15, 30, 45, 39, or 41.

Il Pollaio ★ *Value* ITALIAN/ARGENTINE Simple, affordable, and consistently good is the winning combination at Il Pollaio. When I used to live in the neighborhood I ate here at least once a week and I still can't make chicken this good. Seat yourself in the tiny, unfussy room, order, and wait expectantly for the fresh-from-the-grill lemon-infused chicken, which is so moist it practically falls off the bone. Each meal comes with a choice of salad or fries. If you're not in the mood for chicken, you can opt for rabbit, lamb, pork chop, or Italian sausage. On a sunny day, get your goods to-go and picnic across the street at Washington Square.

555 Columbus Ave. (between Green and Union sts.). ✆ **415/362-7727.** Reservations not accepted. Main courses $8–$15. DISC, MC, V. Mon–Sat 11:30am–9pm. Bus: 15, 30, 39, 41, or 45. Cable car: Powell–Mason line.

L'Osteria del Forno ★★ ITALIAN L'Osteria del Forno might be only slightly larger than a walk-in closet, but it's one of the top three authentic Italian restaurants in North Beach. Peer in the window facing Columbus Avenue, and you'll probably see two Italian women with their hair up, sweating from the heat of the oven, which cranks out the best focaccia (and focaccia sandwiches) in the city. There's no pomp or circumstance here: Locals come strictly to eat. The menu features a variety of superb pizzas, salads, soups, and fresh pastas, plus a good selection of daily specials (pray for the roast pork braised in milk), which includes a roast of the day, pasta, and ravioli. Small baskets of warm focaccia keep you going until the arrival of the entrees, which should always be accompanied by a glass of Italian red. Good news for folks on the go: You can get pizza by the slice. Note that it's cash-only here.

519 Columbus Ave. (between Green and Union sts.). ✆ **415/982-1124.** www.losteriadelforno.com. Reservations not accepted. Sandwiches $6–$7; pizzas $10–$18; main courses $6–$14. No credit cards. Sun–Mon and Wed–Thurs 11:30am–10pm; Fri–Sat 11:30am–10:30pm. Bus: 15, 30, 41, or 45.

Mario's Bohemian Cigar Store ★ *Finds* ITALIAN Across the street from Washington Square is one of North Beach's most venerable neighborhood hangouts. The century-old corner cafe—small, well worn, and perpetually busy—is one of the oldest and best original cappuccino cafes in United States. I stop by at least once a month for a meatball or eggplant focaccia sandwich and a slice of Mario's house-made ricotta cheesecake, then recharge with a cappuccino as I watch the world stroll by the picture windows. And no, they don't sell cigars.

566 Columbus Ave. (at Union St.). ✆ **415/362-0536.** www.mariosbohemiancigarstore.com. Sandwiches $7.75–$8.50. MC, V. Mon–Sat 10am–midnight; Sun 10am–11pm. Bus: 15, 30, 41, or 45.

Mo's Gourmet Burgers ★★ *Kids* AMERICAN This simple diner offers a straightforward but winning combination: big, thick, grilled patties of fresh-ground, best-quality, center-cut chuck; fresh french fries; and choice of cabbage slaw, sautéed garlic mushrooms, or chili. *Voilà!* You've got the city's burger of choice (Zuni Café's is a contender, but at almost twice the price—p. 138). The other food—spicy chicken sandwiches; steak with veggies, garlic bread, and potatoes; and token veggie dishes—is also up to snuff, but that messy, memorable burger is what keeps the carnivores captivated (the sinisterly sweet shakes are fantastic, too). Bargain-diners will appreciate prices, with burgers ranging from $5.95 for a classic to $7.95 for an "Alpine" burger with Gruyère cheese and sautéed mushrooms. Entrees start at $9 for meatloaf with mashed potatoes, garlic bread, and a vegetable, and top out at $17 for New York steak. The classic breakfast menu is also a bargain. A second location at SoMa's Yerba Buena Gardens, 772 Folsom St., between Third and Fourth streets (✆ **415/957-3779**), is open Monday from 10am to 5pm, Tuesday through Friday from 10am to 8pm, Saturday from 9am to 8pm, and Sunday from 9am to 5pm. It features breakfast and burgers.

1322 Grant Ave. (between Vallejo and Green sts.). ✆ **415/788-3779.** Main courses $5.95–$17. MC, V. Mon–Thurs 11:30am–10:30pm; Fri 11:30am–11:30pm; Sat 9am–11:30pm; Sun 9am–10:30pm. Bus: 9X, 15, 30, 39, 41, or 45.

North Beach Pizza ★ *Kids* ITALIAN/PIZZA Whenever I order a North Beach pizza, I'm always disappointed by the measly amount of toppings that they give you. Then I eat the entire damn thing in one sitting. There's something about that uniquely gooey whole-milk mozzarella and hand-spun dough with thick, chewy edges that's so addictive it's been the most awarded and widely beloved pizza in the city for more than 2 decades. You *can* get a better pizza in the city—Pauline's and Little Star has them beat—but not in North Beach, not via free delivery throughout the city, and not at 2:30am on Saturday when you're drunk, stoned, and starving. Either create your own pizza from their list of 20 fresh ingredients (the sausage with black olives is the *bomb*), or choose from the house's 10 specialties such as the San Francisco Special—clams, garlic, cheese, and one brutal case of halitosis. There are numerous satellite NBPs throughout the city offering fast, free delivery until the wee hours.

1499 Grant St. (at Union St.). ✆ **415/433-2444.** www.northbeachpizza.com. Main courses $9–$21. AE, DC, DISC, MC, V. Sun–Thurs 9am–1am; Fri–Sat 9am–3am. Cable car: Powell-Mason line. Bus: 15, 30, 41, or 45.

Pasta Pomodoro ★★ *Kids* *Value* ITALIAN If you're looking for a good, cheap meal in North Beach—or anywhere else in town, for that matter—this San Francisco chain can't be beat. There can be a short wait for a table, but after you're seated, you'll be surprised at how promptly you're served. Every dish is fresh and sizable and, best of all, costs a third of what you'd pay elsewhere. Winners include spaghetti *frutti di mare* made with calamari, mussels, scallops, tomato, garlic, and wine; and smoked rigatoni, with roast chicken, sun-dried tomatoes, cream, mushrooms, and Parmesan—both under $13. When I don't feel like cooking, I often stop here for angel-hair pasta with tomato and basil and a decadent spinach salad with peppered walnuts and bleu cheese. The tiramisu is huge, delicious, and cheap, too.

655 Union St. (at Columbus Ave.). ✆ **415/399-0300.** www.pastapomodoro.com. Reservations not accepted. Main courses $6–$12. AE, MC, V. Sun–Thurs 11am–10:30pm; Fri–Sat 11am–11pm. Bus: 15, 30, 41, or 45. Cable car: Powell–Mason line. There are 7 other locations, including 2304 Market St., at 16th St. (✆ **415/558-8123**); 3611 California St., between Spruce St. and Parker Ave. (✆ **415/831-0900**); and 816 Irving St., between Ninth and 10th sts. (✆ **415/566-0900**).

San Francisco Art Institute Café *Finds* AMERICAN Never in a million years would you stumble upon the Art Institute Café by accident. One of the best-kept secrets in San Francisco, this cafe offers fresh, affordable cafe standards for in-the-know residents and visitors as well as Art Institute students: a wide array of hearty breakfast dishes, fresh salads, sandwiches on homemade bread, daily ethnically inspired specials, and anything with caffeine in it—all priced at or under $7. The view, which extends from Alcatraz Island to Coit Tower and beyond, is so phenomenal that the exterior served as the outside of Sigourney Weaver's chic apartment in the movie *Copycat.* The cafe has an open kitchen, sleek aluminum tables, and weekly rotating student art shows. A large courtyard with cement tables (and the same Hollywood view) is the perfect spot for an alfresco lunch high above the tourist fray.

800 Chestnut St. (between Jones and Leavenworth sts.). ✆ **415/749-4567.** Main courses $4–$6. No credit cards. Fall–spring Mon–Thurs 8am–5pm, Fri 8am–4pm; summer Mon–Fri 9am–2pm. Closed Sat–Sun. Hours dependent on school schedule; please call to confirm. Bus: 30 or 49. Cable car: Powell–Hyde or Powell–Mason line.

Sodini's Green Valley Restaurant ★ ITALIAN Sodini's is everything you would expect from a classic Italian restaurant in North Beach—a family-owned and -operated business run by a friendly, vivacious staff that serves hearty Italian classics on tables topped with wax-encrusted chianti bottle candles while the Chairman of the Board croons love songs in the background. There's usually a wait for a table; fortunately, the bar is a great place to hang out, shoot the breeze with the friendly bartender (most likely one of the owners), and get a little North Beach history lesson. The clientele is a mix of locals and tourists, all getting hungrier by the minute as the aroma of garlic and fresh basil wafts from the kitchen. The large wood-fired pizzas are very good and worth moving that belt one more notch, but their best dish is the light and tender gnocchi. Regardless of what you order, you won't leave hungry or unhappy.

510 Green St. (at Grant St.). ✆ **415/291-0499.** Reservations not accepted. Main courses $10–$23. MC, V. Daily 5–10pm. Cable car: Powell-Mason line. Bus: 15, 30, 41, or 45.

Steps of Rome Caffe ★ ITALIAN All the vibrancy and flavor of Italy can be found at this affordable and casual North Beach eatery. It's known as much as a meeting point for the young and social as it is for its heaping plates of fresh pasta, so if you head here, expect a lively time. Start with tasty bruschetta, carpaccio, or Caesar or caprese salad, but save room for panini (sandwiches of pressed toasted bread with killer fillings like salmon, tomatoes, and citrus sauce or prosciutto and mozzarella), classic pastas—from Alfredo to pomodoro to crab ravioli—pizzas, or entrees ranging from grilled chicken breast over salad to filet mignon. Should you want the taste without the bustle, the more mild and formal Trattoria is next door. Also, keep this spot in mind for late-night hunger pangs; they serve until 2am weekdays, 3am weekends.

348 Columbus Ave. (between Broadway and Vallejo St.). ✆ **415/397-0435.** www.stepsofrome.com. Reservations recommended. Main courses $6.95–$20. No credit cards. Sun–Thurs 10–2am; Fri–Sat 10–3am. Bus: 15 or 41.

Tommaso's ★ *Kids* ITALIAN From the street, Tommaso's looks wholly unappealing—a drab, windowless brown facade sandwiched between sex shops. Then why are people always waiting in line to get in? Because everyone knows that Tommaso's, which opened in 1935, bakes one of San Francisco's best traditional-style pizzas. The center of attention in the downstairs dining room is the chef, who continuously tosses huge hunks of garlic and mozzarella onto pizzas before sliding them into the oak-burning brick oven. Nineteen different toppings make pizza the dish of choice, even though Italian classics such as veal Marsala, chicken cacciatore, superb lasagna, and wonderful calzones are also available. Tommaso's also offers half-bottles of house wines, homemade manicotti, and good Italian coffee. If you can overlook the seedy surroundings, this fun, boisterous restaurant is a great place to take the family.

1042 Kearny St. (at Broadway). ✆ **415/398-9696.** www.tommasosnorthbeach.com. Reservations not accepted. Pasta and pizza $14–$24; main courses $11–$18. AE, DC, DISC, MC, V. Tues–Sat 5–10:30pm; Sun 4–9:30pm. Closed Dec 15–Jan 15. Bus: 15 or 41.

8 Fisherman's Wharf

For a map of restaurants in this section, see the "Dining around Town" map on p. 112.

VERY EXPENSIVE

A. Sabella's ★ SEAFOOD One of the first families to open a restaurant at the wharf continues its old-fashioned hospitality with a genuine sense of place, solid food, and an attentive staff—all packaged in a pretty and spacious room overlooking the wharf. Accessed via an incognito elevator, this hidden restaurant offers something for everyone—classic renditions of steak, lamb, seafood, chicken, and pasta, all made from scratch with fresh local ingredients—but where A. Sabella's really shines is in the shellfish department. Its 1,000-gallon saltwater tank allows for fresh crab, abalone, and lobster year-round, which means no restaurant in the city can touch this spot when it comes to feasting on fresh Dungeness crab and abalone out of season. Of course, such luxuries are anything but cheap. But on the bright side, with the kids' menu, you can fill them up for a mere $7.50.

Fisherman's Wharf, 2766 Taylor St. (at Jefferson St.), 3rd floor. ✆ **415/771-6775.** www.asabellas.com. Reservations recommended. Most main courses $16–$28. AE, DC, DISC, MC, V. Daily 5–10pm. 2-hr. validated parking at the Wharf Garage, 350 Beach St. Streetcar: F. Cable car: Powell–Mason or Powell–Hyde lines.

Forbes Island ★ *Moments* FRENCH Been there and done that in every San Francisco dining room? Then it's time for Forbes Island, a wonderfully ridiculous floating restaurant disguised as an island (complete with lighthouse and real 40-ft. palm trees) and unknown to even most locals. The idea's kitschy, but the execution's actually quite wonderful. Here's how it works: Arrive at the dock next to Pier 39, call the restaurant via the courtesy phone, climb aboard its pontoon boat that takes you on a 4-minute journey to the "island" located 75 feet from the city's famed sea lions, and descend into the island's bowels to find a surprisingly classy, Tudor-like wood-paneled dining room. Warmed by a fireplace and amused by fish swimming past the portholes (yes, the dining room is a wee bit underwater), guests dine on surprisingly well-prepared classic French food such as decadent ragout of wild mushrooms, toasted brioche, and soft goat cheese or roasted half-rack of lamb with herbed flageolet beans, minted edamame, and natural lamb reduction *jus.* The added "Sea Lion" room boasts the closest view you'll ever get of the creatures. ***But be warned:*** The menu is very limited, the wine list features basic big-name producers without listing the vintage, and the "island" does gently rock. (Landlubbers need not apply or should take Dramamine a couple of hours beforehand.) ***One annoyance:*** the mandatory $3 shuttle fee since the only other way to get there is to swim.

Water shuttle is just left of Pier 39. ✆ **415/951-4900.** www.forbesisland.com. Reservations recommended. Main courses $24–$34. AE, DC, MC, V. Wed–Sun arrive 5–10pm. Validated parking at Pier 39 garage, $8 for up to 6 hr.

Restaurant Gary Danko ★★★ FRENCH James Beard Award–winning chef Gary Danko presides over my top pick for fine dining. Eschewing the white-glove formality of yesteryear's fine dining, Danko offers impeccable cuisine and perfectly orchestrated service in an unstuffy environment of wooden paneling and shutters and well-spaced tables (not to mention spa-style bathrooms). The three- to five-course fixed-price seasonal menu is freestyle, so whether you want a sampling of appetizers or a flight of meat courses, you need only ask. I am a devoted fan of his trademark buttery-smooth glazed oysters with lettuce cream, salsify, and Osetra caviar; seared foie gras, which may be accompanied by peaches, caramelized onions, and *verjus* (a classic French sauce); horseradish-crusted salmon medallions with dilled cucumbers; and adventurous Moroccan spiced squab with *chermoula* (a Moroccan sauce made with cilantro) and orange-cumin carrots. Truthfully, I've never had a dish here that wasn't wonderful. And wine? The list is stellar, albeit expensive. If after dinner you have the will to pass on the glorious cheese cart or flambéed dessert of the day, a plate of petit fours reminds you that Gary Danko is one sweet and memorable meal. ***Tip:*** If you can't get a reservation and are set on dining here, slip in and grab a seat at the 10-stool first-come, first-served bar where you can also order a la carte.

800 North Point St. (at Hyde St.). ✆ **415/749-2060**. www.garydanko.com. Reservations required except at walk-in bar. 3- to 5-course fixed-price menu $61–$89. AE, DC, DISC, MC, V. Daily 5:30–10pm; bar open 5pm. Valet parking $10. Bus: 10. Streetcar: F. Cable car: Hyde.

Scoma's ★ SEAFOOD A throwback to the dining of yesteryear, Scoma's eschews trendier trout preparations and fancy digs for good old-fashioned seafood served in huge portions amid a very casual windowed waterfront setting. Gourmands should skip this one. But if your idea of heaven is straightforward seafood classics—fried calamari, raw oysters, pesto pasta with rock shrimp, crab cioppino, lobster thermidor—served with a generous portion of old-time hospitality, then Scoma's is as good as it gets. Unfortunately, a taste of tradition will cost you big time. Prices are as steep as those at some of the finest restaurants in town. Personally, I'd rather splurge at Gary Danko or A. Sabella's. But many of my out-of-town guests insist we meet at Scoma's, which is fine by me since it's a change of pace from today's chic spots, and the parking's free.

Pier 47 and Al Scoma Way (between Jefferson and Jones sts.). ✆ **800/644-5852** or 415/771-4383. www.scomas.com. Reservations not accepted. Most main courses $18–$35. AE, DC, DISC, MC, V. Mon–Thurs 11:30am–10pm; Fri–Sat 11:30am–10:30pm; Sun 11:30am–10pm; bar opens 30 min. prior to lunch daily. Free valet parking. Bus: 10 or 47. Streetcar: F.

EXPENSIVE

Alioto's SEAFOOD One of San Francisco's oldest restaurants, run by one of the city's most prominent families, the Aliotos, this Fisherman's Wharf landmark has a long-standing reputation for great cioppino. The curbside crab stand, Café 8, and the outdoor crab market are great for quick, inexpensive doses of San Francisco's finest. For more formal surroundings, continue up the stairs to the multilevel, harbor-view dining room. Don't mess around with the menu: If you're here, you're after Dungeness crab. Cracked, caked, stuffed, or stewed, it's impossible to get your fill, so bring plenty of money—particularly if you intend to order from Alioto's prodigious (and pricey) wine list. If you don't care for cracked crab, try the griddle-fried sand dabs or the rex sole served with tartar sauce.

Fisherman's Wharf (at Taylor St.). ✆ **415/673-0183**. www.aliotos.com. Reservations recommended. Main courses $15–$30 lunch; most main courses $20–$35 dinner. AE, DC, DISC, MC, V. Daily 11am–11pm. Bus: 10, 15, 39, or 47. Streetcar: F. Cable car: Powell–Hyde line.

Ana Mandara ★ VIETNAMESE Yes, Don Johnson is part owner. But more important, this Fisherman's Wharf favorite serves fine Vietnamese food in an outstandingly beautiful setting. Amid a shuttered room with mood lighting, palm trees, and Vietnamese-inspired decor, diners (mostly tourists) splurge on crispy rolls, lobster ravioli with mango and coconut sauce, and wok-charred tournedos of beef tenderloin with sweet onions and peppercress. There is no more expensive Vietnamese dining room in town, but, along with the enjoyable fare, diners pay for the atmosphere, which, if they're in the neighborhood and want something more exotic than the standby seafood dinner, is worth the price.

891 Beach St. (at Polk St.). ✆ **415/771-6800.** www.anamandara.com. Reservations recommended. Main courses $19–$32. AE, DC, DISC, MC, V. Mon–Fri 11:30am–2pm; Sun–Thurs 5:30–9:30pm; Fri–Sat 5:30–10:30pm; bar until 1am. Valet parking Tues–Sun $9. Bus: 19, 30, or 45.

MODERATE

Cafe Pescatore ★ ITALIAN This cozy trattoria is one of the better bets in Fisherman's Wharf. Two walls of sliding glass doors offer pseudo-sidewalk seating when the weather's warm, although heavy vehicular traffic can detract from the alfresco experience. All the classics are well represented here: crisp Caesar salad; fried calamari; bruschetta; cioppino; pastas; chicken Marsala; and veal saltimbocca (sautéed veal scaloppini) with whipped baby potatoes, spinach, prosciutto and lemon-caper butter sauce. The consensus is to order anything that's cooked in the open kitchen's wood-fired oven, such as pizza (Margherita), roasts (sea bass with pine-nut crust, or Atlantic salmon), or panini (lunch only; grilled chicken or grilled veggies). They serve a darn good breakfast, too.

2455 Mason St. (at North Point St., adjoining the Tuscan Inn). ✆ **415/561-1111.** www.cafepescatore.com. Reservations recommended. Main courses $6.50–$12 breakfast, $9–$22 lunch and dinner. AE, DC, DISC, MC, V. Daily 7am–10pm. Bus: 15, 39, or 42. Streetcar: F. Cable car: Powell–Mason line.

Fog City Diner ★ AMERICAN The Fog City Diner gets a lot of mixed reviews among locals for service and food, but I've always had a satisfying experience dining here. The restaurant looks like a genuine American metallic diner—but only from the outside. Inside, dark polished woods, inspired lighting, and a well-stocked raw bar tell you this is no hash-slinger. Here dressed-up diner dishes include juicy gourmet burgers with house-made pickles, huge salads, "warm breads," soups, sandwiches, cioppino, macaroni and Gouda cheese, and pork chops. Fancier fish and meat meals include grilled catches of the day and thick-cut steaks. Light eaters can make a meal out of the long list of "small plates," which include crab cakes and quesadillas with asparagus and leek. They've recently opened for weekend brunch as well. The food is fine, but if your heart is set on coming here, do so at lunch or early evening cocktails and appetizers—you'll be better off elsewhere if you want a special dinner.

1300 Battery St. (at the Embarcadero.). ✆ **415/982-2000.** www.fogcitydiner.com. Reservations recommended. Main courses $11–$22. DC, DISC, MC, V. Mon–Thurs 11am–10pm; Fri 11am–11pm; Sat 10:30am–11pm; Sun 10:30am–10pm. Bus: 42.

Lou's Pier 47 STEAK/SEAFOOD/CAJUN This popular restaurant and blues club is one of the few establishments on Fisherman's Wharf that locals will admit they've been to at least once. The bottom floor consists of a bar and bistro-style dining room, while the upstairs hosts blues bands every night of the week, with the occasional Motown, country, and R&B act thrown in for variety. Lunch and dinner items range from a variety of Cajun classics such as gumbo ya ya, jambalaya, and shrimp Creole to baby back ribs, steamed Dungeness crab, blackened swordfish, and New York steak. There's a lengthy starters menu if you just want to nosh on a Jamaica jerk salad, Louisiana crawfish bowl, or "peel 'em and eat" shrimp. ***Budget tip:*** The Saturday blues show from noon to 3pm is free; otherwise, the upstairs club cover is $3 to $10.

300 Jefferson St. (near Pier 47). ✆ **415/771-5687.** www.louspier47.com. Main courses $11–$18. AE, DC, MC, V. Daily 11am–11pm (club remains open until 2am). Cable car: Powell-Hyde line. Bus: 32.

INEXPENSIVE

Boudin at the Wharf DELI/AMERICAN This industrial-chic Fisherman's Wharf shrine to the city's famous tangy French-style bread is impossible to miss. Even if you're not hungry, drop in to see bakers at work making 3,000 loaves daily or take the tour and learn about the city sourdough bread's history (Boudin is the city's oldest continually operating business). Good, strong coffee is served at **Peet's Coffee** (another Bay Area great), and at **Bakers Hall** you'll find picnic possibilities such as handcrafted cheeses, fruit spreads, and chocolates, as well as a wall map highlighting the town's best places to spread a blanket and feast. There's also a casual **self-serve cafe** serving sandwiches, clam chowder bowls, salads, and pastries, and the more formal **Bistro Boudin** restaurant, which offers Alcatraz views with its Dungeness crab Louis, pizza, crab cakes, and burgers on sourdough buns.

160 Jefferson St., near Pier 43½. ✆ **415/928-1849.** www.boudinbakery.com. Reservations recommended at bistro. Main courses cafe $6–$10, bistro $11–$33. AE, DC, DISC, MC, V. Cafe daily 8am–10pm; bistro Mon–Fri noon–10pm; Sat 11:30am–10pm; Sun 11:30am–9pm. Bus: 10, 15, or 47. Streetcar: F.

Hard Rock Cafe *Kids* AMERICAN I hate to plug chains, and this loud, rock-nostalgia-laden place would be no exception if it didn't serve a fine burger and overall decent heaping plates of food at such moderate prices. For many, the real draw—more than 20 years past the time when it was hip to wear the restaurant's logo—is the merchandise shop, but a shopper's gotta eat. The menu offers burgers, fajitas, baby back ribs, grilled fish, chicken, salads, and sandwiches, the munching of which tend to be muffled by blaring music. Although nothing unique to San Francisco, the Hard Rock is a fine place to bring the kids and grab a bite.

Pier 39. ✆ **415/956-2013.** www.hardrock.com. Reservations accepted for groups of 25 or more. Main courses $8–$23. AE, DC, DISC, MC, V. Sun–Thurs 11am–11pm; Fri–Sat 11am–midnight. Validated parking for 1 hr. during lunch and 2 hr. after 6pm at Pier 39 lot. Bus: 10, 15, or 47. Streetcar: F.

9 The Marina/Pacific Heights/Cow Hollow

For a map of restaurants in this section, see the "Dining around Town" map on p. 112.

VERY EXPENSIVE

Harris' ★★ STEAKHOUSE Every big city has a great steak restaurant, and in San Francisco it's Harris'—a comfortably elegant establishment where the seriously handsome and atmospheric wood-paneled dining room has high-backed booths, banquettes, high ceilings, hunting murals, stately waiters, a convivial bar scene with live jazz Thursday through Saturday, and even a meat counter for the carnivore on the go. Here, the point, of course, is steak, which can be seen hanging in a glass-windowed aging room off Pacific Avenue. They are cut thick—New York–style or T-bone—and are served with a baked potato and seasonal vegetables. You'll also find classic French onion soup, spinach and Caesar salads, and sides of delicious creamed spinach, sautéed shiitake mushrooms, or caramelized onions. Harris' also offers lamb chops, fresh fish, lobster, and occasionally venison, buffalo, and other seasonal game. Desserts, such as a sculptural beehive-like baked Alaska, are surprisingly good. If you're debating between this place and House of Prime Rib, consider that aside from specializing in aged meats, this place is more "upscale," while HOPR features prime rib and a classic old-school vibe.

2100 Van Ness Ave. (at Pacific Ave.). ✆ **415/673-1888.** www.harrisrestaurant.com. Reservations recommended. Most main courses $24–$42. AE, DC, DISC, MC, V. Mon–Thurs 5:30–9:30pm; Fri 5:30–10pm; Sat 5–10pm; Sun 5–9:30pm. Valet parking $10. Bus: 12, 47, or 49.

EXPENSIVE

Quince ★★ CALIFORNIA/ITALIAN Its discreet location in a quiet residential neighborhood hasn't stopped this tiny and predominantly white-hued restaurant from becoming one of the city's hardest reservations to get. With only 15 tables, diners are clamoring for a seat to savor the nightly changing Italian-inspired menu by Michael Tusk, who mastered the art of pasta while working at the East Bay's famed Chez Panisse and Oliveto restaurants. Regardless, it's worth the effort—especially if you love simple food that honors a few high-quality, organic ingredients. Dining divinity might start with a pillowy spring garlic soufflé or white asparagus with a lightly fried egg and brown butter, but it really hits heavenly notes with the pasta course, be it garganelli with English peas and prosciutto, tagliatelle with veal ragout and fava beans, or artichoke ravioli. Meat and fish selections don't fall short either, with delicately prepared mixed grill plates, tender Alaskan halibut with fava beans, and juicy lamb with fennel and olives. Desserts aren't quite as celestial, but the trio of citrus sorbets make for a light, pleasant finish to a wonderful meal.

1701 Octavia St. (at Bush St.). ✆ **415/775-8500.** www.quincerestaurant.com. Reservations required. Main courses $16–$29. AE, MC, V. Mon–Thurs 5:30–10pm; Fri–Sat 5–10pm. Valet parking $8. Bus: 1, 31, or 38.

MODERATE

Ace Wasabi's Rock 'n' Roll Sushi ★ JAPANESE/SUSHI What differentiates this Marina hot spot from the usual sushi spots around town are the unique combinations, the varied menu, and the young, hip atmosphere. The innovative rolls are a nice change for those bored with traditional styles, but don't worry if someone in your party isn't a raw fish fan: There are also plenty of non-seafood and cooked items on the menu. Don't miss the rainbow "Three Amigos" roll, or the "Flying Kamikaze" with spicy albacore tuna wrapped around asparagus and topped with ponzu and scallions. The service, like the surroundings, is jovial.

3339 Steiner St. (at Chestnut St.). ✆ **415/567-4903.** Reservations not accepted. Sushi $4–$14. AE, MC, V. Mon–Thurs 5:30–10:30pm; Fri–Sat 5:30–11pm; Sun 5–10pm. Bus: 30.

A16 ★★ ITALIAN This sleek, casual, and wonderfully lively spot is one of San Francisco's best and busiest restaurants, featuring Neapolitan-style pizza and cuisine from the region of Campania. Named after the motorway that traverses the region, the divided space boasts a wine and beer bar up front, a larger dining area and open kitchen in the back, and a wall of wines in between. But its secret weapon is the creative menu of outstanding appetizers, pizza, and entrees, which are orchestrated by chef Nate Appleman with the same perfection as they were by opening chef Christophe Hille. Even if you must hoard the insanely good braised pork shoulder to yourself, start by sharing roasted asparagus with walnut cream and pecorino tartuffo or artichoke and tuna conserva with grilled bread and chiles. Co-owner and wine director Shelley Lindgren guides diners through one of the city's most exciting wine lists, featuring 40 wines by the half-glass, glass, and carafe. Oddly enough, their desserts are consistently mediocre, but perhaps that will change by the time you visit.

2355 Chestnut St. (between Divisadero and Scott sts.). ✆ **415/771-2216.** www.a16sf.com. Reservations recommended. Main courses $8–$13 lunch, $14–$20 dinner. AE, DC, MC, V. Wed–Fri 11:30am–2:30pm; Sun–Thurs 5–10pm; Fri–Sat 5–11pm. Bus: 22, 30, or 30X.

Betelnut ★ SOUTHEAST ASIAN Although San Francisco is teeming with Asian restaurants, few offer the posh, fashionable dining environment of this restaurant on upscale Union Street. As the menu explains, the restaurant is themed after Pejui Wu, a traditional Asian beer house offering local brews and savory dishes. But with the bamboo paneling, red Formica countertops, and low-hanging lamps, the place feels less like an authentic harbor restaurant and more like a set out of *Shanghai Surprise.* Still, the atmosphere is en vogue, with dimly lit booths, ringside seating overlooking the bustling stir-fry chefs, sidewalk tables (weather permitting), and body-to-body flirting at the cramped but festive bar. Starters include sashimi and tasty salt-and-pepper whole gulf prawns; main courses offer wok-seared Mongolian beef and Singapore chile crab (seasonal). Whatever you do, order their heavenly signature dessert: a mouthwatering tapioca pudding with sweet red adzuki beans.

2030 Union St. (at Buchanan St.). ✆ **415/929-8855.** www.betelnutrestaurant.com. Reservations recommended. Main courses $9–$16. DC, DISC, MC, V. Sun–Thurs 11:30am–11pm; Fri–Sat 11:30am–midnight. Bus: 22, 41, or 45.

Chez Nous ★★ FRENCH Diners get crammed into the 40-seat dining area of this bright, cheery, small, and bustling dining room, but the eclectic tapas are so delicious and affordable, no one seems to care. Indeed, this friendly and fast-paced neighborhood haunt has become a blueprint for other restaurants that understand the allure of small plates. But Chez Nous stands out as more than a petite-portion trendsetter. The clincher is that most of its Mediterranean dishes taste so clean and fresh you can't wait to come back and dine here again. Start with the soup, whatever it is; don't skip tasty french fries with *harissa* (Tunisian hot sauce) aioli; savor the lamb chops with lavender sea salt; and save room for their famed dessert, the minicustard-cakelike *canneles de Bordeaux.*

1911 Fillmore St. (between Pine and Bush sts.). ✆ **415/441-8044.** Reservations accepted, but walk-ins welcome. Small dishes $5–$13. AE, MC, V. Daily 11:30am–3pm and 5:30–10pm (Fri–Sat until 11pm). Bus: 22, 41, or 45.

E'Angelo Restaurant ★ ITALIAN Back when I was barely making enough to cover my rent, I would often treat myself to a night out at E'Angelo. All the house specialties, pastas, and pizzas cost less than $19; the atmosphere is casual and fun; tables are cozy-cramped; and the Italian staff is friendly. For me, the combination made not only for a hearty meal, but for an opportunity to mingle with San Francisco: to live a little, eavesdrop on neighbors' conversations, and perhaps even run into local celebrities such as Robin Williams with his family. While years have passed, not much has changed at this traditional Italian hot spot: The place still won't take reservations or credit cards. It still serves decent portions of pastas, veal, lamb, chicken, and fish; a carafe of red or white wine for about 18 bucks (thrifty by-the-bottle prices, too); and one heck of a rich eggplant parmigiana. And unlike those at most of the neighboring restaurants, desserts are dirt-cheap.

2234 Chestnut St. (between Pierce and Scott sts.). ✆ **415/567-6164.** Reservations not accepted. Main courses $13–$19. No credit cards. Tues–Sun 5–10pm. Bus: 22, 30, or 30X.

Ella's ★★ AMERICAN/BREAKFAST Well known throughout town as the undisputed queen of breakfasts, this restaurant's acclaim means you're likely to wait in line up to an hour on weekends. But midweek and in the wee hours of morning, it's possible to slide onto a counter or table seat in the colorful split dining room and lose yourself in outstanding and generous servings of chicken hash, crisped to perfection and served with eggs any way you like them, with a side of fluffy buttermilk biscuits. Pancakes, omelets, and the short list of other breakfast essentials are equally revered. Alas, service can be woefully slow, but at least the busboys and -gals are quick to fill coffee cups. Come lunchtime, solid entrees like salads, chicken potpie, and grilled salmon with mashed potatoes remind you what's great about American cooking.

500 Presidio Ave. (at California St.). ✆ **415/441-5669.** www.ellassanfrancisco.com. Reservations accepted for lunch. Main courses $5.50–$10 breakfast, $6–$12 lunch. AE, DISC, MC, V. Mon–Fri 7am–3pm; Sat–Sun 8:30am–2pm. Bus: 1, 3, or 43.

Greens Restaurant ★★ VEGETARIAN In an old waterfront warehouse, with enormous windows overlooking the bridge, boats, and the bay, Greens is one of the most renowned vegetarian restaurants in the country. Executive chef Annie Somerville (author of *Fields of Greens*) cooks with the seasons, using produce from local organic farms. Within the quiet dining room, a weeknight dinner might feature such appetizers as mushroom soup with Asiago cheese and tarragon; or grilled portobello and endive salad. Entrees run the gamut from pizza with wilted escarole, red onions, lemon, Asiago, and Parmesan, to Vietnamese yellow curry or risotto with black trumpet mushrooms, leeks, savory spinach, white-truffle oil, Parmesan Reggiano, and thyme. Those interested in the whole shebang should make reservations for the $48 four-course dinner served on Saturday only. Lunch and brunch are equally fresh and tasty. The adjacent Greens To Go sells sandwiches, soups, salads, and pastries.

Building A, Fort Mason Center (enter Fort Mason opposite the Safeway at Buchanan and Marina sts.). ✆ **415/771-6222.** www.greensrestaurant.com. Reservations recommended. Main courses $9.50–$14 lunch, $15–$20 dinner, fixed-price dinner $48; Sun brunch $8–$14. AE, DISC, MC, V. Tues–Sat noon–2:30pm; Sun 10:30am–2pm; Mon–Sat 5:30–9pm. Greens To Go Mon–Thurs 8am–8pm; Fri–Sat 8am–5pm; Sun 9am–4pm. Parking in hourly lot $4 for up to 2½ hours. Bus: 28 or 30.

Isa ★★ FRENCH Luke Sung, who trained with some of the best French chefs in the city, has captured many locals' hearts by creating the kind of menu we foodies dream of: a smattering of small dishes, served a la carte family-style, that allow you to try numerous items in one sitting. It's a good thing the menu, considered "French tapas," offers small portions at reasonable prices. After all, it's asking a lot to make a diner choose between mushroom ragout with veal sweetbreads, seared foie gras with caramelized apples, potato-wrapped sea bass in brown butter, and rack of lamb. Here, a party of two can choose all of these plus one or two more and not be rolled out the door afterward. Adding to the allure is the warm boutique dining environment—70 seats scattered amid a small dining room in the front, and a large tented and heated patio out back that sets the mood with a warm yellow glow. Take a peek at the "kitchen," a shoebox of a cooking space, to appreciate Sung's accomplishments that much more. Cocktailers, take note: You'll only find beer, wine, and shoju cocktails (shoju is a smooth alcohol made from sweet potato that is used like vodka).

3324 Steiner St. (between Lombard and Chestnut sts.). ✆ **415/567-9588.** www.isarestaurant.com. Reservations recommended. Main courses $9–$16. MC, V. Mon–Thurs 5:30–10pm; Fri–Sat 5:30–10:30pm. Bus: 22, 28, 30, 30X, 43, or 76.

Pane e Vino ★ ITALIAN While the rest of the city tries to modernize their manicotti, this ultracasual Italian spot focuses on huge helpings of classics that are fine for the traditional diner, but not fabulous for the gourmand. That said, prices are reasonable, and the mostly Italian-accented staff is always smooth and efficient under pressure (you'll see). The menu offers a wide selection of appetizers, including a fine carpaccio, *vitello tonnato* (sliced roasted veal and capers in lemony tuna sauce), and the hugely popular chilled artichoke stuffed with bread and tomatoes and served with vinaigrette. The broad selection of pastas includes flavorful *penne putanesca* with tomatoes, capers, anchovies, garlic, and olives. Other specialties are grilled fish and meat dishes, including chicken breast marinated in lime juice and herbs. Top dessert picks are any of the Italian ice creams, panna cotta, and (but of course) creamy tiramisu.

1715 Union St. (between Gough and Octavia sts.). ✆ **415/346-2111.** www.paneevinotrattoria.com. Reservations highly recommended. Main courses $10–$24. AE, MC, V. Mon–Thurs 5–10pm; Fri–Sat 11:30am–10pm; Sun 5–9pm. No parking. Bus: 41 or 45.

PlumpJack Café ★ CALIFORNIA/FRENCH/MEDITERRANEAN Wildly popular among San Francisco's style-setters, this small, 55-seat Cow Hollow restaurant, with a hint of whimsical Shakespearean decor, is one of the neighborhood's most "in" places to dine—partly because the place was founded and is frequented by Mayor Gavin Newsom. A typical dinner may start with Sonoma foie gras sweetened with Khalas dates and sweet vermouth, local Delta asparagus with smoked ham hock rillette, poached and roasted guinea fowl with a side of caramelized endive and parsnips, and for dessert a bananas Foster with vanilla bean ice cream. The extraordinarily extensive California wine list—gleaned from the PlumpJack wine shop down the street—is sold at next to retail prices, with many wines available by the glass.

3127 Fillmore St. (between Filbert and Greenwich sts.). ✆ **415/563-4755.** www.plumpjack.com. Reservations recommended. Main courses $13–$16 lunch, $20–$34 dinner. AE, DC, DISC, MC, V. Mon–Fri 11:30am–2pm; daily 5:30–10pm. Valet parking $14 for 3 hr. after 6pm. Bus: 22, 41, or 45.

INEXPENSIVE

Andalé Taqueria ★ *Kids* *Value* MEXICAN Andalé (Spanish for "hurry up") offers *muy bueno* high-end fast food for the health-conscious and the just plain hungry. As the long menu explains, this small California chain prides itself on its fresh ingredients and low-cal options. Lard, preservatives, and canned items are eschewed; Andalé favors salad dressings made with double virgin olive oil, whole vegetarian beans (not refried), skinless chicken, salsas and *aguas frescas* made from fresh fruits and veggies, and mesquite-grilled meats. Add the location (on a sunny shopping stretch), sophisticated decor, full bar, and check-me-out patio seating (complete with corner fireplace), and it's no wonder that good-looking, fitness-fanatic Marina District residents consider this place home. Cafeteria-style service keeps prices low.

2150 Chestnut St. (between Steiner and Pierce sts.). ✆ **415/749-0506.** Reservations not accepted. Most dishes $4.25–$11. MC, V. Daily 10am–10pm. Bus: 22, 28, 30, 30X, 43, 76, or 82X.

Barney's Gourmet Hamburgers ★ *Kids* HAMBURGERS If you're on a perpetual quest for the best burger in America, a mandatory stop is Barney's Gourmet Hamburgers. Once you get past all the framed awards for the Bay Area's best burger, you're bombarded by a mind-boggling menu of beef, chicken, turkey, and vegetarian burgers to choose from, as well as sandwiches and salads. The ultimate combo is a humungous basket of fries (enough for a party of three), one-third-pound burger, and thick shake. Popular versions are the California Burger with jack cheese, bacon, Ortega chiles, and sour cream, or the Popeye Burger made with chicken, sautéed spinach, and feta cheese. Be sure to dine alfresco in the hidden courtyard in back.

3344 Steiner St. (between Chestnut and Lombard sts.). ✆ **415/563-0307.** www.barneyshamburgers.com. Main courses $5–$8. No credit cards. Mon–Thurs 11am–9:30pm; Fri–Sat 11am–10pm; Sun 11am–9pm. Bus: 22, 28, 30, 30X, 43, 76, or 82X.

The Grove ★ CAFE The Grove is the kind of place you go just to hang out and enjoy the fact that you're in San Francisco. That the heaping salads, lasagna, pasta, sandwiches, and daily specials are predictably good is an added bonus. I like coming here on weekday mornings for the easy-going vibe, strong coffee, and friendly, fast service. Inside you can sit at one of the dark wood tables on the scuffed hardwood floor and people-watch through the large open windows, but on sunny days the most coveted seats are along the sidewalk. It's the perfect place to read the newspaper, sip an enormous mug of coffee, and be glad you're not at work right now. A second Pacific Heights location is at 2016 Fillmore St. between California and Pine Sts (✆ **415/474-1419**).

2250 Chestnut St. (between Scott and Pierce sts.). ✆ **415/474-4843.** Most main courses $6–$7. MC, V. Mon–Fri 7am–11pm; Sat–Sun 8am–11pm. Bus: 22, 28, 30, 30X, 43, 76, or 82X.

Home Plate ★ *Finds* BREAKFAST Dollar for dollar, Home Plate just may be the best breakfast place in San Francisco. Many Marina residents kick off their hectic weekends by carbo-loading here on big piles of buttermilk pancakes and waffles smothered with fresh fruit, or hefty omelets stuffed with everything from apple wood–smoked ham to spinach. You'll always start off with a coveted plate of freshly baked scones, best eaten with a bit of butter and a dab of jam. Be sure to look over the daily specials scrawled on the little green chalkboard before you order. And as every fan of this tiny cafe knows, it's best to call ahead and ask to have your name put on the waiting list before you slide into Home Plate.

2274 Lombard St. (at Pierce St.). ✆ **415/922-HOME.** Main courses $3.95–$7. DC, DISC, MC, V. Daily 7am–4pm. Bus: 28, 30, 43, or 76.

Eliza's ★ *Value* CHINESE Despite the curiously colorful design of modern architecture, whimsy, and glass art, this perennially packed neighborhood haunt serves some of the freshest California-influenced Chinese food in town. Unlike comparable options, here the atmosphere (albeit unintentionally funky) and presentation parallel the food. The fantastically fresh soups, salads, seafood, pork, chicken, duck, and such specials as spicy eggplant are outstanding and are served on beautiful English and Japanese plates. (Get the sea bass with black-bean sauce and go straight to heaven!) I often come at midday and order the wonderful kung pao chicken lunch special (available weekdays only): a mixture of tender chicken, peanuts, chile peppers, subtly hot sauce, and perfectly crunchy vegetables. It's one of 32 main-course choices that come with rice and soup for around $6. The place is also jumping at night, so prepare to stand in line. A second location, in Potrero Hill at 1457 18th St. (✆ **415/648-9999**), is open Monday through Friday 11am to 3pm and daily 5 to 9pm.

2877 California St. (at Broderick St.). ✆ **415/621-4819.** Reservations accepted for parties of 4 or more. Main courses $5.30–$6.15 lunch, $7.15–$15 dinner. MC, V. Mon–Thurs 11am–3pm and 5–9:30pm; Fri 11am–3pm and 5–10pm; Sat 4:30–10pm; Sun 4:30–9pm. Bus: 1 or 24.

La Méditerranée ★ *Value* MEDITERRANEAN With an upscale-cafe ambience and quality food, La Méditerranée has long warranted its reputation as one of most appealing inexpensive restaurants on upper Fillmore. Here you'll find freshly prepared traditional Mediterranean food that's worlds apart from the Euro-eclectic fare many restaurants now call "Mediterranean." Baba ghanouj, tabbouleh, dolmas, and hummus start out the menu. My favorite dish here is the chicken Cilicia, a phyllo-dough dish that's hand-rolled and baked with cinnamony spices, almonds, chickpeas, and raisins. Also recommended are the zesty chicken pomegranate drumsticks on a bed of rice. Both come with green salad, potato salad, or soup for around $9.50. Ground lamb dishes, quiches, and Middle Eastern combo plates round out the affordable menu, and wine comes by the glass and in half- or full liters. A second location is at 288 Noe St., at Market Street (✆ **415/431-7210**).

2210 Fillmore St. (at Sacramento St.). ✆ **415/921-2956.** www.cafelamed.com. Main courses $7–$10 lunch, $8–$12 dinner. AE, MC, V. Sun–Thurs 11am–10pm; Fri–Sat 11am–11pm. Bus: 1, 3, or 22.

Mel's Drive-In ★ *Kids* AMERICAN Sure, it's contrived, touristy, and nowhere near healthy, but when you get that urge for a chocolate shake and banana cream pie at the stroke of midnight—or when you want to entertain the kids—no other place in the city comes through like Mel's Drive-In. Modeled after a classic 1950s diner, right down to the jukebox at each table, Mel's harkens back to the halcyon days when cholesterol and fried foods didn't jab your guilty conscience with every greasy, wonderful bite. Too bad the prices don't reflect the '50s; a burger with fries and a Coke costs about $12.

Another Mel's at 3355 Geary St., at Stanyan Street (✆ **415/387-2244**), is open from 6am to 1am Sunday through Thursday and 6am to 3am Friday and Saturday. Additional locations are: 1050 Van Ness (✆ **415/292-6357**), open Sunday through Thursday 6am to 3am and Friday through Sunday 6am to 4am; and 801 Mission St. (✆ **415/227-4477**), open Sunday through Wednesday 6am to 1am, Thursday 6am to 2am, and Friday and Saturday 24 hours.

2165 Lombard St. (at Fillmore St.). ✆ **415/921-3039.** www.melsdrive-in.com. Main courses $6.50–$12 breakfast, $7–$10 lunch, $8–$15 dinner. MC, V. Sun–Wed 6am–1am; Thurs 6am–2am; Fri–Sat 24 hr. Bus: 22, 30, or 43.

Pluto's ★ *Value* CALIFORNIA Catering to the Marina District's DINK (double income, no kids) crowd, Pluto's combines assembly-line efficiency with high quality. The result is cheap, fresh fare: huge salads with a dozen choices of toppings; oven-roasted poultry and grilled meats (the tri-tip is great); sandwiches; and a wide array of sides like crispy garlic potato rings, seasonal veggies, and barbecued chicken wings. Pluto's serves teas, sodas, bottled brews, and Napa wines as well as homemade desserts. The ordering system is bewildering to newcomers: Grab a checklist, and then hand it to the servers who check off your order and relay it to the cashier. Seating is limited during the rush, but the turnover is fairly fast. A second Inner Sunset location is at 627 Irving St., at Eighth Avenue (✆ **415/753-8867**).

3258 Scott St. (at Chestnut St.). ✆ **415/7-PLUTOS.** www.plutosfreshfood.com. Reservations not accepted. Main courses $3.50–$5.75. MC, V. Mon–Fri 11am–10pm; Sat–Sun 10:30am–10pm. Bus: 28, 30, or 76.

10 Japantown

MODERATE

Takara ★ JAPANESE/SUSHI When I'm in the mood for sushi, I often head to this unassuming restaurant tucked at the eastern end of Japantown. Not only is it large enough that you don't have to wait in a long line (unlike other local sushi spots), but the fish is extremely fresh and affordable and the other offerings are fantastic. Along with standard nigiri, I always go for the seaweed with fabulously tangy vinegar and a floating quail egg. But on the occasions that I can curb my sushi craving, I get more than my fill with their *yosenabe.* A meal for two that's under $20, it's a giant pot of soup brought to the table on a burner accompanied by a plate of fresh raw meat or seafood and vegetables. After you push the food into the liquid and briefly let it cook, you ladle it out and devour it. Even after serving two hungry people, there are always leftovers. Other favorites are anything with shrimp—pulled live from the tank—and sukiyaki, another tableside cooking experience. Bargain hunters should come for a lunch plate.

22 Peace Plaza no. 202 (in Japan Center Miyako Mall). ✆ **415/921-2000.** Reservations recommended. Main courses: $15–$23. MC, V. Daily lunch 11:30am–2:30pm; dinner 5:30–10pm.

11 Civic Center

For a map of restaurants in this section, see the "Dining around Town" map on p. 112.

VERY EXPENSIVE

Jardinière ★★ CALIFORNIA/FRENCH Jardinière is a pre- and post-symphony favorite, and it also happens to be the perfect setting for enjoying a cocktail with your significant other. A culinary dream team created the elegant dining room and sophisticated menu: owner-designer Pat Kuleto, who created the beautiful champagne-inspired decor, and owner-chef Traci Des Jardins, one of the city's most popular chefs. On most evenings the bi-level brick structure is abuzz with an older crowd (including ex-mayor Brown, a regular) who sip cocktails at the centerpiece mahogany bar or watch the scene discreetly from the circular balcony. The restaurant's champagne theme extends to twinkling lights and clever ice buckets built into the balcony railing, making the atmosphere conducive to splurging in the best of style—especially when live jazz is playing (at 7:30pm nightly). The daily changing menu might include seared scallops with truffled potatoes and truffle reduction; sautéed petrale sole with Alsatian cabbage and Riesling sauce; or venison with celery root, red wine, braised cabbage, and juniper sauce. There's also an outstanding cheese selection and superb wine list—many by the glass, and over 500 bottles.

300 Grove St. (at Franklin St.). ✆ **415/861-5555.** www.jardiniere.com. Reservations recommended. Main courses $26–$38; 6-course tasting menu $79. AE, DC, DISC, MC, V. Sun–Wed 5–10:30pm; Thurs–Sat 5–11:30pm. Valet parking $10. Bus: 19 or 21.

MODERATE

Absinthe ★ FRENCH This Hayes Valley hot spot is sexy, fun, reasonably priced, and frequented by everyone from the theatergoing crowd to the young and chic. Decor is all brasserie, with French rattan cafe chairs, copper-topped tables, a pressed-tin ceiling, soft lighting, period art, and a rich use of color and fabric, including leather and mohair banquettes. It's always a pleasure to unwind at the bar with a Ginger Rogers—gin, mint, lemon juice, ginger ale, and a squeeze of lime. The lengthy lunch menu offers everything from oysters and caviar to Caesar salad and a respectable burger, but I always end up getting the same thing: their outstanding open-faced smoked-trout sandwich on grilled Italian bread. In the divided dining room, main courses are equally satisfying, from coq au vin and steak frites to roasted whole Dungeness crab with poached leeks in mustard vinaigrette, salt roasted potatoes, and aioli. The best item on the weekend brunch menu is the creamy polenta with mascarpone, maple syrup, bananas, and toasted walnuts.

398 Hayes St. (at Gough St.). ✆ **415/551-1590.** www.absinthe.com. Reservations recommended. Brunch $8–$14; most main courses $12–$22 lunch, $18–$28 dinner. AE, DC, DISC, MC, V. Tues–Fri 11:30am–midnight (bar until 2am Fri); Sat 11am–midnight (bar until 2am); Sun 11am–10pm (bar until midnight). Valet parking (Tues–Sat after 5pm) $10. Bus: 21.

Hayes Street Grill ★ SEAFOOD For well over a decade, this small, no-nonsense seafood restaurant (owned and operated by revered food writer and chef Patricia

Finds Hidden Treasures

They're on the way to nowhere, but because they're among the city's most unique, it would be a crime to leave out these destination restaurants. If you're not familiar with the streets of San Francisco, be sure to call first to get directions; otherwise, you'll spend more time driving than dining.

Thanh Long ★, 4101 Judah St. (at 46th Ave.; ✆ **415/665-1146;** www.anfamily.com; streetcar: N), is an out-of-the-way Sunset District Vietnamese standout that, long after my mom started taking me here as a tot for excellent roasted crab and addictive garlic noodles, has remained a San Francisco secret. Since the owners, the An family, have become rather famous for their aforementioned signature dishes now that they're served in sister restaurants Crustacean Beverly Hills and S.F., suffice it to say the crab's out of the bag. But this location is still far enough on the outskirts of the city to keep it from becoming overcrowded. The restaurant is more visually pleasing than most Southeast Asian outposts (white tablecloths, tastefully exotic decor), but the extra glitz is reflected in the prices of luxury dishes (main courses run from $14–$34) such as charbroiled tiger prawns with those famed garlic noodles and steamed sea bass with scallions and ginger sauce. On the plus side, unlike the cheaper options around town, there's a full bar here, too, serving fun cocktails such as the Pineapple and Litchi vodka infusion. Reservations are recommended. Thanh Long is open Sunday and Tuesday through Thursday from 4:30 to 10pm, Friday and Saturday from 4:30 to 11pm, and is closed on Mondays.

The Ramp, 855 China Basin (at the end of Mariposa St.; ✆ **415/621-2378;** www.ramprestaurant.com; bus: 22 or 48), is an out-of-the-way mecca for seaside snacks, dancing, and drinking that's at its best when the sun is shining.

Unterman) has maintained a solid reputation among San Francisco's picky epicureans for its impeccably fresh and straightforwardly prepared fish. The concise menu offers a dozen appetizers—most of which are fresh and lively salads—a half-dozen grilled fish selections cooked to perfection and matched with your sauce of choice (Szechuan peanut, tomatillo salsa, herb-shallot butter), and a side of signature fries. Fancier seafood specials, which change with the seasons and range from mahimahi (with Vietnamese dipping sauce, baby spinach, roasted peanuts, and basmati rice) to classic paella, are balanced by a few meat-driven dishes, which may include Niman Ranch (organic and wonderful) flatiron steak with mustard butter and balsamic onions. Finish your meal with the outstanding crème brûlée.

320 Hayes St. (near Franklin St.). ✆ **415/863-5545.** www.hayesstreetgrill.com. Reservations recommended. Main courses $14–$20 lunch, $16–$23 dinner. AE, DISC, MC, V. Mon–Fri 11:30am–2pm; Mon–Thurs 5–9:30pm; Fri 5–10:30pm; Sat 5:30–10:30pm; Sun 5–8:30pm. Bus: 19, 21, 31, or 38.

Zuni Café ★★ *Finds* MEDITERRANEAN Zuni Café embodies the best of San Francisco dining: Its clientele spans young hipsters to hunky gays, the cuisine is consistently terrific, and the atmosphere is electric. Its expanse of windows overlooking

If you're lucky enough to be in San Francisco on one of those rare hot days, head to this bayside hangout. The fare is of the basic pub grub variety—burgers, sandwiches, salads, and soups from $8 to $13—but the rustic boatyard environment and patio seating make this a relaxing place to dine in the sun. In summer, the place really rocks when live bands perform (4:30–8:30pm Fri–Sun Apr–Oct) and tanned, cocktailing singles prowl the area. It's open for lunch Monday through Friday from 11am to 3:30pm, and for brunch Saturday and Sunday from 8:30am to 4pm. The bar is open until 9pm on weekdays and later on weekends. From April to October, an outdoor barbecue is offered Saturday and Sunday from 4 to 7:30pm.

Little Star Pizza ★★, 846 Divisadero St. (at McAllister St.; © **415/441-1118;** www.littlestarpizza.com; bus: 5 or 24), may be on a dreary strip of busy Divisadero Street and feel like a bohemian speak-easy with its dark colored walls, low ceilings, and jukebox, but this joint is cranking out the best pizza in town. You're likely to have to wait for a seat at one of the well-spaced tables and you may have to strain to chat over the music and dining din, but there's little I wouldn't endure for one of Little Star's deep dish cornmeal-crust pizzas ($11–$22). Rather than inches of dough, these pies are thin and crisp with high sides that coddle fillings such as chicken, tomatoes, artichoke hearts, red bell peppers, sausage, and feta. These babies take about 25 minutes to bake, which is a great excuse to order chicken wings and a glass of wine for the wait. The place serves dinner Sunday and Tuesday through Thursday from 5 to 10pm, Friday and Saturday from 5 to 11pm, and is closed on Mondays. ***Note:*** There's a second location in the Mission District at 400 Valencia St. at 15th St. (© **415/551-7827**).

Market Street gives the place a sense of space despite the fact that it's always packed. For the full effect, stand at the bustling, copper-topped bar and order a glass of wine and a few oysters from the oyster menu (a dozen or so varieties are on hand at all times). Then, because *of course* you made advance reservations, take your seat in the stylish exposed-brick two-level maze of little dining rooms or on the outdoor patio. Then do what we all do: Splurge on chef Judy Rodgers' Mediterranean-influenced menu. Although the ever-changing menu always includes meat (such as hanger steak), fish (grilled or braised on the kitchen's wood grill), and pasta (tagliatelle with nettles, applewood-smoked bacon, butter, and Parmesan), it's almost sinful not to order her brick-oven roasted chicken for two with Tuscan-style bread salad. I rarely pass up the polenta with mascarpone and a proper Caesar salad. But then again, if you're there for lunch or after 10pm, the hamburger on grilled rosemary focaccia bread is a strong contender for the city's best. Whatever you decide, be sure to order a stack of shoestring potatoes.

1658 Market St. (at Franklin St.). © **415/552-2522.** www.zunicafe.com. Reservations recommended. Main courses $10–$19 lunch, $15–$29 dinner. AE, MC, V. Tues–Sat 11:30am–midnight; Sun 11am–11pm. Valet parking $10. Bus: 6, 7, or 71. Streetcar: All Market St. streetcars.

INEXPENSIVE

Frjtz Fries ★ BELGIAN Although they serve great sandwiches and salads, this funky-artsy "Belgian fries, crepes, and DJ/Art teahouse" is best known for its addictively crisp french fries, piled high in a paper cone (how Euro) and served with a barrage of exotic dipping sauces such as chipotle rémoulade and balsamic mayo. I'm also a fan of their crepes—try the grilled rosemary chicken and Swiss cheese—their big, leafy salad, or the chunky focaccia sandwich packed with roasted peppers, red onions, pesto mayo, grilled eggplant, and melted Gorgonzola. Wash it down with creamy Chimay Belgian ale.

579 Hayes St. (at Laguna St.). ✆ **415/864-7654.** www.frjtzfries.com. Reservations not accepted. Fries $3–$4.50; crepes $5–$8; sandwiches $7–$8.25. AE, DC, DISC, MC, V. Mon–Thurs 9am–10pm; Fri 9am–midnight; Sat 10am–midnight; Sun 10am–9pm. Bus: 21.

Tommy's Joynt *Value* *Kids* AMERICAN With its colorful mural exterior, it's hard to miss Tommy's Joynt, a 58-year-old haven for cholesterol-be-damned hold-outs from America's halcyon days and a late-night favorite for those in search of a cheap and hearty meal. The restaurant's exterior is tame in comparison to the interior, which looks like a Buffalo Bill museum that imploded: a wild collage of stuffed birds, a mounted buffalo head, an ancient piano, rusty firearms, fading prints, a beer-guzzling lion, and Santa Claus masks. The hofbrau-style buffet offers a cornucopia of rib-clinging a la carte dishes such as their signature buffalo stew (via a buffalo ranch in Wyoming), which resides under heat lamps among the stainless steel trays of turkeys, hams, sloppy Joes, oxtails, corned beef, meatballs, mashed potatoes, and other classics. There's also a slew of seating on two levels, almost 100 varieties of beer, and a most interesting clientele of almost exclusively 50-something pre-cardiac-arrest males (some of whom have been coming to the "Joynt" for more than 40 years). It's all good stuff in a 'merican kind of way, the kind of place you take Grandpappy when he's in town just to show him that San Francisco's not entirely sissy.

1101 Geary Blvd. (at Van Ness Ave.). ✆ **415/775-4216.** www.tommysjoynt.com. Reservations not accepted. Main courses $4–$7. No credit cards. Daily 10am–2am. Bus: 2, 3, 4, or 38.

12 Mission District

For a map of restaurants in this section, see the "Dining around Town" map on p. 112.

MODERATE

Delfina ★★ ITALIAN Unpretentious warehouse-chic atmosphere, reasonable prices, and chef/co-owner Craig Stoll's superb seasonal Italian cuisine have made this family-owned restaurant one of the city's most cherished. Stoll, who was one of *Food & Wine*'s Best New Chefs in 2001 and a 2005 James Beard Award nominee, changes the menu daily, while his wife Annie works the front of the house (when she's not being a mom). Standards include Niman Ranch flatiron steak with french fries, and roasted chicken with Yukon Gold mashed potatoes and royal trumpet mushrooms. The winter menu might include slow-roasted pork shoulder or gnocchi with squash and chestnuts, while spring indulgences can include sand dabs with frisée, fingerling potatoes, and lemon-caper butter; or lamb with polenta and sweet peas. Trust me—order the buttermilk *panna cotta* (custard) if it's available. ***A plus:*** A few tables and counter seating are reserved for walk-in diners. Delfina also has a heated and covered patio that's used mid-March through November.

3621 18th St. (between Dolores and Guerrero sts.). ✆ **415/552-4055.** www.delfinasf.com. Reservations recommended. Main courses $13–$22. MC, V. Mon–Thurs 5:30–10pm; Fri–Sat 5:30–11pm; Sun 5:30–10pm. Parking lot at 18th and Valencia sts, $8. Bus: 26 or 33. Streetcar: J.

Foreign Cinema ★★ MEDITERRANEAN This place is so chic and well-hidden that it eludes me every time I drive past it on Mission Street (***hint:*** look for the valet stand). The "cinema" here is a bit of a gimmick: It's an outdoor dining area (partially covered and heated, but still chilly) where mostly foreign films are projected onto the side of an adjoining building without any audio. What's definitely not a gimmick, however, is the superb Mediterranean-inspired menu created by husband-and-wife team John Clark and Gayle Pirie. Snackers like me find solace at the oyster bar with a half-dozen locally harvested Miyagi oysters and a devilishly good *brandade* (fish purée) gratin. Heartier eaters can opt for grilled halibut with chanterelles and roasted figs in a fig vinaigrette; fried Madras curry-spiced chicken with gypsy peppers; or grilled natural rib-eye with Tuscan-style beans and rosemary-fried peppercorn sauce—all made from seasonal, sustainably farmed, organic ingredients when possible. Truth be told, even if the food weren't so good, I'd still come here—it's just that cool. If you have to wait for your table, consider stepping into their adjoining bar, Laszlo.

2534 Mission St. (between 21st and 22nd sts.). ✆ **415/648-7600.** www.foreigncinema.com. Reservations recommended. Main courses $17–$26. AE, MC, V. Mon–Thurs 6–10pm; Fri–Sat 6–11pm; Sun 5–10pm; brunch Sat–Sun 11am–3pm. Valet parking $10. Bus: 14, 14L, or 49.

Pauline's ★ PIZZA Housed in a cheery yellow double-decker building that stands out like a beacon in a somewhat seedy neighborhood, Pauline's does only three things—pizzas, salads, and desserts—but it does them better than most restaurants in the city. Running the gauntlet of panhandlers for a slice of Louisiana Andouille pizza topped with Andouille sausage, bell peppers, and fontina cheese is completely worth it. Other gourmet toppings include house-made chicken sausage, French goat cheese, roasted eggplant, Danish fontina cheese, and *tasso* (spiced pork shoulder). The salads are equally amazing: certified organic, handpicked by California growers, and topped with fresh and dried herbs (including edible flowers) from Pauline's own gardens in Berkeley. Don't forget to leave room for the house-made ice cream and sorbets or chocolate mousse and butterscotch pudding. The wine list offers a smart selection of low-priced wines, where Star Canyon Vineyards, yet another of the owners' pursuits, is showcased. Yes, prices are a bit steep (small pizzas start at $14), but what a paltry price to pay for perfection.

260 Valencia St. (between 14th St. and Duboce Ave.). ✆ **415/552-2050.** www.paulinespizza.com. Reservations accepted for parties of 8 or more. Pizzas $12–$25. MC, V. Tues–Sat 5–10pm. Bus: 14, 26, or 49.

INEXPENSIVE

Taquerias La Cumbre MEXICAN If San Francisco commissioned a flag honoring its favorite food, we'd probably all be waving a banner of the Golden Gate Bridge bolstering a giant burrito—that's how much we love the mammoth tortilla-wrapped meals. Taquerias La Cumbre has been around forever and still retains its "Best Burrito" title, each deftly constructed using fresh pork, steak, chicken, or vegetables, plus cheese, beans, rice, salsa, and maybe a dash of guacamole or sour cream. The fact that it's served in a cafeteria-like brick-lined room with overly shellacked tables featuring a woman with overflowing cleavage makes it taste even better.

515 Valencia St. (between 16th and 17th sts.). ✆ **415/863-8205.** Reservations not accepted. Tacos and burritos $3.50–$6.50; dinner plates $5–$7. No credit cards. Mon–Sat 11am–9pm; Sun noon–9pm. Bus: 14, 22, 33, 49, or 53. BART: Mission.

Ti Couz ★ CREPES At Ti Couz (pronounced "Tee Cooz"), one of the most architecturally stylish and popular restaurants in the Mission, the headliner is simple: the delicate, paper-thin crepe. More than 30 choices of fillings make for infinite expertly executed combinations. The menu advises you how to enjoy these wraps: Order a light crepe as an appetizer, a heftier one as a main course, and a drippingly sweet one for dessert. Recommended combinations are listed, but you can build your own from the 15 main-course selections (such as smoked salmon, mushrooms, sausage, ham, scallops, and onions) and over 15 dessert options (caramel, fruit, chocolate, Nutella, and more). Soups and salads are equally stellar; the seafood salad, for example, is a delicious and generous compilation of shrimp, scallops, and ahi tuna with veggies and five kinds of lettuce.

3108 16th St. (at Valencia St.). ✆ **415/252-7373.** Reservations not accepted. Crepes $2–$12. MC, V. Mon and Fri 11am–11pm; Tues–Thurs 5–10pm; Sat–Sun 10am–11pm. Bus: 14, 22, 26, 33, 49, or 53. BART: 16th or Mission.

13 The Castro

For a map of restaurants in this section, see the "Dining around Town" map on p. 112.

EXPENSIVE

Mecca ★ NEW AMERICAN In 1996, Mecca entered the San Francisco dining scene in a decadent swirl of chocolate-brown velvet, stainless steel, cement, and brown leather. It's an industrial-chic supper club that makes you want to order a martini just so you'll match the ambience. The eclectic city clientele (with a heavy dash of same-sex couples) mingles at the oval centerpiece bar. A night here promises a live DJ spinning hot grooves, and a globally inspired New American meal prepared by chef Randy Lewis and served at tables tucked into several nooks. Lewis's menu items are as varied and interesting as his clientele: Moroccan-spiced lamb meatballs; "Last-Night's-Red-Wine-by-the-Glass Braised Short Ribs"; pan-seared Scottish salmon served with gnocchi, mustard seed vinaigrette, and pecan-apple relish; and a wickedly good Angus cheeseburger with tomato marmalade and garlic aioli on a brioche bun. When the place is jumping on a weekend night it's a great opportunity for tourists to experience an only-in-San Francisco vibe.

2029 Market St. (by 14th and Church sts.). ✆ **415/621-7000.** www.sfmecca.com. Reservations recommended. Main courses $22–$34. AE, DC, MC, V. Tues–Thurs 5–10pm; Fri–Sat 5pm–midnight; Sun 4–10pm. Valet parking $10. Bus: 8, 22, 24, or 37. Streetcar: F, K, L, or M.

MODERATE

2223 Restaurant & Bar ★ CALIFORNIA Surrounded by hardwood floors, candles, streamlined modern light fixtures, and loud music, a festive mixed crowd comes here for heavy-handed specialty drinks, grilled pork chops, the ever-popular roasted chicken with roasted potatoes, and sour cherry bread pudding. Along with Mecca (see above), this is one of the hottest dining and schmoozing spots in the area—and definitely one of the better Sunday brunch spots.

2223 Market St. (between Sanchez and Noe sts.). ✆ **415/431-0692.** www.2223restaurant.com. Reservations recommended. Main courses $4.75–$11 brunch, $9–$20 dinner. AE, DC, MC, V. Sun–Thurs 5:30–9:30pm; Fri–Sat 5:30–11pm; Sun brunch 10:30am–2:30pm. Bus: 8, 22, 24, or 37. Streetcar: F, K, L, or M.

INEXPENSIVE

Café Flore *Value* CALIFORNIA Because of its large and lively patio overlooking a busy section of Market Street intersection, Café Flore is the top sunny-day meet-me-for-coffee spot within the Castro community. And boy is the people-watching good here—leather-wrapped bears, drag queens, trannies (Dad, is that you?), gym bunnies, and other anti-establishment types saunter down Market Street in full glory. As for dining at the cafe, here's how it works: You order drinks and desserts inside at the bar, then find a seat indoors or outside on the patio or sidewalk and claim a spot. Next, go to the kitchen counter (there are no waiters), place your meal order and get a number, and the food will be delivered to your table. Many of the menu items are composed of mostly organic ingredients, and include a succulent version of roasted chicken over rice, Niman Ranch hamburgers, soups, salads, and pastas. Breeders are always welcome as long as they behave, and breakfast is served until 3pm.

2298 Market St. (at Noe St.). ✆ **415/621-8579.** Reservations not accepted. American breakfast $5.95; main courses $4.50–$10. MC, V. Sun–Thurs 7am–11:30pm; Fri–Sat 7am–midnight. Metro: F.

Chow ★ *Value* AMERICAN Chow claims to serve American cuisine, but the management must be thinking of today's America, because the menu is not exactly meatloaf and apple pie. And that's just fine for eclectic and cost-conscious diners. After all, what's not to like about starting with a Cobb salad before moving on to Thai-style noodles with steak, chicken, peanuts, and spicy lime-chile garlic broth, or cioppino? Better yet, everything except the fish of the day costs under $15, especially the budget-wise daily sandwich specials, which range from meatball with mozzarella (Sun) to grilled tuna with Asian-style slaw, pickled ginger, and a wasabi mayonnaise (Mon); both come with salad, soup, or fries. Although the food and prices alone would be a good argument for coming here, beer on tap, a great inexpensive wine selection, and the fun, tavernlike environment clinch the deal. A second location, **Park Chow,** is at 1240 Ninth Ave. (✆ **415/665-9912**). You can't make reservations unless you have a party of eight or more, but if you're headed their way, you can call ahead to place your name on the wait list (recommended).

215 Church St. (near Market St.). ✆ **415/552-2469.** Reservations not accepted. Main courses $7–$15. DISC, MC, V. Mon–Thurs 11am–11pm; Fri 11am–midnight; Sat 10am–midnight; Sun 10am–11pm; brunch served Sat–Sun 10–2:30pm. Bus: 8, 22, or 37. Streetcar: F, J, K, L, or M.

Firewood Café ★ *Value* AMERICAN/ITALIAN One of the sharpest rooms in the neighborhood, the colorful Firewood put its money in the essentials and eliminated extra overhead. There are no waiters or waitresses; everyone orders at the counter and then relaxes at the single family-style table, at one of the small tables facing the huge street-side windows, or in the cheery back dining room. Management didn't skimp on the cozy-chic atmosphere and inspired but limited menu: The fresh salads come with a choice of three "fixin's," ranging from caramelized onions to spiced walnuts, and three gourmet dressing options. Then there are the pastas—three tortellini selections, such as roasted chicken and mortadella—and gourmet pizzas. Or how about herb-roasted half or whole chicken ($8.25 or $15, respectively) with roasted new potatoes? Wines cost $4.95 to $5.95 by the glass and a reasonable $15 to $22 per bottle. Draft and bottled beers are also available, and desserts top off at $4.

4248 18th St. (at Diamond St.). ✆ **415/252-0999.** www.firewoodcafe.com. Main courses $7–$15. MC, V. Mon–Thurs 11am–11pm; Fri–Sat 11am–11pm; Sun 11am–10pm. Bus: 8, 33, 35, or 37. Streetcar: F, K, L, or M.

14 Haight-Ashbury

For a map of restaurants in this section, see the "Dining around Town" map on p. 112.

MODERATE

RNM ★ AMERICAN Lower Haight is hardly known for glamour, and that's just what makes this hip little restaurant such a pleasant surprise. Beyond the full-length silver mesh curtain is a glitzy dual-level dining room that looks like it belongs in New York City rather than this funky 'hood. Warmly lit with dark-wood floors and tables, a cool full bar, and lounge mezzanine, it's a pleasant setting for an Italian- and French-inspired American meal by chef Justine Miner, who sharpened her culinary skills and knives at San Francisco's Postrio, Café Kati, and Globe. Start with appetizers such as ahi tuna tartare with waffle chips, quail egg, and microgreens; the charcuterie plate; and caramelized onion and wild-mushroom pizza with fontina cheese and truffle oil. Entrees range from porcini-crusted day boat scallops on a purée of artichokes, to pan roasted rib-eye steak with pancetta-wrapped red Irish potatoes and shaved black Himalayan truffles. It's not a destination restaurant, but if you're in the area or want to go off the beaten dining path, this is a good choice. ***Tip:*** A $28 prix fixe menu is offered daily from 5:30 to 7pm.

598 Haight St. (at Steiner St.). ✆ **415/551-7900.** www.rnmrestaurant.com. Reservations recommended. Small plates and pizza $7–$14; main courses $12–$22. AE, MC, V. Tues–Thurs 5:30–10pm; Fri–Sat 5:30–11pm. Valet Thurs–Sat. Closed Sun–Mon. Bus: 7 or 22.

INEXPENSIVE

Cha Cha Cha ★★ *Value* CARIBBEAN This is one of my all-time favorite places to get festive, but it's not for everybody. Dining at Cha Cha Cha is not about a meal, it's about an experience. Put your name on the waiting list, crowd into the minuscule bar, and sip sangria while you wait. When you do get seated (it can take up to two pitchers of sangria, but by then you really don't care), you'll dine in a loud—and I mean *loud*—dining room with Santería altars, banana trees, and plastic tropical-themed tablecloths. The best thing to do is order from the tapas menu and share the dishes family-style. Fried calamari, fried new potatoes, Cajun shrimp, and mussels in saffron broth are all bursting with flavor and accompanied by luscious sauces—whatever you choose, you can't go wrong. This is the kind of place where you take friends in a partying mood and make an evening of it. If you want the flavor without the festivities, come during lunch. Their second, larger location, in the Mission District, at 2327 Mission St., between 19th and 20th streets (✆ **415/648-0504**), is open for dinner only and has a full bar specializing in mojitos.

1801 Haight St. (at Shrader St.). ✆ **415/386-7670.** www.cha3.com. Reservations not accepted. Tapas $5–$9; main courses $12–$15. MC, V. Daily 11:30am–4pm; Sun–Thurs 5–11pm; Fri–Sat 5–11:30pm. Bus: 6, 7, or 71. Streetcar: N.

Citrus Club ★ NOODLES When you're a starving writer you quickly discover that the cheapest, healthiest, and most satisfying things to eat in San Francisco are burritos and noodles. Citrus Club does noodles. Large, heaping bowls of thick Asian noodles, served hot in bone-warming broth or cool, minty, and refreshing. In typical Upper Haight fashion, the Club has sort of a cheap-Polynesian-chic feel—love those Vietnamese straw hat lamps—a young, hip staff and clientele, and the omnipresent world beat rhythms. Most items on the menu are unlike anything you've seen before, so take my advice and walk around the two dining rooms to see what looks good before ordering. A refreshing starter is the citrus salad made with mixed greens, mint, fried noodles, and a tangy citrus vinaigrette. Popular cold noodle selections are the spicy lime and coconut, and the orange-mint. For hot noodles, try the marmalade shrimp or sweet chile-glazed tofu and greens. If you're in a party mood, order a sake margarita; otherwise, a big pot of ginger tea goes well with any of the noodle dishes.

1790 Haight St. (at Shrader St.). ✆ **415/387-6366.** Main courses $6–$10. MC, V. Mon–Thurs and Sun 11:30am–10pm; Fri–Sat 11:30am–11pm. Muni Metro: N. Bus: 6, 7, 66, 71, or 73.

Kan Zaman ★ *Finds* MIDDLE EASTERN An evening dining at Kan Zaman is one of those quintessential Haight-Ashbury experiences that you can't wait to tell your friends about back in Ohio. As you pass through glass-beaded curtains, you're led by the hostess to knee-high tables under a billowed canopy tent. Shoes removed, you sit cross-legged with your friends in cushioned comfort. The most adventurous of your group requests an *argeeleh,* a large hookah pipe filled with fruity honey or apricot tobacco. Reluctantly at first, everyone simultaneously sips the sweet smoke from the cobra-like tendrils emanating from the hookah, then dinner arrives—inexpensive platters offering a variety of classic Middle Eastern cuisine: smoky baba ghanouj, kibbe (cracked wheat with spiced lamb) meat pies, Casablanca beef couscous, spicy hummus with pita bread, succulent lamb and chicken kabobs. The spiced wine starts to take effect, just in time for the beautiful, sensuous belly dancers who glide across the dining room, mesmerizing the rapt audience with their seemingly impossible gyrations. The evening ends, the bill arrives: $17 each. Perfect. ***Note:*** Belly dancing starts at 9pm Thursday though Saturday only.

1793 Haight St. (at Shrader St.). ✆ **415/751-9656.** Main courses $4–$14. MC, V. Mon–Thurs 5pm–midnight; Fri 5pm–2am; Sat noon–2am; Sun noon–midnight. Metro: N. Bus: 6, 7, 66, 71, or 73.

Thep Phanom ★ THAI It's the combination of fresh ingredients, attractive decor, and friendly service, and that heavenly balance of salty, sweet, hot, and sour flavors, that have made Thep Phanom one of the city's most beloved Thai restaurants. Those who like to play it safe will be more than happy with standards such as pad Thai, coconut-lemon-grass soup, and prawns in red curry sauce, but consider diverting from the usual suspects for such house specialties as Thaitanic Beef (stir-fried beef and string beans in a spicy sauce), prawns with eggplant and crisped basil, and *ped sawan*—duck with a delicate honey sauce served over spinach. There's good people-watching here as well—the restaurant's reputation attracts a truly diverse San Francisco crowd. Be sure to make reservations or prepare for a long wait on weekend nights, and don't leave anything even remotely valuable in your car.

400 Waller St. (at Fillmore St.). ✆ **415/431-2526.** www.thepphanom.com. Reservations recommended. Main courses $9–$13. AE, DC, DISC, MC, V. Daily 5:30–10:30pm. Bus: 6, 7, 22, 66, or 71.

15 Richmond/Sunset Districts

Yes, it's a long haul from Downtown to "The Avenues," but these restaurants wouldn't be in the guidebook if they weren't worth the trip. For a map of restaurants in this section, see the "Dining around Town" map on p. 112.

MODERATE

Aziza ★★ MOROCCAN If you're looking for something really different—or a festive spot for a large party—head deep into the Avenues for an exotic taste of Morocco. Chef-owner Mourad Lahlou creates an excellent dining experience through colorful and distinctly Moroccan surroundings combined with a modern yet authentic take on the cuisine of his homeland. In any of the three opulently adorned dining rooms (the front room features private booths, the middle room is more formal, and the back has lower seating and a Moroccan lounge feel), you can indulge in the seasonal five-course tasting menu ($49) or individual treats such as kumquat-enriched lamb shank; saffron guinea hen with preserved lemon and olives; or Paine Farm squab with wild mushrooms, bitter greens, and a *ras el hanout* reduction (a traditional Moroccan blend of 40 or so spices). Consider finishing off with my favorite dessert (if it's in season): rhubarb galette with rose- and geranium-scented crème fraîche, vanilla aspic, and rhubarb consommé.

5800 Geary Blvd. (at 22nd Ave.). ✆ **415/752-2222.** www.aziza-sf.com. Reservations recommended. Main courses $10–$22; 5-course menu $39. MC, V. Wed–Mon 5:30–10:30pm. Valet parking $8 weekdays, $10 weekends. Bus: 29 or 38.

Beach Chalet Brewery & Restaurant ★ AMERICAN While Cliff House (see below) has more historical character and better ocean views, the Beach Chalet down the road has far better food, drinks, and atmosphere (ergo, it's where the locals go). The Chalet occupies the upper floor of a historic public lounge adorned with WPA frescos that originally opened in 1900 and has been fully restored. Dinner is pricey, and the ocean view disappears with the sun, so come for lunch or an early dinner when you can eat your hamburger, buttermilk fried calamari, or grilled Atlantic salmon with one of the best vistas around. It the evening it's a more local crowd, especially on Tuesday through Sunday evenings when live bands accompany the cocktails and house-brewed ales. Breakfast is served here as well. ***Note:*** Be careful getting into the parking lot (accessible only from the northbound side of the highway)—it's a quick, sandy turn.

In early 2004, owners Lara and Greg Truppelli added the adjoining **Park Chalet** restaurant to the Beach Chalet. The 3,000-square-foot glass-enclosed extension behind the original landmark building offers more casual fare—with entrees ranging from $11 to $23—including rib-eye steak, fish and chips, roasted chicken, and pizza. Other reasons to come? Retractable glass walls reveal Golden Gate Park's landmark Dutch windmill, a fireplace warms the room on chillier evenings, and live music is performed Tuesday and Thursday through Sunday evenings. Weather permitting, you can eat out back on the lawn; there's even a weekend barbecue from 11am to dusk in the summer. The restaurant opens at 11am daily in the summer (noon in winter) and, like the Beach Chalet, has varying closing times, so call ahead.

1000 Great Hwy. (at west end of Golden Gate Park, near Fulton St.). ✆ **415/386-8439.** www.beachchalet.com. Main courses $8–$17 breakfast, $11–$27 lunch/dinner. AE, MC, V. Beach Chalet: Breakfast Mon–Fri 9am–11am; lunch daily 11am–5pm; dinner Sun–Thurs 5–10pm, Fri–Sat 5–11pm; brunch Sat–Sun 9am–2pm. Park Chalet: Lunch Mon–Fri noon–9pm; dinner Sun–Thurs 5–9pm, Fri–Sat 5–11pm; brunch Sat–Sun 11am–2pm. Bus: 18, 31, or 38. Streetcar: N.

Cliff House ★ CALIFORNIA/SEAFOOD In the old days (we're talking way back), Cliff House was *the* place to go for a romantic night on the town. Nowadays, the revamped San Francisco landmark caters mostly to tourists who arrive to gander at the Sutro Baths remains next door or dine at the two remodeled restaurants. The more formal (and pricey) **Sutro's** has contemporary decor, spectacular panoramic views, and a fancy seafood-influenced American menu that showcases local ingredients. The food, while nothing revolutionary, is well prepared and features the likes of roasted organic beet salad; lobster and crab cakes with shaved fennel, romesco sauce, and caramelized Meyer lemon; and a mighty fine grilled lamb sirloin sandwich (at lunch). The same spectacular views in less dramatic but still beautiful surroundings can be found at the **Bistro,** which offers big salads, sandwiches, burgers, and other soul-satisfiers. For the most superb ocean views, come for sunset, so long as it looks like the fog will let up.

Alternatively, overindulge to the tune of live harp music at the Sunday champagne buffet in the **Terrace Room.** (Reserve well in advance; it's a popular event.)

1090 Point Lobos (at Merrie Way). ✆ **415/386-3330.** www.cliffhouse.com. Reservations accepted for Sutro's only. Bistro main courses $9–$26 breakfast/lunch, $13–$26 dinner; Sutro main courses $18–$25 lunch, $18–$30 dinner; 3-course prix-fixe $25 lunch and $35 dinner (Mon–Fri only). AE, DC, DISC, MC, V. Bistro: Mon–Sat 9am–9:30pm; Sat–Sun 9am–10pm. Sutro: daily 11:30am–3:30pm and 5–9:30pm; brunch Sun 10am–2pm. Bus: 18 or 38.

Khan Toke Thai House ★★ *Value* THAI Khan Toke Thai is so traditional you're asked to remove your shoes before being seated. Popular for special occasions, this Richmond District fixture is easily the prettiest Thai restaurant in the city; lavishly carved teak interiors evoke the ambience of a Thai temple. To start, I suggest ordering the *tom yam gong* soup of lemon grass, shrimp, mushroom, tomato, and cilantro. Follow with such well-flavored dishes as ground pork with fresh ginger, green onion, peanuts, and lemon juice; prawns with hot chiles, mint leaves, lime juice, lemon grass, and onions; or chicken with cashews, crispy chiles, and onions. For a real treat, have the deep-fried pompano topped with sautéed ginger, onions, peppers, pickled garlic, and yellow-bean sauce; or deep-fried red snapper with "three-flavors" sauce and basil leaves. A complete dinner, including appetizer, soup, salad, two main courses, dessert, and coffee, is a great value.

5937 Geary Blvd. (between 23rd and 24th aves.). ✆ **415/668-6654.** Reservations recommended Fri–Sat for parties of 3 or more. Main courses $6–$13; fixed-price dinner $20. AE, MC, V. Daily 5–10pm. Bus: 38.

INEXPENSIVE

Burma Superstar ★ *Value* BURMESE Despite its gratuitous name, this basic dining room garners two-star status by offering exceptional Burmese food at rock-bottom prices. Unfortunately, the allure of the tealeaf salad, Burmese-style curry with potato, and sweet-tangy sesame beef is one of the city's worst-kept secrets. Add to that a no-reservations policy and you can count on waiting in line for up to an hour. (FYI, parties of two are seated more quickly than larger groups, and it's less crowded at lunch.) On the bright side, you can pencil your cellphone number onto the waiting list and browse the Clement Street shops until you receive a call.

309 Clement St. (at Fourth Ave.). ✆ **415/387-2147.** www.burmasuperstar.com. Reservations not accepted. Main courses $8–$16. MC, V. Mon–Thurs 11am–3:30pm and 5:30–9:30pm; Fri–Sat 11am–3:30pm and 5:30–10pm; Sun 11am–3:30pm and 5:30–9:30pm. Bus: 2, 4, 38, or 44.

Ton Kiang ★★ CHINESE/DIM SUM Ton Kiang is the number one place in the city to have dim sum (served daily), only partially due to the fact that they make all their sauces, pickles, and other delicacies in-house The experience goes like this: Wait in line (which is out the door 11am–1:30pm on weekends), get a table on the first or second floor, and get ready to say yes to dozens of delicacies, which are brought to the table for your approval. From stuffed crab claws, roast Beijing duck, and a gazillion dumpling selections (including scallop and vegetable, shrimp, and beef) to the delicious and hard-to-find *doa miu* (snow pea sprouts flash-sautéed with garlic and peanut oil) and a mesmerizing mango pudding, every tray of morsels coming from the kitchen is an absolute delight. Though it's hard to get past the dim sum, which is served all day every day, the full menu of Hakka cuisine is worth investigation as well—fresh and flavorful soups; an array of seafood, beef, and chicken; and clay-pot specialties.

5821 Geary Blvd. (between 22nd and 23rd aves.). ✆ **415/387-8273.** www.tonkiang.net. Reservations accepted for parties of 8 or more. Dim sum $2–$5.50; main courses $9–$25. AE, DC, DISC, MC, V. Mon–Thurs 10am–10pm; Fri 10am–10:30pm; Sat 9:30am–10:30pm; Sun 9am–10pm. Bus: 38.

7

Exploring San Francisco

San Francisco's parks, museums, tours, and landmarks are favorites for travelers the world over and offer an array of activities to suit every visitor. But no particular activity or place makes the city one of the most popular destinations in the world. It's San Francisco itself—its charm, its atmosphere, its perfect blend of big metropolis with small-town hospitality. No matter what you do while you're here—whether you spend all your time in central areas like Union Square or North Beach, or explore the outer neighborhoods—you're bound to discover the reason millions of visitors keep leaving their hearts in San Francisco.

1 Famous San Francisco Sights

Alcatraz Island ★★★ *Kids* Visible from Fisherman's Wharf, Alcatraz Island (also known as The Rock) has seen a checkered history. Juan Manuel Ayala was the first European to discover it in 1775 and named it after the many pelicans that nested on the island. From the 1850s to 1933, when the army vacated the island, it served as a military post, protecting the bay's shoreline. In 1934, the government converted the buildings of the military outpost into a maximum-security prison. Given the sheer cliffs, treacherous tides and currents, and frigid water temperatures, it was believed to be a totally escape-proof prison. Among the famous gangsters who occupied cell blocks A through D were Al Capone, Robert Stroud, the so-called Birdman of Alcatraz (because he was an expert in ornithological diseases), Machine Gun Kelly, and Alvin Karpis. It cost a fortune to keep them imprisoned here because all supplies, including water, had to be shipped in. In 1963, after an apparent escape in which no bodies were recovered, the government closed the prison. In 1969, a group of Native Americans chartered a boat to the island to symbolically reclaim the island for the Indian people. They occupied the island until 1971, the longest occupation of a federal facility by Native Americans to this day, when they were forcibly removed by the U.S. government (see www.nps.gov/archive/alcatraz/indian.html for more information on the Native American occupation of Alcatraz). The next year the island became part of the Golden Gate National Recreation Area. The wildlife that was driven away during the military and prison years has begun to return—the black-crested night heron and other seabirds are nesting here again—and a trail passes through the island's nature areas. Tours, including an audio tour of the prison block and a slide show, are given by the park's rangers, who entertain guests with interesting anecdotes.

Allow about 2½ hours for the round-trip boat ride and the tour. Wear comfortable shoes (the National Park Service notes that there are a lot of hills to climb on the tour) and take a heavy sweater or windbreaker, because even when the sun's out, it's cold there. You should also bring snacks and drinks with you if you think you'll want them. Although there is a beverage-and-snack bar on the ferry, the options are limited and

Tips **Finding Your Way**

When asking for directions in San Francisco, be careful not to confuse numerical avenues with numerical streets. Numerical avenues (Third *Avenue* and so on) are in the Richmond and Sunset districts in the western part of the city. Numerical streets (Third *Street* and so on) are south of Market St. in the eastern and southern parts of the city. Get this wrong and you'll be an hour late for dinner.

expensive, and only water is available on the island. The excursion to Alcatraz is very popular and space is limited, so purchase tickets as far in advance as possible (up to 90 days) via the **Alcatraz Cruises** website at www.alcatrazcruises.com. You can also purchase tickets in person by visiting the Hornblower Alcatraz Landing ticket office at Pier 33. The first departure, called the "Early Bird," leaves at 9am, and ferries depart about every half-hour afterward until 2pm. Night tours (highly recommended) are also available Thursday through Monday and are a more intimate and wonderfully spooky experience.

For those who want to get a closer look at Alcatraz without going ashore, two boat-tour operators offer short circumnavigations of the island (see "Self-Guided & Organized Tours" on p. 184 for complete information).

Pier 41, near Fisherman's Wharf. ✆ **415/981-7625.** www.alcatrazcruises.com or www.nps.gov/alcatraz. Admission (includes ferry trip and audio tour) $22 adults; $20 seniors 62 and older; $14 children 5–11. Night tours cost $29 adults; $26 seniors 62 and older; $17 children 5–11. Arrive at least 20 min. before departure time.

AT&T Park ★★ *Moments* If you're a baseball fan, you'll definitely want to schedule a visit to the magnificent AT&T Park, home of the San Francisco Giants and hailed by the media as one of the finest ballparks in America. From April through October, a sell-out crowd of 40,800 fans pack the $319-million ballpark for nearly every game—which has a smaller, more intimate feel than Monster Park (where the 49ers play) and prime views of San Francisco Bay—and root for their National League Giants.

During the Major League season, tickets to the game are usually hard to come by (and expensive when you find them), but you can try to join the Bleacher Bums by purchasing one of the 500 bleacher-seat tickets sold every day before the game. They make you work for it, however: You have to show up at the ballpark 4 hours early to get a lottery number, then come back 2 hours before the game to get your tickets (maximum four per person). The upside is that the tickets are only $8.50 to $10.

If you can't even get bleacher sets, you can always join the "knothole gang" at the Portwalk (located behind right field) to catch a free glimpse of the game through cut-out portholes into the ballpark. In the spirit of sharing, Portwalk peekers are encouraged to take in only an inning or two before giving way to fellow fans.

One guaranteed way to get into the ballpark is to take a **guided tour of AT&T Park** and go behind the scenes where you'll see the press box, the dugout, the visitor's clubhouse, a luxury suite, and more. All tours run daily at 10:30am and 12:30pm. Ticket prices are $10 for adults, $8 for seniors over 55, and $6 for kids 12 and under. There are no tours on game days, and limited tours on the day of night games. To buy tickets online log onto www.sfgiants.com, then click on "SBC Park" and "Ballpark Tours" from the drop-down list. You can also buy tour tickets at any Giants Dugout Store or Tickets.com outlet. For more tour information call ✆ **415/972-2400.**

Major San Francisco Attractions

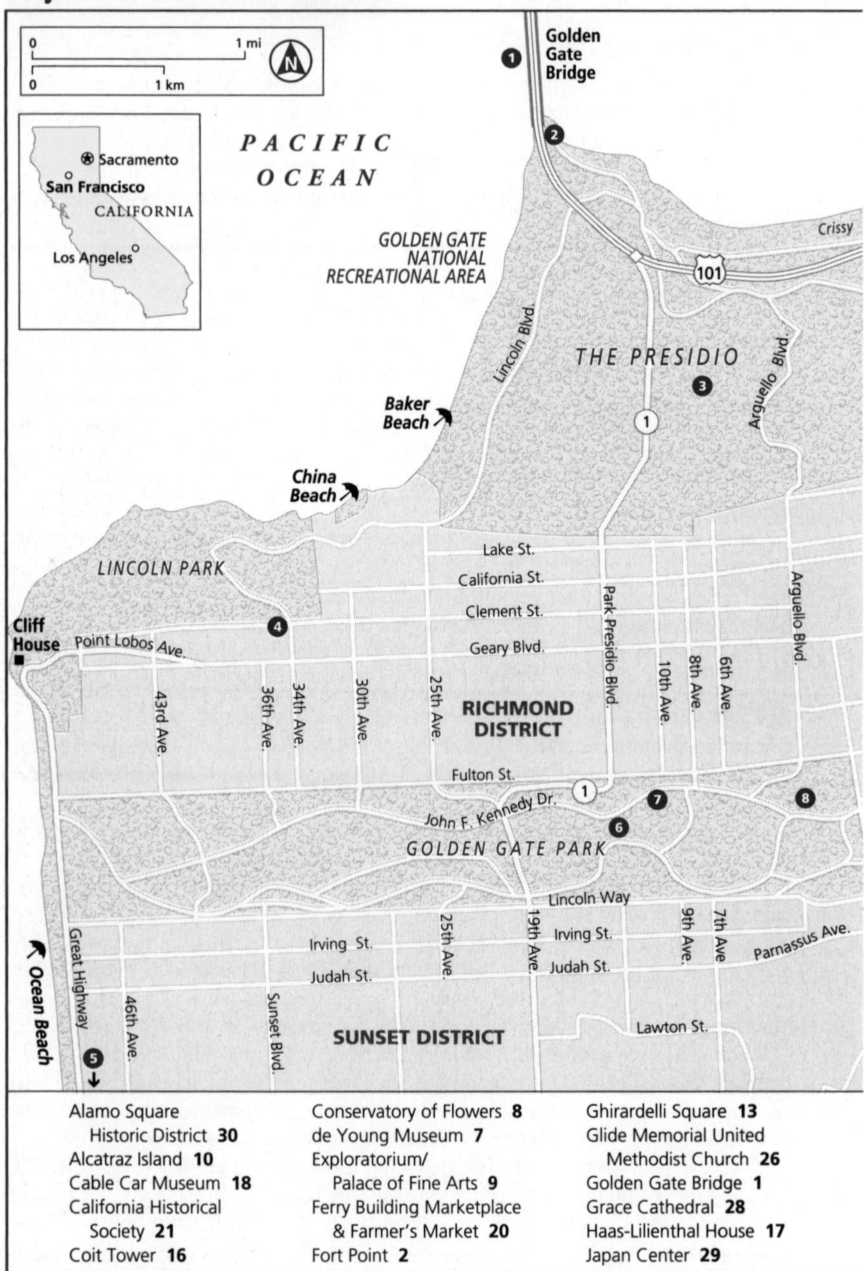

Alamo Square Historic District **30**
Alcatraz Island **10**
Cable Car Museum **18**
California Historical Society **21**
Coit Tower **16**
Conservatory of Flowers **8**
de Young Museum **7**
Exploratorium/ Palace of Fine Arts **9**
Ferry Building Marketplace & Farmer's Market **20**
Fort Point **2**
Ghirardelli Square **13**
Glide Memorial United Methodist Church **26**
Golden Gate Bridge **1**
Grace Cathedral **28**
Haas-Lilienthal House **17**
Japan Center **29**

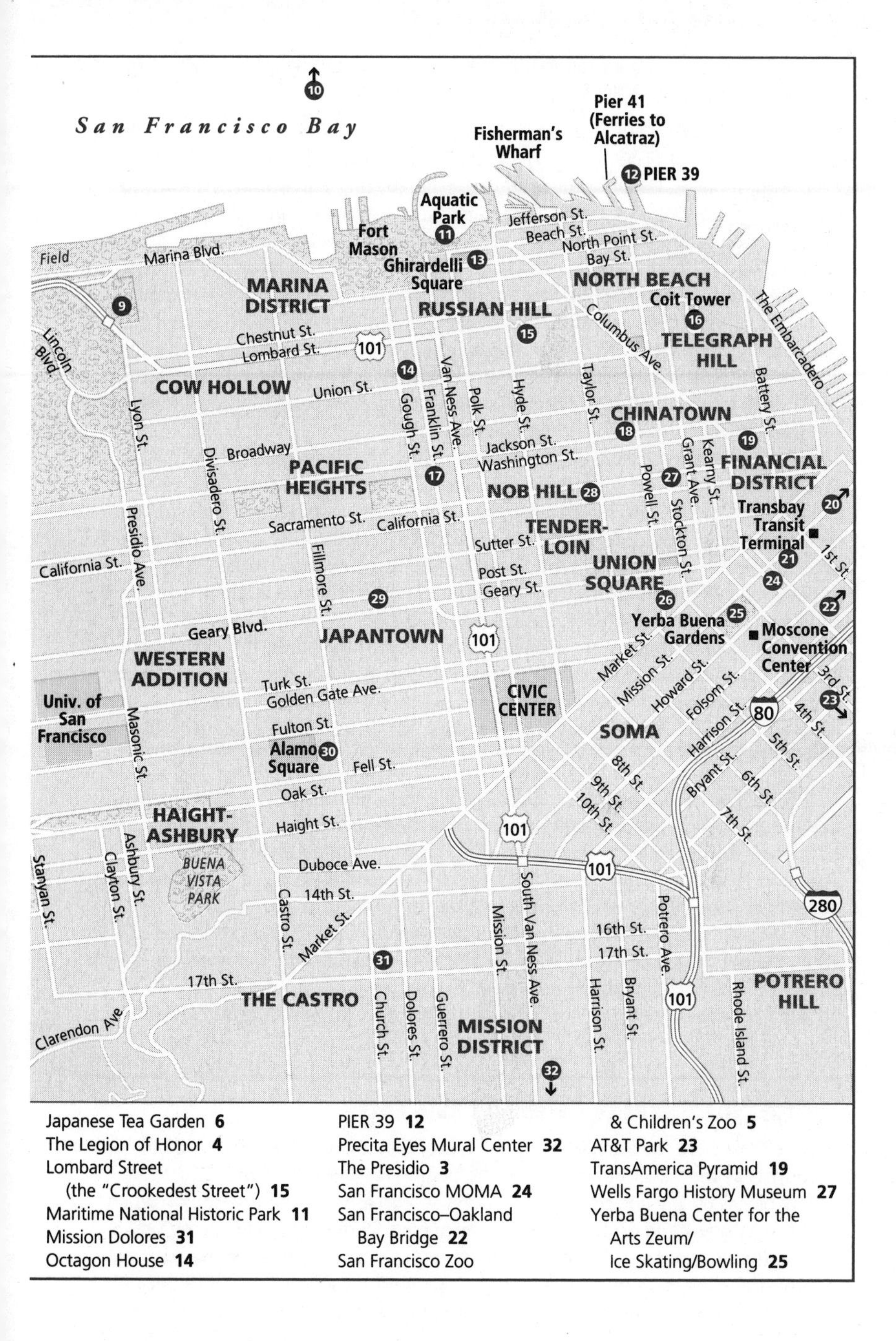
San Francisco Bay
10
Pier 41
(Ferries to
Alcatraz)
Fisherman's
Wharf
12 PIER 39
Aquatic
Park
11
Fort
Mason
Jefferson St.
Beach St.
North Point St.
Bay St.
Field
Marina Blvd.
Ghirardelli
Square
13
MARINA
DISTRICT
NORTH BEACH
Coit Tower
16
RUSSIAN HILL
9
Columbus Ave.
The Embarcadero
15
Chestnut St.
Lombard St.
101
TELEGRAPH
HILL
Lincoln
Blvd.
14
COW HOLLOW
Union St.
Van Ness Ave.
Franklin St.
Gough St.
Polk St.
Hyde St.
Taylor St.
Battery St.
CHINATOWN
18
Lyon St.
Broadway
19
Divisadero St.
PACIFIC
HEIGHTS
Jackson St.
Washington St.
Grant Ave.
Kearny St.
FINANCIAL
DISTRICT
17
27
Powell St.
NOB HILL
28
Stockton St.
Transbay
Transit
Terminal
20
Presidio Ave.
Sacramento St.
California St.
TENDER-
LOIN
Sutter St.
1st St.
21
California St.
Fillmore St.
Post St.
Geary St.
UNION
SQUARE
24
29
26
22
Yerba Buena
Gardens
25
Geary Blvd.
JAPANTOWN
101
Moscone
Convention
Center
WESTERN
ADDITION
Market St.
Mission St.
Howard St.
Folsom St.
3rd St.
Univ. of
San
Francisco
Turk St.
Golden Gate Ave.
CIVIC
CENTER
80
23
4th St.
Harrison St.
Masonic St.
Fulton St.
SOMA
Alamo
Square
30
Fell St.
8th St.
5th St.
Bryant St.
Oak St.
9th St.
6th St.
HAIGHT-
ASHBURY
10th St.
Haight St.
7th St.
101
Stanyan St.
Clayton St.
Ashbury St.
BUENA
VISTA
PARK
Duboce Ave.
101
14th St.
South Van Ness Ave.
Castro St.
Mission St.
280
Potrero Ave.
Market St.
16th St.
17th St.
31
17th St.
101
POTRERO
HILL
THE CASTRO
Church St.
Dolores St.
Guerrero St.
Harrison St.
Bryant St.
Rhode Island St.
Clarendon Ave.
MISSION
DISTRICT
32
Japanese Tea Garden 6
The Legion of Honor 4
Lombard Street
(the "Crookedest Street") 15
Maritime National Historic Park 11
Mission Dolores 31
Octagon House 14
PIER 39 12
Precita Eyes Mural Center 32
The Presidio 3
San Francisco MOMA 24
San Francisco–Oakland
Bay Bridge 22
San Francisco Zoo
& Children's Zoo 5
AT&T Park 23
TransAmerica Pyramid 19
Wells Fargo History Museum 27
Yerba Buena Center for the
Arts Zeum/
Ice Skating/Bowling 25

At the southeast corner of SoMa at the south end of the Embarcadero (bounded by King, 2nd, and 3rd sts.). ✆ **415/972-2000.** www.sfgiants.com. Metro: N line; Bus: 10, 15, 30, 45, and 47.

Boudin at the Wharf ★ After more than 30 years of being an inconspicuous bread shop in the heart of Fisherman's Wharf, the Boudin Bakery has been super-sized. The new, ultra-modern, 26,000-square-foot flagship baking emporium is nearly half a block long, housing not only their signature demonstration bakery but also a museum, gourmet marketplace, cafe, espresso bar, and restaurant. The Boudin (pronounced bo-DEEN) family has been baking sourdough French bread in San Francisco since the Gold Rush, using the same simple recipe and "mother dough" for more than 150 years. About 3,000 loaves a day are baked within the glass-walled bakery; visitors can watch the entire process from a 30-foot observation window along Jefferson Street or from a catwalk suspended directly over the bakery (it's quite entertaining, actually). You'll smell it before you see it, as the heavenly aroma emanating from the bread ovens is purposely blasted down onto the sidewalk.

The best time to arrive is in the morning when the demo bakery is in full swing. Watch (and smell) the action along Jefferson Street; then, when your appetite is stoked, head to the cafe for an inexpensive breakfast of sourdough French toast or their Bread Bowl Scrambler filled with eggs, bacon, cheddar, onions, and bell peppers. After breakfast, spend some time browsing the museum and marketplace. On the upper level is **Bistro Boudin,** a full-service restaurant serving lunch, dinner, and weekend brunch, and there's usually a jazz band playing on Friday and Saturday from 7 to 11pm. Tours of the bakery are available as well. ***Tip:*** If the line at the cafe is too long, walk across the parking lot to the octagon-shaped building, which serves the same items—Boudin chowder bowls, salads, pizzas—in a serve-yourself setting.

160 Jefferson St. (between Taylor and Mason sts.). ✆ **415/928-1849.** www.boudinbakery.com. Bakery/cafe/marketplace daily 10am–7pm.

Cable Cars ★★★ *Moments* *Kids* Although they may not be San Francisco's most practical means of transportation, cable cars are certainly the best loved and are a must-experience when visiting the city. Designated official historic landmarks by the National Park Service in 1964, they clank up and down the city's steep hills like mobile museum pieces, tirelessly hauling thousands of tourists each day to nowhere in particular.

London-born engineer Andrew Hallidie invented San Francisco's cable cars in 1869. He got the idea by serendipity. As the story goes, Hallidie was watching a team of overworked horses haul a heavily laden carriage up a steep San Francisco slope. As he watched, one horse slipped and the car rolled back, dragging the other tired beasts

---

Tips **The Secret to Catching Cable Cars**

Here's the secret to catching a ride on a cable car: Don't wait in line with all the tourists at the turnaround stops at the beginning and end of the lines. Walk a few blocks up the line (follow the tracks) and do as the locals do: Hop on when the car stops, hang on to a pole, and have your $5 ready to hand to the brakeman (hoping, of course, that he'll never ask). On a really busy weekend, however, the cable cars often don't stop to pick up passengers en route because they're full, so you might have to stand in line at the turnarounds.

Tips Earthquake Advice

Earthquakes are fairly common in California, though most are so minor you won't even notice them. However, in case of a significant shaker, there are a few basic precautionary measures to follow: If you are inside a building, do not run outside into falling debris. Seek cover—stand under a doorway or against a wall, and stay away from windows. If you exit a building after a substantial quake, use stairwells, not elevators. If you're in a car, pull over to the side of the road and stop—but not until you are away from bridges, overpasses, telephone poles, and power lines. Stay in your car. If you're out walking, stay outside and away from trees, power lines, and the sides of buildings. If you're in an area with tall buildings, find a doorway in which to stand. And if you're having cocktails find a straw.

with it. At that moment, Hallidie resolved that he would invent a mechanical contraption to replace such horses, and just 4 years later, in 1873, the first cable car made its maiden run from the top of Clay Street. Promptly ridiculed as "Hallidie's Folly," the cars were slow to gain acceptance. One early onlooker voiced the general opinion by exclaiming, "I don't believe it—the damned thing works!"

Even today, many visitors have difficulty believing that these vehicles, which have no engines, actually work. The cars, each weighing about 6 tons, run along a steel cable, enclosed under the street in a center rail. You can't see the cable unless you peer straight down into the crack, but you'll hear its characteristic clickity-clanking sound whenever you're nearby. The cars move when the gripper (not the driver) pulls back a lever that closes a pincerlike "grip" on the cable. The speed of the car, therefore, is determined by the speed of the cable, which is a constant 9½ mph—never more, never less.

The two types of cable cars in use hold a maximum of 90 and 100 passengers, and the limits are rigidly enforced. The best views are from the outer running boards, where you have to hold on tightly when taking curves.

Hallidie's cable cars have been imitated and used throughout the world, but all have been replaced by more efficient means of transportation. San Francisco planned to do so, too, but the proposal met with so much opposition that the cable cars' perpetuation was actually written into the city charter in 1955. The mandate cannot be revoked without the approval of a majority of the city's voters—a distant and doubtful prospect.

San Francisco's three existing cable car lines form the world's only surviving system of cable cars, which you can experience for yourself should you choose to wait in the often long boarding lines (up to a 2-hr. wait in summer). For more information on riding them, see "Getting Around," in chapter 4, p. 51.

Powell–Hyde and Powell–Mason lines begin at the base of Powell and Market sts.; California St. line begins at the foot of Market St. $5 per ride.

The Cannery The Cannery was built by Del Monte in 1907 as the world's largest fruit-canning plant. It was converted into a mall in the 1960s and now contains 30-plus shops and several restaurants, including **Jack's Cannery Bar** (**© 415/931-6400**), one of the few places in the city where you can sample Anchor Steam Brewery's "Old Foghorn Barleywine Style Ale" on draft (wickedly good). Vendors' stalls and sidewalk cafes occupy the courtyard amid a grove of century-old olive trees, and weather permitting, street

San Francisco Segway Tours

Segways are those weird-looking upright scooters you've probably seen on TV. The two-wheeled "human transporter" is an ingenious electric-powered transportation device that uses gyroscopes to emulate human balance. After the free 40-minute lesson, riding a Segway becomes intuitive: lean forward, go forward; lean back, go back; stand upright, stop. Simple. The **San Francisco Electric Tour Company** offers Segway-powered narrated 2-hour tours of the San Francisco waterfront daily, starting from Fisherman's Wharf and heading out all the way to the Marina Green. For $70 it's not a bad deal, and it's the closest you'll come to being a celebrity (*everyone* checks you out). ***Note:*** You have be at least 12 years old to join the tour. For more information log onto www.sfelectrictour.com or call ✆ **415/474-3130.**

performers are usually out in force, entertaining tourists (but very few locals). Shops are open daily at 10am and Sunday at 11am, while the restaurants generally open at 11:30am.

2801 Leavenworth St. (between Beach and Jefferson sts.). ✆ **415/771-3112.** www.thecannery.com. Bus: 30 or 47. Cable car: F-line to Hyde St.

Coit Tower ★★ In a city known for its great views and vantage points, Coit Tower is one of the best. Located atop Telegraph Hill, just east of North Beach, the round stone tower offers panoramic views of the city and the bay.

Completed in 1933, the tower is the legacy of Lillie Hitchcock Coit, a wealthy eccentric who left San Francisco a $125,000 bequest "for the purpose of adding beauty to the city I have always loved" and as a memorial to its volunteer firemen. She had been saved from a fire as a child and held the city's firefighters in particularly high esteem.

Inside the base of the tower are impressive murals titled *Life in California* and *1934,* which were completed under the WPA during the New Deal. They are the work of more than 25 artists, many of whom had studied under Mexican muralist Diego Rivera.

The only bummer: The narrow street leading to the tower is often clogged with tourist traffic. If you can, find a parking spot in North Beach and hoof it. It's actually a beautiful walk—especially if you take the Filbert Street Steps (p. 188).

Telegraph Hill. ✆ **415/362-0808.** Admission is free to enter; elevator ride to the top is $4.50 adults, $3.50 seniors, $2 children 6–12. Daily 10am–6pm. Bus: 39 (Coit).

Farmers' Market ★★★ If you're heading to the Ferry Building Marketplace or just happen to be in the area at the right time (especially a sunny Sat), make a point of visiting the Farmers' Market, which is held in the outdoor areas in front of and behind the marketplace. This is where San Francisco foodies and many of the best local chefs—including the famed Alice Waters of Chez Panisse—gather, hang out, and peruse stalls hawking the finest Northern California fruits, vegetables, breads, dairy, flowers, readymade snacks, and complete meals by local restaurants. You'll be amazed at the variety and quality, and the crowded scene itself is something to behold. You can also pick up locally made vinegars, preserves, olives, and oils here—they make wonderful gifts. Drop by on Saturday from 9am to noon for a serious social fest, including interviews with local farmers and culinary demos by city chefs.

The Embarcadero, at Market St. ✆ **415/291-3276.** www.cuesa.org. Year-round Tues 10am–2pm, Sat 8am–2pm; May–Oct Tues 10am–2pm, Thurs 4–8pm, Sat 8am–2pm, Sun 10am–2pm. Bus: 2, 7, 12, 14, 21, 66, or 71. Streetcar: F. BART: Embarcadero.

Ferry Building Marketplace ★★★ *Finds* There's no better way to enjoy a San Francisco morning than strolling this gourmet marketplace in the Ferry Building and snacking your way through breakfast or lunch. San Franciscans—myself included—can't get enough of this place; we're still amazed at what a fantastic job they did renovating the interior. The Marketplace is open daily and includes much of Northern California's best gourmet bounty: Cowgirl Creamery's Artisan Cheese Shop, Recchiuti Confections (amazing), Scharffen Berger Chocolate, Acme Breads, Wine Country's gourmet diner Taylor's Refresher, famed Vietnamese restaurant The Slanted Door, and myriad other restaurants, delis, gourmet coffee shops, specialty foods, and wine bars. Check out the Imperial Tea Court where you'll be taught the traditional Chinese way to steep and sip your tea; nosh on premium sturgeon roe at Tsar Nicoulai Caviar, a small Parisian-style "caviar cafe"; buy cooking items at the Sur La Table shop; grab a bite and savor the bayfront views from in- and outdoor tables; or browse the Farmers' Market when it's up and running (see above). Trust me, you'll love this place.

The Embarcadero, at Market St. ✆ **415/693-0996.** www.ferrybuildingmarketplace.com. Most stores daily 10am–6pm; restaurant hours vary. Bus: 2, 7, 12, 14, 21, 66, or 71. Streetcar: F. BART: Embarcadero.

Fisherman's Wharf *Kids* Few cities in America are as adept at wholesaling their historical sites as San Francisco, which has converted Fisherman's Wharf into one of the most popular tourist attractions in the world. Unless you come early in the morning to watch the few remaining fishing boats depart, you won't find many traces of the traditional waterfront life that once existed here—the only trolling going on at Fisherman's Wharf these days is for tourists' dollars. Nonetheless, everyone always seems to be enjoying themselves as they stroll down Pier 39 on a sunny day, especially the kids.

Originally called Meigg's Wharf, this bustling strip of waterfront got its present moniker from generations of fishermen who used to dock their boats here. A small fleet of fewer than 30 fishing boats still set out from here, but basically Fisherman's Wharf has been converted into one long shopping and entertainment mall that stretches from Ghirardelli Square at the west end to Pier 39 at the east.

Accommodating a total of 300 boats, two marinas flank Pier 39 and house the sightseeing ferry fleets, including departures to Alcatraz. In recent years, some 900 California sea lions have taken up residence on the adjacent floating docks. Until they abandon their new playground, which seems more and more unlikely, these playful, noisy (some nights you can hear them all the way from Washington Sq.) *Zalophus californianus* are one of the best free attractions on the wharf. Weather permitting, the **Marine Mammal Center** (✆ **415/289-SEAL**) offers an educational talk at Pier 39 on weekends from 11am to 5pm that teaches visitors about the range, habitat, and adaptability of the California sea lion.

Some people love Fisherman's Wharf; others can't get far enough away from it. Most agree that, for better or for worse, it has to be seen at least once in your lifetime. There are still some traces of old-school San Francisco character here that I will always enjoy, particularly the convivial seafood street vendors who dish out piles of fresh Dungeness, clam chowder, and sourdough bread from their steaming stainless steel carts. Fisherman's Wharf is also one of the few places in the city where kids can be unleashed to roam through the aquarium, crawl through a real World War II submarine, play at the

Kids Funky Favorites at Fisherman's Wharf

The following attractions clustered on or near Fisherman's Wharf are great fun for kids, adults, and kitsch-lovers of all ages. My favorite is the ominous-looking World War II submarine **USS *Pampanito,*** Pier 45, Fisherman's Wharf (✆ **415/775-1943;** www.maritime.org), which saw plenty of action in the Pacific. It has been completely restored, and visitors are free to crawl around inside and play Das Boot. Admission, which includes an audio tour, is $9 for those 13 to 61, $5 for seniors 62 and older, $3 for children 6 to 12, and free for children under 6; the family pass (two adults, up to four kids) costs $20. The *Pampanito* is open daily at 9am. Also on Pier 45, the free **Musée Mécanique** (p. 164) is worth a look.

Ripley's Believe It or Not! Museum, 175 Jefferson St. (✆ **415/771-6188;** www.ripleysf.com), has drawn curious spectators through its doors for over 30 years. Inside, you'll experience a world of improbabilities: a 1/3-scale matchstick cable car, a shrunken human torso once owned by Ernest Hemingway, a dinosaur made from car bumpers, a walk through a kaleidoscope tunnel, and video displays and illusions. Robert LeRoy Ripley's infamous arsenal may lead you to ponder whether truth is, in fact, stranger than fiction. What it won't do is blow your mind or feel truly worth the money. That said, with the right attitude, it's easy to enjoy an hour here playing amid the goofy and interactive displays with lots of laughs included in the admission price, which is $15 for adults, $9 for children 5 to 12, and free for children 4 and under. The museum is open Sunday through Thursday from 9am to 11pm, and 9am until midnight on Friday and Saturday (open 10am in winter months).

Conceived and executed in the Madame Tussaud mold, San Francisco's **Wax Museum,** 145 Jefferson St. (✆ **800/439-4305** or 415/202-0402; www.waxmuseum.com), has long been a kitschy tourist trap. The museum's 270 lifelike figures, including Oprah Winfrey, Britney Spears, Marilyn Monroe, John Wayne, former President George Bush and current president George W. Bush, Giants baseball star Barry Bonds, rap artist Eminem, and "Feared Leaders" such as Fidel Castro. The Chamber of Horrors features Dracula, Frankenstein, and a werewolf, along with bloody victims hanging from meat hooks. New additions include pop icons such as Brad Pitt, Angelina Jolie, and Nicole Kidman. Admission is $13 for adults, $9.95 for juniors 12 to 17 and seniors 55 and older, $6.95 for children 6 to 11, and free for children under 5. The complex is open Monday through Friday from 10am to 9pm, Saturday and Sunday from 9am to 11pm.

arcade, ride the carousel, and eat junk food galore. In short, there's something for everyone here, even us snobby locals.

At Taylor St. and The Embarcadero. ✆ **415/674-7503.** www.fishermanswharf.org. Bus: 15, 30, 32, 39, 42, or 82X. Streetcar: F-line. Cable car: Powell–Mason to the last stop and walk to the wharf. If you're arriving by car, park on adjacent streets or on the wharf between Taylor and Jones sts. for $16 per day, $8 with validation from participating restaurants.

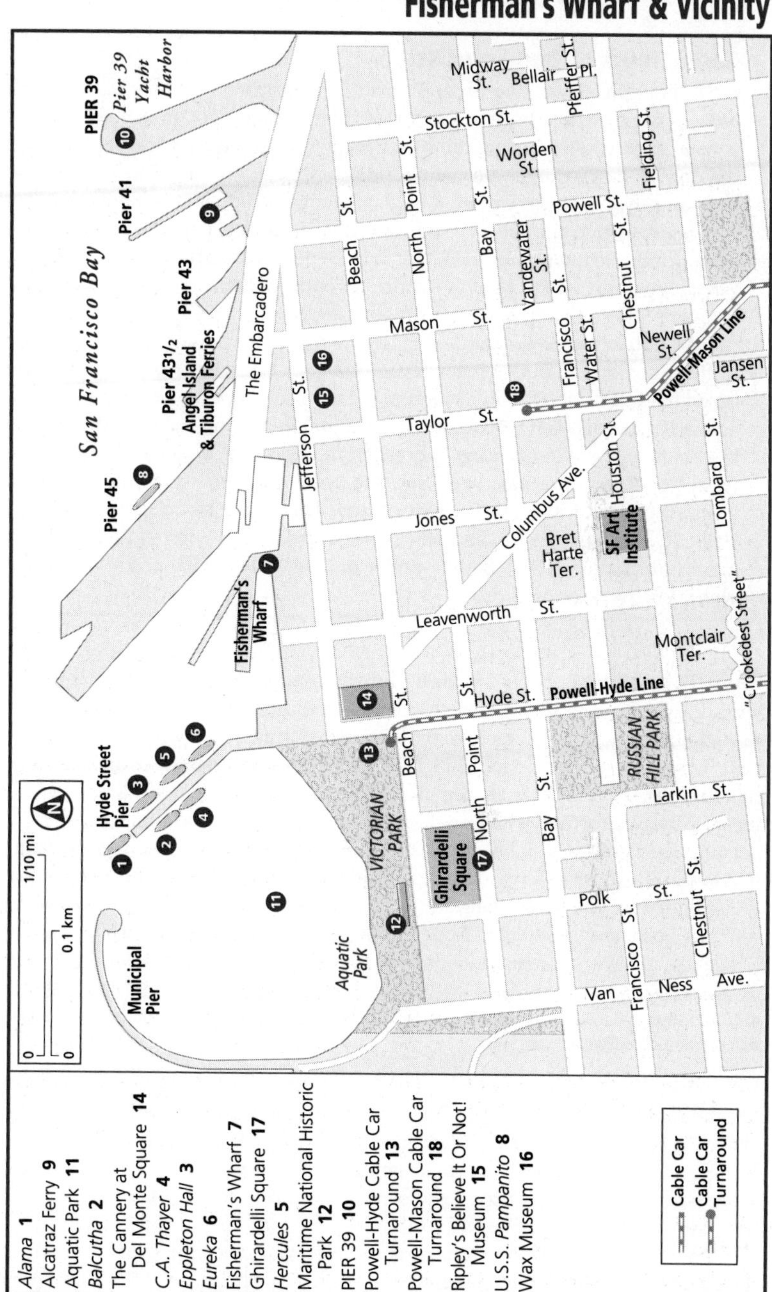
Alama 1
Alcatraz Ferry 9
Aquatic Park 11
Balcutha 2
The Cannery at Del Monte Square 14
C.A. Thayer 4
Eppleton Hall 3
Eureka 6
Fisherman's Wharf 7
Ghirardelli Square 17
Hercules 5
Maritime National Historic Park 12
PIER 39 10
Powell-Hyde Cable Car Turnaround 13
Powell-Mason Cable Car Turnaround 18
Ripley's Believe It Or Not! Museum 15
U.S.S. Pampanito 8
Wax Museum 16
Cable Car
Cable Car Turnaround
0
1/10 mi
0
0.1 km
N
San Francisco Bay
Municipal Pier
Hyde Street Pier
Aquatic Park
VICTORIAN PARK
Ghirardelli Square
Fisherman's Wharf
Pier 45
Pier 43½ Angel Island & Tiburon Ferries
Pier 43
Pier 41
PIER 39
Pier 39 Yacht Harbor
The Embarcadero
Jefferson St.
Beach St.
North Point St.
Bay St.
Francisco St.
Chestnut St.
Lombard St.
Van Ness Ave.
Polk St.
Larkin St.
Hyde St.
Powell-Hyde Line
Leavenworth St.
Jones St.
Taylor St.
Mason St.
Powell St.
Stockton St.
Columbus Ave.
Powell-Mason Line
Midway St.
Bellair Pl.
Pfeiffer St.
Worden St.
Fielding St.
Vandewater St.
Water St.
Newell St.
Jansen St.
Houston St.
SF Art Institute
Bret Harte Ter.
Montclair Ter.
"Crookedest Street"
RUSSIAN HILL PARK

GoCar Tours of San Francisco

If the thought of walking up and down San Francisco's brutally steep streets has you sweating already, considering renting a talking GoCar instead. The tiny yellow three-wheeled convertible cars are easy and fun to drive—every time I see one of these things the people riding in them are grinning from ear to ear—and they're cleverly guided by a talking GPS (Global Positioning System), which means that the car always knows where you are, even if you don't. The most popular computer-guided tour is a 2-hour loop around the Fisherman's Wharf area, out to the Marina District, through Golden Gate Park, and down Lombard Street, the "crookedest street in the world." As you drive, the talking car tells you where to turn and what landmarks you're passing. Even if you stop to check something out, as soon as you turn your GoCar back on, the tour picks up where it left off. Or you can just cruise around wherever you want (but not across the Golden Gate Bridge). There's a lockable trunk for your things, and the small size makes parking a breeze. You can rent a GoCar from 1 hour (about $44) to a full day. You'll have to wear a helmet, and you must be a licensed driver of at least 18-years of age. The GoCar rental shop is at 2715 Hyde St., between Beach and North Point streets at Fisherman's Wharf. For more information call ✆ **800/91-GoCar** or ✆ **415/441-5695,** or log onto their website at www.gocarsf.com.

Ghirardelli Square This National Historic Landmark property dates from 1864, when it served as a factory making Civil War uniforms, but it's best known as the former chocolate and spice factory of Domingo Ghirardelli (pronounced "*Gear*-ardelly"), who purchased it in 1893. The factory has since been converted into an unimpressive three-level mall containing 30-plus stores and five dining establishments. Street performers entertain regularly in the West Plaza and fountain area. Incidentally, the Ghirardelli Chocolate Company still makes chocolate, but its factory is in a lower-rent district in the East Bay. Still, if you have a sweet tooth, you won't be disappointed at the mall's fantastic (and expensive) old-fashioned soda fountain, which is open until midnight. Their "world famous" hot fudge sundae is good, too. (Then again, have you ever had a bad hot fudge sundae?)

900 North Point St. (between Polk and Larkin sts.). ✆ **415/775-5500.** www.ghirardellisq.com. Stores generally open daily 10am–9pm in summer; Sun–Fri 10am–6pm, Sat 10am–9pm rest of year. Parking $2 per 20 min. (1–1½ hr. free with purchase and validation, max. $16).

Golden Gate Bridge ★★★ *Kids* The year 2007 marks the 70th birthday of possibly the most beautiful, and certainly the most photographed, bridge in the world. Often half-veiled by the city's trademark rolling fog, San Francisco's Golden Gate Bridge, named for the strait leading from the Pacific Ocean to the San Francisco Bay, spans tidal currents, ocean waves, and battering winds to connect The City by the Bay with the Redwood Empire to the north.

With its gracefully suspended single span, spidery bracing cables, and zooming twin towers, the bridge looks more like a work of abstract art than one of the 20th century's greatest practical engineering feats. Construction was completed in May 1937 at the then-colossal cost of $35 million (plus another $39 million in interest being financed entirely by bridge tolls).

The 1.7-mile bridge (including the approach), which reaches a height of 746 feet above the water, is awesome to cross. Although kept to a maximum of 45 miles an hour, traffic usually moves quickly, so crossing by car won't give you too much time to see the sights. If you drive from the city, take the last San Francisco exit, right before the toll plaza, park in the southeast parking lot, and make the crossing by foot. Back in your car, continue to Marin's Vista Point, at the bridge's northern end. Look back, and you'll be rewarded with one of the finest views of San Francisco.

Millions of people visit the bridge each year, gazing up at the tall orange towers, out at the vistas of San Francisco and Marin County, and down into the stacks of ocean-going liners. You can walk out onto the span from either end, but be prepared—it's usually windy and cold, and the traffic is noisy. Still, walking even a short distance is one of the best ways to experience the immense scale of the structure.

Hwy. 101 N. www.goldengatebridge.org. $5 cash toll collected when driving south. Bridge-bound Golden Gate Transit buses (✆ **511**) depart hourly during the day for Marin County, starting from Mission and First sts. (across the street from the Transbay Terminal and stopping at Market and Seventh sts., at the Civic Center, along Van Ness Ave., at Lombard and Fillmore sts., and at Francisco and Richardson sts.).

Lombard Street ★ Known (erroneously) as the "crookedest street in the world," this whimsically winding block of Lombard Street draws thousands of visitors each year (much to the chagrin of neighborhood residents, most of whom would prefer to block off the street to tourists). The angle of the street is so steep that the road has to snake back and forth to make a descent possible. The brick-lined street zigzags around the residences' bright flower gardens, which explode with color during warmer months. This short stretch of Lombard Street is one-way, downhill, and fun to drive. Take the curves slowly and in low gear, and expect a wait during the weekend. Save your film for the bottom where, if you're lucky, you can find a parking space and take a few snapshots of the silly spectacle. You can also take staircases (without curves) up or down on either side of the street. In truth, most locals don't understand what the fuss is all about. I'm guessing the draw is the combination of seeing such a famous landmark, the challenge of negotiating so many steep curves, and a classic photo op. ***FYI:*** Vermont Street, between 20th and 22nd streets in Potrero Hill, is even more crooked, but not nearly as picturesque.

Between Hyde and Leavenworth sts.

Pier 39 *Overrated* Pier 39 is a multilevel waterfront complex a few blocks east of Fisherman's Wharf. Constructed on an abandoned cargo pier, it is, ostensibly, a re-creation of a turn-of-the-20th-century street scene, but don't expect a slice of old-time maritime life here: Today, Pier 39 is a busy mall welcoming millions of visitors per year. It has more than 110 stores, 13 bay-view restaurants, a two-tiered Venetian carousel, a Hard Rock Cafe, the Riptide Arcade, and the Aquarium of the Bay (p. 160) for the kids. And everything here is slanted toward helping you part with your travel dollars. This is *the* place that locals love to hate, but kids adore it here. That said, it does have a few perks: absolutely beautiful natural surroundings and bay views, fresh sea air, and hundreds of sunbathing sea lions (about 900 in peak season) lounging along its neighboring docks. (See p. 155 for info about the free weekend talks.)

On the waterfront at The Embarcadero and Beach St. ✆ **415/705-5500**. www.pier39.com. Shops daily 10am–8:30pm, with extended weekend hours during summer.

2 Museums

For information on museums in Golden Gate Park, see the "Golden Gate Park" section, beginning on p. 173.

Aquarium of the Bay *Overrated* This $38-million, 1-million-gallon marine attraction filled with sharks, stingrays, and more, transports visitors through clear acrylic tunnels via a moving footpath. Frankly, however, it's overrated and overpriced, and I recommend you skip it. If you really want to see marine life, take a drive down the coast to the Monterey Bay Aquarium.

The Embarcadero at Beach St. ✆ **888/SEA-DIVE** or 415/623-5333. www.aquariumofthebay.com. Aquarium admission $14 adults, $7 seniors and children 3–11, free for children under 3. Family (two adults, two children) package $34. Behind-the-scenes tour $25 per person, including admission to the aquarium. Mon–Thurs 10am–6pm; Fri–Sun 10am–7pm; summer hours 9am–8pm daily. Closed Dec 25.

Asian Art Museum ★ Previously in Golden Gate Park and reopened in what was once the Civic Center's Beaux Arts–style central library, San Francisco's Asian Art Museum is one of the Western world's largest museums devoted to Asian art. Its collection boasts more than 15,000 art objects, such as world-class sculptures, paintings, bronzes, ceramics, and jade items, spanning 6,000 years of history and regions of south Asia, west Asia, Southeast Asia, the Himalayas, China, Korea, and Japan. Inside you'll find 40,000 square feet of gallery space showcasing 2,500 objects at any given time. Add temporary exhibitions, live demonstrations, learning activities, Cafe Asia, and a store, and you've got one very good reason to head to the Civic Center.

200 Larkin St. (between Fulton and McAllister sts.). ✆ **415/581-3500.** www.asianart.org. Admission $12 adults, $8 seniors 65 and over, $7 youths 13–17 and college students with ID, free for children 12 and under, $5 flat rate for all (except children under 12 who are free) after 5pm Thurs. Free 1st Tues of the month. Tues–Wed and Fri–Sun 10am–5pm; Thurs 10am–9pm. Bus: All Market St. buses. Streetcar: Civic Center.

Cable Car Museum ★ *Value* *Kids* If you've ever wondered how cable cars work, this nifty museum explains (and demonstrates) it all. Yes, this is a museum, but the Cable Car Museum is no stuffed shirt. It's the living powerhouse, repair shop, and storage place of the cable car system and is in full operation. Built for the Ferries and Cliff House Railway in 1887, the building underwent an $18-million reconstruction to restore its original gaslight-era look, install an amazing spectators' gallery, and add a museum of San Francisco transit history.

The exposed machinery, which pulls the cables under San Francisco's streets, looks like a Rube Goldberg invention. Stand in the mezzanine gallery and become mesmerized by the massive groaning and vibrating winches as they thread the cable that hauls the cars through a huge figure-eight and back into the system using slack-absorbing tension wheels. For a better view, move to the lower-level viewing room, where you can see the massive pulleys and gears operating underground.

Also on display here is one of the first grip cars developed by Andrew S. Hallidie, operated for the first time on Clay Street on August 2, 1873. Other displays include an antique grip car and trailer that operated on Pacific Avenue until 1929, and dozens of exact-scale models of cars used on the various city lines. There's also a shop where you can buy a variety of cable car gifts. You can see the whole museum in about 45 minutes.

1201 Mason St. (at Washington St.). ✆ **415/474-1887.** www.cablecarmuseum.org. Free admission. Apr–Sept daily 10am–6pm; Oct–Mar daily 10am–5pm. Closed Thanksgiving, Christmas, and New Year's Day. Cable car: Both Powell St. lines.

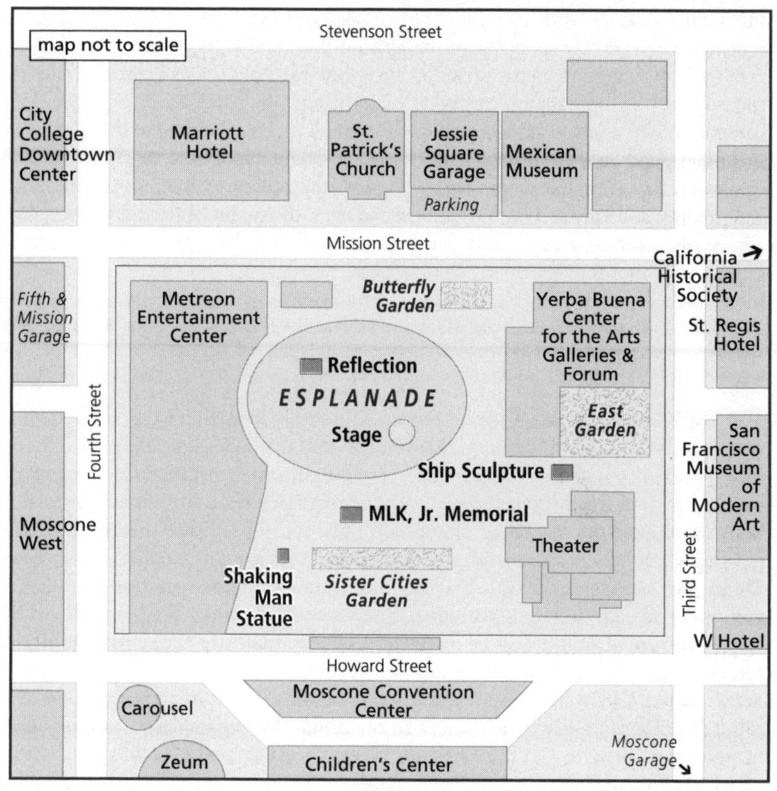

California Historical Society As part of the plan to develop the Yerba Buena Gardens area as the city's cultural hub, the **California Historical Society** opened to house a research library, an ever-changing roster of exhibits that pertain to California's rich history, 2-hour walking tours of the Bay Area given by local eccentric Gary L. Holloway, and a museum store. Call or check the website for current exhibit and walking tour information.

678 Mission St. (between Third and New Montgomery sts.). ✆ **415/357-1848.** www.californiahistoricalsociety.org. North Baker Research Library Wed–Fri noon–4:30pm; Galleries Wed–Sat noon–4:30pm. Bus: 5, 9, 14, 15, 30, or 45. Streetcar: Powell or Montgomery.

de Young Museum ★★★ After closing for several years, San Francisco's oldest museum (founded in 1895) reopened in late 2005 in its new state-of-the-art Golden Gate Park facility. Its vast holdings include one of the finest collections of American paintings in the United States from Colonial times through the 20th century, as well as decorative arts and crafts; western and non-western textiles; and arts from Africa, Oceania, and the Americas. Along with superb revolving exhibitions, the de Young has long been beloved for its educational arts programs for both children and adults, and now it's equally enjoyed for its stunning architecture and sculpture-graced surroundings. The striking facade consists of 950,000 pounds of textured and perforated copper that's intended to patinate with age, while the northeast corner of the building features a 144-foot tower that slowly spirals from the ground floor and culminates with an observation floor offering panoramic views of the entire Bay Area (from a distance it has the surreal look of a rusty aircraft carrier cruising through the park). Surrounding sculpture gardens and lush, grassy expanses are perfect for picnicking. Adding to the allure is surprisingly good and healthy organic fare at the grab-and-go or order-and-wait cafe/restaurant. You'll enjoy browsing through the museum's interesting gift shop as well. ***Note:*** Underground parking is accessed at 10th Avenue and Fulton Street. Also, admission tickets to the de Young may be used on the same day for free entrance to The Legion of Honor (see below).

50 Hagiwara Tea Garden Dr. (inside Golden Gate Park, 2 blocks from the park entrance at Eighth Ave. and Fulton). ✆ **415/863-3330.** www.thinker.org. Adults $10, seniors $7, youths 13–17 and college students with ID $6, children 12 and under free. Free 1st Tues of the month. $2 discount for Muni riders with Fast Pass or transfer receipt. AE, MC, V. Tues–Sun 9:30am–5:15pm. Closed Jan 1, Thanksgiving Day, and Dec 25. Bus: 5, 16AX, 16BX, 21, 44, or 71.

The Exploratorium ★★★ Kids *Scientific American* magazine rated The Exploratorium "the best science museum in the world"—and I couldn't agree more. Inside you'll find hundreds of exhibits that explore everything from giant-bubble blowing to Einstein's theory of relativity. It's like a mad scientist's penny arcade, an educational fun house, and an experimental laboratory all rolled into one. Touch a tornado, shape a glowing electrical current, or take a sensory journey in total darkness in the **Tactile Dome** ($3 extra, and call ✆ 415/561-0362 to make advance reservations)—even if you spent all day here you couldn't experience everything. Every exhibit at The Exploratorium is designed to be interactive, educational, safe and, most importantly, fun. And don't think it's just for kids; parents inevitably end up being the most reluctant to leave. I went here recently and spent 3 hours in just one small section of the museum, marveling like a little kid at all the mind-blowing hands-on exhibits related to light and eyesight. On the way out, be sure to stop in the wonderful gift store, which is chock-full of affordable brain candy.

The museum is in the Marina District at the beautiful **Palace of Fine Arts** ★★, the only building left standing from the Panama-Pacific Exposition of 1915. The adjoining park with lagoon—the perfect place for an afternoon picnic—is home to ducks, swans, seagulls, and grouchy geese, so bring bread.

3601 Lyon St., in the Palace of Fine Arts (at Marina Blvd.). ✆ **415/EXP-LORE,** or 415/561-0360 (recorded information). www.exploratorium.edu. Admission $13 adults; $10 seniors, youth 13–17, visitors with disabilities, and college students with ID; $8 children 4–12; free for children under 4. AE, MC, V. Tues–Sun 10am–5pm. Closed Mon except MLK, Jr., Day, Presidents' Day, Memorial Day, and Labor Day. Free parking. Bus: 28, 30, or Golden Gate Transit.

Haas–Lilienthal House Of the city's many gingerbread Victorians, this handsome Queen Anne house is one of the most flamboyant. The 1886 structure features all the architectural frills of the period, including dormer windows, flying cupolas, ornate trim, and winsome turret. The elaborately styled house is now the only Victorian house museum in the city that has its rooms fully furnished with period pieces. The San Francisco Architectural Heritage maintains the house and offers docent-led 1-hour tours (the only way to see the house), which start every 20 to 30 minutes on Wednesdays, Saturdays, and Sundays.

2007 Franklin St. (at Washington St.). ✆ **415/441-3004.** www.sfheritage.org. 1-hr. guided tour $8 adults, $5 seniors and children 12 and under. Wed and Sat noon–3pm; Sun 11am–4pm. (**Note:** Some Saturdays the house is closed for private functions, so call to confirm.) Bus: 1, 12, 19, 27, 47, or 49. Cable car: California St. line.

Moments **Italian-Style Saturday Sing-Along**

If you haven't completely fallen in love with San Francisco yet, then show up at **Caffè Trieste** in the North Beach on most Saturdays between 1 and 5pm. That's when the stringed instruments are tuned up, the chairs are scooted against the walls, and the locals entertain the crowd with their lively version of classic Italian operas and heartwarming folk songs. Everybody's so high on caffeine that it quickly becomes one big happy party and the highlight of everyone's vacation. (Even lifelong locals still get a kick out of it.) This family-owned corner institution is one of San Francisco's most beloved cafes—a Beat Generation hangout that's been around since 1956 serving locally roasted Italian coffee. You'll find it at 601 Vallejo St. at Grant Ave. (✆ **415/392-6739;** www.caffetrieste.com), next to the row of motorcycles. Call to confirm that the show's on.

The Legion of Honor ★★ Designed as a memorial to California's World War I casualties, this neoclassical structure is an exact replica of The Legion of Honor Palace in Paris, right down to the inscription HONNEUR ET PATRIE above the portal. The exterior's grassy expanses, cliff-side paths, and incredible view of the Golden Gate and downtown make this an absolute must-visit attraction before you even get in the door. The inside is equally impressive: the museum's permanent collection covers 4,000 years of art and includes paintings, sculpture, and decorative arts from Europe, as well as international tapestries, prints, and drawings. The chronological display of 4,000 years of ancient and European art includes one of the world's finest collections of Rodin sculptures. The sunlit Legion Cafe offers indoor and outdoor seating at moderate prices. Plan to spend 2 or 3 hours here.

In Lincoln Park (34th Ave. and Clement St.). ✆ **415/750-3600,** or 415/863-3330 (recorded information). www.thinker.org. Admission $10 adults, $7 seniors 65 and over, $6 youths 13–17 and college students with ID, free for children 12 and under. Fees may be higher for special exhibitions. Free 1st Tues of each month. Tues–Sun 9:30am–5:15pm. Bus: 18.

Octagon House This unusual, eight-sided, cupola-topped house dates from 1861 and is maintained by the National Society of Colonial Dames of America. Its design was based on a past theory that people living in a space of this shape would live longer, healthier lives. Inside is a small museum where you'll find Early American furniture, portraits, silver, pewter, looking glasses, and English and Chinese ceramics. There are also some historic documents, including signatures of 54 of the 56 signers of the Declaration of Independence. Even if you're not able to visit the inside, this atypical structure is worth a look from the outside.

2645 Gough St. (at Union St.). ✆ **415/441-7512.** Free admission; donation suggested. Feb–Dec 2 Sun, and 2nd and 4th Thurs of each month noon–3pm. Tours by appointment are the only way to see the house. Closed holidays. Bus: 41 or 45.

San Francisco Maritime National Historical Park ★ *Kids* This park includes several marine-themed sites within a few blocks of each other. Although the park's signature Maritime Museum—on Beach Street at Polk Street, shaped like an Art Deco ship, and filled with sea-faring memorabilia—is undergoing its planned 2006 to 2009 renovations, it's worth walking by just to admire the building. Head 2 blocks east to the corner of Hyde and Jefferson and you'll find SFMNHP's state-of-the-art Visitor's Center, which offers a fun, interactive look at the City's maritime heritage. Housed in the historic Haslett Warehouse building, the Center tells the stories of voyage, discovery, and cultural diversity. Across the street, at the park's Hyde Street Pier, are several historic ships, which are moored and open to the public.

The ***Balclutha,*** one of the last surviving square-riggers and the handsomest vessel in San Francisco Bay, was built in Glasgow, Scotland, in 1886 and carried grain from California at a near-record speed of 300 miles a day. The ship is now completely restored.

The 1890 ***Eureka*** still carries a cargo of nostalgia for San Franciscans. It was the last of 50 paddle-wheel ferries that regularly plied the bay; it made its final trip in 1957. Restored to its original splendor at the height of the ferryboat era, the sidewheeler is loaded with deck cargo, including antique cars and trucks.

The black-hulled, three-masted ***C. A. Thayer,*** built in 1895 and recently restored, was crafted for the lumber trade and carried logs felled in the Pacific Northwest to the carpentry shops of California.

Other historic ships docked here include the tiny two-masted ***Alma,*** one of the last scow schooners to bring hay to the horses of San Francisco; the ***Hercules,*** a huge 1907 oceangoing steam tug; and the ***Eppleton Hall,*** a side-wheel tugboat built in England in 1914 to operate on London's River Thames.

At the pier's small-boat shop, visitors can follow the restoration progress of historic boats from the museum's collection. It's behind the maritime bookstore on your right as you approach the ships.

Visitor's Center: Hyde and Jefferson sts. (near Fisherman's Wharf). © **415/447-5000.** www.nps.gov/safr. No fee for Visitor's Center. Tickets to board ships $5, free for children under 16. Visitor's Center: Memorial Day to Oct 15 daily 9:30am–7pm; Oct 16–May 30 9:30am–5pm. Ships on Hyde St. Pier: Memorial Day to Oct 15 daily 9:30am–5:30pm; Oct 16–May 30 daily 9:30am–5pm. Bus: 19, 30, or 47. Cable car: Powell–Hyde St. line to the last stop.

San Francisco Museum of Modern Art (SFMOMA) ★ Swiss architect Mario Botta, in association with Hellmuth, Obata, and Kassabaum, designed this $65-million museum, which has made SoMa one of the more popular areas to visit for tourists and residents alike. The museum's permanent collection houses the West Coast's most comprehensive collection of 20th-century art, including painting, sculpture, photography, architecture, design, and media arts. The collection features master works by Ansel

Finds San Francisco's Old-Fashioned Arcade Museum

"Fun for all ages" isn't a trite expression when describing San Francisco's **Musée Mécanique,** a truly unique penny arcade museum containing one of the largest privately owned collections of antique coin-operated mechanical musical instruments in the world—160 machines dating back from the 1880s through the present (and they still work!). You can pay Grand-Ma Fortune Teller a quarter to see what she has to say about your future, or watch little kids cower in fear as Laughing "Fat Lady" Sal gives her infamous cackle of a greeting. Other yesteryear seaside resort games include antique movie machines, 19th-century music boxes, old-school strength testers, and mechanical cranes. The museum is located at Pier 45 at the end of Taylor Street at Fisherman's Wharf. It's open Monday through Friday from 10am to 7pm and Saturday and Sunday from 10am to 8pm. Admission is free (© **415/346-2000;** www.museemechanique.org).

Adams, Bruce Conner, Joseph Cornell, Salvador Dalí, Richard Diebenkorn, Eva Hesse, Frida Kahlo, Ellsworth Kelly, Yves Klein, Sherrie Levine, Gordon Matta-Clark, Henri Matisse, Piet Mondrian, Pablo Picasso, Robert Rauschenberg, Diego Rivera, Cindy Sherman, Alfred Stieglitz, Clyfford Still, and Edward Weston, among many others, as well as an ever-changing program of special exhibits. Unfortunately, few works are on display at one time, and for the money the experience can be disappointing—especially compared to the finer museums of New York. However, this is about as good as it gets in our boutique city, so take it or leave it. Docent-led tours take place daily. Times are posted at the admission desk. Phone or check SFMOMA's website for current details of upcoming special events and exhibitions.

The **Caffè Museo,** to the right of the museum entrance, offers very good-quality fresh soups, sandwiches, and salads. Be sure to visit the **MuseumStore,** which carries a wonderful array of modern and contemporary art books, innovative design objects and furniture, jewelry and apparel, educational children's books and toys, posters, and stationery: It's one of the best shops in town and always carries their famed "FogDome"—a snowglobe with a mini MOMA that gets foggy rather than snowy when you shake it. 151 Third St. (2 blocks south of Market St., across from Yerba Buena Gardens). ✆ **415/357-4000.** www.sfmoma.org. Admission $13 adults, $8 seniors, $7 students over 12 with ID, free for children 12 and under. Half-price for all Thurs 6–9pm; free to all 1st Tues of each month. Thurs 11am–8:45pm; Fri–Tues 11am–5:45pm. Closed Wed and major holidays. Bus: 15, 30, or 45. Streetcar: J, K, L, or M to Montgomery.

San Francisco Zoo (& Children's Zoo) *Kids* Located between the Pacific Ocean and Lake Merced, in the southwest corner of the city, the San Francisco Zoo, which once had a reputation for being a bit shoddy and out-of-date, has come a long way in recent years. Though grown-ups who are into wildlife will enjoy the visit, it's an especially fun trip with kids because they'll really get a kick out of the hands-on Children's Zoo, along with the many other animal attractions. (The flock of shockingly pink flamingos near the entrance is especially appealing.)

Founded at its present site near the ocean in 1929, the zoo is spread over 100 acres and houses more than 930 animals, including some 245 species of mammals, birds, reptiles, amphibians, and invertebrates. Exhibit highlights include the Lipman Family Lemur Forest, a forest setting for five endangered species of lemurs from Madagascar that features interactive components for the visitor; Jones Family Gorilla World, a tranquil setting for a family group of western lowland gorillas; Koala Crossing, which connects to the Australian Walkabout exhibit with its kangaroos, wallaroos, and emu; Penguin Island, home to a large breeding colony of Magellanic Penguins (join them for lunch at 2:30pm daily); and the Primate Discovery Center, home to rare and endangered monkeys. In the South American Tropical Forest building, a large green anaconda can be found as well as other South American reptile and bird species. Puente al Sur (Bridge to the South) has a pair of giant anteaters and some capybaras. The Lion House is home to rare Sumatran and Siberian tigers and African lions. You can see the big cats fed every day at 2pm (except Mon when you are less likely to see them since when they're not eating they like to hang out in secluded areas). African Savanna is a 3-acre mixed-species habitat with giraffes, zebras, antelope, and birds.

The 6-acre Children's Zoo offers kids and their families opportunities for close-up encounters with domestic rare breeds of goats, sheep, ponies, and horses in the Family Farm. Touch and feel small mammals, reptiles, and amphibians along the Nature Trail and gaze at eagles and hawks stationed on Hawk Hill. Visitors can see the inner workings of the Koret Animal Resource Center, a thriving facility that houses the animals used in the educational outreach programs, and visit the incredible Insect Zoo. One of the Children's Zoo's most popular exhibits is the Meerkat and Prairie Dog exhibit, where kids can crawl through tunnels and play in sand, just like these two amazing burrowing species.

Don't miss the Little Puffer miniature steam train, which takes passengers around a ⅓-mile track, and the historic Dentzel Carousel (both $2 per ride). There's a coffee cart by the entrance as well as two decent cafes inside, definitely good enough for a bite with the kids (though the lines can be long and slightly confusing if you're handling food and kid duty at the same time).

Great Highway between Sloat Blvd. and Skyline Blvd. ✆ **415/753-7080.** www.sfzoo.org. Admission to main zoo and Children's Zoo $9 residents, $11 nonresidents for adults; $4.50 residents, $8 nonresidents for seniors 65 and over and youth 12–17; $2.50 for residents, $5 nonresident for children 3–11; free for children 2 and under accompanied by an adult; $1 discount with valid Muni transfer. Free to all 1st Wed of each month, except $2 fee for Children's Zoo. Carousel $2. Daily 10am–5pm, 365 days a year. Bus: 23 or 18. Streetcar: L from downtown Market St. to the end of the line.

Wells Fargo History Museum Wells Fargo, one of California's largest banks, got its start in the Wild West. Its history museum, at the bank's head office, houses hundreds of genuine relics from the company's whip-and-six-shooter days, including pistols, photographs, early banking articles, posters, a stagecoach, and mining equipment.

420 Montgomery St. (at California St.). ✆ **415/396-2619.** www.wellsfargohistory.com. Free admission. Mon–Fri 9am–5pm. Closed bank holidays. Bus: Any to Market St. Cable car: California St. line. BART: Montgomery St.

Yerba Buena Center for the Arts ★ *Finds* *Kids* The **YBCA,** which opened in 1993, is part of the large outdoor complex that takes up a few city blocks across the street from SFMOMA, and sits atop the underground Moscone Convention Center. It's the city's cultural facility, similar to New York's Lincoln Center but far more fun on the outside. The Center's two buildings offer music, theater, dance, and visual arts programs and shows. James Stewart Polshek designed the 755-seat theater, and Fumihiko Maki designed the Galleries and Arts Forum, which features three galleries and a space designed especially for dance. Cutting-edge computer art, multimedia shows, contemporary exhibitions, and performances occupy the center's high-tech galleries.

701 Mission St. ✆ **415/978-ARTS** (box office). www.ybca.org. Admission for gallery $6 adults; $3 seniors, teachers, and students. Free to all 1st Tues of each month. Free for seniors and students with ID every Thurs. Tues–Wed and Sun noon–5pm; Thurs–Sat noon–8pm. Contact YBCA for times and admission to theater. Bus: 5, 9, 14, 15, 30, or 45. Streetcar: Powell or Montgomery.

Yerba Buena Gardens ★ Unless you're at Yerba Buena to catch a performance, you're more likely to visit the 5-acre gardens, a great place to relax in the grass on a sunny day and check out several artworks. The most dramatic outdoor piece is an emotional mixed-media memorial to Martin Luther King, Jr. Created by sculptor Houston Conwill, poet Estella Majozo, and architect Joseph de Pace, it features 12 panels, each inscribed with quotations from King, sheltered behind a 50-foot-high waterfall. There are also several actual garden areas here, including a Butterfly Garden, the Sister Cities Garden (highlighting flowers from the city's 13 sister cities), and The East Garden, blending Eastern and Western styles. May through October, Yerba Buena Arts & Events puts on a series of free outdoor festivals featuring dance, music, poetry, and more by the San Francisco Ballet, Opera, Symphony, and others.

Located on 2 square city blocks bounded by Mission, Folsom, Third, and Fourth sts. www.yerbabuenagardens.com. Daily 6am–10pm. No admission fee. Contact Yerba Buena Arts & Events: ✆ **415/543-1718** or www.ybgf.org for details about the free outdoor festivals. Bus: 5, 9, 14, 15, 30, or 45. Streetcar: Powell or Montgomery.

Value Free Culture

To beef up attendance and give indigent folk like us travel writers a break, almost all of San Francisco's art galleries and museums are open free to the public 1 day of the week or month (or both), and several never charge admission. Use the following list to plan your week around the museums' free-day schedules; refer to the individual attraction listings in this chapter for more information on each museum.

First Tuesday

- California Palace of the Legion of Honor (p. 163)
- Center for the Arts at Yerba Buena Gardens (p. 166)
- de Young Museum (p. 161)
- San Francisco Museum of Modern Art (p. 164)
- Asian Art Museum (p. 160)

First Wednesday

- Exploratorium (p. 162)

Always Free

- Cable Car Museum (p. 160)
- San Francisco Maritime National Historical Park and Museum (there's a fee to board ships) (p. 163)
- Musée Mécanique (p. 164)
- Wells Fargo History Museum (p. 166)
- Glide Memorial United Methodist Church (p. 180)

Zeum/The Yerba Buena Ice Skating and Bowling Center ★ Kids Also in Yerba Buena Gardens you'll find **Zeum,** an innovative, hands-on multimedia, arts and technology museum for kids of all ages. Zeum also features the fabulous 1906 carousel that once graced the city's bygone Oceanside amusement park, Playland-at-the-Beach; the Children's Garden; a cafe; and a fun store. Right behind Zeum, you'll find **The Yerba Buena Ice Skating and Bowling Center,** a great stopover if you're looking for fun, indoor activities with, you guessed it, a 12-lane bowling alley and an ice-skating rink with public sessions daily.

Zeum: 221 Fourth St. (at Howard St.) ✆ **415/820-3320.** www.zeum.com. Adults $8, seniors and students $7, youth 3–18 $6, free for children 2 and under. Summer Tues–Sun 11am–5pm; hours during the school year Wed–Sun 11am–5pm. Carousel $3 per person, each ticket good for 2 rides. Daily 11am–6pm. The Yerba Buena Ice Skating and Bowling Center: 750 Folsom St. ✆ **415/820-3521.** www.skatebowl.com. Bowling alley: $20–$30 per lane/per hour; Sun–Thurs 10am–10pm, Fri–Sat 10am–midnight. Skating rink: call for hours and admission. Bus: 5, 9, 14, 15, 30, or 45. Streetcar: Powell or Montgomery.

Metreon Entertainment Center Kids This 350,000-square-foot hi-tech complex houses great movie theaters, an IMAX theater, the only Sony store in the country devoted to PlayStation, the one-of-a-kind Walk of Game (à la Hollywood's stars in the sidewalk, these steel stars honor the icons of the video game industry), a luxurious arcade (think big screens and a pub), a "Taste of San Francisco" food court with decent "international" fare, and lots more shops, many of which are gaming related. The whole place is wired for Wi-Fi, so if you're a true techie and want to hang out with other techies, grab some lunch, find a comfy spot, and log on.

101 Fourth St. (at the corner of Mission St.) ✆ **415/369-6000.** www.metreon.com. Building 10am–10pm daily; individual businesses may have different hours. Bus: 5, 9, 14, 15, 30, or 45. Streetcar: Powell or Montgomery.

3 Neighborhoods Worth a Visit

To really get to know San Francisco, break out of the downtown and Fisherman's Wharf areas to explore the ethnically and culturally diverse neighborhoods. Walk the streets, browse the shops, grab a bite at a local restaurant—you'll find that San Francisco's beauty and charm are around every corner, not just at the popular tourist destinations.

Note: For information on Fisherman's Wharf, see its entry under "Famous San Francisco Sights," on p. 148. For information on San Francisco neighborhoods and districts that aren't discussed here, see "Neighborhoods in Brief," in chapter 4, beginning on p. 48.

NOB HILL

When the cable car started operating in 1873, this hill became the city's exclusive residential area. Newly wealthy residents who had struck it rich in the gold rush (and were known by names such as the "Big Four" and the "Comstock Bonanza kings") built their mansions here, but they were almost all destroyed by the 1906 earthquake and fire. The only two surviving buildings are the Flood Mansion, which serves today as the **Pacific Union Club,** and **The Fairmont Hotel,** which was under construction when the earthquake struck and was damaged but not destroyed. Today, the burned-out sites of former mansions hold the city's luxury hotels—the InterContinental **Mark Hopkins,** the **Stanford Court, The Huntington Hotel,** and spectacular **Grace Cathedral,** which stands on the Crocker mansion site. Nob Hill is worth a visit if only to stroll around **Huntington Park,** attend a Sunday service at the cathedral, or ooh and aah your way around The Fairmont's spectacular lobby.

SOUTH OF MARKET (SoMa)

From Market Street to Townsend Street and The Embarcadero to Division Street, SoMa has become the city's newest cultural and multimedia center. The process started when alternative clubs began opening in the old warehouses in the area nearly

Finds This City's for the Birds!

If you're walking around San Francisco—especially Telegraph Hill or Russian Hill—and you suddenly hear lots of loud squawking and screeching overhead, look up. You're most likely witnessing a fly-by of the city's famous green flock of wild parrots. These are the scions of a colony that started out as a few wayward house pets—mostly cherry-headed conures, which are indigenous to South America—who found each other, and bred. Years later they've become hundreds strong, traveling in chatty packs through the city (with a few parakeets along for the ride), and stopping to rest on tree branches and delight residents who have come to consider them part of the family. To learn just how special these birds are to the city, check out the book *The Wild Parrots of Telegraph Hill,* see the heart-warming movie of the same name, or log onto www.markbittner.net.

Haight-Ashbury & the Castro

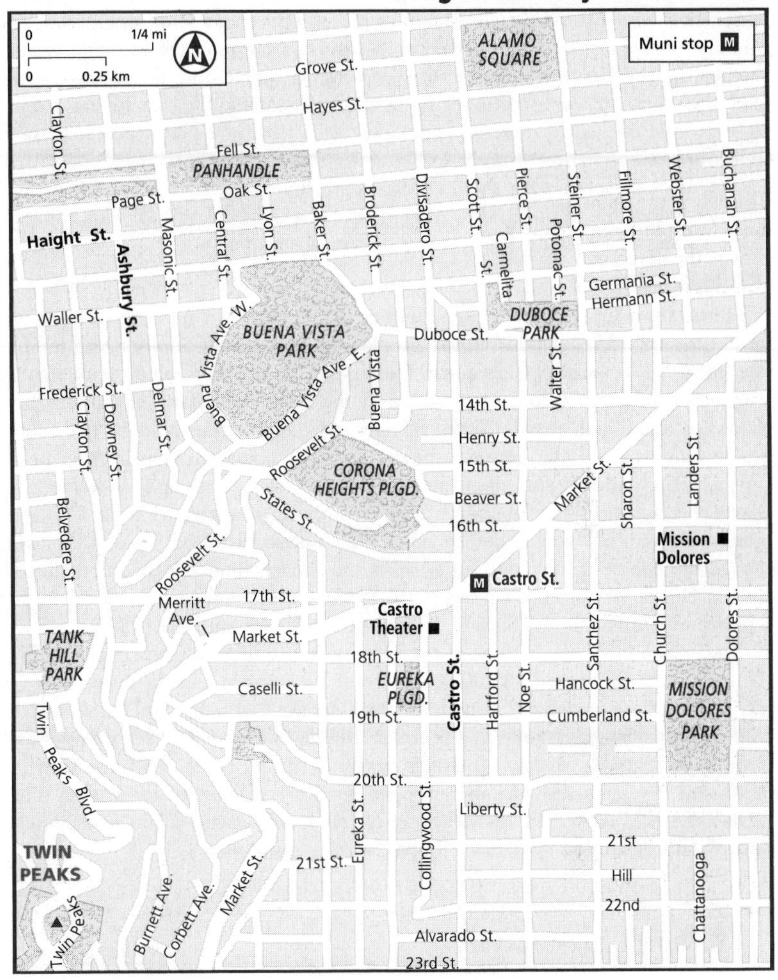

a decade ago. A wave of entrepreneurs followed, seeking to start new businesses in what was once an extremely low-rent area compared to the neighboring Financial District. Today, gentrification and high rents hold sway, spurred by a building boom that started with the **Moscone Convention Center** and continued with the **Yerba Buena Center for the Arts and Yerba Buena Gardens,** the **San Francisco Museum of Modern Art, Four Seasons Hotel, W Hotel, St. Regis Hotel,** and the **Metreon Entertainment Center.** Other institutions, businesses, and museums move into the area on an ongoing basis. A substantial portion of the city's nightlife takes place in warehouse spaces throughout the district.

NORTH BEACH ★★★

In the late 1800s, an enormous influx of Italian immigrants to North Beach firmly established this aromatic area as San Francisco's "Little Italy." Dozens of Italian restaurants and coffeehouses continue to flourish in what is still the center of the city's Italian community. Walk down **Columbus Avenue** on any given morning and you're bound to be bombarded by the wonderful aromas of roasting coffee and savory pasta sauces. Although there are some interesting shops and bookstores in the area, it's the dozens of eclectic little cafes, delis, bakeries, and coffee shops that give North Beach its Italian-bohemian character.

For more perspective on this neighborhood, follow the detailed walking tour in chapter 8 (beginning on p. 198) or sign up for a guided Javawalk with coffee nut Elaine Sosa (see "Walking Tours," on p. 186 in this chapter).

CHINATOWN ★★

The first of the Chinese immigrants came to San Francisco in the early 1800s to work as servants. By 1851, 25,000 Chinese people were working in California, and most had settled in San Francisco's Chinatown. Fleeing famine and the Opium Wars, they had come seeking the good fortune promised by the "Gold Mountain" of California, and hoped to return with wealth to their families in China. For the majority, the reality of life in California did not live up to the promise. First employed as workers in the gold mines during the gold rush, they later built the railroads, working as little more than slaves and facing constant prejudice. Yet the community, segregated in the Chinatown ghetto, thrived. Growing prejudice led to the Chinese Exclusion Act of 1882, which halted all Chinese immigration for 10 years and severely limited it thereafter (the Chinese Exclusion Act was not repealed until 1943). Chinese people were also denied the opportunity to buy homes outside the Chinatown ghetto until the 1950s.

Today, San Francisco has one of the largest communities of Chinese people in the United States. More than 80,000 people live in Chinatown, but the majority of Chinese people have moved out into newer areas like the Richmond and Sunset districts. Although frequented by tourists, the area continues to cater to Chinese shoppers, who crowd the vegetable and herb markets, restaurants, and shops. Tradition runs deep here, and if you're lucky, through an open window you might hear women mixing mah-jongg tiles as they play the centuries-old game. (***Be warned:*** You're likely to hear lots of spitting around here, too—it's part of local tradition.)

Fortune Cookie Factory

At 56 Ross Alley is the Golden Gate Fortune Cookie Factory, a tiny Chinatown storefront where, since 1962, three women sit at a conveyer belt, folding messages into thousands of fortune cookies as the manager invariably calls out to tourists, beckoning them to stroll in, watch the cookies being made, and buy a bag of 40 for about $3. Sure, there are other fortune cookie bakeries in the city, but this is the only one left where the cookies are still made by hand the old-fashioned way. You can purchase regular fortunes, unfolded flat cookies without fortunes, or, if you bring your own fortunes, they can create custom cookies (great for dinner parties) at around $6 for 50 cookies—a very cheap way to impress your friends. The factory is open daily 9am to 8:30pm. Admission is free; ✆ 415/781-3956.

The gateway at Grant Avenue and Bush Street marks the entry to Chinatown. The heart of the neighborhood is Portsmouth Square, where you'll find locals playing board games or just sitting quietly.

On the newly beautified and renovated Waverly Place, a street where the Chinese celebratory colors of red, yellow, and green are much in evidence, you'll find three **Chinese temples:** Jeng Sen (Buddhist and Taoist) at no. 146, Tien Hou (Buddhist) at no. 125, and Norras (Buddhist) at no. 109. If you enter, do so quietly so that you do not disturb those in prayer.

A block west of Grant Avenue, **Stockton Street,** from 1000 to 1200, is the community's main shopping street, lined with grocers, fishmongers, tea sellers, herbalists, noodle parlors, and restaurants. Here, too, is the Buddhist Kong Chow Temple, at no. 855, above the Chinatown post office. Explore at your leisure. A Chinatown walking tour is outlined in chapter 8, beginning on p. 192. Visit www.sanfranciscochinatown.com for more info.

JAPANTOWN

More than 12,000 citizens of Japanese descent (1.4% of the city's population) live in San Francisco, or Soko, as the Japanese who first emigrated here often called it. Initially, they settled in Chinatown and south of Market along Stevenson and Jessie streets from Fourth to Seventh streets. After the earthquake in 1906, SoMa became a light industrial and warehouse area, and the largest Japanese concentration took root in the Western Addition between Van Ness Avenue and Fillmore Street, the site of today's Japantown, now 100 years old. By 1940, it covered 30 blocks.

In 1913, the Alien Land Law was passed, depriving Japanese Americans of the right to buy land. From 1924 to 1952, the United States banned Japanese immigration. During World War II, the U.S. government froze Japanese bank accounts, interned community leaders, and removed 112,000 Japanese Americans—two-thirds of them citizens—to camps in California, Utah, and Idaho. Japantown was emptied of Japanese people, and war workers took their place. Upon their release in 1945, the Japanese found their old neighborhood occupied. Most of them resettled in the Richmond and Sunset districts; some returned to Japantown, but it had shrunk to a mere 6 or so blocks. Today, the community's notable sights include the **Buddhist Church of San Francisco,** 1881 Pine St. (at Octavia St.), www.bcsfweb.org; the **Konko Church of San Francisco,** 1909 Bush St. (at Laguna St.); the **Sokoji–Soto Zen Buddhist Temple,** 1691 Laguna St. (at Sutter St.); **Nihonmachi Mall,** 1700 block of Buchanan Street between Sutter and Post streets, which contains two steel fountains by Ruth Asawa; and the **Japan Center,** an Asian-oriented shopping mall occupying 3 square blocks bounded by Post, Geary, Laguna, and Fillmore streets. At its center stands the five-tiered **Peace Pagoda,** designed by world-famous Japanese architect Yoshiro Taniguchi "to convey the friendship and goodwill of the Japanese to the people of the United States." Surrounding the pagoda, through a network of arcades, squares, and bridges, you can explore dozens of shops and showrooms featuring everything from TVs and tansu chests to pearls, bonsai, and kimonos. **Kabuki Springs & Spa** (see the "Urban Renewal" box on p. 172) is the center's most famous tenant. But locals also head to its numerous restaurants, teahouses, shops, and multiplex movie theater.

There is often live entertainment in this neighborhood on summer weekends, including Japanese music and dance performances, tea ceremonies, flower-arranging demonstrations, martial-arts presentations, and other cultural events. **The Japan Center (© 415/922-6776)** is open daily from 10am to midnight, although most shops

Finds Urban Renewal

- **Kabuki Springs & Spa,** 1750 Geary Blvd. (© **415/922-6000;** www.kabukisprings.com), the Japan Center's most famous tenant, was once an authentic, traditional Japanese bathhouse. The Joie de Vivre hotel group bought and renovated it, however, and it's now more of a pan-Asian spa with a focus on wellness. The deep ceramic communal tubs—at a very affordable $20 to $25 per person—private baths, and shiatsu massages remain. The spa is open from 10am to 10pm daily; joining the baths is an array of massages and ayurvedic treatments, body scrubs, wraps, and facials, which cost from $60 to $150.
- **Spa Radiance,** 3011 Fillmore St. (© **415/346-6281;** www.sparadiance.com), is an utterly San Francisco spa experience due to its unassuming Victorian surroundings and its wonderfully luxurious treatments such as facials, body treatments, massages, manicures, pedicures, Brazilian waxing, spray-tanning, and makeup application by in-house artists.
- A more posh and modern experience is yours at **International Orange,** 2044 Fillmore St., second floor (© **888/894-8811;** www.internationalorange.com). The self-described spa yoga lounge offers just what it says in a chic white-on-white space on the boutique-shopping stretch of Fillmore Street. They've also got a great selection of clothing and face and body products, including one of my personal favorites, locally made In Fiore body balms.
- In the St. Regis Hotel, **Remède Spa,** 125 Third St. (© **415/284-4060;** www.remede.com), has two whole floors dedicated to melting away all your cares, worries, kinks, and knots—not to mention primping. Expect wonderful massage, facials, manis and pedis, waxes, and more. A few doors down in the W Hotel is the city's outpost of New York's **Bliss Spa,** 181 Third St., fourth floor (© **415/281-0990;** www.blissworld.com). The hip version to St. Regis's chic, it offers a similar spa menu, including wedding specialties.

close much earlier. To get there, take bus nos. 2, 3, or 4 (exit at Buchanan and Sutter sts.) or nos. 22 or 38 (exit at the northeast corner of Geary Blvd. and Fillmore St.).

HAIGHT-ASHBURY

Few of San Francisco's neighborhoods are as varied—or as famous—as Haight-Ashbury. Walk along Haight Street, and you'll encounter everything from drug-dazed drifters begging for change to an armada of the city's funky-trendy shops, clubs, and cafes. Turn anywhere off Haight, and instantly you're among the clean-cut, young urban professionals who can afford the steep rents in this hip 'hood. The result is an interesting mix of well-to-do and well-screw-you aging flower children, former Deadheads, homeless people, and throngs of tourists who try not to stare as they wander through this most human of zoos. Some find it depressing, others find it fascinating, but everyone agrees that it ain't what it was in the free-lovin' psychedelic Summer of Love. Is it still worth a visit? Not if you are here for a day or two, but it's certainly worth an excursion on longer trips, if only to enjoy a cone of Cherry Garcia at the now-famous Ben & Jerry's Ice Cream Store on the corner of Haight and Ashbury streets, and then to wander and gawk at the area's intentional freaks.

THE CASTRO

Castro Street, between Market and 18th streets, is the center of the city's gay community as well as a lovely neighborhood teeming with shops, restaurants, bars, and other institutions that cater to the area's colorful residents. Among the landmarks are **Harvey Milk Plaza** and the **Castro Theatre** (www.castrotheatre.com), a 1930s movie palace with a Wurlitzer. The gay community began to move here in the late 1960s and early 1970s from a neighborhood called Polk Gulch, which still has a number of gay-oriented bars and stores. Castro is one of the liveliest streets in the city and the perfect place to shop for gifts and revel in free-spiritedness. Check www.castroonline.com for more info.

THE MISSION DISTRICT

Once inhabited almost entirely by Irish immigrants, The Mission District is now the center of the city's Latino community as well as a mecca for young, hip residents. It's an oblong area stretching roughly from 14th to 30th streets between Potrero Avenue on the east and Dolores on the west. In the outer areas, many of the city's finest Victorians still stand, although they seem strangely out of place in the mostly lower-income neighborhoods. The heart of the community lies along 24th Street between Van Ness and Potrero, where dozens of excellent ethnic restaurants, bakeries, bars, and specialty stores attract people from all over the city. The area surrounding 16th Street and Valencia is a hotbed for impressive—and often impressively cheap—restaurants and bars catering to the city's hip crowd. The Mission District at night doesn't feel like the safest place (although in terms of creepiness, the Tenderloin, a few blocks off Union Sq., beats The Mission by far), and walking around the area should be done with caution, but it's usually quite safe during the day and is highly recommended.

For an even better insight into the community, go to the **Precita Eyes Mural Arts Center,** 2981 24th St., between Harrison and Alabama streets (✆ **415/285-2287;** www.precitaeyes.org), and take one of the 1½- to 2-hour tours conducted on Saturdays and Sundays at 11am and 1:30pm, where you'll see 60 murals in an 8-block walk. Group tours are available during the week by appointment. The 11am tour costs $10 for adults, $8 for students with ID, $5 for seniors, and $2 for children under 18; the 1:30pm tour, which is half an hour longer and includes a slide show, costs $12 for adults, $8 for students with ID, and $5 for seniors and children under 18. All but the Saturday-morning tour (which leaves from 3325 24th St. at the Café Venice) leave from the center's 24th Street location.

Other signs of cultural life in the neighborhood are progressive theaters such as Theatre Rhinoceros (www.therhino.org) and Theater Artaud (www.artaud.org). At 16th Street and Dolores is the Mission San Francisco de Asís, better known as **Mission Dolores** (p. 180). It's the city's oldest surviving building and the district's namesake.

4 Golden Gate Park ★★★

Everybody loves **Golden Gate Park**—people, dogs, birds, frogs, turtles, bison, trees, bushes, and flowers. Literally, everything feels unified here in San Francisco's enormous arboreal front yard. Conceived in the 1860s and 1870s, this great 1,017-acre landmark, which stretches inland from the Pacific coast, took shape in the 1880s and 1890s thanks to the skill and effort of John McLaren, a Scot who arrived in 1887 and began landscaping the park.

When he embarked on the project, sand dunes and wind presented enormous challenges. But McLaren had developed a new strain of grass called "sea bent," which he

Golden Gate Park

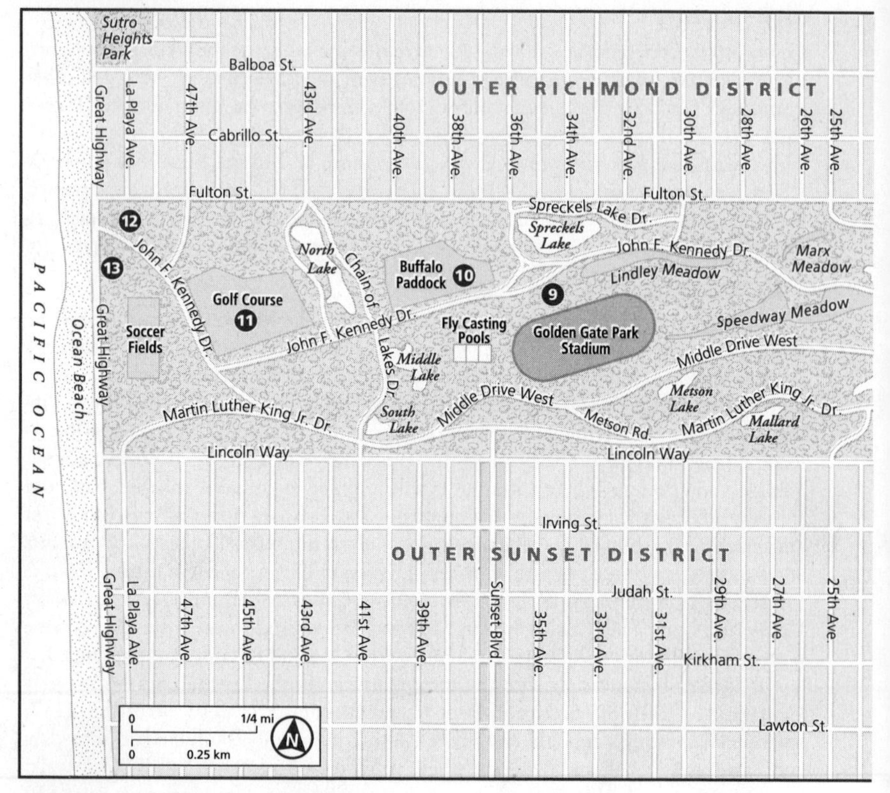

planted to hold the sandy soil along the Firth of Forth back home, and he used it to anchor the soil here, too. Every year the ocean eroded the western fringe of the park, and ultimately he solved this problem, too, though it took him 40 years to build a natural wall, putting out bundles of sticks that the tides covered with sand. He also built the two windmills that stand on the western edge of the park to pump water for irrigation. Under his brilliant eye, the park took shape.

Today the park consists of hundreds of gardens and attractions connected by wooded paths and paved roads. While many worthy sites are clearly visible, there are infinite hidden treasures, so pick up information at **McLaren Lodge and Park Headquarters** (at Stanyan and Fell sts.; ✆ **415/831-2700**) if you want to find the more hidden spots. It's open daily and offers park maps for $3. Of the dozens of special gardens in the park, most recognized are **McLaren Memorial Rhododendron Dell, The Rose Garden, Strybing Arboretum,** and, at the western edge of the park, a springtime array of thousands of tulips and daffodils around the **Dutch windmill.**

In addition to the highlights described in this section, the park contains lots of recreational facilities: tennis courts; baseball, soccer, and polo fields; a golf course; riding stables; and fly-casting pools. The Strawberry Hill boathouse handles boat rentals. The park is also the home of the **M. H. de Young Memorial Museum,** which recently

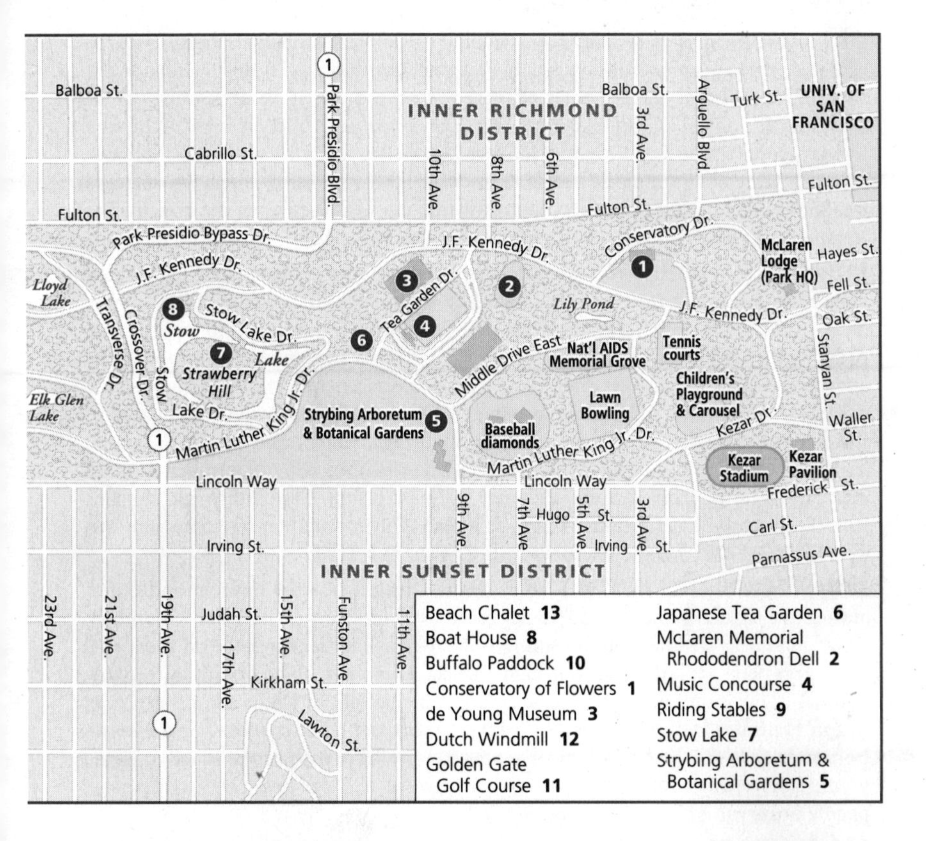

relocated to its spectacular new home at 50 Tea Garden Dr. (✆ **415/750-3600** or 415/863-3330). For more information see p. 161.

For further information, call the San Francisco Visitor Information Center at ✆ **415/283-0177.** Enter the park at Kezar Drive, an extension of Fell Street; bus riders can take no. 5, 6, 7, 16AX, 16BX, 66, or 71.

PARK HIGHLIGHTS

CONSERVATORY OF FLOWERS ★★ Opened to the public in 1879, this glorious Victorian glass structure is the oldest existing public conservatory in the Western Hemisphere. After a bad storm in 1995 and delayed renovations, the conservatory was closed and visitors were only able to imagine what wondrous displays existed within the striking glass assemblage. Thankfully, a $25-million renovation, including a $4-million exhibit upgrade, was completed a few years ago, and now the Conservatory is a cutting-edge horticultural destination with over 1,700 species of plants. Here you can check out the rare tropical flora of the Congo, Philippines, and beyond within the stunning structure. As one of only four public institutions in the U.S. to house a highland tropics exhibit, its five galleries also include the lowland tropics, aquatic plants, the largest Dracula orchid collection in the world, and special exhibits. It doesn't take long to visit, but make a point of staying a while; outside there are good sunny spots for people-watching as well as paths leading to impressive gardens begging to be explored. If you're around during summer and fall, don't miss the Dahlia Garden to the right of the entrance in the center of what was once a carriage roundabout—it's an explosion of colorful Dr. Seuss–like blooms. The conservatory is open Tuesday through Sunday from 9am to 5pm, closed Mondays. Admission is $5 for adults; $3 for youth 12 to 17 years of age, seniors, and students with ID; $1.50 for children 5 to 11; and free for children 4 and under and for all visitors the first Tuesday of the month. For more information, visit www.conservatoryofflowers.org or call ✆ **415/666-7001.**

JAPANESE TEA GARDEN John McLaren, the man who began landscaping Golden Gate Park, hired Makoto Hagiwara, a wealthy Japanese landscape designer, to further develop this garden originally created for the 1894 Midwinter Exposition. It's a quiet place with cherry trees, shrubs, and bonsai crisscrossed by winding paths and high-arched bridges over pools of water. Focal points and places for contemplation include the massive bronze Buddha (cast in Japan in 1790 and donated by the Gump family), the Buddhist wooden pagoda, and the Drum Bridge, which, reflected in the water, looks as though it completes a circle. The garden is open daily November through February from 8:30am to 5pm (teahouse 10am–4:30pm), March through October from 8:30am to 6pm (teahouse 10am–5:30pm). For information on admission, call ✆ **415/752-4227.** For the **teahouse,** call ✆ **415/752-1171.**

STRAWBERRY HILL/STOW LAKE Rent a paddle boat or rowboat and cruise around the circular Stow Lake as painters create still lifes, joggers pass along the grassy shoreline, ducks waddle around waiting to be fed, and turtles sunbathe on rocks and logs. Strawberry Hill, the 430-foot-high artificial island and highest point in the park that lies at the center of Stow Lake, is a perfect picnic spot; it boasts a bird's-eye view of San Francisco and the bay. It also has a waterfall and peace pagoda. For the **boathouse,** call ✆ **415/752-0347.** Boat rentals are available daily from 10am to 4pm, weather permitting; four-passenger rowboats go for $13 per hour, and four-person paddle boats run $17 per hour; fees are cash-only.

STRYBING ARBORETUM & BOTANICAL GARDENS More than 7,000 plant species grow here, among them some ancient plants in a special "primitive garden," rare species, and a grove of California redwoods. Docent tours begin at 1:30pm daily, with an additional 10:20am tour on weekends. Strybing is open Monday through Friday from 8am to 4:30pm, and Saturday, Sunday, and holidays from 10am to 5pm. Admission is free. For more information, call ✆ **415/661-1316** or visit www.strybing.org.

5 The Presidio & Golden Gate National Recreation Area

THE PRESIDIO

In October 1994, the Presidio passed from the U.S. Army to the National Park Service and became one of a handful of urban national parks that combines historical, architectural, and natural elements in one giant arboreal expanse. (It also contains a previously private golf course and a home for George Lucas's production company.) The 1,491-acre area incorporates a variety of terrain—coastal scrub, dunes, and prairie grasslands—that shelter many rare plants and more than 200 species of birds, some of which nest here.

This military outpost has a 220-year history, from its founding in September 1776 by the Spanish under José Joaquin Moraga to its closure in 1994. From 1822 to 1846, the property was in Mexican hands.

During the war with Mexico, U.S. forces occupied the fort, and in 1848, when California became part of the Union, it was formally transferred to the United States. When San Francisco suddenly became an important urban area during the gold rush, the U.S. government installed battalions of soldiers and built Fort Point to protect the entry to the harbor. It expanded the post during the Civil War and during the Indian Wars of the 1870s and 1880s. By the 1890s, the Presidio was no longer a frontier post but a major base for U.S. expansion into the Pacific. During the war with Spain in 1898, thousands of troops camped here in tent cities awaiting shipment to the Philippines, and the Army General Hospital treated the sick and wounded. By 1905, 12 coastal defense batteries were built along the headlands. In 1914, troops under the command of Gen. John Pershing left here to pursue Pancho Villa and his men. The Presidio expanded during the 1920s, when Crissy Army Airfield (the first airfield on the West Coast) was established, but the major action was seen during World War II, after the attack on Pearl Harbor. Soldiers dug foxholes along nearby beaches, and the Presidio became the headquarters for the Western Defense Command. Some 1.75 million men were shipped out from nearby Fort Mason to fight in the Pacific; many returned to the Presidio's hospital, whose capacity peaked one year at 72,000 patients. In the 1950s, the Presidio served as the headquarters for the Sixth U.S. Army and a missile defense post, but its role slowly shrank. In 1972, it was included in new legislation establishing the Golden Gate National Recreation Area; in 1989, the Pentagon decided to close the post and transfer it to the National Park Service.

Today, the area encompasses more than 470 historic buildings, a scenic golf course, a national cemetery, 22 hiking trails (to be doubled over the next decade), and a variety of terrain and natural habitats. The National Park Service offers walking and biking tours around the Presidio (reservations are suggested) as well as a free shuttle "PresidioGo." For more information, call the **Presidio Visitors Center** at © **415/561-4323;** www.nps.gov/prsf or www.presidio.gov. Take bus nos. 28, 45, 76, or 82X to get there.

GOLDEN GATE NATIONAL RECREATION AREA

The largest urban park in the world, GGNRA makes New York's Central Park look like a putting green, covering three counties along 28 miles of stunning, condo-free shoreline. Run by the National Park Service, the Recreation Area wraps around the northern and western edges of the city, and just about all of it is open to the public with no access fees. The Muni bus system provides transportation to the more popular sites, including Aquatic Park, Cliff House, Fort Mason, and Ocean Beach. For more information, contact the **National Park Service** (© **415/561-4700;** www.nps.gov/goga). For more detailed information on particular sites, see the "Getting Outside" section, later in this chapter.

Here is a brief rundown of the salient features of the park's peninsula section, starting at the northern section and moving westward around the coastline:

Aquatic Park, adjacent to the Hyde Street Pier, has a small swimming beach, although it's not that appealing (and darned cold). Far more entertaining is a visit to the San Francisco Maritime National Historical Park's Visitor Center a few blocks away (see p. 163 for more information).

Fort Mason Center, from Bay Street to the shoreline, consists of several buildings and piers used during World War II. Today they hold a variety of museums, theaters, shops, and organizations, and Greens vegetarian restaurant (p. 133), which affords views of the Golden Gate Bridge. For information about Fort Mason events, call © **415/441-3400** or visit www.fortmason.org. The park headquarters is also at Fort Mason.

Golden Gate National Recreation Area

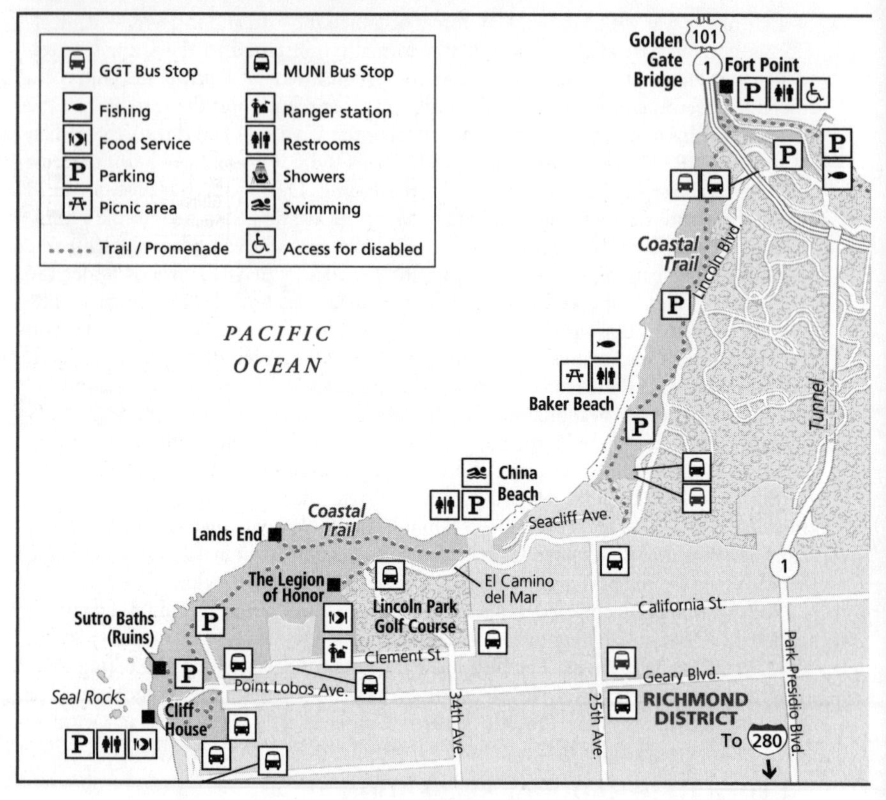

Farther west along the bay at the northern end of Laguna Street is **Marina Green,** a favorite local spot for kite-flying, jogging, and walking along the Promenade. The St. Francis Yacht Club is also here.

Next comes the 3½-mile paved **Golden Gate Promenade** ★, San Francisco's best and most scenic biking, jogging, and walking path. It runs along the shore past **Crissy Field** (www.crissyfield.org) and ends at Fort Point under the Golden Gate Bridge (be sure to stop and watch the gonzo windsurfers and kite surfers, who catch major wind here, and admire the newly restored marshlands). The Crissy Field Café and Bookstore is open from 9am to 5pm Wednesday through Sunday and offers yummy, organic soups, salads, sandwiches, coffee drinks, and a decent selection of outdoor-themed books and cards.

Fort Point ★ (✆ **415/556-1693;** www.nps.gov/fopo) was built in 1853 to 1861 to protect the narrow entrance to the harbor. It was designed to house 500 soldiers manning 126 muzzle-loading cannons. By 1900, the fort's soldiers and obsolete guns had been removed, but the formidable brick edifice remains. Fort Point is open Friday through Sunday only from 10am to 5pm, and guided tours and cannon demonstrations are given at the site once or twice a day on open days, depending on the time of year.

Lincoln Boulevard sweeps around the western edge of the bay to **Baker Beach,** where the waves roll ashore—a fine spot for sunbathing, walking, or fishing. Hikers

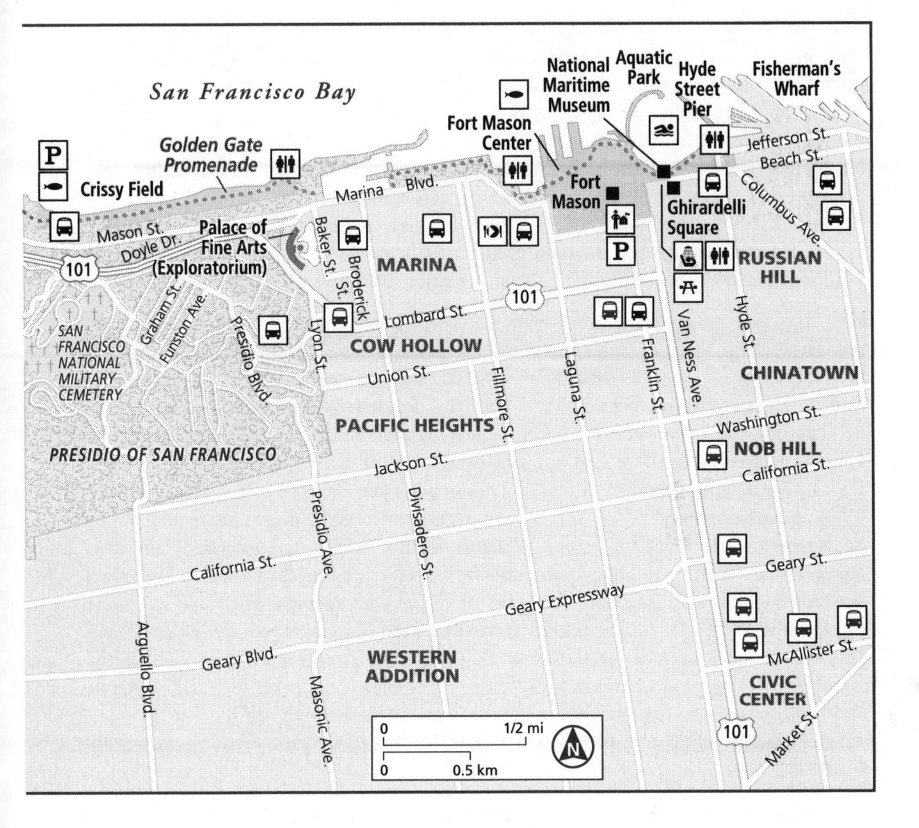

can follow the **Coastal Trail** (www.californiacoastaltrail.org) from Fort Point along this part of the coastline all the way to Lands End.

A short distance from Baker Beach, **China Beach** is a small cove where swimming is permitted. Changing rooms, showers, a sun deck, and restrooms are available.

A little farther around the coast is **Lands End** ★, looking out to Pyramid Rock. A lower and an upper trail offer hiking amid windswept cypresses and pines on the cliffs above the Pacific.

Still farther along the coast lie **Point Lobos,** the **Sutro Baths** (www.sutrobaths.com), and **Cliff House** ★. Cliff House (www.cliffhouse.com), which recently underwent major renovations, has been serving refreshments to visitors since 1863. It's famed for its views of Seal Rocks (a colony of sea lions and many marine birds) and the Pacific Ocean. Immediately northeast of Cliff House you'll find traces of the once-grand Sutro Baths, a swimming facility that was a major summer attraction accommodating up to 24,000 people until it burned down in 1966. (Alas, my favorite Cliff House attraction, the **Musée Mécanique** ★★, an arcade featuring antique games, moved to digs at Pier 45; for more information, call ✆ **415/346-2000** or visit www.museemecanique.org.)

A little farther inland at the western end of California Street is **Lincoln Park,** which contains a golf course and the spectacular Legion of Honor museum (p. 190).

At the southern end of Ocean Beach, 4 miles down the coast, is another area of the park around Fort Funston (✆ **415/561-4700**), where there's an easy loop trail across the cliffs. Here you can watch hang gliders take advantage of the high cliffs and strong winds.

Farther south along Route 280, **Sweeney Ridge** affords sweeping views of the coastline from the many trails that crisscross its 1,000 acres. From here the expedition led by Don Gaspar de Portolá first saw San Francisco Bay in 1769. It's in Pacifica; take Sneath Lane off Route 35 (Skyline Blvd.) in San Bruno.

The GGNRA extends into Marin County, where it encompasses the Marin Headlands, Muir Woods National Monument, and Olema Valley behind the Point Reyes National Seashore. See chapter 11 for information on those areas' highlights.

6 Religious Buildings Worth Checking Out

Glide Memorial United Methodist Church ★★ *Moments* The best way to spend a Sunday morning in San Francisco is to visit this Tenderloin-area church to witness the exhilarating and lively sermons accompanied by an amazing gospel choir. Reverend Cecil Williams's enthusiastic and uplifting preaching and singing with the homeless and poor of the neighborhood has attracted nationwide fame over the past 40-plus years. In 1994, during the pastor's 30th-anniversary celebration, singers Angela Bofill and Bobby McFerrin joined comedian Robin Williams, author Maya Angelou, and talk-show queen Oprah Winfrey to honor him publicly. Even former President Clinton has joined the crowd. Cecil Williams now shares pastor duties with Douglas Fitch and alternates presiding over the roof-raising Sunday services in front of a diverse audience that crosses all socioeconomic boundaries. Go for an uplifting experience and some hand-clapping, shoulder-swaying gospel choir music—it's an experience you'll never forget. ***Tip:*** Arrive about 20 minutes early to make sure you get a seat; otherwise it's SRO.

330 Ellis St. (west of Union Sq.). ✆ **415/674-6000.** www.glide.org. Services Sun at 9 and 11am. Bus: 27. Streetcar: Powell. BART: Powell.

Grace Cathedral Although this Nob Hill cathedral, designed by architect Lewis P. Hobart, appears to be made of stone, it is in fact constructed of reinforced concrete beaten to achieve a stonelike effect. Construction began on the site of the Crocker mansion in 1928 but was not completed until 1964. Among the more interesting features of the building are its stained-glass windows, particularly those by the French Loire studios and Charles Counick, depicting such modern figures as Thurgood Marshall, Robert Frost, and Albert Einstein; the replicas of Ghiberti's bronze *Doors of Paradise* at the east end; the series of religious murals completed in the 1940s by Polish artist John de Rosen; and the 44-bell carillon. Along with its magical ambience, Grace lifts spirits with services, musical performances (including organ recitals on many Sundays), and its weekly Forum (Sun 9:30–10:30am except during summer and major holidays), where guests lead discussions about spirituality in modern times and have community dialogues on social issues.

1100 California St. (between Taylor and Jones sts.). ✆ **415/749-6300.** www.gracecathedral.org.

Mission Dolores San Francisco's oldest standing structure, the Mission San Francisco de Asís (also known as Mission Dolores), has withstood the test of time, as well as two major earthquakes, relatively intact. In 1776, at the behest of Franciscan missionary Junípero Serra, Father Francisco Palou came to the Bay Area to found the sixth in a series of missions that dotted the California coastline. From these humble beginnings grew what was to become the city of San Francisco. The mission's small, simple chapel, built solidly by Native Americans who were converted to Christianity, is a curious mixture of native construction methods and Spanish-colonial style. A statue of Father Serra stands in the mission garden, although the portrait looks somewhat more contemplative, and less energetic, than he must have been in real life. A 45-minute self-guided tour costs $5; otherwise, admission is $3 for adults and $2 for children.

16th St. (at Dolores St.). ✆ **415/621-8203.** www.missiondolores.org. Admission $3 adults, $2 children. Daily 9am–5pm summer; 9am–4pm winter; 9am–4:30pm spring; 9am–noon Good Friday. Closed Thanksgiving, Easter, and Dec 25. Bus: 14, 26, or 33 to Church and 16th sts. Streetcar: J.

7 Architectural Highlights

MUST-SEES FOR ARCHITECTURE BUFFS

ALAMO SQUARE HISTORIC DISTRICT San Francisco's collection of Victorian houses, known as **Painted Ladies,** is one of the city's most famous assets. Most of the 14,000 extant structures date from the second half of the 19th century and are private residences. Spread throughout the city, many have been beautifully restored and ornately painted. The small area bordered by Divisadero Street on the west, Golden Gate Avenue on the north, Webster Street on the east, and Fell Street on the south—about 10 blocks west of the Civic Center—has one of the city's greatest concentrations of Painted Ladies. One of the most famous views of San Francisco—seen on postcards and posters all around the city—depicts sharp-edged Financial District skyscrapers behind a row of Victorians. This fantastic juxtaposition can be seen from Alamo Square, in the center of the historic district, at Fulton and Steiner streets.

CITY HALL & CIVIC CENTER Built between 1913 and 1915, City Hall, located in the Civic Center District, is part of this "City Beautiful" complex done in the Beaux Arts style. The dome rises to a height of 306 feet on the exterior and is ornamented with oculi and topped by a lantern. The interior rotunda soars 112 feet and is finished in oak, marble, and limestone, with a monumental marble staircase leading to the second floor. With a major renovation completed in the late 1990s, the building was returned to its former splendor. No doubt you saw it on TV during early 2004, when much of the hoopla surrounding the short-lived and controversial gay marriage proceedings was depicted on the front steps. (Remember Rosie O'Donnell emerging from this very building after getting married to her girlfriend?) Public tours are given Monday through Friday at 10am, noon, and 2pm. Call ✆ **415/554-4933** for details.

OTHER ARCHITECTURAL HIGHLIGHTS

San Francisco is a center of many architecturally striking sights. This section concentrates on a few highlights.

The Union Square and Financial District areas have a number of buildings worth checking out. One is the former **Circle Gallery,** 140 Maiden Lane. Now a gallery housing Folk Art International, Xanadu Tribal Arts, and Boretti Amber & Design, it's the only building in the city designed by Frank Lloyd Wright (in 1948). The gallery was the prototype for the Guggenheim's seashell-shaped circular gallery space, even though it was meant to serve as a retail space for V. C. Morris, a purveyor of glass and crystal. Note the arresting exterior, a solid wall with a circular entryway to the left. Maiden Lane is just off Union Square between Geary and Post streets.

The **Hallidie Building,** 130–150 Sutter St., designed by Willis Polk in 1917, is an ideal example of a glass-curtain building. The vast glass facade is miraculously suspended

Kids Especially for Kids

The following San Francisco attractions appeal to kids of all ages:

- Alcatraz Island (p. 148)
- Cable Car Museum (p. 160)
- Cable cars (p. 152)
- The Exploratorium (p. 162)
- Golden Gate Bridge (p. 158)
- Golden Gate Park, including the Children's Playground, Bison Paddock, and Japanese Tea Garden (p. 173)
- Maritime Museum (San Francisco Maritime National Historical Park) and the historic ships anchored at Hyde Pier (p. 163)
- The Metreon Entertainment Center (p. 167)
- The San Francisco Zoo (p. 165)

In addition to the sights listed above, a number of playgrounds are of particular interest to kids. One of the most enormous, fun playgrounds for kids is in **Golden Gate Park,** where you'll find a fantastic kids' playground just west of the Stanyan Street entrance. But other playful perks include Stow Lake's boats and peeks at the bison in the bison paddock. Apartment buildings surround the **Cow Hollow Playground,** Baker Street between Greenwich and Filbert streets, on three of four sides. The landscaped playground features a bi-level play area fitted with well-conceived, colorful play structures, including a tunnel, slides, swings, and a miniature cable car. **Huntington Park,** Taylor Street between Sacramento and California streets, sits atop Nob Hill. This tiny play area contains several small structures particularly well suited to children under 5. **Julius Kahn Playground,** West Pacific Avenue at Spruce Street, is a popular playground inside San Francisco's great Presidio Park. Larger play structures and forested surroundings make this area attractive to children and adults alike. Go to www.parks.sfgov.org and click on "Programs" for more info.

between the two cast-iron cornices. The fire escapes that course down each side of the building complete the proscenium-like theatrical effect.

Two prominent pieces of San Francisco's skyline are in the Financial District. The **Transamerica Pyramid,** 600 Montgomery St., between Clay and Washington streets, is one of the tallest structures in San Francisco. This corporate headquarters was completed in 1972, stands 48 stories tall, and is capped by a 212-foot spire. The former **Bank of America World Headquarters,** 555 California St., was designed by Wurster, Bernardi, and Emmons with Skidmore, Owings, and Merrill. This carnelian-marble-covered building dates from 1969. Its 52 stories are topped by a panoramic restaurant and bar, the Carnelian Room. The focal point of the building's formal plaza is an abstract black granite sculpture, known locally as the "Banker's Heart," designed by Japanese architect Masayuki Nagare.

The **Medical Dental Building,** 450 Sutter St., is a steel-frame structure beautifully clad in terra cotta. It was designed by Miller and Pflueger in 1929. The entrance and

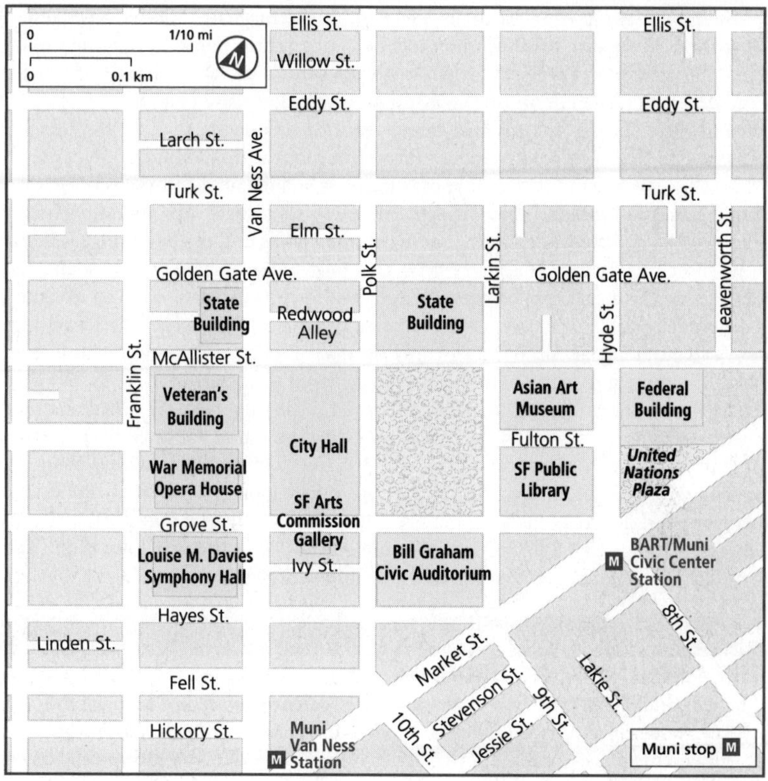

the window frames are elaborately ornamented with Mayan relief work; the lobby ceiling is similarly decorated with gilding. Note the ornate elevators.

At the foot of Market Street you will find the **Ferry Building.** Built between 1895 and 1903, it served as the city's major transportation hub before the Golden Gate and Bay bridges were built; some 170 ferries docked here daily unloading Bay Area commuters until the 1930s. The tower that soars above the building was inspired by the Campanile of Venice and the Cathedral Tower in Seville. In 2003, a 4-year renovation was completed and the building is now a spectacular mixed-use landmark building featuring a 660-foot-long, skylit nave, which had been partially filled in and destroyed in the 1950s. If you stop by the Ferry Building, you might also want to go to **Rincon Center,** 99 Mission St., to see the WPA murals painted by the Russian artist Refregier in the post office.

Several important buildings are on or near Nob Hill. The **Flood Mansion,** 1000 California St., at Mason Street, was built between 1885 and 1886 for James Clair Flood. Thanks to the Comstock Lode, Flood rose from being a bartender to one of the city's wealthiest men. He established the Nevada bank that later merged with Wells Fargo. The house cost $1.5 million to build at the time; the fence alone cost $30,000. It was designed by Augustus Laver and modified by Willis Polk after the 1906 earthquake to accommodate the Pacific Union Club. Unfortunately, you can't go inside: The building is now a private school.

Built by George Applegarth in 1913 for sugar magnate Adolph Spreckels, the **Spreckels Mansion,** 2080 Washington St., is currently home to romance novelist Danielle Steel (don't even try to get in to see her!). The extraordinary building has rounded-arch French doors on the first and second floors and curved balconies on the second floor. Inside, the original house featured an indoor pool in the basement, Adamesque fireplaces, and a circular Pompeian room with a fountain.

Finally, one of San Francisco's most ingenious architectural accomplishments is the **San Francisco–Oakland Bay Bridge.** Although it's visually less appealing than the nearby Golden Gate Bridge (except at night when it's lit up), the Bay Bridge is in many ways more spectacular. The silvery giant that links San Francisco with Oakland is one of the world's longest steel bridges (8¼ miles). It opened in 1936, 6 months before the Golden Gate. Each of its two decks contains five automobile lanes. The Bay Bridge is not a single bridge at all, but a superbly dovetailed series of spans joined mid-bay, at Yerba Buena Island, by one of the world's largest (in diameter) tunnels. To the west of Yerba Buena, the bridge is actually two separate suspension bridges, joined at a central anchorage. East of the island is a 1,400-foot cantilever span, followed by a succession of truss bridges. This east span of the bridge is finally being replaced after being damaged in the 1989 Loma Prieta earthquake and a years-long fight between city residents, planners, and designers. And it looks even more complex than it sounds. You can drive across the bridge (the toll is $3, paid westbound), or you can catch a bus at the Transbay Terminal (Mission at First St.) and ride to downtown Oakland.

8 Self-Guided & Organized Tours

THE 49-MILE SCENIC DRIVE ★★

The self-guided, 49-mile drive is an easy way to orient yourself and to grasp the beauty of San Francisco and its extraordinary location. It's also a flat-out stunning and very worthy excursion. Beginning in the city, it follows a rough circle around the bay and passes virtually all the best-known sights, from Chinatown to the Golden Gate Bridge, Ocean Beach, Seal Rocks, Golden Gate Park, and Twin Peaks. Originally designed for the benefit of visitors to San Francisco's 1939 and 1940 Golden Gate International Exposition, the route is marked by blue-and-white seagull signs. Although it makes an excellent half-day tour, this mini-excursion can easily take longer if you decide, for example, to stop to walk across the Golden Gate Bridge or to have tea in Golden Gate Park's Japanese Tea Garden.

The San Francisco **Visitor Information Center,** at Powell and Market streets (p. 47), distributes free route maps, which are handy since a few of the Scenic Drive marker signs are missing. Try to avoid the downtown area during the weekday rush hours from 7 to 9am and 4 to 6pm.

A BART TOUR

One of the world's best commuter systems, **Bay Area Rapid Transit (BART)** runs along 104 miles of rail, linking 43 stations between San Francisco, Millbrae, and the East Bay. Under the bay, BART runs through one of the longest underwater transit tubes in the world. This link opened in September 1972, 2 years behind schedule and 6 months after the general manager resigned under fire. The train cars are 70 feet long and were designed to represent the latest word in public transport luxury. More than 3 decades later, they no longer seem futuristic, but they're still attractively modern, with carpeted floors, tinted picture windows, air-conditioning, and recessed lighting.

The trains can hit a top speed of 80 mph; a computerized control system monitors and adjusts their speed.

The people who run BART think so highly of their trains and stations that they sell a $4.65 **"Excursion Ticket,"** which allows you, in effect, to "sightsee" the BART system, or basically ride it. "Tour" the entire system as much as you like for up to 3 hours; you must exit at the station where you entered (if you get out anywhere else along the line, the gate instantly computes the normal fare). For more information, call ✆ **415/989-BART** or visit www.bart.gov, where you can also download trip plans directly to your iPod, PDA, or wireless.

BOAT TOURS

One of the best ways to look at San Francisco is from a boat bobbing on the bay. There are several cruises to choose from, and many of them start from Fisherman's Wharf.

Blue & Gold Fleet, Pier 39, Fisherman's Wharf (✆ **415/773-1188;** www.blueandgoldfleet.com), tours the bay year-round in a sleek, 350-passenger sightseeing boat, complete with food and beverage facilities. The fully narrated, 1-hour cruise passes beneath the Golden Gate Bridge and comes within yards of Alcatraz Island. Don a jacket, bring the camera, and make sure it's a clear day for the best bay cruise. Frequent daily departures from Pier 39's West Marina begin at 10:45am daily during winter and 10am daily during summer. Tickets cost $21 for adults, $17 for seniors over 62 and juniors 12 to 18, and $13 for children 5 to 11; children under 5 are admitted free. There's a $2.25 charge for ordering tickets by phone; discounts are available on their website.

The **Red & White Fleet,** Pier 43½ (✆ **415/901-5254;** www.redandwhite.com), offers daily "Bay Cruises" tours that leave from Pier 43½. The tour boats cruise along the city waterfront, beneath the Golden Gate Bridge, past Angel Island, and around Alcatraz and are narrated in eight languages. Prices are $21 for adults, $18 for seniors and teens 12 to 17, and $14 for children 5 to 11. Discounts are available through online purchase.

BUS TOURS

Gray Line (✆ **888/428-6937** or 415/434-8687; www.sanfranciscosightseeing.com) is San Francisco's largest bus-tour operator. It offers numerous itineraries daily (far too many to list here). Free pickup and return are available between centrally located hotels and departure locations. Advance reservations are required for all tours except motorized cable car and trolley tours. Day and evening tours depart from Pier 43½ at Fisherman's Wharf; motorized cable car tours depart from Pier 39 and Pier 41.

SEAPLANE & HELICOPTER TOURS

For those of you seeking a little thrill and adventure during your vacation, consider booking a flight with **San Francisco Seaplane Tours,** the Bay Area's only seaplane tour company. For more than 60 years, this locally owned outfit has provided its customers a bird's-eye view of the city, flying directly over San Francisco at an altitude of about 1,500 feet. Sights you'll see during the narrated excursions include the Golden Gate and Bay Bridges, Alcatraz, Tiburon, and Sausalito. Half the fun, however, is taking off and landing on the water (which is surprisingly smooth). Trips depart from Sausalito, and they offer complimentary shuttle pick-up at Pier 39. Prices range from $139 per person for the 20-minute Golden Gate Tour to $189 for the 30-minute Champagne Sunset Flight, which includes a bottle of bubbly and a cozy backseat for two. Children's rates are also available, and cameras are welcome. (On calm days, the pilot will even roll the window down.) For more information or reservations, log onto www.seaplane.com or call ✆ **415/332-4843.**

Equally thrilling (and perhaps more so if you've never been in a helicopter) is a tour of San Francisco and the bay via **San Francisco Helicopters.** The $140 Vista package includes free shuttle pick-up from your hotel or Pier 39, and a 20-minute tour that takes you under—yes, under—the Golden Gate Bridge, over the city, and past the Bay Bridge and Alcatraz Island. After takeoff, the pilot gives a narrated tour and answers questions while the background music adds a bit of Disney-ride quality to the experience. (***Tip:*** The view from the front seat is the best.) Picnic lunch and sunset dinner packages are available as well. For more information or reservations, log onto www.sfhelicopters.com or call ✆ **800/400-2404** or 650/635-4500.

WALKING TOURS

Javawalk is a 2-hour walking tour by self-described "coffeehouse lizard" Elaine Sosa. As the name suggests, it's loosely a coffee walking tour through North Beach, but there's a lot more going on than drinking cups of brew. Javawalk also serves up a good share of historical and architectural trivia, offering something for everyone. The best part of the tour may be the camaraderie that develops among the participants. Sosa keeps the excursion interactive and fun, and it's obvious she knows a profusion of tales and trivia about the history of coffee and its North Beach roots. It's a guaranteed good time, particularly if you're addicted to caffeine. Javawalk is offered Saturday at 10am. The price is $20 per person, $10 for kids under 12. For information and reservations, call ✆ **415/673-9255;** or visit www.javawalk.com.

Cruisin' the Castro (✆ **415/255-1821;** www.cruisinthecastro.com) is an informative historical tour of San Francisco's most famous gay quarter, which will give you new insight into the contribution of the gay community to the city's political maturity, growth, and beauty. This fun and easy walking tour is for all ages, highlighting gay and lesbian history from 1849 to present. Stops include America's only Pink Triangle Park and Memorial, the original site of the AIDS Quilt Name Project, Harvey Milk's residence and photo shop, the Castro Theatre, and the Human Rights Campaign and Action Center. Tours run Tuesday through Saturday from 10am to noon, and meet at the Rainbow Flag at the Harvey Milk Plaza on the corner of Castro and Market streets above the Castro Muni station. Reservations are required. The tour, with lunch, costs $35 per adult, $25 for children 3 to 12.

On the **Haight-Ashbury Flower Power Walking Tour** (✆ **415/863-1621**), you explore hippie haunts with Pam and Bruce Brennan (the "Hippy Gourmet"). You'll revisit the Grateful Dead's crash pad, Janis Joplin's house, and other reminders of the Summer of Love in 2½ short hours. Tours begin at 9:30am on Tuesdays and Saturdays, and Fridays at 11am. The cost is $20 per person (cash only). Reservations are required. You can purchase tickets online at www.hippygourmet.com (click on the "Walking Tours" link at the bottom left of the webpage) or by calling ✆ 800/979-3370.

San Francisco's Chinatown is always fascinating, but for many visitors with limited time it's hard to know where to search out the "nontouristy" shops, restaurants, and historical spots in this microcosm of Chinese culture. **Wok Wiz Chinatown Walking Tours & Cooking Center,** 250 King St., Suite 268 (✆ **650/355-9657;** www.wokwiz.com), founded over 2 decades ago by author and cooking instructor Shirley Fong-Torres, is the answer. The Wok Wiz tours take you into Chinatown's nooks and crannies. Guides are Chinatown natives, speak fluent Cantonese, and are intimately acquainted with the neighborhood's alleys and small enterprises, as well as Chinatown's history, folklore, culture, and food. Tours are conducted daily from 10am to 1pm and include a 7-course dim sum lunch (a Chinese meal made up of many small plates of food). There's also a less expensive tour that does not include lunch. The walk is easy, as well as fun and fascinating. Groups are generally held to a maximum of 15, and reservations are essential. Prices (including lunch) are $40 for adults and $35 for children under 11; without lunch, prices are $28 and $23, respectively. Tickets can be purchased online at Shirley's website, www.wokwiz.com, or by calling © 212/209-3370. Shirley also operates an **I Can't Believe I Ate My Way Through Chinatown** tour. It starts with breakfast, moves to a wok shop, and stops for nibbles at a vegetarian restaurant, dim sum place, and a marketplace, before taking a break for a sumptuous authentic Cantonese luncheon. It's offered on most Saturdays and costs $80 per person, food included. Tickets to either tour can be purchased online at Shirley's website, www.wokwiz.com, or by calling © 212/209-3370.

Jay Gifford, founder of the **Victorian Homes Historical Walking Tour** (© **415/252-9485;** www.victorianwalk.com) and a San Francisco resident for more than 2 decades, communicates his enthusiasm and love of San Francisco throughout this highly entertaining walking tour. The 2½-hour tour, set at a leisurely pace, starts at the corner of Powell and Post streets at Union Square and incorporates a wealth of knowledge about San Francisco's Victorian architecture and the city's history—particularly the periods just before and after the great earthquake and fire of 1906. You'll stroll through Japantown, Pacific Heights, and Cow Hollow. In the process, you'll see more than 200 meticulously restored Victorians, including the sites where *Mrs. Doubtfire* and *Party of Five* were filmed. Jay's guests often find that they are the only ones on the quiet neighborhood streets, where tour buses are forbidden. The tour ends in Cow Hollow, where you can have lunch on your own, or return via bus to Union Square, passing through North Beach and Chinatown. Tours run daily and start at 11am rain or shine; cost is $20 per person (cash only).

9 Getting Outside

Half the fun in San Francisco takes place outdoors. If you're not in the mood to trek it, there are other things to do that allow you to enjoy the surroundings.

BALLOONING Although you must drive an hour to get to the tour site, hot-air ballooning over the Wine Country is an ethereal experience. **Adventures Aloft,** P.O. Box 2500, Vintage 1870, Yountville, CA 94599 (© **800/944-4408** or 707/944-4408; www.nvaloft.com), is Napa Valley's oldest hot-air balloon company, staffed with full-time professional pilots. Groups are small, and each flight lasts about an hour. The cost of $210 per person includes a post-adventure champagne brunch and a framed "first-flight" certificate. Flights launch daily at sunrise (weather permitting).

BEACHES Most days it's too chilly to hang out at the beach, but when the fog evaporates and the wind dies down, one of the best ways to spend the day is ocean-side in the city. On any truly hot day, thousands flock to the beach to worship the sun, build sandcastles, and throw the ball around. Without a wet suit, swimming is a fiercely cold endeavor and is not recommended. In any case, dip at your own risk—there are no lifeguards on duty and San Francisco's waters are cold and have strong undertows. On the South Bay, **Baker Beach** is ideal for picnicking, sunning, walking, or fishing against the backdrop of the Golden Gate (though pollution makes your catch not necessarily worthy of eating).

Ocean Beach, at the end of Golden Gate Park, on the westernmost side of the city, is San Francisco's largest beach—4 miles long. Just offshore, at the northern end of the beach, in front of Cliff House, are the jagged Seal Rocks, inhabited by various shorebirds and a large colony of barking sea lions (bring binoculars for a close-up view). To the left, Kelly's Cove is one of the more challenging surf spots in town. Ocean Beach is ideal for strolling or sunning, but don't swim here—tides are tricky, and each year bathers drown in the rough surf.

Stop by Ocean Beach bus terminal at the corner of Cabrillo and La Playa to learn about San Francisco's history in local artist Ray Beldner's whimsically historical sculpture garden. Then hike up the hill to explore **Cliff House** and the ruins of the **Sutro Baths.** These baths, once able to accommodate 24,000 bathers, were lost to fire in 1966.

BIKING The San Francisco Parks and Recreation Department maintains two city-designated bike routes. One winds 7.5 miles through Golden Gate Park to Lake Merced; the other traverses the city, starting in the south, and continues over the Golden Gate Bridge. These routes are not dedicated to bicyclists, who must exercise caution to avoid crashing into pedestrians. Helmets are recommended for adults and required by law for kids under 18. A bike map is available from the San Francisco Visitor Information Center, at Powell and Mason streets, for $3 (see "Visitor Information" in chapter 4), and from bicycle shops all around town.

Ocean Beach has a public walk- and bikeway that stretches along 5 waterfront blocks of the Great Highway between Noriega and Santiago streets. It's an easy ride from Cliff House or Golden Gate Park.

Avenue Cyclery, 756 Stanyan St., at Waller Street, in the Haight (✆ **415/387-3155**), rents bikes for $7 per hour or $28 per day. It's open daily, April through September from 10am to 7pm and October through March from 10am to 6pm. For cruising Fisherman's Wharf and the Golden Gate Bridge, your best bet is **Blazing Saddles** (✆ **415/202-8888;** www.blazingsaddles.com), which has five locations around Fisherman's Wharf. Bikes rent for $28 per day, including maps, locks, and helmets; tandem bikes are available as well.

BOATING At the **Golden Gate Park Boat House** (✆ **415/752-0347**) on Stow Lake, the park's largest body of water, you can rent a rowboat or pedal boat by the hour and steer over to Strawberry Hill, a large, round island in the middle of the lake, for lunch. There's usually a line on weekends. The boathouse is open daily from 10am to 4pm, weather permitting.

Cass' Marina, 1702 Bridgeway, Sausalito; P.O. Box 643; Sausalito, CA 94966 (✆ **800/472-4595** or 415/332-6789; www.cassmarina.com), is a certified sailing school that rents sailboats measuring 22 to 38 feet. Sail to the Golden Gate Bridge on your own or with a licensed skipper. In addition, large sailing yachts leave from Sausalito on a regularly scheduled basis. Call or check the website for schedules, prices, and availability of sailboats. The marina is open Wednesday through Monday from 9am to sunset.

CITY STAIR CLIMBING ★★ Many health clubs have stair-climbing machines and step classes, but in San Francisco, you need only go outside. The following city stair climbs will give you not only a good workout, but seriously stunning neighborhood, city, and bay views as well. Check www.sisterbetty.org/stairways for more ideas.

Filbert Street Steps, between Sansome Street and Telegraph Hill, are a particular challenge. Scaling the sheer eastern face of Telegraph Hill, this 377-step climb winds through verdant flower gardens and charming 19th-century cottages. Napier Lane, a narrow, wooden plank walkway, leads to Montgomery Street. Turn right and follow the path to the end of the cul-de-sac, where another stairway continues to Telegraph's panoramic summit.

The **Lyon Street Steps,** between Green Street and Broadway, were built in 1916. This historic stairway street contains four steep sets of stairs totaling 288 steps. Begin at Green Street and climb all the way up, past manicured hedges and flower gardens, to an iron gate that opens into the Presidio. A block east, on Baker Street, another set of 369 steps descends to Green Street.

FISHING **Berkeley Marina Sports Center,** 225 University Ave., Berkeley (✆ **510/237-3474;** www.berkeleysportfishing.com), makes daily trips for ling cod, rock fish, and many other types of game fish year-round, and it makes trips for salmon runs April through October. Fishing equipment is available; the cost, including boat ride and bait, is about $80 per person. Reservations are required, as are licenses for adults. One-day licenses can be purchased for $11 before departure. Find out the latest on the season by contacting their hot line at ✆ **510/486-8300** (press 3). Excursions run daily from 6am to 4pm. Fish are cleaned, filleted, and bagged on the return trip for a small fee (free for salmon fishing).

GOLF San Francisco has a few beautiful golf courses. One of the most lavish is the **Presidio Golf Course** (✆ **415/561-4661;** www.presidiogolf.com). Greens fees are $60 until 12:30pm for residents Monday through Thursday and $96 for nonresidents; rates drop to $50 until 2pm, then to $35 for the rest of the day for residents and non-residents. Friday though Sunday, rates are $96 for residents and $108 for nonresidents from 8 to 11am; from 11am to 12:30pm, the cost is $60 for residents. After that it's $50 for everyone until 2pm and $35 for the rest of the day. Carts are included. There are also two decent municipal courses in town.

The 9-hole **Golden Gate Park Course,** 47th Avenue and Fulton Street (✆ **415/751-8987;** www.goldengateparkgolf.com), charges greens fees of $14 per person Monday through Thursday, $18 Friday through Sunday. The 1,357-yard course is par 27. All holes are par 3, and this course is appropriate for all levels. The course is a little weathered in spots, but it's casual, fun, and inexpensive. It's open daily from sunup to sundown.

The 18-hole **Lincoln Park Golf Course,** 34th Avenue and Clement Street (✆ **415/221-9911;** www.parks.sfgov.org), charges greens fees of $31 per person Monday through Thursday, $36 Friday through Sunday, with rates decreasing after 4pm in summer, 2pm in winter. It's San Francisco's prettiest municipal course, with terrific views and fairways lined with Monterey cypress and pine trees. The 5,181-yard layout plays to par 68, and the 17th hole has a glistening ocean view. This is the oldest course in the city and one of the oldest in the West. It's open daily at daybreak.

HANDBALL The city's best handball courts are in Golden Gate Park, opposite Seventh Avenue, south of Middle Drive East. Courts are available free, on a first-come, first-served basis.

PARKS In addition to **Golden Gate Park** and the **Golden Gate National Recreation Area** (p. 173 and p. 177, respectively), San Francisco boasts more than 2,000 acres of parkland, most of which is perfect for picnicking or throwing around a Frisbee.

Smaller city parks include **Buena Vista Park** (Haight St. between Baker and Central sts.), which affords fine views of the Golden Gate Bridge and the area around it and is also a favored lounging ground for gay lovers; **Ina Coolbrith Park** (Taylor St. between Vallejo and Green sts.), offering views of the Bay Bridge and Alcatraz; and **Sigmund Stern Grove** (19th Ave. and Sloat Blvd.) in the Sunset District, which is the site of a famous free summer music festival.

One of my personal favorites is **Lincoln Park,** a 270-acre green on the northwestern side of the city at Clement Street and 34th Avenue. The Legion of Honor is here (p. 163), as is a scenic 18-hole municipal golf course (see "Golf," above). But the best things about this park are the 200-foot cliffs that overlook the Golden Gate Bridge and San Francisco Bay. To get to the park, take bus no. 38 from Union Square to 33rd and Geary streets, then walk a few blocks.

RUNNING The **ING Bay to Breakers Foot Race** ★ (© **415/359-2800;** www.ingbaytobreakers.com) is an annual 7.5-mile run from downtown to Ocean Beach. About 80,000 entrants take part in it, one of San Francisco's trademark events. Costumed participants and hordes of spectators add to the fun. The event is held on the third Sunday of May.

The San Francisco **Marathon** takes place annually in the middle of July. For more information, visit www.runsfm.com (no phone contact).

Great **jogging paths** include the entire expanse of Golden Gate Park, the shoreline along the Marina, and The Embarcadero.

TENNIS The **San Francisco Parks and Recreation Department** (© **415/753-7001**) maintains more than 132 free courts throughout the city. Almost all are available free, on a first-come, first-served basis. An additional 21 courts are available in **Golden Gate Park,** which cost $5 for 90 minutes during weekdays and $10 on weekends. Check the website for details on rules for reserving courts (www.parks.sfgov.org).

WALKING & HIKING The **Golden Gate National Recreation Area** offers plenty of opportunities. One incredible walk (or bike ride) is along the Golden Gate Promenade, from Aquatic Park to the Golden Gate Bridge. The 3.5-mile paved trail heads along the northern edge of the Presidio out to Fort Point, passing the marina, Crissy Field's new restored wetlands, a small beach, and plenty of athletic locals. You can also hike the Coastal Trail all the way from the Fort Point area to Cliff House. The park service maintains several other trails in the city. For more information or to pick up a map of the Golden Gate National Recreation Area, stop by the park service headquarters at Fort Mason; enter on Franklin Street (© **415/561-4700**).

Although most people drive to this spectacular vantage point, a more rejuvenating way to experience **Twin Peaks** is to walk up from the back roads of U.C. Medical Center (off Parnassus) or from either of the two roads that lead to the top (off Woodside or Clarendon aves.). The best time to trek is early morning, when the city is quiet, the air is crisp, and sightseers haven't crowded the parking lot. Keep an eye out for cars, however, because there's no real hiking trail, and be sure to walk beyond the lot and up to the highest vantage point.

10 Spectator Sports

The Bay Area's sports scene includes several major professional franchises. Check the local newspapers' sports sections for daily listings of local events.

MAJOR LEAGUE BASEBALL

The **San Francisco Giants** ★ play at **AT&T Park,** Third and King streets (✆ **415/972-2000;** www.sfgiants.com), in the China Basin section of SoMa. From April to October, 41,503 fans fill the seats here to root for the National League Giants. Tickets are hard to come by, but you can try to obtain some through **Tickets.com** (✆ **800/225-2277;** www.tickets.com).

The American League's **Oakland Athletics** play across the bay at McAfee Coliseum, at the Hegenberger Road exit from I-880, Oakland (✆ **510/430-8020;** www.athletics.mlb.com). The stadium holds over 50,000 spectators and is accessible through BART's Coliseum station. Tickets are available from the Coliseum Box Office or by phone through **Tickets.com** (✆ **800/225-2277;** www.tickets.com).

PRO BASKETBALL

The **Golden State Warriors** of the NBA play at the Arena in Oakland, a 19,200-seat facility at 7000 Coliseum Way in Oakland (✆ **510/986-2200;** www.nba.com/warriors). The season runs November through April, and most games start at 7:30pm. Tickets are available at the arena, online, and by phone through **Tickets.com** (✆ **800/225-2277;** www.tickets.com).

PRO FOOTBALL

The **San Francisco 49ers** (www.sf49ers.com) play at Monster Park, Giants Drive and Gilman Avenue, on Sundays August through December; kickoff is usually at 1pm. Tickets sell out early in the season but are available at higher prices through ticket agents beforehand and from "scalpers" (illegal ticket-sellers who are usually at the gates). Ask your hotel concierge for the best way to track down tickets.

The 49ers' archenemies, the **Oakland Raiders** (www.raiders.com), play at McAfee Coliseum, off the I-880 freeway (Nimitz). Call ✆ **800/RAIDERS** for ticket information.

COLLEGE FOOTBALL

The **University of California Golden Bears** play at Haas Pavilion, University of California, Berkeley (✆ **800/GO-BEARS** or 510/642-3277; www.calbears.com), on the university campus across the bay. Tickets are usually available at game time. Phone for schedules and information.

HORSE RACING

Ten miles northeast of San Francisco is scenic **Golden Gate Fields,** Buchanan Street off I-80, Albany (✆ **510/559-7300;** www.goldengatefields.com). The racing schedule changes yearly; please call or check the website for current schedule and admission prices. The track is on the seashore.

Bay Meadows, 2600 S. Delaware St., off U.S. 101, San Mateo (✆ **650/574-7223;** www.baymeadows.com), is a thoroughbred track on the peninsula about 20 miles south of downtown San Francisco. Call for admission prices and post times.

8

City Strolls

Hills schmills. Don't let a few steep slopes deter you from one of San Francisco's greatest pleasures—walking around the neighborhoods and exploring the city for yourself. Here are a couple of introductory walks that hit the highlights of my favorite neighborhoods for touring on foot. For more extensive city walking tours, check out ***Frommer's Memorable Walks in San Francisco*** (Wiley Publishing, Inc.).

WALKING TOUR 1 CHINATOWN: HISTORY, CULTURE, DIM SUM & THEN SOME

Start:	**Corner of Grant Avenue and Bush Street.**
Public Transportation:	**Bus nos. 2, 3, 4, 9X, 15, 30, 38, 45, or 76.**
Finish:	**Commercial Street between Montgomery and Kearny streets.**
Time:	**2 hours, not including museum or shopping stops.**
Best Times:	**Daylight hours, when the streets are most active.**
Worst Times:	**Early or late in the day, because shops are closed and no one is milling around.**
Hills That Could Kill:	**None.**

This tiny section of San Francisco, bounded loosely by Broadway and by Stockton, Kearny, and Bush streets, is said to harbor one of the largest Chinese populations outside Asia. Daily proof is the crowds of Chinese residents who flock to the herbal stores, vegetable markets, restaurants, and businesses. Chinatown also marks the spot where the city began its development in the mid-1800s. On this walk, you'll learn why Chinatown remains intriguing to all who wind through its narrow, crowded streets, and how its origins are responsible for the city as we know it.

To begin the tour, make your way to the corner of Bush Street and Grant Avenue, 4 blocks from Union Square and all the downtown buses, where you can't miss the Chinatown Gateway Arch.

❶ Chinatown Gateway Arch

Traditional Chinese villages have ceremonial gates like this one. A lot less formal than those in China, this gate was built more for the benefit of the tourist industry than anything else.

Once you cross the threshold, you'll be at the beginning of Chinatown's portion of Grant Avenue.

❷ Grant Avenue

This is a mecca for tourists who wander in and out of gift shops that offer a variety of unnecessary junk interspersed with quality imports. You'll also find decent restaurants and grocery stores frequented by Chinese residents, ranging from children to the oldest living people you've ever seen.

Walking Tour 1: Chinatown

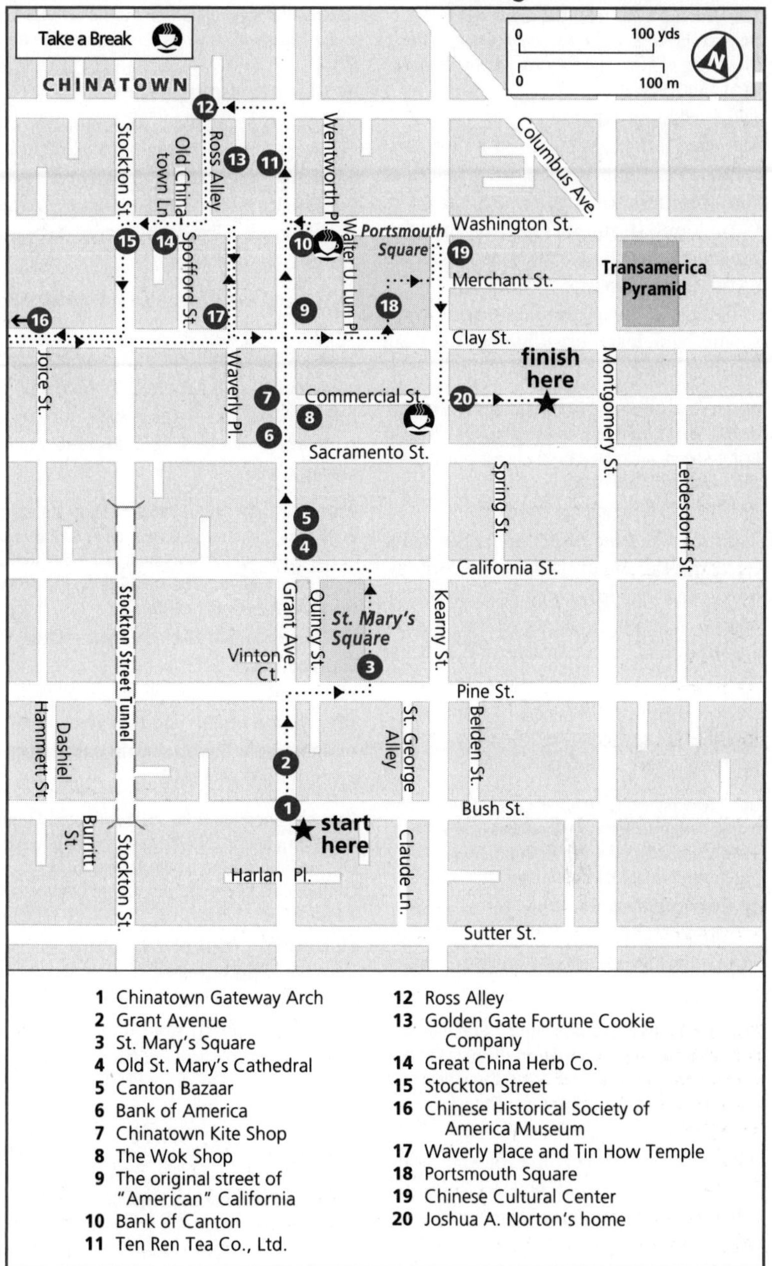

Tear yourself away from the shops and turn right at the corner of Pine Street. Cross to the other side of Pine, and on your left you'll come to St. Mary's Square.

3 St. Mary's Square

Here you'll find a huge metal-and-granite statue of Dr. Sun Yat-sen, the founder of the Republic of China. A native of Guangdong (Canton) Province, Sun Yat-sen led the rebellion that ended the reign of the Qing Dynasty.

Note also the second monument in the square, which honors Chinese-American victims of both World Wars.

Walk to the other end of the square, toward California Street, turn left, cross California Street at Grant Street, and you'll be standing in front of Old St. Mary's Cathedral.

4 Old St. Mary's Cathedral

The first Catholic cathedral in San Francisco and the site of the Chinese community's first English-language school, St. Mary's was built primarily by Chinese laborers and dedicated on Christmas Day 1854.

Step inside to find a written history of the church and turn-of-the-20th-century photos of San Francisco.

Upon leaving the church, take a right and walk to the corner of Grant Avenue and California Street, and then go right on Grant. Here you'll find a shop called Canton Bazaar.

5 Canton Bazaar

Of the knickknack and import shops lining Grant Avenue, this is one of the most popular; it's located at 616 Grant Ave.

Continue in the same direction on Grant Avenue, and cross Sacramento Street to the northwest corner of Sacramento and Grant. You'll be at the doorstep of the Bank of America.

6 Bank of America

This bank is an example of traditional Chinese architectural style. Notice the dragons subtly portrayed on many parts of the building.

Head in the same direction (north) on Grant, and a few doors down is the Chinatown Kite Shop.

7 Chinatown Kite Shop

This store, located at 717 Grant Ave., has an assortment of flying objects, including attractive fish kites, nylon or cotton windsock kites, hand-painted Chinese paper kites, wood-and-paper biplanes, and pentagonal kites.

Cross Grant, and you'll arrive at The Wok Shop.

8 The Wok Shop

Here's where you can purchase just about any cleaver, wok, cookbook, or vessel you might need for Chinese-style cooking in your own kitchen. It's located at 718 Grant Ave.

When you come out of The Wok Shop, go right. Walk past Commercial Street, and you'll arrive at the corner of Grant Avenue and Clay Street; cross Clay, and you'll be standing on the original street of "American" California.

9 Original Street of "American" California

Here an English seaman named William Richardson set up the first tent in 1835, making it the first place that an Anglo set up base in California.

Continue north on Grant to Washington Street. Turn right, and at 743 Washington St. you will be standing in front of the former Bank of Canton, now known as the United Commercial Bank.

10 United Commercial Bank

This building boasts the oldest (from 1909) Asian-style edifice in Chinatown. The three-tiered temple-style building once housed the China Telephone Exchange, known as "China-5" until 1945.

You're probably thirsty by now, so follow Washington Street a few doors down (east); on your right-hand side you will come upon Washington Bakery & Restaurant.

TAKE A BREAK
Washington Bakery & Restaurant is at 733 Washington St. No need to have a full meal here—the service can be abrupt. Do stop in, however, for a little potable adventure: snow red beans with ice cream. The sugary-sweet drink mixed with whole beans and ice cream is not something you're likely to have tried elsewhere, and it happens to be quite tasty. Whatever you do, don't fill up—a few blocks away, some wonderfully fresh dim sum awaits you.

Head back to Grant Avenue, cross Washington Street, cross Grant, and follow the west side of Grant 1 block to Ten Ren Tea Co., Ltd.

⓫ Ten Ren Tea Co., Ltd.

In this amazing shop at 949 Grant Ave., you can sample a freshly brewed tea variety and check out the dozens of drawers and canisters labeled with more than 40 kinds of tea. Like Washington Bakery, Ten Ren offers unusual drinks worth trying: delightful hot or iced milk teas containing giant blobs of jelly or tapioca. Try black tea or green tea and enjoy the outstanding flavors and the giant balls of tapioca slipping around in your mouth.

Leave Ten Ren, make a left, and when you reach Jackson Street, make another left. Follow Jackson Street until you reach Ross Alley, and turn left into the alley.

⓬ Ross Alley

As you walk along this narrow street, just one of the many alleyways that crisscrossed Chinatown to accommodate the many immigrants who jammed into the neighborhood, it's not difficult to believe that this block once was rife with gambling dens.

As you follow the alley south, on the left side of the street you'll encounter the Golden Gate Fortune Cookie Company.

⓭ Golden Gate Fortune Cookie Company

Located at 56 Ross Alley, this store is little more than a tiny place where three women sit at a conveyer belt, folding messages into warm cookies as the manager invariably calls out to tourists, beckoning them to buy a big bag of the fortune-telling treats.

You can purchase regular fortunes, unfolded flat cookies without fortunes, or, if you bring your own fortunes, make custom cookies (I often do this when I'm having dinner parties) at around $6 for 50 cookies—a very cheap way to impress your friends! Or, of course, you can just take a peek and move on.

As you exit the alley, cross Washington Street, take a right heading west on Washington, and you're in front of the Great China Herb Co.

⓮ Great China Herb Co.

For centuries, the Chinese have come to shops like this one, at 857 Washington St., which are full of exotic herbs, roots, and other natural substances. They buy what they believe will cure all types of ailments and ensure good health and long life. Thankfully, unlike owners in many similar area shops, Mr. and Mrs. Ho speak English, so you will not be met with a blank stare when you inquire what exactly is in each box, bag, or jar arranged along dozens of shelves. It is important to note that you should not use Chinese herbs without the guidance of a knowledgeable source such as an herb doctor. They may be natural, but they also can be quite powerful and are potentially harmful if misused.

Take a left upon leaving the store and walk to Stockton Street.

⓯ Stockton Street

The section of Stockton Street between Broadway and Sacramento Street is where most of the residents of Chinatown do their daily shopping.

One noteworthy part of this area's history is **Cameron House** (actually up the hill at 920 Sacramento St., near Stockton St.), which was named after Donaldina Cameron (1869–1968). Called Lo Mo, or "the Mother," by the Chinese, she spent her life trying to free Chinese women who came to America in hopes of marrying well but who found themselves forced into prostitution and slavery. Today, the house still helps women free themselves from domestic violence.

A good stop if you're in the market for some jewelry is **Jade Galore** (1000 Stockton St., at Washington St.). Though the employees aren't exactly warm and fuzzy, they've got the goods. In addition to purveying jade jewelry, the store does a fair trade in diamonds.

After browsing at Jade Galore, you might want to wander up Stockton Street to absorb the atmosphere and street life of this less-tourist-oriented Chinese community before doubling back to Washington Street. At 1068 Stockton St. you'll find **AA Bakery & Café,** an extremely colorful bakery with Golden Gate Bridge–shaped cakes, bright green and pink snacks, moon cakes, and a flow of Chinese diners catching up over pastries. Another fun place at which to peek is **Gourmet Delight B.B.Q.,** at 1045 Stockton St., where barbecued duck and pork are supplemented by steamed pigs' feet and chicken feet. Everything's to go here, so if you grab a snack, don't forget napkins. Head farther north along the street and you'll see live fish and fowl awaiting their fate as the day's dinner.

Meander south on Stockton Street to Clay Street and turn west (right) onto Clay. Continue to 965 Clay St. (Make sure you come Tues–Fri noon–5pm or Sat or Sun noon–4pm.) You've arrived at the museum at 965 Clay St.

⓰ Chinese Historical Society of America Museum

Founded in 1963, this museum (✆ **415/391-1188**) has a small but fascinating collection that illuminates the role of Chinese immigrants in American history, particularly in San Francisco and the rest of California.

The interesting artifacts on display include a shrimp-cleaning machine; 19th-century clothing and slippers of the Chinese pioneers; Chinese herbs and scales; historic hand-carved and painted shop signs; and a series of photographs that document the development of Chinese culture in America.

The goal of this organization is not only to "study, record, acquire, and preserve all suitable artifacts and such cultural items as manuscripts, books, and works of art . . . which have a bearing on the history of the Chinese living in the United States of America," but also to "promote the contributions that Chinese Americans living in this country have made to the United States of America." It's an admirable and much-needed effort, considering what little recognition and appreciation the Chinese have received throughout American history.

The museum is open Tuesday through Friday from noon to 5pm and Saturday and Sunday from noon to 4pm. Admission is $3 for adults, $2 for college students with ID and seniors, and $1 for kids 6 to 17.

Retrace your steps, heading east on Clay Street back toward Grant Avenue. Turn left onto Waverly Place.

⓱ Waverly Place

Also known as "The Street of Painted Balconies," Waverly Place is probably Chinatown's most popular side street or alleyway because of its painted balconies and colorful architectural details—a sort of Chinese-style New Orleans street. And though you can admire the architecture only from the ground, because most of the buildings are private family associations or temples, with a recent beautification and renovation by the City, it's definitely worth checking out.

One temple you can visit (but make sure it's open before you climb the long, narrow stairway) is the **Tin How Temple,** at 125 Waverly Place. Accessible via the stairway three floors up, this incense-laden sanctuary, decorated in traditional black, red, and gold lacquered wood, is a house of worship for Chinese Buddhists, who come here to pray, meditate, and send offerings to their ancestors and to Tin How, the Queen of the Heavens and Goddess of the Seven Seas. There are no scheduled services, but you are welcome to visit. Just remember to quietly respect those who are here to pray, and try to be as unobtrusive as possible. It is customary to give a donation or buy a bundle of incense during your visit.

Once you've finished exploring Waverly Place, walk east on Clay Street, past Grant Avenue, and continue until you come upon the block-wide urban playground that is also the most important site in San Francisco's history.

⓲ Portsmouth Square

This very spot was the center of the region's first township, which was called Yerba Buena before it was renamed San Francisco in 1847. Around 1846, before any semblance of a city had taken shape, this plaza lay at the foot of the bay's eastern shoreline. There were fewer than 50 non–Native American residents in the settlement, there were no substantial buildings to speak of, and the few boats that pulled into the cove did so less than a block from where you're sitting.

In 1846, when California was claimed as a U.S. territory, the marines who landed here named the square after their ship, the USS *Portsmouth.* (Today, a bronze plaque marks the spot where they raised the U.S. flag.)

Yerba Buena remained a modest township until the gold rush of 1849 when, over the next 2 years, the population grew from under 1,000 to over 19,000, as gold seekers from around the world made their way here.

When the square became too crowded, long wharves were constructed to support new buildings above the bay. Eventually, the entire area became landfill. That was almost 150 years ago, but today the square still serves as an important meeting place for neighborhood Chinese—a sort of communal outdoor living room.

Throughout the day, the square is heavily trafficked by children and—in large part—by elderly men, who gamble over Chinese cards. If you arrive early in the morning, you might come across people practicing tai chi.

It is said that Robert Louis Stevenson used to love to sit on a bench here and watch life go by. (At the northeast corner of the square, you'll find a monument to his memory, consisting of a model of the *Hispaniola,* the ship in Stevenson's novel *Treasure Island,* and an excerpt from his "Christmas Sermon.")

Once you've had your fill of the square, exit to the east at Kearny Street. Directly across the street, at 750 Kearny, is the Holiday Inn. Cross the street, enter the hotel, and take the elevator to the third floor, where you'll find the Chinese Culture Center.

⓳ Chinese Culture Center

This center is oriented toward both the community and tourists, offering interesting display cases of Chinese art and a gallery with rotating exhibits of Asian art and writings. The center is open Tuesday through Saturday from 10am to 4pm.

When you leave the Holiday Inn, take a left on Kearny and go 3 short blocks to Commercial Street. Take a left onto Commercial and note that you are standing on the street once known as the site of Joshua A. Norton's Home.

⓴ Joshua A. Norton's Home

Norton, the self-proclaimed "Emperor of the United States and Protector of Mexico," used to walk around the streets in an old brass-buttoned military uniform, sporting a hat with a "dusty plume." He lived in a fantasy world, and San Franciscans humored him at every turn.

Norton was born around 1815 in the British Isles and sailed as a young man to South Africa, where he served as a colonial rifleman. He came to San Francisco in 1849 with $40,000 and proceeded to double and triple his fortune in real estate. Unfortunately for him, he next chose to go into the rice business. While Norton was busy cornering the market and forcing prices up, several ships loaded with rice arrived unexpectedly in San Francisco's harbor. The rice market was suddenly flooded, and Norton was forced into bankruptcy. He left San Francisco for about 3 years and must have experienced a breakdown (or revelation) of some sort, for upon his return, Norton thought he was an emperor.

Instead of ostracizing him, however, San Franciscans embraced him as their own homegrown lunatic and gave him free meals.

When Emperor Norton died in 1880 (while sleeping at the corner of California St. and Grant Ave.), approximately 10,000 people passed by his coffin, which was bought with money raised at the Pacific Union Club, and more than 30,000 people participated in the funeral procession. Today you won't see a trace of his character, but it's fun to imagine him cruising the street.

From here, if you've still got an appetite, you should go directly to 631 Kearny (at Clay St.), home of the R&G Lounge.

TAKE A BREAK
The **R&G Lounge** is a sure thing for tasty $5 rice-plate specials, chicken with black-bean sauce, and gorgeously tender and tangy R&G Special Beef.

Otherwise, you might want to backtrack on Commercial Street to Grant Avenue, take a left, and follow Grant back to Bush Street, the entrance to Chinatown. You'll be at the beginning of the Union Square area, where you can catch any number of buses (especially on Market St.) or cable cars or do a little shopping. Or you might backtrack to Grant, take a right (north), and follow Grant to the end. You'll be at Broadway and Columbus, the beginning of North Beach, where you can venture onward for our North Beach tour (see below).

WALKING TOUR 2 GETTING TO KNOW NORTH BEACH

Start:	**Intersection of Montgomery Street, Columbus Avenue, and Washington Street.**
Public Transportation:	**Bus no. 10, 12, 15, 30X, or 41.**
Finish:	**Washington Square.**
Time:	**3 hours, including a stop for lunch.**
Best Times:	**Monday through Saturday between 11am and 4pm.**
Worst Times:	**Sunday, when shops are closed.**
Hills That Could Kill:	**The Montgomery Street hill from Broadway to Vallejo Street; otherwise, this is an easy walk.**

Along with Chinatown, North Beach is one of the city's oldest neighborhoods. Originally the Latin Quarter, it became the city's Italian district when Italian immigrants moved "uphill" in the early 1870s, crossing Broadway from the Jackson Square area and settling in. They quickly established restaurants, cafes, bakeries, and other businesses familiar to them from their homeland. The "Beat Generation" helped put North Beach on the map, with the likes of Jack Kerouac and Allen Ginsberg holding court in the area's cafes during the 1950s. Although most of the original Beat poets are gone, their spirit lives on in North Beach, which is still a haven for bohemian artists and writers. The neighborhood, thankfully, retains its Italian village feel; it's a place where residents from all walks of life enjoy taking time for conversation over pastries and frothy cappuccinos.

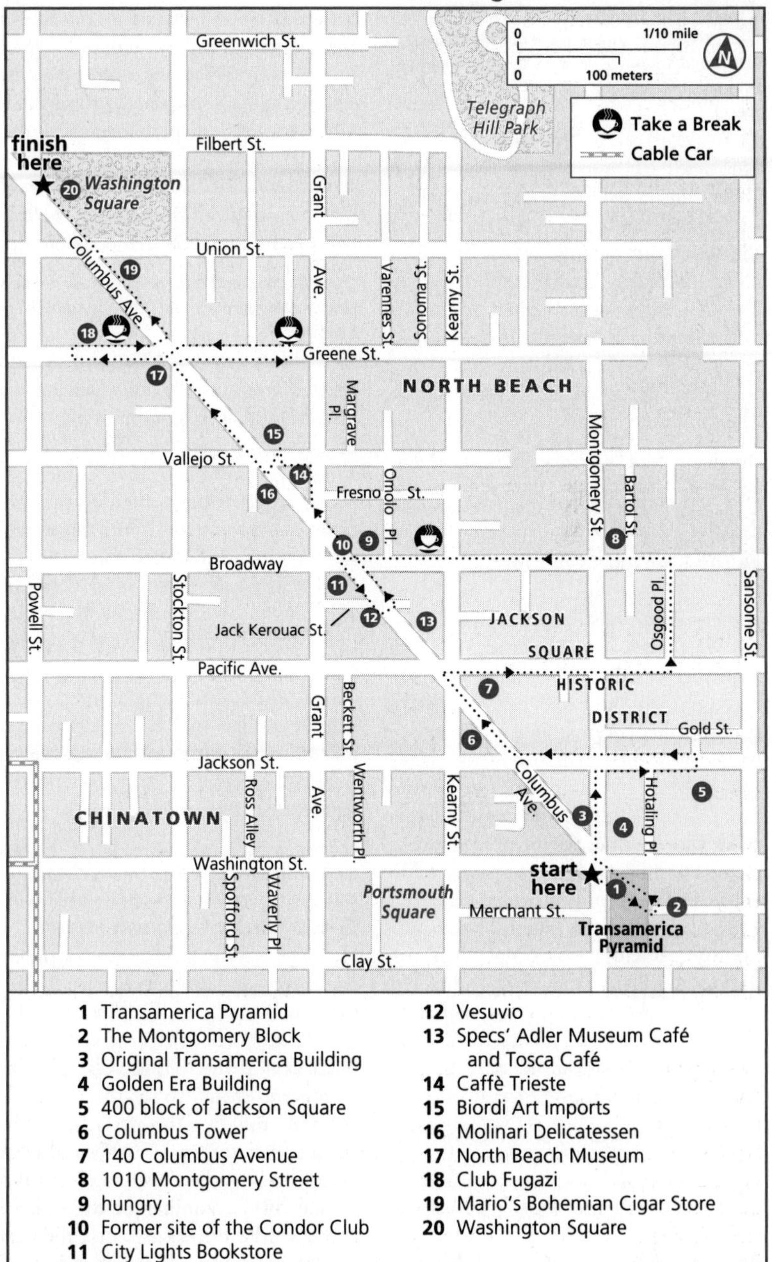
0
1/10 mile
0
100 meters
N
Take a Break
Cable Car
Telegraph Hill Park
Greenwich St.
Filbert St.
finish here
Washington Square
Union St.
Columbus Ave.
Grant Ave.
Varennes St.
Sonoma St.
Kearny St.
Greene St.
NORTH BEACH
Margrave Pl.
Vallejo St.
Fresno St.
Omolo Pl.
Montgomery St.
Bartol St.
Broadway
Powell St.
Stockton St.
Jack Kerouac St.
Osgood Pl.
Sansome St.
JACKSON SQUARE HISTORIC DISTRICT
Pacific Ave.
Beckett St.
Gold St.
Jackson St.
Ross Alley
Wentworth Pl.
Hotaling Pl.
CHINATOWN
Washington St.
Spofford St.
Waverly Pl.
Portsmouth Square
start here
Merchant St.
Transamerica Pyramid
Clay St.
1 Transamerica Pyramid
2 The Montgomery Block
3 Original Transamerica Building
4 Golden Era Building
5 400 block of Jackson Square
6 Columbus Tower
7 140 Columbus Avenue
8 1010 Montgomery Street
9 hungry i
10 Former site of the Condor Club
11 City Lights Bookstore
12 Vesuvio
13 Specs' Adler Museum Café and Tosca Café
14 Caffè Trieste
15 Biordi Art Imports
16 Molinari Delicatessen
17 North Beach Museum
18 Club Fugazi
19 Mario's Bohemian Cigar Store
20 Washington Square

If there's one landmark you can't miss, it's the familiar building on the corner of Montgomery Street and Columbus Avenue, the Transamerica Pyramid (take bus nos. 15, 30X, or 41 to get there).

❶ Transamerica Pyramid

Noted for its spire (which rises 212 ft. above the top floor) and its "wings" (which begin at the 29th floor and stop at the spire), this pyramid is San Francisco's tallest building and a hallmark of the skyline. You might want to take a peek at one of the rotating art exhibits in the lobby or go around to the right and into ½-acre Redwood Park, which is part of the Transamerica Center.

The Transamerica Pyramid occupies part of the 600 block of Montgomery Street, which once held a historic building called the Montgomery Block.

❷ The Montgomery Block

Originally four stories high, the Montgomery Block was the tallest building in the West when it was built in 1853. San Franciscans called it "Halleck's Folly" because it was built on a raft of redwood logs that had been bolted together and floated at the edge of the ocean (which was right at Montgomery St. at that time). The building was demolished in 1959 but is fondly remembered for its historical importance as the power center of the city. Its tenants included artists and writers of all kinds, among them Jack London, George Sterling, Ambrose Bierce, Bret Harte, and Mark Twain. This is a picturesque area, but there's no particular spot to direct you to. It's worth looking around, however, if only for the block's historical importance.

From the southeast corner of Montgomery and Washington streets, look across Washington to the corner of Columbus Avenue, and you'll see the original Transamerica Building, located at 4 Columbus Ave.

❸ Original Transamerica Building

The original Transamerica Building is a Beaux Arts flatiron-shaped building covered in terra cotta; it was also the home of Sanwa Bank and Fugazi Bank. Built for the Banco Populare Italiano Operaia Fugazi in 1909, it was originally a two-story building and gained a third floor in 1916. In 1928, Fugazi merged his bank with the Bank of America, which was started by A. P. Giannini, who also created the Transamerica Corporation. The building now houses a Church of Scientology.

Cross Washington Street and continue north on Montgomery Street to no. 730, the Golden Era Building.

❹ Golden Era Building

Erected around 1852, this San Francisco historic landmark building is named after the literary magazine, *The Golden Era,* which was published here. Some of the young writers who worked on the magazine were known as "The Bohemians"; they included Samuel Clemens (also known as Mark Twain) and Bret Harte (who began as a typesetter here). Backtrack a few dozen feet and stop for a minute to admire the exterior of the annex, at no. 722, which, after years of neglect and lawsuits, has finally been stabilized and is going to be developed. The Belli Annex, as it is currently known, is registered as a historic landmark.

Continue north on Washington Street, and take the first right onto Jackson Street. Continue until you hit the 400 block of Jackson Square.

❺ 400 Block of Jackson Square

Here's where you'll find some of the only commercial buildings to survive the 1906 earthquake and fire. The building at no. 415 Jackson (ca. 1853) served as headquarters for the Ghirardelli Chocolate Company from 1855 to 1894. The Hotaling Building (no. 451) was built in 1866 and features pediments and quoins of cast iron applied over the brick walls. At no. 441 is another of the buildings that survived the disaster of 1906. Constructed between 1850 and 1852 with ship masts for interior supporting columns, it served as the French Consulate from 1865 to 1876.

Cross the street, and backtrack on Jackson Street. Continue toward the intersection of Columbus Avenue and Jackson Street. Turn right on Columbus and look across the street for the small triangular building at the junction of Kearny Street and Columbus Avenue, Columbus Tower (also known as the Sentinel Building).

6 Columbus Tower

If you walk a little farther, and then turn around and look back down Columbus, you'll be able to get a better look at Columbus Tower. The flatiron beauty, a building shaped to a triangular site, went up between 1905 and 1907. Movie director and producer Francis Ford Coppola bought and restored it in the mid-1970s; it is now home to his film production company, American Zoetrope Studios. The building's cafe showcases all things Rubicon (Coppola's winery)—including olive oil, Parmesan cheese, and wine. It's a great place to stop for a glass of wine, an espresso, or a thin-crusted pizza snack.

Across the street from Columbus Tower on Columbus Avenue is 140 Columbus Ave.

7 140 Columbus Ave.

Although it was closed for a few years, the **Purple Onion** (**✆ 415/956-1653**), famous for its many renowned headliners who often played here before they became famous, is again host to an eclectic mix of music and comedy. Let's hope the next Phyllis Diller, who's now so big that she's famous for something as simple as her laugh—and who was still struggling when she played a 2-week engagement here in the late 1950s—will catch her big break here, too.

Continue north on Columbus, and then turn right on Pacific Avenue. After you cross Montgomery Street, you'll find brick-lined Osgood Place on the left. A registered historic landmark, it is one of the few quiet—and car-free—little alleyways left in the city. Stroll up Osgood and go left on Broadway to 1010 Montgomery St. (at Broadway).

8 1010 Montgomery St.

This is where Allen Ginsberg lived when he wrote his legendary poem, "Howl," first performed on October 13, 1955, in a converted auto-repair shop at the corner of Fillmore and Union streets. By the time Ginsberg finished reading, he was crying and the audience was going wild. Jack Kerouac proclaimed, "Ginsberg, this poem will make you famous in San Francisco."

Continue along Broadway toward Columbus Avenue. This stretch of Broadway is San Francisco's answer to New York's Times Square, complete with strip clubs and peep shows that are being pushed aside by restaurants, clubs, and an endless crowd of visitors. It's among the most sought-after locations in the city as more and more profitable restaurants and clubs spring up. Keep walking west on Broadway, and on the right side of the street, you'll come to Black Oak Books, 540 Broadway. It sells new and used discount books and is worth a quick trip inside for a good, cheap read. A few dozen yards farther up Broadway is the current location of the hungry i.

9 hungry i

Now a seedy strip club (at 546 Broadway), the original hungry i (at 599 Jackson St., which is under construction for senior housing) was owned and operated by the vociferous "Big Daddy" Nordstrom. If you had been here while Enrico Banducci was in charge, you would have found only a plain room with an exposed brick wall and director's chairs around small tables. A who's who of nightclub entertainers fortified their careers at the original hungry i, including Lenny Bruce, Billie Holiday (who first sang "Strange Fruit" there), Bill Cosby, Richard Pryor, Woody Allen, and Barbra Streisand.

At the corner of Broadway and Columbus Avenue, you will see the former site of the Condor Club.

10 Former Site of the Condor Club

The Condor Club was located at 300 Columbus Ave.; this is where Carol Doda scandalously bared her breasts and danced topless for the first time in 1964. Note the bronze plaque claiming the Condor Club as BIRTHPLACE OF THE WORLD'S FIRST TOPLESS & BOTTOMLESS ENTERTAINMENT. Go inside what is now the Condor Sports Bar and have a look at the framed newspaper clippings that hang around the dining room. From the elevated back room, you can see Doda's old dressing room and, on the floor below, an outline of the piano that would descend from the second floor with her atop it.

When you leave the Condor Sports Bar, cross to the south side of Broadway. Note the mural of jazz musicians painted on the entire side of the building directly across Columbus Avenue. Diagonally across the intersection from the Condor Sports Bar is the City Lights bookstore.

⓫ City Lights Booksellers & Publishers

Founded in 1953 and owned by one of the first Beat poets to arrive in San Francisco, Lawrence Ferlinghetti, City Lights is now a city landmark and literary mecca. Located at 261 Columbus Ave., it's one of the last of the Beat-era hangouts in operation. An active participant in the Beat movement, Ferlinghetti established his shop as a meeting place where writers and bibliophiles could (and still do) attend poetry readings and other events. A vibrant part of the literary scene, the well-stocked bookshop prides itself on its collection of art, poetry, and political paperbacks.

Upon exiting City Lights bookstore, turn right, cross aptly named Jack Kerouac Street, and stop by Vesuvio, the bar on your right.

⓬ Vesuvio

Because of its proximity to City Lights bookstore, Vesuvio became a favorite hangout of the Beats. Dylan Thomas used to drink here, as did Jack Kerouac, Ferlinghetti, and Ginsberg. Even today, Vesuvio, which opened in 1949, maintains its original bohemian atmosphere. The bar is located at 255 Columbus Ave. (at Jack Kerouac St.) and dates from 1913. It is an excellent example of pressed-tin architecture.

Facing Vesuvio across Columbus Avenue is another favorite spot of the Beat Generation:

⓭ Spec's Adler Museum Café

Located at 12 Saroyan Place, this is one of the city's funkiest bars, a small, dimly lit watering hole with ceiling-hung maritime flags and exposed brick walls crammed with memorabilia. Within the bar is a mini-museum that consists of a few glass cases filled with mementos brought by seamen who frequented the pub from the '40s and onward.

From here, walk back up Columbus across Broadway to Grant Avenue. Turn right on Grant, and continue until you come to Vallejo Street. At 601 Vallejo St. (at Grant Ave.) is Caffè Trieste.

⓮ Caffè Trieste

Yet another favorite spot of the Beats and founded by Gianni Giotta in 1956, Caffè Trieste is still run by family members. The quintessential San Francisco coffeehouse, Trieste features opera on the jukebox, and the real thing, performed by the Giottas, on Saturday afternoons. Any day of the week is a good one to stop in for a cappuccino or espresso—the beans are roasted right next door.

Go left out of Caffè Trieste onto Vallejo Street, turn right on Columbus Avenue, and bump into the loveliest shop in all of North Beach, Biordi Art Imports, located at 412 Columbus Ave.

⓯ Biordi Art Imports

This store has carried imported hand-painted majolica pottery from the hill towns of central Italy for more than 50 years. Some of the colorful patterns date from the 14th century. Biordi hand-picks its artisans, and its catalog includes biographies of those who are currently represented.

Across Columbus Avenue, at the corner of Vallejo Street, is the Molinari Delicatessen.

⓰ Molinari Delicatessen

This deli, located at 373 Columbus Ave., has been selling its pungent, air-dried salamis since 1896. Ravioli and tortellini are made in the back of the shop, but it's the mouthwatering selection of cold salads, cheeses, and marinades up front that captures the attention of most folks. Each Italian sub is big enough for two hearty appetites.

Walk north to the lively intersection of Columbus, Green, and Stockton streets, and look for the U.S. Bank at 1435 Stockton St. On the second floor of the bank, you'll find the North Beach Museum.

⓱ North Beach Museum

The North Beach Museum displays historical artifacts that tell the story of North Beach, Chinatown, and Fisherman's Wharf. Just before you enter the museum, you'll find a framed, handwritten poem by Lawrence Ferlinghetti that captures his impressions of this primarily Italian neighborhood. After passing through the glass doors, visitors see many photographs of some of the first Chinese and Italian immigrants, as well as pictures of San Francisco after the 1906 earthquake. You can visit the museum any time the bank is open (unfortunately, it's closed on weekends), and admission is free.

Now backtrack toward Columbus Avenue and go left on Green Street to Club Fugazi, at 678 Green St.

⓲ Club Fugazi

It doesn't look like much from the outside, but Fugazi Hall was donated to the city (and more important, the North Beach area) by John Fugazi, the founder of the Italian bank that was taken over by A. P. Giannini and turned into the original Transamerica Corporation. For many years, Fugazi Hall has been staging the zany and whimsical musical revue *Beach Blanket Babylon.* The show evolved from Steve Silver's Rent-a-Freak service, which consisted of a group of partygoers who would attend parties dressed as any number of characters in outrageous costumes. The fun caught on and soon became *Beach Blanket Babylon.*

If you love comedy, you'll love this show. We don't want to spoil it for you by telling you what it's about, but if you get tickets and they're in an unreserved-seat section, you should arrive fairly early because you'll be seated around small cocktail tables on a first-come, first-served basis. (Two sections have reserved seating, four don't, and all of them frequently sell out weeks in advance; however, sometimes it is possible to get tickets at the last minute on weekdays.) You'll want to be as close to the stage as possible. This supercharged show (see p. 229 for more information) is definitely worth the price of admission.

TAKE A BREAK
Head back the way you came on Green Street. Before you get to Columbus Avenue, you'll see **O'Reilly's Irish Pub** (622 Green St.), a homey watering hole that dishes out good, hearty Irish food and a fine selection of beers (including Guinness, of course) that are best enjoyed at one of the sidewalk tables. Always a conversation piece is the mural of Irish authors peering from the back wall. How many can you name?

As you come out of O'Reilly's, turn left, cross Columbus Avenue, and then take a left onto Columbus. Proceed 1 block northwest to Mario's Bohemian Cigar Store.

⓳ Mario's Bohemian Cigar Store

Located at 566 Columbus Ave., across the street from Washington Square, this is one of North Beach's most popular neighborhood hangouts. No, it does not sell cigars, but the cramped and casual space overlooking Washington Square does sell killer focaccia sandwiches, coffee drinks, beer, and wine.

Our next stop, directly across Union Street, is Washington Square.

⓴ Washington Square

This is one of the oldest parks in the city. The land was designated a public park in 1847 and has undergone many changes since then. Its current landscaping dates from 1955. You'll notice **Saints Peter and Paul Church** (the religious center for the neighborhood's Italian community) on the northwest end. Take a few moments to go inside and check out the traditional Italian interior. Note that this is the church in which baseball great Joe DiMaggio married his first wife, Dorothy Arnold. He wasn't allowed to marry Marilyn Monroe here because he had been divorced. He married Monroe at City Hall and came here for publicity photos.

Today the park is a pleasant place in which to soak up the sun, read a book, or chat with a retired Italian octogenarian who has seen the city grow and change.

From here, you can see the famous Coit Tower at the top of Telegraph Hill to the northwest. If you'd like to get back to your starting point at Columbus and Montgomery streets, walk south (away from the water) on Columbus.

9

Shopping

Like its population, San Francisco's shopping scene is incredibly diverse. Every style, era, fetish, and financial status is represented here—not in huge, sprawling shopping malls, but in hundreds of boutiques and secondhand stores scattered throughout the city. Whether it's a pair of Jimmy Choo shoes, Chanel knockoff, or Chinese herbal medicine you're looking for, San Francisco's got it. Just pick a shopping neighborhood, wear some sensible shoes, and you're sure to end up with at least a few take-home treasures.

1 The Shopping Scene

MAJOR SHOPPING AREAS

San Francisco has many shopping areas, but the following places are where you'll find most of the action.

UNION SQUARE & ENVIRONS San Francisco's most congested and popular shopping mecca is centered on Union Square and bordered by Bush, Taylor, Market, and Montgomery streets. Most of the big department stores and many high-end specialty shops are here. Be sure to venture to Grant Avenue, Post and Sutter streets, and Maiden Lane. This area is a hub for public transportation; all Market Street and several other buses run here, as do the Powell–Hyde and Powell–Mason cable car lines. You can also take the Muni streetcar to the Powell Street station.

CHINATOWN When you pass through the gate to Chinatown on Grant Avenue, say goodbye to the world of fashion and hello to a swarm of cheap tourist shops selling everything from linen and jade to plastic toys and $2 slippers. But that's not all Chinatown has to offer. The real gems are tucked away on side streets or are small, one-person shops selling Chinese herbs, original art, and jewelry. Grant Avenue is the area's main thoroughfare, and the side streets between Bush Street and Columbus Avenue are full of restaurants, markets, and eclectic shops. Stockton Street is best for grocery shopping (including live fowl and fish). Walking is the way to get around, because traffic through this area is slow and parking is next to impossible. Most stores in Chinatown are open daily from 10am to 10pm. Take bus no. 1, 9X, 15, 30, 41, or 45.

UNION STREET Union Street, from Fillmore Street to Van Ness Avenue, caters to the upper-middle-class crowd. It's a great place to stroll, window-shop the plethora of boutiques, try the cafes and restaurants, and watch the beautiful people parade by. Take bus no. 22, 41, 45, 47, 49, or 76.

Tips Just the Facts: Hours, Taxes & Shipping

Store hours are generally Monday through Saturday from 10am to 6pm and Sunday from noon to 5pm. Most department stores stay open later, as do shops around Fisherman's Wharf, the most heavily visited area (by tourists).

Sales tax in San Francisco is 8.5%, which is added on at the register for all goods and services purchased. If you live out of state and buy an expensive item, you might want to have the store ship it home for you. You'll have to pay for shipping, but you'll escape paying the sales tax.

Most of the city's shops can wrap your purchase and **ship** it anywhere in the world. If they can't, you can send it yourself, either through **UPS** (✆ **800/742-5877**), **FedEx** (✆ **800/463-3339**), or the U.S. Postal Service (see "Fast Facts: San Francisco," in chapter 2).

CHESTNUT STREET Parallel and a few blocks north, Chestnut is a younger version of Union Street. It holds endless shopping and dining choices, and an ever-tanned, superfit population of postgraduate singles who hang around cafes and scope each other out. Take bus no. 22, 28, 30, 43, or 76.

FILLMORE STREET Some of the best shopping in town is packed into 5 blocks of Fillmore Street in Pacific Heights. From Jackson to Sutter streets, Fillmore is the perfect place to grab a bite and peruse the high-priced boutiques, crafts shops, and incredible housewares stores. (Don't miss Zinc Details; p. 219.) Take bus no. 1, 2, 3, 4, 12, 22, or 24.

HAIGHT STREET Green hair, spiked hair, no hair, or mohair—even the hippies look conservative next to Haight Street's dramatic fashion freaks. The shopping in the 6 blocks of upper Haight Street between Central Avenue and Stanyan Street reflects its clientele. It offers everything from incense and European and American street styles to furniture and antique clothing. Bus nos. 6, 7, 66, and 71 run the length of Haight Street, and nos. 33 and 43 run through upper Haight Street. The Muni streetcar N line stops at Waller Street and Cole Street.

SOMA Although this area isn't suitable for strolling, you'll find almost all the discount shopping in warehouse spaces south of Market. You can pick up a discount-shopping guide at most major hotels. Many bus lines pass through this area.

HAYES VALLEY It's not the prettiest area in town, with some of the shadier housing projects a few blocks away. But while most neighborhoods cater to more conservative or trendy shoppers, lower Hayes Street, between Octavia and Gough streets, celebrates anything vintage, chic, artistic, or downright funky. With new shops opening frequently, it's definitely the most interesting new shopping area in town, with furniture and glass stores, thrift shops, trendy shoe stores, and men's and women's clothiers. You can find lots of great antiques shops south on Octavia and on nearby Market Street. Take bus no. 16AX, 16BX, or 21.

FISHERMAN'S WHARF & ENVIRONS *Overrated* The tourist-oriented malls along Jefferson Street include hundreds of shops, restaurants, and attractions. Among them are Ghirardelli Square, PIER 39, The Cannery, and The Anchorage (see "Shopping Centers & Complexes," on p. 221).

2 Shopping A to Z

ANTIQUES

Jackson Square, a historic district just north of the Financial District's Embarcadero Center, is the place to go for the top names in fine furniture and fine art. More than a dozen dealers on the 2 blocks between Columbus and Sansome streets specialize in European furnishings from the 17th to the 19th centuries. Most shops here are open Monday through Friday from 9am to 5pm and Saturday from 11am to 4pm.

Bonhams & Butterfields This renowned auction house holds preview weekends for upcoming auctions of furnishings, silver, antiques, art, and jewelry. Call for auction schedules. 220 San Bruno Ave. (at 16th St.). ✆ **800/223-2854** or 415/861-7500. www.bonhams.com/us.

Therien & Co. For the best in Scandinavian, French, and eastern European antiques, head beyond SoMa's design center to this boutique, where you can find the real thing or antique replicas, as well as made-to-order furniture from their neighboring custom furniture shop. 411 Vermont St. (at 17th St.). ✆ **415/956-8850.** www.therien.com.

ART

The San Francisco Bay Area Gallery Guide, a comprehensive, bimonthly publication listing the city's current shows, is available free by mail. Send a self-addressed, stamped envelope to San Francisco Bay Area Gallery Guide, 1369 Fulton St., San Francisco, CA 94117 (✆ **415/921-1600**); or pick one up at the San Francisco Visitor Information Center at 900 Market St. Most of the city's major art galleries are clustered downtown in the Union Square area.

Catharine Clark Gallery *Value* Catharine Clark's is a different kind of gallery experience. Although many galleries focus on established artists and out-of-this-world prices, Catharine's exhibits works by up-and-coming contemporary as well as established artists (mainly from California). It nurtures beginning collectors by offering a purchasing plan that's almost unheard of in the art business. You can buy a piece on layaway and take up to a year to pay for it—interest free! Prices here make art a realistic purchase for almost everyone for a change, but serious collectors also frequent the shows because Clark has such a keen eye for talent. Shows change every 6 weeks. Open Tuesday through Friday 10:30am to 5:30pm and Saturday 11am to 5:30pm. Closed Sunday and Monday. 150 Minna St. ground floor (between Third St. and New Montgomery sts.). ✆ **415/399-1439.** www.cclarkgallery.com.

Fraenkel Gallery This photography gallery features works by contemporary American and European artists. Excellent shows change every 2 months. Open Tuesday through Friday 10:30am to 5:30pm and Saturday 11am to 5pm. Closed Sunday and Monday. 49 Geary St. (between Grant Ave. and Kearny St.), 4th floor. ✆ **415/981-2661.** www.fraenkelgallery.com.

Hang *Value* Check out this amazingly affordable gallery for attractive pieces by yet-to-be-discovered Bay Area artists. The staff is friendly and helpful, and the gallery is designed to cater to new and seasoned collectors who appreciate original art at down-to-earth prices. 556 Sutter St. ✆ **415/434-4264.** www.hangart.com.

Images of the North The highlight here is one of the most extensive collections of Canadian and Alaskan Inuit art in the United States. There's also a small collection of Native American masks and jewelry. Open Tuesday through Saturday 11am to 5:30pm and by appointment. 2036 Union St. (at Buchanan St.). ✆ **415/673-1273.** www.imagesnorth.com.

San Francisco Shopping

A B fits **53**
Aardvark's **67**
Alabaster **11**
Alessi **42**
All American Boy **18**
Ameoba Records **62**
American Rag Cie **22**
The Anchorage **26**
Art of China **38**
Babushka **26**
Big Pagoda Company **43**
Biordi Art Imports **30**
Bloomingdale's **58**
Bonhams & Butterfield **19**
Book Passage **33**
The Booksmith **64**
Borders Books & Music **48**
Boulangerie **9**
Britex Fabrics **54**
Brooks Brothers **57**
Buffalo Exchange **67**
Bulo **14**
Burlington Coat Factory **21**
Cable Car Clothiers **42**
The Cannery at Del Monte Square **25**
The Canton Bazaar **34**
Catharine Clark Gallery **55**
The Chanel Boutique **45**
The Chinatown Kite Shop **39**
Citizen Clothing **15**
City Lights Booksellers & Publishers **31**
Cost Plus World Market **28**
Cowgirl Creamery Cheese Shop **33**
Crocker Galleria **54**
Dandelion **20**
De Vera Galleries **54**
Dianne's Old & New Estates **2**
Diptyque **51**
The Disney Store **41**
Distractions **65**
emily lee **5**
Flax **15**
Ferry Building Marketplace **33**
Flight 001 **12**
Fraenkel Gallery **55**
Ghirardelli Square **24**
Gimme Shoes **7**
Golden Gate Fortune Cookies Co. **37**
Good Byes **65**
Good Vibrations **18**
Green Apple Books **6**
Gucci America **57**
Gump's **44**
H & M **50**
Hang **49**
Images of the North **3**
Jackson Square **32**
Jeanine Payer **55**
Jeremys **59**
Joseph Schmidt Confections **17**
Kati Koos **41**
Kenneth Cole **58**
La Rosa **63**
Limn **60**
Loehmann's **41**
MAC **13**
Macy's **50**
Métier **43**
Meyerovich Gallery **57**
Minis **1**
Neiman Marcus **57**
Nest **7**
The New Unique Company **36**
Niketown **46**
Nordstrom **58**
Paolo Shoes **9**
Pearl & Jade Empire **49**
Propeller **12**
RAG **10**
Recycled Records **68**
SFMOMA Museum Store **56**
Showroom by In Fiore **23**
Streetlight Records **16**
Sue Fisher King **5**
Sur La Table **57**
Ten Ren Tea Co. **37**
Therien & Co. **19**
Three Bags Full **2**
Tiffany & Co. **47**
True Sake **10**
Union Street Goldsmith **4**
Virgin Megastore **57**
Westfield San Francisco Centre **58**
Wilkes Bashford **46**
William Stout Architectural Books **32**
Wine Club San Francisco **61**
The Wok Shop **35**
Zinc Details **8**

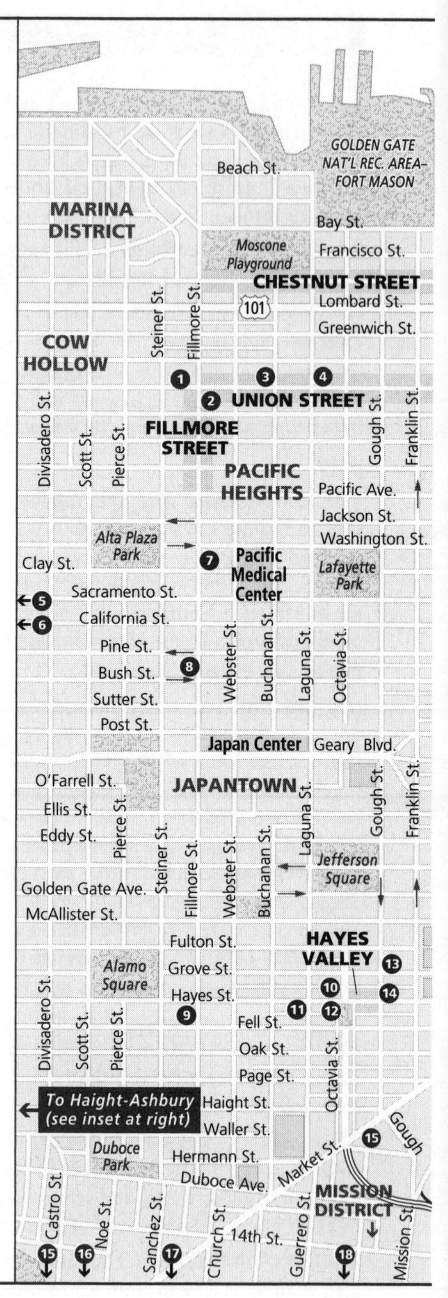

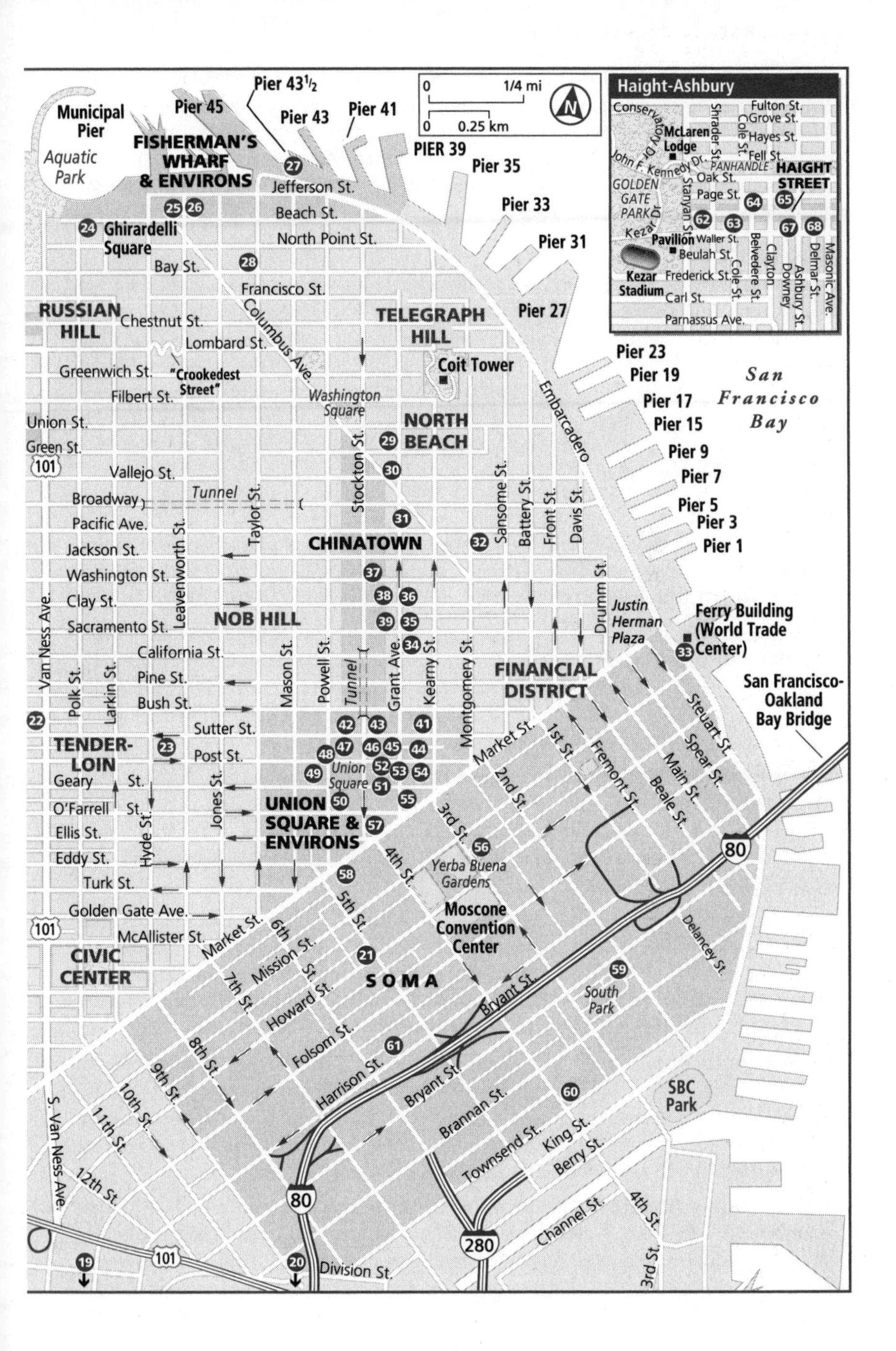

Municipal Pier
Aquatic Park
Pier 45
Pier 43½
Pier 43
Pier 41
PIER 39
Pier 35
Pier 33
Pier 31
Pier 27
Pier 23
Pier 19
Pier 17
Pier 15
Pier 9
Pier 7
Pier 5
Pier 3
Pier 1
0 1/4 mi
0 0.25 km
N
FISHERMAN'S WHARF & ENVIRONS
Jefferson St.
Beach St.
North Point St.
Ghirardelli Square
Bay St.
Francisco St.
RUSSIAN HILL
Chestnut St.
Lombard St.
Columbus Ave.
TELEGRAPH HILL
Greenwich St.
"Crookedest Street"
Filbert St.
Washington Square
Coit Tower
Embarcadero
Union St.
Green St.
NORTH BEACH
Vallejo St.
Broadway
Tunnel
Pacific Ave.
Jackson St.
Washington St.
Clay St.
Sacramento St.
California St.
Pine St.
Bush St.
Sutter St.
Post St.
Geary St.
O'Farrell St.
Ellis St.
Eddy St.
Turk St.
Golden Gate Ave.
McAllister St.
Van Ness Ave.
Polk St.
Larkin St.
Hyde St.
Leavenworth St.
Jones St.
Taylor St.
Mason St.
Powell St.
Stockton St.
Grant Ave.
Kearny St.
Montgomery St.
Sansome St.
Battery St.
Front St.
Davis St.
Drumm St.
CHINATOWN
NOB HILL
TENDER-LOIN
Union Square
UNION SQUARE & ENVIRONS
FINANCIAL DISTRICT
Justin Herman Plaza
Ferry Building (World Trade Center)
San Francisco Bay
San Francisco-Oakland Bay Bridge
Market St.
1st St.
2nd St.
3rd St.
4th St.
5th St.
6th St.
7th St.
8th St.
9th St.
10th St.
11th St.
12th St.
Fremont St.
Beale St.
Main St.
Spear St.
Steuart St.
Delancey St.
Mission St.
Howard St.
Folsom St.
Harrison St.
Bryant St.
Brannan St.
Townsend St.
King St.
Berry St.
Channel St.
Division St.
S. Van Ness Ave.
Yerba Buena Gardens
Moscone Convention Center
SOMA
South Park
SBC Park
CIVIC CENTER
101
80
280
Haight-Ashbury
Conservatory Dr.
McLaren Lodge
John F. Kennedy Dr.
GOLDEN GATE PARK
Kezar Dr.
Pavilion
Kezar Stadium
PANHANDLE
HAIGHT STREET
Fulton St.
Grove St.
Hayes St.
Fell St.
Oak St.
Page St.
Waller St.
Beulah St.
Frederick St.
Carl St.
Parnassus Ave.
Shrader St.
Stanyan St.
Cole St.
Belvedere St.
Clayton
Downey
Ashbury St.
Delmar St.
Masonic Ave.
19 20 21 22 23 24 25 26 27 28 29 30 31 32 33 34 35 36 37 38 39 41 42 43 44 45 46 47 48 49 50 51 52 53 54 55 56 57 58 59 60 61 62 63 64 65 67 68

Meyerovich Gallery Paintings, sculptures, and works on paper here are by modern and contemporary masters, including Chagall, Matisse, Miró, and Picasso. Meyerovich's new Contemporary Gallery, across the hall, features works by Lichtenstein, Stella, Frankenthaler, Dine, and Hockney. Open Monday through Friday 10am to 6pm and Saturday 10am to 5pm. Closed Sunday. 251 Post St. (at Stockton St.), 4th floor. ✆ **415/421-7171**. www.meyerovich.com.

BODY PRODUCTS

Showroom by In Fiore *Finds* I'm totally addicted to In Fiore—a high-end line of body balms, oils, perfumes, and facial serums—so I was especially thrilled when San Francisco–based founder Julie Elliott opened her by-appointment-only shop in what she calls the "Tender-Nob" (on the border of Nob Hill and the Tenderloin near Union Sq.). Come here to check out her whole line, as well as limited-edition balms, and see why celebrities like Julia Roberts and Meg Ryan are fans. Open Tuesday through Saturday and by appointment only. 868 Post St. (between Leavenworth and Hyde sts.). ✆ **415/928-5661**. www.infiore.net.

BOOKS

In addition to the listings below, there's a **Barnes & Noble** superstore at 2550 Taylor St., between Bay and North Point streets, near Fisherman's Wharf (✆ **415/292-6762**); and a four-storied **Borders** at 400 Post St., at Union Square (✆ **415/399-1633**).

Book Passage If you're moseying through the Ferry Building Marketplace, drop into this cozy independent that emphasizes (for tourists and locals alike) local travel, boating on the Bay, food, cooking, sustainable agriculture and ecology, fiction, culinary and regional history and literature, and photo and gift books about the Bay Area. The store also hosts lots of author events: Check their website for details. Ferry Building Marketplace (at The Embarcadero and Market St.). ✆ **415/835-1020**. www.bookpassage.com.

The Booksmith Haight Street's best selection of new books is in this large, well-maintained shop. It carries all the top titles, along with works from smaller presses, and more than 1,000 different magazines. 1644 Haight St. (between Clayton and Cole sts.). ✆ **800/493-7323** or 415/863-8688.

City Lights Booksellers & Publishers *Finds* Brooding literary types browse this famous bookstore owned by Lawrence Ferlinghetti, the renowned Beat Generation poet. The three-level bookshop prides itself on a comprehensive collection of art, poetry, and political paperbacks, as well as more mainstream books. Open daily until midnight. 261 Columbus Ave. (at Broadway). ✆ **415/362-8193**. www.citylights.com.

Green Apple Books *Finds* The local favorite for used books, Green Apple is crammed with titles—more than 60,000 new and 100,000 used books and DVDs. Its extended sections in psychology, cooking, art, and history; collection of modern first editions; and rare graphic comics are superseded only by the staff's superlative service. 506 Clement St. (at Sixth Ave.). ✆ **415/387-2272**. www.greenapplebooks.com.

William Stout Architectural Books *Finds* Step inside this shrine to all things architectural, and even if you think you're not interested in exquisite bathrooms, Southern California's modern homes, or great gardens, you can't help but bury yourself in the thousands of design books. Their recent expansion into a second level means that if they don't have what you're looking for, it probably doesn't exist. 804 Montgomery St. (at Jackson St.). ✆ **415/391-6757**. www.stoutbooks.com.

CHINA, SILVER & GLASS

Gump's *Finds* Founded over a century ago, Gump's offers gifts and treasures ranging from Asian antiquities to contemporary art glass and exquisite jade and pearl jewelry. Many items are made specifically for the store. Gump's also has one of the city's most revered holiday window displays and is a huge wedding registry destination, though the staff can act very affected. 135 Post St. (between Kearny St. and Grant Ave.). ✆ **800/766-7628** or 415/982-1616. www.gumps.com.

CRAFTS

The Canton Bazaar Amid a wide variety of handicrafts, here you'll find an excellent selection of rosewood and carved furniture, cloisonné enamelware, porcelain, carved jade, embroideries, jewelry, and antiques from mainland China. Open daily until 10pm. 616 Grant Ave. (between Sacramento and California sts.). ✆ **415/362-5750.** www.canton bazaar.com.

The New Unique Company Primarily a calligraphy- and watercolor-supplies store, this shop also has a good assortment of books on these topics. In addition, there's a wide selection of carved stones for use as seals on letters and documents. Should you want a special design or group of initials, the store will carve seals to order. 838 Grant Ave. (between Clay and Washington sts.). ✆ **415/981-2036.**

DEPARTMENT STORES (DOWNTOWN)

Bloomingdale's This massive 338,550-square-foot department store is the anchor of the Westfield San Francisco Centre at Fifth and Market streets (see "Shopping Centers & Complexes" on p. 221). It's the largest Bloomies outside of New York's flagship 59th Street store, and even sports the same black-and-white polished checkerboard marble. It's owned by the same company that runs Macy's, but fashions—for both men and women—tend to be more forward. Highlights include '60s-inspired fashions by Biba, knitwear by Sonia Rykiel, handbags by Louis Vuitton, and absurdly expensive shoes by Jimmy Choo. 845 Market St. (at Fifth St.). ✆ **415/856-5300.** www.bloomingdales.com.

Macy's The seven-story Macy's West features contemporary fashions for women, juniors, and children, plus jewelry, fragrances, cosmetics, and accessories. The sixth floor offers a "hospitality suite" where visitors can leave their coats and packages, grab a cup of coffee, or find out more about the city from the concierge. The top floors contain home furnishings, and the Cellar sells kitchenware and gourmet foods. You'll even find a Boudin Cafe (though the food is not as good compared to their food at other locations) and a Wolfgang Puck Cafe on the premises. Across the street, Macy's East has five floors of men's fashions. Stockton and O'Farrell sts., Union Sq. ✆ **415/397-3333.**

Neiman Marcus Some call this Texas-based chain "Needless Mark-ups." But those who can afford the best of everything can't deny that the men's and women's clothes, precious gems, and conservative formalwear are some of the most glamorous in town. The Rotunda Restaurant, located on the fourth floor, is a beautiful place for lunch and afternoon tea that was recently renovated along with the rest of the store. 150 Stockton St. (between Geary and O'Farrell sts.), Union Sq. ✆ **415/362-3900.**

Nordstrom Located and the newly renovated San Francisco Shopping Centre (see "Shopping Centers & Complexes" on p. 221), Nordstrom is renowned for its personalized service. Equally devoted to women's and men's fashions, the store has one of the best shoe selections in the city and thousands of suits in stock. The Bistro, on the fourth floor, has a panoramic view and is ideal for an inexpensive lunch or light snack. Spa Nordstrom, on the fifth floor, is the perfect place to relax after a hectic day of bargain hunting. 845 Market St. (at Fifth St.). ✆ **415/243-8500.**

DISCOUNT SHOPPING

Burlington Coat Factory As its name hints, you'll find hundreds of coats—from cheapies to designer—as well as men's and women's clothing, shoes, and accessories. But the best deal is the home section, where designer bedding, bath accessories, and housewares go for a fraction of their normal retail prices. 899 Howard St. (at Fifth St.). ✆ **415/495-7234.** www.coat.com.

Jeremys *Value* This boutique is a serious mecca for fashion hounds thanks to the wide array of top designer fashions, from shoes to suits, at rock-bottom prices. There are no cheap knockoffs here, just good men's and women's clothes and accessories that the owner scoops up from major retailers who are either updating merchandise or discarding returns. 2 S. Park (between Bryant and Brannan sts. at Second St.). ✆ **415/882-4929.** www.jeremys.com.

Loehmann's San Francisco's branch of Loehmann's—the nation's only upscale off-price specialty retailer—caters to a sophisticated white-collar crowd, offering professional clothing, shoes, and accessories at bargain prices. Be sure to check out the Back Room, where designer clothes are sold for 30% to 65% less than the Union Square department stores. 222 Sutter St. (between Kearny St. and Grant Ave.). ✆ **415/982-3215.** www.loehmanns.com.

FABRICS

Britex Fabrics A San Francisco institution since 1952 and newly renovated, Britex offers an absurd number and variety of fabrics, not to mention a selection of more than 30,000 buttons. Closed Sundays. 146 Geary St. (between Stockton and Grant sts.). ✆ **415/392-2910.** www.britexfabrics.com.

FASHION

See also "Vintage Clothing," later in this section.

CHILDREN'S FASHIONS

Minis Christine Pajunen, who used to design for Banana Republic, opened this children's clothing store to sell her own creations. Every piece, from shirts to pants and dresses, is made from natural fibers. Every outfit perfectly coordinates with everything else in the store. In 2004, Pajunen expanded the store so that it now includes baby gear, including functional and versatile strollers and cribs. Minis also offers educational and creative toys and books with matching dolls as well as maternity wear. 2278 Union St. (between Steiner and Fillmore sts.). ✆ **415/567-9537.** www.minis-sf.com.

MEN'S FASHIONS

All American Boy Long known for setting the mainstream style for gay men, All American Boy is the quintessential Castro clothing shop. 463 Castro St. (between Market and 18th sts.). ✆ **415/861-0444.**

Brooks Brothers In San Francisco, this bulwark of tradition is 1 block east of Union Square. Brooks Brothers introduced the button-down collar and single-handedly changed the standard of the well-dressed businessman. The multilevel shop also sells traditional casual wear, including sportswear, sweaters, and shirts. 150 Post St. (at Grant Ave.). ✆ **415/397-4500.** www.brooksbrothers.com.

Cable Car Clothiers Dapper men head to this fashion institution for traditional attire, such as three-button suits with natural shoulders, Aquascutum coats, McGeorge sweaters, and Atkinson ties. Closed Sundays. 200 Bush St. (at Sansome St.). ✆ **415/397-4740.** www.cablecarclothiers.com.

Citizen Clothing The Castro has some of America's best men's casual clothing stores, and this is one of them. Stylish (but not faddish) pants, tops, and accessories are in stock here. Its sister store, Body, located at 450 Castro St. (between 17th and 18th sts.), carries men's sportswear. 536 Castro St. (between 18th and 19th sts.). ✆ **415/575-3560.**

UNISEX

A B fits Now in Union Square as well as North Beach, this is the place to pop in for jeans to fit all shapes, styles, and sizes, as well as smart and sassy contemporary wear for gals and guys on the go. The snugly fitting stock with over 100 styles of jeans and pants ranges from Chip & Pepper, Earnest Sewn, Edwin, Notify, and Rogan, to chic wear from the likes of Twelfth Street by Cynthia Vincent, Ya-Ya, and Twinkle by Wenlan. There's another location in North Beach at 1519 Grant Ave. (at Union and Filbert sts.) with the same phone number. 40 Grant Ave. (between O'Farrell and Geary sts.). ✆ **415/982-5726.** www.abfits.com.

American Rag Cie *Finds* Fashionistas flock to this find, on an unlikely stretch of busy Van Ness, for vintage and new duds sure to make you look street-swank. Check it out for everything from Juicy Couture to Paul & Joe and from European vintage to modern masters such as Diesel. 1305 Van Ness Ave. (at Sutter St.). ✆ **415/474-5214.**

Gucci America Donning Gucci's golden Gs is not a cheap endeavor. But if you've got the cash, you'll find all the latest lines of shoes, leather goods, scarves, and pricey accessories here, such as a $9,000 handmade crocodile bag. 200 Stockton St. (between Geary and Post sts.). ✆ **415/392-2808.** www.gucci.com.

H & M This ever-trendy and cheap Swedish clothing chain opened in Union Square at the end of 2004, and had lines out the door all through the holiday season—and not just for their collection by Stella McCartney. Drop in anytime for trendy cuts and styles sure to satisfy the hip him and her along on the trip. 150 Powell St. (between Ellis and O'Farrell sts.) ✆ **415/986-4215.**

MAC *Finds* No, we're not talking cosmetics. The more-modern-than-corporate stock at this hip and hidden shop (Modern Apparel Clothing) just combined its men's and women's fashion meccas in a new space next door to pastry pit stop Citizen Cake. Drop in for men's imported tailored suits and women's separates in new and intriguing fabrics as well as gorgeous ties, vibrant sweaters, and a few choice home accouterments. Lines include Belgium's Dries Van Noten and Martin Margiela, New York's John Bartlett, and local sweater sweetheart Laurie B. The best part? Prices are more reasonable than at many of the trendy clothing stores in the area. 387 Grove St. (at Gough St.). ✆ **415/863-3011.**

Niketown Here it's not "I can," but "I can spend." At least that's what the kings of sportswear were banking on when they opened this megastore in 1997. As you'd expect, inside the doors shoppers find themselves in a Nike world offering everything the merchandising team could create. 278 Post St. (at Stockton St.). ✆ **415/392-6453.**

Three Bags Full Snuggling up in a cozy sweater can be a fashionable event if you do your shopping at this pricey boutique, which carries the gamut in handmade, playful, and extravagant knitwear. Other city locations, which are also closed on Sunday, are 500 Sutter St., ✆ **415/398-7987**; and 3314 Sacramento St. (also closed Mon), ✆ **415/923-1454.** 2181 Union St. (at Fillmore St.). ✆ **415/567-5753.** www.threebagsfull.com.

Wilkes Bashford *Finds* Wilkes Bashford is one of the most expensive and best-known clothing stores in the city. In its 3-plus decades in business, the boutique has garnered a reputation for stocking only the finest clothes in the world (which can often be seen on ex-Mayor Willie Brown and current Mayor Gavin Newsom, who do their suit shopping here). Most fashions come from Italy and France; they include women's designer sportswear and couture and men's Kiton and Brioni suits (at $2,500 and up, they're considered the most expensive suits in the world). Closed Sundays. 375 Sutter St. (at Stockton St.). ✆ **415/986-4380.** www.wilkesbashford.com.

WOMEN'S FASHIONS

The Chanel Boutique Ever fashionable and expensive, Chanel is appropriately located on Maiden Lane, the quaint downtown side street where the most exclusive stores and spas cluster. You'll find here what you'd expect from Chanel: clothing, accessories, scents, cosmetics, and jewelry. 155 Maiden Lane (between Stockton St. and Grant Ave.). ✆ **415/981-1550.** www.chanel.com.

emily lee More mature fashionistas head to the quaint shopping street of Laurel Village, a block-long strip mall of shops that includes emily lee, for everything from elegant to artsy-designer garb that tends to be stylish, sensible, and loose-fitting. Designers include the likes of Blanque, Eileen Fisher, Flax, Ivan Grundahl, and Three Dots. 3509 California St. (at Locust St.). ✆ **415/751-3443.**

Métier *Finds* Discerning and well-funded shoppers consider this the best women's clothing shop in town. Within its walls you'll find classic, sophisticated, and expensive creations, which include European ready-to-wear lines and designers: fashions by Italian designers Anna Molinari, Hache, and Blumarine and by French designer Martine Sitbon. You will also find a distinguished collection of antique-style, high-end jewelry from L.A.'s Cathy Waterman as well as ultrapopular custom-designed poetry jewelry by Jeanine Payer. Closed Sunday. 355 Sutter St. (between Stockton and Grant sts.). ✆ **415/989-5395.** www.metiersf.com.

RAG *Finds* If you want to add some truly unique San Francisco designs to your closet, head to RAG, or Residents Apparel Gallery, a co-op shop where around 55 local emerging designers showcase their latest creations. Prices are great; fashions are forward, young, and hip; and if you grab a few pieces, no one at home's going to be able to copy your look. 541 Octavia St. (at Hayes St.). ✆ **415/621-7718.** www.ragsf.com.

FOOD

Boulangerie *Finds* A bit of Paris on Pine Street, this true-blue bakery sells authentically French creations, from delicious and slightly sour French country wheat bread to rustic-style desserts, including the locally famous *cannelés de Bordeaux,* custard baked in a copper mold. And if you're looking for a place to eat Boulangerie bread and pastries, visit their cafes—**Boulange de Polk,** at 2310 Polk St. near Green St. (✆ **415/345-1107**), or **Boulange de Cole,** at 1000 Cole St. at Parnassus St. (✆ **415/242-2442**). Closed Monday. 2325 Pine St. (at Fillmore St.). ✆ **415/440-0356,** ext. 204. www.baybread.com.

Cowgirl Creamery Cheese Shop *Finds* San Francisco is fanatical about cheese, and much of the local enthusiasm can be attributed to the two women who created the small-production Cowgirl Creamery, located in the Ferry Building Marketplace but still imparting the simple neighborhood shop feel. Here's how you do it: Sample, then buy a hefty slice of your favorite cheese, then enjoy it on the waterfront with some crusty Acme Bread and a piece of fruit from Capay Farms (all within the same building). Ferry Building Marketplace, no. 17. ✆ **415/362-9354.** www.cowgirlcreamery.com.

Ferry Building Marketplace *Finds* A one-stop shop for some of the city's finest edibles, the renovated historic Ferry Building is home to the revered Acme Bread Company, Scharffen Berger Chocolate, the Imperial Tea Court, Peet's Coffee, Cowgirl Creamery Cheese Shop (see above), Recchiuti Confections, and more. There's no better place to load up on the Bay Area's outstanding bounty. Ferry Building Plaza (at the foot of Market St. at The Embarcadero). ✆ **415/693-0996.** www.ferrybuildingmarketplace.com.

Golden Gate Fortune Cookies Co. This tiny, touristy factory sells fortune cookies hot off the press. You can purchase them in small bags or in bulk, and you can even bring your own messages and watch them fold them into fresh cookies before your eyes. Even if you're not buying, stop in to see how these sugary treats are made (although the staff can get pushy for you to buy). Open daily until 8:30pm. 56 Ross Alley (between Washington and Jackson sts.). ✆ **415/781-3956.**

Joseph Schmidt Confections *Finds* Here, chocolate takes the shape of exquisite sculptural masterpieces—such as long-stemmed tulips and heart-shaped boxes—that are so beautiful, you'll be hesitant to bite the head off your adorable panda bear. Once you do, however, you'll know why this is the most popular—and reasonably priced—chocolatier in town. 3489 16th St. (at Sanchez St.). ✆ **800/861-8682** or 415/861-8682. www.josephschmidtconfections.com.

Ten Ren Tea Co., Ltd. *Finds* At the Ten Ren Tea Co. shop, you will be offered a steaming cup of tea when you walk in the door. In addition to a selection of almost 50 traditional and herbal teas, the company stocks a collection of cold tea drinks and tea-related paraphernalia, such as pots, cups, and infusers. If you can't make up your mind, take home a mail-order form. The shop is open daily from 9am to 9pm. 949 Grant Ave. (between Washington and Jackson sts.). ✆ **415/362-0656.** www.tentea.com.

GIFTS

Art of China Amid a wide variety of collectibles, this shop features exquisite, hand-carved Chinese figurines. You'll also find a lovely assortment of ivory beads, bracelets, necklaces, and earrings. Pink-quartz dogs, jade figurines, porcelain vases, cache pots, and blue-and-white barrels suitable for use as table bases are just some of the many items stocked here. 839–843 Grant Ave. (between Clay and Washington sts.). ✆ **415/981-1602.** www.artsofchinasf.com.

Babushka Located near Fisherman's Wharf, adjacent to The Anchorage Mall, Babushka sells only Russian products, most of which are wooden nesting dolls. Pier 39. ✆ **415/788-7043.**

Cost Plus World Market At the Fisherman's Wharf cable car turntable, Cost Plus is a vast warehouse crammed to the rafters with Chinese baskets, Indian camel bells, Malaysian batik scarves, and innumerable other items from Algeria to Zanzibar. More than 20,000 items from 50 nations, imported directly from their countries of origin, pack this warehouse. There's also a decent wine shop here. It's open Monday through Saturday from 9am to 9pm and Sunday from 10am to 8pm. 2552 Taylor St. (between North Point and Bay sts.). ✆ **415/928-6200.**

Amazing Grazing

There's no better way to spend a sunny Saturday morning in San Francisco than to stroll the **Ferry Building Marketplace** and **Farmers' Market,** snacking your way through some of America's finest organic produce—it's one of the most highly acclaimed farmers' markets in the United States. While foraging among the dozens of stalls crammed with Northern California fruit, vegetables, bread, shellfish, and dairy items, you're bound to bump elbows with the dozens of Bay Area chefs (such as Alice Waters) who do their shopping here. The enthusiastic vendors are always willing to educate visitors about the pleasures of organic produce, and often provide free samples. It's a unique opportunity for city dwellers to buy freshly picked organic produce directly from small family-operated farms.

On Saturday mornings the market is in its full glory. Nearly the entire building is enrobed with local meat ranchers, artisan cheese makers, bread bakers, specialty food purveyors, and farmers. On Saturdays make sure you arrive by 10:30am to watch Meet The Farmer, a half-hour interview with one of the farmers, food artisans, or other purveyors who give the audience in-depth information about how and where their food is produced. Then, at 11am, Bay Area chefs give cooking demonstrations using ingredients purchased that morning from the market (you get to taste their creations then leave with the recipe in hand). Several local restaurants also have food stalls selling their cuisine—including breakfast items—so don't eat before you arrive. You can also pick up locally made vinegars, preserves, herbs, and oils, which make wonderful gifts.

If you decide you want a local foodie to lead you on a culinary excursion of the Marketplace and Farmers' Market, my friend Lisa Rogovin, an "Epicurean

Dandelion *Finds* Tucked in an out-of-the-way location in SoMa is the most wonderful collection of gifts, collectibles, and furnishings. There's something for every taste and budget here, from an excellent collection of teapots, decorative dishes, and gourmet foods to silver, books, cards, and picture frames. Don't miss the Zen-like second floor, with its peaceful furnishings in Indian, Japanese, and Western styles. The store is closed Sunday and Monday except during November and December, when it's open daily. Hours are 10am to 6pm. 55 Potrero Ave. (at Alameda St.). ✆ **415/436-9500.** www.tampopo.com.

Distractions This is the best of the Haight Street shops selling underground-rave wear, street fashion, and electronica CDs. You'll find pipes, toys, and stickers liberally mixed with lots of cool stuff to look at. 1552 Haight St. (between Ashbury and Clayton sts.). ✆ **415/252-8751.**

Flax If you go into an art store for a special pencil and come out $300 later, don't go near this shop. Flax has everything you can think of in art and design supplies, an amazing collection of blank bound books, children's art supplies, frames, calendars—you name it. There's a gift for every type of person here, especially you. 1699 Market St. (at Valencia and Gough sts.). ✆ **415/552-2355.** www.flaxart.com.

Concierge" and founder of **In The Kitchen With Lisa,** offers guided culinary excursions. Some of Lisa's top noshing tips include:

- Mortgage Lifter heirloom tomatoes dipped in special Rosemary Salt from **Eatwell Farm**
- Creamy and sweet Barhi dates from **Flying Disk Ranch,** spread on an épi baguette from **Acme Bread Company** with a touch of fresh Panir cheese from **Cowgirl Creamery**
- Whatever's in season at **Hamada Farms,** such as their Tahitian pomelos and Oro Blanco grapefruits
- Fleur de Sel chocolates at **Recchiuti Confections**
- **Scharffen Berger's** Bittersweet Mocha chocolate bars made with ground Sumatra coffee beans from Peet's Coffee & Tea
- Warm liquid Valrhona chocolate at **Boulette's Larder** (nirvana, she says).

For more information about Lisa's guided culinary tours, log on to her website at www.inthekitchenwithlisa.com, or call her at ✆ **415/806-5970.**

The Ferry Building Marketplace is open Monday through Friday from 10am to 6pm, Saturday from 9am to 6pm, and Sunday from 11am to 5pm. The Farmers' Market takes place year-round, rain or shine, every Tuesday and Saturday from 10am to 2pm. From spring through fall it also runs on Thursdays from 4 to 8pm and Sundays from 10am to 2pm. The Ferry Building is located on The Embarcadero at the foot of Market Street (about a 15-min. walk from Fisherman's Wharf). Call ✆ **415/693-0996** for more information or log onto www.ferryplazafarmersmarket.com or www.ferrybuildingmarketplace.com.

Good Vibrations A laypersons' sex-toy, book, and video emporium, Good Vibrations is a women-owned, worker-owned cooperative. Unlike most sex shops, it's not a back-alley business, but a straightforward shop with healthy, open attitudes about human sexuality. It also has a vibrator museum. 603 Valencia St. (at 17th St.). ✆ **415/522-5460** or 800/BUY-VIBE (for mail order). www.goodvibes.com. A second location is at 1620 Polk St. (at Sacramento St., ✆ **415/345-0400**); and a third is at 2504 San Pablo Ave., Berkeley (✆ **510/841-8987**).

Kati Koos Need a little humor in your life? Previously called Smile, this store specializes in whimsical art, furniture, clothing, jewelry, and American crafts guaranteed to make you grin. Closed Sunday. 500 Sutter St. (between Powell and Mason sts.). ✆ **415/362-3437.** www.katikoos.com.

SFMOMA MuseumStore *Finds* With an array of artistic cards, books, jewelry, housewares, furniture, knickknacks, and creative tokens of San Francisco, it's virtually impossible not to find something here you'll consider a must-have. (Check out the FogDome!) Aside from being one of the locals' favorite shops, it offers far more tasteful mementos than most Fisherman's Wharf options. Open late (until 9:30pm) on Thursday nights. 151 Third St. (2 blocks south of Market St., across from Yerba Buena Gardens). ✆ **415/357-4035.** www.sfmoma.org.

HOUSEWARES/FURNISHINGS

Alabaster *Finds* Any interior designer who knows Biedermeier from Bauhaus knows that this Hayes Valley shop sets local home accessories trends with its collection of high-end must-haves. Their selection includes everything from lighting—antique and modern Alabaster fixtures, Fortuny silk shades, Venetian glass chandeliers—to other home accessories, like one-of-a-kind antiques, body products from Florence, and more. 597 Hayes St. (at Laguna St.). © **415/558-0482.** www.alabastersf.com.

Alessi Italian designer Alberto Alessi, who's known for his whimsical and colorful kitchen-utensil designs, such as his ever-popular spiderlike lemon squeezer, opened a flagship store here. Drop by for everything from gorgeous stainless-steel double boilers to corkscrews shaped like maidens. 424 Sutter St. (at Stockton St.). © **415/434-0403.** www.alessi.com.

Big Pagoda Company When I need to buy a stylish friend a gift, I head to this downtown Asian-influenced design shop for cool, unique, and contemporary finds. Within the bi-level boutique, East meets West and old meets new in the form of anything from an antique Chinese scholar's chair to a new wave table that hints at Ming or Mondrian. Its furniture and glass art is hardly cheap (an antique Tibetan dragonhead goes for $30,000), but you can get fabulous designer martini glasses at $15 a pop. Open Monday through Saturday 10am to 6pm. 310 Sutter St. (at Grant St.). © **415/296-8881.** www.bigpagoda.com.

Biordi Art Imports *Finds* Whether you want to decorate your dinner table, color your kitchen, or liven up the living room, Biordi's Italian majolica pottery is the most exquisite and unusual way to do it. The owner has been importing these hand-painted collectibles for 60 years, and every piece is a showstopper. Call for a catalog. They'll ship anywhere. Closed Sundays. 412 Columbus Ave. (at Vallejo St.). © **415/392-8096.** www.biordi.com.

Diptyque If the idea of spending $40 on a candle makes you laugh, this isn't the place for you. But if you're the type willing to throw down good money to scentualize your living space, don't skip this French shop offering dozens of spectacular flaming fragrances. I'm such a fan that every time I went to Paris I'd weigh down my luggage with these 50-hour burners. (Before the horrible exchange rate, that is.) But now I can scoop them up in my own backyard. They also make great gifts. 171 Maiden Lane (near Stockton St.). © **415/402-0600.** www.diptyqueusa.com.

Limn For the latest in Europe's trendsetting and ultramodern furniture and lighting, go straight to SoMa celebrity Limn, which also showcases artworks in its adjoining gallery. 290 Townsend St. (at Fourth St.). © **415/543-5466.** www.limn.com.

Nest *Finds* Don't come into Fillmore's cutest French interiors store without your credit cards. Nest carries adorable throws, handmade quilts, must-have slippers and sleepwear, and a number of other things you never knew you needed until now. 2300 Fillmore St. (at Clay St.). © **415/292-6199.**

Propeller *Finds* This airy skylight-lit shop is a must-stop for lovers of the latest in übermodern furniture and home accessories. Owner/designer Lorn Dittfeld handpicks pieces done by emerging designers from as far away as Sweden, Italy, and Canada as well as a plethora of national newbies. Drop in to lounge on the hippest sofas; grab pretty and practical gifts like ultracool magnetic spice racks; or adorn your home with Bev Hisey's throws and graphic pillows, diamond-cut wood tables by William Earle, or hand-tufted graphic rugs by Angela Adams. 555 Hayes St. (between Laguna and Octavia sts.). © **415/701-7767.** www.propeller-sf.com.

Sue Fisher King *Finds* For the ultimate in everything on the traditional side for the tabletop, bedroom, and beyond, head to this exclusive neighborhood boutique known by the society set as the only place to shop. It's filled with items like exquisite table linens, cashmere blankets, towels, china, silver flatware, and more. Closed Sunday. 3067 Sacramento St. (at Baker St.). ✆ **415/922-7276.** www.suefisherking.com.

Sur La Table Cooks should beeline it to this Union Square shop specializing in all things culinary. Its two floors are packed to the rafters with pricey but stylish high-quality pots and pans, utensils, tabletop items, books, and more coupled with an extremely helpful and knowledgeable staff. A second location is at the Ferry Building Marketplace, stall no. 37 (✆ **415/262-9970**). 77 Maiden Lane (at Grant St.). ✆ **415/732-7900.** www.surlatable.com.

The Wok Shop This shop has every conceivable implement for Chinese cooking, including woks, brushes, cleavers, circular chopping blocks, dishes, oyster knives, bamboo steamers, and strainers. It also sells a wide range of kitchen utensils, baskets, handmade linens from China, and aprons. 718 Grant Ave. (at Clay St.). ✆ **415/989-3797** or 888/780-7171 for mail order. www.wokshop.com.

Zinc Details *Finds* This contemporary furniture and knickknack shop has received accolades everywhere from *Elle Decor Japan* to *Metropolitan Home* to *InStyle* for its amazing collection of glass vases, pendant lights, ceramics from all over the world, and furniture from local craftspeople. A portion of these true works of art is made specifically for the store. While you're in the 'hood, check out their new sister store around the corner at 2410 California St. (✆ **415/776-9002**), which showcases contemporary designer furniture. 1905 Fillmore St. (between Bush and Pine sts.). ✆ **415/776-2100.** www.zincdetails.com.

JEWELRY

De Vera Galleries *Finds* Don't come here unless you've got money to spend. Designer Federico de Vera's unique rough-stone jewelry collection, art glass, and vintage knickknacks are too beautiful to pass up and too expensive to be a painless purchase. Still, if you're looking for a keepsake, you'll find it here. Closed Sunday and Monday. 29 Maiden Lane (at Kearny St.). ✆ **415/788-0828.** www.deveraobjects.com.

Dianne's Old & New Estates Many local girls get engagement rings from this fantastic little shop featuring top-of-the-line antique jewelry—pendants, diamond rings, necklaces, bracelets, and pearls. For a special gift, check out the collection of platinum wedding and engagement rings and vintage watches. Don't worry if you can't afford it now—the shop offers 1-year interest-free layaway. And, if you buy a ring, they'll send you off with a thank-you bottle of celebration bubbly. 2181A Union St. (at Fillmore St.). ✆ **888/346-7525** or 415/346-7525.www.diannesestatejewelry.com.

Jeanine Payer If you want to buy a trinket that is truly San Franciscan, stop by this boutique hidden on the street level of the beautifully ornate Phelan Building where designer Jeanine Payer showcases gorgeous, handmade contemporary jewelry that she crafts in sterling silver and 18-karat gold five stories above in her studio. All of her pieces, including fabulous baby gifts, sport engraved poetry—and can even be custom done. Sound familiar? Not surprising. Celebrities such as Sheryl Crow, Debra Messing, and Ellen DeGeneres are fans. 760 Market St., Suite 533 (at O'Farrell St.). ✆ **415/788-2414.** www.jeaninepayer.com.

Pearl & Jade Empire The Pearl & Jade Empire has been importing jewelry from all over the world since 1957. It specializes in unusual pearls and jade and offers restringing on the premises as well as boasts a collection of amber from the Baltic Sea. 427 Post St. (between Powell and Mason sts.). ✆ **415/362-0606.** www.pearlempire.com.

Tiffany & Co. Even if you don't have lots of cash with which to buy an exquisite bauble that comes in Tiffany's famous light-blue box, enjoy this renowned store à la Audrey Hepburn in *Breakfast at Tiffany's.* The designer collection features Paloma Picasso, Jean Schlumberger, and Elsa Peretti in both silver and 18-karat gold, and there's an extensive gift collection in sterling, china, and crystal. 350 Post St. (at Powell St.). ✆ **415/781-7000.** www.tiffany.com.

Union Street Goldsmith A showcase for Bay Area goldsmiths, this exquisite shop sells a contemporary collection of fine custom-designed jewelry in platinum and all karats of gold. Many pieces emphasize colored stones. 1909 Union St. (at Laguna St.). ✆ **415/776-8048.** www.unionstreetgoldsmith.com.

MUSIC

Amoeba Records Don't be scared off by the tattooed, pierced, and fierce-looking employees (and other shoppers!) in this beloved new and used record store highlighting indie labels. They're actually more than happy to recommend some great music to you. If you're looking for the latest from Britney, this might not be the store for you (though they *do* have everything), but if you're into interesting music that's not necessarily on every station all the time, check this place out. You can buy, sell, and trade in this cavernous, loud Haight Street hot spot. 1855 Haight St. (between Shrader and Stanyan sts.). ✆ **415/831-1200.**

Recycled Records *Finds* Easily one of the best used-record stores in the city, this loud shop in the Haight has cases of used "classic" rock LPs, sheet music, and tour programs. It's open from 10am to 8pm daily. 1377 Haight St. (between Central and Masonic sts.). ✆ **415/626-4075.** www.recycled-records.com.

Streetlight Records Overstuffed with used music in all three formats, this place is best known for its records and excellent CD collection. It also carries new and used DVDs and computer games. Rock music is cheap, and the money-back guarantee guards against defects. 3979 24th St. (between Noe and Sanchez sts.). ✆ **415/282-3550.** www.streetlightrecords.com. A second location is at 2350 Market St., between Castro and Noe sts. (✆ **415/282-8000**).

Virgin Megastore With thousands of CDs, including an impressive collection of imports, videos, DVDs, a multimedia department, a cafe, and related books, this enormous Union Square store can make any music-lover blow his or her entire vacation fund. It's open Sunday through Thursday from 10am to 11pm and Friday and Saturday from 10am to midnight. 2 Stockton St. (at Market St.). ✆ **415/397-4525.**

SHOES

Bulo If you have a fetish for foot fashions, you must check out Bulo, which carries nothing but imported Italian shoes. The selection is small but styles run the gamut, from casual to dressy, reserved to wildly funky. New shipments come in every 3 to 4 weeks, so the selection is ever-changing, eternally hip, and, unfortunately, ever-expensive, with many pairs going for close to $200. Men's and women's store: 437A Hayes St. (at Gough St.). ✆ **415/864-3244.** Women's store: across the street, at 418 Hayes St. (✆ **415/255-4939**). www.buloshoes.com.

Gimme Shoes The staff is funky-fashion snobby, the prices are steep, and the European shoes and accessories are utterly chic. 2358 Fillmore St. (at Washington St.). ✆ **415/441-3040.** Additional location at 416 Hayes St. (✆ **415/864-0691.** www.gimmeshoes.com.

Kenneth Cole This trendy shop carries high-fashion footwear for men and women. There is also an innovative collection of handbags and small leather goods and accessories. 865 Market St. (in the San Francisco Shopping Centre). ✆ **415/227-4536.** www.kennethcole.com. Another shop is at 166 Grant St., at Post St. (✆ **415/981-2653**).

Paolo Shoes This Italian import store is run by owner Paolo Iantorno, who actually designs the shoes for his hipster shops. If gorgeous, handcrafted, colorful shoes are what you're looking for, this is the shop for you. You can get your low-heeled slip-ons here—this store features men's and women's footwear and bags—but they might be in silver python. Check out the men's perforated orange slip-ons—not for the faint of heart or fashion-modest. You might not even mind that many shoes are upwards of 200 bucks when you realize that Paolo's women's shoes are so sexy and comfortable, you won't want to take them off. 524 Hayes St. ✆ **415/552-4580.** A second location is at 2000 Fillmore St. (✆ **415/771-1944**). www.paoloshoes.com.

SHOPPING CENTERS & COMPLEXES

The Anchorage This touristy waterfront mall has close to 35 stores that offer everything from music boxes to home furnishings; street performers entertain during open hours. This is not a stop for staples, but more for tourist trinkets. 2800 Leavenworth St. (between Beach and Jefferson sts. on Fisherman's Wharf). ✆ **415/775-6000.**

Crocker Galleria Modeled after Milan's Galleria Vittorio Emanuele, this glass-domed, three-level pavilion, about 3 blocks east of Union Square, features around 40 high-end shops with expensive and classic designer creations. Fashions include Aricie lingerie, Gianni Versace, and Polo/Ralph Lauren. Closed Sunday. 50 Post St. (at Kearny St.). ✆ **415/393-1505.** www.shopatgalleria.com.

Ghirardelli Square This former chocolate factory is one of the city's quaintest shopping malls and most popular landmarks. It dates from 1864, when it served as a factory making Civil War uniforms, but it's best known as the former chocolate and spice factory of Domingo Ghirardelli (say "Gear-ar-delly"). A clock tower, an exact replica of the one at France's Château de Blois, crowns the complex. Inside the tower, on the mall's plaza level, is the fun Ghirardelli soda fountain. It still makes and sells small amounts of chocolate, but the big draw is the old-fashioned ice-cream parlor. If you're coming to shop, think again: It's pretty lame in that department, but you can dine decently at Ana Mandara (p. 128). Main plaza shops' and restaurants' hours are 10am to 6pm Sunday through Thursday and 10am to 9pm Friday and Saturday, with extended hours during the summer. 900 North Point St. (at Polk St.). ✆ **415/775-5500.** www.ghirardellisq.com.

PIER 39 *Overrated* This bayside tourist trap also happens to have stunning views. To residents, that pretty much wraps up PIER 39—an expensive spot where out-of-towners go to waste money on worthless souvenirs and greasy fast food. For vacationers, though, PIER 39 does have some redeeming qualities—fresh crab (in season), playful sea lions, phenomenal views, and plenty of fun for the kids. If you want to get to know the real San Francisco, skip the cheesy T-shirt shops and limit your time here to one afternoon, if at all. Located at Beach St. and The Embarcadero.

Westfield San Francisco Centre Opened in 1988 and given a $460 million expansion in 2006, this ritzy 1.5-million-square-foot urban shopping center is one of the few vertical malls (multilevel rather than sprawling) in the United States. Its most attractive feature is a spectacular atrium with a century-old dome that's 102 feet wide and three stories high. Along with Nordstrom (p. 211) and Bloomingdale's (p. 211) department stores and a Century Theatres multiplex, there are more than 170 specialty stores, including Abercrombie & Fitch, Ann Taylor, bebe, Benetton, Footlocker, J. Crew, and Victoria's Secret. 865 Market St. (at Fifth St.). ✆ **415/512-6776.** www.westfield.com/sanfrancisco.

TOYS

The Chinatown Kite Shop This shop's playful assortment of flying objects includes attractive fish kites, windsocks, hand-painted Chinese paper kites, wood-and-paper biplanes, pentagonal kites, and do-it-yourself kite kits, all of which make great souvenirs or decorations. Computer-designed stunt kites have two or four control lines to manipulate loops and dives. Open daily from 10am to 8pm. 717 Grant Ave. (between Clay and Sacramento sts.). ✆ **415/391-8217.** www.chinatownkite.com.

TRAVEL GOODS

Flight 001 Jetsetters zoom into this space-shuttle-like showroom for hip travel accessories. Check out the sleek luggage, "security friendly" manicure sets, and other mid-air must-haves. 525 Hayes St. (between Laguna and Octavia sts.). ✆ **415/487-1001.** www.flight001.com.

VINTAGE CLOTHING

Aardvark's One of San Francisco's largest secondhand clothing dealers, Aardvark's has seemingly endless racks of shirts, pants, dresses, skirts, and hats from the past 30 years. It's open daily from 11am to 7pm. 1501 Haight St. (at Ashbury St.). ✆ **415/621-3141.**

Buffalo Exchange This large and newly expanded storefront on upper Haight Street is crammed with racks of antique and new fashions from the 1960s, 1970s, and 1980s. It stocks everything from suits and dresses to neckties, hats, handbags, and jewelry. Buffalo Exchange anticipates some of the hottest new street fashions. 1555 Haight St. (between Clayton and Ashbury sts.). ✆ **415/431-7733.** A second shop is at 1210 Valencia St., at 24th St. (✆ **415/647-8332**). www.buffaloexchange.com.

Good Byes *Finds* One of the best new- and used-clothes stores in San Francisco, Good Byes carries only high-quality clothing and accessories, including an exceptional selection of men's fashions at unbelievably low prices (for example, $350 pre-owned shoes for $35). Women's wear is in a separate boutique across the street. 3464 Sacramento St. and 3483 Sacramento St. (between Laurel and Walnut sts.). ✆ **415/346-6388.** www.goodbyessf.com.

La Rosa On a street packed with vintage-clothing shops, this is one of the more upscale options. Since 1978, it has featured a selection of high-quality, dry-cleaned secondhand goods. Formal suits and dresses are its specialty, but you'll also find sport coats, slacks, and shoes. The more moderately priced sister store, **Held Over,** is located at 1543 Haight St., near Ashbury (✆ **415/864-0818**); and their discount store, **Clothes Contact,** is located at 473 Valencia St., at 16th St. (✆ **415/621-3212**). 1711 Haight St. (at Cole St.). ✆ **415/668-3744.**

WINE & SAKE

True Sake Amid woven sea grass flooring, colorful backlit displays, and a so-hip Hayes Valley location are more than 140 varieties of Japanese-produced sake ranging from an $8 300ml bottle of Ohyama to an $180 720ml bottle of Kotsuzumi Rojo-hanaari—which, incidentally, owner Beau Timken (who is on hand to describe each wine), says is available at no other retail store in the U.S. 560 Hayes St. (between Laguna and Octavia sts.). ✆ **415/355-9555.** www.truesake.com.

Wine Club San Francisco *Value* The Wine Club is a discount warehouse that offers bargains on more than 1,200 domestic and foreign wines. Bottles cost between $4 and $1,100. 953 Harrison St. (between Fifth and Sixth sts.). ✆ **415/512-9086.**

10

San Francisco After Dark

For a city with fewer than a million inhabitants, San Francisco boasts an impressive after-dark scene. Dozens of piano bars and top-notch lounges augment a lively dance-club culture, and skyscraper lounges offer dazzling city views. The city's arts scene is also extraordinary: The opera is justifiably world renowned, the ballet is on its toes, and theaters are high in both quantity and quality. In short, there's always something going on in the city, and unlike in Los Angeles or New York you don't have to pay outrageous cover charges or be "picked" to be a part of the scene.

For up-to-date nightlife information, turn to the *San Francisco Weekly* (www.sfweekly.com) and the *San Francisco Bay Guardian* (www.sfbg.com), both of which run comprehensive listings. They are available free at bars and restaurants and from street-corner boxes all around the city. *Where* (www.wheresf.com), a free tourist-oriented monthly, also lists programs and performance times; it's available in most of the city's finer hotels. The Sunday edition of the *San Francisco Chronicle* features a "Datebook" section, printed on pink paper, with information on and listings of the week's events. If you have Internet access, it's a good idea to check out www.citysearch.com or www.sfstation.com for the latest in bars, clubs, and events. And if you want to secure seats at a hot-ticket event, either buy well in advance or contact the concierge of your hotel and see if they can swing something for you.

Tix Bay Area (also known as **TIX;** ✆ **415/433-7827;** www.tixbayarea.org) sells half-price tickets on the day of performance and full-price tickets in advance to select Bay Area cultural and sporting events. TIX is also a Ticketmaster outlet and sells Gray Line tours and transportation passes. Tickets are primarily sold in person with some half-price tickets available on their website. To find out which shows have half-price tickets, call the TIX info line or check out their website. A service charge, ranging from $1.75 to $6, is levied on each ticket depending on its full price. You can pay with cash, traveler's checks, Visa, MasterCard, American Express, or Discover Card with photo ID. TIX, located on Powell Street between Geary and Post streets, is open Tuesday through Thursday from 11am to 6pm, Friday from 11am to 7pm, Saturday from 10am to 7pm, and Sunday from 10am to 3pm. ***Note:*** Half-price tickets go on sale at 11am.

You can also get tickets to most theater and dance events through **City Box Office,** 180 Redwood St., Suite 100, between Golden Gate and McAllister streets off Van Ness Avenue (✆ **415/392-4400;** www.cityboxoffice.com). MasterCard and Visa are accepted.

Tickets.com (✆ **800/225-2277;** www.tickets.com) sells computer-generated tickets (with a hefty service charge of $3–$19 per ticket!) to concerts, sporting events, plays, and special events. **Ticketmaster** (✆ **415/421-TIXS;** www.ticketmaster.com) also offers advance ticket purchases (also with a service charge).

For information on local theater, check out **www.theatrebayarea.org**. For information on major league baseball, pro basketball, pro and college football, and horse racing, see the "Spectator Sports" section of chapter 7, beginning on p. 190.

And don't forget that this isn't New York: Bars close at 2am, so get an early start if you want a full night on the town in San Francisco.

1 The Performing Arts

Special concerts and performances take place in San Francisco year-round. **San Francisco Performances,** 500 Sutter St., Suite 710 (✆ **415/398-6449;** www.performances.org), has brought acclaimed artists to the Bay Area for 27 years. Shows run the gamut from chamber music to dance to jazz. Performances are in several venues, including the Herbst Theater and the Yerba Buena Center for the Arts. The season runs from late September to June. Tickets cost from $12 to $50 and are available through **City Box Office** (✆ **415/392-4400**) or through the San Francisco Performances website.

CLASSICAL MUSIC

Philharmonia Baroque Orchestra This orchestra of baroque, classical, and "early Romantic" music performs in San Francisco and all around the Bay Area. The season lasts September through April. Performing in Herbst Theater, 401 Van Ness Ave. Tickets are sold through City Box Office, ✆ **415/392-4400** (box office), or call 415/252-1288 (administrative offices). www.philharmonia.org. Tickets $29–$67.

San Francisco Symphony Founded in 1911, the internationally respected San Francisco Symphony has long been an important part of the city's cultural life under such legendary conductors as Pierre Monteux and Seiji Ozawa. In 1995, Michael Tilson Thomas took over from Herbert Blomstedt; he has led the orchestra to new heights and crafted an exciting repertoire of classical and modern music. The season runs September through June. Summer symphony activities include a Summer Festival and a Summer in the City series. Tickets are very hard to come by, but if you're desperate, you can usually pick up a few outside the hall the night of the concert. Also, the box office occasionally has a few last-minute tickets. Performing at Davies Symphony Hall, 201 Van Ness Ave. (at Grove St.). ✆ **415/864-6000** (box office). www.sfsymphony.org. Tickets $25–$114.

OPERA

In addition to San Francisco's major opera company, you might check out the amusing **Pocket Opera,** 469 Bryant St. (✆ **415/972-8930;** www.pocketopera.org). From early March to mid-July, the comic company stages farcical performances of well-known operas in English. The staging is intimate and informal, without lavish costumes and sets. The cast ranges from 3 to 16 players, supported by a chamber orchestra. The rich repertoire includes such works as *Don Giovanni, The Barber of Seville,* and over 80 other operas. Performances are Friday at 7:30pm, throughout the day on Saturday, and Sunday at 2pm. Call the box office for complete information, location (which varies), and show times. Tickets cost from $18 (students) to $35.

San Francisco Opera The San Francisco Opera was the second municipal opera in the United States and is one of the city's cultural icons. Brilliantly balanced casts may feature celebrated stars like Frederica Von Stade and Plácido Domingo along with

Value **Free Opera**

Every year, the **San Francisco Opera** stages a number of free performances. Every September, a free performance of Opera in the Park launches the season, followed by occasional free performances throughout the city as part of the Brown Bag Opera program. Schedule details can be found on the company's website at **www.sfopera.com**.

promising newcomers and regular members in productions that range from traditional to avant-garde. All productions have English supertitles. The season starts in September, lasts 14 weeks, takes a break for a few months, and then picks up again in June and July. During the interim winter period, future opera stars are featured in showcases and recitals. Performances are held most evenings, except Monday, with matinees on Sunday. Tickets go on sale as early as June for subscribers and August for the general public, and the best seats sell out quickly. Unless Domingo is in town, some less coveted seats are usually available until curtain time. War Memorial Opera House, 301 Van Ness Ave. (at Grove St.). ✆ **415/864-3330** (box office). www.sfopera.com. Tickets $24–$235; standing room $10 cash only; student rush $15 cash only.

THEATER

American Conservatory Theater (A.C.T.) *Finds* The Tony Award–winning American Conservatory Theater made its debut in 1967 and quickly established itself as the city's premier resident theater group and one of the nation's best. The A.C.T. season runs September through July and features both classic and experimental works. Its home is the fabulous **Geary Theater,** a national historic landmark that is regarded as one of America's finest performance spaces. The 2006–2007 season marks A.C.T.'s 40th anniversary; they haven't been resting on their laurels. In their 4-decade history, they've reached a combined audience of seven million people. Performing at the Geary Theater, 415 Geary St. (at Mason St.). ✆ **415/749-2ACT.** www.act-sf.org. Tickets $14–$82.

Eureka Theatre Company Eureka houses contemporary performances throughout the year, usually Wednesday through Sunday. Check their website or call the theater for information on upcoming shows and how to purchase tickets (but be aware: Since they don't produce the shows themselves, they won't take reservations for any shows at the theater or sell them online). 215 Jackson St. (between Battery and Front sts.). For information, ✆ **415/788-7469;** for tickets ✆ 415/255-8207. www.eurekatheatre.org. Ticket prices vary by company but are generally $22–$38.

Lorraine Hansberry Theatre San Francisco's top African-American theater group performs in a 300-seat state-of-the-art theater. It mounts special adaptations from literature along with contemporary dramas, classics, and music. The year 2006 marks the theater's 25th anniversary and with it will likely come some special performances. Phone for dates and programs. Performing at 620 Sutter St. (at Mason St.). ✆ **415/474-8800.** www.lhtsf.org. Tickets $25–$32.

The Magic Theatre The highly acclaimed Magic Theatre, celebrating its 40th season in 2006, is a major West Coast company dedicated to presenting the works of new plays; over the years it has nurtured the talents of such luminaries as Sam Shepard and David Mamet. Shepard's Pulitzer Prize–winning play *Buried Child* had its premiere

San Francisco After Dark

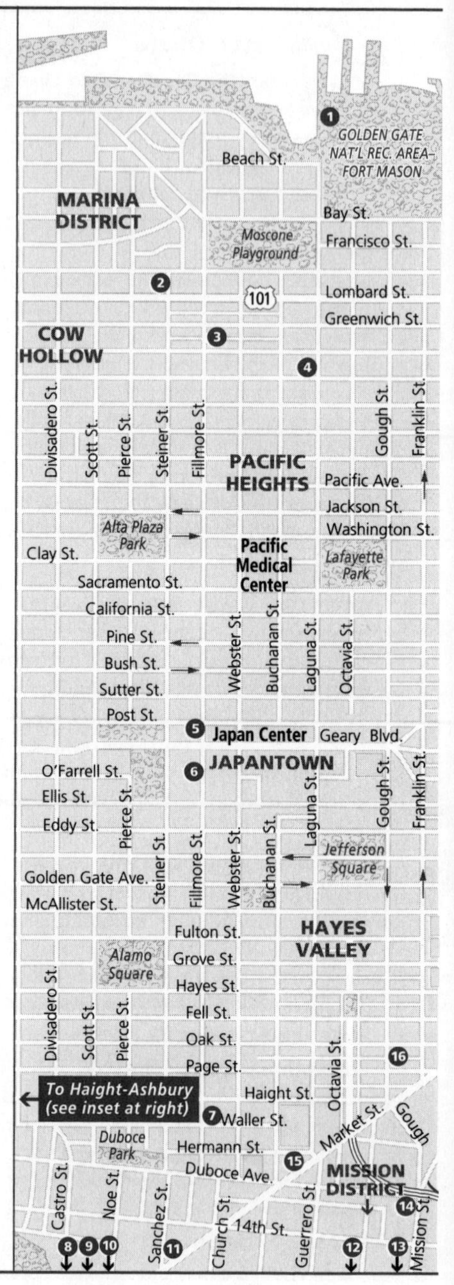

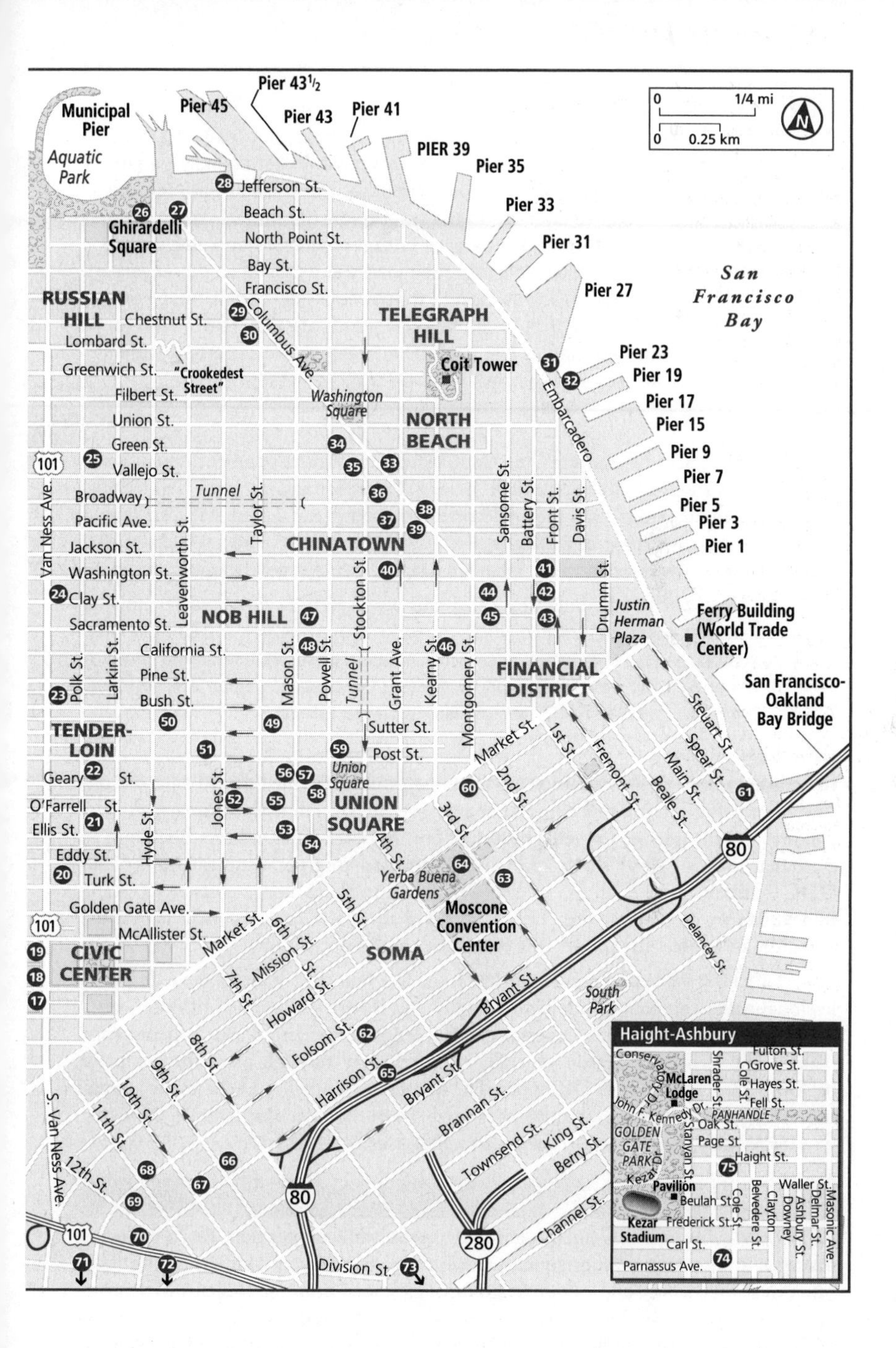

Municipal Pier
Aquatic Park
Pier 45
Pier 43½
Pier 43
Pier 41
PIER 39
Pier 35
Pier 33
Pier 31
Pier 27
Pier 23
Pier 19
Pier 17
Pier 15
Pier 9
Pier 7
Pier 5
Pier 3
Pier 1
0 1/4 mi
0 0.25 km
N
San Francisco Bay
Jefferson St.
Beach St.
North Point St.
Bay St.
Francisco St.
Ghirardelli Square
RUSSIAN HILL
Chestnut St.
Lombard St.
Greenwich St.
"Crookedest Street"
Filbert St.
Union St.
Green St.
Vallejo St.
Broadway
Tunnel
Pacific Ave.
Jackson St.
Washington St.
Clay St.
Sacramento St.
California St.
Pine St.
Bush St.
Columbus Ave.
Washington Square
TELEGRAPH HILL
Coit Tower
NORTH BEACH
CHINATOWN
NOB HILL
Embarcadero
Sansome St.
Battery St.
Front St.
Davis St.
Drumm St.
Justin Herman Plaza
Ferry Building (World Trade Center)
San Francisco-Oakland Bay Bridge
FINANCIAL DISTRICT
Van Ness Ave.
Leavenworth St.
Taylor St.
Stockton St.
Polk St.
Larkin St.
Mason St.
Powell St.
Tunnel
Grant Ave.
Kearny St.
Montgomery St.
Sutter St.
Post St.
Union Square
UNION SQUARE
TENDER-LOIN
Geary St.
O'Farrell St.
Ellis St.
Eddy St.
Turk St.
Golden Gate Ave.
McAllister St.
Hyde St.
Jones St.
Market St.
1st St.
2nd St.
3rd St.
4th St.
5th St.
6th St.
7th St.
8th St.
9th St.
10th St.
11th St.
12th St.
Fremont St.
Beale St.
Main St.
Spear St.
Steuart St.
Delancey St.
Yerba Buena Gardens
Moscone Convention Center
CIVIC CENTER
SOMA
Mission St.
Howard St.
Folsom St.
Harrison St.
Bryant St.
Brannan St.
Townsend St.
King St.
Berry St.
Channel St.
Division St.
South Park
S. Van Ness Ave.
101
80
280
Haight-Ashbury
Conservatory Dr.
McLaren Lodge
John F. Kennedy Dr.
GOLDEN GATE PARK
Kezar Dr.
PANHANDLE
Pavilion
Kezar Stadium
Shrader St.
Cole St.
Stanyan St.
Fulton St.
Grove St.
Hayes St.
Fell St.
Oak St.
Page St.
Haight St.
Waller St.
Beulah St.
Frederick St.
Carl St.
Parnassus Ave.
Belvedere St.
Clayton
Downey
Ashbury St.
Delmar St.
Masonic Ave.

Tips **ZinZany Dinner Party**

Hungry for dinner and a damned good time? It ain't cheap, but Teatro ZinZanni is a rollicking ride of food, whimsy, drama, and song within a stunningly elegant 1926 spiegeltent on The Embarcadero. Part musical theater and part comedy show, the 3-hour dinner theater includes a surprisingly decent five-course meal served by dozens of performers who weave both the audience and astounding physical acts (think Cirque du Soleil) into their wacky and playful world. Anyone in need of a night of lighthearted laughter should definitely book a table here. Shows are held Wednesday through Sunday and tickets are $123 to $147 including dinner. The tent is located at Pier 29 on The Embarcadero at Battery Street. Call ✆ **415/438-2668** or see www.zinzanni.org for more details.

here, as did Mamet's *Dr. Faustus.* The season usually runs from October through June; performances are held Tuesday through Sunday. A perk for anyone who's been in previous years: In 2005 and 2006 they redecorated the lobby and added new seats in one of the theaters. Performing at Building D, Fort Mason Center, Marina Blvd. (at Buchanan St.). ✆ **415/441-8822.** www.magictheatre.org. Tickets $20–$45; discounts for students, educators, and seniors.

Theatre Rhinoceros Founded in 1977, this was America's first (and remains its foremost) theater ensemble devoted solely to works addressing gay, lesbian, bisexual, and transgender issues. The company presents main-stage shows and studio productions of new and classic works each year. The theater is 1 block east of the 16th St./Mission BART station. 2926 16th St. ✆ **415/861-5079.** www.therhino.org. Tickets $15–$25.

DANCE

In addition to the local companies, top traveling troupes like the Joffrey Ballet and the American Ballet Theatre make regular appearances in San Francisco. Primary modern dance spaces include the **Cowell Theater,** at Fort Mason Center, Marina Boulevard at Buchanan Street (✆ **415/345-7575;** www.fortmason.org/performingarts); and the **ODC Theatre,** 3153 17th St., at Shotwell Street in the Mission District (✆ **415/863-9834;** www.odcdance.org. Tickets cost $18 to $25. Check the local papers for schedules or contact the theater box offices for more information.

San Francisco Ballet Founded in 1933, the San Francisco Ballet is the oldest professional ballet company in the United States and is regarded as one of the country's finest. It performs an eclectic repertoire of full-length, neoclassical and contemporary ballets. The Repertory Season generally runs February through May; the company performs the *Nutcracker* in December. The San Francisco Ballet Orchestra accompanies most performances. War Memorial Opera House, 301 Van Ness Ave. (at Grove St.). ✆ **415/865-2000** for tickets and information. www.sfballet.org. Tickets $10–$205.

2 Comedy & Cabaret

BATS Improv ★ *Finds* Combining improvisation with competition, BATS performs hilarious improvisational tournaments in which teams of actors compete against each other in scenes, songs, and games, based on suggestions from the audience. There are also long-form shows throughout the year with improvisations of movies, musicals, and even Shakespeare; audience members supply suggestions for titles and plot points, and characters and dialogue are then made up and performed immediately onstage.

Main Company shows are Fridays and Saturdays at 8pm; student performance ensemble shows on Sundays at 7pm. Reservations and discount tickets available through their website. Remaining tickets are sold at the box office the night of the show. Performing at Bayfront Theatre at the Fort Mason Center, Building B no. 350, 3rd floor. ✆ **415/474-8935.** www.improv.org. Tickets $5–$15.

Beach Blanket Babylon ★★ *Moments* A San Francisco tradition, *Beach Blanket Babylon* evolved from Steve Silver's Rent-a-Freak service—a group of "party guests" extraordinaire who hired themselves out as a "cast of characters" complete with fabulous costumes and sets, props, and gags. After their act caught on, it moved into the Savoy-Tivoli, a North Beach bar. By 1974, the audience had grown too large for the facility, and *Beach Blanket* has been at the 400-seat Club Fugazi ever since. The show is a comedic musical send-up that is best known for outrageous costumes and oversize headdresses. It's been playing for over 30 years, and almost every performance sells out. The show is updated often enough that locals still attend. Those under 21 are welcome at both Sunday matinees (2 and 5pm), when no alcohol is served; photo ID is required for evening performances. Write for weekend tickets at least 3 weeks in advance, or get them through their website or by calling their box office. ***Note:*** Only a handful of tickets per show are assigned seating; all other tickets are within specific sections depending on price, but seating is first-come, first-seated within that section. Performances are Wednesday and Thursday at 8pm, Friday and Saturday at 7 and 10pm, and Sunday at 2 and 5pm. At Club Fugazi, Beach Blanket Babylon Blvd., 678 Green St. (between Powell St. and Columbus Ave.). ✆ **415/421-4222.** www.beachblanketbabylon.com. Tickets $25–$78.

Cobb's Comedy Club Cobb's features such national headliners as Joe Rogan, Brian Regan, and Jake Johannsen. Comedy reigns Wednesday through Sunday, including a 15-comedian All-Pro Wednesday showcase (a 3-hr. marathon). Cobb's is open to those 18 and over, and occasionally to kids 16 and 17 when accompanied by a parent or legal guardian (call ahead). Shows are held Wednesday, Thursday, and Sunday at 8pm, Friday and Saturday at 8 and 10:15pm. 915 Columbus Ave. (at Lombard St.). ✆ **415/928-4320.** www.cobbscomedy.com. Cover $13–$35. 2-beverage minimum.

Punch Line Comedy Club Adjacent to The Embarcadero One office building, this is the largest comedy nightclub in the city. Three-person shows with top national and local talent are featured here Tuesday through Saturday. Showcase night is Sunday, when 15 comics take the mic. There's an all-star showcase or a special event on Monday. Doors always open at 7pm and shows are Sunday through Thursday at 8pm, Friday and Saturday at 8 and 10pm (18 and over; two-drink minimum). They serve a full menu Thursday through Saturday (think wings, chicken sandwiches, and curiously, ravioli), and pizzas, appetizers, and salads Sunday through Wednesday. 444 Battery St. (between Washington and Clay sts.), plaza level. ✆ **415/397-4337** or 415/397-7573 for recorded information. www.punchlinecomedyclub.com. Cover Mon $7.50; Tues–Thurs $13-$15, Fri and Sat $18–$20; Sun $7.50. Prices are subject to change for more popular comics, maxing out at a price of $45.

3 The Club & Music Scene

The greatest legacy from the 1960s is the city's continued tradition of live entertainment and music, which explains the great variety of clubs and music enjoyed by San Francisco. The hippest dance places are South of Market Street (SoMa), in former warehouses; the artsy bohemian scene centers are in the Mission; and the most popular cafe culture is still in North Beach.

Note: The club and music scene is always changing, often outdating recommendations before the ink can dry on a page. Most of the venues below are promoted as different clubs on various nights of the week, each with its own look, sound, and style. Discount passes and club announcements are often available at clothing stores and other shops along upper Haight Street.

Drink prices at most bars, clubs, and cafes range from about $3.50 to $9, unless otherwise noted.

ROCK & BLUES CLUBS

In addition to the following listings, see "Dance Clubs," below, for (usually) live, danceable rock.

Bimbo's 365 Club ★★ Originally located on Market Street when it opened in 1931, this North Beach destination is a fabulous spot to catch outstanding live rock and jazz (think Chris Isaak and the Brian Setzer Orchestra) and dance amid glamorous surroundings. Grab tickets in advance at the box office, which is open Monday through Friday, 10am to 4pm. 1025 Columbus Ave. (at Chestnut St.). ✆ **415/474-0365.** www.bimbos365club.com.

Biscuits and Blues With a crisp, blow-your-eardrums-out sound system, New Orleans–speak-easy (albeit commercial) appeal, and a nightly lineup of live, national acts, there's no better place to muse the blues than this basement-cum-nightclub. From 7pm on, they serve drink specials, along with their signature fried chicken; namesake moist, flaky biscuits; some new small-plate entrees dubbed "Southern tapas"; and a newly expanded wine list. Menu items range from $7.95 to $17. 401 Mason (at Geary St.). ✆ **415/292-2583.** www.biscuitsandblues.com. Cover (during performances) $10–$20.

The Boom Boom Room *Finds* The late John Lee Hooker and his partner Alex Andreas bought this Western Addition club several years back and used Hooker's star power to pull in some of the best blues bands in the country (even the Stones showed up for an unannounced jam session). Though it changed focus and is now a roots music oriented club, it's still a fun, dark, small, cramped, and steamy joint where you can hear good live tunes—ranging from New Orleans funk, soul, and new wave, to trance jazz, live drum 'n' bass, electronica, house, and more—Tuesday through Sunday until 2am. If you're going to The Fillmore (see below) to see a band, stop by here first for a drink and come back after your show for more great music. The neighborhood's a bit rough, so be sure to park in the underground lot across the street. 1601 Fillmore St. (at Geary Blvd.). ✆ **415/673-8000.** www.boomboomblues.com. Cover varies from free to $15.

Bottom of the Hill *Value* Voted one of the best places to hear live rock in the city by the *San Francisco Bay Guardian,* this popular neighborhood club attracts a diverse crowd ranging from rockers to real-estate salespeople; it also offers tons of all-ages

---

Tips Club-Hopping Tour

If you prefer to let someone else take the lead (and the driver's seat) for a night out, contact **3 Babes and a Bus** (✆ **800/414-0158;** www.threebabes.com). The nightclub tour company (the head babe is a stockbroker by day) will take you and a gaggle of 20- to 40-something partiers (mostly single women) out on the town, skipping lines and cover charges, for $39 per person.

Tips Scope-a-Scene

The local newspapers won't direct you to the city's underground club scene, nor will they advise you which of the dozens of clubs are truly hot. To get dialed in, check out reviews from the ravers themselves at www.sfstation.com. The far more commercial **Club Line** (✆ **415/339-8686;** www.sfclubs.com) offers up-to-date schedules for the city's larger dance venues.

shows. The main attraction is an eclectic range of live music almost every night (focusing on indie punk with the occasional country band thrown in), but the club also offers pretty good burgers, a bar menu, and outdoor seating on the back patio Wednesday through Friday from 4pm to 2am, Saturday through Tuesday 8:30pm to 2am. Happy hour runs Wednesday to Friday from 4 to 7pm. 1233 17th St. (at Missouri St.). ✆ **415/621-4455.** www.bottomofthehill.com. Cover $6–$12.

Empire Plush Room *Finds* San Francisco is woefully short on cabaret and jazz venues, but thanks to the Plush Room, there's still one swank little boutique establishment that lures national talent on stage. Check out their schedule and perhaps you'll get to catch acts such as Paula West, Dixie Carter, Maude Maggart, Jane Oliver, or others doing their classic and under-celebrated thing. Come thirsty: There's a two-drink minimum. In the York Hotel, 940 Sutter St. (between Hyde and Leavenworth sts.). ✆ **415/885-2800.** www.empireplushroom.com. Tickets $20–$65. 2 drink minimum.

The Fillmore *Finds* Made famous by promoter Bill Graham in the 1960s, The Fillmore showcases big names in a moderately sized standing-room-only space. Check listings in papers, call the theater, or visit their website for information on upcoming events. And if you make it to a show, check out the fabulous collection of vintage concert posters chronicling the hall's history. 1805 Geary Blvd. (at Fillmore St.). ✆ **415/346-6000.** www.thefillmore.com. Tickets $17–$45.

Grant & Green Saloon The atmosphere at this historic North Beach dive bar is not that special, but Mondays feature jazz, Tuesdays are DJ and karaoke, and the local bands on Thursday through Saturday are decent. All in all, the space is an all-around great place to let your hair down. 1371 Grant Ave. (at Green St.). ✆ **415/693-9565.** www.grantandgreen.com.

Great American Music Hall ★★ Built in 1907 as a restaurant/bordello, the Great American Music Hall is likely one of the most gorgeous rock venues you'll encounter. With ornately carved balconies, frescoed ceilings, marble columns, and huge hanging light fixtures, you won't know whether to marvel at the structure or watch the acts, which have ranged from Duke Ellington and Sarah Vaughan to Arctic Monkeys, The Radiators, and She Wants Revenge. All shows are all ages (6 and up) so you can bring your family, too. You can buy a ticket for just the show and order bar snacks (such as nachos, black bean and cheese flautas, burgers, and sandwiches); or buy a ticket that includes a complete dinner (an extra $25), which changes nightly but always includes a salad and choice of meat, fish, or veggie entree. Alas, you can't buy your ticket via telephone, but you can download a form from their website and fax it to **415/885-5075** with your Visa or MasterCard info; there is a service charge of $2 per ticket. You can also stop by the box office to purchase tickets directly ($1 service

Drinking & Smoking Laws

The drinking age is 21 in California, and bartenders can ask for a valid photo ID, no matter how old you look. Some clubs demand identification at the door, so it's a good idea to carry it at all times. Once you get through the door, however, forget about cigarettes—smoking is banned in all California bars. The law is generally enforced and though San Francisco's police department has not made bar raids a priority, people caught smoking in bars can be—and occasionally are—ticketed and fined. Music clubs strictly enforce the law and will ask you to leave if you light up. If you must smoke, do it outside. Also, the dreaded last call for alcohol usually rings out at around 1:30am, since state laws prohibit the sale of alcohol from 2 to 6am every morning. A very important word of warning: Driving under the influence of alcohol is a serious crime in California, with jail time for the first offense. You are likely to be legally intoxicated (.08% blood alcohol) if you have had as little as one alcoholic drink an hour. When in doubt, take a taxi.

charge), or buy them at virtuous.com or Tickets.com (✆ **800/225-2277**). Valet parking is available for selects shows; check website for additional parking information. 859 O'Farrell (between Polk and Larkin sts.). ✆ **415/885-0750.** www.musichallsf.com. Ticket prices and starting times vary; call or check website for individual show information.

Lou's Pier 47 Club You won't find many locals in the place, but Lou's happens to be good, old-fashioned fun. It's a casual spot where you can relax with Cajun seafood (downstairs) and live blues bands (upstairs) nightly. A vacation attitude makes the place one of the more, um, jovial spots near the wharf. There's a $3 to $5 cover for bands that play between 4 and 8pm and a $3 to $10 cover for bands that play between 8 or 9pm and midnight or 1am. 300 Jefferson St. (at Jones St.). ✆ **415/771-5687.** www.louspier47.com.

Pier 23 If there's one good-time destination that's an anchor for San Francisco's party people, it's The Embarcadero's Pier 23. Part ramshackle patio spot and part dance floor with a heavy dash of dive bar, here it's all about fun for a startlingly diverse clientele (including a one-time visit by Bill Clinton!). The well-worn box of a restaurant with tented patio is a prime sunny-day social spot for white collars, but on weekends, it's a straight-up people zoo where every age and persuasion coexist more peacefully than the cast in a McDonald's commercial. Expect to boogie down shoulder-to-shoulder to 1980s hits and leave with a contagious feel-good vibe. Pier 23, at The Embarcadero (at Battery St.). ✆ **415/362-5125.** www.pier23cafe.com. Cover $5–$10 during performances.

The Saloon An authentic gold rush survivor, this North Beach dive is the oldest bar in the city. Popular with both bikers and daytime pinstripers, it schedules live blues nightly and afternoons Friday through Sunday. 1232 Grant Ave. (at Columbus St.). ✆ **415/989-7666.** Cover $5–$15 Fri–Sat.

Slim's Co-owned by musician Boz Scaggs, this glitzy restaurant and bar serves California cuisine and seats 200, but its usually standing room only during almost nightly shows ranging from performers of homegrown rock, jazz, blues, and alternative music.

Tips Local Talent

Want to see the best of local jazz, cabaret, or blues performers? Check the *San Francisco Chronicle*'s Sunday "Datebook" to see if the following artists are in the house. Better yet, buy their CDs and take San Francisco's music scene home with you:

- **Faith Winthrop,** a veteran cabaret diva with a velvet voice and heartfelt delivery.
- **Ledisi,** a young local blues singer with a penchant for scatting and smoky, deep, soulful, self-written tunes.
- **Jacqui Naylor,** a seductive young talent with a love for standards and reinventing a phrase with her own modern twist.
- **Lavay Smith & Her Red Hot Skillet Lickers,** a sizzling and toe-tapping swing-style crooner, proves that swing hasn't swung this hard since it was invented.

An added bonus for the musically inclined family: All ages are always welcome. Call or check their website for a schedule; hot bands sell out in advance. 333 11th St. (at Folsom St.). ✆ **415/522-0333.** www.slims-sf.com. Cover free to $30.

JAZZ & LATIN CLUBS

Cafe du Nord *Finds* Although it's been around since 1907, this basement supper club is rightfully self-proclaimed as the place for a "slightly lurid indie pop scene set in a beautiful old speakeasy." It's also where an eclectic (and usually younger) crowd flocks to linger at the front room's 40-foot mahogany bar or dine on the likes of phyllo-wrapped prawns with romesco sauce or sip cocktails at the back room tables—while listening to national indie rock bands like Gomez and Arab Strap, and old school acts like Frank Black and the Pixies. 2170 Market St. (at Sanchez St.). ✆ **415/861-5016.** www.cafedunord.com. Cover $5–$25. Food $5–$15.

Rasselas Large, casual, and comfortable with couches and small tables, this is a favorite spot for local jazz, blues, soul, and R&B combos. The adjacent restaurant serves Ethiopian cuisine in a Bedouin tent. Menu items range from $4 to $14. 1534 Fillmore St. (at Geary Blvd.). ✆ **415/567-5010.** www.rasselasjazzclub.com. Cover $10 Fri–Sat. 2-drink minimum.

DANCE CLUBS

Although a lot of clubs allow dancing, the following are the places to go if all you want to do is shake your groove thang.

The Endup This unique party space with a huge, heated outdoor deck (with waterfall and fountain), indoor fireplace, and eclectic clientele has always thrown some of the most kickin' parties in town. There's a different theme every night: Thursday's Wind Up offers up a variety of house DJs; Fag Friday is just what it sounds like, plus lots of throw-down dancing; and The Endup is ever-popular with the sleepless dance-all-day crowd that comes here after the other clubs close (it's open Sat morning 6am–noon and then nonstop from Sat night around 10pm until Sun night/Mon morning at 4am). Call to confirm nights—offerings change from time to time. 401 Sixth St. (at Harrison St.). ✆ **415/357-0827.** www.theendup.com. Cover free–$15.

SF's Underground Entertainment

If you're really in the mood to for some radical entertainment on your vacation, log on to www.LaughingSquid.com. Since 1995 Laughing Squid's **"Squid List"** has been the Bay Area's sine qua non online resource for underground art, culture, and technology. Along with links to local art and culture events, the Laughing Squid also hosts the Squid List, a daily event announcements list. There's some really freaky fringe stuff on this webpage, with plenty of garbage-level entertainment amongst several gems. Either way it makes for entertaining surfing.

1015 Folsom The ginormous party warehouse at 1015 Folsom Street has three levels of dance floors that make for an extensive variety of dancing venues—complete with a 20- and 30-something gyrating mass who live for the DJs' pounding house, disco, and acid-jazz music matched to a full-color laser system. Each night is a different club that attracts its own crowd, ranging from yuppie to hip-hop. Open Thursday through Saturday 10pm to 2am. 1015 Folsom St. (at Sixth St.). ✆ **415/431-1200.** www.1015.com. Cover varies.

Ruby Skye Downtown's most glamorous and gigantic nightspot is all aglitter thanks to a dramatic renovation and the addition of killer light and sound systems within the 1890s Victorian playhouse previously known as The Stage Door. Inside, hundreds of partiers boogie on the ballroom floor to house music, mingle on the mezzanine and around the three bars, and puff freely in the smoking room while DJs or live music bring down the dancing house Thursday through Saturday. Big spenders should book the VIP lounge, which offers a glitzy place to "kick it" and bird's-eye views of the whole club scene. 420 Mason St. (between Geary and Post sts.). ✆ **415/693-0777.** www.rubyskye.com. Cover $10–$25.

SUPPER CLUBS

If you can eat dinner, listen to live music, and dance (or at least wiggle in your chair) in the same room, it's a supper club—those are the criteria here.

Harry Denton's Starlight Room *Moments* Come to this celestial high-rise cocktail lounge and nightclub, where tourists and locals watch the sunset at dusk and boogie down to live '70s '80s music, Motown covers, and jazz and funk Friday through Tuesday nights; '80s vogue DJ on Thursday nights; or the DJs' hip-hop and Top-40 tunes after dark on Wednesdays. The room is classic 1930s San Francisco, with red-velvet banquettes, chandeliers, and fabulous views. But what really attracts flocks of all ages is a night of Harry Denton–style fun, which usually includes plenty of drinking and unrestrained dancing. The full bar stocks a decent collection of single-malt Scotches and champagnes, and you can snack from the pricey Starlight appetizer menu (make a reservation to guarantee a table and you'll also have a place to rest your weary dancing-dogs). Early evening is more relaxed, but come the weekend, this place gets loose. ***Tip:*** Come dressed for success (no casual jeans, open-toed shoes for men, or sneakers), or you'll be turned away at the door. Atop the Sir Francis Drake Hotel, 450 Powell St., 21st floor. ✆ **415/395-8595.** www.harrydenton.com. Cover $10 Wed after 7pm; $10 Thurs–Fri after 8pm; $15 Sat after 8pm.

Jazz at Pearl's A change of ownership in 2003 converted one of the best jazz venues in the city into one of the best supper clubs. Voted Top 30 Club Worldwide by *Condé Nast Traveler* and Best Live Jazz Venue by *San Francisco Magazine,* Jazz at Pearl's combines a 1930s vibe, Spanish tapas, and great live music. With a variety of acts throughout the week (big band on Mon to national acts Thurs–Sat), there's something for everyone at this all-ages club. However, with only 25 tables, advance tickets are recommended if you want to sit; general admission tickets are available as well, but don't guarantee seating. Shows start at 8 and 10pm nightly; doors open at 7pm. Tickets range from $19 to $154 (for VIP seating, which includes preferred seating, champagne, and a meet-and-greet with the artist), and there's a 2-drink minimum. Cash only. 256 Columbus Ave. (at Broadway). ✆ **415/291-8255.** www.jazzatpearls.com.

DESTINATION BARS WITH DJ GROOVES

Bambuddha Lounge *Finds* A hot place for the young and the trendy to feast, flirt, or just be fabulous is this restaurant/bar adjoining the funky-cool Phoenix Hotel. With a 20-foot reclining Buddha on the roof, ultramodern San Francisco–meets–Southeast Asia decor (including waterfalls in the dining room; outdoor poolside cocktail lounge; and *salas,* Balinese-style lounge areas by an outdoor pool), affordable and above-average Southeast Asian cuisine served late into the evening, and a state-of-the-art sound system streaming ambient, down-tempo, soul, funk, and house music, this is the "it" joint of the moment. 601 Eddy St. (at Larkin St.). ✆ **415/885-5088.** www.bambuddhalounge.com. Cover $5–$10, $20 for special events Thurs–Sat.

The Bliss Bar Surprisingly trendy for sleepy family-oriented Noe Valley, this small, stylish, and friendly bar is a great place to stop for a varied mix of locals, colorful cocktail concoctions, and a DJ spinning at the front window from 9pm to 2am every night except Sunday and Monday. If it's open, take your cocktail into the too-cool back Blue Room. And if you're on a budget, stop by from 4 to 7pm when martinis, lemon drops, cosmos, watermelon cosmos, and apple martinis are $4. 4026 24th St. (between Noe and Castro sts.). ✆ **415/826-6200.** www.blissbarsf.com.

Levende Lounge A fusion of fine dining and cocktails, Levende Lounge is one of the Mission's hottest spots and has been noted as the best bar in the city for singles, romance, bar food, and a slew of other accolades. Drop in early for happy hour Monday through Friday from 5 to 7pm; or sit down for a meal of "world-fusion" small plates (think French, Asian, and Nuevo Latino) in a more standard dinner setting amid exposed brick walls and cozy lighting. Later, tables are traded for lounge furnishings for some late-night noshing and grooving. ***Tip:*** Some nights have cover charges, but you can avoid the fee with a dinner reservation, and food is served until 11pm. 1710 Mission St. (at Duboce St.). ✆ **415/864-5585.** www.levendesf.com.

Wish Bar Flirtation, fun, and an attractive staff await at this somewhat mellow, narrow bar in the popular night crawler area around 11th and Folsom streets. Swathed in burgundy and black with exposed cinder-block walls and cement floors, all's aglow à la candlelight and red-shaded sconces. With a bar in the front, DJ spinning upbeat lounge music in the back, and seating—including cushy leather couches—in between, it's often packed with a surprisingly diverse (albeit youthful) crowd and ever filled with eye candy. Closed Sundays. 1539 Folsom St. (between 11th and 12th sts.). ✆ **415/278-9474.** www.wishsf.com.

4 The Bar Scene

Finding your idea of a comfortable bar has a lot to do with picking a neighborhood filled with your kind of people and investigating that area further. There are hundreds of bars throughout San Francisco, and although many are obscurely located and can't be classified by their neighborhood, the following is a general description of what you'll find, and where:

- **Chestnut and Union Street** bars attract a postcollegiate crowd.
- Young alternatives frequent **Mission District** haunts.
- **Upper Haight** caters to eclectic neighborhood cocktailers.
- **Lower Haight** is skate- and snowboarder grungy.
- Tourists mix with theatergoers and thirsty businesspeople in **downtown** pubs.
- **North Beach** serves all types.
- **The Castro** caters to gay locals and tourists.
- **SoMa** offers an eclectic mix.

The following is a list of a few of San Francisco's most interesting bars. Unless otherwise noted, these bars do not have cover charges.

Buddha Lounge *Finds* If you like colorful dive bars you'll love the Buddha Lounge. This heart-of-Chinatown bar is a great glimpse into Chinatown's neighborhood culture. Of course, most tourists shy away from what appears to be yet another dark, seedy watering hole, but it's really just a cheery neighborhood bar. Be brave. Step inside, order a drink, and pretend you're in a Charlie Chan movie. The best part is when the Chinese woman behind the bar answers the phone: "HELLO BUDDHA!!!" No cover. 901 Grant Ave. (at Washington St.). ✆ **415/362-1792.**

Buena Vista Café *Moments* "Did you have an Irish coffee at the Buena Vista?" The myth is that the Irish coffee was invented at the Buena Vista, but the real story is that this popular wharf cafe was the first bar in the country to serve Irish coffee after a local journalist came back from a trip and described the drink to the bartender. Since then, the bar has poured more of these pick-me-up drinks than any other bar in the world, and ordering one has become a San Francisco must-do. Fact is, it's entertaining just to watch the venerable tenders pour up to 10 whiskey-laden coffees at a time (a rather messy event). The cafe is in a prime tourist spot along the wharf, so plan on waiting for a stool or table to free up. And don't worry if you need a little snack to soak up the booze—they serve food here, too. 2765 Hyde St. (at Beach St.). ✆ **415/474-5044.** www.thebuenavista.com.

Edinburgh Castle Since 1958, this legendary Scottish pub has been known for unusual British ales on tap and the best selection of single-malt Scotches in the city. The huge pub is decorated with horse brasses, steel helmets, and an authentic Ballantine caber (a long wooden pole) used in the annual Scottish games. Fish and chips and other traditional foods are available until 11pm. The Edinburgh also features author readings and performances and has hosted such noteworthy writers as Po Bronson, Beth Lisick, and Anthony Swofford. Open 5pm to 2am daily. 950 Geary St. (between Polk and Larkin sts.). ✆ **415/885-4074.** www.castlenews.com.

Gold Dust Lounge *Finds* If you're staying downtown and want to head to a friendly, festive bar loaded with old-fashioned style and revelry, you needn't wander far off Union Square. This classically cheesy watering hole is all that. The red banquettes, gilded walls, dramatic chandeliers, pro bartenders, and "regulars" are the old-school real deal. Add live music and cheap drinks and you're in for a good ol' time. ***Tip:*** It's cash only, so come with some greenbacks. 247 Powell St. (at Geary St.). ✆ **415/397-1695.**

Hemlock Tavern This former gay dance club is now one of the most popular bars on Polk Street and always packed on weekends. There's lots of dark wood, warm colors, a line for the bathroom, and an enclosed back room that's dedicated just to smokers. The crowd is a bit younger than the Edinburgh Castle crew, but there's a similar mix of locals, hipsters, musicians, and visitors who would never think of themselves as tourists. The jukebox is sweet, and you can chow down on warm peanuts (toss the shells on the floor) and wash 'em down with a good selection of beers on tap. No cover. 1131 Polk St. (at Sutter St.). ✆ **415/923-0923.** www.hemlocktavern.com.

Holy Cow Its motto, "Never a cover, always a party" has been the case since 1987 when this industrial SoMa bar opened. This is the spot to come if you really want to do some drinking in a casual environment with DJ music ranging from club classics from the '70s to the '90s to top 40s. Nightly drink specials—$1 well drinks and Buds from 9 to 10pm and half-price drinks from 9 to 11:30pm on Thursdays; $3 drinks from 9 to 10pm on Fridays—make sure no one leaves sober, so plan your transportation accordingly. The bar's only open Thursday through Saturday, 9pm to 2am. 1535 Folsom St. (between 11th and 12th sts.). ✆ **415/621-6087.**

Li Po Cocktail Lounge *Finds* A dim, divey, slightly spooky Chinese bar that was once an opium den, Li Po's alluring character stems from its mishmash clutter of dusty Asian furnishings and mementos, including an unbelievably huge ancient rice-paper lantern hanging from the ceiling and a glittery golden shrine to Buddha behind the bar. The bartenders love to creep out patrons with tales of opium junkies haunting the joint. 916 Grant Ave. (between Washington and Jackson sts.). ✆ **415/982-0072.**

Matrix Fillmore Despite its previous life as the Pierce Street Annex, Matrix Fillmore remains one of the young and yuppies' hottest singles scenes. Those already spoken for can still appreciate the slick lounge atmosphere of candlelight, dyed concrete floors, flatscreen TVs, and free-standing centerpiece fireplace with its "Zen minimalist" mantel. Though it hosts a martini and mojito crowd, the bar also offers 10 wines by the glass and a large by-the-bottle selection including cult classics like Dalla Valle. Drinks range from $7 to $10. Valet parking available at the nearby Balboa Café (Fillmore and Greenwich sts.). 3138 Fillmore St. (between Greenwich and Filbert sts.). ✆ **415/563-4180.** www.plumpjack.com.

Perry's If you read *Tales of the City,* you already know that this bar and restaurant has a colorful history as a pickup place for Pacific Heights and Marina singles. Although the times are not as wild today, locals still come to casually check out the happenings at the dark mahogany bar. A separate dining room offers breakfast, lunch, dinner, and weekend brunch. It's a good place for hamburgers, simple fish dishes, and pasta. Menu items range from $6 to $22. 1944 Union St. (at Laguna St.). ✆ **415/922-9022.**

Pied Piper Bar The huge Pied Piper mural by Edwardian illustrator Maxfield Parrish steals the show at this historic mahogany bar, where high stakes were once won and lost on the roll of the dice. Happy hour Thursday and Friday from 5 to 7pm features a complimentary buffet and 75¢ oysters on Fridays. In the Palace Hotel, 2 New Montgomery (at Market St.). ✆ **415/512-1111.**

The Red Room Ultramodern, small, and deliciously dim, this lounge reflects no other color but ruby red. It's a sexy place to sip the latest cocktail. In the Commodore Hotel, 827 Sutter St. (at Jones St.). ✆ **415/346-7666.**

The Redwood Room When hotelier Ian Schrager and designer Philippe Starck updated the furniture in this historic Art Deco room, they retained its gorgeous redwood paneling, legendarily made from a single 2,000-year-old tree. With its plush yet modern feel, illuminated by beautiful original Deco sconces, the vibe is definitely updated to attract swinging singles, the tragically hip, and posers who mix, mingle, and seem to have a pretty fab and glamorous time here despite steep drink prices ($9–$25). In the Clift Hotel, 495 Geary St. ✆ **415/775-4700.**

Spec's *Finds* The location of Spec's—Saroyan Place, a tiny alley at 250 Columbus Ave.—makes it less of a walk-in bar and more of a lively local hangout. Its funky decor—maritime flags hang from the ceiling; posters, photos, and oddities line the exposed-brick walls—gives it a character that intrigues every visitor. A "museum," displayed under glass, contains memorabilia and items brought back by seamen who drop in between voyages. The clientele is funky enough to keep you preoccupied while you drink a beer. 12 Saroyan Place (at 250 Columbus Ave.). ✆ **415/421-4112.**

The Tonga Room & Hurricane Bar *Finds* It's kitschy as all get-out, but there's no denying the goofy Polynesian pleasures of the Fairmont Hotel's tropical oasis. Drop in and join the crowds for an umbrella drink, a simulated thunderstorm and downpour, and a heavy dose of whimsy that escapes most San Francisco establishments. If you're on a budget, you'll definitely want to stop by for the weekday happy hour from 5 to 7pm, when you can stuff your face at the all-you-can-eat bar-grub buffet (baby back ribs, chow mein, pot stickers) for $8 and the cost of one drink. Settle in and you'll catch live Top-40 music after 8pm Wednesday through Sunday, when there's a $3 to $5 cover. In the Fairmont Hotel, 950 Mason St. (at California St.). ✆ **415/772-5278.** www.tongaroom.com.

Toronado Gritty Lower Haight isn't exactly a charming street, but there's plenty of nightlife here, catering to an artistic/grungy/skateboarding 20-something crowd. While Toronado definitely draws in the young'uns, its 50-plus microbrews on tap and 100 bottled beers also entice a more eclectic clientele in search of beer heaven. The brooding atmosphere matches the surroundings: an aluminum bar, a few tall tables, minimal lighting, and a back room packed with tables and chairs. Happy hour runs 11:30am to 6pm every day for $1 off pints. 547 Haight St. (at Fillmore St.). ✆ **415/863-2276.** www.toronado.com.

Tosca Cafe *Finds* Open Tuesday through Saturday from 5pm to 2am, Sunday 7pm to 2am, Tosca is a low-key and large popular watering hole for local politicos, writers, media types, incognito celebrities such as Johnny Depp or Nicholas Cage, and similar cognoscenti of unassuming classic characters. Equipped with dim lights, red leather booths, and high ceilings, it's everything you'd expect an old North Beach legend to be. No credit cards. 242 Columbus Ave. (between Broadway and Pacific Ave.). ✆ **415/986-9651.**

Vesuvio Situated along Jack Kerouac Alley, across from the famed City Lights bookstore, this renowned literary beatnik hangout is packed to the second-floor rafters with neighborhood writers, artists, songsters, wannabes, and everyone else ranging from longshoremen and cab drivers to businesspeople, all of whom come for the laid-back atmosphere. The convivial space consists of two stories of cocktail tables, complemented by changing exhibitions of local art. In addition to drinks, Vesuvio features an espresso machine. 255 Columbus Ave. (at Broadway). ✆ **415/362-3370.** www.vesuvio.com.

Zeitgeist The front door is black, the back door is adorned with a skeleton Playboy bunny, and inside is packed to the rafters with tattooed, pierced, and hard-core-looking partiers. But forge on. Zeitgeist is such a friendly and fun punk-rock-cum-biker-bar beer garden that even the occasional yuppie can be spotted mingling around the slammin' juke box featuring tons of local bands and huge back patio filled with picnic tables. (There tend to be cute girls here, too.) Along with fantastic dive-bar environs, you'll find 30 beers on draft, a pool table, and pinball machines. The regular crowd, mostly locals and bike messengers, come here to kick back with a pitcher, and welcome anyone else interested in the same pursuit. And if your night turns out, um, better than expected, there's a hotel upstairs. Cash only. 199 Valencia St. (at Duboce). ✆ **415/255-7505.**

BREWPUBS

Gordon Biersch Brewery Restaurant Gordon Biersch Brewery is San Francisco's largest brew restaurant, serving decent food and tasty beer to an attractive crowd of mingling professionals. There are always several house-made beers to choose from, ranging from light to dark. Menu items run $9.50 to $26. (See p. 115 for more information.) 2 Harrison St. (on The Embarcadero). ✆ **415/243-8246.** www.gordonbiersch.com.

San Francisco Brewing Company Surprisingly low key for an alehouse, this cozy brewpub serves its creations with burgers, fries, grilled chicken breast, and the like. The bar is one of the city's few remaining old saloons (ca. 1907), aglow with stained-glass windows, tile floors, skylit ceiling, beveled glass, and mahogany bar. A massive overhead fan runs the full length of the bar—a bizarre contraption crafted from brass and palm fronds. The handmade copper brew kettle is visible from the street. Most evenings the place is packed with everyday folks enjoying music, darts, chess, backgammon, cards, dice, and, of course, beer. Menu items range from $4.15—curiously, for edamame (soybeans)—to $21 for a full rack of baby back ribs with all the fixings. The happy-hour special, an 8½-ounce microbrew beer for $1.50 (or a pint for $2.75), is offered daily from 4 to 6pm and midnight to 1am. 155 Columbus Ave. (at Pacific St.). ✆ **415/434-3344.** www.sfbrewing.com.

ThirstyBear Brewing Company Nine superb, handcrafted varieties of brew are always on tap at this stylish high-ceilinged brick edifice. Good Spanish food is served here, too. Pool tables and dartboards are upstairs, and live flamenco can be heard on Sunday nights. 661 Howard St. (1 block east of the Moscone Center). ✆ **415/974-0905.** www.thirstybear.com.

COCKTAILS WITH A VIEW

See "Supper Clubs," earlier, for a full review of **Harry Denton's Starlight Room.** Unless otherwise noted, these establishments have no cover charge.

Carnelian Room On the 52nd floor of the Bank of America Building, the Carnelian Room offers uninterrupted views of the city. From a window-front table you feel as though you can reach out, pluck up the Transamerica Pyramid, and stir your martini with it. In addition to cocktails, the restaurant serves a four-course meal ($59 per person) as well as a la carte items ($24–$49 for main entrees). Jackets are required and ties are optional for men, but encouraged. ***Note:*** The restaurant has one of the most extensive wine lists in the city—1,600 selections, to be exact. 555 California St., in the Bank of America Building (between Kearny and Montgomery sts.). ✆ **415/433-7500.** www.carnelianroom.com.

Cityscape When you sit under the glass roof and sip a drink here, it's as though you're sitting out under the stars and enjoying views of the bay. Dinner, focusing on California cuisine, is available (though not destination worthy), and there's dancing to a DJ's picks nightly from 10:30pm. The mirrored columns and floor-to-ceiling

Finds Midnight (or Midday) Mochas

If you happen to be wandering around North Beach past your bedtime and need your caffeine fix, seek out these two cafes. They offer not only excellent espresso, but also a glimpse back at the days of the beatniks, when nothing was as crucial as a strong cup of coffee, a good smoke, and a stimulating environment.

Doing the North Beach thing is little more than hanging out in a sophisticated but relaxed atmosphere over a well-made cappuccino. You can do it at **Caffè Greco,** 423 Columbus Ave., between Green and Vallejo streets (✆ **415/397-6261**), and grab a bite, too—until midnight. The affordable cafe fare includes beer and wine as well as a good selection of coffees, focaccia sandwiches, and desserts (try the gelato or homemade tiramisu).

Caffè Trieste, 601 Vallejo St., at Grant Avenue (✆ **415/392-6739;** www.caffetrieste.com), is one of San Francisco's most beloved cafes—very downhome Italian, with espresso drinks, wine, pizza, and pastries at indoor and outdoor seating. Opera is always on the jukebox, unless it's Saturday afternoon, when the family and their friends break out in arias during an operatic performance from 2 to 5pm every other Saturday. Another perk: They offer access to free Wi-Fi with purchase with your own laptop. Check 'em out until 10pm Sunday through Thursday and midnight on Friday and Saturday.

windows help create an elegant and romantic ambience here. ***FYI:*** They also offer a live jazz champagne brunch on Sundays from 10am to 2pm. Hilton San Francisco, Tower One, 333 O'Farrell St. (at Mason St.), 46th floor. ✆ **415/923-5002.** Cover $10 Fri–Sat nights.

Equinox Though locals don't frequent this Fi-Di (Financial District) place, it's very popular with tourists. The hook? The 17-story Hyatt's rooftop restaurant has a revolving floor that gives each table a 360-degree panoramic view of the city every 45 minutes. Equinox serves cocktails Wednesday through Sunday from 5 to 11pm (until 1am Fri–Sat); dinner is served from 6 to 10pm. In the Hyatt Regency Hotel, 5 Embarcadero Center. ✆ **415/788-1234.**

Top of the Mark *Moments* This is one of the most famous cocktail lounges in the world, and for good reason—the spectacular glass-walled room features an unparalleled 19th-floor view. During World War II, Pacific-bound servicemen toasted their goodbyes to the States here. While less dramatic today than they were back then, evenings spent here are still sentimental, thanks to the romantic atmosphere. Live bands play throughout the week; a jazz pianist on Tuesdays starts at 7pm; salsa on Wednesdays begins with dance lessons at 8pm and the band starts up at 9pm; on Thursdays Stompy Jones brings a swing vibe from 7:30pm; and a dance band playing everything from '50s hits through contemporary music keeps the joint hopping Fridays and Saturdays starting at 9pm. Drinks range from $9 to $12. A $59 three-course fixed-price sunset dinner is served Friday and Saturday at 7:30pm. Sunday brunch, served from 10am to 2pm, costs $59 for adults and includes a glass of champagne; for children 4 to 12, the brunch is $30. In the Mark Hopkins Inter-Continental, 1 Nob Hill (California and Mason sts.). ✆ **415/616-6916.** www.topofthemark.com. Cover $5–$10.

A SPORTS BAR

Greens Sports Bar If you think San Francisco sports fans aren't as enthusiastic as those on the East Coast, try to get a seat at Green's during a 49ers game. It's a classic old sports bar, with lots of polished dark wood and windows that open onto Polk Street, but it's loaded with modern appliances (including two large-screen televisions and 25 smaller ones) and modern partiers (read: the mid-20s and -30s set). With 18 beers on tap, a pool table, and a happy hour Monday through Friday from 4 to 7pm, there are reasons to cheer here even when the home team's got a day off. 2239 Polk St. (at Green St.). ✆ **415/775-4287.** www.greenssportsbar.citysearch.com.

WINE & CHAMPAGNE BARS

The Bubble Lounge Toasting the town is a nightly event at this two-level champagne bar. With 300 champagnes and sparkling wines (about 30 by the glass), brick walls, couches, and velvet curtains, there's plenty of pop in this fizzy lounge. 714 Montgomery St. (between Washington and Jackson sts.). ✆ **415/434-4204.** www.bubblelounge.com.

Eos If you're in the Financial District, head for the London Wine Bar (see below). For anything west of there, your top choice should be Eos, a highly successful restaurant in Cole Valley (near the Haight), with an adjoining wine bar where you can sip from the huge by-the-glass selection or choose a bottle from some 200 vintages from around the world. 901 Cole St. (at Carl St.). ✆ **415/566-3063.** www.eossf.com.

First Crush If you're staying downtown and want to sip through regional specialties, stop by this wine-centric restaurant and bar. Amid a sleek and stylish interior, an eclectic clientele noshes on reasonably priced "progressive American cuisine" paired, if desired, with an outstanding selection of California wines. But plenty of people drop in simply to sample wine—especially since there are around three dozen excellent choices for filling your glass, and the joint serves until 11pm (until midnight Thurs–Sat). 101 Cyril Magnin St. (also known as Fifth St., just north of Market St., at Ellis St.). ✆ **415/982-7874.** www.firstcrush.com.

London Wine Bar This British-style wine bar and store is a popular after-work hangout for Financial District suits. It's more of a place to drink and chat, however, than one in which to admire fine wines. Usually 60 wines, mostly from California, are open at any given time, and 800 are available by the bottle. It's a great venue for sampling local Napa Valley wines before you buy. 415 Sansome St. (between Sacramento and Clay sts.). ✆ **415/788-4811.** www.londonwinesf.com.

Nectar Wine Lounge Catering to the Marina's young and beautiful, this ultrahip place to sip—and snack—pours an exciting and well-edited wine selection (plus 900 choices by the bottle) along with creative small plates (pairings optional). Industrial-slick decor includes cube chairs, a long bar, and lounge areas that are often packed with 20- through 40-somethings. 3330 Steiner St. (at Chestnut St.). ✆ **415/345-1377.** www.nectarwinelounge.com.

5 Gay & Lesbian Bars & Clubs

Just like straight establishments, gay and lesbian bars and clubs target varied clienteles. Whether you're into leather or Lycra, business or bondage, San Francisco has something just for you.

Check the free weeklies, the *San Francisco Bay Guardian* and *San Francisco Weekly,* for listings of events and happenings around town. The *Bay Area Reporter* is a gay paper with comprehensive listings, including a weekly community calendar. All these papers are free and distributed weekly on Wednesday or Thursday. They can be found stacked at the corners of 18th and Castro streets and Ninth and Harrison streets, as well as in bars, bookshops, and other stores around town. There are also a number of gay and lesbian guides to San Francisco. See "Gay & Lesbian Travelers," in chapter 2, beginning on p. 27, for further details and helpful information. Also check out the rather homely but very informative site titled "Queer Things to Do in the San Francisco Bay Area" at www.io.com/~larrybob/sanfran.html or www.leatherandbears.com for a plethora of gay happenings.

Listed below are some of the city's most established mainstream gay hangouts.

The Café *Finds* When this place first got jumping, it was the only predominantly lesbian dance club on Saturday nights in the city. Once the guys found out how much fun the girls were having, however, they joined the party. Today, it's a happening mixed gay and lesbian scene with three bars; two pool tables; a steamy, free-spirited dance floor; and a small, heated patio and balcony where smoking and schmoozing are allowed. A perk: They open at 4pm weekdays and 3pm weekends. 2369 Market St. (at Castro St.). ✆ **415/861-3846.** www.cafesf.com.

The Cinch Saloon Part cruisy neighborhood bar, part modern-day penny arcade, The Cinch Saloon features free Wi-Fi, two pool tables, five TVs, video games, an Internet juke box, pinball, and an outdoor smoking patio. They even have their own softball team, The Renegades! With happy hour Monday through Friday 4 to 8pm (all night on Mon), progressive music by DJs after 9pm (except Mon and Tues), and a host of other fun theme nights (like Hot Fudge Sundays, billed as "cocktails, food, fun, and fabulosity"), the bar attracts a mixed crowd of gays, lesbians, and gay-friendly straights. 1723 Polk St. (near Washington St.). ✆ **415/776-4162.** www.thecinch.com.

The Eagle Tavern One of the city's most traditional Levi's 'n' leather bars, The Eagle boasts a heated outdoor patio (where smoking is permitted), a happy hour (Mon–Fri 4–8pm), live bands every Thursday at 9pm, and a popular Sunday afternoon beer fest from 3 to 6pm. 398 12th St. (at Harrison St.). ✆ **415/626-0880.** www.sfeagle.com.

The Endup It's a different nightclub every night of the week, but regardless of who's throwing the party, the place is always jumping to the tunes blasted by DJs. There are two pool tables, a fireplace, an outdoor patio and, on the dance floor, a mob of gyrating souls. Some nights are straight, so call ahead. (See p. 233 for more information.) 401 Sixth St. (at Harrison St.). ✆ **415/357-0827.** www.theendup.com. Cover $5–$15.

Kimo's This gay-owned and -operated neighborhood bar in the seedier gay section of town is a friendly oasis, decorated with plastic plants and random pictures on the walls. The bar provides a relaxing venue for chatting, drinking, and quiet cruising, and livens up with indie, punk rock, and jazz bands nightly at Kimo's Penthouse upstairs. 1351 Polk St. (at Pine St.). ✆ **415/885-4535.** Cover $5–$10 for live music.

Lone Star Saloon Expect lesbians and a heavier, furrier motorcycle crowd (both men and women) here most every night. The Thursday night and Saturday and Sunday afternoon beer busts on the patio are especially popular and cost $7 to $9 per person. 1354 Harrison St. (between 9th and 10th sts.). ✆ **415/863-9999.** www.lonestarsaloon.com.

Metro This bar provides the gay community with high-energy music and the best view of the Castro District from its large balcony. The bar seems to attract people of all ages who enjoy the friendliness of the bartenders and the highly charged, cruising atmosphere. There's a Spanish restaurant on the premises if you get hungry. 3600 16th St. (at Market St.). ✆ **415/703-9751.**

Country-Western Dancing, San Francisco-Style

Country-western dancing is far from hip in San Francisco, but nevertheless there are plenty of cowgirls—of both genders—who like to don their cowboy duds and have a little fun. The best place in town (the only place, actually) is the **Sundance Saloon.** Every Thursday and Sunday night you can get dance lessons in the early evening, then two-step your little pea-pickin' heart out until 10:30pm—all for only $5. Where else but in a fabulous gay-lesbian-bisexual-transgender blender dance hall could you learn line dances like the Tush Push, Backstreet Attitude, Circle Jerk, and Dog Bone Boogie? On a good night, you might just hook up with a cowpoke wearing nothing but chaps. It's located at 550 Barneveld Ave. off Industrial Ave. (✆ **415/820-1403;** www.sundancesaloon.org).

The Mint Karaoke Lounge This is a gay and lesbian karaoke bar—sprinkled with a heavy dash of straight folks on weekends—where you can get up and sing your heart out every night. Along with song, you'll encounter a mixed 20- to 40-something crowd that combines cocktails with do-it-yourself cabaret. Want to eat and listen at the same time? Feel free to bring in the Japanese food from the attached restaurant. Sashimi goes for about $7, main entrees $8, and sushi combo plates about $11. 1942 Market St. (at Laguna St.). ✆ **415/626-4726.** www.themint.net. 2-drink minimum.

The Stud The Stud, which has been around for almost 40 years, is one of the most successful gay establishments in town. The interior has an antiques-shop look. Music is a balanced mix of old and new, and nights vary from cabaret to oldies to discopunk. Check their website in advance for the evening's offerings. Drink prices range from $3.25 to $8. Happy hour runs Monday through Saturday 5 to 9pm with $1 off well drinks. 399 Ninth St. (at Harrison St.). ✆ **415/863-6623** or 415/252-STUD for event info. www.studsf.com. Cover free–$10.

Twin Peaks Tavern Right at the intersection of Castro, 17th, and Market streets is one of the Castro's most famous (at 35 years old) gay hangouts. It caters to an older crowd but often has a mixture of patrons and claims to be the first gay bar in America. Because of its relatively small size and desirable location, the place becomes fairly crowded and convivial by 8pm, earlier than many neighboring bars. 401 Castro St. (at 17th and Market sts.). ✆ **415/864-9470.**

6 Film

Celebrating its 50th anniversary in 2006, the **San Francisco International Film Festival** (✆ **415/561-5000;** www.sffs.org), held at the end of April, is one of America's longest-running film festivals. Entries include new films by new and established directors. Call or surf ahead for a schedule or information, and check out their website for more information on purchasing tickets, which are relatively inexpensive.

If you're not here in time for the festival, don't despair. The classic, independent, and mainstream cinemas in San Francisco are every bit as good as the city's other cultural offerings.

REPERTORY CINEMAS

Castro Theatre *Finds* Built in 1922 by renowned Bay Area architect Timothy Pflueger, and listed as a City of San Francisco registered landmark, the beautiful Castro Theatre is known for its screenings of classics and for its Wurlitzer organ, which is played before each evening show. There's a different feature almost nightly, and more often than not it's a double feature. They also play host to a number of festivals throughout the year. Bargain matinees are usually offered on Wednesday, Saturday, Sunday, and holidays. Phone or visit their website for schedules, prices, and show times. 429 Castro St. (near Market St.). ✆ **415/621-6120.** www.castrotheatre.com.

Red Vic The worker-owned Red Vic movie collective originated in the neighboring Victorian building that gave it its name. The theater specializes in independent releases and premieres and contemporary cult hits, and situates its patrons among an array of couches. Prices are $8.50 for adults ($6.50 for matinees) and $5 for seniors and kids 12 and under. Tickets go on sale 20 minutes before each show. Phone for schedules and show times or look around the city for printouts. 1727 Haight St. (between Cole and Shrader sts.). ✆ **415/668-3994.** www.redvicmoviehouse.com.

The Roxie Film Center Founded in 1909, The Roxie is the oldest continually running theater in San Francisco, and so when it almost went under in 2005, a private donor saved it with a huge donation and a great idea; the theater merged with the New College of California and is now a nonprofit film center serving both students and the general public. Management has promised that the programming will stay the same and that they will continue to screen the best new alternative films anywhere, as well as host filmmakers like Akira Kurosawa and Werner Herzog. The low-budget contemporary features are largely devoid of Hollywood candy coating; many are West Coast premieres. Phone for schedules, prices, and show times. Admission is $8 adults, $4 seniors 65 plus and children under 12; $5 matinee is the first show on weekends. 3117 16th St. (at Valencia St.). ✆ **415/863-1087.** www.roxie.com.

11

Side Trips from San Francisco

The City by the Bay is, without question, captivating, but don't let it ensnare you to the point of ignoring its environs. The surrounding region contains a multitude of natural beauty such as Mount Tamalpais and Muir Woods; scenic bayside communities such as Tiburon and Sausalito; and neighboring cities such as Oakland and Berkeley.

From San Francisco, you can reach any of these points in an hour or less by car. Public transportation options are also listed throughout the chapter. Another option is to hitch a ride with **San Francisco Sightseeing** (© **888/428-6937** or 415/434-8687; www.sanfranciscosightseeing.com), which runs regularly scheduled bus tours to neighboring towns and the countryside. Half-day trips to Muir Woods and Sausalito, and full-day trips to Napa and Sonoma are available, as are excursions to Yosemite and the Monterey Peninsula. Phone for prices and schedules.

1 Berkeley

10 miles NE of San Francisco

Berkeley is best known as the home of the University of California at Berkeley, which is world-renowned for its academic standards, 18 Nobel prize winners (seven are active staff), and protests that led to the most famous student riots in U.S. history. Today, there's still hippie idealism in the air, but the radicals have aged; the 1960s are present only in tie-dye and paraphernalia shops. The biggest change the town is facing is yuppification; as San Francisco's rent and property prices soar out of the range of the average person's budget, everyone with less than a small fortune is seeking shelter elsewhere, and Berkeley is one of the top picks (although Oakland is quickly becoming a favorite, too). Berkeley is a lively city teeming with all types of people, a beautiful campus, vast parks, great shopping, and some incredible restaurants.

ESSENTIALS

The Berkeley **Bay Area Rapid Transit (BART)** station is 2 blocks from the university. The fare from San Francisco is less than $4. Call © **511** or visit www.bart.gov for trip info, or fares, or to download trip planners to your iPod, mobile phone, or PDA.

If you are coming **by car** from San Francisco, take the Bay Bridge (go during the evening commute, and you'll think Los Angeles traffic is a breeze). Follow I-80 east to the University Avenue exit, and follow University until you hit the campus. Parking is tight, so either leave your car at the Sather Gate parking lot at Telegraph Avenue and Durant Street, or expect to fight for a spot.

Pricing Categories

Note: In this chapter, hotels are organized by location, then by price range, as follows: **Very Expensive,** more than $250 per night; **Expensive,** $200 to $250 per night; **Moderate,** $150 to $200 per night; and **Inexpensive,** less than $150 per night.

Restaurants are organized by location, then by price range for a complete dinner (appetizer, entree, dessert, and glass of wine) as follows: **Expensive,** dinner from $50 per person; **Moderate,** dinner from $35 per person; and **Inexpensive,** less than $35 per person for dinner. (***Note:*** The "Very Expensive" category—dinner from $75 per person—has been omitted since no restaurants in this chapter fall under its umbrella.)

WHAT TO SEE & DO

Hanging out is the preferred Berkeley pastime, and the best place to do it is **Telegraph Avenue,** the street that leads to the campus's southern entrance. Most of the action lies between Bancroft Way and Dwight Way, where coffeehouses, restaurants, shops, great book and record stores, and crafts booths (with vendors selling everything from T-shirts and jewelry to I Ching and tarot-card readings) swarm with life. Pretend you're a local: Plant yourself at a cafe, sip a latte, and ponder something intellectual, or survey the town's unique residents.

Bibliophiles must stop at **Cody's Books,** 1730 Fourth St. (✆ **510/559-9500;** www.codysbooks.com), to peruse its gargantuan selection of titles, independent-press books, and magazines. If used and antiquarian books are your thing, stop by **Moe's Books,** 2476 Telegraph Ave. (✆ **510/849-2087;** www.moesbooks.com). After exploring four floors of new, used, and out-of-print books, you're unlikely to leave empty-handed.

UC BERKELEY CAMPUS

The University of California at Berkeley (www.berkeley.edu) is worth a stroll. It's a beautiful campus with plenty of woodsy paths, architecturally noteworthy buildings and, of course, 33,000 students. Among the architectural highlights of the campus are a number of buildings by Bernard Maybeck, Bakewell and Brown, and John Galen Howard.

Contact the **Visitor Information Center,** 101 University Hall, 2200 University Ave., at Oxford Street (✆ **510/642-5215;** www.berkeley.edu/visitors), to join a free 90-minute campus tour. Reservations are required; see website for details. Tours are available year-round Monday through Saturday at 10am and Sunday at 1pm. Weekday tours depart from the Visitor's Center and weekend tours start from Sather Bell Tower in the middle of campus. Electric cart tours are available year-round for travelers with disabilities for $40; 2 weeks' advance reservations required; no tours are given the week between Christmas and New Year's Day. Or stop by the office and pick up a self-guided walking-tour brochure or a free Berkeley map. ***Note:*** The information center is closed on weekends, but you can find the latest information on their website.

The university's southern, main entrance is at the northern end of Telegraph Avenue, at Bancroft Way. Walk through the entrance into Sproul Plaza, and when school is in session, you'll encounter the gamut of Berkeley's inhabitants: colorful street people, rambling political zealots, and ambitious students. You might be lucky

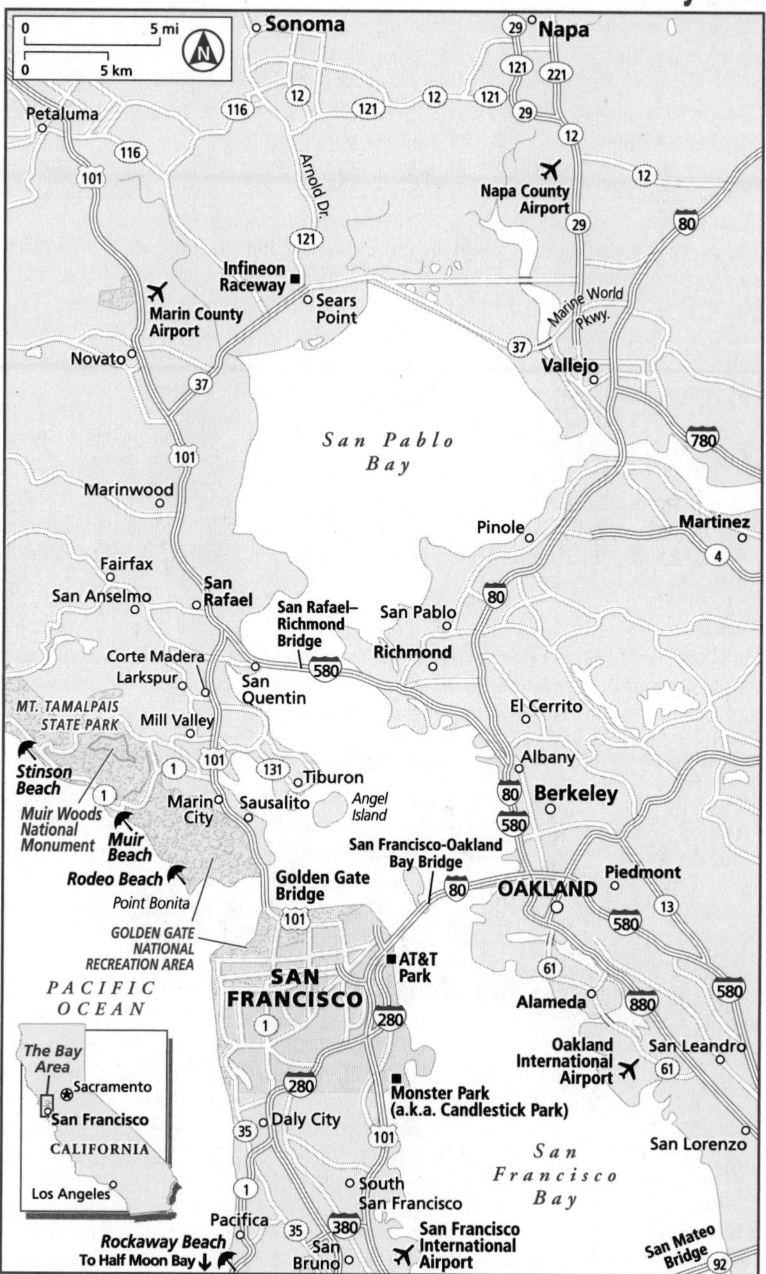
0 5 mi
0 5 km
N
Sonoma
Napa
Petaluma
Arnold Dr.
Napa County Airport
Infineon Raceway
Sears Point
Marin County Airport
Marine World Pkwy.
Novato
Vallejo
San Pablo Bay
Marinwood
Pinole
Martinez
Fairfax
San Anselmo
San Rafael
San Rafael–Richmond Bridge
San Pablo
Richmond
Corte Madera
Larkspur
San Quentin
El Cerrito
MT. TAMALPAIS STATE PARK
Mill Valley
Albany
Stinson Beach
Tiburon
Marin City
Sausalito
Angel Island
Berkeley
Muir Woods National Monument
Muir Beach
San Francisco-Oakland Bay Bridge
Piedmont
Rodeo Beach
Golden Gate Bridge
OAKLAND
Point Bonita
GOLDEN GATE NATIONAL RECREATION AREA
AT&T Park
PACIFIC OCEAN
SAN FRANCISCO
Alameda
The Bay Area
Sacramento
San Francisco
CALIFORNIA
Los Angeles
Oakland International Airport
San Leandro
Monster Park (a.k.a. Candlestick Park)
Daly City
San Lorenzo
San Francisco Bay
South San Francisco
Pacifica
Rockaway Beach
To Half Moon Bay
San Bruno
San Francisco International Airport
San Mateo Bridge
1
4
12
13
29
35
37
61
80
92
101
116
121
131
221
280
380
580
780
880

enough to stumble upon some impromptu musicians or a heated debate. There's always something going on here, so stretch out on the grass for a few minutes and take in the Berkeley vibe. You'll also find the student union, complete with a bookstore, cafes, and an information desk on the second floor where you can pick up the student newspaper (also found in dispensers throughout campus).

For viewing more traditional art forms, there are some noteworthy museums, too. The **Lawrence Hall of Science** ★ (east of campus on Centennial Dr., just above the Botanical Gardens; ✆ **510/642-5132;** www.lawrencehallofscience.org) offers hands-on science exploration. It's open daily from 10am to 5pm, and is a wonderful place to watch the sunset. Included in the admission price is an outdoor science park called Forces That Shape the Bay, which lets visitors explore ongoing geologic forces. The site includes activity stations such as earthquake simulators, a geologic uplift bench, a water feature, telescopes, BayLab programs and demonstrations, an audio tour, and picnic sites. Admission is $9.50 for adults; $7.50 for seniors 62 and over, students, and children 5 to 18; $5.50 for children 3 or 4; and free for kids under 3. The **UC Berkeley Art Museum** ★ (2626 Bancroft Way, between College and Telegraph aves.; ✆ **510/642-0808;** www.bampfa.berkeley.edu) is open Wednesday through Sunday from 11am to 5pm. Admission is $8 for adults; $5 for seniors, non-UCB students, visitors with disabilities, and children 17 and under; and $4 for UCB students. This museum contains a substantial collection of Hans Hofmann paintings, a sculpture garden, and the Pacific Film Archive.

PARKS

Unbeknownst to many travelers, Berkeley has some of the most extensive and beautiful parks around. If you want to wear the kids out or enjoy hiking, swimming, sniffing roses, or just getting a breath of California air, jump in your car and make your way to **Tilden Park** ★. On the way, stop at the colorful terraced **Rose Garden** ★ (✆ **510/981-5151**) in north Berkeley on Euclid Avenue between Bay View and Eunice Street. Then head high into the Berkeley hills to Tilden, where you'll find plenty of flora and fauna, hiking trails, an old steam train and merry-go-round, a farm and nature area for kids, and a chilly tree-encircled lake. The East Bay's public transit system, AC Transit (✆ **511;** www.actransit.org), runs the air-conditioned no. 67 bus line around the edge of the park on weekdays and all the way to the Tilden Visitors Center on Saturdays and Sundays. Call ✆ **510/562-PARK** or see www.ebparks.org for further information.

Another worthy nature excursion is **The University of California Botanical Garden** (✆ **510/643-2755;** www.botanicalgarden.berkeley.edu), which features a vast collection of herbage ranging from cacti to redwoods. It's on campus in Strawberry Canyon on Centennial Drive. Unfortunately no public bus can take you directly there, so driving is the way to go. Call for directions. Open daily from 9am to 5pm; closed the first Tuesday of every month; docent-led tours on Thursdays, Saturdays, and Sundays at 1:30pm. Admission is $5 adults, $3 seniors 65 and over, $1 youth 3 to 17, and free for children under 3 and UC students.

SHOPPING

If you're itching to exercise your credit cards, head to one of two places. **College Avenue** from Dwight Way to the Oakland border overflows with eclectic boutiques, antiques shops, and restaurants. The other option is **Fourth Street,** in west Berkeley, 2 blocks north of the University Avenue exit. This shopping strip is the perfect place

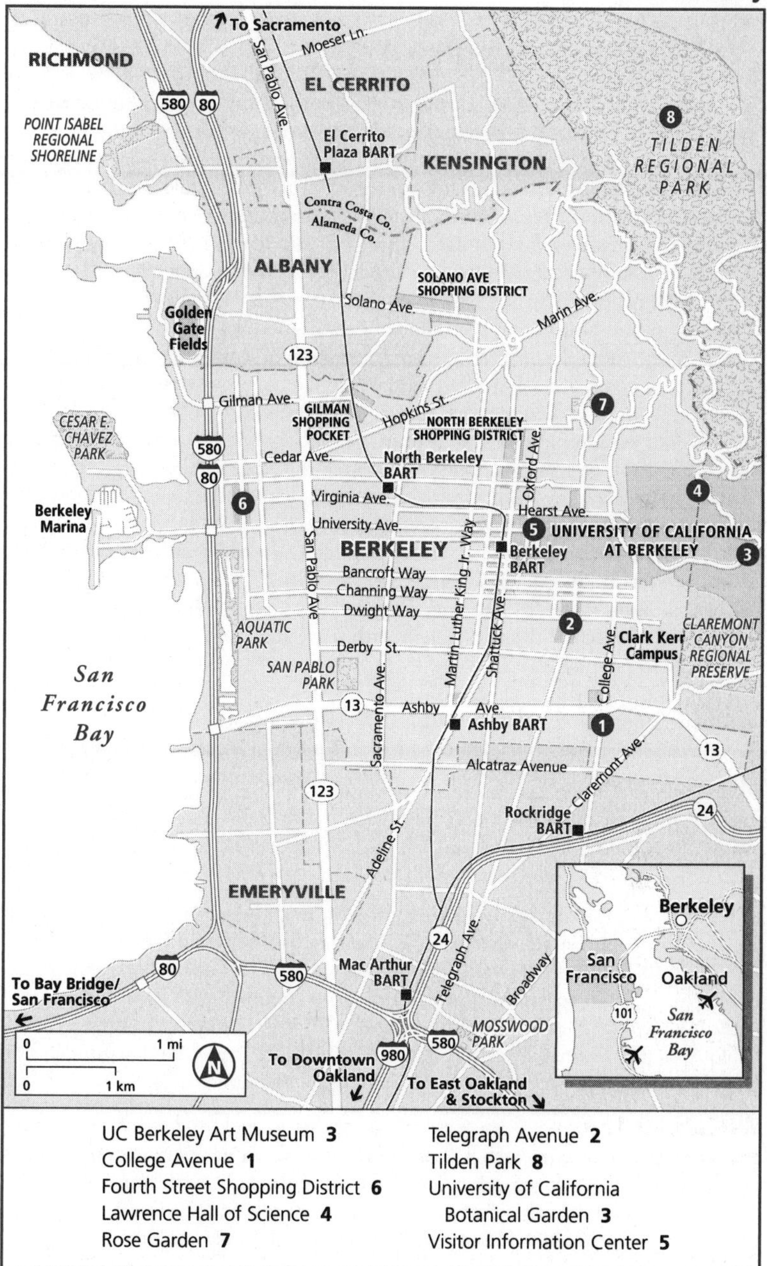
To Sacramento
Moeser Ln.
San Pablo Ave.
RICHMOND
EL CERRITO
580
80
POINT ISABEL REGIONAL SHORELINE
El Cerrito Plaza BART
KENSINGTON
8
TILDEN REGIONAL PARK
Contra Costa Co.
Alameda Co.
ALBANY
SOLANO AVE SHOPPING DISTRICT
Solano Ave.
Marin Ave.
Golden Gate Fields
123
Gilman Ave.
GILMAN SHOPPING POCKET
Hopkins St.
NORTH BERKELEY SHOPPING DISTRICT
7
CESAR E. CHAVEZ PARK
Cedar Ave.
North Berkeley BART
Oxford Ave.
4
6
Virginia Ave.
Hearst Ave.
Berkeley Marina
University Ave.
5 UNIVERSITY OF CALIFORNIA AT BERKELEY
3
BERKELEY
Berkeley BART
Bancroft Way
Channing Way
Dwight Way
Martin Luther King Jr. Way
Shattuck Ave.
2
AQUATIC PARK
College Ave.
Clark Kerr Campus
CLAREMONT CANYON REGIONAL PRESERVE
Derby St.
SAN PABLO PARK
Sacramento Ave.
San Francisco Bay
13
Ashby Ave.
Ashby BART
1
Claremont Ave.
Alcatraz Avenue
Rockridge BART
24
Adeline St.
EMERYVILLE
Telegraph Ave.
Broadway
To Bay Bridge/ San Francisco
Mac Arthur BART
MOSSWOOD PARK
980
To Downtown Oakland
To East Oakland & Stockton
0
1 mi
1 km
N
Berkeley
San Francisco
Oakland
101
San Francisco Bay
UC Berkeley Art Museum 3
College Avenue 1
Fourth Street Shopping District 6
Lawrence Hall of Science 4
Rose Garden 7
Telegraph Avenue 2
Tilden Park 8
University of California Botanical Garden 3
Visitor Information Center 5

People's Park/People's Power

In late 1968, the university demolished an entire block of buildings north of Telegraph Avenue. The destruction, which forced hippies and other "undesirables" from the slum housing that stood there, was done under the guise of university expansion and urban renewal—good liberal causes. But after the lot lay vacant for months, a group of Berkeley radicals, whose names read like a who's who of 1960s leftists, including Jerry Rubin, Bobby Seale, and Tom Hayden, decided to take the land for "the people."

On April 20, 1969, hundreds of activists invaded the vacant lot with gardening tools and tamed the muddy ground into a park. One month later, Berkeley's Republican mayor sent 250 police officers into the park, and 6,000 demonstrators materialized to challenge them. A riot ensued, and the police fired buckshot at the crowd. One rioter was killed and another blinded. Gov. Ronald Reagan sent in the National Guard, and for the next 17 days, the guardsmen repeatedly gassed innocent students, faculty, and passersby. Berkeley was a war zone, and People's Park became the decade's most important symbol of "people power."

The park again sparked controversy in 1992, when university officials decided to build volleyball courts there. In August, a park activist broke into the campus home of the university's chancellor. When a police officer arrived, the activist lunged at him with a machete and was shot dead. On the victim's body was a note with the message: "We are willing to die for this land. Are you?" On news of the contemporary radical's death, more than 150 of her supporters rioted.

Postscript: The volleyball courts didn't get much use, and now basketball courts have taken their place. Visit www.peoplespark.org for more information.

to go on a sunny morning. Grab a cup of java, read the paper at a patio table, then hit the **Crate & Barrel Outlet,** 1785 Fourth St., between Hearst and Virginia (✆ **510/528-5500**). Prices are 30% to 70% off retail. It's open daily from 10am to 6pm. This area also boasts small, wonderful stores crammed with imported and locally made housewares. Nearby is **REI,** the Bay Area's favorite outdoors outfitter, 1338 San Pablo Ave., near Gilman Street (✆ **510/527-4140**). It's open Monday through Friday from 10am to 9pm, Saturday from 10am to 8pm, and Sunday from 10am to 7pm.

WHERE TO STAY

Unfortunately, a little research will prove that Berkeley is not even remotely close to a good hotel town. Most accommodations are extremely basic motels and funky B&Bs. The one exception (though it's overpriced) is **The Claremont Resort & Spa,** 41 Tunnel Rd., Berkeley (✆ **800/551-7266** or 510/843-3000; www.claremontresort.com), a grand Victorian hotel, also on the border of Oakland, with a fancy spa and gym, three restaurants, a hip bar, and grandiose surroundings. Though it's the most luxurious thing going, it's overpriced and rooms aren't nearly as charming as the exterior. Rates range from $290 to $450 for doubles and $460 to $1,050 for suites. Or you can contact the **Berkeley & Oakland Bed and Breakfast Network** (✆ **510/547-6380;** www.bbonline.com/ca/berkeley-oakland), which books visitors into private homes and apartments in the East Bay area.

MODERATE

Rose Garden Inn Like a Merchant-Ivory movie, the accommodations within this 40-room/five-building inn range from English Country to Victorian, making it a favorite for visiting grandparents and vacationing retirees. Despite your age or design sense, the stunning and expansive garden exploding with rose bushes, hydrangeas, and an abundance of flora and fauna is sure to delight as well as erase all memories that you're on a characterless stretch of Telegraph Avenue a few blocks south of the student action. Rooms, many of which have fireplaces, cable TVs, and all the basic amenities, show some wear and tend to be a little dark, but they are spacious, updated, and very clean despite the obvious age of some bathroom nooks and crannies.

2740 Telegraph Ave. (at Stuart St.), Berkeley, CA 94705. www.rosegardeninn.com. ✆ **800/992-9005** or 510/549-2145. Fax 510/549-1085. 40 units. $125–$275 double. Breakfast included. AE, DC, DISC, MC, V. Free parking on a space-available basis. **Amenities:** Wi-Fi in lobby; coffee and afternoon cookies. *In room:* TV, hair dryer, iron upon request, high-speed Internet access in deluxe rooms.

WHERE TO DINE

East Bay dining is a relaxed alternative to San Francisco's gourmet scene. There are plenty of ambitious Berkeley restaurants and, unlike in San Francisco, plenty of parking, provided you're not near the campus.

If you want to dine student-style, eat on campus Monday through Friday. Buy something at a sidewalk stand or in the building directly behind the Student Union. There's also the **Bear's Lair Pub and Coffee House,** the **Terrace,** and the **Golden Bear Restaurant.** All the university eateries have both indoor and outdoor seating.

Telegraph Avenue has an array of small, ethnic restaurants, cafes, and sandwich shops. Follow the students: If the place is crowded, it's good, supercheap, or both.

EXPENSIVE

Chez Panisse ★★★ CALIFORNIA California cuisine is so much a product of Alice Waters's genius that all other restaurants following in her wake should be dated A.A.W. (After Alice Waters). Read the menus posted outside, and you'll understand why. Most of the produce and meat comes from local farms and is organically produced, and after all these years, Alice still tends her restaurant with great integrity and innovation. Chez Panisse is a delightful redwood and stucco cottage with a brick terrace filled with flowering potted plants. The two dining areas, the cafe and the restaurant, both serve Mediterranean-inspired cuisine.

In the upstairs cafe are displays of pastries and fruit and an oak bar adorned with large bouquets of fresh flowers. At lunch or dinner, the menu might feature delicately smoked gravlax or roasted eggplant soup with pesto, followed by lamb ragout garnished with apricots, onions, and spices and served with couscous.

The cozy downstairs restaurant, strewn with blossoming floral bouquets, is an appropriately warm environment in which to indulge in the $65 fixed-price four-course gourmet dinner, which is served Tuesday through Thursday. Friday and Saturday, it's $85 for four courses; and Monday is bargain night, with a three-course dinner for $50.

The restaurant posts the following week's menu, which changes daily, every Saturday. There's also an excellent wine list, with bottles ranging from $28 to $300.

1517 Shattuck Ave. (between Cedar and Vine). ✆ **510/548-5525** for main restaurant reservations, 510/548-5049 for cafe reservations. Fax 510/548-0140. www.chezpanisse.com. Reservations required for the dining room and taken 1 month prior to calendar date requested. Reservations are recommended for the cafe, but walk-ins are welcomed. Restaurant fixed-price menu $50–$85; cafe main courses $15–$25. AE, DC, DISC, MC, V. Restaurant seatings Mon–Sat 6–6:30pm and 8:30–9:15pm most times of the year (in slower months, like Jan–Mar, times vary; please call to confirm). Cafe Mon–Thurs 11:30am–3pm and 5–10:30pm; Fri–Sat 11:30am–3:30pm and 5–11:30pm. BART: Downtown Berkeley. From I-80 N, take the University Ave. exit and turn left onto Shattuck Ave.

MODERATE

Cafe Rouge ★ MEDITERRANEAN After cooking at San Francisco's renowned Zuni Cafe for 10 years, chef-owner Marsha McBride launched her own restaurant, a sort of Zuni East. She brought former staff members and some of the restaurant's flavor with her, and now her sparse, loftlike dining room serves salads, rotisserie chicken with oil and thyme, grilled lamb chops, steaks, and homemade sausages. East Bay carnivores are especially happy with the burger; like Zuni's, it's top-notch. During warm days, outdoor dining overlooking the shopping square is ideal.

1782 Fourth St. (between Delaware and Hearst). ✆ **510/525-1440.** www.caferouge.net. Reservations recommended. Main courses $14–$32. MC, V. Lunch Mon–Fri 11:30am–3pm; dinner Tues–Thurs 5:30–9:30pm; Fri–Sat 5:30–10pm; Sun 5–9:30pm; brunch Sun 10am–2:30pm.

Rivoli ★★ *Finds* CALIFORNIA One of the favored dinner destinations in the East Bay, Rivoli offers top-notch food at amazingly reasonable prices. Aside from a few house favorites, the menu changes entirely every 3 weeks to feature whatever's freshest and in season; the wine list follows suit with around 10 by-the-glass options handpicked to match the food. While many love it, I'm not a fan of the portobello-mushroom fritter, a gourmet variation of the fried zucchini stick. However, plenty of dishes shine, including chicken cooked with prosciutto di Parma, wild mushroom chard and ricotta cannelloni, Marsala *jus,* snap peas, and baby carrots; and braised lamb shank with green garlic risotto, sautéed spinach, and oven-dried tomatoes. Finish the evening with an assortment of cheeses or a warm chocolate truffle torte with hazelnut ice cream, orange crème anglaise, and chocolate sauce.

1539 Solano Ave. ✆ **866/496-2489** or 510/526-2542. www.rivolirestaurant.com. Reservations recommended. Main courses $16–$22. AE, DC, DISC, MC, V. Mon–Thurs 5:30–9:30pm; Fri 5:30–10pm; Sat 5–10pm; Sun 5–9pm.

INEXPENSIVE

Cafe Fanny ★★ FRENCH/ITALIAN Alice Waters's (of Chez Panisse fame) cafe is one of those local must-do East Bay breakfast traditions. Don your Birkenstocks and earth-tone apparel, grab the morning paper, and head here to wait in line for a simple yet masterfully prepared French breakfast. The menu offers such items as soft-boiled farm-fresh eggs on Levain toast, buckwheat crepes with house-made preserves, cinnamon toast, and an assortment of superb pastries. Lunch is more of an Italian experience featuring seasonal selections. Sandwiches—such as Alice's baked ham and watercress on focaccia or grilled chicken breast wrapped in prosciutto, sage, and aioli on Acme bread—might convince you that maybe Berkeley isn't such a crazy place to live after all. There's also a selection of pizzettas, salads, and soup. Eat inside at the stand-up food bar (one bench), or outside at one of the cafe tables.

1603 San Pablo Ave. (at Cedar St.). ✆ **510/524-5447.** Most breakfast items $5; lunch $5–$7. MC, V. Mon–Fri 7am–3pm; Sat 8am–4pm; Sun 8am–3pm. Breakfast until 11am; Sun all day. Closed major holidays.

Finds Sweet Sensations at Berkeley's Chocolate Factory

If you haven't had chocolate nibs, you haven't lived—at least that's what chocoholics are likely to discover upon visiting **Scharffen Berger Chocolate Maker,** California's runaway-success chocolatier that opened its factory and retail-shop doors in Berkeley in mid-2001. Within the brick building, visitors can not only taste the nibs (crunchy roasted and shelled cocoa beans), but also see how the famous chocolate company uses vintage European equipment during regularly scheduled free tours (call or visit their website to reserve a spot as spaces are limited). All manner of chocolate-related products, from candy bars to cocoa powder to chocolate sauce, are also available in the retail shop. You can have coffee, pastries, lunch, or brunch at their restaurant, Café Cacao, which is open Monday through Friday 8am to 5pm (serving lunch 11am–3pm) and Saturday and Sunday 9am to 3pm. The factory is located at 914 Heinz Ave., Berkeley (✆ **510/981-4066;** www.scharffenberger.com). From I-80 E take the Ashby Avenue exit, turn left on Seventh Street, and turn right on Heinz.

O Chamé ★★ JAPANESE Spare and plain in its decor, with ocher-colored walls etched with patterns, this spot has a meditative air to complement the traditional, experimental, and extremely fresh Japanese-inspired cuisine. The menu, which changes daily, offers meal-in-a-bowl dishes ($9–$13) that allow a choice of soba or udon noodles in a clear soup with a variety of toppings—from shrimp and wakame seaweed to beef with burdock root and carrot. Appetizers include a flavorful melding of grilled shiitake mushrooms, as well as portobello mushrooms and green-onion pancakes. Their main entree selection always includes delicious roasted salmon, but you can also easily fill up on a bowl of soba or udon noodles with fresh, wholesome fixings (think roasted oysters, sea bass, and tofu skins).

1830 Fourth St. (near Hearst). ✆ **510/841-8783.** www.themenupage.com/ochame.html. Reservations recommended Fri–Sat dinner. Main courses lunch $9–$19, dinner $18–$24. AE, MC, V. Mon–Sat 11:30am–3pm; Mon–Thurs 5:30–9pm; Fri–Sat 5:30–9:30pm.

2 Oakland

10 miles E of San Francisco

Although it's less than a dozen miles from San Francisco, Oakland is worlds apart from its sister city across the bay. Originally little more than a cluster of ranches and farms, Oakland exploded in size and stature practically overnight, when the last mile of transcontinental railroad track was laid down. Major shipping ports soon followed and, to this day, Oakland remains one of the busiest industrial ports on the West Coast.

The price for economic success, however, is Oakland's lowbrow reputation as a predominantly working-class city; it is forever in the shadow of chic San Francisco. However, as The City by the Bay has become crowded and expensive in the past few years, Oakland has experienced a rush of new residents and businesses. As a result, Oak-town is in the midst of a renaissance, and its future continues to look brighter and brighter.

Rent a sailboat on Lake Merritt, stroll along the waterfront, explore the fantastic Oakland Museum—they're all great reasons to hop the bay and spend a fog-free day exploring one of California's largest and most ethnically diverse cities.

ESSENTIALS

BART connects San Francisco and Oakland through one of the longest underwater transit tunnels in the world. Fares range from $2 to $4, depending on your station of origin; children under 5 ride free. BART trains operate Monday through Friday from 4am to midnight, Saturday from 6am to midnight, and Sunday from 8am to midnight. Exit at the 12th Street station for downtown Oakland. Call ✆ **511** or visit www.bart.gov for more info.

By car from San Francisco, take I-80 across the San Francisco–Oakland Bay Bridge and follow signs to downtown Oakland. Exit at Grand Avenue South for the Lake Merritt area.

For a calendar of events in Oakland, contact the **Oakland Convention and Visitors Bureau,** 463 11th St., Oakland, CA 94607 (✆ **510/839-9000;** www.oaklandcvb.com). The city also sponsors eight free guided tours, including African-American Heritage and downtown tours held Wednesdays and Saturdays May through October; call ✆ **510/238-3234** or visit www.oaklandnet.com/walkingtours for details.

Downtown Oakland lies between Grand Avenue on the north, I-980 on the west, Inner Harbor on the south, and Lake Merritt on the east. Between these landmarks are three BART stations (12th St., 19th St., and Lake Merritt), City Hall, the Oakland Museum, Jack London Square, and several other sights.

WHAT TO SEE & DO

Lake Merritt is Oakland's primary tourist attraction, along with Jack London Square (see below). Three and a half miles in circumference, the tidal lagoon was bridged and dammed in the 1860s and is now a wildlife refuge that is home to flocks of migrating ducks, herons, and geese. The 122-acre **Lakeside Park,** a popular place to picnic, feed the ducks, and escape the fog, surrounds the lake on three sides. Visit www.oaklandnet.com/parks for more info. At the **Municipal Boathouse** ★ (✆ **510/238-2196**), in Lakeside Park along the north shore, you can rent sailboats, rowboats, pedal boats, canoes, or kayaks for $8 to $15 per hour (cash only). Or you can take an hour-long gondola ride with **Gondola Servizio** (✆ **888/737-8494;** www.gondolaservizio.com). Experienced gondoliers will serenade you, June through October, as you glide across the lake; the cost ranges from $45 to $225 for two depending on the time and gondola style.

Another site worth visiting is Oakland's **Paramount Theatre** ★, 2025 Broadway (✆ **510/893-2300;** www.paramounttheatre.com), an outstanding National Historic Landmark and example of Art Deco architecture and decor. Built in 1931 and authentically restored in 1973, it's the city's main performing-arts center, hosting big-name performers like Smokey Robinson and Alicia Keys. Guided tours of the 3,000-seat theater are given the first and third Saturday morning of each month, excluding holidays. No reservations are necessary; just show up at 10am at the box office entrance on 21st Street at Broadway. The tour lasts 2 hours, cameras are allowed, and admission is $5.

If you take pleasure in strolling sailboat-filled wharves or are a die-hard fan of Jack London, you might enjoy a visit to **Jack London Square** ★ (✆ **866/295-9853;** www.jacklondonsquare.com). Oakland's only patently tourist area remains a relatively low-key version of San Francisco's Fisherman's Wharf, which shamelessly plays up the fact that Jack London spent most of his youth along the waterfront. The square fronts the harbor, housing a tourist-tacky complex of boutiques and eateries, as well as a more locals-friendly farmers' market year-round on Sundays from 10am to 2pm. Most shops are open daily from 11am to 6pm (some restaurants stay open later). One of the

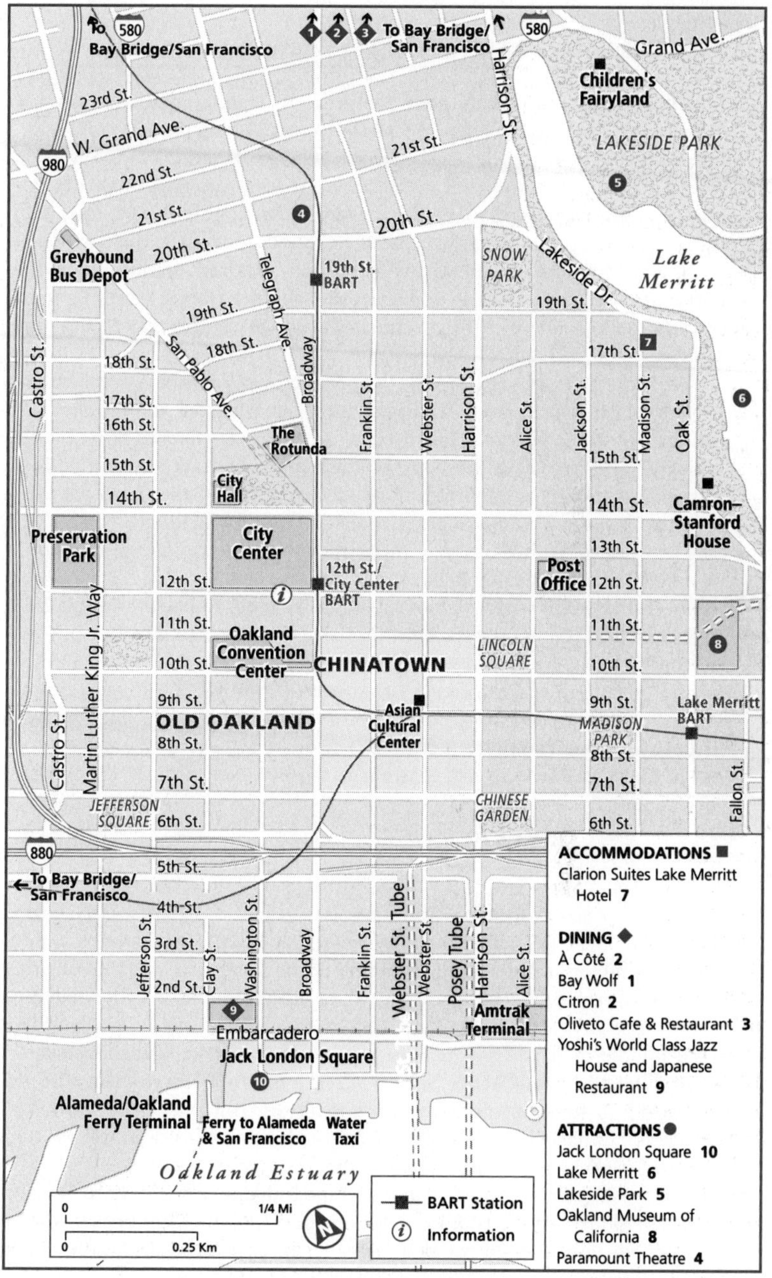

To Bay Bridge/San Francisco
To Bay Bridge/ San Francisco
To Bay Bridge/ San Francisco
580
980
880
Grand Ave.
Children's Fairyland
LAKESIDE PARK
Lake Merritt
Lakeside Dr.
SNOW PARK
23rd St.
W. Grand Ave.
22nd St.
21st St.
20th St.
19th St.
18th St.
17th St.
16th St.
15th St.
14th St.
13th St.
12th St.
11th St.
10th St.
9th St.
8th St.
7th St.
6th St.
5th St.
4th St.
3rd St.
2nd St.
Greyhound Bus Depot
Telegraph Ave.
San Pablo Ave.
Broadway
Franklin St.
Webster St.
Harrison St.
Alice St.
Jackson St.
Madison St.
Oak St.
Castro St.
Martin Luther King Jr. Way
Fallon St.
Jefferson St.
Clay St.
Washington St.
19th St. BART
12th St./ City Center BART
Lake Merritt BART
The Rotunda
City Hall
City Center
Preservation Park
Oakland Convention Center
CHINATOWN
OLD OAKLAND
Asian Cultural Center
Post Office
Camron–Stanford House
LINCOLN SQUARE
MADISON PARK
CHINESE GARDEN
JEFFERSON SQUARE
Webster St. Tube
Posey Tube
Amtrak Terminal
Embarcadero
Jack London Square
Alameda/Oakland Ferry Terminal
Ferry to Alameda & San Francisco
Water Taxi
Oakland Estuary
1/4 Mi
0.25 Km
BART Station
Information
ACCOMMODATIONS
Clarion Suites Lake Merritt Hotel 7
DINING
À Côté 2
Bay Wolf 1
Citron 2
Oliveto Cafe & Restaurant 3
Yoshi's World Class Jazz House and Japanese Restaurant 9
ATTRACTIONS
Jack London Square 10
Lake Merritt 6
Lakeside Park 5
Oakland Museum of California 8
Paramount Theatre 4

The USS *Potomac:* FDR's Floating White House

It took the Potomac Association's hundreds of volunteers more than 12 years—at a cost of $5 million—to restore the 165-foot presidential yacht *Potomac,* President Franklin D. Roosevelt's beloved "Floating White House." Now a proud and permanent memorial berthed at the Port of Oakland's FDR Pier at Jack London Square, the revitalized *Potomac* is open to the public for dockside tours, as well as 2-hour History Cruises along the San Francisco waterfront and around Treasure and Alcatraz islands. Prior to departure, a 15-minute video, shown at the nearby Potomac Visitor Center, provides background on FDR's presidency and FDR's legacy concerning the Bay Area.

The dockside tours are available year-round on Wednesdays and Fridays from 10am to 2:30pm, and on Sundays from noon to 3pm. Admission is $7 for ages 13 to 59, $5 for seniors over 60, and free for children age 12 and under. The History Cruise runs on Thursdays and Saturdays from early May to mid-November; the departure time is 11am. History Cruise fares are $40 for ages 13 to 59, $35 for seniors 60 and older, $20 for children 6 to 12, and free for kids 5 and under. Due to the popularity of the cruises, advance purchase is strongly recommended.

Hours and cruise schedules are subject to change, so be sure to call the Potomac Visitor Center before arriving. Tickets for the Dockside Tour can be purchased at the Visitor Center upon arrival; tickets for the History Cruise can be purchased in advance via **Ticketweb** (**© 866/468-3399;** www.ticketweb.com) or by calling the **Potomac Visitor Center** (**© 510/627-1215;** www.usspotomac.org). The Visitor Center is located at 540 Water St., at the corner of Clay and Water streets adjacent to the FDR pier at the north end of Jack London Square.

best options is live jazz at **Yoshi's World Class Jazz House & Japanese Restaurant** ★, 510 Embarcadero W. (**© 510/238-9200;** www.yoshis.com), which serves some fine sushi in its adjoining restaurant. In the center of the square is a small, reconstructed Yukon cabin in which Jack London lived while prospecting in the Klondike during the gold rush of 1897.

In the middle of Jack London Square you'll find a more authentic memorial, **Heinold's First and Last Chance Saloon** (**© 510/839-6761;** www.heinoldsfirstandlastchance.com), a funky, friendly little bar and historic landmark that's worth a visit. This is where London did some of his writing and most of his drinking; the corner table he used has remained exactly as it was nearly a century ago.

Jack London Square is at Broadway and Embarcadero. Take I-880 to Broadway, turn south, and drive to the end. Or you can ride BART to 12th Street station and then walk south along Broadway (about half a mile). Or take bus no. 72R or 72M to the foot of Broadway.

Oakland Museum of California ★ Two blocks south of Lake Merritt, the Oakland Museum of California incorporates just about everything you'd want to know about the state and its people, history, culture, geology, art, environment, and ecology. Inside a low, modern building set among sweeping gardens and terraces, it's actually three museums in one: exhibitions of works by California artists from Bierstadt to Diebenkorn; collections of historic artifacts, from Pomo Indian basketry to Country Joe McDonald's guitar; and re-creations of California habitats from the coast to the Sierra Mountains. The museum holds major shows of California artists as well as exhibitions dedicated to California's rich nature and history. Recent exhibits included *Aftershock: Personal Stories from the '06 Quake and Fire* and *Baseball as America*, which showcased artifacts and photos of the nation's favorite sport. The museum also frequently shows photography from its huge collections.

Forty-five-minute guided tours leave from the gallery information desks on request or by appointment. There's a fine cafe, a **Collector's Gallery** (✆ **510/834-2296**) that sells works by California artists, and a museum shop. The cafe is open Wednesday through Saturday from 10:30am to 4pm, Sunday from 1:30 to 4pm.

1000 Oak St. (at 10th St.). ✆ **510/238-2200.** www.museumca.org. Admission $8 adults, $5 students and seniors, free for children under 6. 2nd Sun of the month is free (special exhibitions excepted). Wed–Sat 10am–5pm; Sun noon–5pm; open until 9pm 1st Fri of the month. Closed Jan 1, July 4, Thanksgiving, and Dec 25. BART: Lake Merritt station; follow the signs posted in the station. From I-880 N, take the Oak St. exit; the museum is 5 blocks east. Or take I-580 to I-980 and exit at the Jackson St. ramp.

WHERE TO STAY

Two fine midrange hotel options in Oakland are the **Waterfront Plaza Hotel,** 10 Washington St., Jack London Square (✆ **800/729-3638** or 510/836-3800; www.waterfront plaza.com), and the **Oakland Marriott City Center,** 1001 Broadway (✆ **800/228-9290** or 510/451-4000; fax 510/835-3466; www.marriott.com). Most major motel chains also have locations (and budget prices) around town and near the airport. If you want to stay near the fabulous shopping and dining neighborhood of Oakland's Rockridge and pamper yourself with a great gym, outdoor pools, and lit tennis courts, your best hotel bet (though it's undoubtedly overpriced) is **The Claremont Resort & Spa,** 41 Tunnel Rd., Berkeley (✆ **800/551-7266** or 510/843-3000; www.claremontresort.com), a grand Victorian hotel (with modern rooms) that borders both Berkeley and Oakland. It ain't downtown, but it's just a quick drive to all the action, and it is one of the area's prettiest options (see p. 250 for more information).

WHERE TO DINE

EXPENSIVE

Citron ★ FRENCH/CALIFORNIA This petite, adorable French bistro was an instant smash when it opened in 1992, and it continues to earn raves for its small yet enticingly eclectic menu. Chef and owner Chris Rossi draws the flavors of France, Italy, and Spain together with fresh California produce for results you aren't likely to have tasted elsewhere. The menu changes every few weeks; dishes range from succulent roasted Sonoma leg of lamb, served with gigande beans, cardoons, and fennel; to spicy bayou seafood stew brimming with fried oysters, shrimp, snapper, bell peppers, and tomato sauce; to fresh chèvre lasagna with braising greens and truffled crimini mushrooms. They've also added a lunch and brunch menu. ***A word of advice:*** If you're into classic foods you can identify by name, head elsewhere. It's all about creative cooking here.

5484 College Ave. (north of Broadway between Taft and Lawton sts.). ✆ **510/653-5484.** www.citronrestaurant.com. Reservations recommended. Lunch and brunch main courses $8–$15; 3-course fixed-price menu $15; dinner main courses $20–$26; 3- to 5-course fixed-price menu $32–$48. AE, DC, DISC, MC, V. Tues–Fri 11:30am–4:30pm; Sat–Sun 10am–3pm; Mon–Tues 5:30–9pm; Wed–Thurs 5:30–9:30pm; Fri 5:30–10pm; Sat 5–10pm; Sun 5–9pm.

Oliveto Cafe & Restaurant ★★★ ITALIAN Opened 20 years ago by Bob and Maggie Klein, and now under the helm of executive chef Paul Canales (who has been with the Kleins for 11 years, working his way up through the ranks in the kitchen), Oliveto is one of the top Italian restaurants in the Bay Area (and certainly the best in Oakland). Local workers pile in at lunchtime for wood-fired pizzas, simple salads, and sandwiches served in the lower-level cafe. The upstairs restaurant—with suave neo-Florentine decor and a partially open kitchen—is more elegant and packed nightly with fans of the mind-blowing house-made pastas, sausages, and prosciutto. Oliveto has a wood-burning oven, flame-broiled rotisserie, and a full bar which sports a high-end liquor cabinet. An assortment of pricey grills, braises, and roasts anchor the daily changing menu, but the heavenly pastas, pizzettas, and awesome salads offer the most tang for your buck. Still, the Arista (classic Italian pork with garlic and rosemary and pork *jus*) is insanely good; and no one does fried calamari, onion rings, and lemon slices better than Oliveto. ***Tip:*** Free parking is available in the lot at the rear of the Market Hall building.

Rockridge Market Hall, 5655 College Ave. (off the northeast end of Broadway at Shafter/Keith St., across from the Rockridge BART station). ✆ **510/547-5356.** www.oliveto.com. Reservations recommended for restaurant. Main courses cafe $2.50–$12 breakfast, $4–$8 lunch, $12–$15 dinner; restaurant $11–$15 lunch, $16–$30 dinner. AE, DC, MC, V. Cafe Mon 7am–9pm; Tues–Fri 7am–10pm; Sat 8am–10pm; Sun 8am–9pm. Restaurant Mon–Fri 11:30am–2pm; Tues–Wed 5:30–9:30pm; Thurs–Sat 5:30–10pm; Sun 5–9pm.

MODERATE

À Côté ★★ FRENCH TAPAS Jack and Daphne Knowles look to chef Matthew Colgan to serve up superb rustic Mediterranean-inspired small plates at this loud, festive, and warmly lit joint. A "limited reservations" policy means there's usually a long wait during prime dining hours, but once seated, you can join locals in a nosh fest featuring the likes of croque-monsieur; *pommes frites* with aioli; wood-oven cooked mussels in Pernod; grilled pork tenderloin with creamy polenta, and pancetta; and cheese plates—and wash it down with Belgian ales, perky cocktails, or excellent by-the-glass or -bottle selections from the great wine list. ***Note:*** The heated and covered outdoor seating area tends to be quieter.

5478 College Ave. (at Taft Ave.). ✆ **510/655-6469.** www.acoterestaurant.com. Limited reservations accepted. Small plates $5–$14. MC, V. Sun–Tues 5:30–10pm; Wed–Thurs 5:30–11pm; Fri–Sat 5:30pm–midnight.

Bay Wolf ★ CALIFORNIA The lifespan of most Bay Area restaurants is about a year; Bay Wolf, one of Oakland's most revered restaurants, has, fittingly, been going strong for over 3 decades. The converted brown Victorian is a comfortably familiar sight for most East Bay diners, who have come here for years to let executive chef-owner Michael Wilds and his chef de cuisine Louis Le Gassic do the cooking. Bay Wolf enjoys a reputation for simple yet sagacious preparations using only fresh ingredients. Main courses include Liberty Ranch duck three ways (grilled breast, braised leg, and crépinette) with turnips, curly endive, apples, and Calvados; flavorful seafood stew seasoned with saffron; and tender braised *osso buco* with creamy polenta and gremolata. Informal service means you can leave the tie at home. The front deck has heat lamps and a radiant heat floor, allowing for open-air evening dining year-round—a treat that San Franciscans rarely experience.

3853 Piedmont Ave. (off Broadway between 40th St. and MacArthur Blvd.). ✆ **510/655-6004.** www.baywolf.com. Reservations recommended. Main courses $8.50–$18 lunch, $17–$24 dinner. AE, MC, V. Mon–Fri 11:30am–1:45pm; Mon–Thurs 5:30–9pm; Fri–Sat 5:30-10pm; Sun 5:30–9:30pm. Paid parking at Piedmont Ave. and Yosemite St.

3 Angel Island & Tiburon

8 miles N of San Francisco

A California State Park, **Angel Island** is the largest of San Francisco Bay's three islets (the others are Alcatraz and Yerba Buena). The island has been, at various times, a prison, a quarantine station for immigrants, a missile base, and even a favorite site for duels. Nowadays, most visitors are content with picnicking on the large green lawn that fronts the docking area; loaded with the appropriate recreational supplies, they claim a barbecue pit, plop their fannies down on the lush green grass, and while away an afternoon free of phones, televisions, and traffic. Hiking, mountain biking, and guided tram tours are other popular activities here.

Tiburon, situated on a peninsula of the same name, looks like a cross between a fishing village and a Hollywood Western set—imagine San Francisco reduced to toy dimensions. The seacoast town rambles over a series of green hills and ends up at a spindly, multicolored pier on the waterfront, like a Fisherman's Wharf in miniature. In reality, it's an extremely plush patch of yacht-club suburbia, as you'll see by the marine craft and the homes of their owners. Ramshackle, color-splashed old frame houses line Main Street, sheltering chic boutiques, souvenir stores, antiques shops, and art galleries. Other roads are narrow, winding, and hilly and lead up to dramatically situated homes. The view from here of San Francisco's skyline and the islands in the bay is a good enough reason to pay the precious price to live here.

Although there is a hotel in Tiburon, I wouldn't recommend staying there: It's a 1-block town, and the hotel is very expensive. There are no hotels on Angel Island. Both destinations are better as day trips.

ESSENTIALS

Ferries of the **Blue & Gold Fleet** (✆ **415/705-5555;** www.blueandgoldfleet.com) from Pier 41 (Fisherman's Wharf) travel to both Angel Island and Tiburon. Boats run on a seasonal schedule; phone or look online for departure information. The round-trip fare is $15 to Angel Island, $8.50 for kids 6 to 12, and free for kids 5 and under. The fare includes state park fees. Tickets to Tiburon are $8.50 each way for adults, $4.50 for kids 5 to 11, and free for kids 4 and under. Tickets are available at Pier 41, online, or over the phone.

By car from San Francisco, take U.S. 101 to the Tiburon/Highway 131 exit, then follow Tiburon Boulevard all the way downtown, a 40-minute drive from San Francisco. Catch the **Tiburon–Angel Island Ferry** (✆ **415/435-2131;** www.angelisland ferry.com) to Angel Island from the dock at Tiburon Boulevard and Main Street. The 15-minute round-trip costs $10 for adults, $8 for children 5 to 11, and $1 for bikes. One child under 5 is admitted free of charge with each paying adult (after that it's $8 each). Boats run on a seasonal schedule, but usually depart hourly from 10am to 5pm on weekends, with a more limited schedule on weekdays. Call ahead or look online for departure information. Tickets can only be purchased when boarding, and include state park fees. No credit cards.

WHAT TO SEE & DO ON ANGEL ISLAND

Passengers disembark from the ferry at **Ayala Cove,** a small marina abutting a huge lawn area equipped with tables, benches, barbecue pits, and restrooms. During the summer season, there's also a small store, a gift shop, the Cove Cafe (with surprisingly good grub), and an overpriced mountain-bike rental shop at Ayala Cove.

Angel Island's 12 miles of hiking and bike trails include the **Perimeter Road,** a paved path that circles the island. It winds past disused troop barracks, former gun emplacements, and other military buildings; several turnoffs lead to the top of Mount Livermore, 776 feet above the bay. Sometimes referred to as the "Ellis Island of the West," Angel Island was used as a holding area for detained Chinese immigrants awaiting admission papers from 1910 to 1940. You can still see faded Chinese characters on some of the walls of the barracks where the immigrants were held.

The 1-hour audio-enhanced open-air **Tram Tour** of the island costs $14 for adults, $13 for seniors, $9.50 for children 6 to 12, and is free for children 5 and under; schedules vary depending on the time of year. Your best bet is to check in at the Cove Cafe upon arrival on the island for current day's tram schedule.

Guided **Segway tours** of the island are available as well March through November. The 2½ hour interpretive tour circles the island's paved Perimeter Trail and cost $65 (there's a shorter $35 afternoon tour as well). All riders must be 16 years and older. To make tour reservations call ✆ **415/435-3392** or visit www.segwayangelisland.com.

During the warmer months you can camp at a limited number of reserved sites; call **Reserve America** at ✆ **800/444-7275** or visit www.reserveamerica.com to find out about environmental campgrounds at Angel Island. Reservations are taken 2 days to 7 months in advance.

Guided **sea-kayak tours** ★ are also available. The 2½-hour trips combine the thrill of paddling stable, two- or three-person kayaks in an informative, naturalist-led tour around the island (conditions permitting). All equipment is provided, kids are welcome, and no experience is necessary. Rates run about $75 per person. For more information, contact the Sausalito-based **Sea Trek** at ✆ **415/488-1000;** www.seatrekkayak.com. ***Note:*** Tours depart from Sausalito, not Angel Island.

For more information about activities on Angel Island, call ✆ **415/897-0715** or log onto www.angelisland.com.

WHAT TO SEE & DO IN TIBURON

The main thing to do in tiny Tiburon is stroll along the waterfront, pop into the stores, and spend an easy $50 on drinks and appetizers before heading back to the city. For a taste of the Wine Country, stop at **Windsor Vineyards,** 72 Main St. (✆ **415/435-3113;** www.windsorvineyards.com)—its Victorian tasting room dates from 1888. Twenty or more choices are available for a free tasting. Wine accessories and gifts—glasses, cork pullers, carry packs (which hold six bottles), gourmet sauces, posters, and maps—are also available. Ask about personalized labels for your selections. The shop is open Sunday through Thursday from 10am to 6pm, Friday and Saturday from 10am to 7pm.

WHERE TO DINE IN TIBURON

Guaymas MEXICAN Guaymas offers authentic Mexican regional cuisine and a spectacular panoramic view of San Francisco and the bay. In good weather, the two heated outdoor patios are almost always packed with diners soaking in the sun and scene. Inside the very large dining room, colorful Mexican artwork and tons of colored paper cutouts strewn overhead on string brighten the beige walls. Should you feel chilled, to the rear of the dining room is a beehive-shaped adobe fireplace.

Guaymas is named after a fishing village on Mexico's Sea of Cortez, and both the town and the restaurant are famous for their *camarones* (giant shrimp). The restaurant also features ceviche, handmade tamales, and charcoal-grilled beef, seafood, and fowl.

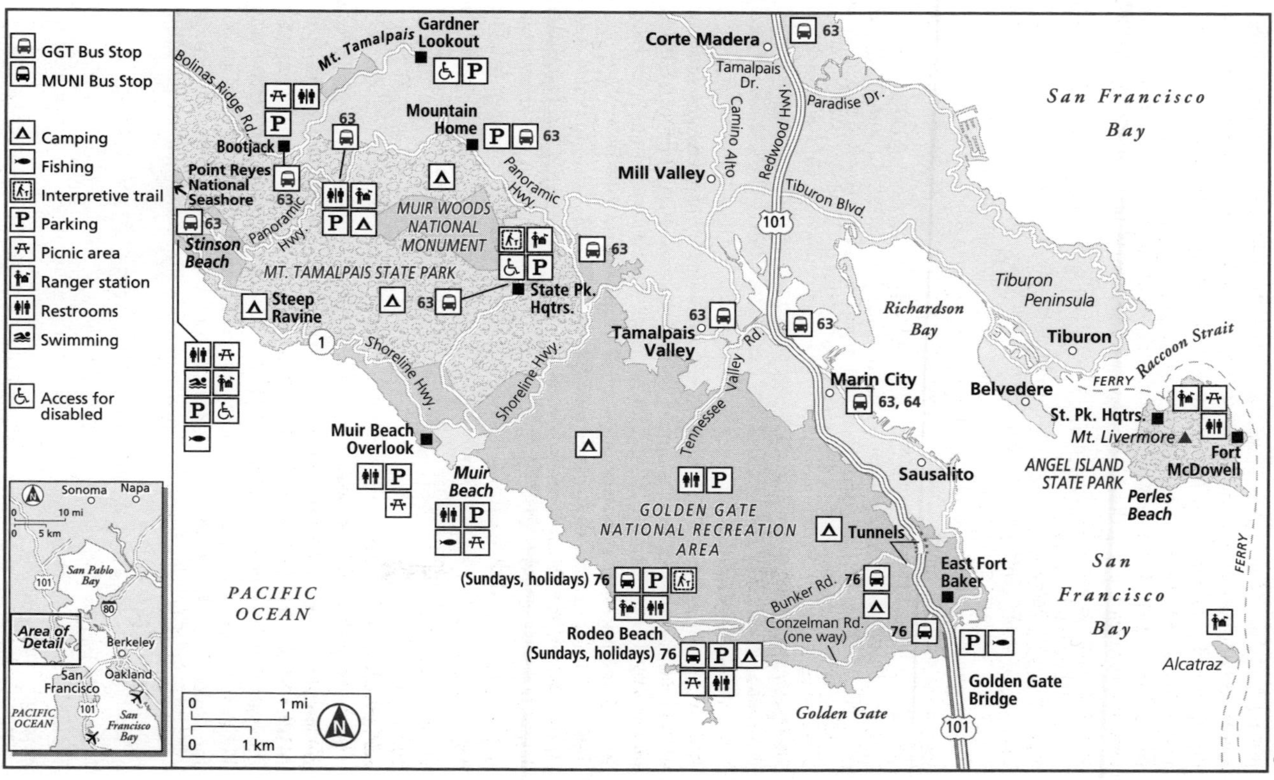
GGT Bus Stop
MUNI Bus Stop
Camping
Fishing
Interpretive trail
Parking
Picnic area
Ranger station
Restrooms
Swimming
Access for disabled
San Francisco Bay
Corte Madera
Mill Valley
Tamalpais Valley
Tamalpais Dr.
Camino Alto
Redwood Hwy.
Paradise Dr.
Tiburon Blvd.
Tiburon Peninsula
Tiburon
Belvedere
Richardson Bay
Marin City
Sausalito
Tennessee Valley Rd.
GOLDEN GATE NATIONAL RECREATION AREA
Tunnels
East Fort Baker
Bunker Rd.
Conzelman Rd. (one way)
Golden Gate
Golden Gate Bridge
Rodeo Beach (Sundays, holidays) 76
(Sundays, holidays) 76
St. Pk. Hqtrs.
Mt. Livermore
ANGEL ISLAND STATE PARK
Perles Beach
Fort McDowell
Raccoon Strait
FERRY
Alcatraz
Mt. Tamalpais
Gardner Lookout
Mountain Home
Panoramic Hwy.
MUIR WOODS NATIONAL MONUMENT
State Pk. Hqtrs.
MT. TAMALPAIS STATE PARK
Shoreline Hwy.
Muir Beach
Muir Beach Overlook
Steep Ravine
Bootjack
Bolinas Ridge Rd.
Point Reyes National Seashore
Stinson Beach
PACIFIC OCEAN
1 mi
1 km
Sonoma
Napa
San Pablo Bay
Berkeley
Oakland
San Francisco
San Francisco Bay
Area of Detail
10 mi
5 km

It's not fancy, nor is it gourmet, but it is a good place to come with large parties or family. In addition to a small selection of California and Central American wines, the restaurant offers an exceptional variety of tequilas and Mexican beers.

5 Main St. ✆ **415/435-6300.** Reservations recommended. Main courses $13–$23. AE, DC, DISC, MC, V. Mon–Thurs 11:30am–10pm; Fri–Sat 11:30am–11pm; Sun 10:30am–10pm. Ferry: Walk about 10 paces from the landing. From U.S. 101, exit at Tiburon/Hwy. 131; follow Tiburon Blvd. 5 miles and turn right onto Main St. Restaurant is behind the bakery.

Sam's Anchor Café ★ *Finds* SEAFOOD Summer Sundays are liveliest in Tiburon, when weekend boaters tie up at the docks of waterside restaurants like this one, and good-time cyclists pedal from the city to kick back here. Sam's is the kind of place where you and your cronies can take off your shoes and have a fun, relaxing time eating burgers and drinking margaritas outside on the pier. The fare is typical—sandwiches, salads, and such—but the quality and selection are inconsequential: Beers, burgers, and a designated driver are all you really need.

27 Main St. ✆ **415/435-4527.** www.samscafe.com. Main courses $9–$17 brunch, $11–$24 lunch, $15–$24 dinner. AE, DC, DISC, MC, V. Mon–Fri 11am–10pm; Sat–Sun 9:30am–10pm. Ferry: Walk from the landing. From U.S. 101, exit at Tiburon/Hwy. 131; follow Tiburon Blvd. 4 miles and turn right onto Main St.

4 Sausalito

5 miles N of San Francisco

Just off the northeastern end of the Golden Gate Bridge is the picturesque little town of Sausalito, a slightly bohemian adjunct to San Francisco. With fewer than 8,000 residents, Sausalito feels rather like St. Tropez on the French Riviera (minus the beach). Next to the pricey bayside restaurants, antiques shops, and galleries you'll see hamburger joints, ice cream shops, and secondhand bookstores. Sausalito's main strip is Bridgeway, which runs along the water; on a clear day the views of San Francisco far across the bay are spectacular. After admiring the view, those in the know make a quick detour to Caledonia Street, 1 block inland; not only is it less congested, but it also has a better selection of cafes and shops. Since the town is all along the waterfront and only stretches a few blocks, it's best explored on foot and easy to find your way around.

ESSENTIALS

The **Golden Gate Ferry Service** fleet, Ferry Building (✆ **415/923-2000;** www.goldengate.org), operates between the San Francisco Ferry Building, at the foot of Market Street, and downtown Sausalito. Service is frequent, running at reasonable intervals every day of the year except January 1, Thanksgiving, and December 25. Phone for an exact schedule. The ride takes a half-hour, and one-way fares are $6.75 for adults; $3.35 for youth 6 to 18, seniors 65 plus, and passengers with disabilities (50% off full fare); children 5 and under ride free (limit two children per full-fare adult). Family rates are available on weekends.

Ferries of the **Blue & Gold Fleet** (✆ **415/705-5555;** www.blueandgoldfleet.com) leave from Pier 41 (Fisherman's Wharf); the one-way cost is $8.50 for adults, $4.50 for kids 5 to 11. Boats run on a seasonal schedule; phone or log onto their website for departure information.

By car from San Francisco, take U.S. 101 N, then take the first right after the Golden Gate Bridge (Alexander exit). Alexander becomes Bridgeway in Sausalito.

WHAT TO SEE & DO

Above all else, Sausalito has scenery and sunshine, for once you cross the Golden Gate Bridge, you're out of the San Francisco fog patch and under blue California sky (we hope). Houses cover the town's steep hills, overlooking a forest of masts on the waters below. Most of the tourist action, which is almost singularly limited to window-shopping and eating, takes place at sea level on Bridgeway.

Sausalito is a mecca for shoppers seeking handmade, original, and offbeat clothes and footwear, as well as arts and crafts. Many of the town's shops are in the alleys, malls, and second-floor boutiques reached by steep, narrow staircases on and off Bridgeway. Caledonia Street, which runs parallel to Bridgeway 1 block inland, is home to more shops.

Bay Area Discovery Museum *Kids* If you just can't stand the thought of one more trip to PIER 39 or Fisherman's Wharf and are looking for something else to do with your kids (infants to 8 years old), check out this museum. Located on 7½ acres in the Golden Gate National Recreation Area at Fort Baker, the museum offers spectacular (jaw-dropping even!) views of the city and Golden Gate Bridge (you're literally at the northern base of the bridge) and is also the ultimate indoor-outdoor interactive kids' adventure. Tot Spot is tops for crawlers and toddlers (up to 42 in.); Lookout Cove is a 2½-acre outdoor area with a scaled-down model of the GGB that kids can add rivets to, a shipwreck to explore, tidal pools, and lovely site-specific art; Art Studios splits kids into age groups 5 and under and 6 and older; and the Wave Workshop re-creates the habitat under the GGB. There's even a small cafe that serves yummy, organic food far better than typical family-friendly fare. Remi Hayashi, a California Culinary Academy grad, is at the helm here, serving up Niman Ranch hot dogs, fresh sandwiches, panini, and pizzas plus a host of snacks. ***One thing to note:*** If you're here alone with two kids of different ages, it can be difficult to navigate, as they do keep the little ones separate from the older ones in the Tot Spot. If you explain your situation, they'll give your older one (12 and up) a "Tot Spot Helper" sticker, and let them in, but they won't be allowed to play and will have to stick by you. But if it's a nice day, you can spend the whole time in Lookout Cove with both kids, have lunch outside, and still feel like you got your money's worth.

E. Fort Baker, 557 McReynolds Rd. © **415/339-3900.** www.baykidsmuseum.org. Admission $8.50 adults, $7.50 children, free for children under 1 and members. Discounts available to AAA members and members of reciprocal museum organizations (see website). Tues–Fri 9am–4pm; Sat–Sun 10am–5pm. Closed Mon and all major holidays. By car: Cross the Golden Gate Bridge and take the Alexander Ave. exit. Follow signs to E. Fort Baker and the Bay Area Discovery Museum.

Bay Model Visitors Center *Kids* The U.S. Army Corps of Engineers once used this high-tech, 1½-acre model of San Francisco's bay and delta to resolve problems and observe the impact of changes in water flow. Today the model is strictly for educational purposes and reproduces (in scale) the rise and fall of tides and the flows and currents of water. There's a 10-minute film, self-guided and audio tours ($3 donation requested), and a 1-hour tour (free; book a reservation), but the most interesting time to visit is when the model is in operation, so call ahead.

2100 Bridgeway. © **415/332-3871.** www.spn.usace.army.mil/bmvc. Free admission. Labor Day to Memorial Day (winter hours) Tues–Sat 9am–4pm; Memorial Day to Labor Day (summer hours) Tues–Fri 9am–4pm, Sat–Sun and holidays 10am–5pm.

WHERE TO STAY

Sausalito is such a desirable enclave that it offers little in the way of affordable lodging. On the bright side, it's so close to San Francisco that it takes only about 15 minutes to get here, traffic permitting. Although the hotels listed below are great destinations in themselves, Sausalito itself is more day trip than destination.

VERY EXPENSIVE

The Inn Above Tide ★★ Perched directly over the bay atop well-grounded pilings, this former luxury-apartment complex underwent a $4-million transformation in 2004 into one of Sausalito's—if not the Bay Area's—finest accommodations. The view clinches it: Every room affords an unparalleled panorama of the San Francisco Bay, including a postcard-quality vista of the city glimmering in the distance. Should you manage to tear yourself away from your private deck, you'll find that 23 of the sumptuously appointed rooms sport romantic little fireplaces. Soothing warm earth tones highlight the decor, which blends in well with the bayscape outside. Be sure to request that your breakfast and newspaper be delivered to your deck, and then cancel your early appointments—on sunny mornings, nobody checks out early.

30 El Portal (next to the Sausalito Ferry Landing), Sausalito, CA 94965. ✆ **800/893-8433** or 415/332-9535. Fax 415/332-6714. www.innabovetide.com. 29 units. $295–$950 double. Rates include continental breakfast and evening wine and cheese. AE, DC, MC, V. Valet parking $12. **Amenities:** Concierge; in-room massage; same-day laundry service/dry cleaning; free shoeshine. *In room:* A/C, TV/DVD, dataport, minibar, fridge, hair dryer, free Wi-Fi access, CD player.

EXPENSIVE

Casa Madrona Hotel & Spa ★★ Sooner or later most visitors to Sausalito look up and wonder at the ornate mansion on the hill. It's part of Casa Madrona, a hideaway by the bay built in 1885 by a wealthy lumber baron. The epitome of luxury in its day, the mansion had slipped into decay when John Gallagher purchased it in 1910 and converted it into a hotel. By 1976 it was damaged and facing the threat of demolition when John Mays acquired the property and revitalized the hotel. Successive renovations and extensions added a rambling, New England–style building to the hillside below the main house. Now listed on the National Register of Historic Places, the hotel offers whimsically decorated rooms, suites, and cottages, which are accessed by steep, gorgeously landscaped pathways. The 16 free-standing units, the seven cottages, and the rooms in the mansion have individual themes such as Lilac and Lace, Renoir, or the Artist's Loft. Some have claw-foot tubs and others have fireplaces. Rooms in the newer adjoining building have a chic contemporary decor, four-poster beds, marble bathrooms, and great marina views from some rooms. The classy Italian Poggio restaurant (see below) has been a Sausalito favorite since opening, and the hotel's full-service spa offers a wide assortment of treatments and getaway packages.

801 Bridgeway, Sausalito, CA 94965. ✆ **415/332-0502.** Fax 415/332-2537. www.casamadrona.com. 63 units. $295–$450 double; $550 suite. AE, DC, DISC, MC, V. Valet parking $20. Ferry: Walk across the street from the landing. From U.S. 101 N, take the 1st right after the Golden Gate Bridge (Alexander exit); Alexander becomes Bridgeway. **Amenities:** Restaurant; spa; concierge; room service; babysitting upon request; laundry service; dry cleaning. *In room:* TV, VCR upon availability, minibar, coffeemaker, hair dryer, robes.

WHERE TO DINE

EXPENSIVE

Horizons ★ SEAFOOD/AMERICAN Eventually, every San Franciscan ends up at Horizons to meet a friend for Sunday Bloody Marys. It's not much to look at from the outside, but it gets better as you head past the 1960s-era dark-wood interior toward

A Picnic Lunch, Sausalito Style

If the crowds are too much or the prices too steep at Sausalito's bay-side restaurants, grab a bite to go for an impromptu picnic in the park fronting the marina. It's one of the best and most romantic ways to spend a warm, sunny day in Sausalito. The best source for a la carte eats is the Mediterranean-style **Venice Gourmet Delicatessen** at 625 Bridgeway, located right on the waterfront just south of the ferry landing. Since 1964 this venerable deli has offered all the makings for a superb picnic: wines, cheeses, fruits, stuffed vine leaves, salami, lox, prosciutto, salads, quiche, made-to-order sandwiches, and fresh-baked pastries. It's open daily from 9am to 6pm (✆ **415/332-3544;** www.venicegourmet.com).

the waterside terrace. On warm days it's worth the wait for alfresco seating if only to watch dreamy sailboats glide past San Francisco's distant skyline. The food here can't touch the view, but it's well portioned and satisfying enough. Seafood dishes are the main items, including steamed clams and mussels, freshly shucked oysters, and a variety of seafood pastas. In fine Marin tradition, Horizons has an "herb tea and espresso" bar.

558 Bridgeway. ✆ **415/331-3232.** www.horizonssausalito.com. Reservations accepted weekdays only. Main courses $9–$21; salads and sandwiches $6–$11. AE, MC, V. Mon–Fri 11:30am–9pm; Sat 10:30am–10pm; Sun 10:30am–9pm. Valet parking $4.

Poggio ★★ ITALIAN Sausalito has long been low on upscale dining options, but all that changed with the late-2003 opening of elegant "Poggio," which is a loose Italian translation for "special hillside place." Adjoining the Casa Madrona hotel and across the street from the marina, everything *is* special here, from the floor-to-ceiling doors opening to the sidewalk; to its interior with arches and earthen colors, mahogany accents, well-directed light, and centerpiece wood-oven manned by a cadre of chefs; to the wine cellar, terra-cotta-tiled floors, comfy mohair banquettes, and white linen-draped tables. The daily changing menu features items like a superb salad of endive, Gorgonzola, walnuts, figs, and honey; pizzas; addictively excellent pastas (try the spinach ricotta gnocchi with beef ragout); and entrees such as whole local petrale sole deboned and served tableside, or grilled lamb chops with roasted fennel and gremolata. With a full bar, well-priced wine list, and great desserts, this is Sausalito's premier dining destination—excluding the more casual Sushi Ran (see below).

777 Bridgeway (at Bay St.). ✆ **415/332-7771.** www.poggiotrattoria.com. Italian-style breakfast a la carte $2.50–$5.50; main courses lunch $8–$18, dinner $13–$25. AE, DC, DISC, MC, V. Continental breakfast daily 6:30–11am; lunch 11:30am–5:30pm; dinner Sun–Thurs 5:30–10pm, Fri–Sat 5:30–11pm. Free valet parking at Casa Madrona Hotel & Spa.

Sushi Ran ★★ SUSHI/JAPANESE San Francisco isn't exactly stellar in its Japanese-food selection, but right across from the Golden Gate Bridge is a compact, but fashionable, destination for seriously delicious sushi and cooked dishes. All walks of sushi-loving life cram into the sushi bar, window seats, and more roomy back dining area for Nori Kusakabe's nigiri sushi and standard and specialty rolls. You'll also find a slew of creative dishes by Executive Chef Scott Whitman, such as generously sized and unbelievably moist and buttery miso-glazed black cod (a must-have), oysters on the half-shell with ponzu sauce and *tobiko* (fish eggs), and a Hawaiian-style ahi *poke* (Hawaiian-style minced raw fish) salad with seaweed dressing that's authentic enough to make you want to hula.

107 Caledonia St. © **415/332-3620.** www.sushiran.com. Reservations recommended. Sushi $5–$14; main courses $8.50–$16. AE, MC, V. Mon–Fri 11:45am–2:30pm; Mon–Sat 5:30–11pm; Sun 5–10:30pm. From U.S. 101 N, take the 1st right after the Golden Gate Bridge (Alexander exit); Alexander becomes Bridgeway in Sausalito. At Johnson St. turn left, then right onto Caledonia.

INEXPENSIVE

Hamburgers BURGERS Like the name says, the specialty at this tiny, narrow cafe is juicy flame-broiled hamburgers, arguably Marin County's best. Look for the rotating grill in the window off Bridgeway, and then stand in line and salivate with everyone else. Chicken burgers are a slightly healthier option. Order a side of fries, grab a bunch of napkins, and head to the park across the street.

737 Bridgeway. © **415/332-9471.** Sandwiches $5.50–$6.50. No credit cards. Daily 11am–5pm. From U.S. 101 N, take the 1st right after the Golden Gate Bridge (Alexander exit); Alexander becomes Bridgeway in Sausalito.

5 Muir Woods & Mount Tamalpais

12 miles N of the Golden Gate Bridge

While the rest of Marin County's redwood forests were being devoured to feed San Francisco's turn-of-the-20th-century building spree, Muir Woods, in a remote ravine on the flanks of Mount Tamalpais, escaped destruction in favor of easier pickings.

MUIR WOODS

Although the magnificent California redwoods have been successfully transplanted to five continents, their homeland is a 500-mile strip along the mountainous coast of southwestern Oregon and Northern California. The coast redwood, or *Sequoia sempervirens,* is one of the tallest living things known to man (!); the largest known specimen in the Redwood National Forest towers 368 feet. It has an even larger relative, the *Sequoiadendron giganteum* of the California Sierra Nevada, but the coastal variety is stunning enough. Soaring toward the sky like a wooden cathedral, Muir Woods is unlike any other forest in the world and an experience you won't soon forget.

Granted, Muir Woods is tiny compared to the Redwood National Forest farther north, but you can still get a pretty good idea of what it must have been like when these giants dominated the entire coastal region. What is truly amazing is that they exist a mere 6 miles (as the crow flies) from San Francisco—close enough, unfortunately, that tour buses arrive in droves on the weekends. You can avoid the masses by hiking up the **Ocean View Trail,** turning left on **Lost Trail,** and returning on the **Fern Creek Trail.** The moderately challenging hike shows off the woods' best sides and leaves the lazy-butts behind.

To reach Muir Woods from San Francisco, cross the Golden Gate Bridge heading north on Highway 101, take the Stinson Beach/Highway 1 exit heading west, and follow the signs (and the traffic). The park is open daily from 8am to sunset, and the admission fee is $5 per person over 16. There's also a small gift shop, educational displays, and ranger talks. For more information, call the **National Parks Service at Muir Woods** (© **415/388-2596**) or visit www.nps.gov.

If you don't have a car, you can book a bus trip with **San Francisco Sightseeing** (© **888/428-6937** or 415/434-8687; www.sanfranciscosightseeing.com), which takes you straight to Muir Woods and makes a short stop in Sausalito on the way back. The

3½-hour tour runs twice daily at 9:15am and 2:15pm and costs $47 for adults, $45 for seniors, $22 for children 5 through 11, and free for kids under 5. Pickup and return are offered from select San Francisco hotels. Call for information and departure times.

MOUNT TAMALPAIS

The birthplace of mountain biking, Mount Tam—as the locals call it—is the Bay Area's favorite outdoor playground and the most dominant mountain in the region. Most every local has his or her secret trail and scenic overlook, as well as an opinion on the raging debate between mountain bikers and hikers (a touchy subject). The main trails—mostly fire roads—see a lot of foot and bicycle traffic on weekends, particularly on clear, sunny days when you can see a hundred miles in all directions, from the foothills of the Sierra to the western horizon. It's a great place to escape from the city for a leisurely hike and to soak in breathtaking views of the bay.

To get to Mount Tamalpais **by car,** cross the Golden Gate Bridge heading north on Highway 101, and take the Stinson Beach/Highway 1 exit. Follow the signs up the shoreline highway for about 2½ miles, turn onto Pantoll Road, and continue for about a mile to Ridgecrest Boulevard. Ridgecrest winds to a parking lot below East Peak. From there, it's a 15-minute hike up to the top. You'll find a visitor center with a small museum, video, fun diorama, and store, as well as enthusiastic and informative "Mount Tam Hosts" who are more than happy to help you plan a hike, identify plants, and generally share their love of the mountain. Visitor center admission is free; it's open Saturday and Sunday from 11am to 4pm (standard time), and Saturday and Sunday 10am to 5:30pm (daylight saving time). Park hours are 7am to 6pm daily in winter; 7am to 9pm for about 1 month during the height of summer. Two-hour, 2-mile moonlight hikes, among many others, are offered (✆ **415/388-2070;** www.mttam.net).

6 Point Reyes National Seashore

35 miles N of San Francisco

The National Seashore system was created to protect rural and undeveloped stretches of the coast from the pressures brought by soaring real-estate values and increasing population. Nowhere is the success of the system more evident than at Point Reyes. Residents of the surrounding towns—Inverness, Point Reyes Station, and Olema—have steadfastly resisted runaway development. You won't find any strip malls or fast-food joints here, just laid-back coastal towns with cafes, country inns, and vast expanses of open, undeveloped space in between, where gentle living prevails.

Although the peninsula's people and wildlife live in harmony above the ground, the situation beneath the soil is much more volatile. The infamous San Andreas Fault separates Point Reyes—the northernmost landmass on the Pacific Plate—from the rest of California, which rests on the North American Plate. Point Reyes is making its way toward Alaska at a rate of about 2 inches per year, but at times it has moved much faster. In 1906, Point Reyes jumped north almost 20 feet in an instant, leveling San Francisco and jolting the rest of the state. The half-mile Earthquake Trail, near the Bear Valley Visitor Center, illustrates this geological drama with a loop through an area torn by the slipping fault. Shattered fences, rifts in the ground, and a barn knocked off its foundation by the quake illustrate how alive the earth is.

ESSENTIALS

Point Reyes is only 30 miles northwest of San Francisco, but it takes at least 90 minutes to reach **by car** (it's all the small towns, not the topography, that slow you down). The easiest route is Sir Francis Drake Boulevard from Highway 101 south of San Rafael; it takes its time getting to Point Reyes, but it does so without any detours. For a much longer but more scenic route, take the Stinson Beach/Highway 1 exit off Highway 101 just south of Sausalito and follow Highway 1 north.

As soon as you arrive at Point Reyes, stop at the **Bear Valley Visitor Center** (**© 415/464-5100;** www.nps.gov/pore) on Bear Valley Road (look for the small sign just north of Olema on Hwy. 1) and pick up a free Point Reyes trail map. The rangers are extremely friendly and helpful and can answer any questions about the National Seashore. Be sure to check out the great natural history and cultural displays while you're there. The center is open weekdays from 9am to 5pm, weekends and holidays from 8am to 5pm.

Entrance to the park is free. **Camping** is $15 per site per night for up to six people, and permits are required. All the sites range from a 1.4- to 5.5-mile hike in from the nearest trail head. Reservations can be made up to 3 months in advance by calling **© 415/663-8054** Monday through Friday from 9am to 2pm.

WHAT TO SEE & DO

When headed to any part of the Point Reyes coast, expect to spend the day surrounded by nature at its finest; however, bear in mind that as beautiful as the wilderness can be, it's also untamable. The bone-chilling waters in these areas are not only home to a vast array of sea life, including sharks, but are unpredictable and dangerous. There are no lifeguards on duty, and swimming is strongly discouraged because of the waves and rip tides. Pets are not permitted on any of the area's trails. However, if you are looking for a place to swim, consider heading toward Tomales Bay during the summer months.

By far the most popular—and crowded—attraction at Point Reyes National Seashore is the venerable **Point Reyes Lighthouse** ★ (**© 415/669-1534**), at the westernmost tip of Point Reyes. Even if you plan to forgo the 308 steps to the lighthouse itself (sorry—no strollers or wheelchairs), the area is still worth a visit. The dramatic scenery includes thousands of common murres and prides of sea lions that bask on the rocks far below (binoculars come in handy). It's open Thursday through Monday from 10am to 4:30pm and admission is free. A parking area is designated for travelers with disabilities at the visitor center. Call **© 415/464-5100** to make arrangements.

The lighthouse is also the top spot on the California coast from which to observe **gray whales** as they make their southward and northward migrations along the coast January through April. The annual round-trip is 10,000 miles—one of the longest known mammal migrations. The whales head south in January and return north in March. There's never a guarantee that you will see a whale, but it's best to come during clear, calm weather. ***Note:*** If you plan to drive to the lighthouse to whale-watch, arrive early because parking is limited. If possible, come on a weekday. On a weekend or holiday January through the beginning of April, you have to park at the Drake's Beach Visitor Center and take the shuttle bus (weather permitting) to the lighthouse and on to Chimney Rock to watch elephant seals; the shuttle bus runs from around New Year's Day to the beginning of April and costs $5 for adults, free for children under 16. Dress warmly when you come here—it's often quite cold and windy—and bring binoculars. Expect to spend about 2½ hours.

Finds **Drake's Bay Oyster Farm**

If you want to escape the crowds and enjoy some man-made entertainment, head to **Drake's Bay Oyster Farm.** Located on the edge of Drakes Estero (a uniquely pristine and nutrient-rich saltwater lagoon on the Point Reyes peninsula that produces some of the finest oysters in the world), the oyster farm doesn't look like much—it's just a cluster of wooden shacks and oyster tanks surrounded by piles of oyster shells—but there's no better place in California to buy delicious fresh-out-of-the-water oysters by the sackful. The owner is very friendly and doles out all the information you'll ever want to know about the bivalves, including a lesson on how to properly shuck them. They also have picnic tables and bottled oyster sauce so you can enjoy your recently purchased bivalves immediately (though I prefer to drive down to Point Reyes Beach), but bring your own oyster knife. Drake's Bay Oyster Farm is located at 17171 Sir Francis Drake Blvd., about 6 miles west(ish) of Inverness on the way to the Point Reyes Lighthouse. It's open daily 8am to 4:30pm (✆ **415/669-1149;** www.drakesbayfamilyfarms.com).

Whale-watching is far from the only activity at the Point Reyes National Seashore. On weekend afternoons or daily during the summer months, many different tours are offered: You can walk along the Bear Valley Trail, spotting the wildlife at the ocean's edge; see the waterfowl at Alamere Falls; explore tide pools; view some of North America's most beautiful ducks in the wetlands of Limantour; hike to the promontory overlooking Chimney Rock to see the sea lions, harbor seals, elephant seals, and seabirds; or take a guided walk along the San Andreas Fault to observe the epicenter of the 1906 earthquake and learn about the regional geology. And this is just a sampling. Tours vary seasonally; for the most up-to-date details, call the **Bear Valley Visitor Center** (✆ **415/464-5100**) or visit the National Park Service's website (www.nps.gov/pore), where you can also get a lay of the land and more details, including area maps, in the "Plan Your Visit" section of the site. ***Note:*** Many tours are suitable for travelers with disabilities.

Some of the park's best—and least crowded—highlights can be approached only on foot. They include **Alamere Falls,** a freshwater stream that cascades down a 40-foot bluff onto Wildcat Beach; and **Tomales Point Trail,** which passes through the Tule Elk Reserve, a protected haven for roaming herds of tule elk that once numbered in the thousands. Hiking most of the trails usually ends up being an all-day outing, however, so it's best to split a 2-day trip into a "by car" day and a "by foot" day.

If you're into bird-watching, you'll definitely want to visit the **Point Reyes Bird Observatory** (✆ **415/868-0655;** www.prbo.org), one of the few full-time ornithological research stations in the United States. At the southeast end of the park on Mesa Road, this is where ornithologists keep an eye on more than 400 feathered species. Admission to the visitor center and nature trail is free, and visitors are welcome to observe the tricky process of catching and banding the birds. The observatory is open daily from sunrise to 5pm. Banding hours vary, so call the field station for exact times.

One of my favorite things to do in Point Reyes is paddle through placid Tomales Bay, a haven for migrating birds and marine mammals. **Blue Waters Kayaking** ★ (✆ **415/669-2600;** www.bwkayak.com) organizes nature tours and hiking and kayak trips, including 3-hour morning or sunset outings, oyster tours, day trips, and longer excursions. Instruction, private groups and classes, clinics, and boat rental are available, and all ages and levels are welcome. Prices for tours start at $68. Rentals begin at $30 per person. Don't worry—the kayaks are very stable, and there aren't any waves to contend with. There are two launching points: One is on Highway 1 at the Marshall Boatworks in Marshall, 8 miles north of Point Reyes Station; and the other is on Sir Francis Drake Boulevard, in Inverness, 5 miles west of Point Reyes Station. The Inverness site is open daily from 9am to 5pm; the Marshall site is open, weather permitting, on weekends from 9am to 5pm and by appointment. Call or visit their website to confirm.

WHERE TO STAY

Inns of Marin, P.O. Box 547, Point Reyes Station, CA 94956 (© **800/887-2880** or 415/663-2000; www.innsofmarin.com), is a free service that can help you find accommodations ranging from one-room cottages to inns to complete vacation homes. Many places have a 2-night minimum, but at slow times they might make an exception. The service can also refer you to restaurants, hiking trails, and area attractions.

EXPENSIVE

Manka's Inverness Lodge & Restaurant ★★★ *Finds* If there was ever a reason to pack your bags and leave San Francisco for a day or two, this is it. A former hunting and fishing lodge, Manka's looks like something out of a Hans Christian Andersen fairy tale, right down to the tree-limb bedstands. It's all terribly romantic in a Jack London-ish sort of way, and tastefully done. The lodge consists of a superb restaurant on the first floor, four rooms upstairs (room nos. 1 and 2 have large private decks), and four rooms in the Redwood Annex. Two spacious one-bedroom cabins, behind the lodge and on the water, have living rooms and bathrooms with vintage 6-foot double-ended tubs and private outdoor showers opening up to the sky. For the ultimate romantic splurge, inquire about the three secluded guesthouses: Boat House, Perch, and Cabin 125. The lodge's reputation was built on its rustic and romantic restaurant, which dominates the bottom floor and continues to make visitors swoon with house specialties of game and fish. The menu is price-fixed, ranging from $58 to $88 (Sat), and features limited selections that might include pheasant with Madeira *jus,* mashed potatoes, and wild-huckleberry jam; black-buck antelope chops with sweet-corn salsa; or, everybody's favorite, pan-seared elk tenderloin. The restaurant is open for dinner Thursday through Sunday for a single seating (7–7:30pm Thurs–Sat; 4–4:30pm Sun) except for the first 6 weeks of the year, when it's closed. ***Note:*** A recent fire did considerable damage to the restaurant and main lodge, but hopefully it will be repaired by the time you read this.

30 Callendar Way (at Argyle St., off Sir Francis Drake Blvd., ¼ mile north of downtown Inverness), P.O. Box 1110, Inverness, CA 94937. © **415/669-1034.** Fax 415/669-1598. www.mankas.com. 14 units, including 4 cabins. $215–$385 double; $365–$565 cabin. AE, MC, V. **Amenities:** Restaurant; in-room massage; room service; movies on request; personal music library; free Wi-Fi access. *In room:* MP3 player with CD library, phones in guesthouses, redwood soaking tubs in some rooms, massage.

INEXPENSIVE

Motel Inverness *Kids* Homey, well-maintained, and fronting Tomales Bay, this is the perfect pick for the spendthrift or the outdoor adventurer who plans to spend as little time indoors as possible. All the guest rooms except one twin-bed option have queen-size beds and skylights. Attached to the hotel is a giant great room, complete with fireplace and pool table to distract the kids; parents can relax and children can play on the back lawn overlooking the bay, bird sanctuary, and rolling green hills beyond. Ideal for families is the Dacha cottage, a few miles away. On the water, it has three bedrooms, a living/dining room, sitting room, and deck with Tomales Bay views.

12718 Sir Francis Drake Blvd., Inverness, CA 94937. ✆ **888/669-6909** or 415/669-1081. www.motelinverness.com. 8 units. $99–$175 double; $225–$275 suite; Dacha Cottage $500. MC, V. *In room:* TV, coffeemaker.

WHERE TO DINE

MODERATE

Station House Café ★ AMERICAN For more than 2 decades, the Station House Café has been a favorite pit stop for Bay Area residents headed to and from Point Reyes. It's a friendly, low-key place with an open kitchen, an outdoor garden dining area, and live music on weekend nights. Breakfast dishes include a Hangtown omelet with local oysters and bacon, and eggs with creamed spinach and mashed-potato pancakes. Lunch and dinner specials might be fettuccine with fresh local mussels steamed in white wine and butter sauce, two-cheese polenta served with fresh spinach sauté and grilled garlic-buttered tomato, or a daily fresh salmon special—all made from local produce, seafood, and organically raised Niman Ranch beef.

11180 Hwy. 1, Main St., Point Reyes Station. ✆ **415/663-1515.** www.stationhousecafe.com. Reservations recommended. Breakfast $5.25–$9.25; main courses $7.50–$18 lunch, $9–$25 dinner. AE, DISC, MC, V. Thurs–Tues 8am–3:30pm and 5–9pm.

INEXPENSIVE

Rosie's Cowboy Cookhouse ★ MEXICAN/AMERICAN Fresh, good, fast, cheap, and healthy: What more could you ask for in a restaurant? Taqueria La Quinta, which was a favorite lunch stop in downtown Point Reyes for years and years, is now known as Rosie's Cowboy Cookhouse. The huge selection of Mexican standards remains on the menu—try the house-made tamales—but now they've added some Tex to their Mex, such as rib-eye steak, pulled-pork sandwiches, and excellent Niman Ranch beef chili, all prepared from scratch in their kitchen using natural, free range, and organic ingredients. Oh, and watch out for the salsa—that sucker's hot.

11285 Hwy. 1 (at Third and Main sts.), Point Reyes Station. ✆ **415/663-8868.** No credit cards. Wed–Mon 11am–9pm.

12

The Wine Country

by Erika Lenkert

If you've got more than a few days in San Francisco or already are well-versed in the city's offerings, I highly recommend at least a quick jaunt to the Wine Country, an hour or so north by car. Amid mountains dipping into grapevine-trellised valleys, you'll experience an entirely different Northern California: fresh country air, mustard-flower–draped hillsides in spring, gloriously hot weather during summer, some of the world's finest wineries, legendary restaurants, cow-studded pastures, and virtually nothing to do but overindulge. With eating, drinking, and lounging the primary attractions, there's virtually no better example of "the good life."

To decide which of the Wine Country's two distinct valleys (Napa and Sonoma) you prefer to visit, you need to consider their differences: The most obvious is size—Napa Valley dwarfs Sonoma Valley in population, number of wineries, and sheer volume of tourism (and traffic). Napa is definitely the more commercial of the two, with many more wineries and spas to choose from, and a superior selection of restaurants, hotels, and quintessential Wine Country activities, like hot-air ballooning, wine-tasting, and shopping. Furthermore, if your goal is to really learn about the world of winemaking, Napa Valley should be your choice. World-class wineries such as Sterling and Robert Mondavi offer the most interesting and edifying wine tours in North America, if not the world (although Sonoma's Benziger Winery does give them a run for their money).

Meanwhile, Sonoma Valley is the answer for those who are in the less-is-more camp. Napa Valley's neighbor has fewer wineries (about 35), fewer big hotels and restaurants, and a less commercial feel. As a result, there are fewer crowds on the low-key country roads; more down-home charm in the country communities, B&Bs, and little family-run restaurants; and, in general, more opportunities for intimate pastoral experiences. For more on Sonoma Valley's offerings (as spectacular as Napa Valley's but more low-key), see the "Sonoma Valley" section.

If you're planning a more extensive trip to the area, consult *Frommer's Portable California Wine Country* (Wiley Publishing, Inc.).

1 Napa Valley

Just 55 miles north of San Francisco, the city of Napa and its neighboring towns have an overall tourist and big-business feel. You'll see plenty of rolling hills, flora and fauna, and vast stretches of vineyards, but they come hand-in-hand with upscale restaurants, designer discount outlets, rows of hotels and, in summer, traffic clustered more tightly than grapes on the vines. Even with hordes of visitors year-round, Napa

The Wine Country

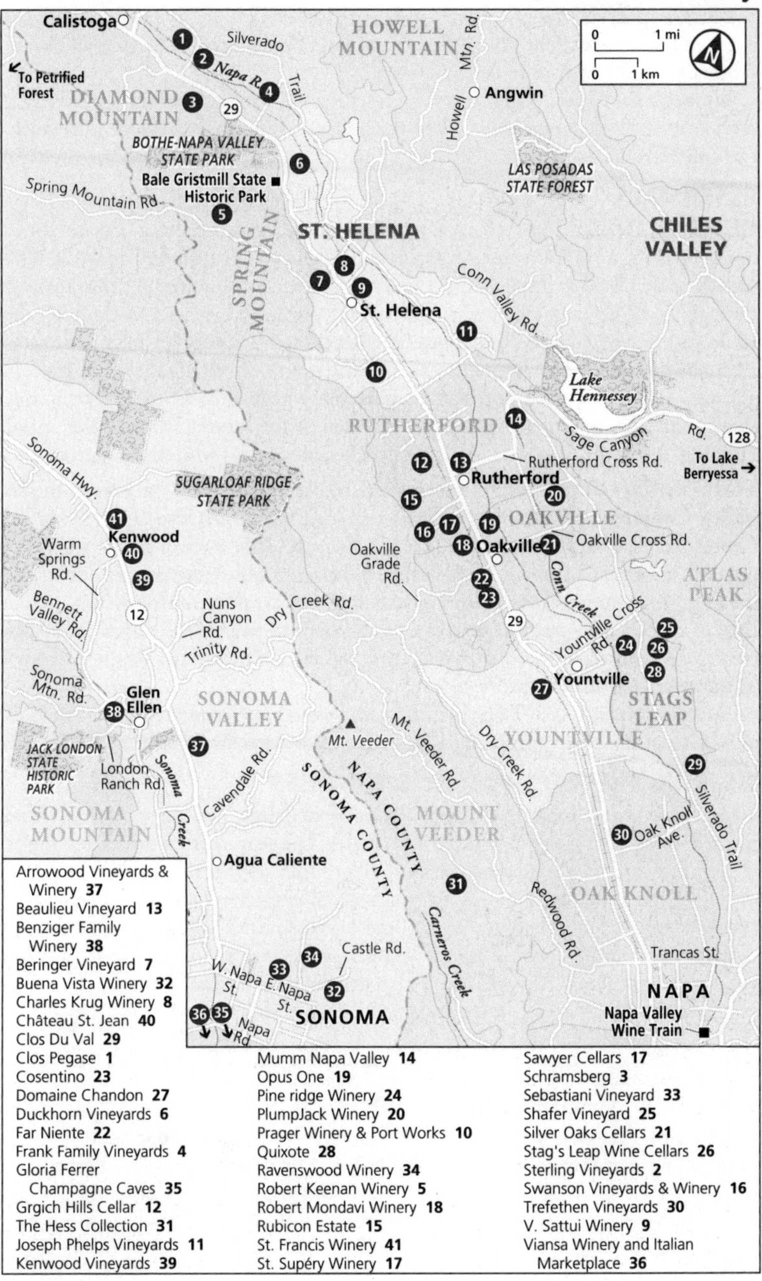

is still pretty sleepy, focusing on daytime attractions (wine, outdoor activities, and spas) and, of course, food. Nightlife is very limited, but after indulging all day, most visitors are ready to turn in early anyway.

Although the name "Napa Valley" is larger than life, the actual area is relatively condensed and only 35 miles long. When the traffic cooperates, you can venture from the town of Napa all the way to Calistoga in half an hour.

ESSENTIALS

GETTING THERE From San Francisco, cross the Golden Gate Bridge and continue north on U.S. 101. Turn east on California Highway 37; turn left onto the 12/121 turnoff and follow it through the Carneros District to Highway 29, the main road through the Wine Country. Head north on 29. Downtown Napa is a few minutes ahead, while Yountville, Oakville, Rutherford, St. Helena, and Calistoga are further along.

Highway 29 (the St. Helena Hwy.) runs the length of Napa Valley. You really can't get lost—there's just one north-south road, on which most of the wineries, hotels, shops, and restaurants are located. The other main thoroughfare, which parallels Highway 29, is the Silverado Trail. You'll find lots of great wineries here, too.

VISITOR INFORMATION Once you're in Napa Valley, you can stop at the **Napa Valley Conference & Visitors Bureau,** open daily 9am to 5pm, 1310 Napa Town Center, Napa, CA 94559 (© **707/226-7459,** ext. 106; www.napavalley.com). You can call or write in for the *Napa Valley Guidebook,* which includes information on lodging, restaurants, wineries, and other things to do, along with a winery map; the Bureau charges a $5 postage fee. If you don't want to pay for the official publication, point your browser to www.napavalley.org, the NVCVB's official site, which has lots of the same information for free.

Another good source is WineCountry.com, where you'll find tons of information on all of California's wine-producing regions as well as a weekly column written by *moi.*

TOURING THE NAPA VALLEY & WINERIES

Napa Valley claims more than 45,000 acres of vineyards, making it the most densely planted winegrowing region in the United States. The venture from one end to the other is easy; you can drive it in around half an hour (but expect it to take closer to 50 min. during high season, Apr–Nov). With more than 300 wineries tucked into the nooks and crannies surrounding Highway 29 and the Silverado Trail—almost all of which offer tastings and sales—it's worthwhile to research which wineries you'd like to visit before you hit the wine trails. If you'd like a map detailing the region's wineries, you can grab one from the visitor center or see *Frommer's Portable California Wine Country.*

Tips Reservations at Wineries

Plenty of wineries' doors are open to everyone between 10am and 4:30pm. Most wineries that require reservations for visits do so because of local permit laws. It's always best to call ahead if you have your heart set on visiting a certain winery. A few wineries limit the number of guests to create a more intimate experience. In many cases, however, they'll be just as happy to see you if you arrive unannounced.

Tips **Napa Valley Traffic**

Travel the Silverado Trail as often as possible to avoid California Highway 29's traffic. It runs parallel to and about 2 miles east of Highway 29. You get there from the city of Napa or by taking any of the "crossroads" from Highway 29. Crossroads are not well signposted, but they're clearly defined on most maps. If you take the Trail, keep us locals happy by driving *at least* the speed limit. Slow rubberneckers are no fun to follow when you're trying to get from one end of the valley to the other. Also, avoid passing through Main Street in St. Helena (on Hwy. 29) during high season. While a wintertime ride from Napa to Calistoga can take 30 minutes, in summer you can expect the trek to take closer to 50 minutes.

Conveniently, most of the large wineries—as well as most of the hotels, shops, and restaurants—are along a single road, Highway 29. It starts at the mouth of the Napa River, near the north end of San Francisco Bay, and continues north to Calistoga and the northern limits of the grape-growing region. When planning your tour, keep in mind that most wineries are closed on major holidays.

Each of the Napa Valley establishments in this chapter—every town, winery, hotel, and restaurant—is organized below from south to north, beginning in the city of Napa, and can be reached from the main thoroughfare of Highway 29.

NAPA

55 miles N of San Francisco

The city of Napa serves as the commercial center of the Wine Country and the gateway to Napa Valley—hence the high-speed freeway that whips you right past it and on to the "tourist" towns of St. Helena and Calistoga. However, if you veer off the highway, you'll be surprised to discover a small but burgeoning community of nearly 75,000 residents with the most cosmopolitan (if you can call it that) atmosphere in the county—and some of the most affordable accommodations in the valley. It is in the process of gentrification, thanks to (relatively) affordable housing and ongoing additions of new restaurants and attractions, the latest of which is Oxbow Market, a culinary destination by the developer behind San Francisco's famed Ferry Building Marketplace. Heading north on either Highway 29 or the Silverado Trail leads you to Napa's wineries and the more quintessential Wine Country atmosphere of vineyards and wide-open country views.

The Hess Collection ★★ *Finds* Tucked into the hillside of rural Mount Veeder, one of the region's sexiest wineries brings art and wine together like no other destination in the valley. Swiss art collector Donald Hess is behind the 1978 transformation of the Christian Brothers' 1903 property into a winery–art gallery exhibiting huge, colorful works by the likes of Frank Stella, Francis Bacon, and Anselm Kiefer, along with a few Andy Goldsworthy pieces. A free self-guided tour leads through the collection and offers glimpses through tiny windows into the winemaking facilities. New guided tours and food and wine pairings, which include four to six wines and seasonal noshes, are available by appointment only Thursday through Saturday and cost $35 to $50 per person. But you can drop by the tasting room anytime, fork over $10, and sample the current cabernet and chardonnay and one other featured wine; $15 to $20 gets you a reserve tasting. For bottles, current-release prices start at $22 and top off at around $115. Definitely check out their gift shop; it always has gifts that go beyond the ubiquitous ceramicware and hand-painted wine goblets.

4411 Redwood Rd., Napa. ✆ **707/255-1144.** www.hesscollection.com. Daily 10am–5pm, except some holidays; call to book a guided tour with food and wine pairing. From Hwy. 29 north, exit at Redwood Rd. west, and follow Redwood Rd. for 6½ miles.

Trefethen Vineyards Listed on the National Register of Historic Places, the vineyard's main building was built in 1886 and is Napa's last example of 19th-century wooden, gravity-flow wineries. Although Trefethen is one of the valley's oldest wineries, it didn't produce its first chardonnay until 1973—but thank goodness it did. The award-winning whites and reds are a pleasure to the palate. Tastings are $10 for four estate wines, but if you want to sample a reserve, it'll cost you $20. A 30-minute tour is available by appointment only.

1160 Oak Knoll Ave. (east of Hwy. 29), Napa. ✆ **707/255-7700.** www.trefethen.com. Daily 10am–4:30pm. From Hwy. 29 N, take a right onto Oak Knoll Ave. Tours by appointment.

Clos Du Val Outside, French and American flags mark the entrance to the ivy-covered building and well-manicured rose garden. Inside, you'll experience a friendly, small-business atmosphere along with a matter-of-fact tasting room pouring California wines made in subtler French style. Cabernet makes up 70% of the winery's production, but other varietals include chardonnay, pinot noir, and merlot. There's a $10 tasting charge (refunded with purchase) for about four wines, and a $20 reserve tasting that includes a logo glass and a library selection or two. Lovely picnic facilities and free access to the lawn game *pétanque* are available in grassy nooks along the grounds.

5330 Silverado Trail (north of Oak Knoll Ave.), Napa. ✆ **707/259-2200.** www.closduval.com. Daily 10am–5pm. Tours by appointment only.

Stag's Leap Wine Cellars Founded in 1972, Stag's Leap shocked the oenological world in 1976 when its 1973 cabernet won first place over French wines in a Parisian blind tasting. Visit the charmingly landscaped, unfussy winery and its very cramped "tasting room" where, for $15 per person, you can try a selection of four current release wines. Be prepared to fork over up to $40 for estate and library selections. A 1 ½-hour tour and tasting runs through everything from the vineyard and production facilities to the ultraswank (by appointment only) wine caves (used to store and age wine).

5766 Silverado Trail, Napa. ✆ **707/944-2020.** www.cask23.com. Daily 10am–4:30pm. Tours by appointment only. From Hwy. 29, go east on Trancas St. or Oak Knoll Ave., then north to the cellars.

Pine Ridge Winery More for the serious wine taster than the casual winery hopper, Pine Ridge welcomes guests with a pretty hillside location, less tourist traffic than most, and good wines. Outside, vineyards surround the well-landscaped property. Across the parking lot is a demonstration vineyard, which is somewhat educational if you know something about grape growing and even more helpful if you take their $25 tour (by appointment), which also covers the cellar and barrel tastings. Otherwise, tastings, which are held inside a modest room, start at $15 for current releases. Their appointment-only cab and reserve barrel-to-bottle tastings are $20 and $35, respectively, and are held at 11am, 1pm, and 3pm. They also offer a $45 Sunday cooking seminar at 11am during which you'll learn about food and wine pairings; in the winter it's held indoors, but during great summer weather it's done alfresco. If you're

Tips Paying to Taste

It used to be unusual to have to pay for wine tasting, and when the tides first started to change, I wasn't really for it. But over the past decade, sipping through the region has become such a pastime that in the more popular—and cheap or free—tasting spots you'll often find yourself competing for room at the bar, never mind a refill or a little wine chatter with your host. As a result, I've changed my view on paying a premium to taste. With the flash of a 10- or 20-spot per person you not only avoid crowding in with the hundreds of tipsy souls who come merely for the fun and the buzz, but you also usually get a more intimate experience, complete with attention from staff and usually far more exclusive (and sometimes even seated) surroundings.

visiting in summer and want to know about food and wine pairing, call to learn whether they're holding their tasty weekend seminars.

5901 Silverado Trail, Napa. ✆ **800/575-9777** or 707/253-7500. www.pineridgewinery.com. Daily 10:30am–4:30pm. Tours by appointment at 10am, noon, and 2pm.

Quixote ★★ *Finds* Due to zoning laws, this spectacular and truly one-of-a-kind Stags' Leap District winery was closed to the public until 2007. Now it welcomes up to eight guests per day, all of whom are likely to find themselves as awestruck by the winery as they are by the powerful petite syrahs and cabernet sauvignons. The hidden hillside property owned by longtime industry power player Carl Doumani is the only U.S. structure designed by late great European artist Friedensreich Hundertwasser. Whimsical and captivating even to those know nothing about architecture, it's a structural fantasy world with undulating lines, a gilded onion dome, and a fearless use of color. During the $25-per-person reservation-only sit-down tasting visitors can fill their agape mouths with tastes of the winery's current releases.

6126 Silverado Trail, Napa. ✆ **707/944-2659.** www.quixotewinery.com. Tastings by appointment only.

Shafer Vineyards ★★ *Finds* For an intimate, off-the-beaten-track wine experience, make an appointment to tour and taste at this newly renovated Stags' Leap destination. Unlike many Napa wineries, this one is family owned—by John and Doug Shafer. After 23 years in publishing, John bought 209 Wine Country hillside acres and planted vines on 50 of them. Today, he and his son Doug, joined by winemaker Elias Fernandez, use sustainable farming and solar energy to make exceptional chardonnay, merlot, cabernet sauvignon, and syrah. Though they produce only 34,000 cases per year, their wines are well known and highly regarded. (So much so, in fact, that anyone who gets their hands on a bottle of their Hillside Select can immediately resell it for more than $100 over the suggested retail price.) But more importantly, they share it and their winemaking philosophy with you during a truly enjoyable and relaxed $25-per-person 1½-hour tour and tasting, which includes sipping, chatting, and perhaps patting their yellow lab, Tucker. Most wines go for $45 to $65, but their Hillside Select cabernet will cost you $200.

6154 Silverado Trail, Napa. ✆ **707/944-2877.** www.shafervineyards.com. By appointment only Mon–Fri 10am and 2pm; closed weekends and holidays.

YOUNTVILLE

70 miles N of San Francisco

Yountville (pop. 2,916) was founded by the first white American to settle in the valley, George Calvert Yount. While it lacks the small-town charm of neighboring St. Helena and Calistoga—primarily because its main street, though filling up with hotels, restaurants, and shops, doesn't feel like a center—it's still a great starting point for valley exploration. It's home to a handful of excellent wineries and inns and a small stretch of fab restaurants, including the world-renowned French Laundry.

Domaine Chandon ★★ *Finds* Founded in 1973 by French champagne house Moët et Chandon, the valley's most renowned sparkling winemaker rises to the grand occasion with truly elegant grounds and atmosphere. Manicured gardens showcase locally made sculpture, and guests linger—their glasses fizzing with bubbly by a table loaded with snacks—in the festive tasting Salon or under its patio's umbrella shade. In the restaurant, diners indulge in a somewhat formal French-inspired meal (a more casual menu is available at lunchtime). If you can pull yourself away from the Salon's bubbly (sold in tastings for $9–$14), the comprehensive tour of the facilities is interesting, very informative, and friendly. There's also a $30 Epicurean Experience Tour that includes stops along the way to taste wine paired with foods prepared by Chandon's chef. The Shop at Domaine Chandon carries some varietal wines not sold elsewhere, along with liqueurs, spa items, and requisite logo mementos. ***Note:*** The restaurant, which is closed on Tuesday and Wednesday, usually requires reservations.

1 California Dr. (at Hwy. 29), Yountville. ✆ **707/944-2280.** www.chandon.com. Daily 10am–6pm; hours vary by season, so call to confirm. Call or check website for free tour schedules and seasonal hours.

Cosentino Known for its friendly, laid-back atmosphere and vast selection of wines, Cosentino's tasting room is a great stop for anyone interested in covering a lot of wine-tasting ground under one roof. Pay $10 ($15 for reserve wines) and you can taste an array of wines from their portfolio, which includes the brands Cosentino, CE2V, Legends, Blockheadia, and Crystal Valley Cellars, and nearly 40 different wines on sale ($12–$125). The long copper-top bar offers a lot of entertainment value. Join the wine club for free tastings and 25% off purchases.

7415 St. Helena Hwy. (Hwy. 29), Yountville. ✆ **707/944-1220.** www.cosentinowinery.com. Daily 10am–5pm.

OAKVILLE

68 miles N of San Francisco

Driving farther north on Highway 29 brings you to Oakville, most easily recognized by Oakville Cross Road.

Far Niente ★ This storybook stone winery is a serious treat for wine, garden, and classic car lovers. Founded in 1885, it was abandoned for 60 years around prohibition, purchased in 1979 by Gil Nickel (of nearby Nickel & Nickel winery), and opened to the public for the first time in spring 2004. The tour includes a walk around the beautiful historic stone property, caves, private car collection (truly stunning!), and a huge azalea garden. It finishes with a sampling of five wines (including a delicious chardonnay, cabernet sauvignon, and "Dolce"—their spectacular semillon and sauvignon blanc dessert blend that's sure to make converts of even sweet-wine naysayers). Tastings are $50 and by appointment only. Wines aren't cheap either—from around $52 for the chardonnay to $115 for their estate cabernet sauvignon.

1350 Acacia Dr., Oakville. ✆ **800-FN-DOLCE** or 707/944-2861. www.farniente.com. Tours and tastings by appointment only daily 10am–4pm.

Silver Oak Cellars Colorado oilman Ray Duncan and former Christian Brothers monk Justin Meyer formed a partnership and a mission to create the finest cabernet sauvignon in the world. The answer was this winery, which produces one of the valley's cabernet kings. Unfortunately, a fire recently destroyed the original Mediterranean-style tasting room. But during rebuilding you can toast with their wines in temporary facilities. Despite the setback, the winery still produces roughly 30,000 cases of Napa Valley Cabernet Sauvignon annually (an additional 70,000 cases are produced annually at their Alexander Valley winery in Geyserville). Tastings, which include a keepsake bordeaux glass, are $10. No picnic facilities are available.

915 Oakville Cross Rd. (at Money Rd.), Oakville. ✆ **800/273-8809** or 707/944-8808. www.silveroak.com. Tasting room Mon–Sat 9am–4pm.

PlumpJack Winery If most wineries are like a Brooks Brothers suit, PlumpJack stands out as the Todd Oldham of wine tasting: chic, colorful, a little wild, and popular with a young, hip crowd as well as a growing number of aficionados. Like the franchise's PlumpJack San Francisco restaurants and wine shop, and its Lake Tahoe resort, this playfully medieval winery is a welcome diversion from the same old same old. With Getty bucks behind what was once Villa Mt. Eden winery, the budget covers far more than just atmosphere: There's some serious winemaking going on here, too. For $5 you can sample current releases. Alas, there are no tours or picnic spots.

620 Oakville Cross Rd. (just west of the Silverado Trail), Oakville. ✆ **707/945-1220.** www.plumpjack.com. Daily 10am–4pm.

Robert Mondavi Winery ★ *Finds* At mission-style Mondavi, computers control almost every variable in the winemaking process—it's fascinating to watch, especially since Mondavi gives the most comprehensive tours in the valley. Basic jaunts, which cost $25 and last about an hour and 15 minutes, take you through the vineyards—complete with examples of varietals—and through their newest winemaking facilities. Ask the guides anything; they know a heck of a lot. After the tour, you taste the results of all this attention to detail in selected current wines. If you're really into learning more about wine, ask about their myriad in-depth tours, such as the $60 "essence tasting," which explores the flavor profiles of wine by sniff-comparing varietals alongside the scents of fresh fruits, spices, and nuts, or their $110 "Celebrating California Wine and Food" tour, which includes a presentation on the history of wine, a tour of the winery, and a three-course luncheon with wine pairing. In summer, the winery also schedules some great outdoor concerts; previous performers included Buena Vista Social Club, Aimee Mann, and Chaka Kahn. Call about upcoming events.

7801 St. Helena Hwy. (Hwy. 29), Oakville. ✆ **888/766-6328,** ext. 2000, or 707/226-1395. www.robertmondaviwinery.com. Daily 10am–5pm. Reservations recommended for guided tour; book 1 week ahead, especially for weekend tours.

Opus One A visit to Opus One is a serious and stately affair that was developed in a partnership between Robert Mondavi and Baron Philippe de Rothschild. Today, the state-of-the-art collaboration continues between Baron Philippe de Rothschild and Constellation Brands, which bought out much of Mondavi's winery empire. Architecture buffs in particular will appreciate the tour, which takes in both the impressive

Greco-Roman-meets-20th-century building and the no-holds-barred ultra-high-tech production and aging facilities.

This entire facility caters to one ultrapremium wine, which is offered here for a whopping $25 per 4-ounce taste (and a painful $165 per bottle). But wine lovers should happily fork over the cash: It's a memorable red. Grab your glass and head to the redwood rooftop deck to enjoy the view.

7900 St. Helena Hwy. (Hwy. 29), Oakville. ✆ **707/944-9442.** www.opusonewinery.com. Daily 10am–4pm. Tours daily by appointment only; in high season, book a month in advance.

RUTHERFORD

3 miles N of Oakville

If you so much as blink after Oakville, you're likely to overlook Rutherford, the next small town that borders on St. Helena. Each town in Napa Valley has its share of spectacular wineries, but you won't see most of them while driving along Highway 29.

Swanson Vineyards & Winery ★ *Finds* The valley's most posh and unique wine tasting is yours with a reservation and a $25 to $55 fee at Swanson. Here the shtick is to treat a tasting more like a private party, which they call a "SA-lon." You and up to seven other guests sit at a centerpiece round table in a vibrant coral parlor adorned with huge paintings, seashells, and a fireplace, and take in the uncommonly refined yet whimsical atmosphere. The table's set more for a dinner party than for a tasting, with Reidel stemware, caviar on potato crisps, slivers of a fine cheese or two, crackers, and one Alexis ganache-filled bonbon, the likes of which you will be glad to know can be purchased on the premises. Over the course of the hour-or-more snack-and-sip event, a winery host will pour four to seven wines, perhaps a bright pinot grigio, merlot, and hearty Alexis, their signature cab-syrah blend, and you're bound to befriend those at the table with you. Definitely a must-do for those who don't mind spending the money.

1271 Manley Lane, Rutherford. ✆ **707/967-3500.** www.swansonvineyards.com. Tasting appointments available Wed–Sun 11am, 1:30pm, and 4pm.

Sawyer Cellars *Finds* The most attractive thing about Sawyer, aside from its clean and tasty wines, is its dedication to extremely high quality while it maintains a humble, accommodating attitude. Step into the simple restored 1920s barn to see what I mean. Whatever you ask, the tasting-room host will answer. Whatever your request, they do their best to accommodate it. Want to picnic on the back patio overlooking the vineyards? Be their guest. Like to participate in a crush? Come on over and get your hands dirty. Fancy reserving their charming wine library for a private luncheon? Pay a minimal fee and make yourself at home. Here you can tour the property on a little tram or learn more about winemaker Brad Warner, who spent 30 years at Mondavi before embarking on this exclusive endeavor. Plunk down $7.50 to taste delicious estate-made wines: sauvignon blanc, merlot, cabernet sauvignon, and Meritage ($18–$46 for current releases), which some argue are worth twice the price. With a total production of only 4,200 cases and a friendly attitude, this winery is a rare treat.

8350 St. Helena Hwy. (Hwy. 29), Rutherford. ✆ **707/963-1980.** www.sawyercellars.com. Tasting by appointment. Tours by appointment. 10am–5pm daily.

St. Supéry Winery *Kids* The outside looks like a modern corporate office building, but inside you'll find a functional, welcoming winery that encourages first-time tasters to learn more about oenology. On the self-guided tour, you can wander through the demonstration vineyard, where you'll learn about growing techniques. Inside, kids gravitate toward coloring books and "SmellaVision," an interactive display that teaches one how to identify different wine ingredients. Adjoining it is the Atkinson House, which chronicles more than 100 years of winemaking history during public tours at 1 and 3pm. For $10, you'll get lifetime tasting privileges and a tour, which includes samples of four wines, which hopefully includes their excellent and very well-priced sauvignon blanc; there's a limited edition reserve tasting for $15. Even the prices make visitors feel at home: Bottles start at $19, although the tag on their high-end bordeaux red blend is $60.

8440 St. Helena Hwy. (Hwy. 29), Rutherford. ✆ **800/942-0809** or 707/963-4507. www.stsupery.com. Daily 10am–5pm (until 5:30pm during summer). $10 tour at 1 and 3pm daily.

Rubicon Estate ★ Founded in 1880, Francis Ford Coppola's historic Inglenook Vineyards, also previously known as Niebaum-Coppola, is now named after the winery's most prestigious wine. You'll have to fork over $25 to visit the estate, but that includes a tasting of five wines, tour of the gorgeous chateau and its Centennial museum and the winery, as well as valet parking. Outside the spectacular 1880s ivy-draped stone winery and grounds are historic grandeur. Inside is a series of intimate tasting rooms and a retail center. Wine, food, and wine-related gift items dominate the tasting area, where wines such as the Estate's flagship wine, Rubicon (a Bordeaux blend), cabernet franc, merlot, and zinfandel made from organically grown grapes are sampled. Bottles range from around $19 to more than $100. Along with the basic tour, you can pay extra for more exclusive, specialized tours as well.

1991 St. Helena Hwy. (Hwy. 29), Rutherford. ✆ **800/RUBICON** or 707/968-1100. www.rubiconestate.com. 10am–5pm daily. Tours daily.

Beaulieu Vineyard Bordeaux native Georges de Latour founded the third-oldest continuously operating winery in Napa Valley in 1900. With the help of legendary oenologist André Tchelistcheff, he produced world-class, award-winning wines that have been served at the White House since Franklin D. Roosevelt was at the helm and is also the official wine of the Academy of Television Arts and Sciences and the Prime-time Emmys. The brick-and-redwood tasting room isn't much to look at, but with Beaulieu's (*Bowl*-you) reputation, it has no need to visually impress. Appellation tastings cost $10, and a variety of bottles sell for under $20. The recently remodeled Reserve Tasting Room offers a "flight" of five reserve wines to taste for $25, but if you want to take a bottle to go, it may cost upwards of $100.

1960 St. Helena Hwy. (Hwy. 29), Rutherford. ✆ **707/967-5233.** www.bvwines.com. Daily 10am–5pm.

Grgich Hills Cellar Croatian émigré Miljenko (Mike) Grgich (*Grr*-gitch) made his presence known to the world when his 1973 Chateau Montelena chardonnay bested the top French white burgundies at the famous 1976 Paris tasting. Since then, the master vintner teamed up with Austin Hills (of the Hills Brothers coffee fortune) and started this extremely successful and respected winery featuring estate grown wines from organically and biodynamically farmed vineyards.

The ivy-covered stucco building isn't much to behold, and the tasting room is even less appealing, but people don't come here for the scenery: As you might expect, Grgich's chardonnays are legendary—and priced accordingly. The smart buys are the outstanding zinfandel and cabernet sauvignon, which cost around $30 and $58, respectively. The winery also produces a fantastic fumé blanc for around $24 a bottle. Before you leave, be sure to poke your head into the barrel-aging room and inhale the divine aroma. Tastings cost $10 (which includes the glass). No picnic facilities are available.

1829 St. Helena Hwy. (Hwy. 29), north of Rutherford Cross Rd., Rutherford. ✆ **707/963-2784.** www.grgich.com. Daily 9:30am–4:30pm. $15 tours by appointment only.

Mumm Napa Valley At first glance, Mumm, housed in a big redwood barn, looks almost humble. Once you're through the front door, however, you'll know that they mean business—big business. Just beyond the extensive gift shop (filled with all sorts of namesake mementos) is the tasting room, where you can purchase sparkling wine flights ($15–$50), or the bottle ($16–$70), and appreciate breathtaking vineyard and mountain views on the open patio. You can also take a 45-minute free educational tour (with your dog—this joint's pooch friendly!) and stroll the impressive fine art photography gallery, which features a permanent Ansel Adams collection and ever-changing photography exhibits. Sorry, there's no food or picnicking here.

8445 Silverado Trail (just south of Rutherford Cross Rd.), Rutherford. ✆ **800/686-6272** or 707/967-7730. www.mummnapa.com. Daily 10am–5pm. Tours offered every hr. daily 10am–3pm.

ST. HELENA

73 miles N of San Francisco

Located 17 miles north of Napa on Highway 29, this former Seventh-day Adventist village maintains a pseudo–Old West feel while catering to upscale shoppers with deep pockets—hence Vanderbilt and Company, purveyor of fine housewares, at 1429 Main St. (✆ **707/963-1010;** www.vanderbiltandcompany.com). St. Helena is a quiet, attractive little town, where you'll find a slew of beautiful old homes and first-rate restaurants and accommodations.

V. Sattui Winery ★ *Kids* *Finds* So what if it's touristy and crowded? This enormous winery is also a fun picnic-party stop thanks to a huge gourmet deli and grassy expanse. It's especially great for families since you can fill up on wine, pâté, and cheese samples without ever reaching for your pocketbook, while the kids romp around the grounds. The gourmet store stocks more than 200 cheeses, sandwich meats, pâtés, breads, exotic salads, and desserts such as white-chocolate cheesecake. (It would be an easier place to graze were it not for the continuous mob scene at the counter.) Meanwhile, the extensive wine offerings flow at the long wine bar in the back. Wines aren't distributed or particularly noteworthy, if you ask me. But if you taste something you simply must have, buy it. (A case purchase will get you membership into their private cellar and its less crowded, private tasting room.) Wine prices start at around $12, with many in the $18 neighborhood; reserves top out at around $65. ***Note:*** To use the picnic area, you must buy food and wine here. On summer weekends, check out the barbecues for $6 to $10.

1111 White Lane (at Hwy. 29), St. Helena. ✆ **707/963-7774.** www.vsattui.com. Daily 9am–6pm; winter daily 9am–5pm.

Prager Winery & Port Works *Finds* If you want an off-the-beaten-track experience, Prager's can't be beat. Turn the corner from Sutter Home winery and roll into the small gravel parking lot; you're on the right track, but when you pull open the creaky old wooden door to this shack of a wine-tasting room, you'll begin to wonder. Don't turn back! Pass the oak barrels, and you'll quickly come upon the clapboard tasting room, made homey with a big Oriental rug, some of the most interesting "wallpaper" you've ever seen, and a Prager family host. Fork over $10 (includes a complimentary glass), and they'll pour you four samples of their wines and ports (which cost $33–$80 per bottle). Also available is "Prager Chocolate Drizzle," a chocolate liqueur sauce that tops ice creams and other desserts. In general the experience is more of a novelty than an incredible wine discovery, but sometimes that's just what the afternoon calls for.

1281 Lewelling Lane (just west of Hwy. 29, behind Sutter Home), St. Helena. ✆ **800/969-PORT** or 707/963-7678. www.pragerport.com. Daily 10:30am–4:30pm.

Joseph Phelps Vineyards ★ Visitors interested in intimate, comprehensive tours and a knockout tasting should schedule a tour at this winery. A quick turn off the Silverado Trail in Spring Valley (there's no sign—watch for Taplin Rd., or you'll blast right by), Joseph Phelps was founded in 1973 and is a major player in both the regional and the worldwide wine market. Phelps himself accomplished a long list of valley firsts, including launching the syrah varietal in the valley and extending the 1970s Berkeley food revolution (led by Alice Waters) to the Wine Country by founding the Oakville Grocery Co. (p. 304).

A favorite stop for serious wine lovers, this modern, state-of-the-art winery and big-city vibe are proof that Phelps's annual 80,000 cases prove fruitful in more ways than one. When you pass the wisteria-covered trellis to the entrance of the redwood building, you'll encounter an air of seriousness that hangs heavier than harvest grapes. Fortunately, the mood lightens during the informal tasting for $20 or any of the "seminars" like the Blending Seminar, Le Nez Seminar, or the Wine Appreciation Seminar (all $30) that include tastings of five or six wines, mostly reds with a few whites. There's also a short film on the history of the winery. Seminars are 1½ hours on weekdays and 1 hour on weekends. Unfortunately, some wines are so popular that they sell out quickly; come late in the season, and you may not be able to taste or buy them. The three excellently located picnic tables, on the terrace overlooking the valley, are available on a first-come, first-served basis, with preference given to Phelps wine club members (join and get wine shipped a certain number of times per year) who are also able to make a reservation.

200 Taplin Rd. (off the Silverado Trail), P.O. Box 1031, St. Helena. ✆ **800/707-5789** or 707/963-4831. www.jpvwines.com. Mon–Fri 10am–5pm; Sat and Sun 10am–4pm. $30 seminars and tastings by appointment only; weekends at 10am, 11:30am, 1pm, and 2:30pm; weekdays at 11am and 2:30pm. $10 per person for 1-oz. pour of Insignia.

Robert Keenan Winery *Finds* It's a winding, uphill drive to reach secluded Robert Keenan, but this far off the tourist track you're guaranteed more elbowroom at the tasting bar and a quieter, less commercial experience. When you drive in, you'll pass a few modest homes and wonder whether one of the buildings is the family winery. It's not. Keep driving (slowly—kids and dogs at play) until you get to the main building and its redwood tasting room.

The 10,000 cases produced here per year are the result of yet another fast-paced professional who left his business behind and headed for the hills. In this case, it's native San Franciscan Robert Keenan, who ran his own insurance agency for 20 years. When his company merged with another firm and was bought out in 1981, he had already purchased his "retirement property," the winery's 176 acres (48 of which are now planted with grapes), and he soon turned his fascination with winemaking into a second career. The renovated stone building has a much older history, dating back to the old Conradi Winery, which was founded in 1890.

Today, Robert Keenan Winery is known for its big, full-bodied reds, such as the Mountain cab and merlot. Chardonnay, cabernet franc, and zin sold exclusively at the winery range from $25 to $42 per bottle. Older vintages, which you won't find elsewhere, are for sale here as well. Take the tour to learn about the vineyards, production facilities, and winemaking in general. Those looking for a pastoral picnic spot should consider spreading their blankets out here. The three tables, situated right outside the winery and surrounded by vineyards, offer stunning views.

3660 Spring Mountain Rd. (off Hwy. 29), St. Helena. © **707/963-9177.** www.keenanwinery.com. Weekends 11am–4pm. Tastings by appointment only, call or email rkw@keenanwinery.com for an appointment.

Beringer Vineyards ★ *Finds* You won't find a personal experience at this tourist-heavy stop. But you will get a taste of history within the regal 1876 estate founded by brothers Jacob and Frederick and hand-dug tunnels in the hillside. The oldest continuously operating winery in Napa Valley, Beringer managed to stay open even during Prohibition by cleverly making sacramental wines. White zinfandel is the winery's most popular seller, but plenty of other varietals are available to enjoy. Tastings of current vintages for $5 are conducted in new facilities, where there's also a large selection of bottles for less than $20. Reserve wines are available for tasting in the remarkable Rhine House for $25 (applied toward purchase), and tours range from the $10 standard or $20 historical to the $35 1½-hour vintage legacy tour. There are several other tours in the $15 to $30 range; check the website for details.

2000 Main St. (Hwy. 29), St. Helena. © **707/963-7115.** www.beringer.com. May 30–Oct 23 daily 10am–6pm; Oct 24–May 29 10am–5pm.

Charles Krug Winery Founded in 1861, Krug was the first winery built in the valley. The family of Peter Mondavi, Sr. (yes, Robert is his brother), owns it today (and at 92 he still comes to work 5 days a week—the story being that he drinks a glass of red wine a day, of course). It's worth paying your respects here by dropping $10 and $15 on a weekend to sip current releases and reserves, respectively, and $12 on weekdays for a combo. On the grounds are picnic facilities with umbrella-shaded tables overlooking vineyards or the wine cellar.

2800 Main St. (St. Helena Hwy.; just north of the tunnel of trees at the northern end of St. Helena), St. Helena. © **707/963-5057.** www.charleskrug.com. Daily 10:30am–5pm. No tours available.

CALISTOGA

81 miles N of San Francisco

Calistoga, the last tourist town in Napa Valley, got its name from Sam Brannan, entrepreneur extraordinaire and California's first millionaire. After making a bundle supplying miners during the gold rush, he went on to take advantage of the natural geothermal springs at the north end of the valley by building a hotel and spa here in 1859. Flubbing up a speech, in which he compared this natural California wonder to New York State's Saratoga Springs resort town, he serendipitously coined the name "Calistoga," and it stuck. Today, this small, simple resort town, with 5,225 residents and an old-time main street (no building along the 6-block stretch is more than two stories high), is popular with city folk who come here to unwind. Calistoga is a great place to relax and indulge in mineral waters, mud baths, Jacuzzis, massages and, of course, wine. The vibe is more casual—and a little groovier—than you find in neighboring towns to the south.

Tips The Ins & Outs of Shipping Wine Home

Perhaps the only things more complex than that $800 case of cabernet you just purchased are the rules and regulations about shipping it home. Because of absurd and forever fluctuating laws—which supposedly protect the business of the country's wine distributors—wine shipping is limited by regulations that vary in each of the 50 states. Shipping rules also vary from winery to winery.

Every single time I write this book, the rules change. This go-round the government is said to be phasing out reciprocity laws and requiring that each state be approved to ship or receive wine. Individual wineries must buy permits for each state they want to ship to, making it difficult for smaller wineries to ship to many states (so most will probably opt only for the states that brandish the most visitors or mail-order demands). There are currently 27 states with permits and 7 with the old reciprocal agreement (that will probably change soon, too), and as this book goes to press, several more are pending. Technically, only wineries with permits are allowed to ship wine; shipping stores are not supposed to ship any wine or liquor. That said, they do it anyway, so don't fret if you want to send wine.

If you do get stuck shipping illegally (not that we're recommending you do that, but believe me, it's done all the time and most shipping companies are well aware of it), you might want to package your wine in an unassuming box and head to a post office, UPS, or other shipping company outside the Wine Country area. It's less obvious that you're shipping wine from Vallejo or San Francisco than from Napa Valley.

However, you can try these companies. They are likely to help you out.

Napa Valley Shipping Companies

The UPS Store, at 3212 Jefferson St. in the Grape Yard Shopping Center (✆ **707/259-1398**), claims to pack and ship anything anywhere. Rates for a case of wine were quoted at approximately $25 for ground shipping to Los Angeles and $60 to New York.

St. Helena Mailing Center, 1241 Adams St., at Highway 29, St. Helena (✆ **707/963-2686**), says they will pack and ship to certain states within the U.S. Rates for pre-wrapped shipments are around $30 per case for ground delivery to Los Angeles.

Sonoma Valley Shipping Companies

The UPS Store, 19229 Sonoma Hwy., in Maxwell Village, Sonoma (✆ **707/935-3438**), has a lot of experience with shipping wine. It claims it will ship your wine to any state. Prices vary from $30 to Los Angeles to as much as $79 to the East Coast and $150 to Hawaii and Alaska.

The **Wine Exchange of Sonoma,** 452 First St. E., between East Napa and East Spain streets, Sonoma (✆ **707/938-1794**), will ship your wine, but there's a catch: You must buy an equal amount of any wine at the store (which they assured me would be in stock, and probably at a better rate). Shipping rates range from $20 to Los Angeles to $72 to the East Coast.

Frank Family Vineyards ★ *Finds* "Wine dudes" Dennis, Tim, Jeff, Rick, and Pat will do practically anything to maintain their rightfully self-proclaimed reputation as the "friendliest winery in the valley." In recent years the name may have changed from Kornell Champagne Cellars to Frank-Rombauer to Frank Family, but the vibe has remained constant; it's all about down-home, friendly fun. No muss, no fuss, no intimidation factor. At Frank Family, you're part of their family—no joke. They'll greet you like a long-lost relative and serve you all the bubbly you want (three to four varieties: blanc de blanc, blanc de noir, reserve, and rouge, at $30–$55 a bottle). Still-wine lovers can slip into the equally casual back room to sample chardonnay and a very well-received cabernet sauvignon. Behind the tasting room is a choice picnic area, situated under the oaks and overlooking the vineyards.

1091 Larkmead Lane (just off the Silverado Trail), Calistoga. ✆ **707/942-0859.** Daily 10am–5pm. No tours; tastings free.

Schramsberg ★★ *Finds* This 217-acre sparkling wine estate, a landmark once frequented by Robert Louis Stevenson and the second-oldest property in Napa Valley, has a wonderful old-world feel and is one of the valley's all-time best places to explore. Schramsberg is the label that presidents serve when toasting dignitaries from around the globe, and there's plenty of historical memorabilia in the front room to prove it. But the real mystique begins when you enter the sparkling wine caves, which wind 2 miles (reputedly the longest in North America) and were partly hand-carved by Chinese laborers in the 1800s. The caves have an authentic Tom Sawyer ambience, complete with dangling cobwebs and seemingly endless passageways; you can't help but feel you're on an adventure. The comprehensive, unintimidating tour ends in a charming, cozy tasting room, where you'll sample four surprisingly varied selections of their high-end bubbly. Tastings are a bit dear ($25 per person), but it's money well spent. Note that tastings are offered only to those who take the free tour, and you must make reservations in advance.

1400 Schramsberg Rd. (off Hwy. 29), Calistoga. ✆ **707/942-2414.** www.schramsberg.com. Daily 10am–4pm. Tours and tastings by appointment only.

Sterling Vineyards ★ *Kids* *Finds* No, you don't need climbing shoes to reach this dazzling white Mediterranean-style winery, perched 300 feet up on a rocky knoll. Just fork over $15 ($20 weekends and holidays and $10 for kids at all times—including juice, crayons, and wine country scene coloring paper) and take the aerial tram, which offers stunning bucolic views along the way. Once you're back on land, follow the self-guided tour (one of the most comprehensive in the Wine Country) of the winemaking process. Wine tastings of five varietals in the panoramic tasting room are included in the tram fare, but more sophisticated sips—limited releases or reserve flights—will set you back anywhere from $3 to $15, respectively. They also offer a guided reserve tasting and tour, limited to 10 people at 11am daily; it's $45 and reservations are highly recommended. Expect to pay anywhere from $14 to $75 for a souvenir bottle.

1111 Dunaweal Lane (off Hwy. 29, just south of downtown Calistoga), Calistoga. ✆ **707/942-3344.** www.sterlingvineyards.com. Daily 10:30am–4:30pm.

Clos Pegase ★ *Finds* Renowned architect Michael Graves designed this incredible oasis, which integrates art, 20,000 square feet of aging caves, and a luxurious hilltop private home. Viewing the art is as much the point as tasting the wines—which, by the way, don't come cheap: Prices range from $15 for the 2000 Vin Gris merlot to as much as $75 for the 2001 Hommage Artist Series Reserve, an extremely limited edition of the winery's finest lots of cabernet sauvignon. Current release tastings cost $10. The grounds at Clos Pegase (Cloh Pey-*goss*) feature an impressive sculpture garden as well as scenic picnic spots.

1060 Dunaweal Lane (off Hwy. 29 or the Silverado Trail), Calistoga. ✆ **707/942-4981.** www.clospegase.com. Daily 10:30am–5pm. Tours daily at 11am and 2pm.

Duckhorn Vineyards With quintessential pastoral surroundings and a unique wine-tasting program, Duckhorn Vineyards has much to offer for visitors interested in spending time to relax and taste. The airy Victorian farmhouse seems very welcoming, not only because you can stand on the veranda and look out on the surrounding meadow, but because the interior affords equally bucolic views. If you're going to taste wine in their surprisingly modern tasting room, complete with cafe tables and a centerpiece bar, you'll pay $10 for a tasting of three wines, $20 for a flight of five limited-release wines, or $30 for a semi-private estate-wine tasting, the latter of which you can book in advance. The fee may sound steep, but this is not your run-of-the-mill drink and dash. You'll get plenty of attention and information on their current releases of sauvignon blanc, merlot, and cabernet sauvignon.

1000 Lodi Lane (at the Silverado Trail), St. Helena. ✆ **707/963-7108.** www.duckhorn.com. Daily 10am–4pm. By appointment only.

BEYOND THE WINERIES: WHAT TO SEE & DO IN NAPA VALLEY

NAPA/ST. HELENA

If you have plenty of time and a penchant for Victorian architecture, seek out the **Napa Valley Conference & Visitors Bureau,** 1310 Napa Town Center, off First Street (✆ **707/226-7459,** ext. 106; www.napavalley.com), which offers self-guided walking tours of the town's historic buildings.

A MUSEUM **COPIA: The American Center for Wine, Food & the Arts,** at 500 First St. (✆ **707/259-1600;** www.copia.org), opened at the end of 2001 with a mission to explore and celebrate how wine and food influence our culture. This $50-million multifaceted facility, which was spearheaded by Robert Mondavi, tackles the topic in a myriad of ways, including visual arts à la rotating exhibitions, vast organic vegetable and demonstration gardens, fun culinary programs, basic and advanced wine classes, concerts, films, and opportunities to dine and drink on the premises. There's not a ton to look at, but youngsters will get a kick out of the Kids' Garden with rabbits and chickens, while connoisseurs might pay extra to slip into seasonal cooking demos by famous chefs. Drop by the cafe for gourmet picnic items or neighboring gift

---

Tips **Sip Tip**

You can cheaply sip your way through downtown Napa without ever getting behind the wheel with the new "Taste Napa Downtown" wine card. For a mere $20, you get 10-cent tasting privileges at 10 local winecentric watering holes and tasting rooms, all of which are within walking distance of each other. Plus you'll get 10% discounts at tasting rooms and half-off admission to Copia. Available at the **Napa Valley Conference & Visitors Bureau** (1310 Napa Town Center, off First St.; ✆ **707/226-7459,** ext. 106) and Copia (see above). Learn more at **www.napadowntown.com.**

Finds Enjoying Art & Nature

Anyone with an appreciation for art absolutely must visit **di Rosa Preserve.** Rene and Veronica di Rosa collected contemporary American art for more than 40 years and then converted their 215 acres of prime property into a monument to Northern California's regional art and nature. Veronica has passed on, but Rene still carries the torch through his world-renowned collection featuring 2,000 works in all media, by more than 900 Greater Bay Area artists. You're not likely to meet him, as the day-to-day operations are now run by a nonprofit staff, but you will be privy to his treasures, which are on display practically everywhere—along the shores of the property's 35-acre lake and in each nook and cranny of their 125-year-old winery-turned-residence, adjoining building, two newer galleries, and gardens. With hundreds of surrounding acres of rolling hills (protected under the Napa County Land Trust), this place is a must-see for both art and nature lovers. It's at 5200 Carneros Hwy. (Hwy. 121/12); look for the gate. Drop-ins are welcome at the Gatehouse Gallery Tuesday through Friday from 9:30am to 3pm; $3 suggested donation. One- and two-hour, docent-led tours are offered Tuesday through Saturday; check www.dirosapreserve.org for times.

Reservations recommended. Call ✆ **707/226-5991** to make reservations.

shop for accessories and food-related finds, or have a full-on feast at the adjoining restaurant Julia's Kitchen. Also, drop by Tuesday or Saturday mornings April through November for the outdoor farmers' market and check out their Thursday Outdoor Summer Concert Series for great affordable alfresco entertainment.

Copia admission is $5 for adults, $4 for seniors and students, and free for children 12 and under. Wednesday admissions are half-price for Napa and Sonoma residents. The center is open Wednesday through Monday from 10am to 5pm. The restaurant stays open until 9:30pm Thursday through Sunday.

Marketplace Across the street from Copia is the new Oxbow Market, which is under construction as this book went to press and is slated to debut in fall 2007. A smaller version of San Francisco's Ferry Building Marketplace, the co-op will feature a cornucopia of tasty tenants, including a new restaurant by the owners of Napa's Bistro Don Giovanni restaurant, a number of organic produce vendors, an exceptional rotisserie chicken joint called RoliRoti (try the potatoes!), a wine bar, yet another outpost of Taylor's Automatic Refresher (see St. Helena restaurants for details), a food-related antique shop, and many other reasons to loosen your belt and your grip on your wallet. This is also the new home to the farmers' market previously held at Copia; it's held seasonally May through August on Tuesdays from 7:30am to noon and Saturday 8am to noon. Check the website below to confirm times, as they are subject to change.
600 First Street, adjacent to Copia. For more information visit www.oxbowpublicmarket.com.

BIKING The quieter northern end of the valley is an ideal place to rent a bicycle and ride the Silverado Trail. **St. Helena Cyclery,** 1156 Main St. (✆ **707/963-7736;** www.sthelenacyclery.com), rents bikes for $10 per hour or $30 a day, including rear rack, helmet, lock, and bag in which you can pack a picnic.

SHOPPING Shopaholics should make a beeline to the **Napa Premium Outlets** (✆ **707/226-9876;** www.premiumoutlets.com), where Barneys New York can inspire even a jaded local to take the First Street exit off Highway 29 and brave the crowds. Unfortunately, Barneys now carries only cheap outlet-store stuff, but, you'll find multiple places to part with your money, including TSE (killer cashmere at bargain prices), Banana Republic, Calvin Klein, Nine West, Benetton, Jones New York, BCBG, more fashion shops, a few kitchenware and gift shops, a food court, and a decent (but expensive) sushi restaurant. Shops are open Monday through Saturday from 10am to 8pm and Sunday from 10am to 6pm. Call for seasonal hours.

St. Helena's Main Street ★ is the best place to go if you're suffering from serious retail withdrawal. Here you'll find trendy fashions at **Pearl** (1428 Main St.; ✆ 707/963-3236), Jimmy Choo shoes at **Footcandy** (1239 Main St.; ✆ 707/963-2040), chic pet gifts at **Fideaux** (1312 Main St.; ✆ 707/967-9935), custom-embroidered French linens at **Jan de Luz** (1219 Main St.; ✆ 707/963-1550), estate jewelry at **Patina** (1342 Main St.; ✆ 707/963-5445), and European home accessories, sample holiday table settings, and free gift-wrapping at **Vanderbilt and Company** (1429 Main St.; ✆ 707/963-1010).

Most stores are open 10am to 5pm daily; the mall is on Main Street, between Pope and Pine streets, St. Helena.

Shopaholics should also take the sharp turn off Highway 29 two miles north of downtown St. Helena to the **St. Helena Premier Outlets** (✆ **707/963-7282;** www.sthelenapremieroutlets.com). Featured designers include Escada, Brooks Brothers, and Tumi. The stores are open daily from 10am to 6pm.

One last favorite stop: **Napa Valley Olive Oil Manufacturing Company,** 835 Charter Oak Ave., at the end of the road behind Tra Vigne restaurant (✆ **707/963-4173**). The tiny market presses and bottles its own oils and sells them at a fraction of the price you'll pay elsewhere. In addition, it has an extensive selection of Italian cooking ingredients, imported snacks, great deals on dried mushrooms, and a picnic table in the parking lot. You'll love the age-old method for totaling the bill, which you simply must find out for yourself.

SPA-ING IT If the Wine Country's slow pace and tranquil vistas aren't soothing enough for you, the region's diverse selection of spas can massage, bathe, wrap, and steam you into an overly pampered pulp. Should you choose to indulge, do so toward the end of your stay—when you've wined and dined to the point where you have only enough energy left to make it to and from the spa. Good choices include **Dr. Wilkinson's Hot Springs,** 1507 Lincoln Ave., Calistoga (✆ 707/942-4102); **Calistoga Spa Hot Springs,** 1006 Washington St., Calistoga (✆ 707/942-6269); and **Meadowood,** 900 Meadowood Lane, St. Helena (✆ 707/963-3646).

CALISTOGA

BIKING Cycling enthusiasts can rent bikes from **Getaway Adventures/Wine Country Adventures** (✆ **800/499-BIKE** or 707/568-3040; www.getawayadventures.com). Full-day group tours cost $125 per person, including lunch and a visit to four or five wineries, $105 per person for private groups of six or more. Bike rental without a tour costs $30 per day plus a $20 delivery fee. You can also inquire about the company's kayaking and hiking tours.

MUD BATHS The one thing you should do while you're in Calistoga is what people have been doing here for the past 150 years: Take a mud bath. The natural baths contain local volcanic ash, imported peat, and naturally boiling mineral hot-springs water, mulled together to produce a thick mud that simmers at a temperature of about 104°F (40°C).

Indulge yourself at any of these Calistoga spas: **Dr. Wilkinson's Hot Springs,** 1507 Lincoln Ave. (© 707/942-4102); **Golden Haven Hot Springs Spa,** 1713 Lake St. (© 707/942-6793); **Calistoga Spa Hot Springs,** 1006 Washington St. (© 707/942-6269); **Calistoga Village Inn & Spa,** 1880 Lincoln Ave. (© 707/942-0991); **Indian Springs Resort,** 1712 Lincoln Ave. (© 707/942-4913); or **Roman Spa Motel,** 1300 Washington St. (© 707/942-4441).

NATURAL WONDERS **Old Faithful Geyser of California,** 1299 Tubbs Lane (© **707/942-6463;** www.oldfaithfulgeyser.com), is one of only three "old faithful" geysers in the world. It's been blowing off steam at regular intervals for as long as anyone can remember. On average, the 350°F (176°C) water spews at a height of about 40 to 60 feet every 40 minutes, day and night, and the performance lasts about 3 minutes (***Note:*** Height and length of time are weather-dependent.)You can bring a picnic lunch to munch on between spews. An exhibit hall, gift shop, and snack bar are open every day. Admission is $8 for adults, $7 for seniors, $3 for children 6 to 12, and free for children under 6. Check the website for discount coupons. The geyser is open daily from 9am to 6pm (to 5pm in winter). To get there, follow the signs from downtown Calistoga; it's between Highway 29 and Calif. 128.

You won't see thousands of trees turned into stone, but you'll still find many interesting petrified specimens at the **Petrified Forest,** 4100 Petrified Forest Rd. (© **707/942-6667;** www.petrifiedforest.org). Volcanic ash blanketed this area after an eruption near Mount St. Helena 3 million years ago. You'll find redwoods that have turned to rock through the slow infiltration of silicas and other minerals, a .25-mile walking trail, a museum, a discovery shop, and picnic grounds. Admission is $6 for adults, $5 for seniors over 60 and juniors 12 to 17, $3 for children 6 to 11, and free for children under 6; look on the website for discount coupons. The forest is open daily from 9am to 7pm (to 5pm in winter). Heading north from Calistoga on Calif. 128, turn left onto Petrified Forest Road, just past Lincoln Street.

WHERE TO STAY IN NAPA VALLEY

Accommodations in Napa Valley run the gamut—from motels and B&Bs to world-class luxury retreats—and all are easily accessible from the main highway. While I recommend staying in the more romantically pastoral areas such as St. Helena, there's no question you're going to find better deals in the towns of Napa or laid-back Calistoga.

When planning your trip, keep in mind that during the high season—April to November—most hotels charge peak rates and sell out completely on weekends; many also have a 2-night minimum. If you need help organizing your Wine Country vacation, contact an agency. **Bed & Breakfast Inns of Napa Valley** (© **707/944-4444;** www.bbinv.com), an association of B&Bs, provides descriptions and lets you know who has rooms available. **Napa Valley Reservations Unlimited** (© **800/251-NAPA**

Pricing Categories

The listings below are arranged first by area, then by price, using the following categories: **Very Expensive,** more than $250 per night; **Expensive,** $200 to $250 per night; **Moderate,** $150 to $200 per night; and **Inexpensive,** less than $150 per night.

or 707/252-1985; www.napavalleyreservations.com) is also a source for booking everything from hot-air balloon rides to wine-tasting tours by limousine.

NAPA

Wherever tourist dollars are to be had, you're sure to find big hotels with familiar names, catering to independent vacationers, business travelers, and groups. **Embassy Suites,** 1075 California Blvd., Napa, CA 94559 (✆ **800/362-2779** or 707/253-9540; www.embassynapa.com), offers 205 of its usual two-room suites. Each includes a galley kitchen complete with coffeemaker, fridge, microwave, and wet bar; they also have a dataport and two TVs and access to indoor and outdoor pools and a restaurant. Rates range from $169 to $289 and include cooked-to-order breakfast, 2-hour beverage reception from 5:30 to 7:30pm, complimentary passes to a nearby health club, and free parking. The 272-room **Napa Valley Marriott,** 3425 Solano Ave., Napa, CA 94558 (✆ **800/228-9290** or 707/253-8600; www.marriott.com), has an exercise room, a heated outdoor pool and spa, and two restaurants; rates range from $119 to $329 for rooms, $350 to $500 for suites.

Very Expensive

Milliken Creek Inn ★★ This riverfront retreat, just north of downtown Napa, combines upscale boutique hotel accommodations with country living. Right off the Silverado Trail and surrounded by tranquil gardens, oaks, and redwoods, the 12 spacious and luxuriously appointed rooms are located in three neighboring buildings (including the restored 1857 Coach House). Soothing shades of brown and beige, greens, and yellows become even warmer and more welcoming when the fireplace is in action. King-size beds are firm and draped in Frette linens, tubs are the whirlpool variety, and fluffy robes await you. Delicious perks include a picnic breakfast delivered to your door, a wine-and-cheese tasting nightly in the equally sophisticated parlor, and the new spa rooms for facials and massages. Live jazz piano accompanies the affair on Fridays and Saturdays. No doubt this hotel is one of Napa's finest choices.

1815 Silverado Trail, Napa, CA 94558. ✆ **888/622-5775** or 707/255-1197. Fax 707/255-3112. www.millikencreekinn.com. 12 units. $395–$695 double. AE, DC, DISC, MC, V. **Amenities:** Yoga deck; spa rooms. *In room:* A/C, plasma-screen TVs with TiVo, dataport, minibar, hair dryer, iron, Wi-Fi throughout entire property, CD player.

Moderate

Cedar Gables Inn ★★ *Finds* This grand, romantic B&B in Old Town Napa is in a stunning Shakespearean/Renaissance style building, built in 1892. Rooms reflect that era, with rich tapestries and stunning gilded antiques. Four have fireplaces, five have whirlpool tubs, and all feature queen-size brass, wood, or iron beds. Guests meet each evening in front of the roaring fireplace in the lower family room for wine and cheese. At other times, the family room is a perfect place to cuddle up and watch the large-screen TV. Bonuses include a gourmet breakfast each morning, port in every room, and VIP treatment at many local wineries.

486 Coombs St. (at Oak St.), Napa, CA 94559. ✆ **800/309-7969** or 707/224-7969. Fax 707/224-4838. www.cedargablesinn.com. 9 units. $209–$329 double. Rates include full breakfast, evening wine and cheese, and port. AE, DISC, MC, V. From Hwy. 29 N, exit onto First St. and follow signs to downtown; turn right onto Jefferson, and left on Oak; house is on the corner. **Amenities:** Dataport (in the shared living room). *In room:* A/C, hair dryer, iron, ironing board, deluxe bathrobes, free Wi-Fi.

Napa River Inn ★★ Downtown Napa's most luxurious hotel manages an old-world boutique feel throughout most of its three buildings. The main building, part of the renovated Historic Napa Mill and Hatt Market Building, is an 1884 historic landmark. Each of its fantastically appointed rooms is exceedingly romantic, with burgundy-colored walls, original brick, wood furnishings, plush fabrics, seats in front of the gas fireplace, and claw-foot tubs in the bathrooms. A newer and more modern themed addition overlooking the river and a patio boasts bright and airy accommodations. Yet another building houses the less luxurious but equally well-appointed mustard-and-brown rooms that also overlook the riverfront, but have a nautical theme and less daylight. Perks abound and include instant access to downtown dining, complimentary vouchers to breakfast at adorable Sweetie Pie's bakery, and wine at the nearby swank wine bar, The Bounty Hunter. A small but excellent spa and outstanding restaurant (Angèle) are located on the property.

500 Main St., Napa, CA 94559. ✆ **877/251-8500** or 707/251-8500. Fax 707/251-8504. www.napariverinn.com. 66 units. $179–$499 double. Rates include vouchers to a full breakfast and wine tasting at the nearby Bounty Hunter. AE, DC, DISC, MC, V. Pets $25 per night. **Amenities:** 2 restaurants; concierge; business services; same-day laundry service/dry cleaning. *In room:* A/C, TV, dataport, fridge, coffeemaker, hair dryer, iron, free Wi-Fi, CD clock radio/MP3 docking station.

Inexpensive

Chablis Inn ★ There's no way around it: If you want to sleep cheaply in a town where the *average* room rate tops $200 per night in high season, you're destined for a motel. Look on the bright side: Because your room is likely to be little more than a crash pad after a day of eating and drinking, a clean bed and a remote control are all you'll really need anyway. And Chablis offers much more than that. All of the motel-style rooms are superclean, and some even boast kitchenettes or whirlpool tubs. Guests have access to a heated outdoor pool and hot tub.

3360 Solano Ave., Napa, CA 94558. ✆ **800/443-3490** or 707/257-1944. Fax 707/226-6862. www.chablisinn.com. 34 units. May to mid-Nov 109–$159 double; mid-Nov to Apr $79–$150 double. AE, DC, DISC, MC, V. **Amenities:** Heated outdoor pool; Jacuzzi. *In room:* A/C, satellite TV, dataport, kitchenette in some rooms, fridge, coffeemaker, hair dryer.

Wine Valley Lodge ★ *Value* Dollar for dollar, the Wine Valley Lodge offers a great deal. At the south end of town in a quiet and funky residential neighborhood, the mission-style motel is extremely well kept and accessible, just a short drive from Highway 29 and the wineries to the north. The reasonably priced one- and two-bedroom suites are great for families. The Lodge is nonsmoking.

200 S. Coombs St. (between S. Franklin St. and Imola Ave.), Napa, CA 94559. ✆ **800/696-7911** or 707/224-7911. www.winevalleylodge.com. 54 units. $89–$169 double; $159–$225 suite. Rates include continental breakfast. AE, DISC, MC, V. **Amenities:** Heated outdoor pool (closed during the winter). *In room:* A/C, TV.

YOUNTVILLE

Very Expensive

Napa Valley Lodge ★ *Finds* Just off Highway 29, beyond a wall that does a good job of blocking the road, this lodge's guest rooms are large, ultraclean, and better appointed than many in the area, especially since all of the rooms were renovated in 2007 and now have spacious bathrooms with dual showerheads. Many also have vaulted ceilings, and 39 have fireplaces. Each comes with a king-size or 2 queen-size beds, wicker furnishings, robes, and a private balcony or a patio. Ground-level units are smaller and get less sunlight than those on the second floor. Suites boast king-size beds and Jacuzzi tubs. Extras are a concierge, afternoon tea and cookies in the lobby, Friday-evening wine tasting in the library, and a continental breakfast—with all this, it's no wonder AAA gave the Napa Valley Lodge the four-diamond award for excellence. Ask about winery tour packages and winter discounts, the latter of which can be as high as 30%.

2230 Madison St., Yountville, CA 94599. ✆ **800/368-2468** or 707/944-2468. Fax 707/944-9362. www.napavalley lodge.com. 55 units. $275–$575 double. Rates include champagne breakfast buffet, afternoon tea and cookies, and Fri-evening wine tasting. AE, DC, DISC, MC, V. **Amenities:** Heated outdoor pool; small exercise room; Jacuzzi; spa; redwood sauna; concierge; in-room massage. *In room:* A/C, ceiling fan, TV w/pay movies, minibar, coffeemaker, hair dryer, iron, free Wi-Fi.

Vintage Inn ★★ This contemporary, French-country complex situated on an old 23-acre winery estate in the heart of Yountville feels far more corporate than "inn" would suggest. But big business does have its perks, like a very professional staff, bright cozy rooms, each of which comes equipped with a fireplace and private veranda, oversize bed, Jacuzzi tub, plush bathrobes, and welcoming bottle of wine. If you're looking for a workout, you may rent a bike, reserve one of the two tennis courts, or take a dip in the 60-foot swimming pool or outdoor whirlpool, both heated year-round. A champagne breakfast buffet and afternoon tea are served daily in the lobby, and wine tastings are held on Fridays. If they're booked, ask about their sister property, the spa-centric Villagio Inn & Spa, a Tuscan-style hotel complex just down the road.

6541 Washington St. (between Humboldt St. and Webber Ave.), Yountville, CA 94599. ✆ **800/351-1133** or 707/944-1112. Fax 707/944-1617. www.vintageinn.com. 80 units. $230–$507 double; $345–$585 minisuite or villa. Rates include champagne breakfast buffet, free wine upon arrival, and afternoon tea. AE, DC, MC, V. Free parking. From Hwy. 29 N, take the Yountville exit and turn left onto Washington St. Pets $40. **Amenities:** Concierge; business center; secretarial services; room service; massage in spa; laundry service; dry cleaning. *In room:* A/C, TV/VCR w/movie library, fridge, coffeemaker, hair dryer, iron, free Wi-Fi access.

Inexpensive

Maison Fleurie ★★ It's impossible not to enjoy your stay at Maison Fleurie. One of the prettiest garden-set B&Bs in the Wine Country, it comprises a trio of beautiful 1873 brick-and-fieldstone buildings overlaid with ivy. The main house—a charming Provençal replica with thick brick walls, terra-cotta tile, and paned windows—holds seven rooms; the rest are in the old bakery building and the carriage house. Some feature private balconies, patios, sitting areas, Jacuzzi tubs, and fireplaces. An above-par breakfast is served in the quaint little dining room; afterward, you're welcome to wander the landscaped grounds or hit the wine-tasting trail, returning in time for afternoon hors d'oeuvres and wine.

6529 Yount St. (between Washington St. and Yountville Cross Rd.), Yountville, CA 94599. ✆ **800/788-0369** or 707/944-2056. Fax 707/944-9342. www.maisonfleurienapa.com. 13 units. $130–$285 double. Rates include full breakfast and afternoon hors d'oeuvres. AE, DC, DISC, MC, V. **Amenities:** Heated outdoor pool; Jacuzzi; free use of bikes. *In room:* A/C, TV, dataport, hair dryer, iron, Wi-Fi.

Napa Valley Railway Inn ★ This is a favorite place to stay in the Wine Country. Why? Because it's inexpensive and it's cute as all get-out. Looking hokey as heck from the outside, the Railway Inn consists of two rows of sun-bleached cabooses and rail cars sitting on a stretch of Yountville's original track and connected by a covered wooden walkway. Things get considerably better when you enter your private caboose or car, especially since they've all been recently redecorated and updated with flatscreen TVs, new furniture, armoires with fridges, and Wi-Fi. Each is appointed with comfy love seat, king- or queen-size black iron bed, and tiled bathroom. The coups de grâce are the bay windows and skylights, which let in plenty of California sunshine. Guests enjoy complimentary passes to the nearby Yountville Fitness Center. Adjacent to the inn is Yountville's main shopping complex.

6523 Washington St., Yountville, CA 94599. © **707/944-2000.** 9 units. $125–$210 double. AE, MC, V. Free parking. *In room:* A/C, TV, coffeemaker, hair dryer upon request, heater, iron, Wi-Fi.

OAKVILLE & RUTHERFORD

Very Expensive

Auberge du Soleil ★★★ *Moments* This spectacular Relais & Châteaux member is one of the most luxurious retreats in all of California. Set high above Napa Valley in a 33-acre olive grove, contemporary California bungalow-like rooms are large enough to get lost in . . . and you might want to, once you discover all the amenities. The bathtub alone—an enormous soaking tub with a skylight overhead—will entice you to grab your complimentary bottle of California wine and settle in for a while. In the private living room, oversize, cushy furniture surrounds a wood-burning fireplace—the ideal place to relax and listen to CDs (the stereo comes with a few selections) or watch one of the room's two flatscreen TVs. Fresh flowers, original art, wood floors, cozy new persimmon-color couches, and a minibar complete with complimentary sodas, espresso machines, and snacks are the best of luxury home-away-from-home. Each sun-washed private deck has views of the valley that are nothing less than spectacular. Alas, some of the main house rooms might not be appropriate for light sleepers, but those with money to burn should opt for one of the $3,000 to $3,750-per-night private "maisons," which were updated in 2006. Each has two fireplaces, a den, a patio Jacuzzi, and a kitchen with wine bar; one even includes a private fitness studio. Now, that's living. All guests have access to a celestial swimming pool, exercise room, and the Wine Country's most fabulous spa. Although only guests can use the spa, you can savor Auberge's romantic grandeur without staying overnight if you have lunch on the terrace of their restaurant overlooking the valley (see p. 303 for more information). Overall, this is one of my favorite Wine Country places. ***Parents take note:*** This is not a kid-friendly place.

180 Rutherford Hill Rd., Rutherford, CA 94573. © **800/348-5406** or 707/963-1211. Fax 707/963-8764. www.aubergedusoleil.com. 50 units. $525–$950 double; $1,000–$1,900 suite; $3,000–$3,750 private cottage. AE, DC, DISC, MC, V. From Hwy. 29 in Rutherford, turn right on Calif. 128 and go 3 miles to the Silverado Trail; turn left and head north about 600 ft. to Rutherford Hill Rd.; turn right. **Amenities:** Restaurant; 3 outdoor pools ranging from hot to cold; tennis court; health club and full-service spa; outdoor Jacuzzi; sauna; steam room; bikes; concierge; secretarial services; room service; massage; same-day laundry service/dry cleaning; free wired Internet or Wi-Fi; art gallery and plain-air art supplies; daily newspapers. *In room:* A/C, TV/DVD w/HBO, dataport, kitchenette, minibar, fridge, coffeemaker, hair dryer, iron, Wi-Fi, stereo, MP3 docking stations.

Moderate

Rancho Caymus Inn ★ This cozy Spanish-style hacienda, with two floors opening onto wisteria-covered balconies, was the creation of sculptor Mary Tilden Morton (whose dad was a forestry baron; Berkeley's Tilden Park is named for him). Morton wanted each room in the hacienda to be a work of art, so she employed the most skilled craftspeople she could find. As a result you'll find Morton-designed adobe fireplaces in 22 of 26 rooms, and artifacts she gathered in Mexico and South America.

Decent-size guest rooms surround a whimsical garden courtyard with an enormous outdoor fireplace. The mix-and-match decor is on the funky side, with braided rugs and overly varnished imported carved wood furnishings. But it's hard to balk when they include wet bars, sitting areas with sofa beds, small private patios and new beds and fresh paint added in 2005. Most of the suites have fireplaces, one has a kitchenette, and five have whirlpool tubs. Breakfast, which includes fresh fruit, granola, orange juice, and pastries, is served in the inn's dining room. The fancy, formal, and French-influenced La Toque restaurant (see p. 305 for complete details) is on-site and is where breakfast is served.

1140 Rutherford Rd., P.O. Box 78, Rutherford, CA 94573. ✆ **800/845-1777** or 707/963-1777. Fax 707/963-5387. www.ranchocaymus.com. 26 suites. $155–$320 double; $215–$410 master suite; $275–$450 2-bedroom suite. Rates include continental breakfast. AE, MC, V. From Hwy. 29 N, turn right onto Rutherford Rd./Calif. 128 east; the hotel is on your left. **Amenities:** Restaurant. *In room:* A/C, TV, dataport, kitchenette in 1 room, minibar, fridge, microwave in master suite, coffeemaker, hair dryer, iron in some rooms, Wi-Fi.

ST. HELENA

Very Expensive

Harvest Inn ★★ One of the valley's few sprawling resorts, this 74-unit property has wonderfully spacious accommodations, all of which are uniquely decorated with warm homey furnishings and nestled into 8 acres of flora; most have fireplaces. Extensive grounds (which include two swimming pools and hot tubs, a spa, and a wine bar) and well-appointed suites make the place popular with wedding parties and families. Although you can't reserve specific rooms in advance, request an abode away from the highway upon arrival. Also, if you're not into climbing stairs, ask for a ground-level room, as some accommodations are on a second story and don't have elevator access.

One Main St., St. Helena, CA 94574. ✆ **800/950-8466** or 707/963-9463. Fax 707/963-5387. www.harvestinn.com. 74 units. $469–$649, suites from $749. Rates include breakfast. AE, MC, V. From Hwy. 29 N, turn left into the driveway at the large HARVEST INN sign. **Amenities:** Complimentary parking and breakfast; evening wine tasting Sat–Sun nights; wine bar; 2 heated outdoor swimming pools; 2 hot tubs; event facilities; mountain bike rentals; in-room massage. *In room:* A/C, TV/DVD, clock radio, Wi-Fi, dataport, fridge, twice-daily maid service, coffeemaker, hair dryer, iron.

The Inn at Southbridge ★ It's expensive for what it is, but if you want to be in St. Helena and prefer upscale Pottery Barn decor to lace and latticework, this is a good place to shack up. Along with modern digs you'll find terry robes, fireplaces, bathroom skylights, down comforters, small balconies, and a host of other luxuries. One notable bummer: The inn is along the highway, so it lacks that reclusive feel offered by many other upscale hotels. Additionally, this isn't an ideal stop for families, but the adjoining casual and cheap Italian restaurant Pizzeria Tra Vigne does lure families with little ones with games, TV, and pizzas.

1020 Main St., St. Helena, CA 94574. ✆ **800/520-6800** or 707/967-9400. www.innatsouthbridge.com. Fax 707/967-9486. 21 units. $255–$625 double. AE, DC, MC, V. **Amenities:** Restaurant; large heated outdoor pool; excellent health club and full-service spa; Jacuzzi; concierge; room service; massage; same-day dry cleaning; Wi-Fi in lobby. *In room:* A/C, TV, dataport, minibar, coffeemaker, hair dryer, iron, high-speed Internet.

Meadowood Napa Valley ★★ *Finds* Originally a private country club for Napa's well-to-do families, Cape Cod–like Meadowood has long been one of California's top-ranked privately owned resorts. Though in past years its rooms have looked a little tired, everything old is new again due to a fantastic renovation in 2006. Surrounded by 250 secluded acres of pristine mountainside dotted with madrones and oaks, the property is still a favorite retreat for celebrities and CEOs. Units, which vary in size tremendously depending on the price, are freshly furnished with warm colors, lush fabrics, and American country classic furnishings and still include beamed ceilings, private patios, stone fireplaces, and views of the forest. Many are individual suite-lodges so far removed from the common areas that you must drive to get to them—and hike a bit to get to the restaurant or spa. Lazier folks can opt for more centrally located rooms.

The resort offers a wealth of activities: golf on a challenging 9-hole course, tennis on seven championship courts, and croquet (yes, croquet) on two international regulation lawns. There are private hiking trails, a health spa, yoga, two heated pools, and two whirlpools. An added bonus for lazy travelers: Their formal restaurant has reopened and the chef is doing a decent job of creating fancy multi-course meals that focus on the seasons and local ingredients.

900 Meadowood Lane, St. Helena, CA 94574. ✆ **800/458-8080** or 707/963-3646. Fax 707/963-3532. www.meadowood.com. 85 units. Double $475–$975; 1-bedroom suite $900–$1,700; 2-bedroom $1,425–$2,675; 3-bedroom $1,950–$3,650; 4-bedroom $2,475–$4,625. Ask about promotional offers and off-season rates. 2-night minimum stay on weekends. AE, DC, DISC, MC, V. **Amenities:** 2 restaurants; 2 large heated outdoor pools (adult and family pools); golf course; 7 tennis courts; health club and full-service spa; Jacuzzi; sauna; concierge; business center; room service; same-day laundry service/dry cleaning weekdays only; 2 croquet lawns. *In room:* A/C, TV, dataport, kitchenette in some rooms, minibar, coffeemaker, hair dryer, iron, free high-speed Internet access and Wi-Fi.

Moderate

Wine Country Inn ★★ Just off the highway behind Freemark Abbey vineyard is one of Wine Country's most personable choices. The attractive wood-and-stone inn, complete with a French-style mansard roof and turret, overlooks a pastoral landscape of vineyards. The individually decorated rooms contain antique furnishings and handmade quilts; most have fireplaces and private terraces overlooking the valley, and others have private hot tubs. The five luxury cottages include king-size beds, a single bed (perfect for the tot in tow), sitting areas, fireplaces, private patios, and three-headed walk-in showers. Two of the inn's best features (besides the absence of TVs) are the heated outdoor pool and hot tub, which are attractively landscaped into the hillside. Another favorite feature is the selection of suites, which come with two-person jetted tubs, stereos, plenty of space, and lots of privacy. The family that runs this place puts personal touches everywhere and makes every guest feel welcome. They serve wine and plenty of appetizers nightly, along with a big dash of hotel-staff hospitality in the inviting living room. A full buffet breakfast is served there, too.

1152 Lodi Lane, St. Helena, CA 94574. ✆ **888/465-4608** or 707/963-7077. Fax 707/963-9018. www.winecountryinn.com. 29 units, 12 w/shower only. $195–$410 double; $270–$485 suite; $505–$590 cottage. Rates include breakfast and appetizers. MC, V. **Amenities:** Heated outdoor pool; Jacuzzi; concierge; free Wi-Fi; big-screen TV in common room; spa services. *In room:* A/C, hair dryer, iron.

Inexpensive

El Bonita Motel ★ *Kids* *Value* This 1940s Art Deco motel is a bit too close to Highway 29 for comfort, but the 2½ acres of beautifully landscaped gardens behind the building (away from the road) help even the score. The rooms, while small and nothing fancy (think motel basic), are spotlessly clean and decorated with newer furnishings and kitchenettes; some have a whirlpool bathtub. It ain't heaven, but it is cheap for St. Helena.

195 Main St. (at El Bonita Ave.), St. Helena, CA 94574. ✆ **800/541-3284** or 707/963-3216. Fax 707/963-8838. www.elbonita.com. 41 units. $89–$259 double. Rates include continental breakfast. AE, DC, DISC, MC, V. **Amenities:** Heated outdoor pool; spa; Jacuzzi; free high-speed Internet access in lobby. *In room:* A/C, TV, fridge, microwave, coffeemaker, hair dryer, iron, free Wi-Fi.

CALISTOGA

Very Expensive

Calistoga Ranch ★★★ Napa Valley's hottest new luxury resort is my absolute favorite. Tucked into the eastern mountainside on 157 pristine hidden-canyon acres, each of the 46 rural-chic free-standing luxury cottages may cost more than $525 per night. But it combines the best of sister property Auberge du Soleil and rival Meadowood, is beautifully decorated, and is packed with every conceivable amenity (including fireplaces, patios along a wooded area, and cushy outdoor furnishings). Reasons not to leave include a giant swimming pool, a reasonably large gym, an incredibly designed indoor-outdoor spa with a natural thermal pool, and individual pavilions with private-garden soaking tubs, as well as a breathtakingly beautiful restaurant with stunning views of the property's Lake Lommel. Need more enticement? They recently added free activities like watercolor painting, yoga, biking, and hiking. Add the startlingly good food (that can be experienced only by guests) to the resort architecture that intentionally tries to blend with the natural surroundings, and you've got a romantically rustic slice of Wine Country heaven.

580 Lommel Rd., Calistoga, CA 94515. ✆ **707/254-2800.** Fax 707/254-2888. www.calistogaranch.com. 46 cottages. $525–$3,200 double. AE, DC, DISC, MC, V. **Amenities:** Restaurant; large heated outdoor pool; gym; activities; spa; Jacuzzi; steam room; concierge; room service; massage; laundry service; dry cleaning (next-day); Wi-Fi throughout. *In room:* A/C, TV/DVD w/DVDs, fax upon request, dataport, 1 lodge w/full kitchen, minibar, fridge, coffeemaker, hair dryer, iron, safe, free Wi-Fi.

Expensive

Cottage Grove Inn ★ Standing in two parallel rows at the end of the main strip in Calistoga is the perfect retreat—adorable cottages that, though on a residential street (with a paved road running between two rows of accommodations), seem removed from the action once you've stepped across the threshold. Each compact guesthouse has a wood-burning fireplace, homey furnishings, a king-size bed with down comforter, and an enormous bathroom with a skylight and a deep, two-person Jacuzzi tub. Guests enjoy such niceties as gourmet coffee, a stereo with CD player, a DVD (the inn has a complimentary DVD library), and a wet bar. Several major spas are within walking distance. This is a top pick if you want to do the Calistoga spa scene in comfort and style. Smoking is allowed only in the gazebos. Bicycles are provided for cruises around town, and guests can recoup a few bucks by using the complimentary tasting passes to more than a dozen nearby wineries.

1711 Lincoln Ave., Calistoga, CA 94515. ✆ **800/799-2284** or 707/942-8400. Fax 707/942-2653. www.cottagegrove.com. 16 cottages. $250–$350 double. Rates include continental breakfast and evening wine and cheese. AE, DC, DISC, MC, V. *In room:* A/C, TV/DVD, dataport, fridge, coffeemaker, hair dryer, iron, safe, robes, wet bar, 40 digital music channels.

Moderate

Christopher's Inn ★ *Kids* A cluster of seven buildings makes up one of Calistoga's more attractive accommodations options. A decade of renovations and expansions by architect-owner Christopher Layton have turned sweet old homes at the entrance to downtown into hotel rooms with a little pizzazz. Options in this non-smoking spot range from somewhat simple but tasteful rooms with colorful and impressive antiques and small bathrooms to huge lavish abodes with four-poster beds, rich fabrics and brocades, and sunken Jacuzzi tubs facing a fireplace. Room no. 3 impresses you with its commanding 9-foot-tall black-wood carved Asian panels. Two of the rooms are "luxury suites" and overlook the fountain courtyard. Most rooms have fireplaces, and some have flatscreen TVs and DVDs (with cable). Outstanding bouquets (during the seasons when flowers abound) attest that the management goes the distance on the details. Those who prefer homey accommodations will feel comfortable here, since the property doesn't have corporate polish or big-business blandness. The lobby features a 6-foot high fireplace and cappuccino machine, making it a great place for an afternoon pick-me-up pit stop. The two rather plain but very functional two-bedroom units are ideal for families, provided you're not expecting the Ritz. An expanded continental breakfast is delivered to your room daily.

1010 Foothill Blvd., Calistoga, CA 94515. ✆ **866/876-5755** or 707/942-5755. Fax 707/942-6895. www.christophersinn.com. 24 units. $150–$445 double; $330–$350 house sleeping 5–6. Rates include expanded continental breakfast. AE, MC, V. **Amenities:** Non-smoking; 2-person massage studio. *In room:* TV, dataport, Wi-Fi, free computer hookups.

Euro Spa & Inn ★★ In a quiet residential section of Calistoga, this small inn and spa provides a level of solitude and privacy that few other spas can match. The horseshoe-shaped inn consists of 13 stucco bungalows, a spa center, and an outdoor patio, where an expanded continental breakfast and snacks are served. The rooms, although small, are pleasantly decorated and come equipped with whirlpool tubs, decks, gas wood stoves, and kitchenettes. Spa treatments range from clay baths and foot reflexology to minifacials.

1202 Pine St. (at Myrtle), Calistoga, CA 94515. ✆ **707/942-6829.** www.eurospa.com. Fax 707/942-1138. 13 units. $89–$239 double. Rates include expanded continental breakfast. 7 package discounts available. AE, DC, DISC, MC, V. **Amenities:** Outdoor heated pool; Jacuzzi. *In room:* A/C, TV, kitchenette, hair dryer, iron, robes, free Wi-Fi.

Silver Rose Inn & Spa ★ If you'd like a big, ranch-style spread complete with a large wine bottle–shaped heated pool, a smaller unheated pool, two hot tubs, dual tennis courts, and even a chipping and putting green, then you'll love the Silver Rose Inn & Spa. Situated on a small oak-covered knoll overlooking the upper Napa Valley, the inn, which is known for its polished hospitality, offers so many amenities that you'll have a tough time searching for reasons to leave (other than to eat dinner). Each of the spacious guest rooms, which surround a centerpiece two-story atrium living room, is individually—and whimsically—decorated in sometimes over-the-top (read: kitschy) themes ranging from the peach-colored Peach Delight to the Oriental room, complete with shoji screens and Oriental rugs, to the Mardi Gras room adorned with colorful masks. Several rooms come with fireplaces, whirlpool baths, and private balconies or terraces. Guests can partake of the exclusive full-service spa as well as an afternoon "hospitality hour" of wine, cheese, and crackers. Also, the winery is open and offers free samples ($10 for outside guests).

351 Rosedale Rd. (off the Silverado Trail), Calistoga, CA 94515. ✆ **800/995-9381** or 707/942-9581. www.silverrose.com. 20 units. $165–$265 double weekdays; $195–$310 double weekends. Rates include continental breakfast. AE, DISC, MC, V. **Amenities:** 2 pools; spa; 2 Jacuzzis; tennis courts; chipping and putting green. *In room:* A/C, dataport, hair dryer, iron upon request.

Inexpensive

Calistoga Spa Hot Springs ★ *Kids* *Value* Very few hotels in the Wine Country cater specifically to families with children, which is why I recommend Calistoga Spa Hot Springs if you're bringing the little ones: They classify themselves as a family resort and are accommodating to visitors of all ages. In any case, it's a great bargain, offering unpretentious yet comfortable rooms, as well as a plethora of spa facilities. All of Calistoga's best shops and restaurants are within easy walking distance, and you can even whip up your own grub at the barbecue grills near the large pool and patio area.

1006 Washington St. (at Gerard St.), Calistoga, CA 94515. ✆ **866/822-5772** or 707/942-6269. www.calistogaspa.com. 57 units. Nov–Feb $115–$175 double; Mar–Oct $136–$196 double. MC, V. **Amenities:** 3 heated outdoor pools; kids' wading pool; exercise room; spa. *In room:* A/C, TV, kitchenette, fridge, coffeemaker, hair dryer, iron.

Dr. Wilkinson's Hot Springs Resort ★ This spa/"resort," located in the heart of Calistoga, is one of the best deals in Napa Valley. The rooms range from attractive Victorian-style accommodations to cozy, recently renovated guest rooms in the main 1960s-style motel. All rooms are spiffier than most of the area's other hotels, with surprisingly tasteful textiles and basic motel-style accouterments. Larger rooms have refrigerators and/or kitchens. Facilities include three mineral-water pools (two outdoor and one indoor), a Jacuzzi, a steam room, and mud baths. All kinds of body treatments are available in the spa, including famed mud baths, steams, and massage—all of which I highly recommend. Be sure to inquire about their excellent packages; their new, fantastic facial held in the facial cottage; and hot stone massage therapy.

1507 Lincoln Ave. (Calif. 29, between Fairway and Stevenson aves.), Calistoga, CA 94515. ✆ **707/942-4102.** www.drwilkinson.com. 42 units. $129–$239 double. Weekly discounts and packages available. AE, MC, V. **Amenities:** 3 pools; Jacuzzi; spa; steam room; mud baths; Wi-Fi in lobby. *In room:* A/C, TV, dataport, coffeemaker, hair dryer, iron, voice mail.

WHERE TO DINE IN NAPA VALLEY

Napa Valley's restaurants draw as much attention to the valley as its award-winning wineries. Nowhere else in the state are kitchens as deft at mixing fresh seasonal, local, organic produce into edible magic, which means that menus change constantly to reflect the best available ingredients. Add that to a great bottle of wine and stunning views, and you have one heck of an eating experience. To best enjoy Napa's restaurant scene, keep one thing in mind: Reserve in advance—especially for a seat in a famous room.

NAPA

Moderate

Angèle ★★ COUNTRY FRENCH I love this riverside spot for two reasons: The food is great, and the surroundings are some of the best in the valley. Its cozy combo of raw wood beams, taupe-tinted concrete-block, concrete slab floors, bright yellow leather bar stools, candlelight, and a heated, shaded patio (weather permitting) has always been great for intimate dining. But chef Tripp Mauldin, previously at Michael Mina and the Ritz-Carlton in San Francisco, who arrived in mid-2005, has upped the culinary ante, offering fabulous crispy roast chicken with summer corn, chanterelles, lardons, baby potatoes, and *jus;* outstanding burgers; and tasty seafood such as king salmon with arugula salad, heirloom tomatoes, olives, basil, and Parmesan. During winter eves, opt for the rustic-chic indoors; for summer, settle into one of the outdoor seats. And if you're a banana fan, definitely try their cobbler version for dessert; with fresh banana slices submerged in pastry cream and topped with crisp crumbly topping, it's deliciously decadent.

540 Main St. (in the Hatt Building). ✆ **707/252-8115.** Reservations recommended. Main courses $18–$28. AE, MC, V. Daily 11:30am–10pm.

Pricing Categories

The restaurants listed in this section are classified first by town, then by price, using the following categories: **Very Expensive,** dinner from $75 per person; **Expensive,** dinner from $50 per person; **Moderate,** dinner from $35 per person; and **Inexpensive,** less than $35 per person for dinner. These categories reflect prices for an appetizer, a main course, a dessert, and a glass of wine.

Bistro Don Giovanni ★★★ Value REGIONAL ITALIAN Donna and Giovanni Scala—who launched Scala's Bistro in San Francisco (but, sadly, are no longer involved with that venture)—own this bright, bustling, and cheery Italian restaurant, which also happens to be one of my favorite restaurants in Napa Valley. Fare prepared by chef/partner Scott Warner highlights quality ingredients and California flair and never disappoints, especially when it comes to the thin-crusted pizzas and house-made pastas. Every time I grab a menu, I can't get past the salad of beets and *haricots verts* or the pasta with duck Bolognese. On the rare occasion that I do, I am equally smitten with outstanding classic pizza Margherita fresh from the wood-burning oven, seared wild salmon filet perched atop a tower of buttermilk mashed potatoes, and steak frites. My only complaint: Over the past few years the appetizers have been getting skimpier and more expensive and the staff has been more aloof. But don't let these drawbacks deter you. Alfresco dining in the vineyards is available—and highly recommended on a warm, sunny day. Midwinter, I'm a fan of ordering a bottle of wine (always expensive here) and dining at the bar. Desserts seriously rock, so be sure to partake.

4110 Howard Lane (at St. Helena Hwy.), Napa. ✆ **707/224-3300.** www.bistrodongiovanni.com. Reservations recommended. Main courses $12–$24. AE, DC, DISC, MC, V. Sun–Thurs 11:30am–10pm; Fri–Sat 11:30am–11pm.

Ristorante Allegria ★ NORTHERN ITALIAN When all I really want is a quality dinner at everyday prices, I go directly to this local spot housed downtown in a beautiful historic bank. High ceilings, faux-finished walls, mood lighting, an accordion player on Mondays and Wednesdays(!), and a sectioned-off full bar create an excellent atmosphere. The staff is very friendly and you won't find a more perfectly prepared grilled salmon over Yukon gold potatoes served with baby spinach hash topped with lemon-caper aioli—especially at 17 bucks! They also make a generous and tasty Caesar salad, offer plenty of antipasti and pastas (the latter of which are not nearly as good as Don Giovanni's), and offer the likes of filet mignon with garlic-mashed potatoes and Gorgonzola compound butter to satisfy red-meat lovers. Plus, you can order their fixed-price menu of three courses plus dessert for a measly $39. You won't get the vineyard-view "wine country" dining experience—or its corresponding high prices—here, but sometimes, that's exactly what the diner ordered. Oh! And one last perk: You can pay $10 to bring and drink your own bottle of wine *and* they waive the fee if you order a bottle from the list as well.

1026 First St. (at Main St.), Napa. ✆ **707/254-8006.** www.ristoranteallegria.com. Most main courses $9–$16 lunch, $11–$22 dinner. AE, DISC, MC, V. Mon–Thurs lunch 11am–2:30pm, dinner 5–10pm; Fri–Sun 10am–11pm.

Inexpensive

Alexis Baking Company ★ BAKERY/CAFE Alexis (also known as ABC) is a quaint, casual stop for residents and in-the-know tourists. On weekend mornings—especially Sunday, which is when you'll find me devouring their out-of-this-world huevos rancheros and classic eggs Benedict—the line stretches out the door. Once you order (from the counter during the week and at the table on Sun) and find a seat, you can relax and enjoy the coffeehouse atmosphere. Start your day with spectacular pastries, coffee drinks, and breakfast goodies like pumpkin pancakes with sautéed pears. Lunch also bustles with locals who come for simple, fresh fare like grilled hamburgers with Gorgonzola, grilled-chicken Caesar salad, roast lamb sandwich with minted mayo and roasted shallots on rosemary bread, and lentil bulgur orzo salad. (Sorry, fries lovers; you won't find any here.) Desserts run the gamut; during the holidays, they include a moist and magical steamed persimmon pudding. Oh, and the pastry counter's cookies and cakes beg you to take something for the road.

1517 Third St. (between Main and Jefferson sts.), Napa. ✆ **707/258-1827**. www.alexisbakingcompany.com. Main courses $5–$12 breakfast, $7–$10 lunch. MC, V. Mon–Fri 6:30am–4pm; Sat 7:30am–3pm; Sun 8am–2pm.

Sweetie Pies ★ *Finds* CAFE/BAKERY Simple breakfasts of granola, egg-and-cheese croissant sandwiches, quiche, and coffee are a perfect and light way to kick off each decadent day at this adorable and aptly named country bakery. But yummy pastries, decadent individual cakes, huge cookies, and lunchtime edibles like ham and fontina panini and pizzettas with mixed green salads are equally good reasons to stop by and linger at one of the few tables. Got a sweet tooth? You can't go wrong with the dark chocolate and caramel ganache fudge cake or mudpie cheesecake.

520 Main St., at the south end, Napa. ✆ **707/257-7280**. Breakfast snacks $2.75–$4.50; pastries $2.25–$2.75; cake $6.75; sandwiches $6.75. MC, V. Mon–Thurs 6:30am–5pm; Fri–Sat 6:30am–6pm; Sun 7am–5pm.

Villa Corona ★ MEXICAN The best Mexican food in town is served in this bright, funky, and colorful restaurant hidden in the southwest corner of a strip mall behind an unmemorable sports bar and restaurant. The winning plan here is simple: Order and pay at the counter, sit at either a table inside or at one of the few sidewalk seats, and wait for the huge burritos, enchiladas, and chimichangas to be delivered to your table. Those with pork preferences shouldn't miss the carnitas, which are abundantly flavorful and juicy. My personal favorites are hard-shell tacos or chicken enchiladas with light savory red sauce, a generous side of beans, and rice. Don't expect to wash down your menudo, or anything else for that matter, with a margarita. The place serves only beer and wine. Don't hesitate to come for a hearty breakfast, too. Excellent *chilaquiles* (eggs scrambled with salsa and tortilla) and huevos rancheros are part of the package.

3614 Bel Aire Plaza, on Trancas St., Napa. ✆ **707/257-8685**. Breakfast, lunch, and dinner $6–$10. MC, V. Tues–Fri 9am–9pm; Sat 8am–9pm; Sun 8am–8pm.

ZuZu ★★ TAPAS A local place to the core, ZuZu lures neighborhood regulars with a no-reservation policy, a friendly cramped wine and beer bar, and affordable Mediterranean/Latin American small plates, which are meant to be shared. The comfortable, warm, and not remotely corporate atmosphere extends from the environment to the food, which includes sizzling miniskillets of tangy and fantastic paella, addictive prawns with chipotle and paprika, light and delicate sea scallop ceviche salad, and Moroccan barbecued lamb chops with a sweet-and-spicy sauce. Desserts aren't as fab, but with a bottle of wine and tastier plates than you can possibly devour, who cares?

829 Main St., Napa. ✆ **707/224-8555**. Reservations not accepted. Tapas $3–$13. MC, V. Mon–Thurs 11:30am–10pm; Fri 11:30am–11pm; Sat 4–11pm; Sun 4–9pm.

YOUNTVILLE

Very Expensive

The French Laundry ★★★ CLASSIC AMERICAN/FRENCH It's almost futile to include this restaurant, because you're about as likely to secure a reservation—or get through on the reservation line, for that matter—as you are to drive Highway 29 without passing a winery. Several years after renowned chef-owner Thomas Keller bought the place and caught the attention of epicureans worldwide (including the judges of the James Beard Awards, who named him "Chef of the Nation" in 1997), this discreet restaurant is one of the hottest dinner tickets *in the world.*

Plainly put, The French Laundry is unlike any other dining experience, period. Part of it has to do with the intricate preparations, often finished tableside and always presented with uncommon artistry and detail, from the food itself to the surface it's delivered on. Other factors are the service (superfluous, formal, and attentive) and the sheer length of time it takes to ride chef Keller's culinary magic carpet. The atmosphere is as serious as the diners who quietly swoon over the ongoing parade of bite-size delights. Seating ranges from downstairs to upstairs to seasonal garden tables, where you also might wait to be seated, sip some champagne, or puff a cigar. Technically, the prix-fixe menu offers a choice of nine courses (including a vegetarian menu), but after a slew of cameo appearances from the kitchen, everyone starts to lose count. Signature dishes include Keller's "tongue in cheek" (a marinated and braised round of sliced lamb tongue and tender beef cheeks) and "macaroni and cheese" (sweet butter-poached Maine lobster with creamy lobster broth and orzo with mascarpone cheese). The truth is, the experience defies description, so if you absolutely love food, you'll simply have to try it for yourself. Portions are small, but only because Keller wants his guests to taste as many things as possible. Trust me, nobody leaves hungry.

The staff is well acquainted with the wide selection of regional wines; there's a $50 corkage fee if you bring your own bottle, which is only welcome if it's not on the list. ***Hint:*** If you can't get a reservation, try walking in as soon as lunch or dinner service begins—on occasion folks don't keep their reservation and tables open up, especially during lunch on rainy days. Reservations are accepted 2 months in advance of the date, starting at 10am. Anticipate hitting redial many times for the best chance. Also, insiders tell me that fewer people call on weekends, so you have a better chance at getting beyond the busy signal.

You can now also try www.opentable.com (but it's still done 2 months in advance).

6640 Washington St. (at Creek St.), Yountville. ✆ **707/944-2380.** www.frenchlaundry.com. Reservations required. 9-course chef's tasting menu or 9-course vegetable menu $210, including service. AE, MC, V. Fri–Sun 11am–1pm; daily 5:30–9pm. Dress code: no jeans, shorts, or tennis shoes; men should wear jackets; ties optional.

Expensive

Redd ★★ CONTEMPORARY AMERICAN Chef Richard Reddington may have put his name on the culinary map at nearby resort Auberge du Soleil, but he secured a spot among the valley's very best chefs when he opened his own restaurant at the end of 2005. Though the modern and stark dining room is a wee too stark and white-on-white for my taste, the menu is definitely full-flavored. Not that I am surprised. Expect exceptional appetizers such as a delicate sashimi hamachi with edamame, cucumber, ginger, and sticky rice, as well as a cold foie gras trio with pistachios and brioche. For entrees, the Atlantic cod with chorizo, clams, and curry sauce is a dream dish that simultaneously manages to be rich *and* light. The new pastry chef promises to sweeten the offerings with the likes of a citrus trio of Meyer lemon cake, tangerine float, and grapefruit s'mores. If your budget allows, definitely let the sommelier wine-pair the meal for you. He's bound to turn you on to some new favorites. Also, if you're looking for a lush brunch spot, this is it!

6480 Washington St., Yountville. ✆ **707/944-2222.** Reservations recommended. Main courses brunch and lunch $14–$25, main courses dinner $23–$29; 5-course tasting menu $70, 9-course tasting menu $105. AE, DISC, MC, V. Mon–Sat 11:30am–2:30pm, Sun 11am–2pm; dinner daily 5:30–10pm; bar menu served 2:30pm–midnight nightly.

Moderate

Bistro Jeanty ★ FRENCH BISTRO This casual, warm bistro, with muted buttercup walls, two dining rooms divided by the bar, and patio seats, is where chef Philippe Jeanty creates seriously rich French comfort food for legions of fans. The all-day menu includes legendary tomato soup in puff pastry, foie gras pâté, steak tartare, and home-smoked trout with potato slices. No meal should start without a paper cone filled with fried smelt (it's often on the list of specials), and none should end without the crème brûlée, made with a thin layer of chocolate cream between classic vanilla custard and a caramelized sugar top. In between, it's a rib-gripping free-for-all including coq au vin; cassoulet; and juicy, thick-cut pork chop with *jus,* spinach, and mashed potatoes. Alas, quality has suffered since Jeanty has branched out to three restaurants, but when the kitchen is on it's still a fine place to sup.

6510 Washington St., Yountville. ✆ **707/944-0103.** www.bistrojeanty.com. Reservations recommended. Appetizers $8.50–$13; most main courses $15–$29. AE, MC, V. Daily 11:30am–10:30pm.

Bouchon ★★ FRENCH BISTRO French Laundry chef Thomas Keller pays tribute to the classic French brasserie in this sexy dining room. Along with a raw bar, expect superb renditions of steak frites, mussels meunière, Croque Madames (fancy grilled-cheese sandwiches with ham, Mornay sauce and a fried egg), and other heavenly French classics (try the expensive and rich foie gras pâté, which is made at Bouchon). My all-time favorite must-orders: the Bibb lettuce salad (seriously, trust me on this), french fries (perhaps the best in the valley), and roasted chicken bathed in wild mushroom ragout. A bonus, especially for restless residents and off-duty restaurant staff, is the late hours, although they offer a more limited menu when the crowds dwindle.

6534 Washington St. (at Humboldt), Yountville. ✆ **707/944-8037.** www.frenchlaundry.com. Reservations recommended during the week, required on weekends. Main courses $15–$27. AE, MC, V. Daily 11:30am–12:30am.

Mustards Grill ★★ CALIFORNIA Mustards is one of those standby restaurants that everyone seems to love because it's dependable and its menu has something that suits any food craving. Housed in a convivial, barn-style space, it offers 300 wines and an ambitious chalkboard list of specials. Options go from exotic offerings like smoked duck or Mongolian style pork chop with hot mustard sauce, to a sautéed lemon-garlic half-chicken with mashed potatoes and fresh herbs. The menu includes something for everyone, from vegetarians to good old burger lovers, and the wine list features nothing but "New World" wines.

7399 St. Helena Hwy. (Hwy. 29), Napa. ✆ **707/944-2424.** www.mustardsgrill.com. Reservations recommended. Main courses $11–$35. AE, DC, DISC, MC, V. Mon–Thurs 11:30am–9pm; Fri 11:30am–10pm; Sat 11am–10pm; Sun 11am–9pm.

Inexpensive

Bouchon Bakery ★ FRENCH BAKERY Another French Laundry chef Thomas Keller creation, this adorable authentic French bakery is next door to his restaurant Bouchon (see above). It ain't cheap, but that doesn't stop locals and visitors from lining up amid the storefront for the outstanding bread baked twice daily, paper-wrapped panini, killer treats (think éclairs, cookies, tarts, and more), coffee drinks, classic sandwiches, and near-perfect pastry. Grab it to go or snack at one of the garden tables, which overlook Yountville's main drag.

6528 Washington St. (between Jefferson and Yount sts.). ✆ **707/944-2253.** Pastries and sandwiches $2.25–$7. AE, MC, V. Daily 7am–7pm.

RUTHERFORD

Expensive

Auberge du Soleil ★ *Finds* WINE COUNTRY CUISINE Perched high atop a hill overlooking Napa Valley, this is the spot to come to if an afternoon or early evening of alfresco romance is on your itinerary. Sure, as part of a luxury resort the restaurant also offers fancy food and expensive wines. But the primary reason to choose this place over other big-ticket restaurants is the view, which is only afforded during the day. In

Tips Where to Stock Up for a Gourmet Picnic

You can easily plan your whole trip around restaurant reservations, but gather one of the world's best gourmet picnics, and the valley's your oyster.

One of the finest gourmet-food stores in the Wine Country, if not all of California, is the **Oakville Grocery Co.,** 7856 St. Helena Hwy., at Oakville Cross Road, Oakville (✆ **707/944-8802;** www.oakvillegrocery.com). You can put together the provisions for a memorable picnic or, with at least 24 hours' notice, the staff can prepare a picnic basket for you. The store, with its small-town vibe and claustrophobia-inducing crowds, can be quite an experience. You'll find shelves crammed with the best breads and choicest cheeses in the northern Bay Area, as well as pâtés, cold cuts, crackers, top-quality olive oils, fresh foie gras (domestic and French, seasonal), smoked Norwegian salmon, and, of course, an exceptional selection of California wines. The store is open daily from 9am to 6pm. There's also an espresso bar tucked in the corner (open Mon–Fri 7am–6pm; Sat and Sun 8am–6pm), offering lunch items, a complete deli, and house-baked pastries.

Another of my favorite places to fill a picnic basket is New York's version of a swank European marketplace, **Dean & DeLuca,** 607 S. St. Helena Hwy. (Hwy. 29), north of Zinfandel Lane and south of Sulphur Springs Road, St. Helena (✆ **707/967-9980;** www.deananddeluca.com). The ultimate in gourmet grocery stores is more like a world's fair of foods, where everything is beautifully displayed and often painfully pricey. As you pace the barn-wood plank floors, you'll stumble upon more high-end edibles than you've probably ever seen under one roof. They include local organic produce (delivered daily); 300 domestic and imported cheeses (with an on-site aging room to ensure proper ripeness); shelves and shelves of tapenades, pastas, oils, hand-packed dried herbs and spices, chocolates, sauces, cookware, and housewares; an espresso bar; one hell of a bakery section; and more. Along the back wall, you can watch the professional chefs prepare gourmet take-out, including salads, rotisserie meats, and sautéed vegetables. You can also snag a pricey bottle from the wine section's 1,500-label collection. The store is open daily from 9am to 8pm (the espresso bar is open daily at 7am.

other words, come for lunch or cocktails and insist on sitting on the heated patio if you can. There, you join the wealthy patrons, many of whom have emerged from their überluxury guest rooms for a casual burger or salad lunch or a more luxe multi-course dinner surrounded by breathtaking views, wisteria, olive trees, and hummingbirds.

Chef Robert Curry, previously at Domaine Chandon and the nearby Culinary Institute, serves well-prepared cuisine that focuses on the very best of local seasonal ingredients. On my last visit, he regaled us with stories of raiding the vendor trucks at local farmers' markets in order to snag the best ingredients for the day's menu. His forage for freshness pays off in dishes such as risotto with lobster, sunchokes, and hazelnut emulsion; or Liberty Farm duck with chestnuts, verjus, braised radicchio, and caramelized shallot sauce. Add to this the impressive (and very pricy) wine list, with over 30 available by the glass, and you're in for a treat. At dinner you can opt for a four-course fixed-price feast (with a vegetarian option) or the tasting menu for the whole table. For lighter fare, grab a seat at the bar, a cozy room wrapped around the remains of an ancient tree, where you can sample ahi tuna tartare, grilled chicken panini, and oysters on the half-shell, along with 25 wines by the glass.

180 Rutherford Hill Rd., Rutherford. ✆ **707/967-3111.** www.aubergedusoleil.com. Reservations required. Main courses $19–$25 lunch; 4-course fixed-price dinner $90; tasting menu for whole table $115 per person; vegetarian tasting menu $90; bar menu $7–$32. AE, DISC, MC, V. Breakfast 7–11am, lunch 11:30am–2:30pm, and dinner 6–9:30pm. Bar open 11am–11pm.

La Toque ★★ FRENCH Renowned chef and owner Ken Frank attracts diners to one of Wine Country's most formal dining rooms with beautifully presented five-course extravaganzas. Well-spaced tables create plenty of room to showcase the chef-owner's memorable and innovative French-inspired cuisine, which might include an incredible seared foie gras with apple and mango; New England spotted skate wing with butternut squash and Brussels sprouts petals; or ravioli with house-cured duck breast, ricotta, and fresh black truffles. But don't count on it. The menu changes weekly, so you might discover a completely different, but equally delicious, selection. Should you find room and an extra few bucks for the cheese course, try a few delicious slabs, served with walnut bread. For an additional $62 per person you can also drink well-paired wines with each course.

1140 Rutherford Rd., Rutherford. ✆ **707/963-9770.** www.latoque.com. Reservations recommended. Fixed-price menu $98. AE, MC, V. Wed–Sun 5:30–9:30pm. Closed Mon–Tues.

ST. HELENA

Expensive

Terra ★★★ CONTEMPORARY AMERICAN Terra is one of my favorite restaurants, because it manages to be humble even though it serves some of the most extraordinary food in Northern California. The creation of Lissa Doumani and her husband, Hiro Sone, a master chef who hails from Japan, is a culmination of talents brought together nearly 20 years ago, after the duo worked at L.A.'s Spago. Today, the menu reflects Sone's full use of the region's bounty and his formal training in classic European and Japanese cuisine. Dishes—all of which are incredible and are served in the rustic-romantic dining room—range from understated and refined (two must-tries: rock shrimp salad, or broiled sake-marinated cod with shrimp dumplings and shiso broth) to rock-your-world flavorful. I cannot express the importance of saving room for dessert (or forcing it even if you don't). The tiramisu is to die for.

1345 Railroad Ave. (between Adams and Hunt sts.), St. Helena. ✆ **707/963-8931.** www.terrarestaurant.com. Reservations recommended. Main courses $19–$32. AE, DC, MC, V. Wed–Mon dinner starting at 6pm. Closed 2 weeks in early Jan.

Moderate

Tra Vigne Restaurant ★ ITALIAN As much as I want to love everything about this famous, absurdly scenic restaurant, I can't—anymore. With lots of chef changes over the years and meals that range from barely so-so to totally rockin', it's just not the sure thing it used to be. If you sit in the Tuscany-evoking courtyard, however, you'll likely enjoy yourself regardless of whether the kitchen is on the money or missing the mark. Inside, the bustling, cavernous dining room and happening bar are fine for chilly days and eves, but they're not nearly as magical. You can also count on wonderful bread (served with house-cured olives); a menu of robust California dishes, cooked

Italian-style; a daily oven-roasted pizza special; lots of pastas; and tried-and-true standbys like short ribs and fritto misto.

1050 Charter Oak Ave., St. Helena. ✆ **707/963-4444.** www.travignerestaurant.com. Reservations recommended. Main courses $15–$36. DC, DISC, MC, V. Summer daily 11:30am–10pm; winter Sun–Thurs 11:30am–9pm, Fri–Sat 11:30am–10pm.

Wine Spectator Greystone Restaurant ★ CALIFORNIA This place offers a visual and culinary feast that's unparalleled in the area, if not the state. The room is an enormous stone-walled former Christian Bros. winery, warmed by the festive decor and heavenly aromas. Cooking islands—complete with scurrying chefs, steaming pots, and rotating chickens—provide entertainment. The menu features creative seasonal dishes such as grilled Angus hanger steak with porcini mushroom-mizuna salad, toasted brioche and sauce poivrade; or steamed Alaskan halibut filet with young ginger, wilted Asian greens, black mushrooms, jasmine rice, and chile soy broth. I recommend that you opt for a barrage of appetizers for your table to share. You might also consider the "Lessons in Wine"—$14 to $25, which allows you to sample three 3-ounce pours of local wines such as white Rhone, pinot, or zinfandel. Although the food is serious, the atmosphere is playful—casual enough that you'll feel comfortable in jeans or shorts. If you want to ensure having a meal here, reserve far in advance (they book 60 days in advance). Personally, I prefer to stop by, have a snack at the bar, and eat big meals elsewhere.

At the Culinary Institute of America at Greystone, 2555 Main St., St. Helena. ✆ **707/967-1010.** www.ciachef.edu. Reservations recommended. Temptations $9; main courses $19–$30. AE, DC, MC, V. Daily 11:15am–10pm.

Inexpensive

Market AMERICAN In past editions I've highly recommended this upscale but cheap ode to American comfort food. But ever since the chef departed to open Cyrus, a high-end sister restaurant in Northern Sonoma County's town of Healdsburg, the food quality has been unpredictable (though it's incredible at Cyrus: 29 North St., Healdsburg—that's a 45-min. drive from St. Helena; ✆ **707/433-3311;** 3- to 5-course menus $58–$95; www.cyrusrestaurant.com). Still, if you're in expensive St. Helena and want some casual glamour with your burger, you'll find it here with fancy stone-wall and Brunswick bar surroundings paired with clunky steak knives and simple white-plate presentations. Skip the lame chopped salad and perhaps go instead for filet mignon with potato leek risotto, Blue Lake beans, and glazed shallots; or toast-it-yourself s'mores with crisp homemade graham crackers. At lunch, you can also opt for a three-course meal—a steal at a measly $20.

1347 Main St., St. Helena. ✆ **707/963-3799.** www.marketsthelena.com. Most main courses $7–$20. AE, MC, V. Daily 11:30am–10pm.

Pizzeria Tra Vigne ★ *Kids* *Value* ITALIAN After spending a week in Wine Country, I usually can't stand the thought of another decadent wine and foie gras meal. That's when I race here for a $6.95 chopped salad, a welcome respite from gluttonous excess. Families and locals come here for another reason: Although the menu is limited, it's a total winner for anyone in search of freshly prepared, wholesome food at atypically cheap Wine Country prices. Try the staff-recommended Positano pizza, smothered in such delights as fresh rock shrimp, Crescenza cheese sauce, scallions, and deep-fried lemons, or try one of the "piadines"—pizzas folded like a soft taco and filled with things like hummus, olives, tomatoes, cucumbers and red onion. The

14 respectable local wines come by the glass starting at a toast-worthy $6.50, or $18 per bottle. Dessert, at just over $4 a pop for gelato, or $6 for tiramisu, is an overall sweet deal. Kids like the pool table and big-screen TV.

At The Inn at Southbridge, 1016 Main St., St. Helena. ✆ **707/967-9999.** www.travignerestaurant.com/pizzaria.htm. Pastas $8–$11; pizzas $9–$17. AE, DC, DISC, MC, V. Daily 11:30am–9pm (Fri–Sat until 9:30pm).

Taylor's Automatic Refresher *Overrated* DINER Yet another winner to slip from sublime status to buyer beware, this gourmet roadside burger shack built in 1949 still draws huge lines of tourists who love the notion of ordering at the counter and feasting alfresco. But the last few meals I had there left me knowing the $80 I coughed up for lunch for five would have been better spent at Oakville Grocery's deli. The burger, onion rings, and fries were mediocre at best, the iceberg salad was unwieldy, and only the shake left me satisfied. (How hard is it to make a great shake, after all?) Perhaps it's that the owners now have a closer eye on their San Francisco outpost, which is great, by the way. No matter. It's still the only casual burger joint in St. Helena (it also offers ahi tuna burgers and various sandwiches, tacos, soups and salads) and its ever-bustling status proves everyone knows it.

933 Main St., St. Helena. ✆ **707/963-3486.** www.taylorsrefresher.com. Main courses $4–$14. AE, MC, V. Daily 10:30am–7:30pm (9pm in summer).

CALISTOGA

Moderate

All Seasons Café ★★ CALIFORNIA All Seasons successfully balances old-fashioned down-home dining charm with today's penchant for sophisticated, seasonally inspired dishes. It also happens to have perhaps the best food in downtown Calistoga. Vibrant bouquets, large framed watercolors, and windows overlooking busy Lincoln Avenue soften the look of the black-and-white checkered flooring, brick-red ceiling, and long, marble wine bar. The laid-back atmosphere and service make the quality of crispy skin chicken with black truffle chicken *jus* and herb-roasted monkfish with fennel nage that much more of a delicious surprise. Don't forget to take advantage of the fact that they have 400-plus wines available from their adjoining wine shop (with a $15 corkage fee, buy next door and drink for far cheaper than at most restaurants). Alas, the kitchen was a wee bit slow on my last visit, but all was forgiven when the food far surpassed my expectations.

1400 Lincoln Ave. (at Washington St.), Calistoga. ✆ **707/942-9111.** www.allseasonsnapavalley.net. Reservations recommended on weekends. Main courses $9–$11 lunch, $19–$28 dinner. DISC, MC, V. Lunch Fri–Sun noon–2:30pm; dinner Tues–Sun 6–9pm (times vary in winter, please call or go online to confirm).

Inexpensive

Wappo Bar & Bistro GLOBAL One of the best alfresco dining venues in the Wine Country is under Wappo's giant jasmine-and-grapevine-covered arbor. I used to shrug off the mediocre food, reasoning that much can be forgiven when the wine's flowing and you're surrounded by pastoral splendor. But the globally influenced menu has been better of late. Anticipate the likes of Thai noodles and green papaya salad, tandoori chicken, rosemary-scented rabbit with gnocchi and mustard cream sauce. Desserts of choice are black-bottom coconut cream pie and strawberry rhubarb pie.

1226 Washington St. (off Lincoln Ave.), Calistoga. ✆ **707/942-4712.** www.wappobar.com. Main courses $14–$24. AE, MC, V. Wed–Mon 11:30am–2:30pm and 6–9:30pm.

2 Sonoma Valley

A pastoral contrast to Napa, Sonoma manages to maintain a backcountry ambience, thanks to its far lower density of wineries, restaurants, and hotels. Small, family-owned wineries are Sonoma's mainstay; tastings are low-key and come with plenty of friendly banter with the winemakers. Basically, this is the valley to target if your ideal vacation includes visiting a handful of wineries along quiet woodsy roads, avoiding shopping outlets and Napa's high-end glitz, and simply enjoying the laid-back country atmosphere.

The valley is some 17 miles long and 7 miles wide, and it's bordered by two mountain ranges: the Mayacamas to the east and the Sonomas to the west. Unlike in Napa Valley, you won't find much in the way of palatial wineries with million-dollar art collections or aerial trams. Rather, the Sonoma Valley offers a refreshing dose of family-owned winery reality, where modestly sized wineries are integrated into the community. If Napa Valley feels like a fantasyland, where everything exists to service the almighty grape and the visitors it attracts, then the Sonoma Valley is its antithesis, an unpretentious gaggle of ordinary towns, ranches, and wineries that welcome tourists but don't necessarily rely on them. The result is a chance to experience what Napa Valley must have been like long before the Seagrams and Moët et Chandons of the world turned the Wine Country into a major tourist destination.

As in Napa, you can pick up *Wine Country Review* throughout Sonoma. It gives you the most up-to-date information on wineries and related area events.

ESSENTIALS

GETTING THERE From San Francisco, cross the Golden Gate Bridge and stay on U.S. 101 north. Exit at Highway 37; after 10 miles, turn north onto Highway 121. After another 10 miles, turn north onto Highway 12 (Broadway), which takes you directly into the town of Sonoma.

VISITOR INFORMATION While you're in Sonoma, stop by the **Sonoma Valley Visitors Bureau,** 453 First St. E. (✆ **866/996-1090** or 707/996-1090; www.sonomavalley.com). It's open Monday through Saturday from 9am to 5pm (6pm in summer) and Sunday 10am to 5pm. An additional **Visitors Bureau** is a few miles south of the square at Cornerstone Festival of Gardens at 23570 Arnold Dr. (Hwy. 121; ✆ **866/996-1090**); it's open daily from 9am to 4pm, 5pm during summer.

If you prefer advance information from the bureau, you can contact the Sonoma Valley Visitors Bureau to order the free *Sonoma Valley Visitors Guide,* which lists almost every lodge, winery, and restaurant in the valley.

TOURING THE SONOMA VALLEY & WINERIES

Sonoma Valley is currently home to about 40 wineries (including California's first winery, Buena Vista, founded in 1857) and 13,000 acres of vineyards. It produces roughly 25 types of wines, totaling more than five million cases a year. Unlike the rigidly structured tours at many of Napa Valley's corporate-owned wineries, on the Sonoma side of the Mayacamas Mountains, tastings are usually low-key and tours are free.

The towns and wineries covered below are organized geographically from south to north, starting at the intersection of Highway 37 and Highway 121 in the Carneros District and ending in Kenwood. The wineries tend to be a little more spread out here than they are in Napa Valley, but they're easy to find. Still, it's best to decide which wineries you're most interested in and devise a touring strategy before you set out, so you don't do too much backtracking.

I've reviewed some of my favorite Sonoma Valley wineries here—more than enough to keep you busy tasting wine for a long weekend. If you'd like a complete list of local wineries, be sure to pick up one of the free guides available at the Sonoma Valley Visitors Bureau (see "Visitor Information," above).

For a map of the wineries below, please see "The Wine Country" map on p. 273.

THE CARNEROS DISTRICT

As you approach the Wine Country from the south, you must first pass through the Carneros District, a cool, windswept region that borders San Pablo Bay and marks the entrance to both the Napa and Sonoma valleys. Until the latter part of the 20th century, this mixture of marsh, sloughs, and rolling hills was mainly used as sheep pasture (*carneros* means "sheep" in Spanish). However, after experimental plantings yielded slow-growing, high-quality grapes—particularly chardonnay and pinot noir—several Napa and Sonoma wineries expanded their plantings here. They eventually established the Carneros District as an American Viticultural Appellation, a legally defined wine-grape growing area. Although about a dozen wineries are spread throughout the region, there are no major towns or attractions—just plenty of gorgeous scenery as you cruise along Highway 121, the major route between Napa and Sonoma.

Viansa Winery and Italian Marketplace ★ *Finds* The first major winery you'll encounter as you enter Sonoma Valley from the south, this sprawling Tuscan-style villa perches atop a knoll overlooking the entire lower valley. Viansa is the brainchild of Sam and Vicki Sebastiani, who left the family dynasty to create their own temple to food and wine. (*Viansa* is a contraction of "Vicki and Sam.") Here you'll find a large room crammed with a cornucopia of high-quality mustards, olive oils, pastas, salads, breads, desserts, Italian tableware, cookbooks, and wine-related gifts as well as tasting opportunities.

The winery, which does an extensive mail-order business through The Tuscan Club, has established a favorable reputation for its Italian varietals. Tastings, which cost $5 per person, are offered at the east and west end of the marketplace, and the self-guided tour includes a trip through the underground barrel-aging cellar adorned with colorful hand-painted murals. Guided tours, held at 11am and 2pm, cost $5.

Viansa is also one of the few wineries in Sonoma Valley that sells deli items—the focaccia sandwiches are delicious. You can dine alfresco under the grape trellis while you admire the bucolic view.

25200 Arnold Dr. (Calif. 121), Sonoma. ✆ **800/995-4740** or 707/935-4700. www.viansa.com. Daily 10am–5pm. Daily self-guided tours. Guided tours daily 11am and 2pm, $5.

Gloria Ferrer Champagne Caves ★ *Finds* When you have had it up to here with chardonnays and pinots, it's time to pay a visit to Gloria Ferrer, the grande dame of the Wine Country's sparkling-wine producers. Who's Gloria? She's the wife of José Ferrer, whose family has made sparkling wine for 5 centuries. The family business, Freixenet, is the largest producer of sparkling wine in the world; Cordon Negro is its most popular brand. That equals big bucks, and certainly a good chunk of them went into building this palatial estate. Glimmering like Oz high atop a gently sloping hill, it overlooks the verdant Carneros District. On a sunny day, enjoying a glass of dry brut while soaking in the magnificent views is a must.

If you're unfamiliar with the term *méthode champenoise,* be sure to take the free 30-minute tour of the fermenting tanks, bottling line, and caves brimming with racks of yeast-laden bottles. Afterward, retire to the elegant tasting room, order a glass of one

Tips A Garden Detour

Garden lovers should pull over for a gander at the latest Sonoma addition, **Cornerstone Festival of Gardens,** 23570 Arnold Dr., Sonoma (✆ **707/933-3010;** www.cornerstonegardens.com). Modeled in part after the International Garden festival at Chaumont-sur-Loire in France's Loire Valley and the Grand-Métis in Quebec, Canada, the 9-acre property is the first gallery-style garden exhibit in the United States and includes a series of 22 ever-changing gardens designed by famed landscape architects and designers. With a recently added children's garden featuring a brightly colored water tower surrounded by a sand moat and buckets, shovels, and plastic plumbing fittings, this is a great spot for the whole family. When you get hungry, stop by the **Blue Tree Café,** which offers light breakfasts, pastries, and espresso drinks along with a seasonal lunch menu including soups, salads, and sandwiches. It's all served on nifty metal trays, perfect for carrying out to the gardens; there's also seating indoors and out in front. Another plus for those with kids: The gardens include a cleverly installed willow reed maze that's about 3 feet high and only has one entrance/exit right in front of the cafe, so if you're sitting out front and the kids get bored, you can safely let them run through the maze. If you get inspired, you can load up on loot here that will help your own garden grow—from furniture and gifts to plants, garden art, and books, as there are several interesting shops here, too. Open 10am-5pm daily, year-round (Café opens at 9am). April through November the price for admission to the gardens is $9 adults, $7.50 seniors 65 plus, $6.50 college students, $3 youth 4 to 17, and free for kids under 3 (check for locals' discounts); December through March, tickets are half-price. You can take a self-guided tour anytime; installations are marked with descriptive plaques. Docent tours are available for groups of 10 or more by appointment.

of seven sparkling wines ($4–$10 a glass) or tastes of their eight still wines ($2–$3 per taste), find an empty chair on the veranda, and say, "Ahhh. *This* is the life." There are picnic tables, but it's usually too windy for them to be comfortable, and you must buy a bottle (from around $18–$50) or glass of sparkling wine to reserve a table.

23555 Carneros Hwy. (Calif. 121), Sonoma. ✆ **707/996-7256.** www.gloriaferrer.com. Daily 10am–5pm. Tours daily; call day of visit to confirm schedule.

SONOMA

At the northern boundary of the Carneros District along Highway 12 is the centerpiece of Sonoma Valley. The midsize town of Sonoma owes much of its appeal to Mexican general Mariano Guadalupe Vallejo, who fashioned this pleasant, slow-paced community after a typical Mexican village—right down to its central plaza, Sonoma's geographical and commercial center. The plaza sits at the top of a T formed by Broadway (Hwy. 12) and Napa Street. Most of the surrounding streets form a grid pattern around this axis, making Sonoma easy to negotiate. The plaza's Bear Flag Monument marks the spot where the crude Bear Flag was raised in 1846, signaling the end of Mexican rule; the symbol was later adopted by the state of California and placed on its flag. The 8-acre park at the center of the plaza, complete with two ponds populated by ducks, is perfect for an afternoon siesta in the cool shade. ***Note:*** As this book goes to press, one of the ponds was in the midst of a 1-year restoration, though it should be open sometime in 2007.

Buena Vista Winery Count Agoston Haraszthy, the Hungarian émigré who is universally regarded as the father of California's wine industry, founded this historic winery in 1857. A close friend of General Vallejo, Haraszthy returned from Europe in 1861 with 100,000 of the finest vine cuttings, which he made available to all growers. Although Buena Vista's winemaking now takes place at an ultramodern facility in the Carneros District, the winery maintains a tasting room inside the restored 1862 Press House. The beautiful stone-crafted room brims with wines, wine-related gifts, and accessories.

Tastings are $5 for four wines, $10 for a flight of three library wines. You can take the self-guided tour any time during operating hours; a "Historical Tour and Tasting" (offered daily at 11am and 2pm during high season; Mon–Fri at 2pm and Sat–Sun at 11am and 2pm during off season) details the life and times of Count Haraszthy and includes a viticultural tour and wine and food pairing. For $50, you can do a wine and cheese tasting, by appointment only; call © **707/265-1460.** After tasting, grab your favorite bottle, a selection of cheeses from the Sonoma Cheese Factory, salami, bread, and spreads (all available in the tasting room), and plant yourself at one of the many picnic tables in the lush, verdant setting.

18000 Old Winery Rd. (off E. Napa St., slightly northeast of downtown), Sonoma. © **800/926-1266** or 707/265-1472. www.buenavistawinery.com. Daily 10am–5pm.

Sebastiani Vineyards & Winery The name Sebastiani is practically synonymous with Sonoma. What started in 1904, when Samuele Sebastiani began producing his first wines, has in three generations grown into a small empire, producing some 350,000 cases a year. After a few years of seismic retrofitting, a face-lift, and a temporary tasting room, the original 1904 winery is now open to the public with more extensive educational tours ($5–$7.50 per person) and seminars such as Wine & Cheese ($15) and Soil to Bottle ($25), an 80-foot S-shaped tasting bar, and lots of shopping opportunities in the gift shop. In the contemporary tasting room's minimuseum area you can see the winery's original turn-of-the-20th-century crusher and press, as well as the world's largest collection of oak-barrel carvings, crafted by bygone local artist Earle Brown. If it's merely wine that interests you, you can sample an extensive selection of wines ranging from a complimentary selection to $18 for a flight of their fancy stuff, the latter of which includes a keepsake glass. Bottle prices are reasonable, ranging from $13 to $75. A picnic area adjoins the cellars; a far more scenic spot is across the parking lot in Sebastiani's Cherryblock Vineyards. They also offer a historical Sonoma trolley tour at 2pm on Fridays and Saturdays (weather permitting) that takes visitors around town and through the vineyards.

389 Fourth St. E., Sonoma. © **800/888-5532** or 707/933-3200. www.sebastiani.com. Daily 10am–5pm. Tours: daily 11am, 1pm, and 3pm, with an additional tour at noon Sat–Sun.

Ravenswood Winery Compared to old heavies like Sebastiani and Buena Vista, Ravenswood is a relative newcomer to the Sonoma wine scene. Nevertheless, it quickly established itself as the sine qua non of zinfandel, the versatile red grape that's known in these parts for being big, ripe, juicy, and powerful. The first winery in the United States to focus primarily on zins, which make up about three-quarters of its astonishing 1 million-case production, Ravenswood underscores zins' zest with their motto, "No Wimpy Wines." But they also produce merlot, cabernet sauvignon, Rhone varietals, and a small amount of chardonnay.

Moments Touring the Sonoma Valley by Bike

Sonoma and its neighboring towns are so small, close together, and relatively flat that it's not difficult to get around on two wheels. In fact, if you're in no great hurry, there's no better way to tour the Sonoma Valley than by bicycle, even though there are no great bike routes (it's all along the road for the most part). You can rent a bike from the **Goodtime Bicycle Company** ★ (✆ **888/525-0453** or 707/938-0453; www.goodtimetouring.com). The staff will happily point you to easy bike trails, or you can take an organized excursion to Kenwood-area wineries, south Sonoma wineries, or even northern Sonoma's Russian River and Dry Creek areas. Goodtime also provides a gourmet lunch featuring local Sonoma products. If you purchase wine along the way, Goodtime will carry it for you and help with shipping arrangements. Lunch rides start at 10:30am and end around 3:30pm. The cost, including food and equipment, is $125 per person (that's a darn good deal). Rentals cost $25 a day, and include helmets, locks, everything else you'll need, and delivery and pickup to and from local hotels.

Mountain bikes, helmets, and locks are also available for rent from **Sonoma Valley Cyclery,** 20093 Broadway, Sonoma (✆ **707/935-3377**), for $35 to $55 a day. Hybrid bikes (better for casual wine-tasting cruisers) are $25 per day, helmet and lock included.

The winery is smartly designed—recessed into the hillside to protect its treasures from the simmering summers. Tours ($15 per person) follow the winemaking process from grape to glass, and include a visit to the aromatic oak-barrel aging rooms. You're welcome to bring your own picnic basket to any of the tables, and don't forget to check their website or call to find out if they're having one of their famous ongoing barbecues or winter celebrations. Regardless, tastings are $8 to $15, which is refundable with purchase.

18701 Gehricke Rd. (off Lovall Valley Rd.), Sonoma. ✆ **888/NO-WIMPY** or 707/933-2332. www.ravenswoodwinery.com. Labor Day to Memorial Day 10am–4:30pm; Memorial Day to Labor Day 10am–5pm. Tours at 10:30am; reservations recommended.

GLEN ELLEN

About 7 miles north of Sonoma on Highway 12 is the town of Glen Ellen. Although just a fraction of the size of Sonoma, Glen Ellen is home to several of the valley's finest wineries, restaurants, and inns. Aside from the addition of a few new restaurants, this charming town hasn't changed much since the days when Jack London settled on his Beauty Ranch, about a mile west. Other than the wineries, you'll find few real signs of commercialism; the shops and restaurants, along one main winding lane, cater to a small, local clientele—that is, until the summer tourist season begins and traffic nearly triples on the weekends. If you haven't decided where you want to set up camp during your visit to the Wine Country, I highly recommend this lovable little rural region.

Arrowood Vineyards & Winery Richard Arrowood had already established a reputation as a master winemaker at Château St. Jean when he and his wife, Alis Demers Arrowood, set out on their own in 1986. Their picturesque winery stands on a gently rising hillside lined with perfectly manicured vineyards. Tastings take place in the Hospitality House, the newer of Arrowood's two stately gray-and-white buildings. They're fashioned after New England farmhouses, complete with wraparound porches. Richard's focus is on making world-class wine with minimal intervention, and his results are impressive: More than one of his recent releases scored over 90 points in *Wine Advocate.* Mind you, excellence isn't free: a taste here is $5 or $10 for four limited-production wines, but if you're curious about what near-perfection tastes like, it's well worth it. ***Note:*** No picnic facilities are available here.

14347 Sonoma Hwy. (Calif. 12), Glen Ellen. ✆ **707/935-2600.** www.arrowoodvineyards.com. Daily 10am–4:30pm. Tours by appointment only.

Benziger Family Winery ★ *Finds* A visit here confirms that this is indeed a family winery. At any given time, two generations of Benzigers (*Ben*-zigger) may be running around tending to chores, and they instantly make you feel as if you're part of the clan. The pastoral, user-friendly property features an exceptional self-guided tour of the certified biodynamic winery ("The most comprehensive tour in the wine industry," according to *Wine Spectator*), gardens, and a spacious tasting room staffed by amiable folks. The $10, 45-minute tram tour, pulled by a beefy tractor, is both informative and fun. It winds through the estate vineyards and to caves, and ends with a tasting. ***Tip:*** Tram tickets—a hot item in the summer—are available on a first-come, first-served basis, so either arrive early or stop by in the morning to pick up afternoon tickets.

Tastings of the standard-release wines are $5. Tastes including several limited-production wines or reserve or estate wines cost $10. The winery also offers several scenic picnic spots.

1883 London Ranch Rd. (off Arnold Dr., on the way to Jack London State Historic Park), Glen Ellen. ✆ **888/490-2739** or 707/935-3000. www.benziger.com. Tasting room daily 10am–5pm. Tram tours daily (weather permitting) $10 adults, $5 children, every half-hour, 10:30am–3:30pm.

KENWOOD

A few miles north of Glen Ellen along Highway 12 is the tiny town of Kenwood, the valley's northernmost outpost. Although Kenwood Vineyards' wines are well known throughout the United States, the town itself consists of little more than a few restaurants, wineries, and modest homes on the wooded hillsides. The nearest lodging, the luxurious Kenwood Inn & Spa (p. 319), is about a mile south of the vineyards. Kenwood makes for a pleasant half-day trip from Glen Ellen or downtown Sonoma. Take an afternoon tour of Château St. Jean (see below) and have dinner at Kenwood Restaurant (p. 324).

Kenwood Vineyards Kenwood's history dates from 1906, when the Pagani brothers made their living selling wine straight from the barrel and into the jug. In 1970 the Lee family bought the property and dumped a ton of money into converting the aging winery into a modern, high-production facility (most of it cleverly concealed in the original barnlike buildings). Since then, Kenwood has earned a solid reputation for consistent quality with each of its varietals: cabernet sauvignon, chardonnay, zinfandel, pinot noir, merlot and, most popular, sauvignon blanc—a crisp, light wine with hints of melon.

Although the winery looks rather modest in size, its output is staggering: nearly 550,000 cases of ultrapremium wines fermented in steel tanks and French and American oak barrels. Popular with collectors is their Artist Series cabernet sauvignon, a limited production from the winery's best vineyards, featuring labels with original artwork by renowned artists. The tasting room, housed in one of the old barns, offers complimentary tastes, $2 to $5 tastings of private reserve wines, and gift items for purchase. ***FYI:*** The Lees no longer own the winery; it is now owned by Gary Heck, a fourth-generation Sonoma County vintner.

9592 Sonoma Hwy. (Calif. 12), Kenwood. ✆ **707/833-5891.** www.kenwoodvineyards.com. Daily 10am–4:30pm. No tours.

Château St. Jean ★ *Finds* Château St. Jean is notable for its exceptionally beautiful buildings, expansive landscaped grounds, and gourmet marketlike tasting room. Among California wineries, it's a pioneer in vineyard designation—the procedure of making wine from, and naming it for, a single vineyard. A private drive takes you to what was once a 250-acre country retreat built in 1920; a well-manicured lawn overlooking the meticulously maintained vineyards is now a picnic area, complete with a fountain and tables.

In the huge tasting room—where there's also a charcuterie shop and plenty of other fun stuff for sale—you can sample Château St. Jean's wide array of wines. They range from chardonnays and cabernet sauvignon to fumé blanc, merlot, Riesling, and gewürztraminer. Tastings are $5 per person, $10 per person for reserve wines.

8555 Sonoma Hwy. (Calif. 12), Kenwood. ✆ **800/543-7572** or 707/833-4134. www.chateaustjean.com. Tasting daily 10am–4:30pm. Tour times vary depending on the weather, so call ahead to confirm. At the foot of Sugarloaf Ridge, just north of Kenwood and east of Hwy. 12.

St. Francis Winery Although St. Francis Winery makes commendable chardonnay, zinfandel, and cabernet sauvignon, they're best known for their highly coveted merlot. Winemaker Tom Mackey, a former high-school English teacher from San Francisco, has been hailed as the "Master of Merlot" by *Wine Spectator* for his uncanny ability to craft the finest merlot in California.

If you've visited before, but haven't been back in a while, don't follow your memory to the front door. In 2001, St. Francis moved a little farther north to digs bordering on the Santa Rosa County line. The original property was planted in 1910 as part of a wedding gift to Alice Kunde (scion of the local Kunde family) and christened St. Francis of Assisi in 1979 when Joe Martin and Lloyd Canton—two white-collar executives turned vintners—completed their long-awaited dream winery. Today the winery still owns the property, but there's new history in the making at their much larger facilities, which include a tasting room and upscale gift shop. Tastings are $5 for current releases, $10 for a reserve tasting of four wines, and $20 for a reserve tasting paired with food, served in the private reserve tasting room (by appointment). Now that St. Francis is planning more special activities, it's worthwhile to call or check their website for their calendar of events.

100 Pythian Rd. (Calif. 12/Sonoma Hwy.), Santa Rosa (at the Kenwood border). ✆ **800/543-7713,** ext. 242; or 707/833-4666. www.stfranciswinery.com. Daily 10am–5pm.

WHERE TO STAY IN SONOMA VALLEY

Keep in mind that during the peak season and on weekends, most B&Bs and hotels require a minimum 2-night stay. Of course, that's assuming you can find a vacancy; make reservations as far in advance as possible. If you are having trouble finding a room, call the **Sonoma Valley Visitors Bureau** (✆ **866/996-1090** or 707/996-1090; www.sonomavalley.com). The staff will try to refer you to a lodging that has a room to spare but won't make reservations for you. Another option is the **Bed and Breakfast Association of Sonoma Valley** (✆ **800/969-4667**), which can refer you to a B&B that belongs to the association. You can also find updated information on their website, **www.sonomabb.com**.

SONOMA

Very Expensive

Fairmont Sonoma Mission Inn & Spa ★★★ As you drive through Boyes Hot Springs, you may wonder why someone decided to build a multimillion-dollar spa resort in this ordinary little town. There's no view to speak of, and it certainly isn't within walking distance of any wineries or fancy restaurants. So what's the deal? It's the naturally heated artesian mineral water, piped from directly underneath the spa into the temperature-controlled pools and whirlpools. Set on 12 meticulously groomed acres, the Fairmount Sonoma Mission Inn consists of a massive three-story replica of a California mission (well, aside from the pink paint job) built in 1927, an array of satellite wings housing numerous superluxury suites, and world-class spa facilities. It's a popular retreat for the wealthy and well known, so don't be surprised if you see a famous face (I bumped into Tiffany Amber Thiessen of "90210" in the spa dressing room during my last visit). Big changes have occurred here since Fairmont took over the resort in 2002. It has gained 60 suites, updated its spa to the tune of $25 million, and just finished a $62-million renovation, which included completely redoing the Heritage Rooms in understated country elegance. Fancier digs include more modern rooms with plantation-style shutters, ceiling fans, down comforters, and oversize bath towels. The Wine Country rooms feature king-size beds, desks, refrigerators, and huge limestone and marble bathrooms; some offer wood-burning fireplaces, too, and many have balconies or patios. For the ultimate in luxury, the opulently appointed Mission Suites are the way to go. Golfers will be glad to know the resort is also home to the nearby Sonoma Golf Club, host of the PGA championship every October.

101 Boyes Blvd., corner of Boyes Blvd. and Calif. 12, P.O. Box 1447, Sonoma, CA 95476. ✆ **800/441-1414** or 707/938-9000. Fax 707/938-4250. www.fairmont.com/sonoma. 226 units. $259–$1,259 double. AE, DC, MC, V. Valet parking is free for day use (spa-goers) and $14 for overnight guests. From central Sonoma, drive 3 miles north on Hwy. 12 and turn left on Boyes Blvd. **Amenities:** 2 restaurants; 3 large, heated outdoor pools; golf course; health club and spa (see box, "The Super Spa," on p. 317 for the complete rundown); Jacuzzi; sauna; bike rental; concierge; business center; salon; room service; babysitting; same-day laundry service/dry cleaning; free wine tasting (4:30–5:30pm). *In room:* A/C, TV, dataport, minibar, hair dryer, iron, safe, high-speed Internet access ($13 per day), free bottle of wine upon arrival.

MacArthur Place ★★ A recommended alternative to the Fairmont Sonoma Mission Inn & Spa (see above) is this much smaller and more intimate luxury property and spa located 4 blocks south of Sonoma's plaza. Once a 300-acre vineyard and ranch, MacArthur Place has since been whittled down to a 5½-acre "country estate" replete with landscaped gardens and tree-lined pathways, various free-standing accommodations, a spa, and heated swimming pool and whirlpool. Most of the individually decorated guest rooms are Victorian-modern attached cottages scattered throughout the resort; all are exceedingly well stocked with custom linens, oversize comforters, and original artwork; most have flatscreen TVs. Some suites come with fireplaces, porches, wet bars, six-speaker surround sound, and whirlpool tubs that often have

---

Pricing Categories

Hotel listings are arranged in this section first by area, then by price, using the following categories: **Very Expensive,** more than $250 per night; **Expensive,** $200 to $250 per night; **Moderate,** $150 to $200 per night; and **Inexpensive,** less than $150 per night.

shutters opening to the bedroom. As of 2007 two newly converted suites are all about spa living and include private gardens, teak outdoor soaking tubs, and Japanese tea houses with outdoor showers. Everyone has access to complimentary wine and cheese in the evening and the DVD library anytime. The full-service spa offers a fitness center, body treatments, skin care, and massages. Within the resort's restored century-old barn is Saddles, Sonoma's only steakhouse specializing in grass-fed beef, organic and sustainably farmed produce, and whimsically classy Western decor. An array of other excellent restaurants—as well as shops, wineries, and bars—is within biking distance. ***Note:*** All rooms are nonsmoking.

29 E. MacArthur St., Sonoma, CA 95476. ✆ **800/722-1866** or 707/938-2929. www.macarthurplace.com. 64 units. Sun–Thurs $299–$550 double; Fri–Sat $349–$595 double. Rates include continental breakfast. AE, MC, V. Free parking. **Amenities:** Restaurant and bar specializing in martinis; outdoor heated pool; exercise room; full-service spa; outdoor Jacuzzi; steam room; rental bikes; concierge; room service; massage; laundry service; same-day dry cleaning. *In room:* A/C, TV/DVD, dataport, hair dryer, iron, Wi-Fi throughout; minibar, wet bar and coffeemaker in suites.

Expensive

Best Western Sonoma Valley Inn *Kids* Perfect for the traveling family, this simple inn with recently updated rooms offers plenty for kids along for the ride. There's room to run around, plus a large, heated outdoor saltwater pool, gazebo-covered spa, and sauna to play in. The rooms come with a few nice perks, such as continental breakfast delivered to your room each morning, and satellite TV with HBO (they also offer a host of paid movies). Most rooms have either a balcony or a deck overlooking the inner courtyard. An added bonus: If you need someone to help you get the kinks out, you can reserve one of the two new spa rooms and have the staff book an outside company to come in and give you an on-site massage. The inn is also in a convenient location, just a block from Sonoma's plaza.

550 Second St. W. (1 block from the plaza), Sonoma, CA 95476. ✆ **800/334-5784** or 707/938-9200. Fax 707/938-0935. www.sonomavalleyinn.com. 80 units. $114–$361 double. Rates include continental breakfast. AE, DC, DISC, MC, V. **Amenities:** Heated outdoor pool; exercise room; Jacuzzi; sauna; steam room; free Wi-Fi access. *In room:* A/C, TV, dataport, fridge, coffeemaker, hair dryer, iron, Wi-Fi.

Moderate

El Dorado Hotel ★★ This 1843 mission revival building may look like a 19th-century Wild West relic from the outside, but inside it's all 21st-century deluxe. Each modern, handsomely appointed guest room has French windows and tiny balconies. Some rooms offer lovely views of the plaza; others overlook the private courtyard and heated lap pool. Most rooms are on the second floor and there's no elevator. However, if you're against hoofing it you can request one of the four so-called bungalows on the ground floor, which were upgraded in 2006 and have partially enclosed patios. A new "market," slated for completion at the end of 2007, will serve light breakfast and lunch fare, coffee, and ice cream. Though prices reflect its prime location on Sonoma Square, this is still one of the more charming options within its price range—especially when you factor in instant access to the ground-floor El Dorado Kitchen, which is one of the valley's best restaurants.

405 First St. W., Sonoma, CA 95476. ✆ **800/289-3031** or 707/996-3030. Fax 707/996-3148. www.hoteleldorado.com. 27 units. Summer $195–$225 double; winter $145–$185 double. 2-night minimum weekends and holidays. AE, MC, V. **Amenities:** Restaurant; daily newspapers; coffee and organic teas; heated outdoor pool; fireplace lodge; laundry service. *In room:* A/C, environmentally safe bath products, flatscreen TV, DVD/CD player, cordless phone, voice mail, dataport, fridge, hair dryer, iron.

Finds The Super Spa

The **Fairmount Sonoma Mission Inn, Spa & Country Club,** 18140 Sonoma Hwy. (✆ **800/862-4945** or 707/938-9000; www.fairmont.com/sonoma), has always been the most complete—and the most luxurious—spa in the entire Wine Country. But after its $25-million, 43,000-square-foot facility upgrade, this super spa is justifiably one of the best in the country. The Spanish mission–style retreat offers more than 50 spa treatments, ever-popular natural mineral baths, and virtually every facility and activity imaginable. You can pamper yourself silly: Take a sauna or herbal steam, have a facial set to music, indulge in a grape-seed body wrap, relax with a massage, go for a dip in the outdoor pool, or soak away your worries in the celestial indoor mineral pool area—the list goes on and on (and, alas, so will the bill). You can also work off those wicked Wine Country meals with aerobics, weights, and cardio machines; get loose in a yoga class (all complimentary for guests); or just lounge and lunch by the pool. For non-guests, they offer personalized day spa packages, which range in price from $159 to $459 depending on what you request, and include use of the pool, classes, and hot tub. If you don't mind splurging and are a fan of luxury living, you'll agree that the Fairmount Sonoma Mission Inn Spa is one of the best ways to unwind in the Wine Country.

Inexpensive

Sonoma Hotel ★★ This cute little historic hotel on Sonoma's tree-lined town plaza emphasizes 19th-century elegance and comfort. Built in 1880 by Swiss immigrant Henry Weyl, it has attractive guest rooms decorated in early California style, with French country furnishings, wood and iron beds, and pine armoires. In a bow to modern luxuries, recent additions include private bathrooms, cable TV, phones with dataports, and (this is crucial) air-conditioning. Perks include fresh coffee and pastries in the morning and wine in the evening. Its lovely restaurant, the girl & the fig (p. 320) serves California-French cuisine.

110 W. Spain St., Sonoma, CA 95476. ✆ **800/468-6016** or 707/996-2996. Fax 707/996-7014. www.sonomahotel.com. 16 units. Summer $110–$248 double; winter $95–$200 double. 2-night minimum required for summer weekends. Rates include continental breakfast and evening wine. AE, DC, MC, V. *In room:* A/C, TV, dataport.

GLEN ELLEN

Expensive

Gaige House Inn ★★★ *Finds* Since Thompson Hotels recently purchased this property I can't say just yet whether they will be able to maintain the heart and soul of what is undoubtedly Wine Country's finest B&B. But I can tell you that they're striving to keep the level of service, amenities, and decor normally associated with four-star resorts. Every nook and cranny of the 1890 Queen Anne–Italianate building and Garden Annex remains swathed with fashionable articles from the world over, and the spacious rooms offer everything you could want—firm mattresses, wondrously silky-soft Sferra linens, and premium comforters gracing the beds; even the furniture and artwork are the kind you'd like to take home with you. All 23 rooms, artistically decorated in a plantation theme with Asian and Indonesian influences (trust me, they're beautiful), have king- or queen-size beds; four rooms have Jacuzzi tubs, one has a Japanese soaking tub, and the 13 newer superfancy spa garden suites have, among other delights, granite soaking tubs. For chilly country nights, fireplaces (in 17 rooms) definitely come in handy. Bathrooms are equally luxe and are stocked with fancy toiletries and slippers. Attention to detail means you'll be treated to a robe I liked so much I had to buy it. For the ultimate retreat, reserve one of the suites, which have patios overlooking a stream or private gardens.

But wait, it gets better. The inn is set on a 3-acre oasis with perfectly manicured lawns and gardens, a 40-foot-long heated pool, and an inviting creek-side hammock shaded by a majestic Heritage oak. Evenings are best spent in the reading parlor, sipping premium wines. Appetizers at wine hour might include freshly shucked oysters or a sautéed scallop served ready-to-slurp on a Chinese soupspoon. Breakfast is a momentous event, accented with herbs from the inn's garden and prepared by a chef who cooked at the James Beard House in 2001.

13540 Arnold Dr., Glen Ellen, CA 95442. ✆ **800/935-0237** or 707/935-0237. Fax 707/935-6411. www.thompsonhotels.com. 23 units. Summer $300–$595 double, $500–$595 suite; winter $195–$275 double, $325–$525 suite. Rates include evening wines. AE, DC, DISC, MC, V. **Amenities:** Large heated pool; in-room massage; free Wi-Fi. *In room:* A/C, TV/DVD, dataport, fridge, hair dryer, iron, safe, DSL and Wi-Fi.

Inexpensive

Beltane Ranch ★ *Finds* The word *ranch* conjures up a big ole' two-story house in the middle of hundreds of rolling acres, the kind of place where you laze away the day in a hammock watching the grass grow or in the garden pitching horseshoes. Well, friend, you can have all that and more at the well-located Beltane Ranch, a century-old buttercup-yellow manor that's been everything from a bunkhouse to a brothel to a turkey farm. You simply can't help but feel your tensions ease away as you prop your feet up on the shady wraparound porch overlooking the quiet vineyards, sipping a cool, fruity chardonnay while reading *Lonesome Dove* for the third time. Each room is uniquely decorated with American and European antiques; all have sitting areas and separate entrances. A big and creative country breakfast is served in the garden or on the porch overlooking the vineyards. For exercise, you can play tennis on the private court or hike the trails meandering through the 105-acre estate. The staff here is knowledgeable and helpful. ***Tip:*** Request one of the upstairs rooms, which have the best views.

11775 Sonoma Hwy./Hwy. 12, P.O. Box 395, Glen Ellen, CA 95442. ✆ **707/996-6501**. www.beltaneranch.com. 5 units, 1 cottage. $140–$190 double; $220 cottage. Rates include full breakfast. No credit cards; personal checks accepted. **Amenities:** Outdoor, unlit tennis court. *In room:* No phone.

Glenelly Inn and Cottages ★ Perhaps the best thing about this rustic retreat is its reasonable rates. But equally important, this former railroad inn, built in 1916, is positively drenched in serenity. Located well off the main highway on an oak-studded hillside, the peach-and-cream inn comes with everything you would expect from a country retreat. Long verandas offer Adirondack-style chairs and views of the verdant Sonoma hillsides; breakfast is served beside a large cobblestone fireplace; and bright units contain old-fashioned claw-foot tubs, Scandinavian down comforters, and ceiling fans (though cottages have whirlpool tubs and air-conditioning). Downsides include thin walls, the usual laugh lines that come with age, and depending on your perspective, lack of TV and phone in every room. However, the staff understands that it's the little things that make the difference—hence the firm mattresses, good reading lights, and a simmering hot tub in a grapevine- and rose-covered arbor. All rooms are decorated with antiques and country furnishings, and have terry robes and private entrances. Top picks are the Vallejo and Jack London family suites, both with large private patios, although I also like the rooms on the upper veranda—particularly in the spring, when the terraced gardens below are in full bloom. The new free-standing garden cottages (the best option) are for those who want to splurge; they come with fireplaces, TV/VCRs, CD players, coffeemakers, and fridges.

5131 Warm Springs Rd. (off Arnold Dr.), Glen Ellen, CA 95442. ✆ **707/996-6720.** Fax 707/996-5227. www.glenelly.com. 9 units. $155–$205 double/suite; $325 cottage. Rates include full breakfast. AE, DISC, MC, V. **Amenities:** Outdoor Jacuzzi; TV in common room. *In room:* TV in some rooms, Wi-Fi.

KENWOOD

Very Expensive

Kenwood Inn & Spa ★★ Inspired by the villas of Tuscany, the Kenwood Inn's honey-colored Italian-style buildings, flower-filled flagstone courtyard, and pastoral views of vineyard-covered hills are enough to make any northern Italian homesick. The friendly staff and luxuriously restful surroundings made this California girl feel right at home. What's not to like about a spacious room lavishly and exquisitely decorated with imported tapestries, velvets, and antiques, plus a fireplace, balcony (except on the ground floor), private bathroom (many with spa tubs), feather bed, CD player, and down comforter? With no TV in the rooms, relaxation is inevitable—especially if you book treatments at their Caudalie Vinotherapie Spa, which uses exclusive Caudalie products highlighting wine and grape seed extracts. A minor caveat is road noise, which you're unlikely to hear from your room but can be slightly audible over the tranquil pumped-in music around the courtyard and decent-size pool. Longtime guests will be surprised to find more bodies around the pool—18 guest rooms, a steam room and a wine bar joined this slice of pastoral heaven in June 2003.

An impressive three-course gourmet breakfast is served in the courtyard or in the Mediterranean-style dining room. A note for traveling families: Kenwood Inn doesn't welcome kids under 16.

10400 Sonoma Hwy., Kenwood, CA 95452. ✆ **800/353-6966** or 707/833-1293. Fax 707/833-1247. www.kenwoodinn.com. 30 units. Apr–Oct $325–$750 double; Nov–Mar $250–$600 double. Rates include gourmet breakfast and bottle of wine. 2-night minimum on weekends. AE, MC, V. No pets allowed. children under 16 not recommended. **Amenities:** Heated outdoor pool; 2 outdoor hot tubs; indoor steam room and soaking tub; full-service spa; concierge. *In room:* A/C, phone, hair dryer, iron, high-speed Internet access, Caudalie bath products, CD player.

WHERE TO DINE IN SONOMA VALLEY

SONOMA

Moderate

Cafe La Haye ★★ ECLECTIC Well-prepared and wholesome food, an experienced waitstaff, friendly owners, a soothing atmosphere, and reasonable prices—including a modestly priced wine list—make La Haye a favorite. In truth, everything about this cafe-like restaurant is charming. The atmosphere within the small split-level dining room is smart and intimate. The vibe is small business—a welcome departure from Napa Valley's big-business restaurants. The straightforward, seasonally inspired cuisine, which chefs bring forth from the tiny open kitchen, is delicious and wonderfully well-priced. Although the menu is small, it offers just enough options. Expect a risotto special; pasta such as fresh tagliarini with butternut squash, prosciutto, sage,

Pricing Categories

The restaurants listed here are classified first by town, then by price, using the following categories: **Expensive,** dinner from $50 per person; **Moderate,** dinner from $35 per person; and **Inexpensive,** dinner less than $35 per person. (***Note:*** The "Very Expensive" category—dinner from $75 per person—has been omitted since no restaurants in this chapter fall under its umbrella.) These categories reflect prices for an appetizer, a main course, a dessert, and a glass of wine.

and garlic cream; and pan-roasted chicken breast, perhaps with goat cheese–herb stuffing, caramelized shallot *jus,* and fennel mashed potatoes. Meat eaters are sure to be pleased with filet of beef seared with black pepper and lavender and served with Gorgonzola-potato gratin; and no one can resist the creative salads.

140 E. Napa St., Sonoma. ✆ **707/935-5994.** Reservations recommended. Main courses $14–$24. AE, MC, V. Tues–Sat 5:30–9pm.

Harvest Moon ★★ REGIONAL SEASONAL AMERICAN Napa may have better restaurants in general, but the feasts to the east have nothing on this new downtown Sonoma restaurant. Chef/owner Nick Demarest's experience at Berkeley's world-famous Chez Panisse is evidenced by his use of outstanding ingredients combined into dishes of clean, pure, and glorious flavors. His chicory salad with mustard vinaigrette, house-cured bacon, and Gruyère is a case-in-point appetizer that's easily backed up by entrees such as pan-fried local rock cod with Swiss chard, fingerling potatoes, and beurre rouge. Sweetening the already delicious deal, his wife Jen is a pedigreed pastry chef with experience at Napa's fancy La Toque. The space itself hasn't changed much since its previous incarnation as foie gras-centric Sonoma Saveurs, which means you can expect great seats at the wine bar and a quirky scattering of tables tucked within a cramped and warm historic adobe room. Inside you'll see the chef hard at work within the shoebox open kitchen. Outside, weather permitting, is garden dining. Regardless, if it's a good meal you're after, you will not find a better one this side of the Mayacamas.

487 1st St W, Sonoma. ✆ **707/933-8160,** www.harvestmoonsonoma.com. Reservations recommended. Main courses $17–$25. AE, DISC, MC, V. Sun–Thurs 5:30–9pm; Fri–Sat 5:30–9:30pm.

the girl & the fig ★ COUNTRY FRENCH Well established in its downtown Sonoma digs (it used to be in Glen Ellen), this modern, attractive, and cozy eatery, with lovely patio seating, is the home for Sondra Bernstein's (the girl) beloved restaurant. Here the cuisine, orchestrated by chef de cuisine Matt Murray, is nouveau country with French nuances, and yes, figs are sure to be on the menu in one form or another. The wonderful fig and arugula salad contains pancetta, pecans, dried figs, Laura Chenel goat cheese, and fig-and-port vinaigrette. Murray uses garden-fresh produce and local meats, poultry, and fish whenever possible, in dishes such as grilled pork chops or duck confit. For dessert, try the butterscotch pot de creme, a glass of Cave des Vigneron muscat, and a sliver of one of their delicious offerings from the cheese list. Sondra knows her wines, features Rhone varietals, and will be happy to choose the best accompaniment for your meal. Looking for brunch? Head here on Sunday when it's served until 3pm.

110 W. Spain St., Sonoma. ✆ **707/938-3634.** www.thegirlandthefig.com. Reservations recommended. Main courses $13–$24. AE, DISC, MC, V. Mon–Thurs 11:30am–10pm; Fri–Sat 11:30am–11pm; Sun 10am–10pm.

Shiso ★ ASIAN/SUSHI Open since May 2006, this newcomer has been a welcome addition to the Sonoma food scene with its bright dining room and addictive "modern" Asian fare (with French influences). It's named for a Japanese mint leaf, and you'll find reference to that throughout from a subtle logo to the pretty green splashes in the furniture and on the walls. Grab a table or sit at the sushi bar and go directly to the fresh, seasonal shared plates—miso-glazed butterfish with Chinese long beans and miso emulsion, or braised beef short ribs with glazed daikon and carrots would be good places to start. The specials menu changes nightly and highlights the chefs' love of locally grown ingredients with exotic and tasty ventures such as local skate with sautéed stinging nettles and uni cream sauce. You'll find good sushi here, too, from traditional nigiri, sashimi, hand rolls, and rolls (tuna, negi hama, California) to creative combinations (the Oregon roll has salmon, cream cheese, and cucumber). If it's on the specials menu (it usually is), don't miss the tempura-fried Kobe beef roll with hot Chinese mustard aioli, spinach, and avocado. Although the food is satisfying, it's the little touches like coffee served in French press pots that makes this place a real standout. Finish the evening with ginger snap and macadamia nut–crusted tempura-fried coconut ice cream or ginger crème brûlée.

522 Broadway (just off the plaza), Sonoma. ✆ **707/933-9331.** www.shisorestaurant.com. Reservations accepted. Main courses $7–$14 lunch, $15–$40 dinner; $3.75–$50 sushi and sashimi. AE, DISC, MC, V. Winter hours Wed–Sun 5:30–9:30pm; summer hours Wed–Sun noon–2pm and Tues–Sun 5:30–9:30pm; hours are seasonal, so please call to confirm.

Meritage ★ SOUTHERN FRENCH/NORTHERN ITALIAN Learning from the previous occupants' mistakes—that Sonoma ain't New York and shouldn't treat its customers that way—chef-owner Carlo Cavallo eliminated the big-city attitude and prices at his restaurant without diminishing style, service, or quality. The former executive chef for Giorgio Armani, Cavallo combines the best of southern French and northern Italian cuisines (hence "Meritage," after a blend made with traditional bordeaux varieties), giving Sonomans yet another reason to eat out. The menu, which changes twice daily, is a good read: foie gras ravioli with sage truffle sauce; seafood stew with tiger prawns, Manila clams, mussels, and mixed fresh fish in a spicy tomato saffron broth; and wild boar chops in white truffle sauce with mashed potatoes. Shellfish fans can't help but love the oyster raw bar with options of fresh crab and lobster, and cocktailers revel in the new martini bar. A lovely garden patio is prime positioning for sunny brunches and lunches and summer dinners. Such edible enticement—combined with reasonable prices, excellent service, a stellar wine list, and Carlo's practiced charm—make Meritage a trustworthy option.

165 W. Napa St., Sonoma. ✆ **707/938-9430.** www.sonomameritage.com. Reservations recommended. Main courses $13–$30. AE, MC, V. Mon and Wed–Fri 11:30am–9:30pm; Sat–Sun 10:30am–9:30pm.

Swiss Hotel ★ CONTINENTAL/NORTHERN ITALIAN With its slanting floors and beamed ceilings, the historic Swiss Hotel, located right in the town center, is a Sonoma landmark and very much the local favorite for fine food served at reasonable prices. The turn-of-the-20th-century oak bar at the left of the entrance is adorned with black-and-white photos of pioneering Sonomans. The bright white dining room and sidewalk patio seats are pleasant spots to enjoy lunch specials such as penne with chicken, mushrooms, and tomato cream; hot sandwiches; and California-style pizzas fired in a wood-burning oven. But the secret spot is the atmospheric back garden patio, a secluded oasis shaded by a wisteria-covered trellis and adorned with plants, a fountain, gingham tablecloths, and a fireplace. Dinner might start with a warm winter salad of radicchio and frisée with pears, walnuts, and bleu cheese. Main courses run the gamut; I like the linguine and prawns with garlic, hot pepper, and tomatoes; the bleu cheese–encrusted filet mignon; and roasted rosemary chicken. The food may not knock your socks off, but it's all simply satisfying.

18 W. Spain St (at First St. W.), Sonoma. ✆ **707/938-2884.** www.swisshotelsonoma.com. Reservations recommended. Main courses lunch $8.50–$16, dinner $13–$28. AE, MC, V. Daily 11:30am–2:30pm; Sun–Thurs 5–9pm; Fri–Sat 5–10pm. (Bar daily 11:30am–2am.)

Inexpensive

Black Bear Diner *Kids* DINER When you're craving a classic American breakfast with all the cholesterol and the fixin's (perhaps to counterbalance that wine hangover), make a beeline for this old-fashioned diner. First, it's fun, with its over-the-top bear paraphernalia, gazette-style menu listing local news from 1961 and every possible diner favorite, and absurdly friendly waitstaff. Second, it's darned cheap. Third, helpings are huge. What more could you want? Kids get a kick out of coloring books, old-timers reminisce over Sinatra playing on the jukebox, and everyone leaves stuffed on omelets, scrambles, and pancakes. Lunch and dinner feature steak sandwiches, salads, and comfort food faves like barbecued pork ribs, Cobb salad, fish and chips, and burgers—they grind their own beef. But unless you like old-school run-of-the-mill diner fare, your best bet is to dine elsewhere.

201 W. Napa St. (at Second St.), Sonoma. ✆ **707/935-6800.** www.blackbeardiner.com. Main courses breakfast $5–$8.50, lunch and dinner $5.50–$17. AE, DISC, MC, V. Daily 6am–9:30pm (closing varies on weekends, depending on business).

Della Santina's ★★ TUSCAN For those of you who just can't swallow another expensive, chichi California meal, follow the locals to this friendly, traditional Italian restaurant. How traditional? Ask father-and-son team Dan and Robert: When I last dined here, they pointed out Signora Santina's hand-embroidered linen doilies as they proudly told me about her Tuscan recipes. And their pride is merited: Every dish my party tried was refreshingly authentic and well flavored, without overbearing sauces or one *hint* of California pretentiousness. Be sure to start with traditional antipasti, particularly sliced mozzarella and tomatoes, or delicious, traditional tortellini in brodo (homemade tortellini in broth). The nine pasta dishes are, again, wonderfully authentic (gnocchi lovers, rejoice!). The spit-roasted meat dishes are a local favorite (although I found them a bit overcooked); for those who can't choose between chicken, pork, turkey, rabbit, or duck, there's a selection that offers a choice of three. Don't worry about breaking your bank on a bottle of wine, because many choices here go for under $40. Portions are huge, but be sure to save room for a wonderful dessert, like the creamy panna cotta. Though the inside's small, there's a pretty huge back patio covered in blooming trellises that's full practically every night in the summer (the wait's never too bad), and they've recently tented part of it, so you can eat back there in winter, too, weather permitting.

133 E. Napa St. (just east of the square), Sonoma. ✆ **707/935-0576.** www.dellasantinas.com. Reservations recommended. Main courses $10–$20. AE, DISC, MC, V. Daily 11:30am–3pm and 5–9:30pm.

Rin's Thai ★ THAI When valley residents or visitors get a hankering for Pad Thai, curry chicken, or *tom yum* (classic spicy soup), they head to this adorable little restaurant just off Sonoma Plaza. The atmosphere itself—contemporary, warm environs within an old house—is tasteful and the staff is extremely accommodating. After you settle into one of the well-spaced tables within or outside on the patio (weather permitting), go for your favorites—satay with peanut sauce and cucumber salad; spicy red curry with a choice of pork, beef, chicken, vegetables, or seafood; yummy *larb gai salad* (minced chicken, chiles, onion, and lemon sauce); or charbroiled vegetables or ribs with chile-garlic dipping sauce. They've got it all covered, including that oh-so-sweet Thai iced tea, fried bananas with coconut ice cream, and fresh mango with sticky rice (seasonal).

139 E. Napa St. (just east of the plaza), Sonoma. ✆ **707/938-1462.** www.rinsthai.com. Reservations recommended. Main courses $7.50–$12. MC, V. Daily 11:30am–9pm.

GLEN ELLEN

Moderate

the fig café & wine bar ★★ NEW AMERICAN The girl & the fig's (p. 320) sister restaurant is more casual than its downtown Sonoma sibling. But don't let the bucolic neighborhood vibe, airy environs, and soothing sage-and-mustard color scheme fool you. From his open kitchen, general manager and chef de cuisine Bryan Jones brings you the kind of rustic sophistication more commonly associated with urban restaurants. Consider starting with a thin-crust pizza, fried calamari with spicy lemon aioli, a cheese plate, or the signature fig and arugula salad; move on to braised pot roast with mashed potatoes or mussels in a garlic, leek, and tarragon sauce with fries; and finish with a fantastic chocolate brownie with vanilla ice cream. A perk: the "Rhone Alone" wine selections are available by the flight, glass, or bottle, free corkage.

13690 Arnold Dr. (at Madrone Rd). ✆ **707/938-2130.** www.thefigcafe.com. Reservations not accepted. Main courses $10–$18. AE, DISC, MC, V. Sun–Thurs 5:30–9pm; Fri–Sat until 9:30pm. Brunch offered Sat–Sun 9:30am–2:30pm.

Glen Ellen Inn Oyster Grill & Martini Bar ★ CALIFORNIA Christian and Karen Bertrand have made this place so quaint and cozy that you feel as if you're dining in their home, and that's exactly the place's charm. Garden seating is the favored choice on sunny days, but the covered, heated patio is also always welcoming. The first course from Christian's open kitchen might be a ginger tempura calamari with wasabi or a brie fondue with sourdough toast points. Main courses, which change with the seasons, range from spinach and Stilton ravioli to grilled salmon with blood oranges, watercress, and lemon aioli. Other favorites include pork tenderloin with sun-dried cranberries, mozzarella, caramelized onions, and polenta; and utterly tender filet mignon with Maytag blue cheese and garlic frites. On my last visit, the Sonoma Valley mixed-green salad, seared ahi tuna, and homemade French vanilla ice cream floating in bittersweet caramel sauce made a lovely meal. They've recently added the eponymous oyster grill and martini bar, including half-size taster martinis and, of course, oysters any way you want 'em. If that doesn't do it for you, the 550-plus wine selection list offers numerous bottles from Sonoma, as well as more than a dozen wines by the glass. ***Tip:*** There's a small parking lot behind the restaurant.

13670 Arnold Dr. (at O'Donnell Lane), Glen Ellen. ✆ **707/996-6409.** www.glenelleninn.com. Reservations recommended. Main courses $16–$25. AE, DISC, MC, V. Fri–Tues 11:30am–9pm (dinner from 5pm); Wed–Thurs 5:30–9pm. Closed 1 week in Jan.

Wolf House ★ ECLECTIC The most polished-looking dining room in Glen Ellen is elegant yet relaxed whether you're seated in the handsome dining room—smartly adorned with maple floors, gold walls, dark-wood wainscoting, and a corner fireplace—or outside on the multilevel terrace under the canopy of trees with serene views of adjacent Sonoma Creek. The lunch menu adds fancy finishes to old favorites such as the excellent chicken Caesar salad, fresh grilled ahi tuna niçoise sandwich, or juicy half-pound burger with Point Reyes Original Blue cheese. During dinner, skip the soggy beer-battered prawns and head straight for seared Roasted Liberty farms duck breast with wild stewed plums, cipollini onions, barley risotto, baked pears, and plum demi; or pan-roasted salmon with sweet asparagus, baby arugula salad, and sunchoke mash. The reasonably priced wine list offers many by-the-glass options as well as a fine selection of Sonoma wines. At brunch locals love the *nepalas rancheros* (chorizo, pinto beans, roasted chiles, and fried eggs), Dungeness crab cake Benedict, omelets, and brioche French toast. During my visits, service was rather languid, but well meaning.

13740 Arnold Dr. (at London Ranch Rd.), Glen Ellen. ✆ **707/996-4401**. www.jacklondonlodge.com/rest.html. Reservations recommended. Main courses brunch and lunch $8–$15, dinner $17–$32. AE, MC, V. Lunch Tues–Fri 11am–3pm; dinner Tues–Sun 5:30–9pm; brunch Sat 11am–3pm, Sun 10am–3pm.

KENWOOD

Moderate

Kenwood Restaurant & Bar ★★ CALIFORNIA/CONTINENTAL This is what Wine Country dining should be—but often, disappointingly, is not. From the terrace of the Kenwood Restaurant, diners enjoy a view of the vineyards set against Sugarloaf Ridge as they imbibe Sonoma's finest at umbrella-covered tables. On nippy days, you can retreat inside to the Sonoma-style roadhouse, with its vibrant artwork and cushioned rattan chairs at white cloth–covered tables. Regardless of where you pull up a chair, expect first-rate cuisine, perfectly balanced between tradition and innovation, complemented by a reasonably priced wine list. Great starters are Dungeness crab cake with herb mayonnaise; superfresh sashimi with ginger, soy, and wasabi; and a wonderful Caesar salad. The main dish might be poached salmon in creamy caper sauce, or prawns with saffron Pernod sauce. But the Kenwood doesn't take itself too seriously: Great sandwiches and burgers are also available.

9900 Sonoma Hwy. (just north of Dunbar Rd.), Kenwood. ✆ **707/833-6326**. www.kenwoodrestaurant.com. Reservations recommended. Main courses $13–$30. MC, V. Wed–Sat noon–9pm; Sun noon-8pm.

Inexpensive

Café Citti NORTHERN ITALIAN If you're this far north into the Wine Country, then you're probably doing some serious wine tasting. If that's the case, then you don't want to spend half the day at a fancy, high-priced restaurant. What you need is Café Citti (pronounced *Cheat*-ee), a roadside do-it-yourself Italian trattoria that is both good and cheap. You order from the huge menu board displayed above the open kitchen. Afterward, you grab a table (the ones on the patio, shaded by umbrellas, are the best on warm afternoons), and a server will bring your meal. It's all hearty, home-cooked Italian. Standout dishes are the green-bean salad, tangy Caesar salad, focaccia sandwiches, and roasted rotisserie chicken stuffed with rosemary and garlic. Wine is available by the bottle, and the espresso is plenty strong. Everything on the menu board is available to go, which makes Café Citti an excellent resource for picnic supplies.

9049 Sonoma Hwy., Kenwood. ✆ **707/833-2690**. Prices $7–$22. MC, V. Lunch daily 11am–3:30pm; dinner Sun–Thurs 5–8:30pm, Fri–Sat 5–9pm.

El Dorado Kitchen ★★ CALIFORNIA With its Napa Valley pedigree, El Dorado Kitchen is upping the ante for Sonoma dining within the open, airy dining room, which is sleek and comfortable, if not overly cozy; outdoor seating is available on warm Sonoma nights. Executive Chef Ryan Fancher, who worked at Napa's French Laundry and Auberge du Soleil, brings a much-needed dose of modern fare to town. The seasonal menu ("Mediterranean-inspired bistro cuisine") changes often but always flaunts Fancher's talent at elevating everyday lunch options, perhaps grilled cheese and tomato soup or griddled prosciutto and Vermont cheddar with San Marzano tomato soup. There's always a fritto misto on the menu, such as the surprising and delicious curry fritto misto of lightly battered apples, cauliflower and fall squash served with curry salt and aioli. You'll also find a classic charcuterie plate and a Caesar that pays homage to Southern France with the addition of niçoise olives. Entrees might include Pacific salmon with white bean cassoulet, prosciutto, and sage; or lamb loin with rosemary polenta, piquillo peppers, Swiss chard, and niçoise olive sauce. Don't hesitate to order the white truffle and parmesan French fries and one of their house drinks. In an area where dinner prices can run upwards the cost of some people's monthly house payments, El Dorado Kitchen's prices are surprisingly reasonable and portions are generous.

405 First St. W., Sonoma. ✆ **707/996-3030.** Reservations recommended. Lunch $7–$15, dinner $8–$25, brunch $6–$15. 11:30am–10pm Mon-Sat; 11am–2:30pm Sun brunch, and lunch and dinner menu 2:30–10pm.

Follini & Eichenbaum Café DELI When I'm looking for picnic goods, a deliciously fresh and inexpensive meal, or a kid-friendly spot for the family meal—indoors or out—this is one of my top picks. Jules Abate joined her aunts (Follini and Eichenbaum) in Sonoma to bring her unique take on "Jewish-Italian deli" food to Sonoma. Yes, that means you can find quality hot pastrami in Sonoma. There's also a large selection of fresh salads, unusual sodas and chips, and habit-forming homemade chocolate chip cookies. You can drop by any morning for coffee and pastries, but on Sundays the offerings tempt further with a brunch buffet that includes potato pancakes, deep-dish quiches, eggs Benedict, breads, baked goods, salads, and desserts, plus a lot more. Oy! Too many choices.

19100 Arnold Dr., Sonoma ✆ **707/996-3287.** Reservations recommended for brunch. Sandwiches and main courses $4.95–$9.95. Mon–Fri 6am–2:30pm; Sat 8am–2:30pm; Sun brunch 10am–2pm.

Saddles ★ AMERICAN STEAK HOUSE You won't find any culinary trailblazing at Saddles, but you will get fresh, innovative versions of your favorite comfort food. With firelight dancing on the wall murals of horses, wainscoting painted to look like a picket fence, and yes, well-worn saddles perched around the entrance, this place does things on a grand scale. Get the night going with one of their signature martinis, offered in either a 6- or 10-ounce serving, from the Classic (gin and vermouth) to the Jolly Rancher (Absolut citron vodka and sour apple liqueur). Then tuck into an order of the red cornmeal haystack onion rings with blue cheese aioli, a giant mound of thinly sliced, lightly-battered goodness; or stuffed mushrooms with housemade Italian sausage. Entrees run the gamut from ribs, chicken, burgers, fish, and pasta, to the 14 or so choices of red meat. The barbecued baby back ribs with steak fries do not disappoint, falling off the bone and smothered in a housemade sweet, tangy barbecue sauce. You can also choose from prime rib, signature steaks, and specialty cuts. Try the Niman Ranch filet mignon for a buttery, tender option. Many of the steaks are served a la carte, so you'll want to add a few of the numerous sides, including creamed spinach (it's made with fresh, whole baby spinach leaves, a surprising touch) and potatoes au gratin, perfectly crunchy on top and creamy in the middle. All of these are big enough to share, of course. Desserts are good here too, so try the caramel apple crisp with vanilla ice cream or the cheesecake with fresh berries. The wine list is big too, with close to 215 mostly Californian wines, and lots of options by the glass.

29 E. MacArthur St., Sonoma ✆ **707/933-3191.** Reservations recommended. Main courses $9.95–$49. Sun–Thurs 5:30–9pm; Fri–Sat 5:30–9:30pm.

Taste of the Himalayas ★ NEPALESE/INDIAN You might wonder how this group of Nepalese friends (including a sherpa!), ended up in this small restaurant just off the square in Sonoma, but then you taste their food and you're just happy they did. If you're looking for something other than the usual pizzas, pastas and burritos, this is your spot. Just what does a Nepalese meal entail? Start with crisp *samosas* (a mild blend of potatoes and peas served with mint sauce,) or *momos* (small steamed dumplings stuffed with either lamb or veggies). Move on to entrees such as curry or Tandoori dishes, which wash down nicely with Indian Taj Mahal beer. All entrees come with a delicious bowl of mild *daal bhat,* the traditional Indian lentil soup, your choice of basmati rice or naan, and casual but attentive service.

464 First St. E., Sonoma ✆ **707/996-1161.** Reservations recommended, but walk-ins welcome. Main courses $10–$18. Daily 11am–3pm and 5–10pm.

Index

See also Accommodations and Restaurant indexes, below.

General Index

ACCOMMODATIONS

RESTAURANTS

Frommer's® Complete Travel Guides

Alaska
Amalfi Coast
American Southwest
Amsterdam
Argentina & Chile
Arizona
Atlanta
Australia
Austria
Bahamas
Barcelona
Beijing
Belgium, Holland & Luxembourg
Belize
Bermuda
Boston
Brazil
British Columbia & the Canadian Rockies
Brussels & Bruges
Budapest & the Best of Hungary
Buenos Aires
Calgary
California
Canada
Cancún, Cozumel & the Yucatán
Cape Cod, Nantucket & Martha's Vineyard
Caribbean
Caribbean Ports of Call
Carolinas & Georgia
Chicago
China
Colorado
Costa Rica
Croatia
Cuba
Denmark
Denver, Boulder & Colorado Springs
Edinburgh & Glasgow
England
Europe
Europe by Rail
Florence, Tuscany & Umbria
Florida
France
Germany
Greece
Greek Islands
Hawaii
Hong Kong
Honolulu, Waikiki & Oahu
India
Ireland
Israel
Italy
Jamaica
Japan
Kauai
Las Vegas
London
Los Angeles
Los Cabos & Baja
Madrid
Maine Coast
Maryland & Delaware
Maui
Mexico
Montana & Wyoming
Montréal & Québec City
Moscow & St. Petersburg
Munich & the Bavarian Alps
Nashville & Memphis
New England
Newfoundland & Labrador
New Mexico
New Orleans
New York City
New York State
New Zealand
Northern Italy
Norway
Nova Scotia, New Brunswick & Prince Edward Island
Oregon
Paris
Peru
Philadelphia & the Amish Country
Portugal
Prague & the Best of the Czech Republic
Provence & the Riviera
Puerto Rico
Rome
San Antonio & Austin
San Diego
San Francisco
Santa Fe, Taos & Albuquerque
Scandinavia
Scotland
Seattle
Seville, Granada & the Best of Andalusia
Shanghai
Sicily
Singapore & Malaysia
South Africa
South America
South Florida
South Pacific
Southeast Asia
Spain
Sweden
Switzerland
Tahiti & French Polynesia
Texas
Thailand
Tokyo
Toronto
Turkey
USA
Utah
Vancouver & Victoria
Vermont, New Hampshire & Maine
Vienna & the Danube Valley
Vietnam
Virgin Islands
Virginia
Walt Disney World® & Orlando
Washington, D.C.
Washington State

Frommer's® Day by Day Guides

Amsterdam
Chicago
Florence & Tuscany
London
New York City
Paris
Rome
San Francisco
Venice

Pauline Frommer's Guides! See More. Spend Less.

Hawaii
Italy
New York City

Frommer's® Portable Guides

Acapulco, Ixtapa & Zihuatanejo
Amsterdam
Aruba
Australia's Great Barrier Reef
Bahamas
Big Island of Hawaii
Boston
California Wine Country
Cancún
Cayman Islands
Charleston
Chicago
Dominican Republic
Dublin
Florence
Las Vegas
Las Vegas for Non-Gamblers
London
Maui
Nantucket & Martha's Vineyard
New Orleans
New York City
Paris
Portland
Puerto Rico
Puerto Vallarta, Manzanillo & Guadalajara
Rio de Janeiro
San Diego
San Francisco
Savannah
St. Martin, Sint Maarten, Anguila & St. Bart's
Turks & Caicos
Vancouver
Venice
Virgin Islands
Washington, D.C.
Whistler

Frommer's® Cruise Guides

Alaska Cruises & Ports of Call
Cruises & Ports of Call
European Cruises & Ports of Call

Frommer's® National Park Guides

Algonquin Provincial Park
Banff & Jasper
Grand Canyon
National Parks of the American West
Rocky Mountain
Yellowstone & Grand Teton
Yosemite and Sequoia & Kings Canyon
Zion & Bryce Canyon

Frommer's® Memorable Walks

London
New York
Paris
Rome
San Francisco

Frommer's® With Kids Guides

Chicago
Hawaii
Las Vegas
London
National Parks
New York City
San Francisco
Toronto
Walt Disney World® & Orlando
Washington, D.C.

Suzy Gershman's Born to Shop Guides

France
Hong Kong, Shanghai & Beijing
Italy
London
New York
Paris
San Francisco

Frommer's® Irreverent Guides

Amsterdam
Boston
Chicago
Las Vegas
London
Los Angeles
Manhattan
Paris
Rome
San Francisco
Walt Disney World®
Washington, D.C.

Frommer's® Best-Loved Driving Tours

Austria
Britain
California
France
Germany
Ireland
Italy
New England
Northern Italy
Scotland
Spain
Tuscany & Umbria

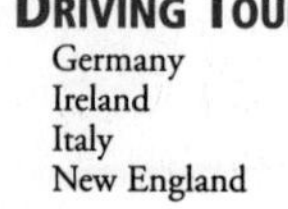

The Unofficial Guides®

Adventure Travel in Alaska
Beyond Disney
California with Kids
Central Italy
Chicago
Cruises
Disneyland®
England
Florida
Florida with Kids
Hawaii
Ireland
Las Vegas
London
Maui
Mexico's Best Beach Resorts
Mini Mickey
New Orleans
New York City
Paris
San Francisco
South Florida including Miami & the Keys
Walt Disney World®
Walt Disney World® for Grown-ups
Walt Disney World® with Kids
Washington, D.C.

Special-Interest Titles

Athens Past & Present
Best Places to Raise Your Family
Cities Ranked & Rated
500 Places to Take Your Kids Before They Grow Up
Frommer's Best Day Trips from London
Frommer's Best RV & Tent Campgrounds in the U.S.A.
Frommer's Exploring America by RV
Frommer's NYC Free & Dirt Cheap
Frommer's Road Atlas Europe
Frommer's Road Atlas Ireland
Great Escapes From NYC Without Wheels
Retirement Places Rated

Frommer's® PhraseFinder Dictionary Guides

French
Italian
Spanish

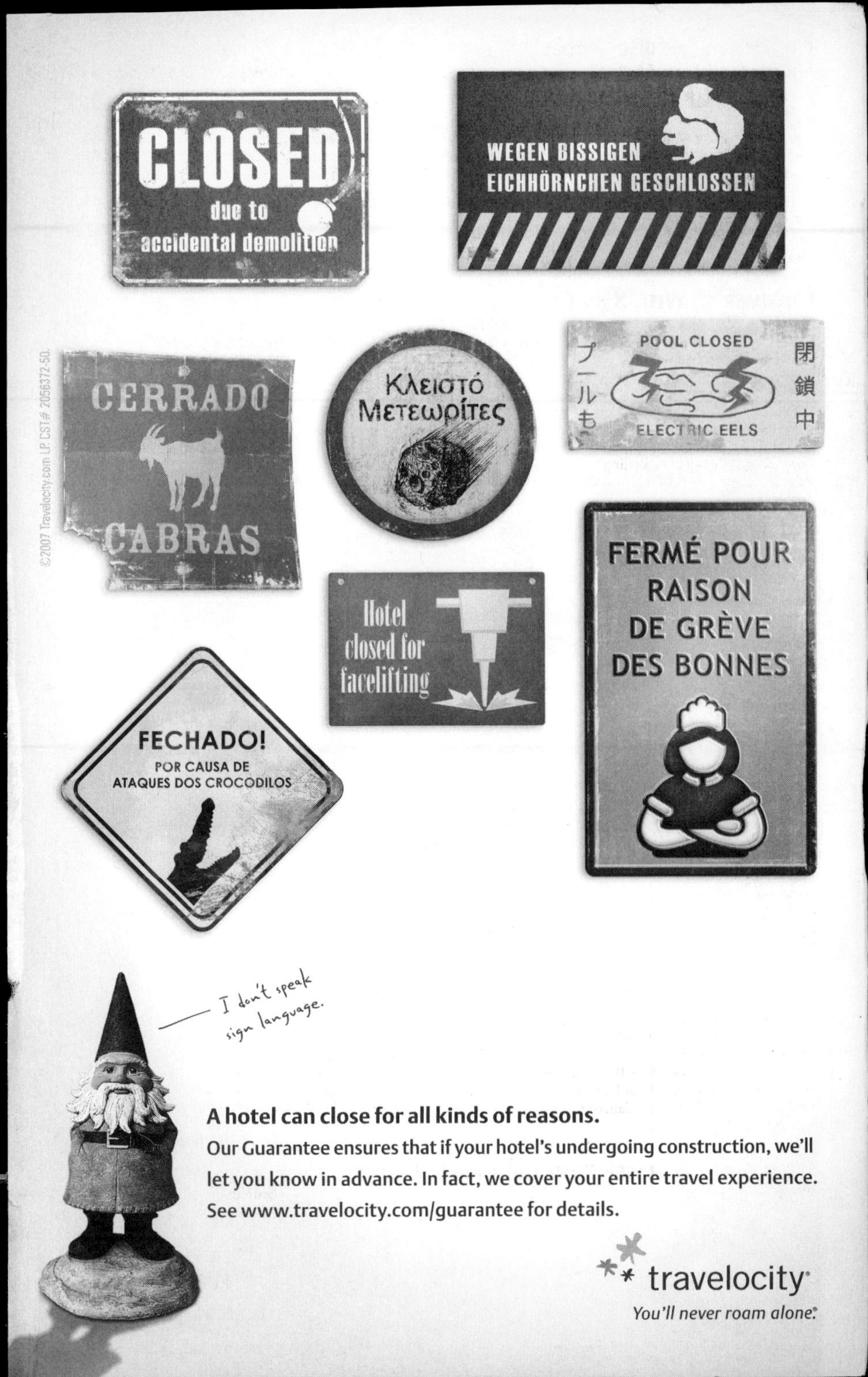
CLOSED
due to
accidental demolition
WEGEN BISSIGEN
EICHHÖRNCHEN GESCHLOSSEN
CERRADO
CABRAS
Κλειστό
Μετεωρίτες
POOL CLOSED
プールも
閉鎖中
ELECTRIC EELS
FERMÉ POUR
RAISON
DE GRÈVE
DES BONNES
Hotel
closed for
facelifting
FECHADO!
POR CAUSA DE
ATAQUES DOS CROCODILOS
I don't speak
sign language.
A hotel can close for all kinds of reasons.
Our Guarantee ensures that if your hotel's undergoing construction, we'll let you know in advance. In fact, we cover your entire travel experience. See www.travelocity.com/guarantee for details.
travelocity®
You'll never roam alone®
©2007 Travelocity.com LP. CST# 2056372-50.